The Complete Works of
WASHINGTON
IRVING

Richard Dilworth Rust
General Editor

THE SKETCH BOOK
OF
GEOFFREY CRAYON, GENT.

E R R A T A

<u>The Sketch Book of Geoffrey Crayon, Gent.</u>

Page 33 line 21: <u>for</u> which <u>read</u> when

Page 63 line 2: <u>for</u> little better than carrion, and apparently the lawless plunderers of the
<u>read</u> little. The contents of his book seemed to be as heterogeneous as those

Page 117 line 10: <u>for</u> my <u>read</u> thy

Page 326 line 16: <u>for</u> v <u>read</u> V

In the diagram "A History of Relevant Forms" which appears following page 348, please note:

Lower left corner: <u>for</u> GOARE <u>read</u> 60ARE

In MS listing in lower left: <u>for</u> "The Widow/ Her Son" Fragment <u>read</u> "The Widow & Her Son" Fragment

At approximate midpoint in diagram: <u>for</u>

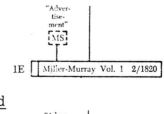

<u>read</u>

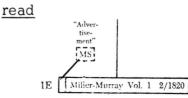

Washington Irving
1820

WASHINGTON IRVING

THE SKETCH BOOK
OF
GEOFFREY CRAYON, GENT.

Edited by

Haskell Springer

Twayne Publishers

Boston

1978

Published by Twayne Publishers

A Division of G. K. Hall & Co.

Copyright © 1978 by

G. K. Hall & Co.

The Complete Works of Washington Irving

Volume VIII

CENTER FOR EDITIONS OF
AMERICAN AUTHORS

AN APPROVED TEXT

MODERN LANGUAGE
ASSOCIATION OF AMERICA

®

Library of Congress Cataloging in Publication Data

Irving, Washington, 1783–1859.
The sketch book of Geoffrey Crayon, gent.

(The complete works of Washington Irving; v. 8)
Includes bibliographical references.
I. Springer, Haskell II. Title.
PS2066.A2S6   1978   818'.2'07   77–13413
ISBN 0–8057–8510–8

Manufactured in the United States of America

ACKNOWLEDGMENTS

An editor's indebtedness in a project extending over many years of active work is too extensive to record in full—and I extend my thanks to those I could not mention by name here. Primarily, two grants from the University of Kansas General Research Fund made possible most of the collations, by machine and hand; and Work-study monies from The University of Kansas and the University of Virginia provided the remainder of paid collation assistance. Both universities also contributed to the cost of photocopying Irving's manuscripts and the manuscript of this edition. To the Center for Editions of American Authors and the National Endowment for the Humanities I owe one semester's paid leave, during which I was able to convert several reams of data into a textual apparatus and commentary. And to my fellow Irving editors, as well as to the staffs of the Alderman Library, University of Virginia, Houghton Library, Harvard University, and Spencer Research Library, University of Kansas I am indebted for their willing and expert assistance.

I must particularly record my debt to my wife, Marlene, who contributed the invaluable criticism of a nontextualist literary scholar, which repeatedly saved me from narrowness and excessive technicality. In addition, the unflagging help of the late Henry A. Pochmann, and the dedicated, intelligent work of my student research assistant, Joel Crown, deserve special mention.

H. S.

University of Kansas

ILLUSTRATIONS

FRONTISPIECE

Portrait of Washington Irving at 37

An oil on canvas portrait by Gilbert Stuart Newton (1794–1835)
Spring, 1820

INTERIOR ILLUSTRATIONS

CONTENTS

EDITORIAL APPENDIX

INTRODUCTION

HISTORY OF THE TEXT

When Washington Irving took ship for England in May of 1815 he apparently had no literary plans in mind. He was " 'weary of every thing' " including himself, and he wanted to escape the idle, meaningless life he was leading in New York so he could later return with the determination (so he said) to " 'settle [himself] down to useful and honourable application.' "[1] He was not, however, to return to America for seventeen years. His British experiences of 1815–1818, moreover, eventually inspired his best-known work, which in its great success gave Irving his life's occupation. This *chef d'oeuvre, The Sketch Book*, was born in tribulation and economic necessity. Irving had come to England with plans for travel to Italy and Greece, to be financed by his apparently prosperous brothers. But almost as soon as he arrived in Liverpool he saw that the family import business was in serious trouble. As the firm of P & E Irving slowly but inevitably went bankrupt, as his mother died and his brother Peter seemed to approach death, Irving lived through perhaps the gloomiest, most self-critical years of his life. He made his escape from this emotional morass by writing.

Except for the two Indian sketches, published in 1814 in the *Analectic Magazine* when Irving was its editor, the essays in *The Sketch Book* (published 1819–1820) were all written in England. Just when he began this process of composition it is impossible to say; although some notes later used in *The Sketch Book* are to be found as early as a notebook of 1810, and jottings in other journals and notebooks can be pointed to as sources of material, the most significant preliminary document is of later date. Kernels and sometimes whole passages of *Sketch Book* essays are to be found in a notebook entitled "Notes While Preparing Sketch Book &c., 1817."[2] In this manuscript book of jottings and notes on all sorts of matters, personal and literary (some of which may possibly antedate 1817), notations relating to at least eight *Sketch Book* essays can be identified. A single phrase, "sees old 'woman totter-

1. Stanley T. Williams, *The Life of Washington Irving* (New York: Oxford University Press, 1935), I, 144; hereafter cited as STW.
2. See *Notes While Preparing Sketch Book &c., 1817*, ed. Stanley T. Williams (New Haven: Yale University Press, 1927).

ing to the grave of a son—'" reveals the central idea and even the language of "The Widow and Her Son" (84); "devouring melancholy that eats into my very soul" becomes "silent and devouring melancholy that had entered into her very soul," in "The Broken Heart" (59). Names and an inscription from "The Boar's Head Tavern," a page of notes concerning King Philip and other Indian matters, some observations suggesting the source of a simile in "Rip Van Winkle," a comment on D'Israeli's ideas of formal gardening, which are the same as those of Squire Bracebridge—these are most of the relevant "Notes." Two essays are represented more fully, however. At least four scattered notations embody words, phrases, and ideas later incorporated into "Roscoe," as, for example, "Sweet reflections and elevated abstractions that visit the mind in the hour of solitude—Sent from heaven like manna in the wilderness[.] They are the proper aliment of noble minds," which in final form read: "The solitude of such a mind is its state of highest enjoyment. It is then visited by those elevated meditations which are the proper aliment of noble souls, and are like manna, sent from heaven in the wilderness of this world" (18). For "The Wife" in particular Irving's notes were detailed. The conclusion of the essay itself, compared with the corresponding passage in the "Notes," shows him expanding and intensifying, substituting the less expected word for the obvious one, and in the last phrase rewriting to remove a cliché:

"Notes, 1817"

—As we approached the cottage she came tripping down to the gate dressed in a simple white rural dress a few flowers twisted in her hair—a bright bloom on her face and her whole countenance beaming with smiles. I never saw her look so lovely My dear Charles said she I am glad youve come—Ive set out the table in one of the sweetest little bowers, and Ive got a dish of the most delicious strawberrys & cream and every thing here is so sweet & beautiful its like a little paradise my poor friend was over come he clasped her to his bosom—he folded his arms

Printer's Copy Manuscript

I felt Leslie's hand tremble on my arm. He stepped forward to hear more distinctly—His step made a noise on the gravel walk—a bright beautiful face glanced out at the window and vanished—a light footstep was heard, and Mary came tripping forth to meet us. She was in a pretty rural dress of white; a few wild flowers were twisted in her fine hair; a fresh bloom was on her cheek; her whole countenance beamed with smiles—I had never seen her look so lovely.

"My dear George," cried she, "I am so glad you are come—I've been watching and watching for you; and running down the lane, and looking round her—he kissed her again and again—the tears started into his eyes—but I saw at that moment he was the happiest man in the world

out for you. I've set out a table under a beautiful tree behind the cottage—and I've been gathering some of the most delicious strawberries, for I know you are fond of them—and we have such excellent cream—and every thing is so sweet and still here—Oh!" said she, putting her arm within his, and looking up brightly in his face—"oh, we shall be so snug!"

Poor Leslie was overcome—He caught her to his bosom—He folded his arms around her—he kissed her again and again—he could not speak, but the tears gushed into his eyes—And he has often assured me that though the world has since gone prosperously with him, and his life has been a happy one; yet never has he experienced a moment of such unutterable felicity.

All the essays themselves were probably written between early 1817 and June, 1820, some (such as "Rip Van Winkle") initially struck off in the heat of inspiration, others laboriously constructed from notes on personal experiences and reading.[3] By August, 1817, he had perhaps nine unfinished essays, and by July, 1818, ten sketches were more or less completed.[4] In early 1819, in reaction to the offer of a government position secured for him through the influence of his brother William he finally determined to try to make a profession of writing and thus be his own man. Accordingly, on March 1, 1819, he sent from London, to his brother Ebenezer in New York, a parcel containing manuscript for the first number of *The Sketch Book*.[5]

This manuscript for *Sketch Book* Number I, plus those for Numbers II and III and a small fragment of "The Legend of Sleepy Hollow," are all that survive of Irving's inscription of the original seven numbers. They are quite legible except (as Irving realized) for a number of instances where punctuation is missing, incomplete, or confused, or

3. See the Explanatory Notes (pp. 305–39) for details on individual sketches.
4. STW, I, 168, 169.
5. Not March 3, as has often been stated. See the unpublished letter from Washington to Ebenezer Irving (March 1, 1819) in the Seligman Collection of the New York Public Library. For contents of the separate numbers, see chart, p. 355.

THE SKETCH BOOK OF GEOFFREY CRAYON, GENT.

where his capitalization and word-division are unclear. Irving did quite a bit of insertion, cancellation, and mending of these inscriptions (all reported in Alterations in the Manuscripts beginning on p. 467). He often reinscribed words for the sake of clarity—a detail which, in conjunction with other evidence, shows these surviving manuscripts to be fair copy, deriving from a rougher form of the text no longer extant.

Accompanying the manuscript of *Sketch Book* Number I was a sheet entitled "Directions for the Printer," in the course of which Irving wrote: "Great care must be taken in the correction of the press, as there may be errors in my Mss: particularly in the punctuation." His subsequent dissatisfaction, five months later, with the excessive punctuation of *Sketch Book* Number I, was due to the over-scrupulousness of the printer, to which this note probably contributed. Two days later he wrote to his old New York friend, Henry Brevoort, asking him to be his agent in all matters relating to the publication of his manuscript:

> Will you, as you are a literary man and a man of leisure, take it under your care. I wish the copy right secured for me, and the work printed, and then sold to one or more booksellers. . . . If the work is printed in N. York will you correct the proof sheets, as I fear the Mss: will be obscure & occasionally incorrect, & you are well acquainted with my handwriting.[6]

Judging from this letter to Brevoort and Irving's subsequent instructions to him to exercise his own initiative, one would suppose that Brevoort's influence on the text of *The Sketch Book* was great.[7] But all evidence indicates that if he did edit the text, it was only to correct errors in the proof sheets; the surviving manuscripts show no evidence of non-authorial correction or alteration.

Irving did depend heavily on Brevoort at least emotionally, however, because, as he later reiterated in one form or another, he felt "great diffidence about this reappearance in literature." "I am conscious of my imperfections," he wrote, "and my mind has been for a long time past so preyed upon and agitated by various cares and anxieties, that I fear it has lost much of its cheerfulness and some of its activity."[8] He even felt it necessary, in the same letter to his old friend, to defend the sort of writing he had produced:

6. *The Letters of Washington Irving to Henry Brevoort*, ed. George S. Hellman (New York: G. P. Putnam's Sons, 1915), II, 87; hereafter cited as Irv-Bvt.

7. Several scholars have made such an assumption. See, for example, STW, I, 174.

8. Irv-Bvt, II, 87.

I have attempted no lofty theme, nor sought to look wise and learned, which appears to be very much the fashion among our American writers, at present. I have preferred addressing myself to the feeling and fancy of the reader more than to his judgment. My writing, therefore, may appear light and trifling in our country of philosophers and politicians; but if they possess merit in the class of literature to which they belong, it is all to which I aspire in the work.

He followed these comments with a promise to try to send a second number as soon as possible, but again expressed his insecurity: "some time may intervene—for my writing moods are very precarious, and I have been rendered exceedingly nervous by the kind of life I have led for some time past."

Irving did not delay long, however. He sent the second number on April 1, and the third on May 13.[9] In the letter accompanying Number III he observed that it was not as large as the first because he had been unable to put more sketches into finished form, but asserted his lack of concern for the uniformity of the different numbers.[10] At the conclusion of this letter he demonstrated his understandable interest in producing what the market wanted: he asked Brevoort to give him "hints" about the popularity in America of particular themes and subjects. Brevoort, however, apparently did not respond with specific suggestions, though he did give his opinion of the various sketches.

The fourth number was, it seems, delayed by Irving's admitted lack of self-confidence, and was not dispatched to Ebenezer Irving until August 2, a few days after Irving had seen *Sketch Book* Number I (published on June 23, 1819) and had expressed his pleasure in a letter to Brevoort:

I have seen a copy of the first number of the Sketch Book, which was sent out to a gentleman of my acquaintance. I cannot but express how much more than ever I feel myself indebted to you for the manner in which you have attended to my concerns. The work is got up in a beautiful style. I should scarcely have ventured to have made so elegant an *entrée* had it been left to myself, for I had lost confidence in my writings. I have not discovered an

9. The third was sent to Ebenezer, and so, probably, was Number II. The letters concerning these numbers, though, were addressed to Brevoort. See the letter from Irving to Brevoort, May 13, 1819, Seligman Collection of the New York Public Library. This letter has not yet been published in its entirety.

10. Pierre M. Irving, *The Life and Letters of Washington Irving* (New York: G. P. Putnam, 1862–1864), I, 420.

error in the printing, and indeed have felt delighted at my genteel appearance in print.[11]

He had good reason to be pleased. *Sketch Book* Number I (and the six succeeding installments) appeared in a 9 x 5½ inch octavo format in both greyish-brown and tan paper covers with shaded letters in the titles. As his "Directions for the Printer" had specified, the paper was good, the printed page contained about as much text as the manuscript page, and the type, which Longfellow judged to be a symbol of the style, and later adopted for *Outre-Mer*, was clear and beautiful.[12]

In the same enthusiastic letter Irving politely complained, "the work appears to be a little too *highly* pointed. I don't know whether my manuscript was so, or whether it is the scrupulous precision of the printer. High pointing is apt to injure the fluency of the style if the reader attends to all the stops." Brevoort assured him, in a letter of September 9, that the excess pointing was not due to the manuscript, but the scrupulousness of the printer, C. S. Van Winkle.[13] He had objected to it himself, said Brevoort, for the very reasons Irving had mentioned, and he would see that the punctuation in the second edition of Number I, due to go to press in a few days, would be "somewhat diminished."[14]

On the day Brevoort was writing these assurances, Irving was examining *Sketch Book* Number II (published July 31) and expressing once again his gratitude to Brevoort, as well as his approval of Van Winkle's job of printing: "I cannot express to you how much I am delighted with the very tasteful manner in which it is executed. You may tell Mr. Van Winkle that it does him great credit and has been much admired here as a specimen of American typography."[15]

Irving was also pleased with Brevoort's business arrangements in bringing these and the succeeding numbers before the American public. The individual numbers were printed in New York by Van Winkle and distributed simultaneously by booksellers in New York, Philadelphia, Boston, and Baltimore. Two thousand copies each of Numbers I and II

11. Irv-Bvt, II, 101.

12. See STW, I, 173.

13. *Letters of Henry Brevoort to Washington Irving, Together With Other Un-published Brevoort Papers,* ed. George S. Hellman (New York: G. P. Putnam's Sons, 1918), p. 110; hereafter cited as Bvt-Irv.

14. Brevoort never got the chance to "diminish" the punctuation, since printing of the second edition of *Sketch Book* Number I did not begin until mid-November, by which time Irving had sent a revised Number I to serve as printer's copy.

15. Irv-Bvt, I, 114.

were printed, and though concrete information is not available for the later ones, it is highly probable that the same number of copies of Numbers III–VII were run off. Van Winkle took out the copyrights in Irving's name while Irving (or rather the Irving brothers acting as his agents) paid for the manufacture of the pamphlets, thus retaining control of sales and financial arrangements with the booksellers.

Irving's first letter to Brevoort concerning *The Sketch Book* (March 3, 1819) had asked that a rather high price be put on his work: he correctly judged that his name would sell. His directions were heeded, and Number I sold for 75 cents. When he sent the shorter Number II he indicated that the price should be less than the first number. It accordingly sold for 62½ cents (though one copy has been seen with a printed 50 cent price mended in ink to 62½ cents). Numbers III, IV, and V also sold for 75 cents, but VI and VII went up to 87½ cents.[16] Thus the whole work cost the reader $5.37½, a high price on the American market where, in the absence of an international copyright law, the retail buyer could get one of Scott's novels for two dollars.[17] As one might expect, the reading public complained. When Irving was informed of these grumblings he responded with some trenchant comments: "You observe that the public complains of the price of my work—this is the disadvantage of coming in competition with re-published English works for which the Booksellers have not to pay any thing to the authors. If the American public wish to have literature of their own they must consent to pay for the support of authors."[18] This American author, according to Brevoort's calculations, should have cleared five hundred dollars on the two thousand copies of Number I and the same for II, a profit of 33⅓ percent of the retail price of Number I and 38.7 percent on Number II—while William Charvat has estimated that *Sketch Book* Number V yielded Irving a profit of forty percent of selling price.[19]

Because of the time-consuming Atlantic crossing, Irving's enthusiastic comments on Number II were made at the same time Brevoort was reading manuscript for *Sketch Book* Number IV. Number III was already printed and due to be published on September 13; and now Brevoort had in hand "The Mutability of Literature," "The Spectre Bridegroom," and "John Bull," dispatched by Irving on August 2. In

16. Some wrappers of Number III were printed with a price of 62½ cents, but according to Henry Brevoort (Bvt-Irv, p. 111, September 9, 1819) only a few copies were printed before the error was corrected.

17. William Charvat, *Literary Publishing in America, 1790–1850* (Philadelphia: University of Pennsylvania, 1959), p. 40.

18. Irv-Bvt, II, 107 (August 12, 1819).

19. Charvat, p. 39.

the letter concerning Number IV he gave Brevoort great license in handling the *Sketch Book* materials: "Should you, at any time think any article so indifferent as to be likely to affect the reputation of the work, you may use your discretion in omitting it, and delaying the number until the arrival of my next number, out of which you can take an article to supply the deficiency."[20] But it was Irving who made the only substitution. First, on August 12, he sent a correction for "John Bull," and then on August 16 sent "Rural Funerals," instructing Brevoort to substitute it for "John Bull," which would in turn go into Number V. In the letter accompanying "Rural Funerals" he again expressed his diffidence about the correctness of his manuscript: "I have not had time to give this article a proper finishing, and wish you to look sharp that there are not blunders and tautologies in it."[21] "John Bull," displaced because Irving thought the humor of Number IV too prominent, did not, however, become part of Number V (published January 1, 1820). That number had a unifying theme—Christmas and its customs—so "John Bull" had to wait for inclusion in Number VI.

It was on October 28 and December 29 respectively that he sent the manuscripts for *Sketch Book* Numbers V and VI to Ebenezer. Number IV had been published (on November 10), but Brevoort was leaving New York on November 20 to spend the winter in Charleston, South Carolina, and turned all *Sketch Book* duties over to Ebenezer. Two other Irving brothers, William and John T., were to help correct proofs.[22] But at this point the system of transmission from England and first publication in America was disrupted.

Before *Sketch Book* Number III had appeared in the United States, the British papers had been getting wind of Irving's success. The *Kaleidoscope* of Liverpool reprinted "The Wife" on August 24, 1819, and the London *Literary Gazette* printed *Sketch Book* selections in its issues of September 25 and October 5. Six months later, on April 8, 1820, the *Gazette*, in a notice of the British *Sketch Book*, reported having received a "polite" letter from the author of these selections during the previous October, in which he had stated his intention to publish *The Sketch Book* in London. The paper, as it said, had then given up its plan to publish the book piecemeal. But Irving had also heard rumors that a British publisher planned to bring out an unauthorized volume of the essays. Thus, at about the same time he wrote his letter to the *Literary Gazette* he took the first two or three

20. PMI, I, 428.
21. Irv-Bvt, II, 112.
22. PMI, I, 446–47.

American numbers to John Murray for consideration.[23] Murray politely refused to publish them, and Irving, after trying briefly to secure John Constable for his publisher, decided to pay the entire cost of bringing out a volume in England. He would not have done so, he later wrote Ebenezer, "had there not been a likelihood of these works being re-published here from incorrect American numbers."[24] Consequently, in mid-February 1820, John Miller, Burlington Arcade, published a volume of the first four numbers in an edition of one thousand copies. But within two months, just as the book was beginning to be noticed by the literati, Miller's small business failed.

At this point Irving's friendship with Walter Scott (soon to become Sir Walter) saved him from great financial—and no doubt emotional—difficulty. As his "Preface to the Revised Edition" of 1848 relates in some detail, Irving had earlier written to Scott for advice on publishing in England and then had written again, sending him three numbers of *The Sketch Book* and asking him to recommend them to Constable. Scott had given the advice and also, by his own testimony, had spoken to Constable in favor of the work. Now Scott proved of such service that Irving later dedicated the second volume of the British edition to him. When Miller failed, Scott urged Murray to reconsider. Murray did, and to Irving's relief took over publication by buying Miller's stock of five hundred sets of unbound sheets and printing a new title page for them, reading "Second Edition" over his imprint.[25] Irving was pleased with the financial arrangements, and also with Murray's publication of one thousand copies of a second volume of three numbers in July.

Two months before, on May 13, 1820, Irving had written to Brevoort: "I shall not send any more manuscript to America, until I put it to press here, as the second volume might be delayed, and the number

23. Irving's story of his attempt to publish in England is told in the "Preface" to the Author's Revised Edition, 1848. For a detailed, balanced account see Ben Harris McClary, *Washington Irving and the House of Murray* (Knoxville: University of Tennessee Press, 1969), 16–20, 120; hereafter cited as McClary.

24. PMI, I, 436, 449. It is unclear whether or not Irving thought that by publishing the work before any other British appearance he would protect his rights in England, as well as insure the publication of a correct, personally revised text. The law at the time was held to mean that in Irving's case, where the work had already appeared abroad, he could not expect British copyright protection.

25. Irving's comment in his "Preface" to the Author's Revised Edition, that "a further edition of the first volume was struck off," is misleading. On p. 262 of John Murray's Ledger B, under "The Sketch Book," is the item "Printing Titles vol 1 13/6." Ledger B also records the sale of five hundred copies of Volume I under April, 1820.

come out here from America."[26] In accordance with Irving's plan, he resumed American publication on June 28, after the printing of the second Murray volume had begun, most likely by sending Ebenezer manuscript for the seventh number.[27] Thus, after long delay, Sketch Book Number VII finally appeared in America on September 13, 1820, six months after Number VI and fifteen months from the publication of Number I.

Long before the last number of the first American edition (1A) of The Sketch Book was published, however, a second edition (2A) had been launched in the United States.[28] Irving had begun sending random corrections and alterations in his letters, beginning on July 28, 1819, and asking Brevoort to make the changes should a second edition be printed. But his first systematic revisions were sent to the United States on September 21, 1819, when he mailed annotated copies of Sketch Book Numbers I and II to Brevoort and requested that any second editions be printed from those copies. Brevoort reported on November 9 that he had received the copies and that the second editions would be put to press within the week. Irving eventually sent back revised copies of Numbers III, IV, V, VI, and probably VII, from which the second editions were printed. The first number of this second edition is dated 1819 and the other six, 1820. For this edition, also printed and published by Van Winkle, Irving heavily revised parts of his book but left others untouched: "A Royal Poet" is virtually a new essay in the second edition because of rearrangement of its parts and extensive rewriting, whereas all of Sketch Book Number VI contains only four substantive differences, all single words.

Van Winkle began a third edition (3A) in parts two years later. The third editions of Sketch Book Numbers I and II read 1822 and Number III is dated 1823, but no other individual parts are known to have been published. After this incomplete third edition came a "Fourth American Edition" (1824) from Van Winkle, in two volumes. The advent of these printings put an end to the "American" text of The Sketch Book, for they both derive not from the earlier 1A and 2A, but from the distinct British text which had since the Miller-Murray first edition of 1820 (1E) appeared in England in at least six more editions, and had been separately revised by the author in 1822.[29]

---

26. Irv-Bvt, II, 126–27.

27. The complex relationship between the British and American versions of these sketches is discussed below in the Textual Commentary, p. 348.

28. See the list of symbols on p. 380.

29. "Philip of Pokanoket," "Traits of Indian Character," and "L'Envoy" first appeared in America in this fourth edition, which derives from the authorially revised Murray edition of 1822.

This first composite British edition of 1820 (1E) had had such a swift sale that shortly after the appearance of Volume II Murray had proposed printing a new, uniform two-volume edition at *his* expense. Irving, however, perhaps because of his professed dislike for keeping accounts or being bothered with financial matters, offered to sell him the copyright. Murray accepted: his ledger reads, "Paid Copyright for 1 & 2 262/10"; that is, Irving received 250 guineas. This small payment, only one fourth the amount Murray paid for *Bracebridge Hall* in 1822, is explained not only by Murray's lack of certainty about future sales, but by the tenuousness of the rights he paid for. He must, however, have had some hope of defending his claim against possible poachers, and that hope no doubt rested on the fact that the British and American *Sketch Books* were not quite the same work: the British *Sketch Book* contained four items not included in the American edition. They were the "Advertisement," the two Indian sketches, "Traits of Indian Character" and "Philip of Pokanoket," as well as the brief "L'Envoy" which closed the second volume.[30] In addition, Irving had made numerous small changes throughout the whole book. At any rate, Murray bought the rights, printed the new edition (2E), and on August 10, 1820, deposited eleven copies at Stationer's Hall as he registered copyright.[31] The first volume of this supposedly uniform edition reads "Third Edition," but the second volume is called "Second Edition." This confusing discrepancy is accounted for by the fact that Murray had labeled his copies of the remainder of Miller's Volume I "Second Edition." Consequently, he called this new Volume I "Third Edition" while correctly calling Volume II "Second Edition."

Within a week of Murray's taking out copyright, Irving left for a year in Paris, temporarily free of *Sketch Book* responsibilities. In the next three years Murray published five editions of *The Sketch Book*: three in 1821, another in 1822, and one in 1823. During this period Irving worked over his text once again, making perhaps one hundred substantive changes. He apparently did this work sometime between July, 1821, and July, 1822, when he was back in England to oversee the publication of *Bracebridge Hall*, since the alterations first appear in Murray's "New Edition" of 1822 (22E).

Irving returned to Paris in July, 1822, and the next important stage in *The Sketch Book*'s textual history is announced by an entry in his journal for April 10, 1823: "Dr. Montucci calls on me to request

30. "Traits" and "Philip" had appeared in 1814 in the *Analectic Magazine* when Irving was its editor, but both were heavily revised for *The Sketch Book*.

31. See McClary, p. 220. McClary also prints valuable material bearing on the question of British copyright for Irving's other works published by Murray.

permission to publish an edition of the Sketch Book in English."[32] By May 4 the journal reads, "corrected Sketch Book for Montucci between 6 & 7"; and on May 5, 11, 19, and 20 Irving records reading more proof. Montucci, a professor of Italian and English, published this edition of *The Sketch Book* (1G) in Dresden in the latter part of 1823. Collation shows that Irving used one of the 1821 Murray editions for printer's copy, and made a number of alterations in phraseology. That is, the Montucci edition does not contain the revisions made for the Murray edition of 1822, but has a set of changes all its own. These emendations, however, were not perpetuated: the Montucci edition did not serve as the basis for any other edition of *The Sketch Book* in which Irving had a hand. We return, rather, to Paris to pursue this textual history.

On August 16, 1823, Irving wrote in his journal: "After dinner stroll to the quais—on the way find a Book shop where they have a pretty edition of Sketch Book in the press...."[33] The edition he refers to is no doubt the one published by Baudry and Didot in 1823, the first publication of *The Sketch Book* in France (1F). Irving had nothing to do with this edition; it was based, however, on the 1823 Murray text and so incorporated the revisions Irving had made in 1821–1822. Looking ahead twenty-five years, though, we can see the importance of this Baudry-Didot edition to *The Sketch Book*'s history. When, in 1848, Irving began going over his books for the collected Author's Revised Edition (ARE) to be published by Putnam, he made many major changes and numerous minor ones in *The Sketch Book*. Still extant are a few annotated leaves from the printer's copy, and these pages, as far as we can tell, come from a later, page-for-page reprinting of the Baudry-Didot edition of 1823.[34]

We can only conjecture why Irving should have used this unauthoritative edition as the basis for the Author's Revised Edition. Most likely, it was the one he had at hand on his shelf at Sunnyside. Since he would revise it and then read proof, he apparently felt he need not worry about the French edition's inaccuracy in small details. Here Irving demonstrates, as do so many other authors, a disregard for the minutiae of his text. It did not matter to him, as it does to a textual editor, that the spelling and punctuation of the French edition were unauthoritative. Whereas in 1819 he had worried about over-

32. Washington Irving, *Journals and Notebooks*, Vol. III, ed. Walter A. Reichart (Madison: University of Wisconsin Press, 1970), p. 137; hereafter cited as Reichart.

33. Reichart, p. 212.

34. The exact edition has not yet been identified because the editor has been unable to locate all the known subsequent printings and resettings of this edition, some of which are quite scarce.

punctuation in the first of his works printed without his supervision of the press, in 1848 it concerned him less. Like most writers he did not want the bother of attending to it; and except for that one recorded, understated comment on the overpointing of the Van Winkle edition, he seems to have been perfectly willing to leave accidentals to the printers and their readers.[35]

This Author's Revised Edition of Irving's works was first advertised in the New York *Literary World* for June 10, 1848, at which time George P. Putnam announced that the twelve-volume uniform edition (which grew to fifteen volumes and sold for $1.25 per volume) would commence publication on September 1 with *The Sketch Book*, followed on October 1 by Knickerbocker's *History of New York*. The same full-page advertisement promised for October appearance an illustrated *Sketch Book* with designs by F. O. C. Darley. By August 19, however, Putnam had changed his publication schedule: *A History of New York* would appear on September 1, and *The Sketch Book* would be Volume II in the series, published on the first of October. One would assume from this change of plans that despite his extensive rewriting of *Knickerbocker*, Irving had it ready for the printer before the less heavily revised *Sketch Book*. Alternatively, author and publisher may have decided that *Knickerbocker*, as the earlier of the two books, should lead the way.

The Putnam *Sketch Book* included seventeen pages of new material, and numerous revisions. It appeared, as advertised, in two formats, printed from the same plates, and was reprinted all through the 1850's. Irving's contract called for him to receive 12½ percent of the retail price of each volume sold.[36] How much this amounted to before his death is unknown because Putnam's records are no longer extant, but by 1853, according to one account, Putnam had sold 144,000 volumes (all titles included), yielding Irving a five-year profit of approximately $22,464.[37]

Irving died a national celebrity in 1859, and editions of *The Sketch Book* proliferated through the rest of the century. No authoritative

35. A letter from Irving to G. P. Putnam, August 3, 1848, can be interpreted as revealing his unconcern for his own accidentals. He wrote: "I will thank you to send me the proof of the introduction to the Sketch Book by mail. . . . You need not send the copy with the proof" (Clifton Waller Barrett Library, University of Virginia).

36. PMI, IV, 41.

37. See STW, II, 395. PMI reports that six thousand copies of the unillustrated *Sketch Book* had been sold in less than four months, and that the illustrated version had had a very brisk holiday sale.

changes, however, were introduced into the book after 1848, though a number of its errors were corrected and some new ones created.

This is the basic history of the key editions of *The Sketch Book*. Even a list of the other printings published between 1820 and 1859 would take pages—the Williams and Edge bibliography cites forty-three of them. Selective collation fails to reveal, however, any evidence that Irving had anything to do with the texts of any of these other printings: they are merely reprints and do not affect the establishment of an authoritative text.

RECEPTION

Irving's previous works, especially the *History of New York*, had greatly pleased the American public. Thus, in 1819 he had reason to expect that *The Sketch Book* would get a good reception in the United States. A somewhat overenthusiastic contemporary notice spoke of his American reputation:

> "When the first number of this beautiful work was announced, it was sufficient to induce an immediate and importunate demand, that the name of Mr. Irving was attached to it in the popular mind. With his name so much of the honor of our national literature is associated, that our pride as well as our better feelings is interested in accumulating the gifts of his genius."[38]

Irving had no idea, however, that from the very beginning *The Sketch Book* would be a critical as well as popular success both in England and in the States. Though Irving's faults were noticed on both sides of the ocean, critical approbation and even eulogy abounded. A long article in the *Edinburgh Monthly Review* closed with a quotation from "Stratford-on-Avon" and this high praise: "The author himself, if he should ever chance to see our journal, would assuredly know how to appreciate the compliment we mean to pay, when we leave him in company with Shakespeare."[39]

Two early notices of *The Sketch Book* were written at the instigation of friends, and no doubt helped smooth the way in both countries. In the American *Analectic Magazine* for July, 1819, G. C. Verplanck, who, just six months earlier had been moved by his Dutch heritage to attack the "coarse caricature" in *A History of New York*, congratulated "the American public that one of their choicest favourites has, after so long

38. PMI, I, 418.
39. *Edinburgh Monthly Review*, September, 1820, p. 333.

interval, again resumed the pen." Verplanck made clear his intention in writing the notice: he wanted to "announce" the appearance of *Sketch Book* Number I and to "stimulate the curiosity of our readers. . . ." The few appreciative comments he made, appearing only days after the publication of Number I, made his brief article much more than an announcement:

It will be needless to inform any who have read the book, that it is from the pen of Mr. Irving. His rich, and sometimes extravagant humour, his gay and graceful fancy, his peculiar choice and felicity of original expression, as well as the pure and fine moral feelings which imperceptibly pervades [*sic*] every thought and image, without being any where ostentatious or dogmatic, betray the author in every page; even without the aid of those minor peculiarities of style, taste, and local allusions, which at once identify the travelled Geoffrey Crayon with the venerable Knickerbocker.[40]

For this encomium Irving could thank Henry Brevoort, who had encouraged Verplanck to do Irving the good service. In England it was Walter Scott who filled a similar role. Scott decorously told Irving about it: "If you ever see a witty but rather local publication called *Blackwood's Edinburgh Magazine*, you will find some notice of your works in the last number: the author is a friend of mine, to whom I have introduced you in your literary capacity."[41] The author was John Gibson Lockhart, soon to become Scott's son-in-law. His article, "On the Writings of Charles Brockden Brown and Washington Irving," appeared in February, 1820, the month in which John Miller published Volume I of the British *Sketch Book* (1E). Lockhart had read the first three American numbers, and, unaware of Irving's arrangements for British publication, promised "great and eager acceptance" of his work in England were he to publish it there. The review specifically cited "Rip Van Winkle," "Rural Life in England," "The Voyage," and "The Broken Heart" as "exquisite and classical pieces of writing," while calling Irving's serious style "very graceful—infinitely more so than any piece of American writing that ever came from any other hand, and well entitled to be classed with the best English writings of our day."[42]

Another laudatory article appeared in the August 3, 1819, New York *Evening Post*. Irving assumed it to be by William Coleman, editor and

---

40. *Analectic Magazine*, July, 1819, p. 78.
41. See Irving's "Preface," p. 6.
42. *Blackwood's Edinburgh Magazine*, February, 1820, p. 559.

owner of the paper, and was rather touched, he wrote Henry Brevoort, by this tribute from someone he had expected to be hostile.[43] He must have been somewhat chagrined to read, in a subsequent letter from Brevoort: "The article in the E Post was written by me, at Coleman's request, and published under the Editorial head as his own.... he assured me that the article expressed exactly what he felt and would have written. Had it been otherwise depend on it he would have shaped the notice to his own liking."[44] Perhaps Coleman would have challenged Brevoort's sentiments just as he had disagreed with an earlier *Evening Post* notice contributed "by a literary friend" (Brevoort again?) which had judged "Rip Van Winkle" "the master-piece" of *Sketch Book* Number I.[45] But Irving well knew that the Brevoort article as well as the ones by Verplanck and Lockhart all deserved the same response: "So much for an author's egotism."[46]

Brevoort's notice in the *Evening Post* was one in a packet of clippings from American journals and newspapers sent to Irving by Brevoort and received September 9, 1819. On reading them Irving was almost instantly released from the six months of recurring dissatisfaction with his writing which had begun with the sending of the manuscript for *Sketch Book* Number I and had been only slightly alleviated by the personal, enthusiastic responses of his brother Ebenezer and, of course, Brevoort: "The manner in which the work has been received and the eulogiums that have been passed upon it in the American papers and periodical works have completely overwhelmed me. They go far, far beyond my most sanguine expectations and indeed are expressed with such peculiar warmth and kindness as to affect me in the tenderest manner."[47] Irving admitted in the same letter that he felt "almost appalled by such success" and was afraid that he would be unable later to fulfill "the expectations which may be formed" by his readers.

43. See Irv-Bvt, II, 117 (September 9, 1819).

44. Bvt-Irv, p. 120 (November 9, 1819). Irving could have seen that the review was probably by Brevoort had he noted the familiar sound of a particular passage. "The literary ambition of Mr. I.," said the review, "aims simply at a flute accompaniment, in our national concert of authors, leaving to the more aspiring the management of the louder instruments." In his March 3 letter asking Brevoort to superintend publication Irving had written, "I seek only to blow a flute accompaniment in the national concert, and leave others to play the fiddle and French horn" (PMI, I, 416).

45. New York *Evening Post*, June 26, 1819. Coleman demonstrated a deplorable sense of humor by criticizing the "probability" of "Rip Van Winkle" and thus becoming perhaps the model for the "dry looking old gentleman" in the postscript to "The Legend of Sleepy Hollow" who averred that "there were one or two points on which he had his doubts."

46. Irv-Bvt, II, 121.

47. Irv-Bvt, II, 115 (September 9, 1819).

The doubts were, of course, verified: he was never again to produce work to match the best in *The Sketch Book*, nor to be so warmly and universally praised. His corollary fear, perhaps largely rhetorical, that the critical praise was "not fully merited" was also unfortunately justified, for many of the reviews, like those of his friends, were uncritically enthusiastic. Brevoort summarized the burden of most of these laudatory American critiques: "It is a point universally agreed upon, that your work is an honor to American literature as well as an example to those who aspire to a correct and eloquent style of composition."[48]

While there were very few attacks on *The Sketch Book*, some thoughtful critics who judged the book a success nevertheless faulted Irving on points of style and content. One such article was written by Richard Henry Dana in the *North American Review* for September, 1819, and is particularly noteworthy because Irving revised his text in accordance with at least four of Dana's specific criticisms. Selected for censure because of the misuse of figurative language were phrases from "Roscoe," "The Broken Heart," and "Rural Life in England." From the first sketch the review (not too accurately) quoted "he has planted bowers by the way-side for the refreshment of the pilgrim and sojourner, and has *established* pure *fountains* which, etc." Apparently Irving agreed that one really did not "establish" fountains, and so emended the word to "opened" in 1E. From "The Broken Heart" Dana quoted (again italicizing the offending words) "She is like some tender *tree*, the pride and beauty of the grove; graceful in its form, bright in its foliage, but with the worm preying at its *core*." Irving changed "core" to "heart" in 1E. And from "Rural Life in England" two passages were also cited for improper figures of speech. The first, "various *strata* of society . . . ," Irving altered to "various orders of society. . . ." The criticism of "while it has thus banded society together, has *implanted* in each intermediate *link* a *spirit* of independence," led Irving to substitute in 1E "infused" for "implanted" and "rank" for "link." He let "spirit" stand. These instances, then, document Irving's frequently mentioned sensitivity to criticism.

The special effects of Dana's more general criticisms and the comments of other reviewers are impossible to isolate and identify, but certainly many of the authorial emendations in 1E (the most heavily revised of all the editions) derive not only from Irving's finally being able to read and correct proof, but also from his sense of error or deficiency, aroused by adverse critical comment. He was not, however, slavish in his acceptance of this criticism. Dana's review, for example,

48. Bvt-Irv, p. 110 (September 9, 1819).

makes several disparaging comments on Irving's taste and decorum, especially in "The Broken Heart" and "The Wife"; but no corresponding emendations appear in the text.

Dana held, in general, that *The Sketch Book* was inferior to Irving's earlier works because of its increased sophistication. In style Irving "has given up something of his direct, simple manner and plain phraseology, for a more studied, periphrastical mode of expression." His former style was "masculine—good bone and muscle—this is feminine—*dressy*, elegant and languid."[49] In using "elegant" Dana was finding fault in what most rejoiced over. Perhaps the most repeated word in the contemporary reviews was "elegant." While Dana lamented the lack of "natural irregularity," the more conservative—for whom Irving had knowingly written—praised the correctness and refinement. Dana heaped compliments, however, on "English Writers on America," "Rural Life in England," and especially "Rip Van Winkle," which demonstrated "a free, spirited touch."[50]

The British reviewers, within a year or so of *The Sketch Book's* appearance in England, liked it for some of the same reasons most Americans did, though they expressed themselves differently. They too thought the style correct and refined—so much so that they in effect judged Irving the best British writer America had yet produced; and although their comments tended toward chauvinism, they were in essence correct when noting, as did *The Quarterly Review*, that Irving "seems to have studied our language where alone it can be studied in all its strength and perfection—in the writings of our old sterling authors; and in working these precious mines of literature he has refined for himself the ore which there so richly abounds."[51] The reviewer did not see the numerous entries in Irving's notebooks which document his interest in earlier English literature, but even a swift survey of his allusions and quotations in *The Sketch Book* reveals how much he loved English medieval and Renaissance literature, and with what assiduity he had indeed mined in the British Museum.[52]

Though Irving's English audience was no doubt somewhat nearsighted in attributing his stylistic success to his great British models, on matters

49. *North American Review*, September, 1819, p. 348.

50. The *North American Review* for July, 1822, judged the whole *Sketch Book* in similar terms. Edward Everett thought the book inferior to Irving's earlier work "because it wants the raciness of originality."

51. *The Quarterly Review*, April, 1821, p. 67.

52. See the Explanatory Notes, pp. 305–39. Irving's references span six centuries of British literature and are from the obscure as much as the famous. Their use is pervasive, and essential to the tone of many sketches, as well as to the delineation of Geoffrey Crayon as an anglophilic American antiquarian.

of style in general the British critics were more thoughtfully compli-
mentary than many of the author's own countrymen. Even though *The
Quarterly Review* justly observed that Irving's attempts to be "sweet"
sometimes become almost "cloying," and the *British Critic* said that
"Roscoe" was written in a "ranting manner,"[53] Irving's style was, except
for a few such random criticisms, highly praised: "playful and picturesque," "great beauty of expression," "best transatlantic we have yet
seen," "chaste," "poetic," and of course "elegant," ran the British chorus.
His lighter style was compared to Addison's, his "spirit" brought
Scott to mind.[54]

The content of the work was also repeatedly commended in England,
but with definite qualifications. Unlike the large numbers of American
readers who felt that Irving's power lay in evoking pathos, some British
reviewers found fault with the sentimental pieces. The comment in
The Edinburgh Magazine and Literary Miscellany was representative
in its criticism of Irving's "affected imitations of the weaker and more
sickly parts of our pathetic writers...."[55] Another reiterated complaint
dealt with the excessive length of the Christmas sketches, while several
of the critiques also touched in passing on the slightness of the book's
content. Though only one critic thought that *The Sketch Book* "attempts
to make something out of nothing," others also observed Irving's intellectual lightness.[56] Some who hoped that Irving would take up weightier
matters in future nevertheless recognized that this book, written under
the pseudonym Geoffrey Crayon, Gent., was as it should be. Thus they
did not condemn him for lack of depth or significance.

The miscellaneous character of *The Sketch Book* led the critics to
comment on the individual essays, sometimes at length. The general
agreement at the time was that "Rip" and "Sleepy Hollow" were probably
the best in the book; and "The Spectre Bridegroom," "The Voyage,"
"Little Britain," and "Rural Life in England" were also particularly noted
and admired. The essay most often singled out for comment, however,
was—as one might expect—"English Writers on America." In the United
States this piece had been highly praised for its patriotism, its firm
rebuke of English slanders, and its warmhearted liberality. In England,
despite repeated flag-wavings, and admonitions to upstart America,
Irving's essay was also highly regarded. *The Quarterly Review, Blackwood's, The Edinburgh Monthly Review, The Investigator, The New*

---

53. *The Quarterly Review*, April, 1821, p. 66; *The British Critic and Quarterly
Theological Review*, June, 1820, p. 646.

54. *The Investigator; or, Quarterly Magazine*, May, 1820, p. 157; *The Quarterly
Review*, April, 1821, p. 53.

55. September, 1819, p. 207.

56. *The British Critic and Quarterly Theological Review*, November, 1820, p. 515.

Monthly Magazine, and *The British Critic* were among those which joined in praise of its moderation and good sense. As *The Investigator* observed, after quoting from the essay, "such is the judicious admonition given by Mr. Irvine [*sic*] to his countrymen, such the merited reproof administered more in kindness than in wrath to ours."[57] But the *Literary Gazette,* focusing on one page of "English Writers" to the exclusion of the rest, loftily held that "there the author ... complains ... without reason, boasts without foundation, and threatens without effect."[58]

The critical esteem which *The Sketch Book* initially enjoyed in England gradually faded as years passed and the book was admitted to contain more dross and less gold than at first believed. Godwin's enthusiastic response to *Sketch Book* Number II and Byron's "Crayon is very good" were countered by Hazlitt's judgment in 1825 that Irving had merely *"skimmed the cream,* and taken off patterns with great skill and cleverness, from our best known and happiest writers, so that their thoughts and almost their reputations are indirectly transferred to his page...."[59]

Yet, *The Sketch Book* continued to receive some critical acceptance in England. In 1844, *Chambers' Cyclopaedia of English Literature* asserted that "'Rip Van Winkle,' and 'Sleepy Hollow' are perhaps the finest pieces of original fictitious writing that this century has produced next to the works of Scott." As late as 1863 (in the March 21 issue) the *Spectator* gave it high tribute; and though the critics were no longer writing about it very much after 1859, its lasting popularity with the reading public well beyond Irving's death is documented by the long list of reprints in England, on the Continent—and of course in America.[60]

In the United States *The Sketch Book* had a long life both in popular esteem and in its influence on other writers. Bryant thought it seminal; Longfellow's work demonstrates its effect; Poe, Hawthorne, Holmes, Whittier, Lowell all responded to it favorably; and minor writers imitated it.[61] After the first group of editions by Van Winkle (1819–1820 [2 editions], 1822–1823, 1824, 1826), *The Sketch Book* was reprinted in America in 1828, 1829, 1831, 1832, 1833, 1834, 1835, 1836, and 1842, before the Author's Revised Edition appeared in 1848. During these

57. May, 1820, p. 162.
58. April 8, 1820, p. 228.
59. William Godwin in a letter to James Ogilvie, quoted in PMI, I, 422; for Byron's remarks see STW, I, 188, 432; for Hazlitt, STW, II, 278. A more detailed account of *The Sketch Book*'s later reputation may be found in STW, II, 277–80.
60. See Stanley T. Williams and Mary A. Edge, *A Bibliography of the Writings of Washington Irving: A Check List* (New York: Oxford University Press, 1936).
61. See STW, II, 277–78.

years, as further works came from the prolific Irving, critics used the occasions to review his former achievements.[62] While *The Sketch Book* as a whole suffered by comparison to *Knickerbocker* and even to *Columbus* in some of these pieces, the appeal of its best essays was, as in England, undiminished.

When in 1848 Putnam announced his contract with Irving for the "new, uniform, and complete edition" of the works, the event was loudly applauded in the journals and newspapers. *The Sketch Book* came in for its share of eager anticipation and then commendation, both for its beautiful new format and for its well-known content. One notice after another greeted it as an old and valued friend. " 'It is needless to refer to the work itself,' " said one reviewer, " 'for who that reads at all has failed to make acquaintance with its pages?' "[63] Bryant's *Evening Post*, on October 13, 1848, alluded to Rip Van Winkle and Ichabod Crane as "universal heroes," recalled the appeal of "The Widow and her Son," and observed that "every American traveller in England divides the enjoyment and the reminiscences of his pilgrimage to Stratford-on-Avon between Shakespeare and Irving...."[64]

The history of *The Sketch Book*'s reputation in England and America had one common denominator which was unaltered by time. Nearly everyone, no matter what his opinions on the literary worth of the book in whole or in part, was captivated by the personality of its author as it lay revealed on the printed page. In the reviews of 1850 no less than in those of 1820 his geniality, humanity, warmth of character and moral strength were repeatedly noted and admired. From temperament and experience Irving had made mutability the dominant theme of his book. He strongly and sincerely felt the diverse effects of the "dilapidations of time," and successfully communicated them to an audience generally willing to contemplate the varieties of this theme as exemplified in Westminster Abbey, in East Cheap, or in the highlands of the Hudson. In responding to the personality as well as the style of the Geoffrey Crayon who described the scenes he observed and at the same time imparted the feelings they should inspire, his readers made him as well known as any of his contemporaries, and established his book as an undoubted American classic for one hundred years. In the 1820's *The Sketch Book* was the first internationally respected work of literature by an American author; in the 1950's it was still being read as a model for English composition in Taiwan and Korea. In between, it went through enough printings to place it high

62. See, for example, *The North American Review*, January, 1829, pp. 103–34.
63. PMI, IV, 46.
64. Quoted in PMI, IV, 47.

on the list of universally popular American books. *The Sketch Book* takes up thirty-nine pages in the Williams and Edge bibliography, almost three times as many as *The Alhambra* or *Columbus*, its closest rivals among Irving's works. Extracts were printed in great numbers, while, in whole or in part, *The Sketch Book* appeared in fourteen foreign languages as well as in Esperanto, shorthand, and Braille. If this popularity and longevity are largely due to the achievement of only a few sketches, and partly to conservative or archaic taste, those sketches are nevertheless of a very high order, and not many works have become so much a part of our culture.

THE
SKETCH BOOK
OF
GEOFFREY CRAYON, GENT.

"I have no wife nor children, good or bad, to provide for. A mere spectator of other men's fortunes and adventures, and how they play their parts; which methinks are diversely presented unto me, as from a common theatre or scene."

BURTON

PREFACE TO THE REVISED EDITION

The following papers, with two exceptions, were written in England, and formed but part of an intended series for which I had made notes and memorandums. Before I could mature a plan, however, circumstances compelled me to send them piecemeal to the United States, where they were published from time to time in portions or numbers. It was not my intention to publish them in England, being conscious that much of their contents could be interesting only to American readers, and in truth, being deterred by the severity with which American productions had been treated by the British press.

By the time the contents of the first volume had appeared in this occasional manner, they began to find their way across the Atlantic, and to be inserted, with many kind encomiums, in the London Literary Gazette. It was said, also, that a London bookseller intended to publish them in a collective form. I determined, therefore, to bring them forward myself, that they might at least have the benefit of my superintendence and revision. I accordingly took the printed numbers which I had received from the United States, to Mr. John Murray, the eminent publisher, from whom I had already received friendly attentions, and left them with him for examination, informing him that should he be inclined to bring them before the public, I had materials enough on hand for a second volume. Several days having elapsed without any communication from Mr. Murray, I addressed a note to him, in which I construed his silence into a tacit rejection of my work, and begged that the numbers I had left with him might be returned to me. The following was his reply.

My dear Sir,

I entreat you to believe that I feel truly obliged by your kind intentions towards me, and that I entertain the most unfeigned respect for your most tasteful talents. My house is completely filled with workpeople at this time, and I have only an office to transact business in; and yesterday I was wholly occupied, or I should have done myself the pleasure of seeing you.

If it would not suit me to engage in the publication of your present work, it is only because I do not see that scope in the nature of it

3

which would enable me to make those satisfactory accounts between us, without which I really feel no satisfaction in engaging—but I will do all I can to promote their circulation, and shall be most ready to attend to any future plan of yours.

With much regard, I remain, dear sir,

Your faithful servant,

JOHN MURRAY.

This was disheartening, and might have deterred me from any further prosecution of the matter, had the question of republication in Great Britain rested entirely with me; but I apprehended the appearance of a spurious edition. I now thought of Mr. Archibald Constable as publisher, having been treated by him with much hospitality during a visit to Edinburgh; but first I determined to submit my work to Sir Walter (then Mr.) Scott, being encouraged to do so by the cordial reception I had experienced from him at Abbotsford a few years previously, and by the favourable opinion he had expressed to others of my earlier writings. I accordingly sent him the printed numbers of the Sketch Book in a parcel by coach, and at the same time wrote to him, hinting that since I had had the pleasure of partaking of his hospitality, a reverse had taken place in my affairs which made the successful exercise of my pen all important to me; I begged him, therefore, to look over the literary articles I had forwarded to him, and, if he thought they would bear European republication, to ascertain whether Mr. Constable would be inclined to be the publisher.

The parcel containing my work went by coach to Scott's address in Edinburgh; the letter went by mail to his residence in the country. By the very first post I received a reply, before he had seen my work.

"I was down at Kelso," said he, "when your letter reached Abbotsford. I am now on my way to town, and will converse with Constable, and do all in my power to forward your views—I assure you nothing will give me more pleasure."

The hint, however, about a reverse of fortune had struck the quick apprehension of Scott, and, with that practical and efficient good will which belonged to his nature, he had already devised a way of aiding me. A weekly periodical, he went on to inform me, was about to be set up in Edinburgh, supported by the most respectable talents, and amply furnished with all the necessary information. The appointment of the editor, for which ample funds were provided, would be five hundred pounds sterling a year, with the reasonable prospect of further advantages. This situation, being apparently at his disposal, he frankly offered to me. The work, however, he intimated, was to have somewhat of a political bearing, and he expressed an apprehension that the tone it was desired to adopt might not suit me. "Yet I risk the question," added he, "because I know no man so well qualified for this important task, and perhaps because it will necessarily bring you to Edinburgh. If my proposal does not suit, you need only keep the matter secret and there is no harm done. 'And for my love I pray you wrong me not.' If on the contrary you think it could be made to suit you, let me know as soon as possible, addressing Castle street, Edinburgh."

In a postscript, written from Edinburgh, he adds, "I am just come here, and have glanced over the Sketch Book. It is positively beautiful, and increases my desire to *crimp* you, if it be possible. Some difficulties there always are in managing such a matter, especially at the outset; but we will obviate them as much as we possibly can."

The following is from an imperfect draught of my reply, which underwent some modifications in the copy sent.

"I cannot express how much I am gratified by your letter. I had begun to feel as if I had taken an unwarrantable liberty; but, somehow or other, there is a genial sunshine about you that warms every creeping thing into heart and confidence. Your literary proposal both surprises and flatters me, as it evinces a much higher opinion of my talents than I have myself."

I then went on to explain that I found myself peculiarly unfitted for the situation offered to me, not merely by my political opinions, but by the very constitution and habits of my mind. "My whole course of life," I observed, "has been desultory, and I am unfitted for any periodically recurring task, or any stipulated labor of body or mind. I have no command of my talents, such as they are, and have to watch the varyings of my mind as I would those of a weather cock. Practice and training may bring me more into rule; but at present I am as useless for regular service as one of my own country Indians, or a Don Cossack.

"I must, therefore, keep on pretty much as I have begun; writing when I can, not when I would. I shall occasionally shift my residence and write whatever is suggested by objects before me, or whatever rises in my imagination; and hope to write better and more copiously by and by.

"I am playing the egotist, but I know no better way of answering your proposal than by showing what a very good for nothing kind of being I am. Should Mr. Constable feel inclined to make a bargain for the wares I have on hand, he will encourage me to further enterprise; and it will be something like trading with a gipsy for the fruits of his prowlings, who may at one time have nothing but a wooden bowl to offer, and at another time a silver tankard."

In reply, Scott expressed regret, but not surprise, at my declining what might have proved a troublesome duty. He then recurred to the original subject of our correspondence; entered into a detail of the various terms upon which arrangements were made between authors and booksellers, that I might take my choice; expressing the most encouraging confidence of the success of my work, and of previous works which I had produced in America. "I did no more," added he, "than open the trenches with Constable; but I am sure if you will take the trouble to write to him, you will find him disposed to treat your overtures with every degree of attention. Or, if you think it of consequence in the first place to see me, I shall be in London in the course of a month, and whatever my experience can command is most heartily at your command. But I can add little to what I have said above, except my earnest recommendation to Constable to enter into the negotiation."*

Before the receipt of this most obliging letter, however, I had determined to look to no leading bookseller for a launch, but to throw my work before the public at my own risk, and let it sink or swim according to its merits. I wrote to that effect to Scott, and soon received a reply:

"I observe with pleasure that you are going to come forth in Britain. It is certainly not the very best way to publish on one's own accompt; for the booksellers set their face against the circulation of such works as do not pay an amazing toll to themselves. But they have lost the art of altogether damming up the road in such cases between the author and the public, which they were once able to do as effectually as Diabolus in John Bunyan's Holy War closed up the windows of my Lord Understanding's mansion. I am sure of one thing, that you have only to be known to the British public to be admired by them, and I would not say so unless I really was of that opinion.

"If you ever see a witty but rather local publication called Blackwood's Edinburgh Magazine, you will find some notice of your works in the last number: the author is a friend of mine, to whom I have introduced you in your literary capacity. His name is Lockhart, a young man of very considerable talent, and who will soon be intimately connected with

---

*I cannot avoid subjoining in a note a succeeding paragraph of Scott's letter, which, though it does not relate to the main subject of our correspondence, was too characteristic to be omitted. Some time previously I had sent Miss Sophia Scott small duodecimo American editions of her father's poems published in Edinburgh in quarto volumes; showing the "nigromancy" of the American press, by which a quart of wine is conjured into a pint bottle. Scott observes: "In my hurry, I have not thanked you in Sophia's name for the kind attention which furnished her with the American volumes. I am not quite sure I can add my own, since you have made her acquainted with much more of papa's folly than she would ever otherwise have learned; for I had taken special care they should never see any of those things during their earlier years. I think I told you that Walter is sweeping the firmament with a feather like a maypole and indenting the pavement with a sword like a scythe— in other words, he has become a whiskered hussar in the 18th dragoons."

Sunnyside

An engraving reproduced in the Geoffrey Crayon edition of *The Sketch Book* (New York: G. P. Putnam's Sons, 1880).

my family. My faithful friend Knickerbocker is to be next examined and illustrated. Constable was extremely willing to enter into consideration of a treaty for your works, but I foresee will be still more so when

> Your name is up, and may go
> From Toledo to Madrid.

————And that will soon be the case. I trust to be in London about the middle of the month, and promise myself great pleasure in once again shaking you by the hand."

The first volume of the Sketch Book was put to press in London as I had resolved, at my own risk, by a bookseller unknown to fame, and without any of the usual arts by which a work is trumpeted into notice. Still some attention had been called to it by the extracts which had previously appeared in the Literary Gazette, and by the kind word spoken by the editor of that periodical, and it was getting into fair circulation, when my worthy bookseller failed before the first month was over, and the sale was interrupted.

At this juncture Scott arrived in London. I called to him for help, as I was sticking in the mire, and, more propitious than Hercules, he put his own shoulder to the wheel. Through his favourable representations, Murray was quickly induced to undertake the future publication of the work which he had previously declined. A further edition of the first volume was struck off and the second volume was put to press, and from that time Murray became my publisher, conducting himself in all his dealings with that fair, open, and liberal spirit which had obtained for him the well merited appellation of the Prince of Booksellers.

Thus, under the kind and cordial auspices of Sir Walter Scott, I began my literary career in Europe; and I feel that I am but discharging, in a trifling degree, my debt of gratitude to the memory of that golden hearted man in acknowledging my obligations to him.—But who of his literary contemporaries ever applied to him for aid or counsel that did not experience the most prompt, generous, and effectual assistance!

W.I.

Sunnyside, 1848.

THE AUTHOR'S ACCOUNT OF HIMSELF

I am of this mind with Homer, that as the snaile that crept out
of her shel was turned eftsoones into a Toad, and thereby was forced
to make a stoole to sit on; so the traveller that stragleth from his
owne country is in a short time transformed into so monstrous a
shape that he is faine to alter his mansion with his manners and to
live where he can, not where he would.

LYLY'S EUPHUES.

I was always fond of visiting new scenes and observing strange
characters and manners. Even when a mere child I began my travels
and made many tours of discovery into foreign parts and unknown
regions of my native city; to the frequent alarm of my parents and
the emolument of the town cryer. As I grew into boyhood I extended the
range of my observations. My holyday afternoons were spent in rambles
about the surrounding country. I made myself familiar with all its
places famous in history or fable. I knew every spot where a murder or
robbery had been committed or a ghost seen. I visited the neighbouring
villages and added greatly to my stock of knowledge, by noting their
habits and customs, and conversing with their sages and great men.
I even journeyed one long summer's day to the summit of the most
distant hill, from whence I stretched my eye over many a mile of
terra incognita, and was astonished to find how vast a globe I inhabited.

This rambling propensity strengthened with my years. Books of voyages and travels became my passion, and in devouring their contents
I neglected the regular exercises of the school. How wistfully would I
wander about the pier heads in fine weather, and watch the parting
ships, bound to distant climes. With what longing eyes would I gaze
after their lessening sails, and waft myself in imagination to the ends
of the earth.

Further reading and thinking, though they brought this vague inclination into more reasonable bounds, only served to make it more
decided. I visited various parts of my own country, and had I been
merely a lover of fine scenery, I should have felt little desire to seek
elsewhere its gratification, for on no country have the charms of nature
been more prodigally lavished. Her mighty lakes, like oceans of liquid
silver; her mountains with their bright aerial tints; her valleys teeming
with wild fertility; her tremendous cataracts thundering in their solitudes;
her boundless plains waving with spontaneous verdure; her broad deep
rivers, rolling in solemn silence to the ocean; her trackless forests, where
vegetation puts forth all its magnificence; her skies kindling with the
magic of summer clouds and glorious sunshine—no, never need an

American look beyond his own country for the sublime and beautiful of natural scenery.

But Europe held forth the charms of storied and poetical association. There were to be seen the masterpieces of art, the refinements of highly cultivated society, the quaint peculiarities of ancient and local custom. My native country was full of youthful promise; Europe was rich in the accumulated treasures of age. Her very ruins told the history of times gone by, and every mouldering stone was a chronicle. I longed to wander over the scenes of renowned achievement—to tread as it were in the footsteps of antiquity—to loiter about the ruined castle—to meditate on the falling tower—to escape in short, from the commonplace realities of the present, and lose myself among the shadowy grandeurs of the past.

I had, beside all this, an earnest desire to see the great men of the earth. We have, it is true, our great men in America—not a city but has an ample share of them. I have mingled among them in my time, and been almost withered by the shade into which they cast me; for there is nothing so baleful to a small man as the shade of a great one, particularly the great man of a city. But I was anxious to see the great men of Europe; for I had read in the works of various philosophers, that all animals degenerated in America, and man among the number. A great man of Europe, thought I, must therefore be as superior to a great man of America, as a peak of the Alps to a highland of the Hudson; and in this idea I was confirmed by observing the comparative importance and swelling magnitude of many English travellers among us; who, I was assured, were very little people in their own country.—I will visit this land of wonders, thought I, and see the gigantic race from which I am degenerated.

It has been either my good or evil lot to have my roving passion gratified. I have wandered through different countries and witnessed many of the shifting scenes of life. I cannot say that I have studied them with the eye of a philosopher, but rather with the sauntering gaze with which humble lovers of the picturesque stroll from the window of one print shop to another; caught sometimes by the delineations of beauty, sometimes by the distortions of caricature and sometimes by the loveliness of landscape. As it is the fashion for modern tourists to travel pencil in hand, and bring home their portfolios filled with sketches, I am disposed to get up a few for the entertainment of my friends. When I look over, however, the hints and memorandums I have taken down for the purpose, my heart almost fails me at finding how my idle humour has led me aside from the great objects studied by every regular traveller who would make a book. I fear I shall give equal disappointment with an unlucky landscape painter, who had travelled on the continent, but following the bent of his vagrant inclination, had sketched in nooks and corners and bye places. His sketch book was accordingly crowded with cottages, and landscapes, and obscure ruins; but he had neglected to paint St. Peter's or the Coliseum; the cascade of Terni or the Bay of Naples; and had not a single Glacier or Volcano in his whole collection.

THE VOYAGE

Ships, ships, I will descrie you
            Amidst the main,
I will come and try you
What you are protecting
And projecting,
            What's your end and aim.
One goes abroad for merchandize and trading,
Another stays to keep his country from invading,
A third is coming home with rich and wealthy lading.
            Hallo my fancie, whither wilt thou go?

OLD POEM.

To an American visiting Europe the long voyage he has to make is an excellent preparative. The temporary absence of worldly scenes and employments produces a state of mind peculiarly fitted to receive new and vivid impressions. The vast space of waters, that separates the hemispheres is like a blank page in existence. There is no gradual transition by which as in Europe the features and population of one country blend almost imperceptibly with those of another. From the moment you lose sight of the land you have left, all is vacancy until you step on the opposite shore, and are launched at once into the bustle and novelties of another world.

In travelling by land there is a continuity of scene and a connected succession of persons and incidents, that carry on the story of life, and lessen the effect of absence and separation. We drag, it is true, "a lengthening chain" at each remove of our pilgrimage; but the chain is unbroken—we can trace it back link by link; and we feel that the last still grapples us to home. But a wide sea voyage severs us at once.—It makes us conscious of being cast loose from the secure anchorage of settled life and sent adrift upon a doubtful world. It interposes a gulph, not merely imaginary, but real, between us and our homes—a gulph subject to tempest and fear and uncertainty, rendering distance palpable and return precarious.

Such at least was the case with myself. As I saw the last blue line of my native land fade away like a cloud in the horizon, it seemed as if I had closed one volume of the world and its concerns, and had time for meditation before I opened another. That land too, now vanishing from my view; which contained all that was most dear to me in life; what vicissitudes might occur in it—what changes might take place in me, before I should visit it again.—Who can tell when he sets forth to wander,

11

whither he may be driven by the uncertain currents of existence; or when he may return; or whether it may ever be his lot to revisit the scenes of his childhood?

I said that at sea all is vacancy—I should correct the expression. To one given to day dreaming and fond of losing himself in reveries, a sea voyage is full of subjects for meditation: but then they are the wonders of the deep and of the air, and rather tend to abstract the mind from worldly themes. I delighted to loll over the quarter railing or climb to the main top of a calm day, and muse for hours together, on the tranquil bosom of a summer's sea. To gaze upon the piles of golden clouds just peering above the horizon; fancy them some fairy realms and people them with a creation of my own. To watch the gently undulating billows, rolling their silver volumes as if to die away on those happy shores.

There was a delicious sensation of mingled security and awe with which I looked down from my giddy height on the monsters of the deep at their uncouth gambols. Shoals of porpoises tumbling about the bow of the ship; the grampus slowly heaving his huge form above the surface, or the ravenous shark darting like a spectre through the blue waters. My imagination would conjure up all that I had heard or read of the watery world beneath me. Of the finny herds that roam its fathomless valleys; of the shapeless monsters that lurk among the very foundations of the earth and of those wild phantasms that swell the tales of fishermen and sailors.

Sometimes a distant sail, gliding along the edge of the ocean would be another theme of idle speculation. How interesting this fragment of a world, hastening to rejoin the great mass of existence. What a glorious monument of human invention; which has in a manner triumphed over wind and wave; has brought the ends of the earth into communion; has established an interchange of blessings,—pouring into the sterile regions of the north all the luxuries of the south; has diffused the light of knowledge and the charities of cultivated life, and has thus bound together those scattered portions of the human race, between which nature seemed to have thrown an insurmountable barrier.

We one day descried some shapeless object drifting at a distance. At sea every thing that breaks the monotony of the surrounding expanse attracts attention. It proved to be the mast of a ship that must have been completely wrecked; for there were the remains of handkerchiefs, by which some of the crew had fastened themselves to this spar to prevent their being washed off by the waves. There was no trace by which the name of the ship could be ascertained. The wreck had evidently drifted about for many months: clusters of shell fish had fastened about it; and long sea weeds flaunted at its sides.

But where, thought I, is the crew!—Their struggle has long been over —they have gone down amidst the roar of the tempest—their bones lie whitening among the caverns of the deep. Silence—oblivion, like the waves, have closed over them, and no one can tell the story of their end. What sighs have been wafted after that ship; what prayers offered up at the deserted fireside of home. How often has the mistress, the wife, the mother pored over the daily news to catch some casual intelligence of this rover of the deep. How has expectation darkened into anxiety— anxiety into dread and dread into despair. Alas! not one memento may ever return for love to cherish. All that may ever be known is, that she sailed from her port, "and was never heard of more!"

The sight of this wreck, as usual, gave rise to many dismal anecdotes. This was particularly the case in the evening when the weather, which had hitherto been fair began to look wild and threatening, and gave indications of one of those sudden storms which will sometimes break in upon the serenity of a summer voyage. As we sat round the dull light of a lamp in the cabin, that made the gloom more ghastly, every one had his tale of shipwreck and disaster. I was peculiarly struck with a short one related by the captain.

"As I was once sailing," said he, "in a fine stout ship across the banks of Newfoundland, one of those heavy fogs which prevail in those parts rendered it impossible for us to see far ahead even in the day time; but at night the weather was so thick that we could not distinguish any object at twice the length of the ship. I kept lights at the mast head and a constant watch forward to look out for fishing smacks, which are accustomed to lie at anchor on the banks. The wind was blowing a smacking breeze and we were going at a great rate through the water. Suddenly the watch gave the alarm of 'a sail ahead!'—it was scarcely uttered before we were upon her. She was a small schooner at anchor, with the broad side toward us. The crew were all asleep and had neglected to hoist a light. We struck her just a mid-ships. The force, the size and weight of our vessel bore her down below the waves—we passed over her and were hurried on our course. As the crashing wreck was sinking beneath us I had a glimpse of two or three halfnaked wretches, rushing from her cabin—they just started from their beds to be swallowed shrieking by the waves. I heard their drowning cry mingling with the wind. The blast that bore it to our ears swept us out of all further hearing—I shall never forget that cry!—It was some time before we could put the ship about; she was under such headway. We returned as nearly as we could guess to the place where the smack had anchored. We cruised about for several hours in the dense fog. We fired signal guns and listened if we might hear the halloo of any survivors; but all was silent—we never saw or heard any thing of them more!—"

I confess these stories for a time put an end to all my fine fancies. The storm encreased with the night. The sea was lashed up into tremendous confusion. There was a fearful sullen sound of rushing waves and broken surges. Deep called unto deep. At times the black volume of clouds over head seemed rent asunder by flashes of lightning which quivered along the foaming billows, and made the succeeding darkness doubly terrible. The thunders bellowed over the wild waste of waters and were echoed and prolonged by the mountain waves. As I saw the ship staggering and plunging among these roaring caverns, it seemed miraculous that she regained her balance or preserved her buoyancy. Her yards would dip into the water; her bow was almost buried beneath the waves. Sometimes an impending surge appeared ready to overwhelm her, and nothing but a dextrous movement of the helm preserved her from the shock.

When I retired to my cabin the awful scene still followed me. The whistling of the wind through the rigging sounded like funereal wailings. The creaking of the masts; the straining and groaning of bulk heads as the ship laboured in the weltering sea were frightful. As I heard the waves rushing along the side of the ship and roaring in my very ear, it seemed as if death were raging round this floating prison, seeking for his prey—the mere starting of a nail—the yawning of a seam might give him entrance.

A fine day, however, with a tranquil sea and favouring breeze soon put all these dismal reflections to flight. It is impossible to resist the gladdening influence of fine weather and fair wind at sea. When the ship is decked out in all her canvass, every sail swelled, and careering gaily over the curling waves, how lofty, how gallant she appears—how she seems to lord it over the deep!

I might fill a volume with the reveries of a sea voyage, for with me it is almost a continual reverie—but it is time to get to shore.

It was a fine sunny morning when the thrilling cry of Land! was given from the mast head. None but those who have experienced it can form an idea of the delicious throng of sensations which rush into an American's bosom, when he first comes in sight of Europe. There is a volume of associations with the very name. It is the land of promise, teeming with every thing of which his childhood has heard, or on which his studious years have pondered.

From that time until the moment of arrival it was all feverish excitement. The ships war that prowled like guardian giants along the coast—the headlands of Ireland stretching out into the channel—the Welsh mountains towering into the clouds, all were objects of intense interest. As we sailed up the Mersey I reconnoitered the shores with a telescope. My eye dwelt with delight on neat cottages with their trim shrubberies and green grass plots. I saw the mouldering ruin of an abbey over run with ivy, and the taper spire of a village church rising from the brow of a neighbouring hill—all were characteristic of England.

The tide and wind were so favourable that the ship was enabled to come at once to the pier. It was thronged with people; some idle lookers-on, others eager expectants of friends or relatives. I could distinguish the merchant to whom the ship was consigned. I knew him by his calculating brow and restless air. His hands were thrust into his pockets; he was whistling thoughtfully and walking to and fro, a small space having been accorded him by the crowd in deference to his temporary importance. There were repeated cheerings and salutations interchanged between the shore and the ship, as friends happened to recognize each other. I particularly noticed one young woman of humble dress, but interesting demeanour. She was leaning forward from among the crowd; her eye hurried over the ship as it neared the shore, to catch some wished for countenance. She seemed disappointed and agitated; when I heard a faint voice call her name. It was from a poor sailor who had been ill all the voyage and had excited the sympathy of every one on board. When the weather was fine his messmates had spread a mattress for him on deck in the shade, but of late his illness had so encreased, that he had taken to his hammock, and only breathed a wish that he might see his wife before he died. He had been helped on deck as we came up the river, and was now leaning against the shrouds, with a countenance so wasted, so pale, so ghastly that it was no wonder even the eye of affection did not recognize him. But at the sound of his voice her eye darted on his features—it read at once a whole volume of sorrow—she clasped her hands; uttered a faint shriek and stood wringing them in silent agony.

All now was hurry and bustle. The meetings of acquaintances—the greetings of friends—the consultations of men of business. I alone was solitary and idle. I had no friend to meet, no cheering to receive. I stepped upon the land of my forefathers—but felt that I was a stranger in the land.

ROSCOE

—In the service of mankind to be
A guardian god below; still to employ
The mind's brave ardour in heroic aims,
Such as may raise us o'er the groveling herd,
And make us shine forever—that is life.
                                    THOMSON.

One of the first places to which a stranger is taken in Liverpool is the Athenæum. It is established on a liberal and judicious plan; contains a good library and spacious reading room and is the great literary resort of the place. Go there at what hour you may, you are sure to find it filled with grave looking personages, deeply absorbed in the study of newspapers.

As I was once visiting this haunt of the learned my attention was attracted to a person just entering the room. He was advanced in life, tall, and of a form that might once have been commanding, but it was a little bowed by time—perhaps by care. He had a noble Roman style of countenance; a head that would have pleased a painter; and though some slight furrows on his brow shewed that wasting thought had been busy there, yet his eye still beamed with the fire of a poetic soul. There was something in his whole appearance that indicated a being of a different order from the bustling race around him.

I inquired his name and was informed that it was Roscoe. I drew back with an involuntary feeling of veneration. This then was an Author of celebrity; this was one of those men, whose voices have gone forth to the ends of the earth; with whose minds I have communed even in the solitudes of America. Accustomed as we are in our country to know European writers only by their works, we cannot conceive of them, as of other men, engrossed by trivial or sordid pursuits, and jostling with the crowd of common minds in the dusty paths of life. They pass before our imaginations like superior beings, radiant with the emanations of their genius, and surrounded by a halo of literary glory.

To find, therefore, the elegant historian of the Medici, mingling among the busy sons of traffic at first shocked my poetical ideas; but it is from the very circumstances and situation in which he has been placed, that Mr. Roscoe derives his highest claims to admiration. It is interesting to notice how some minds seem almost to create themselves; springing up under every disadvantage, and working their solitary but irresistible way through a thousand obstacles. Nature seems to delight in disappointing the assiduities of art, with which it would rear legitimate dullness to maturity, and to glory in the vigour and luxuriance of her chance productions. She scatters the seeds of genius to the winds, and though some may perish among the stony places of the world, and some be choked by the thorns and brambles of early adversity, yet others will now and then strike root even in the clefts of the rock, struggle bravely up into sunshine, and spread over their sterile birth place all the beauties of vegetation.

Such has been the case with Mr. Roscoe. Born in a place apparently ungenial to the growth of literary talent; in the very market place of trade; without fortune, family connexions or patronage; self prompted, self sustained and almost self taught, he has conquered every obstacle, achieved his way to eminence, and having become one of the ornaments of the nation, has turned the whole force of his talents and influence to advance and embellish his native town.

Indeed it is this last trait in his character which has given him the greatest interest in my eyes, and induced me particularly to point him out to my countrymen. Eminent as are his literary merits, he is but one among the many distinguished authors of this intellectual nation. They, however, in general live but for their own fame, or their own pleasures. Their private history presents no lesson to the world, or perhaps a humiliating one of human frailty and inconsistency. At best, they are prone to steal away from the bustle and commonplace of busy existence; to indulge in the selfishness of lettered ease, and to revel in scenes of mental but exclusive enjoyment.

Mr. Roscoe on the contrary has claimed none of the accorded privileges of talent. He has shut himself up in no garden of thought nor elysium of fancy; but has gone forth into the highways and thoroughfares of life; he has planted bowers by the wayside for the refreshment of the pilgrim and the sojourner, and has opened pure fountains where the labouring man may turn aside from the dust and heat of the day, and drink of the living streams of knowledge. There is a "daily beauty in his life," on which mankind may meditate and grow better. It exhibits no lofty and almost useless, because inimitable example of excellence; but presents a picture of active yet simple and imitable virtues, which are within every man's reach, but which, unfortunately, are not exercised by many, or this world would be a paradise.

But his private life is peculiarly worthy the attention of the citizens of our young and busy country, where literature and the elegant arts must grow up side by side with the coarser plants of daily necessity; and must depend for their culture, not on the exclusive devotion of time and wealth, nor the quickening rays of titled patronage, but on hours and seasons snatched from the pursuit of worldly interests, by intelligent and public spirited individuals.

He has shown how much may be done for a place in hours of leisure, by one master spirit, and how completely it can give its own impress to surrounding objects. Like his own Lorenzo De Medici, on whom he seems to have fixed his eye as on a pure model of antiquity, he has interwoven the history of his life with the history of his native town, and has made the foundations of its fame the monuments of his virtues. Wherever you go in Liverpool you perceive traces of his footsteps in all that is elegant and liberal. He found the tide of wealth flowing merely in the channels of traffic, he has diverted from it invigorating rills to refresh the gardens of literature. By his own example and constant exertions he has effected that union of commerce and the intellectual pursuits so eloquently recommended in one of his latest writings;* and has practically proved how beautifully they may be brought to harmonize and to benefit each other. The noble institutions for literary and scientific purposes, which reflect such credit on Liverpool, and are giving such an impulse to the public mind, have mostly been originated, and have all been effectively promoted by Mr. Roscoe; and when we consider the rapidly encreasing opulence and magnitude of that town, which promises to vie in commercial importance with the metropolis; it will be perceived that in awakening an ambition of mental improvement among its inhabitants, he has effected a great benefit to the cause of British literature.

In America we know Mr. Roscoe only as the Author—in Liverpool he is spoken of as the Banker, and I was told of his having been unfortunate in business. I could not pity him as I heard some rich men do. I considered him far above the reach of my pity. Those who live only for the world and in the world, may be cast down by the frowns of adversity; but a man like Roscoe is not to be overcome by the reverses of fortune. They do but drive him in upon the resources of his own mind, to the superior society of his own thoughts, which the best of men are apt sometimes to neglect, and to roam abroad in search of less worthy associates. He is independent of the world around him. He lives with antiquity and with posterity. With antiquity, in the sweet communions of studious retirement, and with posterity in the generous aspirings after future renown. The solitude of such a mind is its state of highest enjoyment. It is then visited by those elevated meditations which are the proper aliment of noble souls, and are like manna, sent from heaven in the wilderness of this world.

While my feelings were yet alive on the subject it was my fortune to light on further traces of Mr. Roscoe. I was riding out with a gentleman to view the environs of Liverpool when he turned off through a

*Address on the opening of the Liverpool Institution.

gate into some ornamented grounds. After riding a short distance we came to a spacious mansion of freestone, built in the Grecian style. It was not in the purest taste, yet it had an air of elegance and the situation was delightful. A fine lawn sloped away from it, studded with clumps of trees, so disposed as to break a soft fertile country into a variety of Landscapes. The Mersey was seen winding a broad quiet sheet of water through an expanse of green meadow land, while the Welsh mountains, blending with clouds and melting into distance, bordered the horizon.

This was Roscoe's favourite residence during the days of his prosperity. It had been the seat of elegant hospitality and literary retirement—The house was now silent and deserted. I saw the windows of the study, which looked out upon the soft scenery I have mentioned. The windows were closed—the library was gone. Two or three ill favoured beings were loitering about the place, whom my fancy pictured into retainers of the law. It was like visiting some classic fountain that had once welled its pure waters in a sacred shade, but finding it dry and dusty, with the lizard and the toad brooding over the shattered marbles.

I enquired after the fate of Mr. Roscoe's library which had consisted of scarce and foreign books, from many of which he had drawn the materials for his Italian histories. It had passed under the hammer of the auctioneer and was dispersed about the country. The good people of the vicinity thronged like wreckers to get some part of the noble vessel that had been driven on shore. Did such a scene admit of ludicrous associations, we might imagine something whimsical in this strange irruption into the regions of learning. Pigmies rummaging the armoury of a giant, and contending for the possession of weapons which they could not wield. We might picture to ourselves some knot of speculators debating with calculating brow over the quaint binding and illuminated margin of an obsolete author; or the air of intense but baffled sagacity with which some successful purchaser attempted to dive into the black letter bargain he had secured.

It is a beautiful incident in the story of Mr. Roscoe's misfortunes, and one which cannot fail to interest the studious mind, that the parting with his books seems to have touched upon his tenderest feelings; and to have been the only circumstance that could provoke the notice of his muse. The scholar only knows how dear these silent, yet eloquent companions of pure thoughts and innocent hours become in the season of adversity. When all that is worldly turns to dross around us, these only retain their steady value. When friends grow cold and the converse of intimates languishes into vapid civility and commonplace, these only continue the unaltered countenance of happier days, and cheer us with that true friendship which never deceived hope nor deserted sorrow.

I do not wish to censure, but surely if the people of Liverpool had been properly sensible of what was due to Mr. Roscoe and themselves, his library would never have been sold. Good worldly reasons may doubtless be given for the circumstance, which it would be difficult to combat with others that might seem merely fanciful; but it certainly appears to me such an opportunity as seldom occurs, of cheering a noble mind, struggling under misfortunes, by one of the most delicate but most expressive tokens of public sympathy. It is difficult, however, to estimate a man of genius properly, who is daily before our eyes. He becomes mingled up and confounded with other men. His great qualities lose their novelty and we become too familiar with the common materials which form the basis even of the loftiest character. Some of Mr. Roscoe's townsmen may regard him merely as a man of business; others as a politician; all find him engaged like themselves in ordinary occupations and surpassed, perhaps, by themselves on some points of worldly wisdom. Even that amiable and unostentatious simplicity of character, which gives the nameless grace to real excellence, may cause him to be undervalued by some coarse minds, who do not know that true worth is always void of glare and pretension. But the man of letters who speaks of Liverpool, speaks of it as the residence of Roscoe. The intelligent traveller who visits it, enquires where Roscoe is to be seen. He is the literary land mark of the place, indicating its existence to the distant Scholar. He is like Pompey's column at Alexandria, towering alone in classic dignity.

The following sonnet, addressed by Mr. Roscoe to his books on parting with them, is alluded to in the preceding article. If any thing can add effect to the pure feeling and elevated thought here displayed, it is the conviction, that the whole is no effusion of fancy, but a faithful transcript from the writer's heart.

TO MY BOOKS

As one, who, destined from his friends to part,
Regrets his loss, but hopes again erewhile
To share their converse and enjoy their smile,
And tempers as he may, affliction's dart;

Thus, loved associates, chiefs of elder art,
Teachers of wisdom, who could once beguile
My tedious hours and lighten every toil—
I now resign you; nor with fainting heart;

For pass a few short years, or days, or hours,
And happier seasons may their dawn unfold,
And all your sacred fellowship restore;
When, freed from earth, unlimited its powers,
Mind shall with mind direct communion hold,
And kindred spirits meet to part no more.

THE WIFE

The treasures of the deep are not so precious
As are the conceal'd comforts of a man
Lock'd up in woman's love. I scent the air
Of blessings, when I come but near the house.
What a delicious breath marriage sends forth,
The violet bed's not sweeter!

MIDDLETON.

I have often had occasion to remark the fortitude with which women sustain the most overwhelming reverses of fortune. Those disasters which break down the spirits of a man, and prostrate him in the dust, seem to call forth all the energies of the softer sex, and give such intrepidity and elevation to their character, that at times it approaches to sublimity. Nothing can be more touching than to behold a soft and tender female, who had been all weakness and dependence, and alive to every trivial roughness while treading the prosperous paths of life, suddenly rising in mental force, to be the comforter and supporter of her husband under misfortune, and abiding, with unshrinking firmness, the bitterest blasts of adversity.

As the vine which has long twined its graceful foliage about the oak, and been lifted by it into sunshine, will, when the hardy plant is rifted by the thunderbolt, cling round it with its carressing tendrils and bind up its shattered boughs; so is it beautifully ordered by providence, that woman, who is the mere dependent and ornament of man in his happier hours, should be his stay and solace when smitten with sudden calamity, winding herself into the rugged recesses of his nature; tenderly supporting the drooping head, and binding up the broken heart.

I was once congratulating a friend, who had around him a blooming family knit together in the strongest affection. "I can wish you no better lot," said he, with enthusiasm, "than to have a wife and children. If you are prosperous, there they are to share your prosperity; and if otherwise, there they are to comfort you.—" And indeed I have observed that a married man falling into misfortune, is more apt to retrieve his situation in the world than a single one; partly because he is more stimulated to exertion by the necessities of the helpless and beloved beings who depend upon him for subsistence; but chiefly because his spirits are soothed and relieved by domestic endearments, and his self respect kept alive by finding, that though all abroad is darkness and humiliation, yet there is still a little world of love at home, of which he is the monarch. Whereas a single man is apt to run to waste and self neglect; to fancy himself lonely and abandoned, and his heart to fall to ruin like some deserted mansion for want of an inhabitant.

These observations call to mind a little domestic story, of which I was once a witness. My intimate friend Leslie had married a beautiful and accomplished girl, who had been brought up in the midst of fashionable life. She had, it is true, no fortune, but that of my friend was ample and he delighted in the anticipation of indulging her in every elegant pursuit; and administering to those delicate tastes and fancies, that spread a kind of witchery about the sex—"her life," said he, "shall be like a fairy tale."

The very difference in their characters produced an harmonious combination. He was of a romantic and somewhat serious cast; she was all life and gladness. I have often noticed the mute rapture with which he would gaze upon her in company, of which her sprightly powers made her the delight; and how in the midst of applause, her eye would still turn to him, as if there alone she sought favour and acceptance. When leaning on his arm her slender form contrasted finely with his tall, manly person. The fond confiding air with which she looked up to him, seemed to call forth a flush of triumphant pride and cherishing tenderness; as if he doted on his lovely burthen, for its very helpless-ness.—Never did a couple set forward on the flowery path of early and well suited marriage, with a fairer prospect of felicity.

It was the misfortune of my friend, however, to have embarked his property in large speculations, and he had not been married many months, when, by a succession of sudden disasters, it was swept from him, and he found himself reduced almost to penury. For a time he kept his situation to himself and went about with a haggard countenance and a breaking heart. His life was but a protracted agony, and what rendered it more insupportable was the necessity of keeping up a smile in the presence of his wife; for he could not bring himself to overwhelm her with the news. She saw, however, with the quick eyes of affection, that all was not well with him. She marked his altered looks and stifled sighs, and was not to be deceived by his sickly and vapid attempts at cheerfulness. She tasked all her sprightly powers and tender blandish-ments to win him back to happiness; but she only drove the arrow deeper into his soul—the more he saw cause to love her the more torturing was the thought that he was soon to make her wretched. A little while, thought he, and the smile will vanish from that cheek— the song will die away from those lips—the lustre of those eyes will be quenched with sorrow; and the happy heart which now beats lightly in that bosom, will be weighed down like mine by the cares and miseries of the world.

At length he came to me, one day, and related his whole situation in a tone of the deepest despair. When I had heard him through I enquired, "Does your wife know all this?"—at the question he burst into an agony of tears—"For God's sake!" cried he, "if you have any pity on me don't mention my wife—it is the thought of her that drives me almost to madness!"

"And why not?" said I, "she must know it sooner or later: you cannot keep it long from her, and the intelligence may break upon her in a more startling manner than if imparted by yourself; for the accents of those we love soften the harshest tidings. Besides you are depriving yourself of the comforts of her sympathy and not merely that, but also endangering the only bond that can keep hearts together, an unreserved community of thought and feeling. She will soon perceive that something is secretly preying upon your mind, and true love will not brook reserve: it feels undervalued and outraged when even the sorrows of those it loves are concealed from it."

"Oh but my friend! to think what a blow I am to give to all her future prospects—how I am to strike her very soul to the earth, by telling her that her husband is a beggar!—That she is to forego all the elegancies of life—all the pleasures of society—to shrink with me into indigence and obscurity!—To tell her that I have dragged her down from the sphere in which she might have continued to move in constant brightness—the light of every eye—the admiration of every heart!——How can she bear poverty!—she has been brought up in all the refinements of opulence.—How can she bear neglect!—she has been the idol of society—oh, it will break her heart!—it will break her heart!—"

I saw his grief was eloquent and I let it have its flow, for sorrow relieves itself by words. When his paroxysm had subsided and he had relapsed into moody silence, I resumed the subject gently, and urged him to break his situation at once to his wife. He shook his head mournfully, but positively.

"But how are you to keep it from her? It is necessary she should know it, that you may take the steps proper to the alteration of your circumstances. You must change your style of living——nay," observing a pang to pass across his countenance—"don't let that afflict you. I am sure you have never placed your happiness in outward shew—you have yet friends, warm friends, who will not think the worse of you for being less splendidly lodged;—and surely it does not require a palace to be happy with Mary—"

"I could be happy with her," cried he convulsively, "in a hovel!—I could go down with her into poverty and the dust!—I could—I could ——God bless her!—God bless her!—" cried he, bursting into a transport of grief and tenderness.

"And believe me my friend," said I stepping up and grasping him warmly by the hand—"believe me, she can be the same with you. Aye, more—it will be a source of pride and triumph to her—it will call forth all the latent energies and fervent sympathies of her nature; for she will rejoice to prove that she loves you for yourself. There is in every true woman's heart a spark of heavenly fire which lies dormant in the broad daylight of prosperity; but which kindles up, and beams and blazes in the dark hour of adversity. No man knows what the wife of his bosom is—no man knows what a ministering angel she is—until he has gone with her through the fiery trials of this world."

There was something in the earnestness of my manner, and the figurative style of my language that caught the excited imagination of Leslie. I knew the auditor I had to deal with; and following up the impression I had made, I finished by persuading him to go home and unburthen his sad heart to his wife.

I must confess, notwithstanding all I had said, I felt some little solicitude for the result. Who can calculate on the fortitude of one whose whole life has been a round of pleasures?—Her gay spirits might revolt at the dark downward path of low humility suddenly pointed out before her, and might cling to the sunny regions in which they had hitherto revelled. Besides, ruin in fashionable life is accompanied by so many galling mortifications to which in other ranks it is a stranger—in short, I could not meet Leslie the next morning without trepidation. He had made the disclosure.

—"And how did she bear it?"

"Like an angel! It seemed rather to be a relief to her mind, for she threw her arms round my neck, and asked if this was all that had lately made me unhappy—but, poor girl,"—added he, "she cannot realize the change we must undergo. She has no idea of poverty but in the abstract—she has only read of it in poetry, where it is allied to love. She feels as yet no privation—she suffers no loss of accustomed conveniences nor elegancies. When we come practically to experience its sordid cares, its paltry wants, its petty humiliations—then will be the real trial."

"But," said I, "now that you have got over the severest task, that of breaking it to her, the sooner you let the world into the secret the better. The disclosure may be mortifying, but then it is a single misery and soon over, whereas you otherwise suffer it in anticipation, every hour in the day. It is not poverty so much as pretence, that harrasses a ruined man. The struggle between a proud mind and an empty purse—the keeping up a hollow shew that must soon come to an end. Have the courage to appear poor and you disarm poverty of its sharpest sting."—On this point I found Leslie perfectly prepared. He had no false pride himself, and as to his wife she was only anxious to conform to their altered fortunes.

Some days afterwards he called upon me in the evening. He had disposed of his dwelling house and taken a small cottage in the country, a few miles from town. He had been busied all day in sending out furniture. The new establishment required few articles, and those of the simplest kind. All the splendid furniture of his late residence had been sold excepting his wife's Harp. That, he said, was too closely associated with the idea of herself—it belonged to the little story of their loves—for some of the sweetest moments of their courtship were those when he had leant over that instrument and listened to the melting tones of her voice.—I could not but smile at this instance of romantic gallantry in a doting husband.

He was now going out to the cottage, where his wife had been all day, superintending its arrangement. My feelings had become strongly interested in the progress of this family story and as it was a fine evening I offered to accompany him.

He was wearied with the fatigues of the day, and as we walked out, fell into a fit of gloomy musing.

"Poor Mary!" at length broke with a heavy sigh from his lips.

"And what of her," asked I, "has any thing happened to her?"

"What," said he, darting an impatient glance, "is it nothing to be reduced to this paltry situation—to be caged in a miserable cottage—to be obliged to toil almost in the menial concerns of her wretched habitation?"

"Has she then repined at the change?"

"Repined!—she has been nothing but sweetness and good humour. Indeed she seems in better spirits than I have ever known her—she has been to me all love and tenderness and comfort!"

"Admirable girl!" exclaimed I. "You call yourself poor my friend; you never were so rich—you never knew the boundless treasures of excellence you possessed in that woman."

"Oh, but my friend—if this first meeting at the cottage were over—I think I could then be comfortable. But this is her first day of real experience. She has been introduced into our humble dwelling. She has been employed all day in arranging its miserable equipments. She has for the first time known the fatigues of domestic employment—She has for the first time looked around her on a home destitute of every thing elegant,—almost of every thing convenient, and may now be sitting down exhausted and spiritless, brooding over a prospect of future poverty."

There was a degree of probability in this picture that I could not gainsay—so we walked on in silence.

After turning from the main road up a narrow lane so thickly shaded by forest trees as to give it a complete air of seclusion, we came in sight of the cottage. It was humble enough in its appearance for the most pastoral poet; and yet it had a pleasing rural look. A wild vine had over run one end with a profusion of foliage—a few trees threw their branches gracefully over it, and I observed several pots of flowers taste-fully disposed about the door and on the grass plot in front. A small wicket gate opened upon a foot path that wound through some shrubbery to the door. Just as we approached we heard the sound of music.— Leslie grasped my arm—we paused and listened. It was Mary's voice singing, in a style of the most touching simplicity, a little air of which her husband was peculiarly fond.

I felt Leslie's hand tremble on my arm. He stepped forward to hear more distinctly—His step made a noise on the gravel walk—a bright beautiful face glanced out at the window and vanished—a light foot-step was heard, and Mary came tripping forth to meet us. She was in a pretty, rural dress of white; a few wild flowers were twisted in her fine hair; a fresh bloom was on her cheek; her whole countenance beamed with smiles—I had never seen her look so lovely.

"My dear George," cried she, "I am so glad you are come—I've been watching and watching for you; and running down the lane, and looking out for you. I've set out a table under a beautiful tree behind the cottage —and I've been gathering some of the most delicious strawberries, for I know you are fond of them—and we have such excellent cream—and every thing is so sweet and still here—Oh!" said she, putting her arm within his, and looking up brightly in his face—"oh, we shall be so happy!"

Poor Leslie was overcome—He caught her to his bosom—he folded his arms round her—he kissed her again and again—he could not speak, but the tears gushed into his eyes—And he has often assured me that though the world has since gone prosperously with him, and his life has, indeed, been a happy one; yet never has he experienced a moment of more exquisite felicity.

RIP VAN WINKLE

The following Tale was found among the papers of the late Diedrich Knickerbocker, an old gentleman of New York, who was very curious in the Dutch history of the province, and the manners of the descendants from its primitive settlers. His historical researches, however, did not lie so much among books, as among men; for the former are lamentably scanty on his favourite topics; whereas he found the old burghers, and still more, their wives, rich in that legendary lore so invaluable to true history. Whenever, therefore, he happened upon a genuine Dutch family, snugly shut up in its low roofed farm house, under a spreading sycamore, he looked upon it as a little clasped volume of black letter, and studied it with the zeal of a bookworm.

The result of all these researches was a history of the province, during the reign of the Dutch governors, which he published some years since. There have been various opinions as to the literary character of his work and, to tell the truth, it is not a whit better than it should be. Its chief merit is its scrupulous accuracy, which indeed was a little questioned on its first appearance, but has since been completely established; and it is now admitted into all historical collections as a book of unquestionable authority.

The old gentleman died shortly after the publication of his work, and now that he is dead and gone, it cannot do much harm to his memory to say that his time might have been much better employed in weightier labours. He, however, was apt to ride his hobby his own way; and though it did now and then kick up the dust a little in the eyes of his neighbours, and grieve the spirit of some friends for whom he felt the truest deference and affection; yet his errors and follies are remembered "more in sorrow than in anger," and it begins to be suspected that he never intended to injure or offend. But however his memory may be appreciated by criticks, it is still held dear by many folk whose good opinion is well worth having; particularly by certain biscuit bakers, who have gone so far as to imprint his likeness on their new year cakes, and have thus given him a chance for immortality, almost equal to being stamped on a Waterloo medal, or a Queen Anne's farthing.

RIP VAN WINKLE

A Posthumous Writing of Diedrich Knickerbocker

By Woden, God of Saxons,
From whence comes Wensday, that is Wodensday,
Truth is a thing that ever I will keep
Unto thylke day in which I creep into
My sepulchre—

CARTWRIGHT.

Whoever has made a voyage up the Hudson must remember the Kaatskill mountains. They are a dismembered branch of the great Appalachian family, and are seen away to the west of the river swelling up to noble height and lording it over the surrounding country. Every change of season, every change of weather, indeed every hour of the day, produces some change in the magical hues and shapes of these mountains, and they are regarded by all the good wives far and near as perfect barometers. When the weather is fair and settled they are clothed in blue and purple, and print their bold outlines on the clear evening sky; but sometimes, when the rest of the landscape is cloudless, they will gather a hood of grey vapours about their summits, which, in the last rays of the setting sun, will glow and light up like a crown of glory.

At the foot of these fairy mountains the voyager may have descried the light smoke curling up from a village, whose shingle roofs gleam among the trees, just where the blue tints of the upland melt away into the fresh green of the nearer landscape. It is a little village of great antiquity, having been founded by some of the Dutch colonists in the early times of the province, just about the beginning of the government of the good Peter Stuyvesant, (may he rest in peace!) and there were some of the houses of the original settlers standing within a few years; built of small yellow bricks brought from Holland, having latticed windows and gable fronts, surmounted with weathercocks.

In that same village, and in one of these very houses (which to tell the precise truth was sadly time worn and weather beaten) there lived many years since, while the country was yet a province of Great Britain, a simple good natured fellow of the name of Rip Van Winkle. He was a descendant of the Van Winkles who figured so gallantly in the chivalrous days of Peter Stuyvesant, and accompanied him to the siege of Fort Christina. He inherited, however, but little of the martial character of his ancestors. I have observed that he was a simple good natured man; he was moreover a kind neighbour, and an obedient, henpecked husband. Indeed to the latter circumstance might be owing that meekness of spirit which gained him such universal popularity; for those men are most apt to be obsequious and conciliating abroad, who are under the discipline of shrews at home. Their tempers doubtless are rendered pliant and malleable in the fiery furnace of domestic tribulation, and a curtain lecture is worth all the sermons in the world for teaching the virtues of patience and long suffering. A termagant wife may therefore in some respects be considered a tolerable blessing—and if so, Rip Van Winkle was thrice blessed.

Certain it is that he was a great favourite among all the good wives of the village, who as usual with the amiable sex, took his part in all family squabbles, and never failed, whenever they talked those matters over in their evening gossippings, to lay all the blame on Dame Van Winkle. The children of the village too would shout with joy whenever he approached. He assisted at their sports, made their play things, taught them to fly kites and shoot marbles, and told them long stories of ghosts, witches and Indians. Whenever he went dodging about the village he was surrounded by a troop of them hanging on his skirts, clambering on his back and playing a thousand tricks on him with impunity; and not a dog would bark at him throughout the neighbourhood.

The great error in Rip's composition was an insuperable aversion to all kinds of profitable labour. It could not be from the want of assiduity or perseverance; for he would sit on a wet rock, with a rod as long and heavy as a Tartar's lance, and fish all day without a murmur, even though he should not be encouraged by a single nibble. He would carry a fowling piece on his shoulder for hours together, trudging through woods, and swamps and up hill and down dale, to shoot a few squirrels or wild pigeons; he would never refuse to assist a neighbour even in the roughest toil, and was a foremost man at all country frolicks for husking Indian corn, or building stone fences; the women of the village too used to employ him to run their errands and to do such little odd jobs as their less obliging husbands would not do for them— in a word Rip was ready to attend to any body's business but his own; but as to doing family duty, and keeping his farm in order, he found it impossible.

In fact he declared it was of no use to work on his farm; it was the most pestilent little piece of ground in the whole country; every thing about it went wrong and would go wrong in spite of him. His fences were continually falling to pieces; his cow would either go astray or get among the cabbages, weeds were sure to grow quicker in his fields than any where else; the rain always made a point of setting in just as he had some outdoor work to do. So that though his patrimonial estate had dwindled away under his management, acre by acre until there was little more left than a mere patch of Indian corn and potatoes, yet it was the worst conditioned farm in the neighbourhood.

His children too were as ragged and wild as if they belonged to nobody. His son Rip, an urchin begotten in his own likeness, promised to inherit the habits with the old clothes of his father. He was generally seen trooping like a colt at his mother's heels, equipped in a pair of his father's cast off galligaskins, which he had much ado to hold up with one hand, as a fine lady does her train in bad weather.

Rip Van Winkle, however, was one of those happy mortals of foolish, well oiled dispositions, who take the world easy, eat white bread or brown, whichever can be got with least thought or trouble, and would rather starve on a penny than work for a pound. If left to himself, he would have whistled life away in perfect contentment, but his wife kept continually dinning in his ears about his idleness, his carelessness and the ruin he was bringing on his family. Morning noon and night her tongue was incessantly going, and every thing he said or did was sure to produce a torrent of household eloquence. Rip had but one way of replying to all lectures of the kind, and that by frequent use had grown into a habit. He shrugged his shoulders, shook his head, cast up his eyes, but said nothing. This, however, always provoked a fresh volley from his wife, so that he was fain to draw off his forces and take to the outside of the house—the only side which in truth belongs to a hen-pecked husband.

Rip's sole domestic adherent was his dog Wolf who was as much henpecked as his master, for Dame Van Winkle regarded them as companions in idleness, and even looked upon Wolf with an evil eye as the cause of his master's going so often astray. True it is, in all points of spirit befitting an honourable dog, he was as courageous an animal as ever scoured the woods—but what courage can withstand the ever during and all besetting terrors of a woman's tongue? The moment Wolf entered the house his crest fell, his tail drooped to the ground or curled between his legs, he sneaked about with a gallows air, casting many a sidelong glance at Dame Van Winkle, and at the least flourish of a broomstick or ladle he would fly to the door with yelping precipitation.

Times grew worse and worse with Rip Van Winkle as years of matrimony rolled on; a tart temper never mellows with age, and a sharp tongue is the only edged tool that grows keener with constant use. For a long while he used to console himself when driven from home, by frequenting a kind of perpetual club of the sages, philosophers and other idle personages of the village which held its sessions on a bench before a small inn, designated by a rubicund portrait of his majesty George the Third. Here they used to sit in the shade, through a long lazy summer's day, talking listlessly over village gossip, or telling endless sleepy stories about nothing. But it would have been worth any statesman's money to have heard the profound discussions that sometimes took place, when by chance an old newspaper fell into their hands from some passing traveller. How solemnly they would listen to the contents as drawled out by Derrick Van Bummel the schoolmaster, a dapper, learned little man, who was not to be daunted by the most gigantic word in the dictionary; and how sagely they would deliberate upon public events some months after they had taken place.

The opinions of this junto were completely controlled by Nicholaus Vedder, a patriarch of the village, and landlord of the inn, at the door of which he took his seat from morning till night, just moving sufficiently to avoid the sun and keep in the shade of a large tree; so that the neighbours could tell the hour by his movements as accurately as by a sun dial. It is true he was rarely heard to speak, but smoked his pipe incessantly. His adherents, however (for every great man has his adherents), perfectly understood him and knew how to gather his opinions. When any thing that was read or related displeased him, he was observed to smoke his pipe vehemently and to send forth short, frequent and angry puffs; but when pleased he would inhale the smoke slowly and tranquilly and emit it in light and placid clouds, and sometimes taking the pipe from his mouth and letting the fragrant vapour curl about his nose, would gravely nod his head in token of perfect approbation.

From even this strong hold the unlucky Rip was at length routed by his termagant wife who would suddenly break in upon the tranquility of the assemblage and call the members all to naught; nor was that august personage Nicholaus Vedder himself sacred from the daring tongue of this terrible virago, who charged him outright with encouraging her husband in habits of idleness.

Poor Rip was at last reduced almost to despair; and his only alternative to escape from the labour of the farm and the clamour of his wife, was to take gun in hand and stroll away into the woods. Here he would sometimes seat himself at the foot of a tree and share the contents of his wallet with Wolf, with whom he sympathised as a fellow sufferer in persecution. "Poor Wolf," he would say, "thy mistress leads thee a dog's life of it, but never mind my lad, whilst I live thou shalt never want a friend to stand by thee!" Wolf would wag his tail, look wistfully in his master's face, and if dogs can feel pity I verily believe he reciprocated the sentiment with all his heart.

In a long ramble of the kind on a fine autumnal day, Rip had unconsciously scrambled to one of the highest parts of the Kaatskill mountains. He was after his favourite sport of squirrel shooting and the still solitudes had echoed and re-echoed with the reports of his gun. Panting and fatigued he threw himself, late in the afternoon, on a green knoll, covered with mountain herbage, that crowned the brow of a precipice. From an opening between the trees he could overlook all the lower country for many a mile of rich woodland. He saw at a distance the lordly Hudson, far, far below him, moving on its silent but majestic course, with the reflection of a purple cloud, or the sail of a lagging bark here and there sleeping on its glassy bosom, and at last losing itself in the blue highlands.

On the other side he looked down into a deep mountain glen, wild, lonely and shagged, the bottom filled with fragments from the impending cliffs and scarcely lighted by the reflected rays of the setting sun. For some time Rip lay musing on this scene, evening was gradually advancing, the mountains began to throw their long blue shadows over the valleys, he saw that it would be dark, long before he could reach the village, and he heaved a heavy sigh when he thought of encountering the terrors of Dame Van Winkle.

As he was about to descend he heard a voice from a distance hallooing "Rip Van Winkle! Rip Van Winkle!" He looked around, but could see nothing but a crow winging its solitary flight across the mountain. He thought his fancy must have deceived him and turned again to descend, which he heard the same cry ring through the still evening air: "Rip Van Winkle! Rip Van Winkle!"—at the same time Wolf bristled up his back and giving a low growl, skulked to his master's side, looking fearfully down into the glen. Rip now felt a vague apprehension stealing over him; he looked anxiously in the same direction and perceived a strange figure slowly toiling up the rocks and bending under the weight of something he carried on his back. He was surprised to see any human being in this lonely and unfrequented place, but supposing it to be some one of the neighbourhood in need of his assistance he hastened down to yield it.

On nearer approach he was still more surprised at the singularity of the stranger's appearance. He was a short, square built old fellow, with thick bushy hair and a grizzled beard. His dress was of the antique Dutch fashion, a cloth jerkin strapped round the waist, several pair of breeches, the outer one of ample volume decorated with rows of buttons down the sides and bunches at the knees. He bore on his shoulder a stout keg that seemed full of liquor, and made signs for Rip to approach and assist him with the load. Though rather shy and distrustful of this new acquaintance Rip complied with his usual alacrity, and mutually relieving each other they clambered up a narrow gully apparently the dry bed of a mountain torrent. As they ascended Rip every now and then heard long rolling peals like distant thunder, that seemed to issue out of a deep ravine or rather cleft between lofty rocks, toward which their rugged path conducted. He paused for an instant, but supposing it to be the muttering of one of those transient thunder showers which often take place in mountain heights, he proceeded. Passing through the ravine they came to a hollow like a small amphitheatre, surrounded by perpendicular precipices, over the brinks of which impending trees shot their branches, so that you only caught glimpses of the azure sky and the bright evening cloud. During the whole time Rip and his companion had laboured on in silence, for though the former marvelled greatly what could be the object of carrying a keg of liquor up this wild mountain, yet there was something strange and incomprehensible about the unknown, that inspired awe and checked familiarity.

On entering the amphitheatre new objects of wonder presented themselves. On a level spot in the centre was a company of odd looking personages playing at ninepins. They were dressed in a quaint outlandish fashion—some wore short doublets, others jerkins with long knives in their belts and most of them had enormous breeches of similar style with that of the guide's. Their visages too were peculiar. One had a large head, broad face and small piggish eyes. The face of another seemed to consist entirely of nose, and was surmounted by a white sugarloaf hat, set off with a little red cock's tail. They all had beards of various shapes and colours. There was one who seemed to be the Commander. He was a stout old gentleman, with a weatherbeaten countenance. He wore a laced doublet, broad belt and hanger, high crowned hat and feather, red stockings and high heel'd shoes with roses in them. The whole group reminded Rip of the figures in an old Flemish painting, in the parlour of Dominie Van Schaick the village parson, and which had been brought over from Holland at the time of the settlement.

What seemed particularly odd to Rip was, that though these folks were evidently amusing themselves, yet they maintained the gravest faces, the most mysterious silence, and were, withal, the most melancholy party of pleasure he had ever witnessed. Nothing interrupted the stillness of the scene, but the noise of the balls, which, whenever they were rolled, echoed along the mountains like rumbling peals of thunder.

As Rip and his companion approached them they suddenly desisted from their play and stared at him with such fixed statue like gaze, and such strange uncouth, lack lustre countenances, that his heart turned within him, and his knees smote together. His companion now emptied the contents of the keg into large flagons and made signs to him to wait upon the company. He obeyed with fear and trembling; they quaffed the liquor in profound silence and then returned to their game.

By degrees Rip's awe and apprehension subsided. He even ventured, when no eye was fixed upon him, to taste the beverage, which he found had much of the flavour of excellent hollands. He was naturally a thirsty soul and was soon tempted to repeat the draught. One taste provoked another, and he reiterated his visits to the flagon so often that at length his senses were overpowered, his eyes swam in his head—his head gradually declined and he fell into a deep sleep.

On awaking he found himself on the green knoll from whence he had first seen the old man of the glen. He rubbed his eyes—it was a bright, sunny morning. The birds were hopping and twittering among the bushes, and the eagle was wheeling aloft and breasting the pure mountain breeze. "Surely," thought Rip, "I have not slept here all night." He recalled the occurrences before he fell asleep. The strange man with a keg of liquor—the mountain ravine—the wild retreat among the rocks—the woe begone party at ninepins—the flagon—"ah! that flagon! that wicked flagon!" thought Rip—"what excuse shall I make to Dame Van Winkle?"

He looked round for his gun, but in place of the clean well oiled fowling piece he found an old firelock lying by him, the barrel encrusted with rust; the lock falling off and the stock worm eaten. He now suspected that the grave roysters of the mountain had put a trick upon him, and having dosed him with liquor, had robbed him of his gun. Wolf too had disappeared, but he might have strayed away after a squirrel or partridge. He whistled after him and shouted his name—but all in vain; the echoes repeated his whistle and shout, but no dog was to be seen.

He determined to revisit the scene of the last evening's gambol, and if he met with any of the party, to demand his dog and gun. As he arose to walk he found himself stiff in the joints and wanting in his usual activity. "These mountain beds do not agree with me," thought Rip, "and if this frolick should lay me up with a fit of the rheumatism, I shall have a blessed time with Dame Van Winkle." With some difficulty he got down into the glen; he found the gully up which he and his companion had ascended the preceding evening, but to his astonishment a mountain stream was now foaming down it; leaping from rock to rock, and filling the glen with babbling murmurs. He, however, made shift to scramble up its sides working his toilsome way through thickets of birch, sassafras and witch hazel, and sometimes tripped up or entangled by the wild grape vines that twisted their coils and tendrils from tree to tree, and spread a kind of net work in his path.

At length he reached to where the ravine had opened through the cliffs, to the amphitheatre—but no traces of such opening remained. The rocks presented a high impenetrable wall over which the torrent came tumbling in a sheet of feathery foam, and fell into a broad deep basin black from the shadows of the surrounding forest. Here then poor Rip was brought to a stand. He again called and whistled after his dog—

he was only answered by the cawing of a flock of idle crows, sporting high in air about a dry tree that overhung a sunny precipice; and who, secure in their elevation seemed to look down and scoff at the poor man's perplexities.

What was to be done? The morning was passing away and Rip felt famished for want of his breakfast. He grieved to give up his dog and gun; he dreaded to meet his wife; but it would not do to starve among the mountains. He shook his head, shouldered the rusty fire lock and with a heart full of trouble and anxiety, turned his steps homeward.

As he approached the village he met a number of people, but none whom he knew, which somewhat surprised him, for he had thought himself acquainted with every one in the country round. Their dress too was of a different fashion from that to which he was accustomed. They all stared at him with equal marks of surprise, and whenever they cast their eyes upon him, invariably stroked their chins. The constant recurrence of this gesture induced Rip involuntarily to do the same, when to his astonishment he found his beard had grown a foot long!

He had now entered the skirts of the village. A troop of strange children ran at his heels, hooting after him and pointing at his grey beard. The dogs too, not one of which he recognized for an old acquaintance, barked at him as he passed. The very village was altered —it was larger and more populous. There were rows of houses which he had never seen before, and those which had been his familiar haunts had disappeared. Strange names were over the doors—strange faces at the windows—every thing was strange. His mind now misgave him; he began to doubt whether both he and the world around him were not bewitched. Surely this was his native village which he had left but the day before. There stood the Kaatskill mountains—there ran the silver Hudson at a distance—there was every hill and dale precisely as it had always been—Rip was sorely perplexed—"That flagon last night," thought he, "has addled my poor head sadly!"

It was with some difficulty that he found the way to his own house, which he approached with silent awe, expecting every moment to hear the shrill voice of Dame Van Winkle. He found the house gone to decay—the roof fallen in, the windows shattered and the doors off the hinges. A half starved dog that looked like Wolf was skulking about it. Rip called him by name but the cur snarled, shewed his teeth and passed on. This was an unkind cut indeed—"My very dog," sighed poor Rip, "has forgotten me!"

He entered the house, which, to tell the truth, Dame Van Winkle had always kept in neat order. It was empty, forlorn and apparently abandoned. This desolateness overcame all his connubial fears—he called loudly for his wife and children—the lonely chambers rung for a moment with his voice, and then all again was silence.

He now hurried forth and hastened to his old resort, the village inn—but it too was gone. A large, rickety wooden building stood in its place, with great gaping windows, some of them broken, and mended with old hats and petticoats, and over the door was printed "The Union Hotel, by Jonathan Doolittle." Instead of the great tree, that used to shelter the quiet little Dutch inn of yore, there now was reared a tall naked pole with something on top that looked like a red night cap, and from it was fluttering a flag on which was a singular assemblage of stars and stripes—all this was strange and incomprehensible. He recognized on the sign, however, the ruby face of King George under which he had smoked so many a peaceful pipe, but even this was singularly metamorphosed. The red coat was changed for one of blue and buff; a sword was held in the hand instead of a sceptre; the head was decorated with a cocked hat, and underneath was printed in large characters GENERAL WASHINGTON.

There was as usual a crowd of folk about the door; but none that Rip recollected. The very character of the people seemed changed. There was a busy, bustling disputatious tone about it, instead of the accustomed phlegm and drowsy tranquility. He looked in vain for the sage Nicholaus Vedder with his broad face, double chin and fair long pipe, uttering clouds of tobacco smoke instead of idle speeches. Or Van Bummel the schoolmaster doling forth the contents of an ancient newspaper. In place of these a lean bilious looking fellow with his pockets full of hand bills, was haranguing vehemently about rights of citizens—elections—members of Congress—liberty—Bunker's hill—heroes of seventy six—and other words which were a perfect babylonish jargon to the bewildered Van Winkle.

The appearance of Rip with his long grizzled beard, his rusty fowling piece his uncouth dress and an army of women and children at his heels soon attracted the attention of the tavern politicians. They crowded around him eying him from head to foot, with great curiosity. The orator bustled up to him, and drawing him partly aside, enquired "on which side he voted?"—Rip stared in vacant stupidity. Another short but busy little fellow, pulled him by the arm and rising on tiptoe, enquired in his ear "whether he was Federal or Democrat?"—Rip was equally at a loss to comprehend the question—when a knowing, self important old gentleman, in a sharp cocked hat, made his way through the crowd, putting them to the right and left with his elbows as he passed, and planting himself before Van Winkle, with one arm akimbo, the other resting on his cane, his keen eyes and sharp hat penetrating as it were into his very soul, demanded in an austere tone—"what brought him to the election with a gun on his shoulder and a mob at his heels, and whether he meant to breed a riot in the village?"—"Alas gentlemen," cried Rip, somewhat dismayed, "I am a poor quiet man, a native of the place, and a loyal subject of the King—God bless him!"

Here a general shout burst from the byestanders—"A tory! a tory! a spy! a Refugee! hustle him! away with him!"—It was with great difficulty that the self important man in the cocked hat restored order; and having assumed a ten fold austerity of brow demanded again of the unknown culprit, what he came there for and whom he was seeking. The poor man humbly assured him that he meant no harm; but merely came there in search of some of his neighbours, who used to keep about the tavern.

"—Well—who are they?—name them."

Rip bethought himself a moment and enquired, "Where's Nicholaus Vedder?"

There was a silence for a little while, when an old man replied, in a thin, piping voice, "Nicholaus Vedder? why he is dead and gone these eighteen years! There was a wooden tombstone in the church yard that used to tell all about him, but that's rotted and gone too."

"Where's Brom Dutcher?"

"Oh he went off to the army in the beginning of the war; some say he was killed at the storming of Stoney Point—others say he was drowned in a squall at the foot of Antony's Nose—I don't know—he never came back again."

"Where's Van Bummel the schoolmaster?"

"He went off to the wars too—was a great militia general, and is now in Congress."

Rip's heart died away at hearing of these sad changes in his home and friends, and finding himself thus alone in the world—every answer puzzled him too by treating of such enormous lapses of time and of matters which he could not understand—war—Congress, Stoney Point— he had no courage to ask after any more friends, but cried out in despair, "Does nobody here know Rip Van Winkle?"

"Oh. Rip Van Winkle?" exclaimed two or three—"oh to be sure!— that's Rip Van Winkle—yonder—leaning against the tree."

Rip looked and beheld a precise counterpart of himself, as he went up the mountain: apparently as lazy and certainly as ragged! The poor fellow was now completely confounded. He doubted his own identity, and whether he was himself or another man. In the midst of his bewilderment the man in the cocked hat demanded who he was,— what was his name?

"God knows," exclaimed he, at his wit's end, "I'm not myself.—I'm somebody else—that's me yonder—no—that's somebody else got into

my shoes—I was myself last night; but I fell asleep on the mountain—
and they've changed my gun—and every thing's changed—and I'm
changed—and I can't tell what's my name, or who I am!"

The byestanders began now to look at each other, nod, wink significantly and tap their fingers against their foreheads. There was a
whisper also about securing the gun, and keeping the old fellow from
doing mischief—at the very suggestion of which, the self important man
in the cocked hat retired with some precipitation. At this critical
moment a fresh likely looking woman pressed through the throng to get
a peep at the greybearded man. She had a chubby child in her arms,
which frightened at his looks began to cry. "Hush Rip," cried she, "hush
you little fool, the old man won't hurt you." The name of the child, the
air of the mother, the tone of her voice all awakened a train of
recollections in his mind. "What is your name my good woman?"
asked he.

"Judith Gardenier."

"And your father's name?"

"Ah, poor man, Rip Van Winkle was his name, but it's twenty years
since he went away from home with his gun and never has been
heard of since—his dog came home without him—but whether he shot
himself, or was carried away by the Indians no body can tell. I was
then but a little girl."

Rip had but one question more to ask, but he put it with a faltering
voice—

"Where's your mother?"—

Oh she too had died but a short time since—she broke a blood vessel
in a fit of passion at a New England pedlar.—

There was a drop of comfort at least in this intelligence. The honest
man could contain himself no longer—he caught his daughter and her
child in his arms.—"I am your father!" cried he—"Young Rip Van Winkle
once—old Rip Van Winkle now!—does nobody know poor Rip Van
Winkle!"

All stood amazed, until an old woman tottering out from among the
crowd put her hand to her brow and peering under it in his face for
a moment exclaimed—"Sure enough!—it is Rip Van Winkle—it is himself—welcome home again old neighbour—why, where have you been
these twenty long years?"

Rip's story was soon told, for the whole twenty years had been to him
but as one night. The neighbours stared when they heard it; some were
seen to wink at each other and put their tongues in their cheeks, and
the self important man in the cocked hat, who when the alarm was
over had returned to the field, screwed down the corners of his mouth

and shook his head—upon which there was a general shaking of the head throughout the assemblage.

It was determined, however, to take the opinion of old Peter Vanderdonk, who was seen slowly advancing up the road. He was a descendant of the historian of that name, who wrote one of the earliest accounts of the province. Peter was the most ancient inhabitant of the village and well versed in all the wonderful events and traditions of the neighbourhood. He recollected Rip at once, and corroborated his story in the most satisfactory manner. He assured the company that it was a fact handed down from his ancestor the historian, that the Kaatskill mountains had always been haunted by strange beings. That it was affirmed that the great Hendrick Hudson, the first discoverer of the river and country, kept a kind of vigil there every twenty years, with his crew of the Half Moon—being permitted in this way to revisit the scenes of his enterprize and keep a guardian eye upon the river and the great city called by his name. That his father had once seen them in their old Dutch dresses playing at nine pins in a hollow of the mountain; and that he himself had heard one summer afternoon the sound of their balls, like distant peals of thunder.

To make a long story short—the company broke up, and returned to the more important concerns of the election. Rip's daughter took him home to live with her; she had a snug well furnished house, and a stout cheery farmer for a husband whom Rip recollected for one of the urchins that used to climb upon his back. As to Rip's son and heir, who was the ditto of himself seen leaning against the tree; he was employed to work on the farm; but evinced an hereditary disposition to attend to any thing else but his business.

Rip now resumed his old walks and habits; he soon found many of his former cronies, though all rather the worse for the wear and tear of time; and preferred making friends among the rising generation, with whom he soon grew into great favour. Having nothing to do at home, and being arrived at that happy age when a man can be idle, with impunity, he took his place once more on the bench at the inn door and was reverenced as one of the patriarchs of the village and a chronicle of the old times "before the war." It was some time before he could get into the regular track of gossip, or could be made to comprehend the strange events that had taken place during his torpor. How that there had been a revolutionary war—that the country had thrown off the yoke of Old England and that instead of being a subject of his majesty George the Third, he was now a free citizen of the United States. Rip in fact was no politician; the changes of states and empires made but little impression on him; but there was one species of despotism under which he had long groaned and that was petticoat government. Happily that was at an end—he had got his neck out of the yoke of matrimony, and could go in and out whenever he pleased without dreading the tyranny of Dame Van Winkle. Whenever her name was mentioned, however, he shook his head, shrugged his shoulders and cast up his eyes; which might pass either for an expression of resignation to his fate or joy at his deliverance.

He used to tell his story to every stranger that arrived at Mr. Doolittle's Hotel. He was observed at first to vary on some points, every time he told it, which was doubtless owing to his having so recently awaked. It at last settled down precisely to the tale I have related and not a man woman or child in the neighbourhood but knew it by heart. Some always pretended to doubt the reality of it, and insisted that Rip had been out of his head, and that this was one point on which he always remained flighty. The old Dutch inhabitants, however, almost universally gave it full credit—Even to this day they never hear a thunder storm of a summer afternoon about the Kaatskill, but they say Hendrick Hudson and his crew are at their game of nine pins; and it is a common wish of all henpecked husbands in the neighbourhood, when life hangs heavy on their hands, that they might have a quieting draught out of Rip Van Winkle's flagon.

NOTE

The foregoing tale one would suspect had been suggested to Mr. Knickerbocker by a little German superstition about the emperor Frederick *der Rothbart* and the Kypphauser Mountain; the subjoined note, however, which he had appended to the tale, shews that it is an absolute fact, narrated with his usual fidelity.—

"The story of Rip Van Winkle may seem incredible to many, but nevertheless I give it my full belief, for I know the vicinity of our old Dutch settlements to have been very subject to marvellous events and appearances. Indeed I have heard many stranger stories than this, in the villages along the Hudson; all of which were too well authenticated to admit of a doubt. I have even talked with Rip Van Winkle myself, who when last I saw him was a very venerable old man and so perfectly rational and consistent on every other point, that I think no conscientious person could refuse to take this into the bargain—nay I have seen a certificate on the subject taken before a country justice and signed with a cross in the justice's own hand writing. The story therefore is beyond the possibility of doubt. D.K."

POSTSCRIPT

The following are travelling notes from a memorandum book of Mr. Knickerbocker.

The Kaatsberg or Catskill mountains have always been a region full of fable. The Indians considered them the abode of spirits who influenced the weather, spreading sunshine or clouds over the landscape and sending good or bad hunting seasons. They were ruled by an old squaw spirit, said to be their mother. She dwelt on the highest peak of the Catskills and had charge of the doors of day and night to open and shut them at the proper hour. She hung up the new moons in the skies and cut up the old ones into stars. In times of drought, if properly propitiated, she would spin light summer clouds out of cobwebs and morning dew, and send them off, from the crest of the mountain, flake after flake, like flakes of carded cotton to float in the air: until, dissolved by the heat of the sun, they would fall in gentle showers, causing the grass to spring, the fruits to ripen and the corn to grow an inch an hour. If displeased, however, she would brew up clouds black as ink, sitting in the midst of them like a bottle bellied spider in the midst of its web; and when these clouds broke—woe betide the valleys!

In old times say the Indian traditions, there was a kind of Manitou or Spirit, who kept about the wildest recesses of the Catskill mountains, and took a mischievous pleasure in wreaking all kinds of evils and vexations upon the red men. Sometimes he would assume the form of a bear a panther or a deer, lead the bewildered hunter a weary chace through tangled forests and among rugged rocks; and then spring off with a loud ho! ho! leaving him aghast on the brink of a beetling precipice or raging torrent.

The favorite abode of this Manitou is still shewn. It is a great rock or cliff in the loneliest part of the mountains, and, from the flowering vines which clamber about it, and the wild flowers which abound in its neighborhood, is known by the name of the Garden Rock. Near the foot of it is a small lake the haunt of the solitary bittern, with water snakes basking in the sun on the leaves of the pond lillies which lie on the surface. This place was held in great awe by the Indians, insomuch that the boldest hunter would not pursue his game within its precincts. Once upon a time, however, a hunter who had lost his way, penetrated to the garden rock where he beheld a number of gourds placed in the crotches of trees. One of these he seized and made off with it, but in the hurry of his retreat he let it fall among the rocks, when a great stream gushed forth which washed him away and swept him down precipices where he was dashed to pieces, and the stream made its way to the Hudson and continues to flow to the present day; being the identical stream known by the name of the Kaaters-kill.

ENGLISH WRITERS ON AMERICA

Methinks I see in my mind a noble and puissant nation rousing herself, like a strong man after sleep, and shaking her invincible locks: methinks I see her as an eagle mewing her mighty youth, and kindling her endazzled eyes at the full midday beam.

MILTON, ON THE LIBERTY OF THE PRESS.

It is with feelings of deep regret that I observe the literary animosity daily growing up between England and America. Great curiosity has been awakened of late with respect to the United States, and the London press has teemed with volumes of travels through the republic; but they seem intended to diffuse error rather than knowledge; and so successful have they been, that, notwithstanding the constant intercourse between the nations, there is no people concerning whom the great mass of the British public have less pure information, or entertain more numerous prejudices.

English travellers are the best, and the worst in the world. Where no motives of pride or interest intervene, none can equal them for profound and philosophical views of society, or faithful, and graphical descriptions of external objects; but when either the interest or reputation of their own country comes in collision with that of another, they go to the opposite extreme, and forget their usual probity and candour in the indulgence of splenetic remark and an illiberal spirit of ridicule.

Hence their travels are more honest and accurate the more remote the country described. I would place implicit confidence in an Englishman's description of the regions beyond the cataracts of the Nile; of unknown islands in the Yellow Sea; of the interior of India, or of any other tract which other travellers might be apt to picture out with the illusions of their fancies; but I would cautiously receive his account of his immediate neighbours, and of those nations with which he is in habits of most frequent intercourse. However I might be disposed to trust his probity I dare not trust his prejudices.

It has also been the peculiar lot of our country to be visited by the worst kind of English travellers. While men of philosophical spirit and cultivated minds have been sent from England to ransack the poles, to penetrate the deserts, and to study the manners and customs of barbarous nations, with which she can have no permanent intercourse of profit or pleasure; it has been left to the broken down tradesman, the scheming adventurer, the wandering mechanic, the Manchester and Birmingham agent, to be her oracles respecting America. From such sources she is content to receive her information respecting a country in a singular state of moral and physical development; a country in which one of the greatest political experiments in the history of the world is now performing, and which presents the most profound and momentous studies to the statesman and the philosopher.

That such men should give prejudiced accounts of America is not a matter of surprize. The themes it offers for contemplation are too vast and elevated for their capacities. The national character is yet in a state of fermentation: it may have its frothings and sediment, but its ingredients are sound and wholesome; it has already given proofs of powerful and generous qualities, and the whole promises to settle down into something substantially excellent. But the causes which are operating to strengthen and ennoble it, and its daily indications of admirable properties, are all lost upon these pur-blind observers; who are only affected by the little asperities incident to its present situation. They are capable of judging only of the surface of things; of those matters which come in contact with their private interests and personal gratifications. They miss some of the snug conveniences and petty comforts which belong to an old, highly finished, and overpopulous state of society, where the ranks of useful labour are crowded, and many earn a painful and servile subsistence, by studying the very caprices of appetite and self indulgence. These minor comforts, however, are all important in the estimation of narrow minds, which either do not perceive, or will not acknowledge, that they are more than counterbalanced among us, by great and generally diffused blessings.

They may, perhaps, have been disappointed in some unreasonable expectation of sudden gain. They may have pictured America to themselves, an El Dorado, where gold and silver abounded, and the natives were lacking in sagacity; and where they were to become strangely and suddenly rich, in some unforeseen, but easy manner. The same weakness of mind that indulges absurd expectations, produces petulance in disappointment. Such persons become embittered against the country on finding that there, as every where else, a man must sow before he can reap; must win wealth by industry and talent; and must contend with the common difficulties of nature, and the shrewdness of an intelligent and enterprizing people.

Perhaps, through mistaken, or ill directed hospitality, or from the prompt disposition to cheer and countenance the stranger, prevalent among my countrymen, they may have been treated with unwonted respect in America; and having been accustomed all their lives to consider themselves below the surface of good society; and brought up in a servile feeling of inferiority; they become arrogant on the common boon of civility; they attribute to the lowliness of others, their own elevation; and under rate a society, where there are no artificial distinctions, and where, by any chance, such individuals as themselves can rise to consequence.

One would suppose, however, that information coming from such sources, on a subject where the truth is so desirable, would be received with caution by the censors of the press. That the motives of these men, their veracity, their opportunities of enquiry and observation and their capacities for judging correctly would be rigorously scrutinized, before their evidence was admitted in such sweeping extent, against a kindred nation. The very reverse, however, is the case, and it furnishes a striking instance of human inconsistency. Nothing can surpass the vigilance with which English critics will examine the credibility of the traveller, who publishes an account of some distant, and comparatively unimportant, country. How warily will they compare the measurements of a pyramid, or the descriptions of a ruin, and how sternly will they censure any inaccuracy in these contributions of merely curious knowledge; while they will receive, with eagerness and unhesitating faith, the gross misrepresentations of coarse and obscure writers, concerning a country with which their own is placed in the most important and delicate relations. Nay, they will even make these apocryphal volumes text books, on which to enlarge, with a zeal and an ability worthy of a more generous cause.

I shall not, however, dwell on this irksome and hackney'd topic; nor should I have adverted to it but for the undue interest apparently taken in it by my countrymen, and certain injurious effects, which I apprehended it might produce upon the national feeling. We attach too much consequence to these attacks. They cannot do us any essential injury. The tissue of misrepresentations attempted to be woven round us are like cobwebs, woven round the limbs of an infant giant. Our country continually outgrows them. One falsehood after another falls off of itself. We have but to live on, and every day we live a whole volume of refutation. All the writers of England united, if we could for a moment suppose their great minds stooping to so unworthy a combination, could not conceal our rapidly growing importance and matchless prosperity. They could not conceal that these are owing, not merely to physical and local, but also to moral causes. To the political liberty, the general diffusion of knowledge, the prevalence of sound moral and religious principles, which give force and sustained energy to the character of a people; and which, in fact have been the acknowledged and wonderful supporters of their own national power and glory.

But why are we so exquisitely alive to the aspersions of England? Why do we suffer ourselves to be so affected by the contumely she has endeavoured to cast upon us? It is not in the opinion of England alone that honor lives and reputation has its being. The world at large is the arbiter of a nation's fame; with its thousand eyes it witnesses a nation's deeds, and from their collective testimony is national glory or national disgrace established.

For ourselves, therefore, it is comparatively of but little importance whether England does us justice or not—it is perhaps of far more importance to herself. She is instilling anger and resentment into the bosom of a youthful nation, to grow with its growth and strengthen with its strength. If in America, as some of her writers are labouring to convince her, she is hereafter to find an invidious rival and a gigantic foe, she may thank those very writers, for having provoked rivalship, and irritated hostility. Every one knows the all pervading influence of literature at the present day, and how much the opinions and passions of mankind are under its control. The mere contests of the sword are temporary; their wounds are but in the flesh, and it is the pride of the generous to forgive and forget them: but the slanders of the pen pierce to the heart; they rankle longest in the noblest spirits; they dwell ever present in the mind; and render it morbidly sensitive to the most trifling collision. It is but seldom that any one overt act produces hostilities between two nations; there exists, most commonly, a previous jealousy and ill will; a predisposition to take offence. Trace these to their cause, and how often will they be found to originate in the mischievous effusions of mercenary writers, who, secure in their closets, and for ignominious bread, concoct and circulate the venom, that is to inflame the generous and the brave.

I am not laying too much stress upon this point; for it applies most emphatically to our particular case. Over no nation does the press hold a more absolute control than over the people of America; for the universal education of the poorest classes, makes every individual a reader. There is nothing published in England on the subject of our country that does not circulate through every part of it. There is not a calumny dropt from an English pen, nor an unworthy sarcasm uttered by an English statesman, that does not go to blight good will and add to the mass of latent resentment. Possessing then as England does, the fountain head from whence the literature of the language flows, how completely is it in her power, and how truly is it her duty, to make it the medium of amiable and magnanimous feeling—a stream where the two nations might meet together and drink in peace and kindness. Should she, however, persist in turning it to waters of bitterness, the time may come when she may repent her folly. The present friendship of America may be of but little moment to her; but the future destinies of that country do not admit of a doubt; over those of England there lower some shadows of uncertainty. Should then a day of gloom arrive; should those reverses overtake her, from which the proudest empires have not been exempt, she may look back with regret at her infatuation, in repulsing from her side a nation she might have grappled to her bosom, and thus destroying her only chance for real friendship beyond the boundaries of her own dominions.

There is a general impression in England that the people of the United States are inimical to the parent country. It is one of the errors which has been diligently propagated by designing writers. There is doubtless considerable political hostility, and a general soreness at the illiberality of the English press, but, generally speaking, the prepossessions of the people are strongly in favour of England. Indeed at one time they amounted, in many parts of the union, to an absurd degree of bigotry. The bare name of Englishman was a passport to the confidence and hospitality of every family, and too often gave a transient currency to the worthless and the ungrateful. Throughout the country there was something of enthusiasm connected with the idea of England. We looked to it with a hallowed feeling of tenderness and veneration as the land of our forefathers—the august repository of the monuments and antiquities of our race—the birth place and mausoleum of the sages and heroes of our paternal history. After our own country there was none in whose glory we more delighted—none whose good opinion we were more anxious to possess—none towards which our hearts yearned with such throbbings of warm consanguinity. Even during the late war, whenever there was the least opportunity for kind feelings to spring forth it was the delight of the generous spirits of our country to shew that in the midst of hostilities they still kept alive the sparks of future friendship.

Is all this to be at an end? Is this golden band of kindred sympathies, so rare between nations, to be broken forever?—Perhaps it is for the best —It may dispel an illusion which might have kept us in mental vassallage; which might have interfered occasionally with our true interests, and prevented the growth of proper national pride. But it is hard to give up the kindred tie!—and there are feelings dearer than interest—closer to the heart than pride—that will still make us cast back a look of regret, as we wander farther and farther from the paternal roof, and lament the waywardness of the parent, that would repel the affections of the child.

Short sighted and injudicious, however, as the conduct of England may be in this system of aspersion, recrimination on our part would be equally ill judged. I speak not of prompt and spirited vindication of our country, nor the keenest castigation of her slanderers—but I allude to a disposition to retaliate in kind; to retort sarcasm and inspire prejudice, which seems to be spreading widely among our writers. Let us guard particularly against such a temper, for it would double the evil instead of redressing the wrong. Nothing is so easy and inviting as the retort of abuse and sarcasm; but it is a paltry and an unprofitable contest. It is the alternative of a morbid mind fretted into petulance rather than warmed into indignation. If England is willing to permit the mean jealousies of trade or the rancorous animosities of politics to deprave the integrity of her press, and poison the fountain of public opinion, let us beware of her example. She may deem it her interest to diffuse error and engender antipathy, for the purpose of checking emigration; we have no purpose of the kind to serve. Neither have we any spirit of national jealousy to gratify, for as yet, in all our rivalships with England we are the rising and the gaining party. There can be no end to answer, therefore, but the gratification of resentment; a mere spirit of retaliation, and even that is impotent. Our retorts are never republished in England; they fall short, therefore, of their aim—but they foster a querulous and peevish temper among our writers—they sour the sweet flow of our early literature, and sow thorns and brambles among its blossoms. What is still worse they circulate through our own country, and, as far as they have effect, excite virulent national prejudices. This last is the evil most especially to be deprecated. Governed as we are entirely by public opinion, the utmost care should be taken to preserve the purity of the public mind. Knowledge is power, and truth is knowledge; whoever therefore knowingly propagates a prejudice, wilfully saps the foundation of his country's strength.

The members of a republic, above all other men, should be candid and dispassionate. They are individually portions of the sovereign mind and sovereign will, and should be enabled to come to all questions of national concern with calm and unbiassed judgements. From the peculiar nature of our relations with England, we must have more frequent questions of a difficult and delicate character with her, than with any other nation; questions that affect the most acute and excitable feelings; and as in the adjusting of these, our national measures must ultimately be determined by popular sentiment, we cannot be too anxiously attentive to purify it from all latent passion or prepossession.

Opening too, as we do, an asylum for strangers from every portion of the earth, we should receive all with impartiality. It should be our pride to exhibit an example of one nation at least, destitute of national antipathies, and exercising, not merely the overt acts of hospitality but those more rare and noble courtesies which spring from liberality of opinion.

What have we to do with national prejudices? They are the inveterate diseases of old countries, contracted in rude and ignorant ages, when nations knew but little of each other, and looked beyond their own boundaries with distrust and hostility. We, on the contrary, have sprung into national existence in an enlightened and philosophic age; when the different parts of the habitable world, and the various branches of the human family, have been indefatigably studied and made known to each other; and we forego the advantages of our birth, if we do not shake off the national prejudices, as we would the local superstitions, of the old world.

But above all, let us not be influenced by any angry feelings so far as to shut our eyes to the perception of what is really excellent and amiable in the English character. We are a young people, necessarily an imitative one, and must take our examples and models, in a great degree, from the existing nations of Europe. There is no country more worthy of our study than England. The spirit of her constitution is most analogous to ours. The manners of her people,—their intellectual activity —their freedom of opinion—their habits of thinking on those subjects which concern the dearest interests and most sacred charities of private life, are all congenial to the American character; and in fact are all intrinsically excellent: for it is in the moral feeling of the people that the deep foundations of British prosperity are laid; and however the superstructure may be time worn, or over run by abuses, there must be something solid in the basis, admirable in the materials, and stable in the structure of an edifice that so long has towered unshaken amidst the tempests of the world.

Let it be the pride of our writers, therefore, discarding all feelings of irritation and disdaining to retaliate the illiberality of British authors, to speak of the English nation without prejudice, and with determined candour. While they rebuke the undiscriminating bigotry with which some of our countrymen admire and imitate every thing english, merely because it is english, let them frankly point out what is really worthy of approbation. We may thus place England before us as a perpetual volume of reference, wherein are recorded sound deductions from ages of experience; and while we avoid the errors and absurdities which may have crept into the page, we may draw from thence golden maxims of practical wisdom, wherewith to strengthen and to embellish our national character.

RURAL LIFE IN ENGLAND

Oh! friendly to the best pursuits of man,
Friendly to thought, to virtue and to peace,
Domestic life in rural pleasure pass'd!

COWPER.

The stranger who would form a correct opinion of the English character must not confine his observations to the metropolis. He must go forth into the country; he must sojourn in villages and hamlets; he must visit castles, villas, farm houses, cottages; he must wander through parks and gardens; along hedges and green lanes; he must loiter about country churches, attend wakes and fairs and other rural festivals, and cope with the people in all their conditions, and all their habits and humours.

In some countries the large cities absorb the wealth and fashion of the nation; they are the only fixed abodes of elegant and intelligent society and the country is inhabited almost entirely by boorish peasantry. In England, on the contrary, the metropolis is a mere gathering place, or general rendezvous of the polite circles, where they devote a small portion of the year to a hurry of gaiety and dissipation, and having indulged this kind of carnival, return again to the apparently more congenial habits of rural life. The various orders of society are therefore diffused over the whole surface of the kingdom, and the most retired neighbourhoods afford specimens of the different ranks.

The English, in fact, are strongly gifted with the rural feeling. They possess a quick sensibility to the beauties of nature, and a keen relish for the pleasures and employments of the country. This passion seems inherent in them. Even the inhabitants of cities born and brought up among brick walls and bustling streets, enter with facility into rural habits and evince a tact for rural occupation. The merchant has his snug retreat in the vicinity of the metropolis, where he often displays as much pride and zeal in the cultivation of his flower garden and the maturing of his fruits as he does in the conduct of his business and the success of a commercial enterprise. Even those less fortunate individuals, who are doomed to pass their lives in the midst of din and traffic, contrive to have something that shall remind them of the green aspect of nature. In the most dark and dingy quarters of the city, the drawing room window resembles frequently a bank of flowers; every spot capable of vegetation, has its grass plot and flower bed; and every square its mimic park, laid out with picturesque taste, and gleaming with refreshing verdure.

Those who see the Englishman only in town are apt to form an unfavourable opinion of his social character. He is either absorbed in business, or distracted by the thousand engagements that dissipate time, thought and feeling, in this huge metropolis. He has therefore too commonly a look of hurry and abstraction. Wherever he happens to be, he is on the point of going somewhere else; at the moment he is talking on one subject his mind is wandering to another; and while paying a friendly visit, he is calculating how he shall economize time so as to pay the other visits allotted in the morning. An immense metropolis like London is calculated to make men selfish and uninteresting. In their casual and transient meetings they can but deal briefly in commonplaces. They present but the cold superficies of character—its rich and genial qualities have no time to be warmed into a flow.

It is in the country that the Englishman gives scope to his natural feelings. He breaks loose gladly from the cold formalities and negative civilities of town; throws off his habits of shy reserve, and becomes joyous and freehearted. He manages to collect around him all the conveniencies and elegancies of polite life, and to banish its restraints. His country seat abounds with every requisite either for studious retirement, tasteful gratification or rural exercise. Books, paintings, music, horses, dogs, and sporting implements of all kinds are at hand. He puts no constraint either upon his guests or himself, but in the true spirit of hospitality, provides the means of enjoyment, and leaves every one to partake according to his inclination.

The taste of the English in the cultivation of land and in what is called landscape gardening is unrivalled. They have studied nature intently and discover an exquisite sense of her beautiful forms and harmonious combinations. Those charms which in other countries she lavishes in wild solitudes are here assembled round the haunts of domestic life. They seem to have caught her coy and furtive graces, and spread them, like witchery, about their rural abodes.

Nothing can be more imposing than the magnificence of English park scenery. Vast lawns that extend like sheets of vivid green, with here and there clumps of gigantic trees heaping up rich piles of foliage. The solemn pomp of groves and woodland glades, with the deer trooping in silent herds across them, the hare bounding away to the covert or the pheasant suddenly bursting upon the wing. The brook, taught to wind in natural meanderings or expand into a glassy lake—The sequestered pool reflecting the quivering trees, with the yellow leaf sleeping on its bosom, and the trout roaming fearlessly about its limpid waters, while some rustic temple, or sylvan statue grown green and dank with age, gives an air of classic sanctity to the seclusion.

These are but a few of the features of park scenery; but what most delights me is the creative talent with which the English decorate the unostentatious abodes of middle life. The rudest habitation; the most un-promising and scanty portion of land, in the hands of an Englishman of taste, becomes a little paradise. With a nicely discriminating eye he seizes at once upon its capabilities, and pictures in his mind the future landscape. The sterile spot grows into loveliness under his hand; and yet the operations of art which produce the effect are scarcely to be perceived. The cherishing and training of some trees; the cautious pruning of others; the nice distribution of flowers and plants of tender and graceful foliage; the introduction of a green slope of velvet turf; the partial opening to a peep of blue distance or silver gleam of water—all these are managed with a delicate tact, a pervading yet quiet assiduity, like the magic touchings with which a painter finishes up a favourite picture.

The residence of people of fortune and refinement in the country has diffused a degree of taste and elegance in rural economy, that descends to the lowest class. The very labourer, with his thatched cottage and nar-row slip of ground, attends to their embellishment. The trim hedge, the grass plot before the door, the little flower bed bordered with snug box; the woodbine trained up against the wall and hanging its blossoms about the lattice; the pot of flowers in the window; the holly providently planted about the house to cheat winter of its dreariness, and to throw in a semblance of green summer to cheer the fire side—all these bespeak the influence of taste, flowing down from high sources, and pervading the lowest levels of the public mind. If ever love, as poets sing, delights to visit a cottage, it must be the cottage of an English peasant.

The fondness for rural life among the higher classes of the English has had a great and salutary effect upon the national character. I do not know a finer race of men than the English gentlemen. Instead of the softness and effeminacy which characterize the men of rank in most countries, they exhibit a union of elegance and strength, a robustness of frame and freshness of complexion, which I am inclined to attribute to their living so much in the open air, and pursuing so eagerly the in-vigorating recreations of the country. These hardy exercises produce also a healthful tone of mind and spirits, a manliness and simplicity of manners, which even the follies and dissipations of the town cannot easily pervert, and can never entirely destroy. In the country too, the different orders of society seem to approach more freely, to be more disposed to blend and operate favourably upon each other. The distinc-tions between them do not appear to be so marked and impassable as in the cities. The manner in which property has been distributed into small estates and farms has established a regular gradation from the nobleman, through the classes of gentry, small landed proprietors, and substantial farmers, down to the labouring peasantry; and while it has thus banded the extremes of society together, has infused in each intermediate rank a spirit of independence. This, it must be confessed, is not so universally the case at present as it was formerly; the larger estates having in late years of distress, absorbed the smaller, and in some parts of the country almost annihilated the sturdy race of small farmers. These, however, I believe, are but casual breaks in the general system I have mentioned.

In rural occupation there is nothing mean and debasing. It leads a man forth among scenes of natural grandeur and beauty; it leaves him to the workings of his own mind operated upon by the purest and most elevating of external influences. Such a man may be simple and rough, but he cannot be vulgar. The man of refinement, therefore, finds nothing revolting in an intercourse with the lower orders in rural life, as he does when he casually mingles with the lower orders of cities. He lays aside his distance and reserve, and is glad to wave the distinctions of rank, and to enter into the honest heartfelt enjoyments of common life. Indeed the very amusements of the country bring men more and more together; and the sound of hound and horn blend all feelings into harmony. I believe this is one great reason why the nobility and gentry are more popular among the inferior orders in England than they are in any other country; and why the latter have endured so many excessive pressures and extremities, without repining more generally at the unequal distribution of fortune and privilege.

To this mingling of cultivated and rustic society may also be attributed the rural feeling that runs through British literature: the frequent use of illustrations from rural life: those incomparable descriptions of nature that abound in the British poets; that have continued down from "The Flower and the Leaf" of Chaucer, and have brought into our closets all the freshness and fragrance of the dewy landscape. The pastoral writers of other countries appear as if they had paid nature an occasional visit, and become acquainted with her general charms; but the British poets have lived and revelled with her—they have wooed her in her most secret haunts, they have watched her minutest caprices. A spray could not tremble in the breeze; a leaf could not rustle to the ground; a diamond drop could not patter in the stream; a fragrance could not exhale from the humble violet, nor a daisy unfold its crimson tints to the morning, but it has been noticed by these impassioned and delicate observers, and wrought up into some beautiful morality.

The effect of this devotion of elegant minds to rural occupations has been wonderful on the face of the country. A great part of the island is rather level, and would be monotonous were it not for the charms of culture, but it is studded and gemmed, as it were, with castles and palaces, and embroidered with parks and gardens. It does not abound in grand and sublime prospects, but rather in little, home scenes of rural repose and sheltered quiet. Every antique farm house and moss grown cottage is a picture, and as the roads are continually winding, and the view shut in by groves and hedges, the eye is delighted by a continual succession of small landscapes of captivating loveliness.

The great charm, however, of English scenery is the moral feeling that seems to pervade it. It is associated in the mind with ideas of order, of quiet, of sober well established principles, of hoary usage and reverend custom. Every thing seems to be the growth of ages of regular, and peaceful existence. The old church of remote architecture, with its low massive portal; its gothic tower; its windows rich with tracery and painted glass in scrupulous preservation; its stately monuments of warriors and worthies of the olden time, ancestors of the present lords of the soil; its tombstones recording successive generations of sturdy yeomanry, whose progeny still plow the same fields and kneel at the same altar. The parsonage, a quaint irregular pile, partly antiquated, but repaired and altered in the tastes of various ages and occupants. The style and footpath leading from the church yard, across pleasant fields and along shady hedge rows, according to an immemorial right of way. The neighbouring village, with its venerable cottages, its public green sheltered by trees under which the forefathers of the present race have sported. The antique family mansion, standing apart in some little rural domain, but looking down with a protecting air on the surrounding scene. —All these common features of English landscape evince a calm and settled security, and hereditary transmission of home bred virtues and local attachments, that speak deeply and touchingly for the moral character of the nation.

It is a pleasing sight of a Sunday morning, when the bell is sending its sober melody across the quiet fields, to behold the peasantry in their best finery, with ruddy faces and modest cheerfulness, thronging tranquilly along the green lanes to church: but it is still more pleasing to see them in the evenings, gathering about their cottage doors, and appearing to exult in the humble comforts and embellishments, which their own hands have spread around them.

It is this sweet home feeling; this settled repose of affection in the domestic scene, that is, after all, the parent of the steadiest virtues and purest enjoyments, and I cannot close these desultory remarks better, than by quoting the words of a modern English poet, who has depicted it with remarkable felicity.

> Through each gradation, from the castled hall,
> The city dome, the villa crown'd with shade,
> But chief from modest mansions numberless,

In town or hamlet shelt'ring middle life,
Down to the cottag'd vale and straw-roof'd shed,
This western isle hath long been fam'd for scenes
Where bliss domestic finds a dwelling place:
Domestic bliss, that, like a harmless dove,
(Honour and sweet endearment keeping guard)
Can centre in a little quiet nest
All that desire would fly for through the earth;
That can, the world eluding, be itself
A world enjoy'd; that wants no witnesses
But its own sharers, and approving heaven.
That, like a flower deep hid in rocky cleft,
Smiles, though 'tis looking only at the sky.*

*From a poem on the death of the Princess Charlotte, by the Reverend Rann
Kennedy, A. M.

THE BROKEN HEART

I never heard
Of any true affection but 'twas nipt
With care, that, like the caterpillar, eats
The leaves of the spring's sweetest book, the rose.
MIDDLETON.

It is a common practice with those who have outlived the susceptibility of early feeling, or have been brought up in the gay heartlessness of dissipated life, to laugh at all love stories, and to treat the tales of romantic passion as mere fictions of novelists and poets. My observations on human nature have induced me to think otherwise. They have convinced me, that however the surface of the character may be chilled and frozen by the cares of the world, or cultivated into mere smiles by the arts of society, still there are dormant fires lurking in the depths of the coldest bosom, which, when once enkindled, become impetuous and are sometimes desolating in their effects. Indeed, I am a true believer in the blind deity, and go to the full extent of his doctrines—Shall I confess it?— I believe in broken hearts and the possibility of dying of disappointed love!—I do not, however, consider it a malady often fatal to my own sex; but I firmly believe that it withers down many a lovely woman into an early grave.

Man is the creature of interest and ambition. His nature leads him forth into the struggle and bustle of the world. Love is but the embellishment of his early life, or a song piped in the intervals of the acts. He seeks for fame, for fortune, for space in the world's thought, and dominion over his fellow men. But a woman's whole life is a history of the affections. The heart is her world: it is there her ambition strives for empire: it is there her avarice seeks for hidden treasures. She sends forth her sympathies on adventure; she embarks her whole soul in the traffic of affection, and if shipwrecked her case is hopeless, for it is a bankruptcy of the heart.

To a man the disappointment of love may occasion some bitter pangs— it wounds some feelings of tenderness—it blasts some prospects of felicity; but he is an active being—he may dissipate his thoughts in the whirl of varied occupation; or may plunge into the tide of pleasure. Or if the scene of disappointment be too full of painful associations, he can shift his abode at will, and, taking as it were the wings of the morning, can "fly to the uttermost parts of the earth and be at rest."

But woman's is comparatively a fixed, a secluded, and a meditative life. She is more the companion of her own thoughts and feelings; and if they are turned to ministers of sorrow, where shall she look for consolation! Her lot is to be wooed and won; and if unhappy in her love, her heart is like some fortress that has been captured, and sacked, and abandoned and left desolate.

How many bright eyes grow dim—how many soft cheeks grow pale—how many lovely forms fade away into the tomb, and none can tell the cause that blighted their loveliness. As the dove will clasp its wings to its side, and cover and conceal the arrow that is preying on its vitals; so is it the nature of woman to hide from the world the pangs of wounded affection. The love of a delicate female is always shy and silent. Even when fortunate, she scarcely breathes it to herself; but when otherwise, she buries it in the recesses of her bosom, and there lets it cower and brood among the ruins of her peace. With her the desire of the heart has failed. The great charm of existence is at an end. She neglects all the cheerful exercises which gladden the spirits, quicken the pulses and send the tide of life in healthful currents through the veins. Her rest is broken—the sweet refreshment of sleep is poisoned by melancholy dreams —"dry sorrow drinks her blood," until her enfeebled frame sinks under the slightest external injury. Look for her, after a little while, and you find friendship weeping over her untimely grave, and wondering that one, who but lately glowed with all the radiance of health and beauty, should so speedily be brought down to "darkness and the worm." You will be told of some wintry chill, some casual indisposition that laid her low—but no one knows of the mental malady which previously sapped her strength and made her so easy a prey to the spoiler.

She is like some tender tree, the pride and beauty of the grove; graceful in its form; bright in its foliage, but with the worm preying at its heart. We find it suddenly withering when it should be most fresh and luxuriant. We see it drooping its branches to the earth and shedding leaf by leaf; until wasted and perished away, it falls even in the stillness of the forest; and as we muse over the beautiful ruin, we strive in vain to recollect the blast or thunderbolt that could have smitten it with decay.

I have seen many instances of women running to waste and self neglect, and disappearing gradually from the earth, almost as if they had been exhaled to heaven; and have repeatedly fancied that I could trace their deaths through the various declensions of consumption, cold, debility, languor, melancholy, until I reached the first symptom of disappointed love. But an instance of the kind was lately told to me; the circumstances are well known in the country where they happened, and I shall but give them in the manner in which they were related.

Every one must recollect the tragical story of young E——— the Irish patriot; it was too touching to be soon forgotten. During the troubles in Ireland he was tried, condemned and executed on a charge of treason. His fate made a deep impression on public sympathy. He was so young—so intelligent—so generous—so brave—so every thing that we are apt to like in a young man. His conduct under trial too was so lofty and intrepid. The noble indignation with which he repelled the charge of treason against his country—the eloquent vindication of his name, his pathetic appeal to posterity in the hopeless hour of condemnation—all these entered deeply into every generous bosom, and even his enemies lamented the stern policy that dictated his execution.

But there was one heart, whose anguish it would be impossible to describe. In happier days and fairer fortunes he had won the affections of a beautiful and interesting girl, the daughter of a late celebrated Irish Barrister. She loved him with the disinterested fervour of a woman's first and early love. When every worldly maxim arrayed itself against him; when blasted in fortune, and disgrace and danger darkened around his name, she loved him the more ardently for his very sufferings. If then his fate could awaken the sympathy even of his foes, what must have been the agony of her whose whole soul was occupied by his image! Let those tell who have had the portals of the tomb suddenly closed between them, and the being they most loved on earth—who have sat at its threshold, as one shut out in a cold and lonely world, from whence all that was most lovely and loving had departed.

But then the horrors of such a grave! so frightful—so dishonoured!—There was nothing for memory to dwell on that could soothe the pang of separation—none of those tender though melancholy circumstances which endear the parting scene—nothing to melt sorrow into those blessed tears, sent like the dews of heaven, to revive the heart in the parching hour of anguish.

To render her widowed situation more desolate, she had incurred her father's displeasure by her unfortunate attachment, and was an exile from the paternal roof. But could the sympathy and kind offices of friends have reached a spirit so shocked and driven in by horror, she would have experienced no want of consolation, for the Irish are a people of quick and generous sensibilities. The most delicate and cherishing attentions were paid her by families of wealth and distinction. She was led into society; and they tried by all kinds of occupations and amusements to dissipate her grief and wean her from the tragical story of her loves. But it was all in vain. There are some strokes of calamity which scathe and scorch the soul; which penetrate to the vital seat of happiness, and blast it, never again to put forth bud or blossom. She never objected to frequent the haunts of pleasure, but was as much alone there, as in the depths of solitude; walking about in a sad reverie, apparently unconscious of the world around her. She carried with her an inward woe that mocked at all the blandishments of friendship, and "heeded not the song of the charmer, charm he never so wisely."

The person who told me her story had seen her at a masquerade. There can be no exhibition of far gone wretchedness more striking and painful than to meet it in such a scene. To find it wandering like a spectre, lonely and joyless, where all around is gay—To see it dressed out in the trappings of mirth, and looking so wan and woe begone, as if it had tried in vain to cheat the poor heart into a momentary forgetfulness of sorrow. After strolling through the splendid rooms and giddy crowd with an air of utter abstraction, she sat herself down on the steps of an orchestra, and looking about for some time with a vacant air that shewed her insensibility to the garish scene, she began, with the capriciousness of a sickly heart, to warble a little plaintive air. She had an exquisite voice; but on this occasion it was so simple, so touching, it breathed forth such a soul of wretchedness, that she drew a crowd mute and silent around her, and melted every one into tears.

The story of one so true and tender could not but excite great interest in a country remarkable for enthusiasm. It completely won the heart of a brave officer, who paid his addresses to her, and thought that one so true to the dead, could not but prove affectionate to the living. She declined his attentions, for her thoughts were irrevocably engrossed by the memory of her former lover. He, however, persisted in his suit. He solicited not her tenderness, but her esteem. He was assisted by her conviction of his worth, and her sense of her own destitute and dependent situation, for she was existing on the kindness of friends—In a word he at length succeeded in gaining her hand, though with the solemn assurance that her heart was unalterably another's.

He took her with him to Sicily, hoping that a change of scene might wear out the remembrance of early woes. She was an amiable and exemplary wife, and made an effort to be a happy one; but nothing could cure the silent and devouring melancholy that had entered into her very soul. She wasted away in a slow but hopeless decline, and at length sunk into the grave, the victim of a broken heart.

It was on her that Moore the distinguished Irish poet composed the following lines.

> She is far from the land where her young hero sleeps,
>   And lovers around her are sighing;
> But coldly she turns from their gaze and weeps,
>   For her heart in his grave is lying.
>
> She sings the wild song of her dear native plains,
>   Every note which he lov'd awaking—

Ah! little they think, who delight in her strains,
 How the heart of the minstrel is breaking!

He had liv'd for his love, for his country he died;
 They were all that to life had entwin'd him—
Nor soon shall the tears of his country be dried,
 Nor long will his love stay behind him!

Oh! make her a grave where the sunbeams rest,
 When they promise a glorious morrow;
They'll shine o'er her sleep, like a smile from the west,
 From her own lov'd island of sorrow!

THE ART OF BOOK MAKING

If that severe doom of Synesius be true, "it is a greater offence to steal dead men's labors, than their clothes," what shall become of most writers?

BURTON'S ANATOMY OF MELANCHOLY.

I have often wondered at the extreme fecundity of the press, and how it comes to pass that so many heads, on which nature seemed to have inflicted the curse of barrenness, should teem with voluminous productions. As a man travels on, however, in the journey of life his objects of wonder daily diminish, and he is continually finding out some very simple cause, for some great matter of marvel. Thus have I chanced, in my peregrinations about this great metropolis, to blunder upon a scene which unfolded to me some of the mysteries of the bookmaking craft, and at once put an end to my astonishment.

I was one summer's day loitering through the great saloons of the British Museum, with that listlessness with which one is apt to saunter about a museum in warm weather; sometimes lolling over the glass cases of minerals, sometimes studying the hieroglyphics on an Egyptian Mummy, and sometimes trying, with nearly equal success, to comprehend the allegorical paintings on the lofty ceilings. Whilst I was gazing about in this idle way my attention was attracted to a distant door, at the end of a suite of apartments. It was closed, but every now and then it would open and some strange favoured being, generally clothed in black, would steal forth and glide through the rooms without noticing any of the surrounding objects. There was an air of mystery about this that piqued my languid curiosity, and I determined to attempt the passage of that strait and to explore the unknown regions beyond. The door yielded to my hand, with that facility with which the portals of enchanted castles yield to the adventurous Knight errant. I found myself in a spacious chamber, surrounded with great cases of venerable books. Above the cases, and just under the cornice, were arranged a great number of black looking portraits of ancient authors. About the room were placed long tables, with stands for reading and writing, at which sat many pale, studious personages, poring intently over dusty volumes, rummaging among mouldy manuscripts, and taking copious notes of their contents. A hushed stillness reigned through this mysterious apartment, excepting that you might hear the racing of pens over sheets of paper; or occasionally the deep sigh of one of these sages as he shifted his position to turn over the page of an old folio; doubtless arising from that hollowness and flatulency incident to learned research.

Now and then one of these personages would write something on a
small slip of paper and ring a bell, whereupon a familiar would appear,
take the paper in profound silence, glide out of the room and return
shortly loaded with ponderous tomes, upon which the other would fall,
tooth and nail, with famished voracity. I had no longer a doubt that I
had happened upon a body of Magi, deeply engaged in the study of
occult sciences. The scene reminded me of an old Arabian tale, of a
philosopher shut up in an enchanted library, in the bosom of a mountain,
which opened only once a year; where he made the spirits of the place
bring him books of all kinds of dark knowledge, so that at the end
of the year, when the magic portal once more swung open on its hinges,
he issued forth so versed in forbidden lore, as to be able to soar above
the heads of the multitude, and to control the powers of nature.

My curiosity being now fully aroused I whispered to one of the
familiars, as he was about to leave the room, and begged an interpreta-
tion of the strange scene before me. A few words were sufficient for the
purpose. I found that these mysterious personages whom I had mistaken
for Magi, were principally authors and in the very act of manufacturing
books. I was, in fact, in the reading room of the great British library,
an immense collection of volumes of all ages and languages, many of
which are now forgotten, and most of which are seldom read: one of
these sequestered pools of obsolete literature, to which modern authors
repair, and draw buckets full of classic lore, or "pure English undefiled"
wherewith to swell their own scanty rills of thought.

Being now in possession of the secret, I sat down in a corner and
watched the process of this book manufactory. I noticed one lean,
bilious looking wight, who sought none but the most worm eaten volumes,
printed in black letter. He was evidently constructing some work of
profound erudition, that would be purchased by every man who wished
to be thought learned, placed upon a conspicuous shelf of his library, or
laid open upon his table—but never read. I observed him now and then
draw a large fragment of biscuit out of his pocket, and gnaw; whether it
was his dinner, or whether he was endeavouring to keep off that exhaustion
of the stomach, produced by much pondering over dry works, I leave to
harder students than myself to determine.

There was one dapper little gentleman in bright coloured clothes,
with a chirping, gossipping expression of countenance, who had all
the appearance of an author on good terms with his bookseller. After
considering him attentively, I recognized in him a diligent getter up of
miscellaneous works, which bustled off well with the trade. I was curious
to see how he manufactured his wares. He made more stir and shew of
business than any of the others; dipping into various books, fluttering over
the leaves of manuscripts, taking a morsel out of one, a morsel out of

another, line upon line, precept upon precept, here a little and there a little better than carrion, and apparently the lawless plunderers of the of the witches' cauldron in Macbeth. It was, here a finger and there a thumb; toe of frog and blind worm's sting, with his own gossip poured in like "baboon's blood," to make the medley "slab and good."

After all, thought I, may not this pilfering disposition be implanted in authors for wise purposes; may it not be the way in which providence has taken care that the seeds of knowledge and wisdom shall be preserved from age to age, in spite of the inevitable decay of the works in which they were first produced. We see that nature has wisely, though whimsically, provided for the conveyance of seeds from clime to clime in the maws of certain birds; so that animals which in themselves are little better than carrion, and apparently the lawless plunderers of the orchard and the corn field, are in fact nature's carriers to disperse and perpetuate her blessings. In like manner the beauties and fine thoughts of ancient and obsolete writers, are caught up by these flights of predatory authors, and cast forth again to flourish and bear fruit in a remote and distant tract of time. Many of their works, also, undergo a kind of metempsychosis and spring up under new forms. What was formerly a ponderous history, revives in the shape of a romance—an old legend changes into a modern play, and a sober philosophical treatise, furnishes the body for a whole series of bouncing and sparkling essays. Thus it is in the clearing of our American woodlands; where we burn down a forest of stately pines, a progeny of dwarf oaks start up in their place; and we never see the prostrate trunk of a tree, mouldering into soil, but it gives birth to a whole tribe of fungi.

Let us not then lament over the decay and oblivion into which ancient writers descend; they do but submit to the great law of nature, which declares that all sublunary shapes of matter shall be limited in their duration, but which decrees also that their elements shall never perish. Generation after generation, both in animal and vegetable life, passes away, but the vital principle is transmitted to posterity, and the species continues to flourish. Thus also do authors beget authors, and having produced a numerous progeny, in a good old age they sleep with their fathers; that is to say, with the authors who preceded them—and from whom they had stolen.

Whilst I was indulging in these rambling fancies I had leaned my head against a pile of reverend folios. Whether it was owing to the soporific emanations from these works, or to the profound quiet of the room; or to the lassitude arising from much wandering, or to an unlucky habit of napping at improper times and places, with which I am grievously afflicted, so it was that I fell into a doze. Still however my imagination continued busy, and indeed the same scene remained before my mind's eye, only a little changed in some of the details. I dreamt that the chamber was still decorated with the portraits of ancient authors, but that the number was encreased. The long tables had disappeared and in place of the sage Magi I beheld a ragged, thread bare throng, such as may be seen plying about the great repository of cast off clothes Monmouth Street. Whenever they seized upon a book, by one of those incongruities common to dreams, methought it turned into a garment of foreign or antique fashion, with which they proceeded to equip themselves. I noticed, however, that no one pretended to clothe himself from any particular suit, but took a sleeve from one, a cape from another, a skirt from a third, thus decking himself out piece meal, while some of his original rags would peep out from among his borrowed finery.

There was a portly, rosy, well fed parson whom I observed ogling several mouldy polemical writers through an eye glass. He soon contrived to slip on the voluminous mantle of one of the old fathers, and having purloined the grey beard of another, endeavoured to look exceeding wise, but the smirking commonplace of his countenance set at naught all the trappings of wisdom. One sickly looking gentleman was busied embroidering a very flimsy garment with gold thread drawn out of several old court dresses of the reign of Queen Elizabeth. Another had trimmed himself magnificently from an illuminated manuscript, had stuck a nosegay in his bosom, culled from "The Paradise of dainty Devices," and having put Sir Philip Sidney's hat on one side of his head, strutted off with an exquisite air of vulgar elegance. A third, who was but of puny dimensions, had bolstered himself out bravely with the spoils from several obscure tracts of philosophy, so that he had a very imposing front, but he was lamentably tattered in rear, and I perceived that he had patched his small clothes with scraps of parchment from a Latin author.

There were some well dressed gentlemen, it is true, who only helped themselves to a gem or so, which sparkled among their own ornaments, without eclipsing them. Some too, seemed to contemplate the costumes of the old writers merely to imbibe their principles of taste, and catch their air and spirit; but I grieve to say that too many were apt to array themselves from top to toe, in the patch work manner I have mentioned. I should not omit to speak of one genius in drab breeches and gaiters, and an arcadian hat, who had a violent propensity to the pastoral, but whose rural wanderings had been confined to the classic haunts of Primrose hill and the solitudes of the Regent's Park. He had decked himself in wreaths and ribbands from all the old pastoral poets, and hanging his head on one side, went about with a fantastical, lack-a-daisical air, "babbling about green fields." But the personage that most struck my attention was a pragmatical old gentleman in clerical robes, with a remarkably large and square, but bald head. He entered

The Plagiarist

An engraving reproduced in the Geoffrey Crayon edition of *The Sketch Book* (New York: G. P. Putnam's Sons, 1880).

the room wheezing and puffing, elbowed his way through the throng with a look of sturdy self confidence, and having laid hands upon a thick Greek quarto, clapped it upon his head, and swept majestically away in a formidable frizzled wig.

In the height of this literary masquerade a cry suddenly resounded from every side of "Thieves! Thieves!" I looked, and lo the portraits about the walls became animated! The old authors thrust out first a head, then a shoulder from the canvass, looked down curiously for an instant upon the motley throng, and then descended, with fury in their eyes, to claim their rifled property. The scene of scampering and hubbub that ensued baffles all description. The unhappy culprits endeavoured in vain to escape with their plunder. On one side might be seen half a dozen old monks stripping a modern professor—on another there was sad devastation carried into the ranks of modern dramatic writers. Beaumont and Fletcher side by side, raged round the field like Castor and Pollux, and sturdy Ben Jonson enacted more wonders than when a volunteer with the army in Flanders. As to the dapper little compiler of farragoes mentioned sometime since, he had arrayed himself in as many patches and colours as harlequin, and there was as fierce a contention of claimants about him, as about the dead body of Patroclus. I was grieved to see many men, to whom I had been accustomed to look up with awe and reverence, fain to steal off with scarce a rag to cover their nakedness. Just then my eye was caught by the pragmatical old gentleman in the Greek grizzled wig, who was scrambling away in sore affright with half a score of authors in full cry after him. They were close upon his haunches; in a twinkling off went his wig; at every turn some strip of raiment was peeled away, until in a few moments, from his domineering pomp, he shrunk into a little, pursy "chopped bald shot," and made his exit with only a few tags and rags fluttering at his back.

There was something so ludicrous in the catastrophe of this learned Theban that I burst into an immoderate fit of laughter, which broke the whole illusion. The tumult and the scuffle were at an end. The chamber resumed its usual appearance. The old authors shrunk back into their picture frames and hung in shadowy solemnity along the walls. In short, I found myself wide awake in my corner, with the whole assemblage of Bookworms gazing at me with astonishment. Nothing of the dream had been real but my burst of laughter, a sound never before heard in that grave sanctuary, and so abhorrent to the ears of wisdom as to electrify the fraternity.

The librarian now stepped up to me and demanded whether I had a card of admission. At first I did not comprehend him, but I soon found that the library was a kind of literary "preserve," subject to game laws, and that no one must presume to hunt there without special licence and permission. In a word, I stood convicted of being an arrant poacher, and was glad to make a precipitate retreat, lest I should have a whole pack of authors let loose upon me.

A ROYAL POET

Though your body be confin'd,
  And soft love a prisoner bound,
Yet the beauty of your mind,
  Neither check nor chain hath found.
  Look out nobly, then, and dare
  Even the fetters that you wear.
                              FLETCHER.

On a soft sunny morning in the genial month of May, I made an
excursion to Windsor castle. It is a place full of storied and poetical
associations. The very external aspect of the proud old pile is enough
to inspire high thought. It rears its irregular walls and massive towers,
like a mural crown, round the brow of a lofty ridge, waves its royal
banner in the clouds, and looks down, with a lordly air, upon the surrounding world.

On this morning the weather was of that voluptuous vernal kind,
which calls forth all the latent romance of a man's temperament, filling
his mind with musick, and disposing him to quote poetry and dream of
beauty. In wandering through the magnificent saloons, and long echoing
galleries of the castle, I passed with indifference by whole rows of
portraits of warriors and statesmen, but lingered in the chamber, where
hang the likenesses of the beauties that graced the gay court of Charles
the Second; and as I gazed upon them, depicted with amorous, half
dishevelled tresses, and the sleepy eye of love, I blessed the pencil of
Sir Peter Lely which had thus enabled me to bask in the reflected rays
of beauty. In traversing also the "large green courts," with sunshine
beaming on the gray walls, and glancing along the velvet turf, my mind
was engrossed with the image of the tender, the gallant, but hapless
Surrey, and his account of his loiterings about them in his stripling
days when enamoured of the Lady Geraldine—

"With eyes cast up unto the maiden's tower,
With easie sighs, such as men draw in love."

In this mood of mere poetical susceptibility, I visited the ancient Keep
of the Castle, where James the First of Scotland, the pride and theme of
Scottish poets and historians, was for many years of his youth detained
a prisoner of state. It is a large gray tower, that has stood the brunt of
ages, and is still in good preservation. It stands on a mound, which

elevates it above the other parts of the castle, and a great flight of steps leads to the interior. In the armoury, which is a gothic hall furnished with weapons of various kinds and ages, I was shewn a coat of armour hanging against the wall, which had once belonged to James. From hence I was conducted up a staircase to a suite of apartments of faded magnificence, hung with storied tapestry, which formed his prison, and the scene of that passionate and fanciful amour, which has woven into the web of his story the magical hues of poetry and fiction.

The whole history of this amiable but unfortunate prince is highly romantic. At the tender age of eleven he was sent from home by his father, Robert III. and destined for the French court, to be reared under the eye of the French monarch, secure from the treachery and danger that surrounded the royal house of Scotland. It was his mishap in the course of his voyage to fall into the hands of the English, and he was detained prisoner by Henry IV., notwithstanding that a truce existed between the two countries.

The intelligence of his capture, coming in the train of many sorrows and disasters, proved fatal to his unhappy father. "The news," we are told, "was brought to him while at supper, and did so overwhelm him with grief, that he was almost ready to give up the ghost into the hands of the servants that attended him. But being carried to his bed chamber, he abstained from all food, and in three days died of hunger and grief, at Rothesay."*

James was detained in captivity above eighteen years; but, though deprived of personal liberty, he was treated with the respect due to his rank. Care was taken to instruct him in all the branches of useful knowledge cultivated at that period, and to give him those mental and personal accomplishments deemed proper for a prince. Perhaps, in this respect, his imprisonment was an advantage, as it enabled him to apply himself the more exclusively to his improvement, and quietly to imbibe that rich fund of knowledge, and to cherish those elegant tastes, which have given such a lustre to his memory. The picture drawn of him in early life, by the Scottish historians, is highly captivating, and seems rather the description of a hero of romance, than of a character in real history. He was well learnt, we are told, "to fight with the sword, to joust, to tournay, to wrestle, to sing and dance; he was an expert mediciner, right crafty in playing both of lute and harp and sundry other instruments of musick, and was expert in grammar, oratory, and poetry."†

With this combination of manly and delicate accomplishments, fitting him to shine both in active and elegant life, and calculated to give him

*Buchanan.
†Ballenden's Translation of Hector Boyce.

an intense relish for joyous existence, it must have been a severe trial, in an age of bustle and chivalry, to pass the spring time of his years in monotonous captivity. It was the good fortune of James, however, to be gifted with a powerfully poetic fancy, and to be visited in his prison by the choicest inspirations of the muse. Some minds corrode and grow inactive, under the loss of personal liberty; others grow morbid and irritable; but it is the nature of the poet to become tender and imaginative in the loneliness of confinement. He banquets upon the honey of his own thoughts, and, like the captive bird, pours forth his soul in melody.

> Have you not seen the nightingale
>   A pilgrim coop'd into a cage,
> How doth she chant her wonted tale,
>   In that her lonely hermitage!
> Even there her charming melody doth prove
> That all her boughs are trees, her cage a grove.*

Indeed, it is the divine attribute of the imagination, that it is irrepressible, unconfinable. That when the real world is shut out, it can create a world for itself, and with a necromantic power, can conjure up glorious shapes and forms, and brilliant visions, to make solitude populous, and irradiate the gloom of the dungeon. Such was the world of pomp and pageant that lived round Tasso in his dismal cell at Ferrara, when he conceived the splendid scenes of his Jerusalem; and we may consider the "King's Quair," composed by James during his captivity at Windsor, as another of those beautiful breakings forth of the soul from the restraint and gloom of the prison house.

The subject of the poem is his love for the Lady Jane Beaufort, daughter of the Earl of Somerset, and a princess of the blood royal of England, of whom he became enamoured in the course of his captivity. What gives it peculiar value is, that it may be considered a transcript of the royal bard's true feelings, and the story of his real loves and fortunes. It is not often that sovereigns write poetry, or that poets deal in fact. It is gratifying to the pride of a common man, to find a monarch thus suing, as it were, for admission into his closet, and seeking to win his favour by administering to his pleasures. It is a proof of the honest equality of intellectual competition, which strips off all the trappings of factitious dignity, brings the candidate down to a level with his fellow men, and obliges him to depend on his own native powers for distinction. It is curious, too, to get at the history of a monarch's heart, and to

*Roger l'Estrange.

find the simple affections of human nature throbbing under the ermine. But James had learnt to be a poet before he was a king: he was schooled in adversity, and reared in the company of his own thoughts. Monarchs have seldom time to parley with their hearts, or meditate their minds into poetry; and had James been brought up amidst the adulation and gaiety of a court, we should never, in all probability, have had such a poem as the Quair.

I have been particularly interested by those parts of the poem which breathe his immediate thoughts concerning his situation, or which are connected with the apartment in the tower. They have thus a personal and local charm, and are given with such circumstantial truth, as to make the reader present with the captive in his prison, and the companion of his meditations.

Such is the account which he gives of his weariness of spirit, and of the incident which first suggested the idea of writing the poem. It was the still mid-watch of a clear moonlight night; the stars, he says, were twinkling as fire in the high vault of heaven; and "Cynthia rinsing her golden locks in Aquarius." He lay in bed, wakeful and restless, and took a book to beguile the tedious hours. The book he chose was Boetius' Consolations of Philosophy, a work popular among the writers of that day, and which had been translated by his great prototype Chaucer. From the high eulogium in which he indulges, it is evident this was one of his favourite volumes while in prison; and indeed it is an admirable text book for meditation under adversity. It is the legacy of a noble and enduring spirit, purified by sorrow and suffering, bequeathing to its successors in calamity, the maxims of sweet morality, and the trains of eloquent but simple reasoning, by which it was enabled to bear up against the various ills of life. It is a talisman, which the unfortunate may treasure up in his bosom, or like the good King James, lay upon his nightly pillow.

After closing the volume, he turns its contents over in his mind, and gradually falls into a fit of musing on the fickleness of fortune, the vicissitudes of his own life, and the evils that had overtaken him even in his tender youth. Suddenly he hears the bell ringing to matins; but its sound chiming in with his melancholy fancies, seems to him like a voice exhorting him to write his story. In the spirit of poetic errantry he determines to comply with this intimation; he therefore takes pen in hand, makes with it a sign of the cross to implore a benediction, and sallies forth into the fairy land of poetry. There is something extremely fanciful in all this, and it is interesting as furnishing a striking and beautiful instance of the simple manner in which whole trains of poetical thought are sometimes awakened, and literary enterprises suggested to the mind.

In the course of his poem he more than once bewails the peculiar hardness of his fate; thus doomed to lonely and inactive life, and shut up from the freedom and pleasure of the world, in which the meanest animal indulges unrestrained. There is a sweetness however in his very complaints; they are the lamentations of an amiable and social spirit at being denied the indulgence of its kind and generous propensities; there is nothing in them harsh nor exaggerated; they flow with a natural and touching pathos, and are perhaps rendered more touching by their simple brevity. They contrast finely with those elaborate and iterated repinings, which we sometimes meet with, in poetry;—the effusions of morbid minds, sickening under miseries of their own creating, and venting their bitterness upon an unoffending world. James speaks of his privations with acute sensibility, but having mentioned them passes on, as if his manly mind disdained to brood over unavoidable calamities. When such a spirit breaks forth into complaint, however brief, we are aware how great must be the suffering that extorts the murmur. We sympathize with James, a romantic, active, and accomplished prince, cut off in the lustihood of youth from all the enterprise, the noble uses, and vigorous delights of life; as we do with Milton, alive to all the beauties of nature and glories of art, when he breathes forth brief, but deep toned lamentations, over his perpetual blindness.

Had not James evinced a deficiency of poetic artifice, we might almost have suspected that these lourings of gloomy reflection were meant as preparative to the brightest scene of his story; and to contrast with that refulgence of light and loveliness, that exhilarating accompaniment of bird and song, and foliage and flower, and all the revel of the year, with which he ushers in the lady of his heart. It is this scene in particular, which throws all the magic of romance about the old castle keep. He had risen, he says, at day break, according to custom, to escape from the dreary meditations of a sleepless pillow. "Bewailing in his chamber thus alone," despairing of all joy and remedy, "fortired of thought and wo begone," he had wandered to the window, to indulge the captive's miserable solace of gazing wistfully upon the world from which he is excluded. The window looked forth upon a small garden which lay at the foot of the tower. It was a quiet, sheltered spot, adorned with arbours and green alleys, and protected from the passing gaze by trees and hawthorn hedges.

> Now was there made fast by the tower's wall,
>   A garden faire, and in the corners set,
> An arbour green with wandis long and small
>   Railed about, and so with leaves beset

> Was all the place and hawthorn hedges knet,
>   That lyf* was none, walkyng there forbye,
>   That might within scarce any wight espye.
>
> So thick the branches and the leves grene,
>   Beshaded all the alleys that there were,
> And midst of every arbour might be seen
>   The sharpe, grene, sweet juniper,
> Growing so fair, with branches here and there,
>   That as it seemed to a lyf without,
>   The boughs did spread the arbour all about.
>
> And on the small grene twistis† set
>   The lytel swete nightingales and sung
> So loud and clere, the hymnis consecrate
>   Of lovis use, now soft, now loud among,
> That all the garden and the wallis rung
> Right of their song——

It was the month of May, when every thing was in bloom; and he interprets the song of the nightingale into the language of his enamoured feeling:

> Worship all ye that lovers be this May,
>   For of your bliss the kalends are begun,
> And sing with us, away, winter away,
>   Come, summer come, the sweet season and sun.

As he gazes on the scene, and listens to the notes of the birds, he gradually lapses into one of those tender and undefinable reveries, which fill the youthful bosom in this delicious season. He wonders what this love may be, of which he has so often read, and which thus seems breathed forth in the quickening breath of May, and melting all nature into ecstacy and song. If it really be so great a felicity, and if it be a boon thus generally dispensed to the most insignificant beings, why is he alone cut off from its enjoyments?

> Oft would I think, O Lord, what, may this be
>   That love is of such noble myght and kynde?

*Lyf, person.
†Twistis, small boughs or twigs.
Note.—The language of the quotations is generally modernized.

Loving his folk, and such prosperitee
Is it of him, as we in books do find:
    May he oure hertes setten* and unbynd:
Hath he upon our hertes such maistrye?
Or is all this but feynit fantasye?

For giff he be of so grete excellence,
    That he of every wight hath care and charge,
What have I gilt† to him, or done offense?
    That I am thral'd, and birdis go at large.

In the midst of his musing, as he casts his eye downward, he beholds "the fairest and the freshest young floure," that ever he had seen. It is the lovely lady Jane walking in the garden to enjoy the beauty of that "fresh May morrowe." Breaking thus suddenly upon his sight in the moment of loneliness and excited susceptibility, she at once captivates the fancy of the romantic prince, and becomes the object of his wandering wishes, the sovereign of his ideal world.

There is, in this charming scene, an evident resemblance to the early part of Chaucer's Knight's Tale; where Palamon and Arcite fall in love with Emilia, whom they see walking in the garden of their prison. Perhaps the similarity of the actual fact to the incident which he had read in Chaucer, may have induced James to dwell on it in his poem. His description of the Lady Jane is given in the picturesque and minute manner of his master; and being doubtless taken from the life, is a perfect portrait of a beauty of that day. He dwells, with the fondness of a lover, on every article of her apparel, from the net of pearl, splendent with emeralds and sapphires, that confined her golden hair, even to the "goodly chaine of small orfeverye‡" about her neck, whereby there hung a ruby in shape of a heart, that seemed, he says, like a spark of fire burning upon her white bosom. Her dress of white tissue was looped up to enable her to walk with more freedom. She was accompanied by two female attendants, and about her sported a little hound decorated with bells; probably the small Italian hound of exquisite symmetry, which was a parlour favourite and pet among the fashionable dames of ancient times. James closes his description by a burst of general eulogium.

In her was youth, beauty, with humble port,
    Bountee, richesse, and womanly feature;

*Setten, incline.
†Gilt, what injury have I done, &c.
‡Wrought gold.

> God better knows than my pen can report,
>   Wisdom, largesse,° estate,† and cunning‡ sure,
> In every point so guided her mesure,
>   In word, in deed, in shape, in countenance,
>   That nature might no more her child advance.

The departure of the lady Jane from the garden, puts an end to this transient riot of the heart. With her departs the amorous illusion that had shed a temporary charm over the scene of his captivity, and he relapses into loneliness, now rendered tenfold more intolerable by this passing beam of unattainable beauty. Through the long and weary day he repines at his unhappy lot, and when evening approaches, and Phœbus, as he beautifully expresses it, had "bad farewell to every leaf and flower," he still lingers at the window, and laying his head upon the cold stone, gives vent to a mingled flow of love and sorrow, until gradually lulled by the mute melancholy of the twilight hour, he lapses "half sleeping, half swoon," into a vision which occupies the remainder of the poem, and in which is allegorically shadowed out the history of his passion.

When he wakes from his trance, he rises from his stony pillow, and, pacing his apartment, full of dreary reflections, questions his spirit whither it has been wandering; whether, indeed, all that has passed before his dreaming fancy, has been conjured up by preceding circumstances; or whether it is a vision, intended to comfort and assure him in his despondency. If the latter, he prays that some token may be sent to confirm the promise of happier days, given him in his slumbers. Suddenly a turtle dove, of the purest whiteness, comes flying in at the window and alights upon his hand, bearing in her bill a branch of red gilliflower, on the leaves of which is written, in letters of gold, the following sentence:

> Awake! awake! I bring, lover, I bring
>   The newis glad that blissful is, and sure
> Of thy comfort; now laugh, and play, and sing,
>   For in the heaven decretit is thy cure.

He receives the branch with mingled hope and dread; reads it with rapture: and this, he says, was the first token of his succeeding happiness. Whether this is a mere poetic fiction, or whether the Lady Jane did actually send him a token of her favour in this romantic way, remains

°*Largesse*, bounty.
†*Estate*, dignity.
‡*Cunning*, discretion.

to be determined according to the faith or fancy of the reader. He concludes his poem, by intimating that the promise conveyed in the vision and by the flower, is fulfilled, by his being restored to liberty, and made happy in the possession of the sovereign of his heart.

Such is the poetical account given by James of his love adventures in Windsor Castle. How much of it is absolute fact, and how much the embellishment of fancy, it is fruitless to conjecture: let us not, however, reject every romantic incident as incompatible with real life; but let us sometimes take a poet at his word. I have noticed merely those parts of the poem immediately connected with the Tower, and have passed over a large part, written in the allegorical vein, so much cultivated at that day. The language, of course, is quaint and antiquated, so that the beauty of many of its golden phrases will scarcely be perceived at the present day; but it is impossible not to be charmed with the genuine sentiment, the delightful artlessness and urbanity, which prevail throughout it. The descriptions of nature, too, with which it is embellished, are given with a truth, a discrimination, and a freshness, worthy of the most cultivated periods of the art.

As an amatory poem it is edifying, in these days of coarser thinking, to notice the nature, refinement, and exquisite delicacy which pervade it; banishing every gross thought or immodest expression, and presenting female loveliness, clothed in all its chivalrous attributes of almost supernatural purity and grace.

James flourished nearly about the time of Chaucer and Gower, and was evidently an admirer and studier of their writings. Indeed in one of his stanzas he acknowledges them as his masters; and in some parts of his poem we find traces of similarity to their productions, more especially to those of Chaucer. There are always, however, general features of resemblance in the works of contemporary authors, which are not so much borrowed from each other as from the times. Writers, like bees, toll their sweets in the wide world; they incorporate with their own conceptions the anecdotes and thoughts current in society; and thus each generation has some features in common, characteristic of the age in which it lives.

James belongs to one of the most brilliant eras of our literary history, and establishes the claims of his country to a participation in its primitive honours. Whilst a small cluster of English writers are constantly cited as the fathers of our verse, the name of their great Scottish compeer is apt to be passed over in silence; but he is evidently worthy of being enrolled in that little constellation of remote but never failing luminaries, who shine in the highest firmament of literature, and who, like morning stars, sang together at the bright dawning of British poesy.

Such of my readers as may not be familiar with Scottish history (though the manner in which it has of late been woven with captivating fiction, has made it a universal study), may be curious to learn something of the subsequent history of James, and the fortunes of his love. His passion for the Lady Jane, as it was the solace of his captivity, so it facilitated his release, it being imagined by the court that a connection with the blood royal of England would attach him to its interests. He was ultimately restored to his liberty and crown, having previously espoused the Lady Jane, who accompanied him to Scotland, and made him a most tender and devoted wife.

He found his kingdom in great confusion, the feudal chieftains having taken advantage of the troubles and irregularities of a long interregnum to strengthen themselves in their possessions, and place themselves above the power of the laws. James sought to found the basis of his power in the affections of his people. He attached the lower orders to him by the reformation of abuses, the temperate and equable administration of justice, the encouragement of the arts of peace, and the promotion of every thing that could diffuse comfort, competency, and innocent enjoyment through the humblest ranks of society. He mingled occasionally among the common people in disguise; visited their fire sides; entered into their cares, their pursuits, and their amusements; informed himself of the mechanical arts, and how they could best be patronized and improved; and was thus an all pervading spirit, watching with a benevolent eye over the meanest of his subjects. Having in this generous manner, made himself strong in the hearts of the common people, he turned himself to curb the power of the factious nobility; to strip them of those dangerous immunities which they had usurped; to punish such as had been guilty of flagrant offences; and to bring the whole into proper obedience to the crown. For some time they bore this with outward submission, but secret impatience and brooding resentment. A conspiracy was at length formed against his life, at the head of which was his own uncle, Robert Stewart Earl of Athol, who, being too old himself for the perpetration of the deed of blood, instigated his grandson Sir Robert Stewart, together with Sir Robert Graham, and others of less note, to commit the deed. They broke into his bed chamber at the Dominican Convent near Perth, where he was residing, and barbarously murdered him by oft repeated wounds. His faithful queen rushing to throw her tender body between him and the sword, was twice wounded in the ineffectual attempt to shield him from the assassin, and it was not until she had been forcibly torn from his person, that the murder was accomplished.

It was the recollection of this romantic tale of former times, and of the golden little poem which had its birth place in this tower, that made me visit the old pile with more than common interest. The

suit of armour hanging up in the hall, richly gilt and embellished as if
to figure in the tournay, brought the image of the gallant and romantic
prince vividly before my imagination. I paced the deserted chambers
where he had composed his poem; I leaned upon the window and
endeavoured to persuade myself it was the very one where he had been
visited by his vision; I looked out upon the spot where he had first seen
the Lady Jane. It was the same genial and joyous month; the birds were
again vying with each other in strains of liquid melody; every thing was
bursting into vegetation, and budding forth the tender promise of the
year. Time, which delights to obliterate the sterner memorials of human
pride, seems to have passed lightly over this little scene of poetry and
love, and to have withheld his desolating hand. Several centuries have
gone by, yet the garden still flourishes at the foot of the tower. It occupies what was once the moat of the keep; and though some parts
have been separated by dividing walls, yet others have still their arbours
and shaded walks, as in the days of James, and the whole is sheltered,
blooming, and retired. There is a charm about a spot that has been
printed by the footsteps of departed beauty, and consecrated by the
inspirations of the poet, which is heightened, rather than impaired, by
the lapse of ages. It is, indeed, the gift of poetry to hallow every place
in which it moves; to breathe round nature an odour more exquisite
than the perfume of the rose, and to shed over it a tint more magical
than the blush of morning.

Others may dwell on the illustrious deeds of James as a warrior and a
legislator; but I have delighted to view him merely as the companion
of his fellow man, the benefactor of the human heart, stooping from
his high estate to sow the sweet flowers of poetry and song in the paths
of common life. He was the first to cultivate the vigorous and hardy
plant of Scottish genius, which has since become so prolific of the
most wholesome and highly flavoured fruit. He carried with him into the
sterner regions of the north, all the fertilizing arts of southern refinement. He did every thing in his power to win his countrymen to the gay,
the elegant, and gentle arts, which soften and refine the character of a
people, and wreathe a grace round the loftiness of a proud and warlike
spirit. He wrote many poems, which, unfortunately for the fullness of
his fame, are now lost to the world; one which is still preserved, called
"Christ's Kirk of the Green," shews how diligently he had made himself
acquainted with the rustic sports and pastimes, which constitute such
a source of kind and social feeling among the Scottish peasantry; and
with what simple and happy humour he could enter into their enjoyments. He contributed greatly to improve the national music; and traces
of his tender sentiment, and elegant taste, are said to exist in those
witching airs, still piped among the wild mountains and lonely glens

of Scotland. He has thus connected his image with whatever is most gracious and endearing in the national character; he has embalmed his memory in song, and floated his name to after ages in the rich stream of Scottish melody. The recollection of these things was kindling at my heart, as I paced the silent scene of his imprisonment. I have visited Vaucluse with as much enthusiasm as a pilgrim would visit the shrine at Loretto; but I have never felt more poetical devotion than when contemplating the old tower and the little garden at Windsor, and musing over the romantic loves of the Lady Jane and the Royal Poet of Scotland.

THE COUNTRY CHURCH

A gentleman?
What, o'the woolpack? or the sugar chest?
Or lists of velvet? which is't pound, or yard,
You vend your gentry by?

BEGGAR'S BUSH.

There are few places more favourable to the study of character than
an English country church. I was once passing a few weeks at the seat
of a friend who resided in the vicinity of one the appearance of which
particularly struck my fancy. It was one of those rich morsels of
quaint antiquity which give such a peculiar charm to English landscape. It stood in the midst of a county filled with ancient families,
and contained within its cold and silent aisles, the congregated dust of
many noble generations. The interior walls were encrusted with monuments of every age and style. The light streamed through windows
dimmed with armorial bearings, richly emblazoned in stained glass. In
various parts of the church were tombs of knights and high born dames
of gorgeous workmanship, with their effigies in coloured marble. On
every side the eye was struck with some instance of aspiring mortality;
some haughty memorial which human pride had erected over its kindred
dust, in this temple of the most humble of all religions.

The congregation was composed of the neighbouring people of rank,
who sat in pews sumptuously lined and cushioned, furnished with richly
gilded prayer books, and decorated with their arms upon the pew doors;
—the villagers and peasantry, who filled the back seats, and a small gallery beside the organ, and the poor of the parish, who were ranged
on benches in the aisles.

The service was performed by a snuffling well fed vicar, who had
a snug dwelling near the church. He was a privileged guest at all the
tables of the neighbourhood and had been the keenest foxhunter in
the county, until age and good living had disabled him from doing
any thing more than ride to see the hounds throw off, and make one
at the hunting dinner.

Under the ministry of such a pastor I found it impossible to get into
the train of thought suitable to the time and place, so having, like many
other feeble christians, compromised with my conscience by laying the
sin of my own delinquency at another person's threshold, I occupied
myself by making observations of my neighbours.

I was as yet a stranger in England, and curious to notice the manners of its fashionable classes. I found, as usual, that there was the least pretension where there was the most acknowledged title to respect. I was particularly struck for instance, with the family of a nobleman of high rank, consisting of several sons and daughters. Nothing could be more simple and unassuming than their appearance. They generally came to church in the plainest equipage, and often on foot. The young ladies would stop and converse in the kindest manner with the peasantry, caress the children, and listen to the stories of the humble cottagers. Their countenances were open, beautifully fair, with an expression of high refinement, but at the same time a frank cheerfulness and an engaging affability. Their brothers were tall and elegantly formed. They were dressed fashionably but simply; with strict neatness and propriety, but without any mannerism or foppishness. Their whole demeanour was easy and natural, with that lofty grace and noble frankness, which bespeak free born souls that have never been checked in their growth by feelings of inferiority. There is a healthful hardiness about real dignity, that never dreads contact and communion with others, however humble. It is only spurious pride that is morbid and sensitive and shrinks from every touch. I was pleased to see the manner in which they would converse with the peasantry about those rural concerns and field sports, in which the gentlemen of this country so much delight. In these conversations there was neither haughtiness on the one part, nor servility on the other; and you were only reminded of the difference of rank by the habitual respect of the peasant.

In contrast to these was the family of a wealthy citizen, who had amassed a vast fortune, and having purchased the estate and mansion of a ruined nobleman in the neighbourhood, was endeavouring to assume all the style and dignity of an hereditary lord of the soil. The family always came to church *en prince*. They were rolled majestically along in a carriage emblazoned with arms. The crest glittered in silver radiance from every part of the harness where a crest could possibly be placed. A fat coachman in a three cornered hat, richly laced, and a flaxen wig, curling close around his rosy face, was seated on the box, with a sleek Danish dog beside him. Two footmen in gorgeous liveries, with huge boquets and gold headed canes lolled behind. The carriage rose and sunk on its long springs with peculiar stateliness of motion. The very horses champed their bits, arched their necks and glanced their eyes more proudly than common horses, either because they had caught a little of the family feeling, or were reined up more tightly than ordinary.

I could not but admire the style with which this splendid pageant was brought up to the gate of the church yard. There was a vast effect produced at the turning of an angle of the wall. A great cracking of

the whip—straining and scrambling of the horses—glistering of harness
and flashing of wheels through gravel. This was the moment of
triumph and vain glory to the Coachman. The horses were urged and
checked until they were fretted into a foam. They threw out their feet
in a prancing trot, dashing about pebbles at every step. The crowd of
villagers sauntering quietly to church opened precipitately to the right
and left, gaping in vacant admiration—On reaching the gate the horses
were pulled up with a suddenness that produced an immediate stop
and almost threw them on their haunches.

There was an extraordinary hurry of the footmen to alight, open the
door, pull down the steps and prepare every thing for the descent on
earth of this august family. The old citizen first emerged his round
red face from out the door, looking about him with the pompous
air of a man accustomed to rule on change and shake the stock market
with a nod. His consort, a fine, fleshy, comfortable dame followed him.
There seemed, I must confess, but little pride in her composition. She
was the picture of broad, honest, vulgar enjoyment. The world went
well with her—and she liked the world. She had fine clothes, a fine
house, a fine carriage, fine children, every thing was fine about her: it
was nothing but driving about, and visiting, and feasting. Life was to
her a perpetual revel; it was one long, lord mayor's day.

Two daughters succeeded to this goodly couple. They certainly were
handsome but had a supercilious air, that chilled admiration and disposed the spectator to be critical. They were ultra-fashionables in dress,
and though no one could deny the richness of their decorations, yet
their appropriateness might be questioned amidst the simplicity of a
country church. They descended loftily from the carriage and moved up
the line of peasantry, with a step that seemed dainty of the soil it trod
on. They cast an excursive glance around that passed coldly over the
burly faces of the peasantry, until they met the eyes of the nobleman's
family, when their countenances immediately brightened into smiles
and they made the most profound and elegant courtsies; which were
returned in a manner that shewed they were but slight acquaintances.

I must not forget the two sons of this aspiring citizen, who came to
church in a dashing curricle with outriders. They were arrayed in the
extremity of the mode, with all that pedantry of dress, which marks
the man of questionable pretensions to style. They kept entirely by
themselves, eying every one askance that came near them; as if measuring his claims to respectability; yet they were without conversation, except
the exchange of an occasional cant phrase. They even moved artificially,
for their bodies, in compliance with the caprice of the day, had been
disciplined into the absence of all ease and freedom. Art had done
every thing to accomplish them as men of fashion, but nature had

denied the nameless grace. They were vulgarly shaped, like men formed for the common purposes of life and had that air of supercilious assumption which is never seen in the true gentleman.

I have been rather minute in drawing the pictures of these two families, because I considered them specimens of what is often to be met with in this country—the unpretending great and the arrogant little. I have no respect for titled rank, unless it be accompanied by true nobility of soul; but I have remarked, in all countries where artificial distinctions exist, the very highest classes are always the most courteous and unassuming—Those who are well assured of their own standing are least apt to trespass on that of others; whereas nothing is so offensive as the aspirings of vulgarity, which thinks to elevate itself by humiliating its neighbour.

As I have brought these families into contrast I must notice their behaviour in church. That of the nobleman's family was quiet, serious and attentive. Not that they appeared to have any fervour of devotion but rather a respect for sacred things and sacred places, inseparable from good breeding. The others on the contrary were in a perpetual flutter and whisper; they betrayed a continual consciousness of finery, and a sorry ambition of being the wonders of a rural congregation.

The old gentleman was the only one really attentive to the service. He took the whole burthen of family devotion upon himself; standing bolt upright and uttering the responses with a loud voice that might be heard all over the church. It was evident that he was one of those thorough Church and King men who connect the idea of devotion and loyalty; who consider the deity somehow or other, of the government party, and religion "a very excellent sort of thing that ought to be countenanced and kept up."

When he joined so loudly in the service it seemed more by way of example to the lower orders, to shew them, that though so great and wealthy, he was not above being religious, as I have seen a turtle fed alderman swallow publicly a basin of charity soup, smacking his lips at every mouthful and pronouncing it "excellent food for the poor."

When the service was at an end I was curious to witness the several exits of my groups. The young noblemen and their sisters as the day was fine preferred strolling home across the fields, chatting with the country people as they went. The others departed as they came, in grand parade. Again were the equipages wheeled up to the gate. There was again the smacking of whips, the clattering of hoofs and the glittering of harness. The horses started off almost at a bound; the villagers again hurried to right and left; the wheels threw up a cloud of dust, and the aspiring family was rapt out of sight in a whirlwind.

THE WIDOW AND HER SON

Pittie olde age, within whose silver haires
Honour and reverence ever more have raign'd.
MARLOWE'S TAMBURLAINE.

Those who are in the habit of remarking such matters must have noticed the pensive quiet of an English landscape on Sunday. The clacking of the mill, the regularly recurring stroke of the flail; the din of the blacksmith's hammer; the whistling of the plowman; the rattling of the cart, and all other sounds of rural labor are suspended. The very farm dogs bark less frequently, being less disturbed by passing travellers. At such times I have almost fancied the winds sunk into quiet and that the sunny landscape, with its fresh green tints melting into blue haze, enjoyed the hallowed calm.

Sweet day, so pure, so calm, so bright,
The bridal of the earth and sky.

Well was it ordained that the day of devotion should be a day of rest. The holy repose which reigns over the face of nature, has its moral influence; every restless passion is charmed down, and we feel the natural religion of the soul gently springing up within us. For my part there are feelings that visit me, in a country church, amid the beautiful serenity of nature, which I experience no where else; and if not a more religious, I think I am a better man on Sunday than on any other day of the seven.

During my recent residence in the country I used frequently to attend at the old village church. Its shadowy aisles; its mouldering monuments; its dark oaken panelling, all reverend with the gloom of departed years, seemed to fit it for the haunt of solemn meditation; but being in a wealthy aristocratic neighborhood, the glitter of fashion penetrated even into the sanctuary; and I felt myself continually thrown back upon the world by the frigidity and pomp of the poor worms around me. The only being in the whole congregation who appeared thoroughly to feel the humble and prostrate piety of a true christian, was a poor, decrepid old woman, bending under the weight of years and infirmities. She bore the traces of something better than abject poverty. The lingerings of decent pride were visible in her appearance. Her dress, though humble in the extreme, was scrupulously clean. Some trivial respect too had been awarded her, for she did not take her seat among the village poor, but sat alone on the steps of the altar. She seemed to have survived all love, all friendship, all society, and to have nothing left her but the hopes of heaven. When I saw her feebly rising and bending her aged form in prayer; habitually conning her prayer book, which her palsied hand and failing eyes would not permit her to read, but which she evidently knew by heart—I felt persuaded that the faltering voice of that poor woman arose to heaven far before the responses of the clerk, the swell of the organ or the chaunting of the choir.

I am fond of loitering about country churches, and this was so delight-fully situated that it frequently attracted me. It stood on a knoll, round which a small stream made a beautiful bend and then wound its way through a long reach of soft meadow scenery. The church was sur-rounded by yew trees, which seemed almost coeval with itself. Its tall gothic spire shot up lightly from among them, with rooks and crows generally wheeling about it. I was seated there one still sunny morning watching two labourers who were digging a grave. They had chosen one of the most remote and neglected corners of the church yard, where, from the number of nameless graves around, it would appear that the indigent and friendless were huddled into the earth. I was told that the new made grave was for the only son of a poor widow. While I was meditating on the distinctions of worldly rank, which extend thus down into the very dust, the toll of the bell announced the approach of the funeral. They were the obsequies of poverty, with which pride had nothing to do. A coffin of the plainest materials, without pall or other covering, was borne by some of the villagers. The sexton walked before with an air of cold indifference. There were no mock mourners in the trappings of affected woe, but there was one real mourner who feebly tottered after the corpse. It was the aged mother of the deceased—the poor old woman whom I had seen seated on the steps of the altar. She was supported by a humble friend, who was endeavouring to comfort her. A few of the neighbouring poor had joined the train, and some children of the village were running, hand in hand, now shouting with unthinking mirth, and now pausing to gaze with childish curiosity on the grief of the mourner.

As the funeral train approached the grave the parson issued from the church porch arrayed in the surplice, with prayer book in hand and attended by the clerk. The service, however, was a mere act of charity. The deceased had been destitute and the survivor was penniless. It was shuffled through, therefore, in form, but coldly and unfeelingly. The well fed priest moved but a few steps from the church door—his voice could scarcely be heard at the grave, and never did I hear the funeral service, that sublime and touching ceremony, turned into such a frigid mummery of words.

The Widow and Her Son

An engraving reproduced in the Geoffrey Crayon edition of *The Sketch Book* (New York: G. P. Putnam's Sons, 1880).

I approached the grave. The coffin was placed on the ground. On it were inscribed the name and age of the deceased. "George Somers, aged 26 Years." The poor mother had been assisted to kneel down at the head of it. Her withered hands were clasped as if in prayer, but I could perceive by a feeble rocking of the body, and a convulsive motion of the lips, that she was gazing on the last reliques of her son with the yearnings of a mother's heart.

Preparations were made to deposit the coffin in the earth. There was that bustling stir, which breaks so harshly on the feelings of grief and affection—directions given in the cold tones of business—the striking of spades into sand and gravel, which, at the grave of those we love, is of all sounds the most withering. The bustle around seemed to awaken the mother from a wretched reverie. She raised her glazed eyes, and looked about, with a faint wildness. As the men approached with cords to lower the coffin into the grave she wrung her hands and broke into an agony of grief. The poor woman who attended her took her by the arm, endeavouring to raise her from the earth and to whisper something like consolation—"Nay now—nay now—don't take it so sorely to heart—" She could only shake her head and wring her hands, as one not to be comforted.

As they lowered the body into the earth the creaking of the cords seemed to agonize her; but when, on some accidental obstruction there was a justling of the coffin, all the tenderness of the mother burst forth; as if any harm could come to him, who was far beyond the reach of worldly suffering.

I could see no more—my heart swelled into my throat—my eyes filled with tears—I felt as if I were acting a barbarous part in standing by and gazing idly on this scene of maternal anguish. I wandered to another part of the church yard where I remained until the funeral train had dispersed.

When I saw the mother slowly and painfully quitting the grave, leaving behind her the remains of all that was dear to her on earth, and returning to silence and destitution, my heart ached for her—What, thought I, are the distresses of the rich!—they have friends to soothe; pleasures to beguile; a world to divert and dissipate their griefs—What are the sorrows of the young! Their growing minds soon close above the wound—their elastic spirits soon rise beneath the pressure—their green and ductile affections soon twine around new objects—But the sorrows of the poor, who have no outward appliances to soothe—the sorrows of the aged with whom life at best is but a wintry day, and who can look for no aftergrowth of joy—the sorrows of a widow, aged, solitary, destitute, mourning over an only son the last solace of her years—these are indeed sorrows which make us feel the impotency of consolation.

It was some time before I left the church yard—on my way homeward I met with the woman who had acted as comforter: she was just returning from accompanying the mother to her lonely habitation, and I drew from her some particulars connected with the affecting scene I had witnessed.

The parents of the deceased had resided in the village from childhood. They had inhabited one of the neatest cottages, and by various rural occupations and the assistance of a small garden, had supported themselves creditably and comfortably, and led a happy and a blameless life. They had one son who had grown up to be the staff and pride of their age—"Oh sir!" said the good woman, "he was such a likely lad; so sweet tempered; so kind to every one round him; so dutiful to his parents! It did one's heart good to see him of a Sunday, drest out in his best, so tall, so straight, so cheery—supporting his old mother to church—for she was always fonder of leaning on George's arm than on her good man's—and, poor soul, she might well be proud of him, for a finer lad, there was not in the country round."

Unfortunately the son was tempted during a year of scarcity and agricultural hardship, to enter into the service of one of the small craft that plied on a neighbouring river. He had not been long in this employ when he was entrapped by a press gang and carried off to sea. His parents received tidings of his seizure, but beyond that they could learn nothing. It was the loss of their main prop. The father who was already infirm, grew heartless and melancholy and sunk into his grave. The widow left lonely in her age and feebleness could no longer support herself, and came upon the parish. Still there was a kind feeling towards her throughout the village and a certain respect as being one of the oldest inhabitants. As no one applied for the cottage in which she had passed so many happy days, she was permitted to remain in it, where she lived solitary and almost helpless—The few wants of nature were chiefly supplied from the scanty productions of her little garden, which the neighbours would now and then cultivate for her. It was but a few days before the time at which these circumstances were told me, that she was gathering some vegetables for her repast, when she heard the cottage door which faced the garden suddenly opened. A stranger came out and seemed to be looking eagerly and wildly around. He was dressed in seaman's clothes, was emaciated and ghastly pale, and bore the air of one broken by sickness and hardships. He saw her and hastened towards her, but his steps were faint and faltering—he sank on his knees before her and sobbed like a child. The poor woman gazed upon him with a vacant and wondering eye—"Oh my dear-dear mother! don't you know your son!—your poor boy George!" It was indeed the wreck of her once noble lad; who, shattered by wounds, by sickness and foreign imprisonment, had at length dragged his wasted limbs homeward to repose among the scenes of his childhood.

I will not attempt to detail the particulars of such a meeting, where joy and sorrow were so completely blended—Still he was alive!—he was come home!—he might yet live to comfort and cherish her old age!— Nature, however, was exhausted in him, and if any thing had been wanting to finish the work of fate, the desolation of his native cottage would have been sufficient. He stretched himself on the pallet on which his widowed mother had passed many a sleepless night, and he never rose from it again.

The villagers, when they heard that George Somers had returned, crowded to see him, offering every comfort and assistance that their humble means afforded. He was too weak, however, to talk—he could only look his thanks. His mother was his constant attendant; and he seemed unwilling to be helped by any other hand.

There is something in sickness that breaks down the pride of manhood; that softens the heart and brings it back to the feelings of infancy. Who that has languished, even in advanced life, in sickness and despondency— who that has pined on a weary bed in the neglect and loneliness of a foreign land—but has thought on the mother "that looked on his child- hood," that smoothed his pillow and administered to his helplessness.— Oh! there is an enduring tenderness in the love of a mother to her son that transcends all other affections of the heart. It is neither to be chilled by selfishness—nor daunted by danger—nor weakened by worthlessness— nor stifled by ingratitude. She will sacrifice every comfort to his con- venience—she will surrender every pleasure to his enjoyment—she will glory in his fame and exult in his prosperity. And if misfortune overtake him he will be the dearer to her from misfortune—and if dis- grace settle upon his name, she will still love and cherish him in spite of his disgrace—and if all the world beside cast him off, she will be all the world to him—

Poor George Somers had known what it was to be in sickness and none to soothe, lonely and in prison and none to visit him. He could not endure his mother from his sight—if she moved away, his eye would follow her. She would sit for hours by his bed watching him as he slept. Sometimes he would start from a feverish dream, and look anxiously up until he saw her bending over him, when he would take her hand, lay it on his bosom and fall asleep with the tranquility of a child—In this way he died.

My first impulse on hearing this humble tale of affliction, was to visit the cottage of the mourner and administer pecuniary assistance, and, if possible comfort. I found, however, on enquiry, that the good feelings of the villagers had prompted them to do every thing that the case admitted: and as the poor know best how to console each other's sorrows, I did not venture to intrude.

The next Sunday I was at the village church; when to my surprize, I saw the poor old woman tottering down the aisle to her accustomed seat on the steps of the altar.

She had made an effort to put on something like mourning for her son; and nothing could be more touching than this struggle between pious affection and utter poverty—A black ribband, or so—a faded black handkerchief—and one or two more such humble attempts to express by outward signs that grief which passes shew—When I looked round upon the storied monuments—the stately hatchments—the cold marble pomp, with which grandeur mourned magnificently over departed pride; and turned to this poor widow bowed down by age and sorrow at the altar of her god, and offering up the prayers and praises of a pious, though a broken heart, I felt that this living monument of real grief was worth them all.

I related her story to some of the wealthy members of the congregation and they were moved by it. They exerted themselves to render her situation more comfortable, and to lighten her afflictions. It was, however, but smoothing a few steps to the grave. In the course of a Sunday or two after she was missed from her usual seat at church, and before I left the neighbourhood I heard with a feeling of satisfaction that she had quietly breathed her last, and had gone to rejoin those she loved, in that world where sorrow is never known, and friends are never parted.

A SUNDAY IN LONDON*

In a preceding paper I have spoken of an English Sunday in the country and its tranquilizing effect upon the landscape; but where is its sacred influence more strikingly apparent than in the very heart of that great Babel, London? On this sacred day the gigantic monster is charmed into repose. The intolerable din and struggle of the week are at an end. The shops are shut. The fires of forges and manufactories are extinguished; and the sun, no longer obscured by murky clouds of smoke, pours down a sober yellow radiance into the quiet streets. The few pedestrians we meet, instead of hurrying forward with anxious countenances, move leisurely along; their brows are smoothed from the wrinkles of business and care; they have put on their Sunday looks, and Sunday manners, with their Sunday clothes, and are cleansed in mind as well as in person.

And now the melodious clangor of bells from church towers summons their several flocks to the fold. Forth issues from his mansion the family of the decent tradesman; the small children in the advance; then the citizen and his comely spouse, followed by the grown up daughters, with small morocco bound prayerbooks laid in the folds of their pocket-handkerchiefs. The housemaid looks after them from the window, admiring the finery of the family, and receiving, perhaps, a nod and smile from her young mistresses, at whose toilette she has assisted.

Now rumbles along the carriage of some magnate of the city; peradventure an Alderman or a Sheriff; and now the patter of many feet announces a procession of charity scholars in uniforms of antique cut, and each with a prayerbook under his arm.

The ringing of bells is at an end; the rumbling of the carriage has ceased; the pattering of feet is heard no more: the flocks are folded in ancient churches cramped up in bye lanes and corners of the crowded city; where the vigilant beadle keeps watch, like the shepherd's dog, round the threshhold of the sanctuary. For a time every thing is hushed; but soon is heard the deep pervading sound of the organ, rolling and vibrating through the empty lanes and courts; and the sweet chaunting of the choir making them resound with melody and praise. Never have I been more sensible of the sanctifying effect of church music than when I have heard it thus poured forth, like a river of joy through the inmost recesses of this great metropolis, cleansing it, as it were, from all the sordid pollutions of the week; and bearing the poor world worn soul on a tide of triumphant harmony to heaven.

*Part of a sketch omitted in the preceding editions.

The morning service is at an end. The streets are again alive with the congregations returning to their homes, but soon again relapse into silence. Now comes on the Sunday dinner, which to the city tradesman, is a meal of some importance. There is more leisure for social enjoyment at the board. Members of the family can now gather together, who are separated by the laborious occupations of the week. A school boy may be permitted on that day to come to the paternal home; an old friend of the family takes his accustomed Sunday seat at the board, tells over his well known stories and rejoices young and old with his well known jokes.

On Sunday afternoon the city pours forth its legions to breathe the fresh air and enjoy the sunshine of the parks and rural environs. Satyrists may say what they please about the rural enjoyments of a London citizen on Sunday, but to me there is something delightful in beholding the poor prisoner of the crowded and dusty city enabled thus to come forth once a week and throw himself upon the green bosom of nature. He is like a child restored to the mother's breast; and they who first spread out these noble parks and magnificent pleasure grounds which surround this huge metropolis, have done at least as much for its health and morality as if they had expended the amount of cost in hospitals, prisons and penitentiaries.

THE BOAR'S HEAD TAVERN, EAST CHEAP
A Shakespearian Research

A tavern is the rendezvous, the Exchange, the staple of good fellows. I have heard my great grandfather tell, how his great, great grandfather should say, that it was an old proverb when his great grandfather was a child, that "it was a good wind that blew a man to the wine."

MOTHER BOMBIE.

It is a pious custom in some Catholic countries to honour the memory of saints, by votive lights burnt before their pictures. The popularity of a saint, therefore, may be known by the number of these offerings. One perhaps is left to moulder in the darkness of his little chapel; another may have a solitary lamp to throw its blinking rays athwart his effigy; while the whole blaze of adoration is lavished at the shrine of some beatified father of renown. The wealthy devotee brings his huge luminary of wax, the eager zealot his seven branched candlestick, and even the mendicant pilgrim is by no means satisfied that sufficient light is thrown upon the deceased, unless he hang up his little lamp of smoking oil. The consequence is, that in the eagerness to enlighten they are often apt to obscure; and I have occasionally seen an unlucky saint, almost smoked out of countenance by the officiousness of his followers.

In like manner has it fared with the immortal Shakespeare. Every writer considers it his bounden duty to light up some portion of his character or works, and to rescue some merit from oblivion. The commentator, opulent in words, produces vast tomes of dissertations; the common herd of editors send up mists of obscurity from their notes at the bottom of each page, and every casual scribbler brings his farthing rush light of eulogy or research, to swell the cloud of incense and of smoke.

As I honour all established usages of my brethren of the quill, I thought it but proper to contribute my mite of homage to the memory of the illustrious bard. I was for some time, however, sorely puzzled in what way I should discharge this duty. I found myself anticipated in every attempt at a new reading; every doubtful line had been explained a dozen different ways and perplexed beyond the reach of elucidation; and as to fine passages, they had all been amply praised by previous admirers; nay, so completely had the bard of late been overlarded with panegyrick by a great German critick, that it was difficult now to find even a fault that had not been argued into a beauty.

In this perplexity I was one morning turning over his pages, when

I casually opened upon the comic scenes of Henry the Fourth, and was in a moment completely lost in the mad cap revelry of the Boar's head Tavern. So vividly and naturally are these scenes of humour depicted, and with such force and consistency are the characters sustained, that they become mingled up in the mind with the facts and personages of real life. To few readers does it occur that these are all ideal creations of a poet's brain, and that, in sober truth, no such knot of merry roysters ever enlivened the dull neighbourhood of East cheap.

For my part I love to give myself up to the illusions of poetry. A Hero of fiction who never existed, is just as valuable to me as a hero of history who existed a thousand years since; and, if I may be excused such an insensibility to the common ties of human nature, I would not give up fat Jack, for half the great men of ancient chronicle. What have the heroes of yore done for me, or men like me?—They have conquered countries of which I do not enjoy an acre—or they have gained laurels of which I do not inherit a leaf—or they have furnished examples of hairbrained prowess, which I have neither the opportunity nor the inclination to follow. But old Jack Falstaff!—kind Jack Falstaff!—sweet Jack Falstaff!—has enlarged the boundaries of human enjoyment; he has added vast regions of wit and good humour, in which the poorest man may revel; and has bequeathed a never failing inheritance of jolly laughter to make mankind merrier and better to the latest posterity.

A thought suddenly struck me—"I will make a pilgrimage to East cheap," said I, closing the book, "and see if the old Boar's head Tavern still exists. Who knows but I may light upon some legendary traces of Dame Quickly and her guests; at any rate, there will be a kindred pleasure in treading the halls once vocal with their mirth, to that the toper enjoys, in smelling to the empty cask, once filled with generous wine."

The resolution was no sooner formed than put in execution. I forbear to treat of the various adventures and wonders I encountered in my travels—of the haunted regions of Cock-lane—of the faded glories of Little Britain and the parts adjacent; what perils I ran in Cateaton Street and Old Jewry; of the renowned Guildhall and its two stunted Giants, the pride and wonder of the city and the terror of all unlucky urchins—and how I visited London Stone and struck my staff upon it in imitation of that arch rebel Jack Cade.

Let it suffice to say, that I at length arrived in merry East cheap, that ancient region of wit and wassail, where the very names of the streets relished of good cheer, as Pudding Lane bears testimony even at the present day. For East cheap says old Stow, "was always famous for its convivial doings. The cookes cried hot ribbes of beef rosted, pies well baked and other victuals: there was clattering of pewter pots, harpe, pipe and sawtrie." Alas! how sadly is the scene changed since the roaring days of Falstaff and old Stow. The mad cap royster has given place to the plodding tradesman—the clattering of pots and the sound of "harp and sawtry" to the din of carts and the accursed dinging of the dustman's bell; and no song is heard save haply the strain of some syren from Billingsgate chaunting the eulogy of deceased mackrel.

I sought in vain for the ancient abode of Dame Quickly. The only relique of it is a boar's head carved in relief in stone, which formerly served as the sign, but at present is built into the parting line of two houses which stand on the scite of the renowned old Tavern.

For the history of this little empire of good fellowship I was referred to a Tallow chandler's widow opposite, who had been born and brought up on the spot, and was looked up to as the indisputable chronicler of the neighbourhood. I found her seated in a little back parlour, the window of which looked out upon a yard about eight feet square, laid out as a flower garden; while a glass door opposite afforded a distant peep of the street through a vista of soap and tallow candles: the two views which comprised in all probability her prospects of life, and the little world in which she had lived, and moved, and had her being, for the better part of a century.

To be versed in the history of East cheap, great and little, from London Stone even unto the Monument, was doubtless in her opinion to be acquainted with the history of the universe. Yet with all this she possessed the simplicity of true wisdom, and that liberal, communicative disposition, which I have generally remarked in intelligent old ladies, knowing in the concerns of their neighbourhood.

Her information, however, did not extend far back into antiquity. She could throw no light upon the history of the Boar's head from the time that Dame Quickly espoused the valiant Pistol, until the great fire of London, when it was unfortunately burnt down. It was soon rebuilt, and continued to flourish under the old name and sign, until a dying Landlord, struck with remorse for double scores, bad measures, and other iniquities which are incident to the sinful race of Publicans, endeavoured to make his peace with heaven by bequeathing the tavern to St. Michael's church, Crooked Lane, towards the supporting of a chaplain. For some time the vestry meetings were regularly held there, but it was observed that the old Boar never held up his head under church government. He gradually declined, and finally gave his last gasp about thirty years since. The tavern was then turned into shops, but she informed me that a picture of it was still preserved in St. Michael's church, which stood just in the rear. To get a sight of this picture was now my determination, so having informed myself of the abode of the sexton I took my leave of the venerable chronicler of East cheap, my visit having doubtless raised greatly her opinion of her legendary lore, and furnished an important incident in the history of her life.

It cost me some difficulty and much curious enquiry to ferret out the humble hanger on to the church. I had to explore Crooked Lane and divers little alleys and elbows and dark passages, with which this old city is perforated, like an ancient cheese, or a worm eaten chest of drawers. At length I traced him to a corner of a small court, surrounded by lofty houses, where the inhabitants enjoy about as much of the face of heaven, as a community of frogs at the bottom of a well. The sexton was a meek acquiescing little man, of a bowing lowly habit; yet he had a pleasant twinkle in his eye, and if encouraged would now and then hazard a small pleasantry, such as a man of his low estate might venture to make in the company of high church wardens, and other mighty men of the earth. I found him in company with the deputy organist, seated apart, like Milton's angels discoursing no doubt on high doctrinal points, and settling the affairs of the church over a friendly pot of ale—for the lower classes of English seldom deliberate on any weighty matter without the assistance of a cool tankard to clear their understandings. I arrived at the moment when they had finished their ale and their argument, and were about to repair to the church to put it in order, so having made known my wishes I received their gracious permission to accompany them.

The church of St. Michael, Crooked Lane, standing a short distance from Billingsgate, is enriched with the tombs of many Fishmongers of renown, and as every profession has its galaxy of glory and its constellation of great men, I presume the monument of a mighty Fishmonger of the olden time, is regarded with as much reverence by succeeding generations of the craft as poets feel on contemplating the tomb of Virgil, or soldiers the monument of a Marlborough or a Turenne.

I cannot but turn aside, while thus speaking of illustrious men, to observe that St. Michael's Crooked Lane contains also the ashes of that doughty champion William Walworth, knight, who so manfully clove down the sturdy wight Wat Tyler in Smithfield, a hero worthy of honorable blazon as almost the only Lord Mayor on record, famous for deeds of arms:—the Sovereigns of Cockney being generally renowned, as the most pacific of all potentates.*

Note

*The following was the ancient inscription on the monument of this worthy—which unhappily was destroyed in the great conflagration—

> Hereunder lyth a man of Fame
> William Walworth callyd by name:
> Fishmonger he was in Lyfftime here

Adjoining the church, in a small cemetery, immediately under the back windows of what was once the Boar's head stands the tomb stone of Robert Preston, whilom drawer at the Tavern. It is now nearly a century since this trusty drawer of good liquor closed his bustling career, and was thus quietly deposited within call of his customers. As I was clearing away the weeds from his epitaph the little sexton drew me on one side with a mysterious air, and informed me in a low voice, that once upon a time on a dark wintry night, when the wind was unruly, howling and whistling, banging about doors and windows and twirling weather cocks so that the living were frightened out of their beds and even the dead could not sleep quietly in their graves, the ghost of honest Preston, which happened to be airing itself in the church yard, was attracted by the well known call of "waiter" from the Boar's head, and made its sudden appearance in the midst of a roaring club, just as the parish clerk was singing a stave from the "mirrie garland of captain Death"—to the discomfiture of sundry train-band captains and the conversion of an infidel attorney, who became a zealous christian on the spot and was never known to twist the truth afterwards except in the way of business.

I beg it may be remembered that I do not pledge myself for the authenticity of this anecdote, though it is well known that the church yards and bye corners of this old metropolis are very much infested with perturbed spirits and every one must have heard of the Cock Lane Ghost, and the apparition that guards the regalia in the Tower, which has frightened so many bold sentinels almost out of their wits.

Be all this as it may, this Robert Preston seems to have been a worthy successor to the nimble tongued Francis who attended upon the revels of Prince Hal, to have been equally prompt with his "anon, anon, sir"

And twise Lord Maior, as in Books appere;
Who with courage stout and manly myght
Slew Jackstraw in King Richards syght.
For which act done and trew Entent
The Kyng made him Knyght incontinent;
And gave him armes, as here you see,
To declare his Fact and chivaldrie.
He left this Lyff the yere of our God
Thirteen hondred fourscore and three odd.

An error in the foregoing inscription has been corrected by the venerable Stow— "Whereas," saith he, "it hath been far spread abroad by vulgar opinion, that the rebel smitten down so manfully by Sir William Walworth, the then worthy Lord Maior was named Jack Straw and not Wat Tyler, I thought good to reconcile this rash conceived doubt by such testimony as I find in ancient and good records. The principal Leaders or captains of the commons were Wat Tyler as the first man; the second was John or Jack Straw &c &c." Stow's London.

and to have transcended his predecessor in honesty, for Falstaff, the veracity of whose taste no man will venture to impeach, flatly accuses Francis of putting lime in his sack: whereas honest Preston's epitaph lauds him for the sobriety of his conduct, the soundness of his wine and the fairness of his measure.* The worthy dignitaries of the church, however, did not appear much captivated by the sober virtues of the Tapster; the deputy organist, who had a moist look out of the eye, made some shrewd remark on the abstemiousness of a man brought up among full hogsheads, and the little sexton corroborated his opinion by a significant wink and a dubious shake of the head.

Thus far my researches, though they threw much light on the history of Tapsters, Fishmongers and Lord Mayors, yet disappointed me in the great object of my quest, the picture of the Boar's head Tavern. No such painting was to be found in the church of St. Michael. "Marry and amen!" said I, "here endeth my research!" So I was giving the matter up with the air of a baffled antiquary, when my friend the sexton, perceiving me to be curious in every thing relative to the old Tavern, offered to shew me the choice vessels of the vestry, which had been handed down from remote times, when the parish meetings were held at the Boar's head. These were deposited in the Parish club room, which had been transferred, on the decline of the ancient establishment, to a tavern in the neighbourhood.

A few steps brought us to the house which stands No. 12. Miles Lane, bearing the title of The Mason's arms, and is kept by Master Edward Honeyball, the "bully Rock" of the establishment. It is one of those little taverns which abound in the heart of the city and form the centre of gossip and intelligence of the neighbourhood.

We entered the bar room, which was narrow and darkling; for in these close lanes but few rays of reflected light are enabled to struggle down

<hr>

Note.

*As this inscription is rife with excellent morality, I transcribe it for the admonition of delinquent Tapsters. It is no doubt the production of some choice spirit who once frequented the Boar's head.

> "Bacchus to give the toping world surprize
> Produced one sober son, and here he lies.
> Though rear'd among full hogsheads he defy'd
> The charms of wine, and every one beside.
> O reader if to justice thou'rt inclin'd
> Keep honest Preston daily in thy mind.
> He drew good wine, took care to fill his pots
> Had sundry virtues that excus'd his faults.
> You that on Bacchus have the like dependance,
> Pray copy Bob, in measure and attendance."

to the inhabitants, whose broad day is at best but a tolerable twilight. The room was partitioned into boxes, each containing a table spread with a clean white cloth ready for dinner. This shewed that the guests were of the good old stamp, and divided their day equally; for it was but just one O'clock. At the lower end of the room was a clear coal fire, before which a breast of lamb was roasting. A row of bright brass candlesticks and pewter mugs glistened along the mantle piece, and an old fashioned clock ticked in one corner. There was something primitive in this medley of Kitchen, Parlour and Hall, that carried me back to earlier times and pleased me. The place indeed was humble, but every thing had that look of order and neatness which bespeaks the superintendance of a notable English housewife. A group of amphibious looking beings, who might be either fishermen or sailors were regaling themselves in one of the boxes. As I was a visitor of rather higher pretensions I was ushered into a little misshapen back room having at least nine corners. It was lighted by a sky light, furnished with an-tiquated leathern chairs and ornamented with the portrait of a fat pig. It was evidently appropriated to particular customers, and I found a shabby gentleman, in a red nose and oil cloth hat, seated in one corner, meditating on a half empty pot of porter.

The old sexton had taken the landlady aside and with an air of profound importance imparted to her my errand. Dame Honeyball was a likely, plump, bustling little woman, and no bad substitute for that paragon of hostesses Dame Quickly. She seemed delighted with an op-portunity to oblige, and hurrying up stairs to the archives of her house, where the precious vessels of the parish club were deposited, she returned smiling and curtseying with them in her hands.

The first she presented me was a japanned iron Tobacco box of gigantic size, out of which I was told the vestry had smoked at their stated meet-ings since time immemorial; and which was never suffered to be profaned by vulgar hands or used on common occasions. I received it with becoming reverence, but what was my delight on beholding on its cover the identical painting of which I was in quest. There was dis-played the outside of the Boar's head Tavern, and before the door was to be seen the whole convivial group at table in full revel; pictured with that wonderful fidelity and force, with which the portraits of re-nowned generals and commodores are illustrated on Tobacco boxes, for the benefit of posterity. Lest, however, there should be any mistake, the cunning limner had warily inscribed the names of Prince Hal and Falstaff on the bottoms of their chairs.

On the inside of the cover was an inscription, nearly obliterated, recording that this box was the gift of Sir Richard Gore, for the use of the vestry meetings at the Boar's head Tavern, and that it was "repaired and beautified by his successor Mr. John Packard 1767." Such is a faithful description of this august and venerable relique, and I question whether the learned Scriblerius contemplated his Roman shield, or the Knights of the Round Table the long sought san-greal with more exultation.

While I was meditating on it with enraptured gaze, Dame Honeyball, who was highly gratified by the interest it excited, put in my hands a drinking cup or goblet, which also belonged to the vestry, and was descended from the old Boar's head. It bore the inscription of having been the gift of Francis Wythers, Knight, and was held, she told me, in exceeding great value, being considered very "antyke." This last opinion was strengthened by the shabby gentleman in the red nose and oil cloth hat, and whom I strongly suspected of being a lineal descendant from the valiant Bardolph. He suddenly aroused from his meditation on the pot of porter, and casting a knowing look at the goblet exclaimed— "Aye-aye, the head don't ache now, that made that there article."—

The great importance attached to this memento of ancient revelry by modern church wardens, at first puzzled me; but there is nothing sharpens the apprehension so much as antiquarian research; for I immediately perceived that this could be no other than the identical "parcel-gilt goblet" on which Falstaff made his loving but faithless vow to Dame Quickly; and which would of course be treasured up with care among the regalia of her domains, as a testimony of that solemn contract.*

Mine hostess indeed gave me a long history how the goblet had been handed down from generation to generation. She also entertained me with many particulars concerning the worthy vestrymen who have seated themselves thus quietly on the stools of the ancient roysters of East cheap, and, like so many commentators, utter clouds of smoke in honour of Shakespeare. These I forbear to relate, lest my readers should not be as curious in these matters as myself. Suffice it to say, the neighbours one and all about East cheap, believe that Falstaff and his merry crew actually lived and revelled there. Nay there are several legendary anecdotes concerning him still extant among the oldest frequenters of the Mason's arms; which they give, as transmitted down from their forefathers; and Mr. McKash, an Irish hair dresser, whose shop stands on

Note.

*Thou didst swear to me, upon a *parcel-gilt goblet*, sitting in my Dolphin chamber, at the round table, by a sea coal fire, on Wednesday in Whitsunweek, when the prince broke thy head for likening his father to a singing man of Windsor; thou didst swear to me then, as I was washing thy wound, to marry me, and make me my lady thy wife. Canst thou deny it? II⁰ Part. Henry IV.

the scite of the old Boar's head, has several dry jokes of Fat Jack's, not laid down in the books, with which he makes his customers ready to die of laughter.

I now turned to my friend the sexton to make some further enquiries, but I found him sunk in pensive meditation. His head had declined a little on one side—a deep sigh heaved from the very bottom of his stomach, and though I could not see a tear trembling in his eye, yet a moisture was evidently stealing from a corner of his mouth. I followed the direction of his eye through the door which stood open and found it fixed wistfully on the savoury breast of lamb, roasting in dripping richness before the fire.

I now called to mind, that in the eagerness of my recondite investigation I was keeping the poor man from his dinner. My bowels yearned with sympathy, and, putting in his hand a small token of my gratitude and good will, I departed with a hearty benediction on him, Dame Honeyball and the parish club of Crooked Lane—not forgetting my shabby, but sententious friend, in the oil cloth hat and copper nose.

Thus have I given a "tedious brief" account of this interesting research, for which, if it prove too short and unsatisfactory, I can only plead my inexperience in this branch of literature so deservedly popular at the present day. I am aware that a more skillful illustrator of the immortal bard would have swelled the materials I have but touched upon, to a good merchantable bulk—comprizing the biographies of William Walworth, Jack Straw and Robert Preston—some notice of the Eminent Fishmongers of St. Michael's—the history of East cheap, great and little—private anecdotes of Dame Honeyball and her pretty daughter, whom I have not even mentioned, to say nothing of a damsel tending the breast of lamb (and whom, by the way, I remarked to be a comely lass, with a neat foot and ancle)—the whole enlivened by the riots of Wat Tyler, and illuminated by the great fire of London.

All this I leave as a rich mine to be worked by future commentators; nor do I despair of seeing the Tobacco box and the "parcel-gilt goblet" which I have thus brought to light, the subjects of future engravings and almost as fruitful of voluminous dissertations and disputes as the shield of Achilles, or the far famed Portland vase.

THE
MUTABILITY OF LITERATURE
A COLLOQUY IN WESTMINSTER ABBEY

I know that all beneath the moon decays,
And what by mortals in this world is brought,
In time's great period shall return to nought.
I know that all the muses' heavenly layes,
With toil of sprite which are so dearly bought,
As idle sounds of few or none are sought,
That there is nothing lighter than mere praise.
DRUMMOND OF HAWTHORNDEN.

There are certain half dreaming moods of mind, in which we naturally steal away from noise and glare, and seek some quiet haunt, where we may indulge our reveries and build our air castles undisturbed. In such a mood I was loitering about the old gray cloisters of Westminster Abbey, enjoying that luxury of wandering thought which one is apt to dignify with the name of reflection, when suddenly an irruption of madcap boys from Westminster school playing at football broke in upon the monastic stillness of the place, making the vaulted passages and mouldering tombs echo with their merriment. I sought to take refuge from their noise by penetrating still deeper into the solitudes of the pile, and applied to one of the vergers for admission to the library. He conducted me through a portal rich with the crumbling sculpture of former ages, which opened upon a gloomy passage leading to the chapter house and the chamber in which doomsday book is deposited. Just within the passage is a small door on the left. To this the verger applied a key; it was double locked, and opened with some difficulty, as if seldom used. We now ascended a dark narrow staircase, and passing through a second door, entered the library.

I found myself in a lofty antique hall, the roof supported by massive joists of old English oak. It was soberly lighted by a row of Gothic windows at a considerable height from the floor, and which apparently opened upon the roofs of the cloisters. An ancient picture of some reverend dignitary of the church in his robes hung over the fire place. Around the hall and in a small gallery were the books, arranged in carved oaken cases. They consisted principally of old polemical writers, and were much more worn by time than use. In the centre of the library was a solitary table with two or three books on it; an inkstand without ink, and a few pens parched by long disuse. The place seemed

100

fitted for quiet study and profound meditation. It was buried deep among the massive walls of the abbey, and shut up from the tumult of the world. I could only hear now and then the shouts of the schoolboys faintly swelling from the cloister, and the sound of a bell tolling for prayers, echoing soberly along the roofs of the abbey. By degrees the shouts of merriment grew fainter and fainter, and at length died away. The bell ceased to toll, and a profound silence reigned through the dusky hall.

I had taken down a little thick quarto, curiously bound in parchment, with brass clasps, and seated myself at the table in a venerable elbow chair. Instead of reading, however, I was beguiled by the solemn monastic air, and lifeless quiet of the place, into a train of musing. As I looked around upon the old volumes in their mouldering covers, thus ranged on the shelves, and apparently never disturbed in their repose, I could not but consider the library a kind of literary catacomb, where authors, like mummies, are piously entombed, and left to blacken and moulder in dusty oblivion.

How much, thought I, has each of these volumes, now thrust aside with such indifference, cost some aching head; how many weary days— how many sleepless nights. How have their authors buried themselves in the solitude of cells and cloisters; shut themselves up from the face of man, and the still more blessed face of nature, and devoted themselves to painful research and intense reflection. And all for what! to occupy an inch of dusty shelf—to have the title of their works read now and then in a future age, by some drowsy churchman, or casual straggler like myself; and in another age to be lost, even to remembrance. Such is the amount of this boasted immortality.—A mere temporary rumour, a local sound, like the tone of that bell which has just tolled among these towers, filling the ear for a moment—lingering transiently in echo—and then passing away, like a thing that was not!

While I sat half murmuring, half meditating these unprofitable speculations, with my head resting on my hand, I was thrumming with the other hand upon the quarto, until I accidentally loosened the clasps, when, to my utter astonishment, the little book gave two or three yawns, like one awakening from a deep sleep; then a husky hem, and at length began to talk. At first its voice was very hoarse and broken, being much troubled by a cobweb which some studious spider had woven across it; and having probably contracted a cold from long exposure to the chills and damps of the abbey. In a short time, however, it became more distinct, and I soon found it an exceedingly fluent conversable little tome. Its language, to be sure, was rather quaint and obsolete, and its pronunciation, what, in the present day, would be deemed barbarous; but I shall endeavour, as far as I am able, to render it in modern parlance.

It began with railings about the neglect of the world—about merit being suffered to languish in obscurity, and other such common place topics of literary repining, and complained bitterly that it had not been opened for more than two centuries. That the Dean only looked now and then into the library, sometimes took down a volume or two, trifled with them for a few moments, and then returned them to their shelves. "What a plague do they mean," said the little quarto, which I began to perceive was somewhat choleric, "what a plague do they mean by keeping several thousand volumes of us shut up here, and watched by a set of old vergers like so many beauties in a harem, merely to be looked at now and then by the Dean? Books were written to give pleasure and to be enjoyed; and I would have a rule passed that the Dean should pay each of us a visit at least once a year; or if he is not equal to the task, let them once in a while turn loose the whole school of Westminster among us, that at any rate we may now and then have an airing."

"Softly, my worthy friend," replied I, "you are not aware how much better you are off than most books of your generation. By being stored away in this ancient library, you are like the treasured remains of those saints and monarchs which lie enshrined in the adjoining chapels, while the remains of your contemporary mortals, left to the ordinary course of nature, have long since returned to dust."

"Sir," said the little tome, ruffling his leaves and looking big, "I was written for all the world, not for the bookworms of an abbey. I was intended to circulate from hand to hand, like other great contemporary works; but here have I been clasped up for more than two centuries, and might have silently fallen a prey to these worms that are playing the very vengeance with my intestines, if you had not by chance given me an opportunity of uttering a few last words before I go to pieces."

"My good friend," rejoined I, "had you been left to the circulation of which you speak, you would long ere this have been no more. To judge from your physiognomy, you are now well stricken in years: very few of your contemporaries can be at present in existence; and those few owe their longevity to being immured like yourself in old libraries; which, suffer me to add, instead of likening to harems, you might more properly and gratefully have compared to those infirmaries attached to religious establishments, for the benefit of the old and decrepid, and where, by quiet fostering and no employment, they often endure to an amazingly good for nothing old age. You talk of your contemporaries as if in circulation—where do we meet with their works? what do we hear of Robert Grosteste of Lincoln? No one could have toiled harder than he for immortality. He is said to have written nearly two hundred volumes. He built, as it were, a pyramid of books to perpetuate his name: but, alas! the pyramid has long since fallen, and only a few fragments are scattered in various libraries, where they are scarcely disturbed even by the antiquarian. What do we hear of Gyraldus Cambrensis, the historian, antiquary, philosopher, theologian, and poet? He declined two bishoprics that he might shut himself up and write for posterity; but posterity never inquires after his labours. What of Henry of Huntingdon, who, beside a learned history of England, wrote a treatise on the contempt of the world, which the world has revenged by forgetting him. What is quoted of Joseph of Exeter, styled the miracle of his age in classical composition? Of his three great heroic poems one is lost forever, excepting a mere fragment; the others are known only to a few of the curious in literature, and as to his love verses and epigrams, they have entirely disappeared. What is in current use of John Wallis, the Franciscan, who acquired the name of the tree of life? Of William of Malmsbury;—of Simeon of Durham; of Benedict of Peterborough; of John Hanvill of St. Albans; of——"

"Prithee, friend," cried the quarto in a testy tone, "how old do you think me? You are talking of authors that lived long before my time, and wrote either in Latin or French, so that they in a manner expatriated themselves, and deserved to be forgotten;* but I, sir, was ushered into the world from the press of the renowned Wynkyn de Worde. I was written in my own native tongue at a time when the language had become fixed, and indeed I was considered a model of pure and elegant English."

(I should observe that these remarks were couched in such intolerably antiquated terms, that I have had infinite difficulty in rendering them into modern phraseology.)

"I cry you mercy," said I, "for mistaking your age; but it matters little; almost all the writers of your time have likewise passed into forgetfulness; and De Worde's publications are mere literary rarities among book collectors. The purity and stability of language, too, on which you found your claims to perpetuity, have been the fallacious dependence of authors of every age, even back to the times of the worthy Robert of Gloucester, who wrote his history in rhymes of mongrel Saxon.† Even now, many talk

---

*In Latin and French hath many soueraine wittes had great delyte to endite, and have many noble thinges fulfilde, but certes there ben some that speaken their poisye in French, of which speche the French men have as good a fantasye as we have in heryng of Frenchemen's Englishe.   *Chaucer's Testament of Love.*

†Holinshed, in his Chronicle, observes, "afterward, also, by diligent travell of Geffray Chaucer and John Gowre, in the time of Richard the second, and after them of John Scogan and John Lydgate, monke of Berrie, our said toong was brought to an excellent passe, notwithstanding that it never came unto the type of perfection until the time of Queen Elizabeth, wherein John Jewell, Bishop of Sarum, John Fox, and sundrie learned and excellent writers, have fully accomplished the ornature of the same, to their great praise and immortal commendation."

of Spenser's 'well of pure English undefiled,' as if the language ever sprang
from a well or fountain head, and was not rather a mere confluence
of various tongues, perpetually subject to changes and intermixtures.
It is this which has made English literature so extremely mutable, and
the reputation built upon it so fleeting. Unless thought can be committed
to something more permanent and unchangeable than such a medium,
even thought must share the fate of every thing else, and fall into decay.
This should serve as a check upon the vanity and exultation of the most
popular writer. He finds the language in which he has embarked his
fame gradually altering, and subject to the dilapidations of time and
the caprice of fashion. He looks back and beholds the early authors
of his country, once the favourites of their day, supplanted by modern
writers. A few short ages have covered them with obscurity, and their
merits can only be relished by the quaint taste of the bookworm. And
such, he anticipates, will be the fate of his own work, which, however
it may be admired in its day, and held up as a model of purity, will
in the course of years grow antiquated and obsolete, until it shall become almost as unintelligible in its native land as an Egyptian obelisk,
or one of those Runic inscriptions said to exist in the deserts of Tartary.
I declare," added I with some emotion, "when I contemplate a modern
library, filled with new works in all the bravery of rich gilding and
binding, I feel disposed to sit down and weep, like the good Xerxes
when he surveyed his army, pranked out in all the splendour of military
array, and reflected that in one hundred years not one of them would
be in existence!"

"Ah," said the little quarto, with a heavy sigh, "I see how it is; these
modern scribblers have superseded all the good old authors. I suppose
nothing is read now-a-days but Sir Philip Sidney's Arcadia, Sackville's
stately plays, and Mirror for Magistrates, or the fine spun euphuisms of
the "unparalelled John Lyly."

"There you are again mistaken," said I, "the writers whom you suppose in vogue, because they happened to be so when you were last in
circulation, have long since had their day. Sir Philip Sydney's Arcadia,
the immortality of which was so fondly predicted by his admirers,* and
which, in truth, is full of noble thoughts, delicate images, and graceful
turns of language, is now scarcely ever mentioned. Sackville has strutted into obscurity; and even Lyly, though his writings were once the

---

*Live ever sweete booke; the silver image of his gentle witt, and the golden
pillar of his noble courage; and ever notify unto the world that thy writer was the
secretary of eloquence, the breath of the muses, the honey bee of the dayntiest
flowers of witt and arte, the pith of morale and intellectual virtues, the arme of
Bellona in the field, the tongue of Suada in the chamber, the spirite of Practise in
esse, and the paragon of excellency in print. *Harvey's Pierce's Supererogation.*

delight of a court, and apparently perpetuated by a proverb, is now scarcely known even by name. A whole crowd of authors who wrote and wrangled at the time, have likewise gone down with all their writings and their controversies. Wave after wave of succeeding literature has rolled over them, until they are buried so deep, that it is only now and then that some industrious diver after the fragments of antiquity brings up a specimen for the gratification of the curious.

"For my part," I continued, "I consider this mutability of language a wise precaution of Providence for the benefit of the world at large, and of authors in particular. To reason from analogy, we daily behold the varied and beautiful tribes of vegetables springing up, flourishing, adorning the fields for a short time, and then fading into dust, to make way for their successors. Were not this the case, the fecundity of nature would be a grievance instead of a blessing. The earth would groan with rank and excessive vegetation, and its surface become a tangled wilderness. In like manner, the works of genius and learning decline and make way for subsequent productions. Language gradually varies, and with it fade away the writings of authors who have flourished their allotted time; otherwise the creative powers of genius would overstock the world, and the mind would be completely bewildered in the endless mazes of literature. Formerly there were some restraints on this excessive multiplication. Works had to be transcribed by hand, which was a slow and laborious operation; they were written either on parchment, which was expensive, so that one work was often erased to make way for another; or on papyrus, which was fragile and extremely perishable. Authorship was a limited and unprofitable craft, and pursued chiefly by monks in the leisure and solitude of their cloisters. The accumulation of manuscripts was slow and costly, and confined almost entirely to monasteries. To these circumstances it may in some measure be owing that we have not been inundated by the intellect of antiquity; that the fountains of thought have not been broken up, and modern genius drowned in the deluge. But the inventions of paper and the press have put an end to all these restraints. They have made every one a writer, and enabled every mind to pour itself into print, and diffuse itself over the whole intellectual world. The consequences are alarming. The stream of literature has swoln into a torrent—augmented into a river—expanded into a sea. A few centuries since, five or six hundred manuscripts constituted a great library; but what would you say to libraries, such as actually exist, containing three and four hundred thousand volumes; legions of authors at the same time busy, and the press going on with fearfully increasing activity, to double and quadruple the number? Unless some unforeseen mortality should break out among the progeny of the muse, now that she has become so prolific, I tremble for posterity.

I fear the mere fluctuation of language will not be sufficient. Criticism may do much; it increases with the increase of literature, and resembles one of those salutary checks on population spoken of by economists. All possible encouragement, therefore, should be given to the growth of critics, good or bad. But I fear all will be in vain; let criticism do what it may, writers will write, printers will print, and the world will inevitably be overstocked with good books. It will soon be the employment of a life time merely to learn their names. Many a man of passable information at the present day reads scarce any thing but reviews, and before long a man of erudition will be little better than a mere walking catalogue."

"My very good sir," said the little quarto, yawning most drearily in my face, "excuse my interrupting you, but I perceive you are rather given to prose. I would ask the fate of an author who was making some noise just as I left the world. His reputation, however, was considered quite temporary. The learned shook their heads at him, for he was a poor half educated varlet, that knew little of Latin, and nothing of Greek, and had been obliged to run the country for deer stealing. I think his name was Shakspeare. I presume he soon sunk into oblivion."

"On the contrary," said I, "it is owing to that very man that the literature of his period has experienced a duration beyond the ordinary term of English literature. There arise authors now and then, who seem proof against the mutability of language, because they have rooted themselves in the unchanging principles of human nature. They are like gigantic trees that we sometimes see on the banks of a stream; which, by their vast and deep roots, penetrating through the mere surface, and laying hold on the very foundations of the earth, preserve the soil around them from being swept away by the everflowing current, and hold up many a neighbouring plant, and, perhaps, worthless weed, to perpetuity. Such is the case with Shakspeare, whom we behold, defying the encroachments of time, retaining in modern use the language and literature of his day, and giving duration to many an indifferent author, merely from having flourished in his vicinity. But even he, I grieve to say, is gradually assuming the tint of age, and his whole form is overrun by a profusion of commentators, who, like clambering vines and creepers, almost bury the noble plant that upholds them."

Here the little quarto began to heave his sides and chuckle, until at length he broke out into a short plethoric fit of laughter that had well nigh choked him, by reason of his excessive corpulency. "Mighty well!" cried he, as soon as he could recover breath, "mighty well! and so you would persuade me that the literature of an age is to be perpetuated by a vagabond deer stealer! by a man without learning! by a poet, forsooth—a poet!" And here he wheezed forth another fit of laughter.

I confess I felt somewhat nettled at this rudeness, which, however, I pardoned on account of his having flourished in a less polished age. I determined, nevertheless, not to give up my point.

"Yes," resumed I positively, "a poet; for of all writers he has the best chance for immortality. Others may write from the head, but he writes from the heart, and the heart will always understand him. He is the faithful portrayer of nature, whose features are always the same, and always interesting. Prose writers are voluminous and unwieldy; their pages are crowded with common places, and their thoughts expanded into tediousness. But with the true poet every thing is terse, touching, or brilliant. He gives the choicest thoughts in the choicest language. He illustrates them by every thing that he sees most striking in nature and art. He enriches them by pictures of human life, such as it is passing before him. His writings, therefore, contain the spirit, the aroma, if I may use the phrase, of the age in which he lives. They are caskets which inclose within a small compass the wealth of the language—its family jewels, which are thus transmitted in a portable form to posterity. The setting may occasionally be antiquated, and require now and then to be renewed, as in the case of Chaucer; but the brilliancy and intrinsic value of the gems continue unaltered. Cast a look back over the long reach of literary history. What vast valleys of dulness, filled with monkish legends and academical controversies. What bogs of theological speculations; what dreary wastes of metaphysics. Here and there only do we behold the heaven illumined bards, elevated like beacons on their widely separated heights, to transmit the pure light of poetical intelligence from age to age."*

I was just about to launch forth into eulogiums upon the poets of the day, when the sudden opening of the door caused me to turn my head. It was the verger, who came to inform me that it was time to close the library. I sought to have a parting word with the quarto, but the worthy little tome was silent; the clasps were closed, and it

*Thorow earth, and waters deepe,
   The pen by skill doth passe:
And featly nyps the worldes abuse,
   And shoes us in a glasse,
The vertu and the vice
   Of every wight alyve;
The honey combe that bee doth make,
   Is not so sweete in hyve,
As are the golden leves
   That drop from poets head:
Which doth surmount our common talke
   As farre as dros doth lead.
                 CHURCHYARD.

looked perfectly unconscious of all that had passed. I have been to the library two or three times since, and have endeavoured to draw it into farther conversation, but in vain. And whether all this rambling colloquy actually took place, or whether it was another of those odd day dreams to which I am subject, I have never, to this moment, been able to discover.

RURAL FUNERALS

Here's a few flowers; but about midnight more:
The herbs that have on them cold dew o' the night
Are strewings fitt'st for graves.———
You were as flowers now wither'd: even so
These herb'lets shall, which we upon you strow.

CYMBELINE.

Among the beautiful and simple hearted customs of rural life which
still linger in some parts of England, are those of strewing flowers before the funerals, and planting them at the graves, of departed friends.
These, it is said, are the remains of some of the rites of the primitive
church; but they are of still higher antiquity, having been observed
among the Greeks and Romans, and frequently mentioned by their
writers, and were no doubt the spontaneous tributes of unlettered
affection, originating long before art had tasked itself to modulate sorrow into song, or story it on the monument. They are now only to be
met with in the most distant and retired places of the kingdom, where
fashion and innovation have not been able to throng in, and trample out
all the curious and interesting traces of the olden time.

In Glamorganshire, we are told, the bed whereon the corpse lies,
is covered with flowers, a custom alluded to in one of the wild and
plaintive ditties of Ophelia:

White his shroud as the mountain snow
   Larded all with sweet flowers;
Which be-wept to the grave did go,
   With true-love showers.

There is also a most delicate and beautiful rite observed in some of
the remote villages of the south, at the funeral of a female who has
did young and unmarried. A chaplet of white flowers is borne before
the corpse by a young girl nearest in age, size, and resemblance, and
is afterwards hung up in the church over the accustomed seat of the
deceased. These chaplets are sometimes made of white paper, in
imitation of flowers, and inside of them is generally a pair of white
gloves. They are intended as emblems of the purity of the deceased, and
the crown of glory which she has received in heaven.

In some parts of the country, also, the dead are carried to the grave
with the singing of psalms and hymns: a kind of triumph, "to show,"

says Bourne, "that they have finished their course with joy, and are become conquerors." This, I am informed, is observed in some of the
northern counties, particularly in Northumberland, and it has a pleasing,
though melancholy effect, to hear, of a still evening, in some lonely
country scene, the mournful melody of a funeral dirge swelling from a
distance, and to see the train slowly moving along the landscape.

> Thus, thus, and thus, we compass round
> Thy harmlesse and unhaunted ground,
> And as we sing thy dirge, we will
> > The Daffodill,
> And other flowers lay upon
> The altar of our love, thy stone.*

There is also a solemn respect paid by the traveller to the passing
funeral in these sequestered places, for such spectacles, occurring among
the quiet abodes of nature, sink deep into the soul. As the mourning
train approaches, he pauses, uncovered, to let it go by; he then follows
silently in the rear; sometimes quite to the grave, at other times for a
few hundred yards, and having paid this tribute of respect to the
deceased, turns and resumes his journey.

The rich vein of melancholy which runs through the English character,
and gives it some of its most touching and ennobling graces, is finely
evidenced in these pathetic customs, and in the solicitude shown by
the common people for an honoured and a peaceful grave. The humblest
peasant, whatever may be his lowly lot while living, is anxious that
some little respect may be paid to his remains. Sir Thomas Overbury,
describing the "faire and happy milkmaid," observes, "thus lives she,
and all her care is, that she may die in the spring time, to have store
of flowers stucke upon her winding sheet." The poets, too, who always
breathe the feeling of a nation, continually advert to this fond solicitude
about the grave. In "The Maid's Tragedy," by Beaumont and Fletcher,
there is a beautiful instance of the kind, describing the capricious
melancholy of a broken hearted girl:

> When she sees a bank
> Stuck full of flowers, she, with a sigh, will tell
> Her servants, what a pretty place it were
> To bury lovers in; and make her maids
> Pluck 'em, and strew her over like a corse.

*Herrick

The custom of decorating graves was once universally prevalent: osiers were carefully bent over them to keep the turf uninjured, and about them were planted evergreens and flowers. "We adorn their graves," says Evelyn, in his Sylva, "with flowers and redolent plants, just emblems of the life of man, which has been compared in holy scriptures to those fading beauties, whose roots being buried in dishonour, rise again in glory." This usage has now become extremely rare in England; but it may still be met with in the church yards of retired villages, among the Welsh mountains; and I recollect an instance of it at the small town of Ruthen, which lies at the head of the beautiful vale of Clewyd. I have been told also by a friend, who was present at the funeral of a young girl in Glamorganshire, that the female attendants had their aprons full of flowers, which, as soon as the body was interred, they stuck about the grave. He noticed several graves which had been decorated in the same manner. As the flowers had been merely stuck in the ground, and not planted, they had soon withered, and might be seen in various states of decay; some drooping others quite perished. They were afterwards to be supplanted by holly, rosemary, and other evergreens; which on some graves had grown to great luxuriance, and overshadowed the tomb stones.

There was formerly a melancholy fancifulness in the arrangement of these rustic offerings that had something in it truly poetical. The rose was sometimes blended with the lily, to form a general emblem of frail mortality. "This sweet flower," says Evelyn, "borne on a branch set with thorns, and accompanied with the lily, are natural hieroglyphics of our fugitive, umbratile, anxious, and transitory life, which, making so fair a shew for a time, is not yet without its thorns and crosses." The nature and colour of the flowers, and of the ribbands with which they were tied, had often a particular reference to the qualities or story of the deceased, or were expressive of the feelings of the mourner. In an old poem, entitled "Corydon's Doleful Knell," a lover specifies the decorations he intends to use:

> A garland shall be framed
>   By art and nature's skill,
> Of sundry-coloured flowers,
>   In token of good will.
>
> And sundry-coloured ribbands
>   On it I will bestow;
> But chiefly blacke and yellowe
>   With her to grave shall go.

> I'll deck her tomb with flowers
> The rarest ever seen;
> And with my tears as showers
> I'll keepe them fresh and green.

The white rose, we are told, was planted at the grave of a virgin; her chaplet was tied with white ribbands, in token of her spotless innocence, though sometimes black ribbands were intermingled, to bespeak the grief of the survivors. The red rose was occasionally used in remembrance of such as had been remarkable for benevolence; but roses in general were appropriated to the graves of lovers. Evelyn tells us that the custom was not altogether extinct in his time, near his dwelling in the county of Surrey, "where the maidens yearly planted and decked the graves of their defunct sweethearts with rose-bushes." And Camden, likewise, remarks in his Britannia: "Here is also a certain custom, observed time out of mind, of planting rose trees upon the graves, especially by the young men and maids who have lost their loves; so that this church yard is now full of them."

When the deceased had been unhappy in their loves, emblems of a more gloomy character were used, such as the yew and cypress; and if flowers were strewn they were of the most melancholy colours. Thus, in poems by Thomas Stanley, Esq. (published in 1651) is the following stanza:

> Yet strew
> Upon my dismall grave
> Such offerings as you have,
> Forsaken cypresse and sad yewe;
> For kinder flowers can take no birth
> Or growth from such unhappy earth.

In "The Maid's Tragedy," a pathetic little air is introduced, illustrative of this mode of decorating the funerals of females who had been disappointed in love:

> Lay a garland on my hearse
> Of the dismall yew,
> Maidens willow branches wear,
> Say I died true.
>
> My love was false, but I was firm
> From my hour of birth,
> Upon my buried body lie
> Lightly, gentle earth.

The natural effect of sorrow over the dead is to refine and elevate
the mind, and we have a proof of it in the purity of sentiment and
the unaffected elegance of thought which pervaded the whole of these
funereal observances. Thus, it was an especial precaution, that none
but sweet scented evergreens and flowers should be employed. The
intention seems to have been to soften the horrors of the tomb, to
beguile the mind from brooding over the disgraces of perishing mortality, and to associate the memory of the deceased with the most
delicate and beautiful objects in nature. There is a dismal process
going on in the grave, ere dust can return to its kindred dust, which
the imagination shrinks from contemplating; and we seek still to think
of the form we have loved, with those refined associations which it
awakened when blooming before us in youth and beauty. "Lay her
i'the earth," says Laertes of his virgin sister,

> And from her fair and unpolluted flesh
> May violets spring!

Herrick, also, in his "Dirge of Jeptha," pours forth a fragrant flow
of poetical thought and image, which in a manner embalms the dead
in the recollections of the living.

> Sleep in thy peace, thy bed of spice,
> And make this place all Paradise:
> May sweets grow here! and smoke from hence,
>   Fat frankinscence.
> Let balme and cassia send their scent
> From out thy maiden monument.
>
>   *   *   *   *   *
>
> May all shie maids at wonted hours
> Come forth to strew thy tombe with flowers;
> May virgins when they come to mourn,
>   Male incense burn
> Upon thine altar! then return
> And leave thee sleeping in thine urn.

I might crowd my pages with extracts from the older British poets,
who wrote when these rites were more prevalent, and delighted frequently to allude to them; but I have already quoted more than is
necessary. I cannot however refrain from giving a passage from
Shakspeare, even though it should appear trite, which illustrates the
emblematical meaning often conveyed in these floral tributes, and at

the same time possesses that magic of language and appositeness of imagery for which he stands pre-eminent:

> With fairest flowers,
> Whilst summer lasts, and I live here, Fidele,
> I'll sweeten thy sad grave; thou shalt not lack
> The flower that's like thy face, pale primrose; nor
> The azur'd harebell like thy veins; no, nor
> The leaf of eglantine; whom not to slander,
> Outsweetened not thy breath.

There is certainly something more affecting in these prompt and spontaneous offerings of nature, than in the most costly monuments of art; the hand strews the flower while the heart is warm, and the tear falls on the grave as affection is binding the osier around the sod; but pathos expires under the slow labour of the chisel, and is chilled among the cold conceits of sculptured marble.

It is greatly to be regretted, that a custom so truly elegant and touching has disappeared from general use, and exists only in the most remote and insignificant villages. But it seems as if poetical custom always shuns the walks of cultivated society. In proportion as people grow polite they cease to be poetical. They talk of poetry, but they have learnt to check its free impulses, to distrust its sallying emotions, and to supply its most affecting and picturesque usages, by studied form and pompous ceremonial. Few pageants can be more stately and frigid than an English funeral in town. It is made up of show and gloomy parade: mourning carriages, mourning horses, mourning plumes, and hireling mourners, who make a mockery of grief. "There is a grave digged," says Jeremy Taylor, "and a solemn mourning, and a great talk in the neighbourhood, and when the daies are finished, they shall be, and they shall be remembered no more." The associate in the gay and crowded city is soon forgotten; the hurrying succession of new intimates and new pleasures effaces him from our minds, and the very scenes and circles in which he moved are incessantly fluctuating. But funerals in the country are solemnly impressive. The stroke of death makes a wider space in the village circle, and is an awful event in the tranquil uniformity of rural life. The passing bell tolls its knell in every ear; it steals with its pervading melancholy over hill and vale, and saddens all the landscape.

The fixed and unchanging features of the country also, perpetuate the memory of the friend with whom we once enjoyed them, who was the companion of our most retired walks, and gave animation to every

Children in the Church-Yard

An engraving reproduced in the Geoffrey Crayon edition of *The Sketch Book* (New York: G. P. Putnam's Sons, 1880).

lonely scene. His idea is associated with every charm of nature; we hear his voice in the echo which he once delighted to awaken; his spirit haunts the grove which he once frequented; we think of him in the wild upland solitude, or amidst the pensive beauty of the valley. In the freshness of joyous morning, we remember his beaming smiles and bounding gayety; and when sober evening returns with its gathering shadows and subduing quiet, we call to mind many a twilight hour of gentle talk and sweet souled melancholy.

> Each lonely place shall him restore,
> For him the tear be duly shed,
> Belov'd till life can charm no more,
> And mourn'd, till pity's self be dead.

Another cause that perpetuates the memory of the deceased in the country, is, that the grave is more immediately in sight of the survivors. They pass it on their way to prayer; it meets their eyes when their hearts are softened by the exercises of devotion; they linger about it on the sabbath, when the mind is disengaged from worldly cares, and most disposed to turn aside from present pleasures and present loves, and to sit down among the solemn mementos of the past. In North Wales the peasantry kneel and pray over the graves of their deceased friends for several Sundays after the interment; and where the tender rite of strewing and planting flowers is still practised, it is always renewed on Easter, Whitsuntide, and other festivals, when the season brings the companion of former festivity more vividly to mind. It is also invariably performed by the nearest relatives and friends; no menials nor hirelings are employed, and if a neighbour yields assistance, it would be deemed an insult to offer compensation.

I have dwelt upon this beautiful rural custom, because, as it is one of the last, so is it one of the holiest offices of love. The grave is the ordeal of true affection. It is there that the divine passion of the soul manifests its superiority to the instinctive impulse of mere animal attachment. The latter must be continually refreshed and kept alive by the presence of its object, but the love that is seated in the soul can live on long remembrance. The mere inclinations of sense languish and decline with the charms which excited them, and turn with shuddering disgust from the dismal precincts of the tomb; but it is thence that truly spiritual affection rises purified from every sensual desire, and returns, like a holy flame, to illumine and sanctify the heart of the survivor.

The sorrow for the dead is the only sorrow from which we refuse

to be divorced. Every other wound we seek to heal—every other affliction to forget; but this wound we consider it a duty to keep open—
this affliction we cherish and brood over in solitude. Where is the
mother who would willingly forget the infant that perished like a
blossom from her arms, though every recollection is a pang? Where
is the child that would willingly forget the most tender of parents,
though to remember be but to lament? Who, even in the hour of
agony, would forget the friend over whom he mourns? Who, even
when the tomb is closing upon the remains of her he most loved, when
he feels his heart, as it were, crushed in the closing of its portal, would
accept of consolation that must be bought by forgetfulness?—No, the
love which survives the tomb is one of the noblest attributes of the
soul. If it has its woes, it has likewise its delights; and when the
overwhelming burst of grief is calmed into the gentle tear of recollection; when the sudden anguish and the convulsive agony over the
present ruins of all that we most loved, is softened away into pensive
meditation on all that it was in the days of its loveliness—who would
root out such a sorrow from the heart? Though it may sometimes
throw a passing cloud over the bright hour of gayety; or spread a
deeper sadness over the hour of gloom; yet who would exchange it
even for the song of pleasure, or the burst of revelry? No, there is a
voice from the tomb sweeter than song. There is a remembrance of
the dead to which we turn even from the charms of the living. Oh
the grave!—the grave!—It buries every error—covers every defect—ex-
tinguishes every resentment. From its peaceful bosom spring none but
fond regrets and tender recollections. Who can look down upon the
grave even of an enemy, and not feel a compunctious throb, that he
should ever have warred with the poor handful of earth that lies
mouldering before him!

But the grave of those we loved—what a place for meditation! There
it is that we call up in long review the whole history of virtue and
gentleness, and the thousand endearments lavished upon us almost
unheeded in the daily intercourse of intimacy;—there it is that we
dwell upon the tenderness, the solemn, awful tenderness of the parting
scene—the bed of death, with all its stifled griefs, its noiseless attendance, its mute, watchful assiduities—the last testimonies of expiring
love—the feeble, fluttering, thrilling, oh! how thrilling! pressure of the
hand—the faint, faltering accents struggling in death to give one more
assurance of affection—the last fond look of the glazing eye, turning
upon us even from the threshold of existence!

Aye, go to the grave of buried love, and meditate! There settle the
account with thy conscience for every past benefit unrequited—every

past endearment unregarded, of that departed being, who can never—never—never return to be soothed by thy contrition!

If thou art a child, and hast ever added a sorrow to the soul, or a furrow to the silvered brow of an affectionate parent—if thou art a husband, and hast ever caused the fond bosom that ventured its whole happiness in thy arms, to doubt one moment of thy kindness or thy truth—if thou art a friend, and hast ever wronged, in thought, or word, or deed, the spirit that generously confided in thee—if thou art a lover, and hast ever given one unmerited pang to that true heart which now lies cold and still beneath my feet;—then be sure that every unkind look, every ungracious word, every ungentle action, will come thronging back upon thy memory, and knocking dolefully at thy soul—then be sure that thou wilt lie down sorrowing and repentant on the grave, and utter the unheard groan, and pour the unavailing tear, more deep, more bitter, because unheard and unavailing.

Then weave thy chaplet of flowers, and strew the beauties of nature about the grave; console thy broken spirit, if thou canst, with these tender, yet futile tributes of regret;—but take warning by the bitterness of this thy contrite affliction over the dead, and henceforth be more faithful and affectionate in the discharge of thy duties to the living.

In writing the preceding article, it was not intended to give a full detail of the funeral customs of the English peasantry, but merely to furnish a few hints and quotations illustrative of particular rites; to be appended, by way of note, to another paper, which has been withheld. The article swelled insensibly into its present form, and this is mentioned as an apology for so brief and casual a notice of these usages, after they have been amply and learnedly investigated in other works.

I must observe, also, that I am well aware that this custom of adorning graves with flowers prevails in other countries besides England. Indeed, in some it is much more general, and is observed even by the rich and fashionable, but it is then apt to lose its simplicity, and to degenerate into affectation. Bright, in his travels in Lower Hungary, tells of monuments of marble, with recesses formed for retirement, with seats placed among bowers of green house plants; and that the graves generally are covered with the gayest flowers of the season. He gives a casual picture of filial piety, which I cannot but transcribe; for I trust it is as useful as it is delightful to illustrate the amiable virtues of the sex. "When I was at Berlin," says he, "I followed the celebrated Iffland to the grave. Mingled with some pomp, you might trace much real feeling. In the midst of the ceremony, my attention was attracted by a young woman who stood on a mound of earth, newly covered with turf, which she anxiously protected from the feet of the passing crowd. It was the tomb of her parent; and the figure of this affectionate daughter presented a monument more striking than the most costly work of art."

I will barely add an instance of sepulchral decoration that I once met with among the mountains of Switzerland. It was at the village of Gersau, which stands on the borders of the lake of Lucerne, at the foot of Mount Rigi. It was once the capital of a miniature republic, shut up between the Alps and the lake, and accessible on the land side only by foot paths. The whole force of the republic did not exceed six hundred fighting men; and a few miles of circumference, scooped out as it were from the bosom of the mountains, comprised its territory. The village of Gersau seemed separated from the rest of the world, and retained the golden simplicity of a purer age. It had a small church, with a burying ground adjoining. At the heads of the graves were placed crosses of wood or iron. On some were affixed miniatures, rudely executed, but evidently attempts at likenesses of the deceased. On the crosses were hung chaplets of flowers, some withering, others fresh, as if occasionally renewed. I paused with interest at this scene; I felt that I was at the source of poetical description, for these were the beautiful but unaffected offerings of the heart which poets are fain to record. In a gayer and more populous place, I should have suspected them to have been suggested by factitious sentiment, derived from books; but the good people of Gersau knew little of books; there was not a novel nor a love poem in the village; and I question whether any peasant of the place dreamt, while he was twining a fresh chaplet for the grave of his mistress, that he was fulfilling one of the most fanciful rites of poetical devotion, and that he was practically a poet.

THE INN KITCHEN

Shall I not take mine ease in mine inn?
FALSTAFF.

During a journey that I once made through the Netherlands, I had arrived one evening at the *Pomme d'Or*, the principal inn of a small Flemish village. It was after the hour of the *table d'hote*, so that I was obliged to make a solitary supper from the reliques of its ampler board. The weather was chilly; I was seated alone in one end of a great gloomy dining room, and my repast being over, I had the prospect before me of a long dull evening, without any visible means of enlivening it. I summoned mine host, and requested something to read; he brought me the whole literary stock of his household, a Dutch family bible, an almanack in the same language, and a number of old Paris newspapers. As I sat dozing over one of the latter, reading old news and stale criticisms, my ear was now and then struck with bursts of laughter which seemed to proceed from the kitchen. Every one that has travelled on the continent, must know how favourite a resort the kitchen of a country inn is to the middle and inferior order of travellers, particularly in that equivocal kind of weather, when a fire becomes agreeable toward evening. I threw aside the newspaper, and explored my way to the kitchen, to take a peep at the group that appeared to be so merry. It was composed partly of travellers who had arrived some hours before in a diligence, and partly of the usual attendants and hangers on of inns. They were seated around a great burnished stove, that might have been mistaken for an altar, at which they were worshipping. It was covered with various kitchen vessels of resplendent brightness; among which steamed and hissed a huge copper tea kettle. A large lamp threw a strong mass of light upon the group, bringing out many odd features in strong relief. Its yellow rays partially illumined the spacious kitchen, dying duskily away into remote corners, except where they settled in mellow radiance on the broad side of a flitch of bacon, or were reflected back from well scoured utensils, that gleamed from the midst of obscurity. A strapping Flemish lass, with long golden pendants in her ears, and a necklace with a golden heart suspended to it, was the presiding priestess of the temple.

Many of the company were furnished with pipes, and most of them with some kind of evening potation. I found their mirth was occasioned

119

by anecdotes which a little swarthy Frenchman, with a dry weazen face and large whiskers, was giving of his love adventures; at the end of each of which there was one of those bursts of honest unceremonious laughter, in which a man indulges in that temple of true liberty, an Inn.

As I had no better mode of getting through a tedious blustering evening, I took my seat near the stove, and listened to a variety of travellers' tales, some very extravagant, and most very dull. All of them, however, have faded from my treacherous memory except one, which I will endeavour to relate. I fear, however, it derived its chief zest from the manner in which it was told, and the peculiar air and appearance of the narrator. He was a corpulent old Swiss, who had the look of a veteran traveller. He was dressed in a tarnished green travelling jacket, with a broad belt round his waist, and a pair of overalls, with buttons from the hips to the ankles. He was of a full, rubicund countenance, with a double chin, aquiline nose, and a pleasant twinkling eye. His hair was light, and curled from under an old green velvet travelling cap stuck on one side of his head. He was interrupted more than once by the arrival of guests, or the remarks of his auditors; and paused now and then to replenish his pipe; at which times he had generally a roguish leer, and a sly joke for the buxom kitchen maid.

I wish my readers could imagine the old fellow lolling in a huge arm chair, one arm akimbo, the other holding a curiously twisted tobacco pipe, formed of genuine *écume de mer*, decorated with silver chain and silken tassel—his head cocked on one side, and a whimsical cut of the eye occasionally, as he related the following story.

THE
SPECTRE BRIDEGROOM

A Traveller's Tale*

He that supper for is dight,
He lyes full cold, I trow, this night!
Yestreen to chamber I him led,
This night Gray-steel has made his bed!
SIR EGER, SIR GRAHAME, AND SIR GRAY-STEEL.

On the summit of one of the heights of the Odenwald, a wild and romantic tract of upper Germany, that lies not far from the confluence of the Main and the Rhine, there stood, many, many years since, the Castle of the Baron Von Landshort. It is now quite fallen to decay, and almost buried among beech trees and dark firs, above which, however, its old watch tower may still be seen struggling, like the former possessor I have mentioned, to carry a high head, and look down upon the neighbouring country.

The Baron was a dry branch of the great family of Katzenellenbogen,† and inherited the reliques of the property, and all the pride of his ancestors. Though the warlike disposition of his predecessors had much impaired the family possessions, yet the Baron still endeavoured to keep up some show of former state. The times were peaceable, and the German nobles, in general, had abandoned their inconvenient old castles, perched like eagles' nests among the mountains, and had built more convenient residences in the valleys: still the Baron remained proudly drawn up in his little fortress, cherishing with hereditary inveteracy, all the old family feuds; so that he was on ill terms with some of his nearest neighbours, on account of disputes that had happened between their great great grandfathers.

The Baron had but one child, a daughter; but nature, when she grants but one child, always compensates by making it a prodigy; and so it was with the daughter of the Baron. All the nurses, gossips, and country cousins, assured her father that she had not her equal for

---

*The erudite reader, well versed in good for nothing lore, will perceive that the above tale must have been suggested to the old Swiss by a little French anecdote, of a circumstance said to have taken place at Paris.

†i.e. CATSELBOW. The name of a family of those parts very powerful in former times. The appellation, we are told, was given in compliment to a peerless dame of the family, celebrated for a fine arm.

beauty in all Germany; and who should know better than they. She
had, moreover, been brought up with great care under the superintendance of two maiden aunts, who had spent some years of their
early life at one of the little German courts, and were skilled in all
the branches of knowledge necessary to the education of a fine lady.
Under their instructions, she became a miracle of accomplishments.
By the time she was eighteen she could embroider to admiration, and
had worked whole histories of the saints in tapestry, with such strength
of expression in their countenances, that they looked like so many
souls in purgatory. She could read without great difficulty, and had
spelled her way through several church legends, and almost all the
chivalric wonders of the Heldenbuch. She had even made considerable
proficiency in writing, could sign her own name without missing a
letter, and so legibly, that her aunts could read it without spectacles.
She excelled in making little elegant good for nothing lady like nick-nacks
of all kinds; was versed in the most abstruse dancing of the day;
played a number of airs on the harp and guitar; and knew all the
tender ballads of the Minne-lieders by heart.

Her aunts, too, having been great flirts and coquettes in their younger
days, were admirably calculated to be vigilant guardians and strict
censors of the conduct of their niece; for there is no duenna so rigidly
prudent, and inexorably decorous, as a superannuated coquette. She
was rarely suffered out of their sight; never went beyond the domains
of the castle, unless well attended, or rather, well watched; had continual lectures read to her about strict decorum and implicit obedience;
and, as to the men—pah!—she was taught to hold them at such distance
and in such absolute distrust, that, unless properly authorized, she
would not have cast a glance upon the handsomest cavalier in the
world—no, not if he were even dying at her feet!

The good effects of this system were wonderfully apparent. The
young lady was a pattern of docility and correctness. While others
were wasting their sweetness in the glare of the world, and liable to
be plucked and thrown aside by every hand, she was coyly blooming
into fresh and lovely womanhood under the protection of those im-
maculate spinsters, like a rose bud blushing forth among guardian
thorns. Her aunts looked upon her with pride and exultation, and
vaunted that though all the other young ladies in the world might
go astray, yet thank heaven, nothing of the kind could happen to the
heiress of Katzenellenbogen.

But, however scantily the Baron Von Landshort might be provided
with children, his household was by no means a small one, for providence had enriched him with abundance of poor relations. They, one

and all, possessed the affectionate disposition common to humble relatives: were wonderfully attached to the Baron, and took every possible occasion to come in swarms and enliven the castle. All family festivals were commemorated by these good people at the Baron's expense; and when they were filled with good cheer, they would declare that there was nothing on earth so delightful as these family meetings, these jubilees of the heart.

The Baron, though a small man, had a large soul, and it swelled with satisfaction at the consciousness of being the greatest man in the little world about him. He loved to tell long stories about the stark old warriors whose portraits looked grimly down from the walls around, and he found no listeners equal to those who fed at his expense. He was much given to the marvellous, and a firm believer in all those supernatural tales with which every mountain and valley in Germany abounds. The faith of his guests exceeded even his own: they listened to every tale of wonder with open eyes and mouth, and never failed to be astonished, even though repeated for the hundredth time. Thus lived the Baron Von Landshort, the oracle of his table, the absolute monarch of his little territory, and happy above all things, in the persuasion that he was the wisest man of the age.

At the time of which my story treats, there was a great family gathering at the Castle, on an affair of the utmost importance. It was to receive the destined bridegroom of the Baron's daughter. A negotiation had been carried on between the father, and an old nobleman of Bavaria, to unite the dignity of their houses by the marriage of their children. The preliminaries had been conducted with proper punctilio. The young people were betrothed without seeing each other, and the time was appointed for the marriage ceremony. The young Count Von Altenburg had been recalled from the army for the purpose, and was actually on his way to the Baron's to receive his bride. Missives had even been received from him, from Wurtzburg, where he was accidentally detained, mentioning the day and hour when he might be expected to arrive.

The castle was in a tumult of preparation to give him a suitable welcome. The fair bride had been decked out with uncommon care. The two aunts had superintended her toilet, and quarrelled the whole morning about every article of her dress. The young lady had taken advantage of their contest to follow the bent of her own taste; and fortunately it was a good one. She looked as lovely as youthful bridegroom could desire; and the flutter of expectation heightened the lustre of her charms.

The suffusions that mantled her face and neck, the gentle heaving of the bosom, the eye now and then lost in reverie, all betrayed the soft tumult that was going on in her little heart. The aunts were continually hovering around her; for maiden aunts are apt to take great interest in affairs of this nature. They were giving her a world of staid counsel how to deport herself, what to say, and in what manner to receive the expected lover.

The Baron was no less busied in preparations. He had, in truth, nothing exactly to do; but he was naturally a fuming, bustling little man, and could not remain passive when all the world was in a hurry. He worried from top to bottom of the castle, with an air of infinite anxiety; he continually called the servants from their work to exhort them to be diligent, and buzzed about every hall and chamber, as idly restless and importunate as a blue bottle fly of a warm summer's day.

In the mean time, the fatted calf had been killed; the forests had rung with the clamour of the huntsmen; the kitchen was crowded with good cheer; the cellars had yielded up whole oceans of *Rhein-wein* and *Ferne-wein*, and even the great Heidelberg tun had been laid under contribution. Every thing was ready to receive the distinguished guest with *Saus und Braus* in the true spirit of German hospitality—but the guest delayed to make his appearance. Hour rolled after hour. The sun that had poured his downward rays upon the rich forests of the Odenwald, now just gleamed along the summits of the mountains. The Baron mounted the highest tower, and strained his eyes in hopes of catching a distant sight of the Count and his attendants. Once he thought he beheld them; the sound of horns came floating from the valley, prolonged by the mountain echoes. A number of horsemen were seen far below, slowly advancing along the road; but when they had nearly reached the foot of the mountain, they suddenly struck off in a different direction. The last ray of sunshine departed— the bats began to flit by in the twilight—the road grew dimmer and dimmer to the view; and nothing appeared stirring in it, but now and then a peasant lagging homeward from his labour.

While the old castle of Landshort was in this state of perplexity, a very interesting scene was transacting in a different part of the Odenwald.

The young Count Von Altenburg was tranquilly pursuing his route in that sober jog trot way in which a man travels towards matrimony, when his friends have taken all the trouble and uncertainty of courtship off his hands, and a bride is waiting for him, as—certainly as a dinner, at the end of his journey. He had encountered, at Wurtzburg, a youthful companion in arms, with whom he had seen some service on the frontiers; Herman Von Starkenfaust, one of the stoutest hands, and worthiest hearts, of German chivalry, who was now returning from the army. His father's castle was not far distant from the old fortress of Landshort, although an hereditary feud rendered the families hostile, and strangers to each other.

In the warm hearted moment of recognition, the young friends related all their past adventures and fortunes, and the count gave the whole history of his intended nuptials with a young lady whom he had never seen, but of whose charms he had received the most enrapturing descriptions.

As the route of the friends lay in the same direction, they agreed to perform the rest of their journey together; and that they might do it the more leisurely, set off from Wurtzburg at an early hour, the count having given directions for his retinue to follow and overtake him.

They beguiled their wayfaring with recollections of their military scenes and adventures; but the count was apt to be a little tedious, now and then, about the reputed charms of his bride, and the felicity that awaited him.

In this way they had entered among the mountains of the Odenwald, and were traversing one of its most lonely and thickly wooded passes. It is well known that the forests of Germany have always been as much infested by robbers as its castles by spectres; and, at this time, the former were particularly numerous from the hordes of disbanded soldiers wandering about the country. It will not appear extraordinary, therefore, that the cavaliers were attacked by a gang of these stragglers, in the midst of the forest. They defended themselves with bravery, but were nearly overpowered, when the count's retinue arrived to their assistance. At sight of them the robbers fled, but not until the count had received a mortal wound. He was slowly and carefully conveyed back to the city of Wurtzburg, and a friar summoned from a neighbouring convent, who was famous for his skill in administering to both soul and body. But half of his skill was superfluous; the moments of the unfortunate count were numbered.

With his dying breath he entreated his friend to repair instantly to the castle of Landshort, and explain the fatal cause of his not keeping his appointment with his bride. Though not the most ardent of lovers, he was one of the most punctilious of men; and appeared earnestly solicitous that this mission should be speedily and courteously executed. "Unless this is done," said he, "I shall not sleep quietly in my grave!" He repeated these last words with peculiar solemnity. A request, at a moment so impressive, admitted no hesitation. Starkenfaust endeavoured to soothe him to calmness, promised faithfully to execute his wish, and gave him his hand in solemn pledge. The dying man pressed it in acknowledgment, but soon lapsed into delirium—

raved about his bride—his engagement—his plighted word; ordered his horse, that he might ride to the castle of Landshort, and expired in the fancied act of vaulting into the saddle.

Starkenfaust bestowed a sigh, and a soldier's tear, on the untimely fate of his comrade; and then pondered on the awkward mission he had undertaken. His heart was heavy, and his head perplexed; for he was to present himself an unbidden guest among hostile people, and to damp their festivity with tidings fatal to their hopes. Still there were certain whisperings of curiosity in his bosom to see this far famed beauty of Katzenellenbogen, so cautiously shut up from the world; for he was a passionate admirer of the sex, and there was a dash of eccentricity and enterprize in his character that made him fond of all singular adventure.

Previous to his departure, he made all due arrangements with the holy fraternity of the convent for the funeral solemnities of his friend, who was to be buried in the cathedral of Wurtzburg, near some of his illustrious relatives; and the mourning retinue of the count took charge of his remains.

It is now high time that we should return to the ancient family of Katzenellenbogen, who were impatient for their guest, and still more for their dinner; and to the worthy little Baron, whom we left airing himself on the watch tower.

Night closed in, but still no guest arrived. The Baron descended from the tower in despair. The banquet, which had been delayed from hour to hour could no longer be postponed. The meats were already overdone; the cook in an agony; and the whole household had the look of a garrison that had been reduced by famine. The Baron was obliged reluctantly to give orders for the feast without the presence of the guest. All were seated at table, and just on the point of commencing, when the sound of a horn from without the gate gave notice of the approach of a stranger. Another long blast filled the old courts of the castle with its echoes, and was answered by the warder from the walls. The Baron hastened to receive his future son in law.

The drawbridge had been let down, and the stranger was before the gate. He was a tall gallant cavalier, mounted on a black steed. His countenance was pale, but he had a beaming, romantic eye, and an air of stately melancholy. The Baron was a little mortified that he should have come in this simple, solitary style. His dignity for a moment was ruffled, and he felt disposed to consider it a want of proper respect for the important occasion, and the important family with which he was to be connected. He, however, pacified himself with the conclusion that it must have been youthful impatience which had induced him thus to spur on sooner than his attendants.

"I am sorry," said the stranger, "to break in upon you thus unseasonably—"

Here the Baron interrupted him with a world of compliments and greetings; for, to tell the truth, he prided himself upon his courtesy and his eloquence. The stranger attempted, once or twice, to stem the torrent of words, but in vain, so he bowed his head and suffered it to flow on. By the time the Baron had come to a pause, they had reached the inner court of the castle; and the stranger was again about to speak, when he was once more interrupted by the appearance of the female part of the family, leading forth the shrinking and blushing bride. He gazed on her for a moment as one entranced; it seemed as if his whole soul beamed forth in the gaze, and rested upon that lovely form. One of the maiden aunts whispered something in her ear; she made an effort to speak; her moist blue eye was timidly raised, gave a shy glance of inquiry on the stranger, and was cast again to the ground. The words died away; but there was a sweet smile playing about her lips, and a soft dimpling of the cheek, that showed her glance had not been unsatisfactory. It was impossible for a girl of the fond age of eighteen, highly predisposed for love and matrimony, not to be pleased with so gallant a cavalier.

The late hour at which the guest had arrived, left no time for parley. The Baron was peremptory, and deferred all particular conversation until the morning, and led the way to the untasted banquet.

It was served up in the great hall of the castle. Around the walls hung the hard favoured portraits of the heroes of the house of Katzenellenbogen, and the trophies which they had gained in the field and in the chase. Hacked corslets; splintered jousting spears, and tattered banners, were mingled with the spoils of sylvan warfare: the jaws of the wolf, and the tusks of the boar, grinned horribly among cross bows and battle axes, and a huge pair of antlers branched immediately over the head of the youthful bridegroom.

The cavalier took but little notice of the company, or the entertainment. He scarce tasted the banquet, but seemed absorbed in admiration of his bride. He conversed in a low tone that could not be overheard—for the language of love is never loud; but where is the female ear so dull that it cannot catch the softest whisper of the lover? There was a mingled tenderness and gravity in his manner, that appeared to have a powerful effect upon the young lady. Her colour came and went as she listened with deep attention. Now and then she made some blushing reply, and when his eye was turned away, she would steal a side long glance at his romantic countenance, and heave a gentle sigh of tender happiness. It was evident that the young couple were completely enamoured. The aunts, who were deeply versed in the mysteries of the heart, declared that they had fallen in love with each other at first sight.

The feast went on merrily, or at least noisily, for the guests were all blessed with those keen appetites that attend upon light purses and mountain air. The Baron told his best and longest stories, and never had he told them so well, or with such great effect. If there was any thing marvellous, his auditors were lost in astonishment; and if any thing facetious, they were sure to laugh exactly in the right place. The Baron, it is true, like most great men, was too dignified to utter any joke but a dull one; it was always enforced, however, by a bumper of excellent Hoch-heimer; and even a dull joke at one's own table, served up with jolly old wine, is irresistible. Many good things were said by poorer and keener wits, that would not bear repeating, except on similar occasions; many sly speeches whispered in ladies' ears, that almost convulsed them with suppressed laughter; and a song or two roared out by a poor, but merry and broad faced cousin of the Baron, that absolutely made the maiden aunts hold up their fans.

Amidst all this revelry, the stranger guest maintained a most singular and unseasonable gravity. His countenance assumed a deeper cast of dejection as the evening advanced, and, strange as it may appear, even the Baron's jokes seemed only to render him the more melancholy. At times he was lost in thought, and at times there was a perturbed and restless wandering of the eye that bespoke a mind but ill at ease. His conversations with the bride became more and more earnest and mysterious. Lowering clouds began to steal over the fair serenity of her brow, and tremors to run through her tender frame.

All this could not escape the notice of the company. Their gayety was chilled by the unaccountable gloom of the bridegroom; their spirits were infected; whispers and glances were interchanged, accompanied by shrugs and dubious shakes of the head. The song and the laugh grew less and less frequent; there were dreary pauses in the conversation, which were at length succeeded by wild tales, and supernatural legends. One dismal story produced another still more dismal, and the Baron nearly frightened some of the ladies into hysterics with the history of the goblin horseman that carried away the fair Leonora; a dreadful, but true story, which has since been put into excellent verse, and is read and believed by all the world.

The bridegroom listened to this tale with profound attention. He kept his eyes steadily fixed on the Baron, and as the story drew to a close, began gradually to rise from his seat, growing taller and taller, until, in the Baron's entranced eye, he seemed almost to tower into a giant. The moment the tale was finished, he heaved a deep sigh, and took a solemn farewell of the company. They were all amazement. The Baron was perfectly thunderstruck.

"What! going to leave the castle at midnight? why, every thing was prepared for his reception: a chamber was ready for him if he wished to retire."

The stranger shook his head mournfully, and mysteriously; "I must lay my head in a different chamber tonight!"

There was something in this reply, and the tone in which it was uttered, that made the Baron's heart misgive him; but he rallied his forces and repeated his hospitable entreaties.

The stranger shook his head silently, but positively, at every offer, and waving his farewell to the company, stalked slowly out of the hall. The maiden aunts were absolutely petrified—the bride hung her head, and a tear stole to her eye.

The Baron followed the stranger to the great court of the castle, where the black charger stood pawing the earth, and snorting with impatience. When they had reached the portal, whose deep archway was dimly lighted by a cresset, the stranger paused, and addressed the Baron in a hollow tone of voice, which the vaulted roof rendered still more sepulchral.

"Now that we are alone," said he, "I will impart to you the reason of my going. I have a solemn, an indispensable engagement—"

"Why," said the Baron, "cannot you send some one in your place?"

"It admits of no substitute—I must attend it in person—I must away to Wurtzburg cathedral—"

"Aye," said the Baron, plucking up spirit, "but not until tomorrow—tomorrow you shall take your bride there."

"No! no!" replied the stranger, with tenfold solemnity, "my engagement is with no bride—the worms! the worms expect me! I am a dead man—I have been slain by robbers—my body lies at Wurtzburg—at midnight I am to be buried—the grave is waiting for me—I must keep my appointment!"

He sprang on his black charger, dashed over the drawbridge, and the clattering of his horse's hoofs was lost in the whistling of the night blast.

The Baron returned to the hall in the utmost consternation, and related what had passed. Two ladies fainted outright, others sickened at the idea of having banquetted with a spectre. It was the opinion of some, that this might be the wild huntsman famous in German legend.

Some talked of mountain sprites, of wood demons, and of other supernatural beings, with which the good people of Germany have been
so grievously harassed since time immemorial. One of the poor relations
ventured to suggest that it might be some sportive evasion of the
young cavalier, and that the very gloominess of the caprice seemed
to accord with so melancholy a personage. This, however, drew on
him the indignation of the whole company, and especially of the
Baron, who looked upon him as little better than an infidel; so that
he was fain to abjure his heresy as speedily as possible, and come
into the faith of the true believers.

But, whatever may have been the doubts entertained, they were
completely put to an end by the arrival, next day, of regular missives,
confirming the intelligence of the young Count's murder, and his
interment in Wurtzburg cathedral.

The dismay at the castle may well be imagined. The Baron shut
himself up in his chamber. The guests who had come to rejoice with
him, could not think of abandoning him in his distress. They wandered
about the courts, or collected in groups in the hall, shaking their
heads and shrugging their shoulders, at the troubles of so good a
man; and sat longer than ever at table, and ate and drank more stoutly
than ever, by way of keeping up their spirits. But the situation of
the widowed bride was the most pitiable. To have lost a husband
before she had even embraced him—and such a husband! if the very
spectre could be so gracious and noble, what must have been the living
man! She filled the house with lamentations.

On the night of the second day of her widowhood she had retired
to her chamber, accompanied by one of her aunts, who insisted on
sleeping with her. The aunt, who was one of the best tellers of ghost
stories in all Germany, had just been recounting one of her longest,
and had fallen asleep in the very midst of it. The chamber was remote,
and overlooked a small garden. The niece lay pensively gazing at
the beams of the rising moon, as they trembled on the leaves of an
aspen tree before the lattice. The castle clock had just tolled midnight,
when a soft strain of music stole up from the garden. She rose hastily
from her bed, and stepped lightly to the window. A tall figure stood
among the shadows of the trees. As it raised its head, a beam of
moonlight fell upon the countenance. Heaven and earth! she beheld
the Spectre Bridegroom! A loud shriek at that moment burst upon
her ear, and her aunt, who had been awakened by the music, and had
followed her silently to the window, fell into her arms. When she
looked again, the spectre had disappeared.

Of the two females, the aunt now required the most soothing, for she was perfectly beside herself with terror. As to the young lady, there was something, even in the spectre of her lover, that seemed endearing. There was still the semblance of manly beauty; and though the shadow of a man is but little calculated to satisfy the affections of a love sick girl, yet, where the substance is not to be had, even that is consoling. The aunt declared she would never sleep in that chamber again; the niece, for once, was refractory, and declared as strongly that she would sleep in no other in the castle: the consequence was, that she had to sleep in it alone; but she drew a promise from her aunt not to relate the story of the spectre, lest she should be denied the only melancholy pleasure left her on earth—that of inhabiting the chamber over which the guardian shade of her lover kept its nightly vigils.

How long the good old lady would have observed this promise is uncertain, for she dearly loved to talk of the marvellous, and there is a triumph in being the first to tell a frightful story; it is, however, still quoted in the neighbourhood, as a memorable instance of female secrecy, that she kept it to herself for a whole week, when she was suddenly absolved from all further restraint, by intelligence brought to the breakfast table one morning, that the young lady was not to be found. Her room was empty—the bed had not been slept in—the window was open, and the bird had flown!

The astonishment and concern with which the intelligence was received, can only be imagined by those who have witnessed the agitation which the mishaps of a great man cause among his friends. Even the poor relations paused for a moment from the indefatigable labours of the trencher; when the aunt, who had at first been struck speechless, wrung her hands, and shrieked out, "the goblin! the goblin! she's carried away by the goblin!"

In a few words, she related the fearful scene of the garden, and concluded that the spectre must have carried off his bride. Two of the domestics corroborated the opinion, for they had heard the clattering of a horse's hoofs down the mountain about midnight, and had no doubt that it was the spectre on his black charger, bearing her away to the tomb. All present were struck with the direful probability; for events of the kind are extremely common in Germany, as many well authenticated histories bear witness.

What a lamentable situation was that of the poor Baron! What a heartrending dilemma for a fond father, and a member of the great family of Katzenellenbogen! His only daughter had either been rapt away to the grave, or he was to have some wood demon for a son in law, and, perchance, a troop of goblin grand children. As usual, he was completely bewildered, and all the castle in an uproar. The men were ordered to take horse, and to scour every road, and path, and glen of the Odenwald. The Baron himself had just drawn on his jack boots, girded on his sword, and was about to mount his steed to sally forth on the doubtful quest, when he was brought to a pause by a new apparition. A lady was seen approaching the castle, mounted on a palfrey, attended by a cavalier on horseback. She galloped up to the gate, sprang from her horse, and falling at the Baron's feet, embraced his knees. It was his lost daughter, and her companion—the Spectre Bridegroom! The Baron was astounded. He looked at his daughter, then at the Spectre, and almost doubted the evidence of his senses. The latter, too, was wonderfully improved in his appearance, since his visit to the world of spirits. His dress was splendid, and set off a noble figure of manly symmetry. He was no longer pale and melancholy. His fine countenance was flushed with the glow of youth, and joy rioted in his large dark eye.

The mystery was soon cleared up. The cavalier (for in truth, as you must have known all the while, he was no goblin) announced himself as Sir Herman Von Starkenfaust. He related his adventure with the young Count. He told how he had hastened to the castle to deliver the unwelcome tidings, but that the eloquence of the Baron had interrupted him in every attempt to tell his tale. How the sight of the bride had completely captivated him, and that to pass a few hours near her, he had tacitly suffered the mistake to continue. How he had been sorely perplexed in what way to make a decent retreat, until the Baron's goblin stories had suggested his eccentric exit. How, fearing the feudal hostility of the family, he had repeated his visits by stealth—had haunted the garden beneath the young lady's window—had wooed—had won—had borne away in triumph—and, in a word, had wedded the fair.

Under any other circumstances, the Baron would have been inflexible, for he was tenacious of paternal authority, and devoutly obstinate in all family feuds; but he loved his daughter; he had lamented her as lost; he rejoiced to find her still alive; and, though her husband was of a hostile house, yet, thank heaven, he was not a goblin. There was something, it must be acknowledged, that did not exactly accord with his notions of strict veracity, in the joke the knight had passed upon him of his being a dead man; but several old friends present, who had served in the wars, assured him that every stratagem was excusable in love, and that the cavalier was entitled to especial privilege, having lately served as a trooper.

Matters, therefore, were happily arranged. The Baron pardoned the young couple on the spot. The revels at the castle were resumed. The poor relations overwhelmed this new member of the family with loving kindness; he was so gallant, so generous, and so rich. The aunts, it is true, were somewhat scandalized that their system of strict seclusion, and passive obedience, should be so badly exemplified, but attributed it all to their negligence in not having the windows grated. One of them was particularly mortified at having her marvellous story marred, and that the only spectre she had ever seen should turn out a counter-feit; but the niece seemed perfectly happy at having found him substantial flesh and blood—and so the story ends.

WESTMINSTER ABBEY

When I behold, with deepe astonishment,
To famous Westminster how there resorte,
Living in brasse or stoney monyment,
The princes and the worthies of all sorte:
Doe not I see reformde nobilitie,
Without contempt, or pride, or ostentation,
And looke upon offenselesse majesty,
Naked of pompe or earthly domination?
And how a play-game of a painted stone,
Contents the quiet now and silent sprites,
Whome all the world which late they stood upon,
Could not content nor quench their appetites.
    Life is a froste of cold felicitie
    And death the thaw of all our vanitie.
        CHRISTOLERO'S EPIGRAMS, BY T. B. 1598.

On one of those sober and rather melancholy days, in the latter part of Autumn, when the shadows of morning and evening almost mingle together, and throw a gloom over the decline of the year, I passed several hours in rambling about Westminster Abbey. There was something congenial to the season in the mournful magnificence of the old pile; and as I passed its threshold, it seemed like stepping back into the regions of antiquity, and losing myself among the shades of former ages.

I entered from the inner court of Westminster School, through a long, low, vaulted passage, that had an almost subterranean look, being dimly lighted in one part by circular perforations in the massy walls. Through this dark avenue I had a distant view of the cloisters, with the figure of an old verger, in his black gown, moving along their shadowy vaults, and seeming like a spectre from one of the neighbouring tombs. The approach to the abbey through these gloomy monastic remains prepares the mind for its solemn contemplation. The cloisters still retain something of the quiet and seclusion of former days. The grey walls are discoloured by damps, and crumbling with age; a coat of hoary moss has gathered over the inscriptions of the mural monuments, and obscured the death's heads, and other funereal emblems. The sharp touches of the chisel are gone from the rich tracery of the arches; the roses which adorned the key stones have lost their leafy beauty; every thing bears marks of the gradual dilapidations of time, which yet has something touching and pleasing in its very decay.

The sun was pouring down a yellow autumnal ray into the square of the cloisters; beaming upon a scanty plot of grass in the centre, and lighting up an angle of the vaulted passage with a kind of dusty splendour. From between the arcades the eye glanced up to a bit of blue sky or a passing cloud; and beheld the sun gilt pinnacles of the abbey towering into the azure heaven.

As I paced the cloisters, sometimes contemplating this mingled picture of glory and decay, and sometimes endeavouring to decipher the inscriptions on the tombstones, which formed the pavement beneath my feet, my eye was attracted to three figures, rudely carved in relief, but nearly worn away by the footsteps of many generations. They were the effigies of three of the early abbots; the epitaphs were entirely effaced; the names alone remained, having no doubt been renewed in later times; (Vitalis. Abbas. 1082, and Gislebertus Crispinus. Abbas. 1114, and Laurentius. Abbas. 1176). I remained some little while, musing over these casual reliques of antiquity, thus left like wrecks upon this distant shore of time, telling no tale but that such beings had been, and had perished; teaching no moral but the futility of that pride which hopes still to exact homage in its ashes, and to live in an inscription. A little longer and even these faint records will be obliterated, and the monument will cease to be a memorial. Whilst I was yet looking down upon these gravestones, I was roused by the sound of the abbey clock, reverberating from buttress to buttress, and echoing among the cloisters. It is almost startling to hear this warning of departed time sounding among the tombs, and telling the lapse of the hour, which like a billow has rolled us onward towards the grave.

I pursued my walk to an arched door opening to the interior of the abbey. On entering here, the magnitude of the building breaks fully upon the mind, contrasted with the vaults of the cloisters. The eye gazes with wonder at clustered columns of gigantic dimensions, with arches springing from them to such an amazing height; and man wandering about their bases, shrunk into insignificance in comparison with his own handywork. The spaciousness and gloom of this vast edifice produce a profound and mysterious awe. We step cautiously and softly about, as if fearful of disturbing the hallowed silence of the tomb; while every footfall whispers along the walls, and chatters among the sepulchres, making us more sensible of the quiet we have interrupted.

It seems as if the awful nature of the place presses down upon the soul, and hushes the beholder into noiseless reverence. We feel that we are surrounded by the congregated bones of the great men of past times; who have filled history with their deeds, and the earth with their renown. And yet it almost provokes a smile at the vanity of human ambition, to see how they are crowded together and justled in the dust: what parsimony is observed in doling out a scanty nook; a gloomy corner; a little portion of earth, to those, whom, when alive, kingdoms could not satisfy: and how many shapes, and forms and artifices, are devised to catch the casual notice of the passenger, and save from forgetfulness, for a few short years, a name which once aspired to occupy ages of the world's thought and admiration.

I passed some time in Poets' Corner, which occupies an end of one of the transepts or cross aisles of the Abbey. The monuments are generally simple; for the lives of literary men afford no striking themes for the sculptor. Shakespeare and Addison have statues erected to their memories; but the greater part have busts, medallions, and sometimes mere inscriptions. Notwithstanding the simplicity of these memorials, I have always observed that the visitors to the abbey remain longest about them. A kinder and fonder feeling takes place of that cold curiosity or vague admiration with which they gaze on the splendid monuments of the great and the heroic. They linger about these as about the tombs of friends and companions; for indeed there is some-thing of companionship between the author and the reader. Other men are known to posterity only through the medium of history, which is continually growing faint and obscure; but the intercourse between the author and his fellow men is ever new, active and immediate. He has lived for them more than for himself; he has sacrificed surrounding enjoyments, and shut himself up from the delights of social life, that he might the more intimately commune with distant minds and distant ages. Well may the world cherish his renown; for it has been purchased, not by deeds of violence and blood, but by the diligent dispensation of pleasure. Well may posterity be grateful to his memory; for he has left it an inheritance, not of empty names and sounding actions, but whole treasures of wisdom, bright gems of thought, and golden veins of language.

From Poets' Corner I continued my stroll towards that part of the abbey which contains the sepulchres of the kings. I wandered among what once were chapels, but which are now occupied by the tombs and monuments of the great. At every turn I met with some illustrious name; or the cognizance of some powerful house renowned in history. As the eye darts into these dusky chambers of death, it catches glimpses of quaint effigies; some kneeling in niches, as if in devotion; others stretched upon the tombs, with hands piously pressed together; war-riors in armour, as if reposing after battle; prelates with croziers and mitres; and nobles in robes and coronets, lying as it were in state. In glancing over this scene, so strangely populous, yet where every form is so still and silent, it seems almost as if we were treading a mansion of that fabled city, where every being had been suddenly transmuted into stone.

I paused to contemplate a tomb on which lay the effigy of a knight in complete armour. A large buckler was on one arm; the hands were pressed together in supplication upon the breast; the face was almost covered by the morion; the legs were crossed in token of the warrior's having been engaged in the holy war. It was the tomb of a crusader; of one of those military enthusiasts, who so strangely mingled religion and romance, and whose exploits form the connecting link between fact and fiction; between the history and the fairy tale. There is something extremely picturesque in the tombs of these adventurers, decorated as they are with rude armorial bearings and gothic sculpture. They comport with the antiquated chapels in which they are generally found; and in considering them, the imagination is apt to kindle with the legendary associations, the romantic fictions, the chivalrous pomp and pageantry which poetry has spread over the wars for the Sepulchre of Christ. They are the reliques of times utterly gone by; of beings passed from recollection; of customs and manners with which ours have no affinity. They are like objects from some strange and distant land, of which we have no certain knowledge, and about which all our conceptions are vague and visionary. There is something extremely solemn and awful in those effigies on gothic tombs, extended as if in the sleep of death, or in the supplication of the dying hour. They have an effect infinitely more impressive on my feelings than the fanciful attitudes, the overwrought conceits, and allegorical groups, which abound on modern monuments. I have been struck, also, with the superiority of many of the old sepulchral inscriptions. There was a noble way, in former times, of saying things simply, and yet saying them proudly; and I do not know an epitaph that breathes a loftier consciousness of family worth and honourable lineage, than one which affirms, of a noble house, that "all the brothers were brave, and all the sisters virtuous."

In the opposite transept to Poets' Corner stands a monument which is among the most renowned achievements of modern art; but which, to me, appears horrible rather than sublime. It is the tomb of Mrs. Nightingale, by Roubillac. The bottom of the monument is represented as throwing open its marble doors, and a sheeted skeleton is starting forth. The shroud is falling from his fleshless frame as he launches his dart at his victim. She is sinking into her affrighted husband's arms, who strives, with vain and frantic effort, to avert the blow. The whole is executed with terrible truth and spirit; we almost fancy we hear the gibbering yell of triumph, bursting from the distended jaws of the spectre.—But why should we thus seek to clothe death with unnecessary terrors, and to spread horrors round the tomb of those we love? The grave should be surrounded by every thing that might inspire tenderness and veneration for the dead; or that might win the living to virtue. It is the place, not of disgust and dismay, but of sorrow and meditation.

While wandering about these gloomy vaults and silent aisles, studying the records of the dead, the sound of busy existence from without occasionally reaches the ear;—the rumbling of the passing equipage; the murmur of the multitude; or perhaps the light laugh of pleasure. The contrast is striking with the deathlike repose around: and it has a strange effect upon the feelings, thus to hear the surges of active life hurrying along and beating against the very walls of the sepulchre.

I continued in this way to move from tomb to tomb, and from chapel to chapel. The day was gradually wearing away; the distant tread of loiterers about the abbey grew less and less frequent; the sweet tongued bell was summoning to evening prayers; and I saw at a distance the choristers, in their white surplices, crossing the aisle and entering the choir. I stood before the entrance to Henry the Seventh's chapel. A flight of steps leads up to it, through a deep and gloomy, but magnificent arch. Great gates of brass, richly and delicately wrought, turn heavily upon their hinges, as if proudly reluctant to admit the feet of common mortals into this most gorgeous of sepulchres.

On entering, the eye is astonished by the pomp of architecture, and the elaborate beauty of sculptured detail. The very walls are wrought into universal ornament, encrusted with tracery, and scooped into niches, crowded with the statues of saints and martyrs. Stone seems, by the cunning labour of the chisel, to have been robbed of its weight and density, suspended aloft, as if by magic, and the fretted roof achieved with the wonderful minuteness and airy security of a cobweb.

Along the sides of the chapel are the lofty stalls of the Knights of the Bath, richly carved of oak, though with the grotesque decorations of gothic architecture. On the pinnacles of the stalls are affixed the helmets and crests of the knights, with their scarfs and swords; and above them are suspended their banners, emblazoned with armorial bearings, and contrasting the splendour of gold and purple and crimson, with the cold grey fretwork of the roof. In the midst of this grand mausoleum stands the sepulchre of its founder,—his effigy, with that of his queen, extended on a sumptuous tomb, and the whole surrounded by a superbly wrought brazen railing.

There is a sad dreariness in this magnificence; this strange mixture of tombs and trophies; these emblems of living and aspiring ambition, close beside mementos which show the dust and oblivion in which all must sooner or later terminate. Nothing impresses the mind with a deeper feeling of loneliness, than to tread the silent and deserted scene of former throng and pageant. On looking round on the vacant stalls of the knights and their esquires; and on the rows of dusty but gorgeous banners that were once borne before them, my imagination conjured up the scene when this hall was bright with the valour and beauty of the land; glittering with the splendour of jewelled rank and military array; alive with the tread of many feet and the hum of an admiring multitude. All had passed away: the silence of death had settled again upon the place; interrupted only by the casual chirping of birds, which had found their way into the chapel, and built their nests among its friezes and pendants—sure signs of solitariness and desertion.

When I read the names inscribed on the banners, they were those of men scattered far and wide about the world; some tossing upon distant seas; some under arms in distant lands; some mingling in the busy intrigues of courts and cabinets: all seeking to deserve one more distinction in this mansion of shadowy honours; the melancholy reward of a monument.

Two small aisles on each side of this chapel present a touching instance of the equality of the grave; which brings down the oppressor to a level with the oppressed, and mingles the dust of the bitterest enemies together. In one is the sepulchre of the haughty Elizabeth, in the other is that of her victim, the lovely and unfortunate Mary. Not an hour in the day but some ejaculation of pity is uttered over the fate of the latter, mingled with indignation at her oppressor. The walls of Elizabeth's sepulchre continually echo with the sighs of sympathy heaved at the grave of her rival.

A peculiar melancholy reigns over the aisle where Mary lies buried. The light struggles dimly through windows darkened by dust. The greater part of the place is in deep shadow, and the walls are stained and tinted by time and weather. A marble figure of Mary is stretched upon the tomb, round which is an iron railing, much corroded, bearing her national emblem the thistle. I was weary with wandering, and sat down to rest myself by the monument, revolving in my mind the chequered and disastrous story of poor Mary.

The sound of casual footsteps had ceased from the abbey. I could only hear, now and then, the distant voice of the priest repeating the evening service, and the faint responses of the choir; these paused for a time, and all was hushed. The stillness, the desertion and obscurity that were gradually prevailing around, gave a deeper and more solemn interest to the place:

> For in the silent grave no conversation,
> No joyful tread of friends, no voice of lovers,
> No careful father's counsel—nothing's heard,
> For nothing is, but all oblivion,
> Dust and an endless darkness.

Suddenly the notes of the deep labouring organ burst upon the ear, falling with doubled and redoubled intensity, and rolling, as it were, huge billows of sound. How well do their volume and grandeur accord with this mighty building! With what pomp do they swell through its vast vaults, and breathe their awful harmony through these caves of death, and make the silent sepulchre vocal!—And now they rise in triumphant acclamation, heaving higher and higher their accordant notes, and piling sound on sound.—And now they pause, and the soft voices of the choir break out into sweet gushes of melody; they soar aloft, and warble along the roof, and seem to play about these lofty vaults like the pure airs of heaven. Again the pealing organ heaves its thrilling thunders, compressing air into music, and rolling it forth upon the soul. What long drawn cadences! What solemn sweeping concords! It grows more and more dense and powerful—it fills the vast pile, and seems to jar the very walls—the ear is stunned—the senses are overwhelmed. And now it is winding up in full jubilee—it is rising from the earth to heaven—the very soul seems rapt away and floated upwards on this swelling tide of harmony!

I sat for some time lost in that kind of reverie which a strain of music is apt sometimes to inspire: the shadows of evening were gradually thickening around me; the monuments began to cast deeper and deeper gloom; and the distant clock again gave token of the slowly waning day.

I rose and prepared to leave the abbey. As I descended the flight of steps which lead into the body of the building, my eye was caught by the shrine of Edward the Confessor, and I ascended the small staircase that conducts to it, to take from thence a general survey of this wilderness of tombs. The shrine is elevated upon a kind of platform, and close around it are the sepulchres of various kings and queens. From this eminence the eye looks down between pillars and funeral trophies to the chapels and chambers below, crowded with tombs; where warriors, prelates, courtiers and statesmen lie mouldering in their "beds of darkness." Close by me stood the great chair of coronation, rudely carved of oak, in the barbarous taste of a remote and gothic age. The scene seemed almost as if contrived, with theatrical artifice, to produce an effect upon the beholder. Here was a type of the beginning and the end of human pomp and power; here it was literally but a step from the throne to the sepulchre. Would not one think that these incongruous mementos had been gathered together as a lesson to living greatness?—to show it, even in the moment of its proudest exaltation, the neglect and dishonour to which it must soon arrive; how soon that crown which encircles its brow must pass away; and it must lie down in the dust and disgraces of the tomb, and be trampled upon by the feet of the meanest of the multitude. For, strange to tell, even the grave is here no longer a sanctuary. There is a shocking levity in some natures, which leads them to sport with awful and hallowed things; and there are base minds, which delight to revenge on the illustrious dead the abject homage and grovelling servility which they pay to the living. The coffin of Edward the Confessor has been broken open, and his remains despoiled of their funeral ornaments; the sceptre has been stolen from the hand of the imperious Elizabeth, and the effigy of Henry the Fifth lies headless. Not a royal monument but bears some proof how false and fugitive is the homage of mankind. Some are plundered; some mutilated; some covered with ribaldry and insult—all more or less outraged and dishonoured!

The last beams of day were now faintly streaming through the painted windows in the high vaults above me: the lower parts of the abbey were already wrapped in the obscurity of twilight. The chapels and aisles grew darker and darker. The effigies of the kings faded into shadows; the marble figures of the monuments assumed strange shapes in the uncertain light; the evening breeze crept through the aisles like the cold breath of the grave; and even the distant footfall of a verger, traversing the Poets' Corner, had something strange and dreary in its sound. I slowly retraced my morning's walk, and as I passed out at the portal of the cloisters, the door, closing with a jarring noise behind me, filled the whole building with echoes.

I endeavoured to form some arrangement in my mind of the objects I had been contemplating, but found they were already falling into indistinctness and confusion. Names, inscriptions, trophies, had all become confounded in my recollection, though I had scarcely taken my foot from off the threshold. What, thought I, is this vast assemblage of sepulchres but a treasury of humiliation; a huge pile of reiterated homilies on the emptiness of renown, and the certainty of oblivion! It is, indeed, the empire of death; his great shadowy palace; where he sits in state, mocking at the reliques of human glory, and spreading dust and forgetfulness on the monuments of princes. How idle a boast, after all, is the immortality of a name! Time is ever silently turning over his pages; we are too much engrossed by the story of the present, to think of the characters and anecdotes that gave interest to the past; and each age is a volume thrown aside to be speedily forgotten. The idol of today pushes the hero of yesterday out of our recollection; and will, in turn, be supplanted by his successor of tomorrow. "Our fathers," says Sir Thomas Brown, "find their graves in our short memories, and sadly tell us how we may be buried in our survivors." History fades into fable; fact becomes clouded with doubt and controversy; the inscription moulders from the tablet; the statue falls from the pedestal. Columns, arches, pyramids, what are they but heaps of sand; and their epitaphs, but characters written in the dust? What is the security of a tomb, or the perpetuity of an embalmment? The remains of Alexander the Great have been scattered to the wind, and his empty sarcophagus is now the mere curiosity of a museum. "The Egyptian mummies, which Cambyses or time hath spared, avarice now consumeth; Mizraim cures wounds, and Pharaoh is sold for balsams."*

What then is to insure this pile which now towers above me from sharing the fate of mightier mausoleums? The time must come when its gilded vaults, which now spring so loftily, shall lie in rubbish beneath the feet; when, instead of the sound of melody and praise, the wind shall whistle through the broken arches, and the owl hoot from the shattered tower—when the garish sun beam shall break into those gloomy mansions of death; and the ivy twine round the fallen column; and the fox glove hang its blossoms about the nameless urn, as if in mockery of the dead. Thus man passes away; his name perishes from record and recollection; his history is as a tale that is told, and his very monument becomes a ruin.

NOTES CONCERNING WESTMINSTER ABBEY

Toward the end of the sixth century when Britain, under the dominion of the Saxons, was in a state of barbarism and idolatry Pope Gregory the Great, struck with the beauty of some Anglo Saxon youths, exposed for sale in the Market place at Rome, conceived a fancy for the race and determined to send missionaries to preach the Gospel among these comely but benighted islanders. He was encouraged to this by

*Sir T. Brown.

learning that Ethelbert King of Kent and the most potent of the Anglo Saxon princes, had married Bertha a christian princess, only daughter of the King of Paris, and that she was allowed by stipulation, the full exercise of her religion.

The shrewd Pontiff knew the influence of the sex in matters of religious faith. He forthwith dispatched Augustine a Roman Monk with forty associates to the Court of Ethelbert at Canterbury, to effect the conversion of the King and to obtain through him a foothold in the island.

Ethelbert received them warily and held a conference in the open air; being distrustful of foreign priest craft, and fearful of spells and magic. They ultimately succeeded in making him as good a christian as his wife; the conversion of the King of course produced the conversion of his loyal subjects. The zeal and success of Augustine were rewarded by his being made archbishop of Canterbury and being endowed with authority over all the British churches.

One of the most prominent converts was Segebert or Sebert, King of the East Saxons a nephew of Ethelbert. He reigned at London, of which Mellitus, one of the Roman Monks who had come over with Augustine was made bishop.

Sebert, in 605, in his religious zeal founded a monastery by the river side to the west of the city on the ruins of a temple of Apollo, being in fact the origin of the present pile of Westminster Abbey. Great preparations were made for the consecration of the church which was to be dedicated to St. Peter. On the morning of the appointed day Mellitus the bishop proceeded with great pomp and solemnity to perform the ceremony. On approaching the edifice he was met by a fisherman who informed him that it was needless to proceed as the ceremony was over. The bishop stared with surprise when the fisherman went on to relate that the night before, as he was in his boat on the Thames St. Peter appeared to him and told him that he intended to consecrate the church himself that very night. The Apostle accordingly went into the church which suddenly became illuminated. The ceremony was performed in sumptuous style accompanied by strains of heavenly music and clouds of fragrant incense. After this the Apostle came onto the boat and ordered the fisherman to cast his net. He did so and had a miraculous draft of fishes; one of which he was commanded to present to the Bishop, and to signify to him that the Apostle had relieved him from the necessity of consecrating the church.

Mellitus was a wary man, slow of belief, and required confirmation of the fisherman's tale. He opened the church doors and beheld wax candles, crosses, holy water; oil sprinkled in various places and various other traces of a grand ceremonial. If he had still any lingering doubts they were completely removed on the fisherman's producing the identical fish which he had been ordered by the Apostle to present to him. To resist this would have been to resist ocular demonstration. The good bishop accordingly was convinced that the church had actually been consecrated by St. Peter in person; so he reverently abstained from proceeding further in the business.

The foregoing tradition is said to be the reason why King Edward the Confessor chose this place as the scite of a religious house which he meant to endow. He pulled down the old church and built another in its place in 1045. In this his remains were deposited in a magnificent shrine.

The sacred edifice again underwent modifications if not a reconstruction by Henry III in 1220 and began to assume its present appearance.

Under Henry VIII it lost its conventual character, that monarch turning the monks away and seizing upon the revenues.

Reliques of Edward the Confessor

A curious narrative was printed in 1688 by one of the choiristers of the Cathedral, who appears to have been the Paul Pry of the sacred edifice, giving an account of his rummaging among the bones of Edward the Confessor, after they had quietly reposed in their sepulchre upwards of six hundred years, and of his drawing forth the crucifix and golden chain of the deceased monarch. During eighteen years that he had officiated in the choir it had been a common tradition, he says, among his brother choiristers and the grey headed servants of the abbey that the body of King Edward was deposited in a kind of chest or coffin which was indistinctly seen in the upper part of the shrine erected to his memory. None of the abbey gossips, however, had ventured upon a nearer inspection, until the worthy narrator to gratify his curiosity mounted to the coffin by the aid of a ladder and found it to be made of wood, apparently very strong and firm, being secured by bands of iron.

Subsequently, in 1685, on taking down the scaffolding used in the coronation of James II, the coffin was found to be broken, a hole appearing in the lid, probably made through accident, by the workmen. No one ventured, however, to meddle with the sacred depository of royal rest, until, several weeks afterwards, the circumstance came to the knowledge of the aforesaid choirister. He forthwith repaired to the abbey in company with two friends of congenial tastes who were desirous of inspecting the tombs. Procuring a ladder he again mounted to the coffin and found, as had been represented, a hole in the lid about six inches long and four inches broad, just in front of the left breast. Thrusting in his hand and groping among the bones he drew from underneath the shoulder a crucifix, richly adorned and enamelled affixed to a gold chain twenty four inches long. These he shewed to his inquisitive friends, who were equally surprized with himself.

"At the time," says he, "when I took the cross and chain out of the coffin, *I drew the head to the hole and viewed it*, being very sound and firm with the upper and nether jaws whole and full of teeth, and a list of gold above an inch broad, in the nature of a coronet, surrounding the temples. There was also in the coffin, white linen and gold coloured flowered silk, that looked indifferent fresh but the least stress put thereto shewed it was well nigh perished. There were all his bones and much dust likewise which I left as I found." It is difficult to conceive a more grotesque lesson to human pride than the scull of Edward the Confessor thus irreverently pulled about in its coffin by a prying choirister, and brought to grin face to face with him through a hole in the lid!

Having satisfied his curiosity the choirister put the crucifix and chain back again into the coffin and sought the Dean, to apprize him of his discovery. The Dean not being accessible at the time; and fearing that the "holy treasure" might be taken away by other hands, he got a brother choirister to accompany him to the shrine about two or three hours afterwards and in his presence again drew forth the reliques. These he afterwards delivered on his knees to King James. The King subsequently had the old coffin enclosed in a new one of great strength: "each plank being two inches thick and cramped together with large iron wedges, where it now remains (1688) as a testimony of his pious care that no abuse might be offered to the sacred ashes therein reposited."

As the history of this shrine is full of moral I subjoin a description of it in modern times. "The solitary and forlorn shrine," says a British writer, "now stands a mere skeleton of what it was. A few faint traces of its sparkling decorations inlaid on solid mortar catch the rays of the sun, forever set on its splendor * * * * Only two of the spiral pillars remain. The wooden Ionic top is much broken and covered with dust. The mosaic is picked away in every part within reach, only the lozenges of about a foot square and five circular pieces of the rich marble remain."   Malcolm. Lond. Rediv.

Inscription on a monument alluded to in the Sketch.

Here lyes the Loyal Duke of Newcastle, and his Dutchess his
second wife, by whom he had no issue. Her name was Margaret
Lucas, youngest sister to the Lord Lucas of Colchester, a noble
Family; for all the brothers were valiant and all the sisters virtuous.
This Dutchess was a wise, witty, and learned Lady, which her
many Bookes do well testify: she was a most virtuous, and loving
and careful wife, and was with her lord all the time of his banish-
ment and miseries, and when he came home, never parted from
him in his solitary retirements.

In the winter time, when the days are short, the service in the afternoon is performed by the light of tapers. The effect is fine of the choir
partially lighted up; while the main body of the cathedral and the
transepts are in profound and cavernous darkness. The white dresses
of the choiristers gleam amidst the deep brown of the oaken slatts
and canopies; the partial illumination makes enormous shadows from
columns and screens, and darting into the surrounding gloom catches
here and there upon a sepulchral decoration, or monumental effigy. The
swelling notes of the organ accord well with the scene.

When the service is over the Dean is lighted to his dwelling, in
the old conventual part of the pile, by the boys of the choir in their
white dresses, bearing tapers, and the procession passes through the
abbey and along the shadowy cloisters, lighting up angles and arches
and grim sepulchral monuments and leaving all behind in darkness.

On entering the cloisters at night from what is called the Dean's
Yard the eye ranging through a dark vaulted passage catches a distant
view of a white marble figure reclining on a tomb, on which a strong
glare thrown by a gas light, has quite a spectral effect. It is a mural
monument of one of the Pultneys.

The cloisters are well worth visiting by moonlight, when the moon
is in the full.

Christmas

But is old, old, good old Christmas gone? Nothing but the hair of his good, gray old head and beard left? Well, I will have that, seeing I cannot have more of him.

HUE AND CRY AFTER CHRISTMAS.

CHRISTMAS

A man might then behold
  At Christmas, in each hall,
Good fires to curb the cold,
  And meat for great and small:
The neighbours were friendly bidden,
  And all had welcome true,
The poor from the gates were not chidden,
  When this old cap was new.

OLD SONG.

Nothing in England exercises a more delightful spell over my imagination, than the lingerings of the holyday customs and rural games of former times. They recall the pictures my fancy used to draw in the May morning of life, when as yet I only knew the world through books, and believed it to be all that poets had painted it; and they bring with them the flavour of those honest days of yore, in which, perhaps with equal fallacy, I am apt to think the world was more homebred, social, and joyous, than at present. I regret to say that they are daily growing more and more faint, being gradually worn away by time, but still more obliterated by modern fashion. They resemble those picturesque morsels of Gothic architecture, which we see crumbling in various parts of the country, partly dilapidated by the waste of ages, and partly lost in the additions and alterations of latter days. Poetry, however, clings with cherishing fondness about the rural game and holyday revel, from which it has derived so many of its themes— as the ivy winds its rich foliage about the gothic arch and mouldering tower, gratefully repaying their support, by clasping together their tottering remains, and, as it were, embalming them in verdure.

Of all the old festivals, however, that of Christmas awakens the strongest and most heartfelt associations. There is a tone of solemn and sacred feeling that blends with our conviviality, and lifts the spirit to a state of hallowed and elevated enjoyment. The services of the church about this season are extremely tender and inspiring. They dwell on the beautiful story of the origin of our faith, and the pastoral scenes that accompanied its announcement. They gradually increase in fervour and pathos during the season of Advent, until they break forth in full jubilee on the morning that brought peace and good will to men. I do not know a grander effect of music on the moral feelings, than to hear the full choir and the pealing organ performing a Christmas anthem in a cathedral, and filling every part of the vast pile with triumphant harmony.

It is a beautiful arrangement, also, derived from days of yore, that this festival, which commemorates the announcement of the religion of peace and love, has been made the season for gathering together of family connexions, and drawing closer again those bands of kindred hearts, which the cares and pleasures and sorrows of the world are continually operating to cast loose; of calling back the children of a family, who have launched forth in life, and wandered widely asunder, once more to assemble about the paternal hearth, that rallying place of the affections, there to grow young and loving again among the endearing mementos of childhood.

There is something in the very season of the year that gives a charm to the festivity of Christmas. At other times we derive a great portion of our pleasures from the mere beauties of nature. Our feelings sally forth and dissipate themselves over the sunny landscape, and we "live abroad and every where." The song of the bird, the murmur of the stream, the breathing fragrance of spring, the soft voluptuousness of summer, the golden pomp of autumn, earth with its mantle of refreshing green, and heaven with its deep delicious blue and its cloudy magnificence, all fill us with mute but exquisite delight, and we revel in the luxury of mere sensation. But in the depth of winter, when nature lies despoiled of every charm, and wrapped in her shroud of sheeted snow, we turn for our gratifications to moral sources. The dreariness and desolation of the landscape, the short gloomy days and darksome nights, while they circumscribe our wanderings, shut in our feelings also from rambling abroad, and make us more keenly disposed for the pleasures of the social circle. Our thoughts are more concentrated, our friendly sympathies more aroused. We feel more sensibly the charm of each other's society, and are brought more closely together by dependence on each other for enjoyment. Heart calleth unto heart, and we draw our pleasures from the deep wells of living kindness which lie in the quiet recesses of our bosoms, and which, when resorted to, furnish forth the pure element of domestic felicity.

The pitchy gloom without, makes the heart dilate on entering the room filled with the glow and warmth of the evening fire. The ruddy blaze diffuses an artificial summer and sunshine through the room, and lights up each countenance into a kindlier welcome. Where does the honest face of hospitality expand into a broader and more cordial smile—where is the shy glance of love more sweetly eloquent—than by the winter fireside;—and as the hollow blast of wintry wind rushes through the hall, claps the distant door, whistles about the casement, and rumbles down the chimney—what can be more grateful than that feeling of sober and sheltered security, with which we look round upon the comfortable chamber, and the scene of domestic hilarity?

The English, from the great prevalence of rural habits throughout every class of society, have always been fond of those festivals and holydays which agreeably interrupt the stillness of country life; and they were, in former days, particularly observant of the religious and social rites of Christmas. It is inspiring to read even the dry details which some antiquaries have given of the quaint humours, the burlesque pageants, the complete abandonment to mirth and good fellowship, with which this festival was celebrated. It seemed to throw open every door, and unlock every heart. It brought the peasant and the peer together, and blended all ranks in one warm generous flow of joy and kindness. The old halls of castles and manor houses re-sounded with the harp and the Christmas carol, and their ample boards groaned under the weight of hospitality. Even the poorest cottage welcomed the festive season with green decorations of bay and holly—the cheerful fire glanced its rays through the lattice, inviting the passenger to raise the latch, and join the gossip knot huddled round the hearth, beguiling the long evening with legendary jokes, and oft told Christmas tales.

One of the least pleasing effects of modern refinement is the havoc it has made among the hearty old holyday customs. It has completely taken off the sharp touchings and spirited reliefs of these embellishments of life, and has worn down society into a more smooth and polished, but certainly a less characteristic surface. Many of the games and ceremonials of Christmas have entirely disappeared, and, like the sherris sack of old Falstaff, are become matters of speculation and dispute among commentators. They flourished in times full of spirit and lustihood, when men enjoyed life roughly, but heartily and vigorously: times wild and picturesque, which have furnished poetry with its richest materials, and the drama with its most attractive variety of characters and manners. The world has become more worldly. There is more of dissipation, and less of enjoyment. Pleasure has expanded into a broader, but a shallower stream, and has forsaken many of those deep and quiet channels where it flowed sweetly through the calm bosom of domestic life. Society has acquired a more enlightened and elegant tone; but it has lost many of its strong local peculiarities, its homebred feelings, its honest fireside delights. The traditionary customs of golden hearted antiquity, its feudal hospitalities, and lordly wassailings, have passed away with the baronial castles and stately manor houses in which they were celebrated. They comported with the shadowy hall, the great oaken gallery, and the tapestried parlour, but were unfitted to the light showy saloons and gay drawing rooms of the modern villa.

Shorn, however, as it is, of its ancient and festive honours, Christmas is still a period of delightful excitement in England. It is gratifying to see that home feeling completely aroused which holds so powerful a place in every English bosom. The preparations making on every side for the social board that is again to unite friends and kindred—the presents of good cheer passing and repassing, those tokens of regard and quickeners of kind feelings—the evergreens distributed about houses and churches, emblems of peace and gladness—all these have the most pleasing effect in producing fond associations, and kindling benevolent sympathies. Even the sound of the Waits, rude as may be their minstrelsy, breaks upon the midwatches of a winter night with the effect of perfect harmony. As I have been awakened by them in that still and solemn hour "when deep sleep falleth upon man," I have listened with a hushed delight, and connecting them with the sacred and joyous occasion, have almost fancied them into another celestial choir, announcing peace and good will to mankind.

How delightfully the imagination, when wrought upon by these moral influences, turns every thing to melody and beauty. The very crowing of the cock, heard sometimes in the profound repose of the country, "telling the night watches to his feathery dames," was thought by the common people to announce the approach of this sacred festival:

> Some say that ever 'gainst that season comes
> Wherein our Saviour's birth is celebrated,
> This bird of dawning singeth all night long:
> And then, they say, no spirit dares stir abroad;
> The nights are wholesome—then no planets strike,
> No fairy takes, no witch hath power to charm,
> So hallowed and so gracious is the time.

Amidst the general call to happiness, the bustle of the spirits, and stir of the affections, which prevail at this period, what bosom can remain insensible? It is, indeed, the season of regenerated feeling—the season for kindling not merely the fire of hospitality in the hall, but the genial flame of charity in the heart.

The scene of early love again rises green to memory beyond the sterile waste of years, and the idea of home, fraught with the fragrance of home dwelling joys, reanimates the drooping spirit—as the Arabian breeze will sometimes waft the freshness of the distant fields to the weary pilgrim of the desert.

Stranger and sojourner as I am in the land—though for me no social hearth may blaze, no hospitable roof throw open its doors, nor the warm grasp of friendship welcome me at the threshold—yet I feel the influence of the season beaming into my soul from the happy looks of those around me. Surely happiness is reflective, like the light of heaven; and every countenance bright with smiles, and glowing with innocent enjoyment, is a mirror transmitting to others the rays of a supreme and ever shining benevolence. He who can turn churlishly away from contemplating the felicity of his fellow beings, and can sit down darkling and repining in his loneliness when all around is joyful, may have his moments of strong excitement and selfish gratification, but he wants the genial and social sympathies which constitute the charm of a merry Christmas.

THE STAGE COACH

Omne benè
Sine poenâ
Tempus est ludendi.
Venit hora
Absque morâ
Libros deponendi.

OLD HOLYDAY SCHOOL SONG.

In the preceding paper I have made some general observations on the Christmas festivities of England, and am tempted to illustrate them by some anecdotes of a Christmas passed in the country: in perusing which, I would most courteously invite my reader to lay aside the austerity of wisdom, and to put on that genuine holyday spirit, which is tolerant of folly, and anxious only for amusement.

In the course of a December tour in Yorkshire, I rode for a long distance in one of the public coaches, on the day preceding Christmas. The coach was crowded, both inside and out, with passengers, who, by their talk, seemed principally bound to the mansions of relations or friends, to eat the Christmas dinner. It was loaded also with hampers of game, and baskets and boxes of delicacies; and hares hung dangling their long ears about the coachman's box, presents from distant friends for the impending feast. I had three fine rosy cheeked school boys for my fellow passengers inside, full of the buxom health and manly spirit which I have observed in the children in this country. They were returning home for the holydays, in high glee, and promising themselves a world of enjoyment. It was delightful to hear the gigantic plans of pleasure of the little rogues, and the impracticable feats they were to perform during their six weeks' emancipation from the abhorred thraldom of book, birch, and pedagogue. They were full of anticipations of the meeting with the family and household, down to the very cat and dog, and of the joy they were to give their little sisters by the presents with which their pockets were crammed; but the meeting to which they seemed to look forward with the greatest impatience was with Bantam, which I found to be a pony, and, according to their talk, possessed of more virtues than any steed since the days of Bucephalus. How he could trot! how he could run! and then such leaps as he would take—there was not a hedge in the whole country that he could not clear.

They were under the particular guardianship of the coachman, to whom, whenever an opportunity presented, they addressed a host of questions, and pronounced him one of the best fellows in the whole world. Indeed, I could not but notice the more than ordinary air of bustle and importance of the coachman, who wore his hat a little on one side, and had a large bunch of Christmas greens stuck in the button hole of his coat. He is always a personage full of mighty care and business, but he is particularly so during this season, having so many commissions to execute in consequence of the great interchange of presents. And here, perhaps, it may not be unacceptable to my untravelled readers, to have a sketch that may serve as a general representation of this very numerous and important class of function-aries, who have a dress, a manner, a language, an air, peculiar to themselves, and prevalent throughout the fraternity, so that, wherever an English stage coachman may be seen, he cannot be mistaken for one of any other craft or mystery.

He has commonly a broad full face, curiously mottled with red, as if the blood had been forced by hard feeding into every vessel of the skin; he is swelled into jolly dimensions by frequent potations of malt liquors, and his bulk is still further increased by a multiplicity of coats, in which he is buried like a cauliflower, the upper one reaching to his heels. He wears a broad brimmed low crowned hat, a huge roll of coloured handkerchief about his neck, knowingly knotted and tucked in at the bosom, and has in summer time a large boquet of flowers in his buttonhole, the present, most probably of some enamoured country lass. His waistcoat is commonly of some bright colour, striped, and his small clothes extend far below the knees, to meet a pair of jockey boots which reach about half way up his legs.

All this costume is maintained with much precision; he has a pride in having his clothes of excellent materials, and notwithstanding the seeming grossness of his appearance, there is still discernible that neatness and propriety of person, which is almost inherent in an Englishman. He enjoys great consequence and consideration along the road; has frequent conferences with the village housewives, who look upon him as a man of great trust and dependence; and he seems to have a good understanding with every bright eyed country lass. The moment he arrives where the horses are to be changed, he throws down the reins with something of an air, and abandons the cattle to the care of the hostler: his duty being merely to drive them from one stage to another. When off the box, his hands are thrust in the pockets of his great coat, and he rolls about the inn yard with an air of the most absolute lordliness. Here he is generally surrounded by an admiring throng of hostlers, stable boys, shoeblacks, and those nameless

hangers on, that infest inns and taverns, and run errands, and do all
kind of odd jobs, for the privilege of battening on the drippings of
the kitchen and the leakage of the tap room. These all look up to him
as to an oracle; treasure up his cant phrases; echo his opinions about
horses and other topics of jockey lore; and above all, endeavour to
imitate his air and carriage. Every ragamuffin that has a coat to his
back, thrusts his hands in the pockets, rolls in his gait, talks slang, and
is an embryo Coachey.

Perhaps it might be owing to the pleasing serenity that reigned in
my own mind, that I fancied I saw cheerfulness in every countenance
throughout the journey. A Stage Coach, however, carries animation
always with it, and puts the world in motion as it whirls along. The
horn, sounded at the entrance of a village, produces a general bustle.
Some hasten forth to meet friends; some with bundles and bandboxes
to secure places, and in the hurry of the moment can hardly take leave
of the group that accompanies them. In the mean time, the coachman
has a world of small commissions to execute; sometimes he delivers
a hare or pheasant; sometimes jerks a small parcel or newspaper to
the door of a public house, and sometimes, with knowing leer, and
words of sly import, hands to some half blushing, half laughing housemaid, an odd shaped billet-doux from some rustic admirer. As the
Coach rattles through the village, every one runs to the window, and
you have glances on every side of fresh country faces, and blooming,
giggling girls. At the corners are assembled juntos of village idlers
and wise men, who take their stations there for the important purpose
of seeing company pass: but the sagest knot is generally at the
blacksmith's, to whom the passing of the coach is an event fruitful of
much speculation. The smith, with the horse's heel in his lap, pauses
as the vehicle whirls by; the cyclops round the anvil suspend their
ringing hammers, and suffer the iron to grow cool; and the sooty spectre
in brown paper cap, labouring at the bellows, leans on the handle for
a moment, and permits the asthmatic engine to heave a long drawn
sigh, while he glares through the murky smoke and sulphureous gleams
of the smithy.

Perhaps the impending holyday might have given a more than
usual animation to the country, for it seemed to me as if every body
was in good looks and good spirits; game, poultry, and other luxuries
of the table, were in brisk circulation in the villages; the grocer's,
butcher's, and fruiterer's shops were thronged with customers. The
housewives were stirring briskly about, putting their dwellings in order,
and the glossy branches of holly, with their bright red berries, began
to appear at the windows. The scene brought to mind an old writer's

account of Christmas preparations. "Now capons and hens, besides turkeys, geese, and ducks, with beef and mutton—must all die—for in twelve days a multitude of people will not be fed with a little. Now plums and spice, sugar and honey, square it among pies and broath. Now or never must music be in tune, for the youth must dance and sing to get them a heat, while the aged sit by the fire. The country maid leaves half her market, and must be sent againe, if she forgets a pack of cards on Christmas even. Great is the contention of Holly and Ivy, whether master or dame wears the breeches. Dice and cards benefit the butler; and if the cook do not lack wit, he will sweetly lick his fingers."

I was roused from this fit of luxurious meditation, by a shout from my little travelling companions. They had been looking out of the coach windows for the last few miles, recognising every tree and cottage as they approached home, and now there was a general burst of joy. "There's John! and there's old Carlo! and there's Bantam!" cried the happy little rogues, clapping their hands.

At the head of a lane there was an old sober looking servant in livery, waiting for them; he was accompanied by a superannuated pointer, and by the redoubtable Bantam, a little old rat of a pony, with a shagged mane and long rusty tail, who stood dozing quietly by the road side, little dreaming of the bustling times that awaited him.

I was pleased to see the fondness with which the little fellows leaped about the steady old footman, and hugged the pointer, who wriggled his whole body for joy. But Bantam was the great object of interest; all wanted to mount at once, and it was with some difficulty that John arranged that they should ride by turns, and the eldest should ride first.

Off they set at last, one on the pony with the dog bounding and barking before him, and the others holding John's hands, both talking at once, and overpowering him with questions about home, and with school anecdotes. I looked after them with a feeling in which I do not know whether pleasure or melancholy predominated; for I was reminded of those days when, like them, I had neither known care nor sorrow, and a holyday was the summit of earthly felicity. We stopped a few moments afterwards to water the horses; and on resuming our route, a turn of the road brought us in sight of a neat country seat. I could just distinguish the forms of a lady and two young girls in the portico, and I saw my little comrades, with Bantam, Carlo, and old John, trooping along the carriage road. I leaned out of the coach window, in hopes of witnessing the happy meeting, but a grove of trees shut it from my sight.

In the evening we reached a village where I had determined to pass the night. As we drove into the great gateway of the inn, I saw on one side, the light of a rousing kitchen fire beaming through a window. I entered and admired, for the hundredth time, that picture of convenience, neatness, and broad honest enjoyment, the kitchen of an English inn. It was of spacious dimensions, hung round with copper and tin vessels highly polished, and decorated here and there with a Christmas green. Hams, tongues, and flitches of bacon, were suspended from the ceiling; a smoke jack made its ceaseless clanking beside the fire place, and a clock ticked in one corner. A well scoured deal table extended along one side of the kitchen, with a cold round of beef, and other hearty viands, upon it, over which two foaming tankards of ale seemed mounting guard. Travellers of inferior order were preparing to attack this stout repast, whilst others sat smoking and gossipping over their ale on two high backed oaken seats beside the fire. Trim housemaids were hurrying backwards and forwards under the directions of a fresh bustling landlady; but still seizing an occasional moment to exchange a flippant word, and have a rallying laugh, with the group around the fire. The scene completely realized Poor Robin's humble idea of the comforts of mid-winter:

> Now trees their leafy hats do bare
> To reverence Winter's silver hair;
> A handsome hostess, merry host,
> A pot of ale now and a toast,
> Tobacco and a good coal fire,
> Are things this season doth require.*

I had not been long at the inn when a post chaise drove up to the door. A young gentleman stepped out, and by the light of the lamps I caught a glimpse of a countenance which I thought I knew. I moved forward to get a nearer view, when his eye caught mine. I was not mistaken; it was Frank Bracebridge, a sprightly good humoured young fellow, with whom I had once travelled on the continent. Our meeting was extremely cordial, for the countenance of an old fellow traveller always brings up the recollection of a thousand pleasant scenes, odd adventures, and excellent jokes. To discuss all these in a transient interview at an inn was impossible, and finding that I was not pressed for time, and was merely making a tour of observation, he insisted that I should give him a day or two at his father's country seat, to which he was going to pass the Holydays, and which lay at a few

*Poor Robin's Almanack, 1684.

miles distance. "It is better than eating a solitary Christmas dinner at an inn," said he, "and I can assure you of a hearty welcome in something of the old fashioned style." His reasoning was cogent, and I must confess the preparation I had seen for universal festivity and social enjoyment, had made me feel a little impatient of my loneliness. I closed, therefore, at once with his invitation; the chaise drove up to the door, and in a few moments I was on my way to the family mansion of the Bracebridges.

CHRISTMAS EVE

Saint Francis and Saint Benedight
Blesse this house from wicked wight;
From the night-mare and the goblin,
That is hight good fellow Robin;
Keep it from all evil spirits,
Fairies, weezels, rats, and ferrets:
    From curfew-time
    To the next prime.

CARTWRIGHT.

It was a brilliant moonlight night, but extremely cold: our chaise whirled rapidly over the frozen ground; the post boy cracked his whip incessantly, and a part of the time his horses were upon a gallop. "He knows where he is going," said my companion, laughing, "and is eager to arrive in time for some of the merriment and good cheer of the servants' hall. My father, you must know, is a bigoted devotee of the old school, and prides himself upon keeping up something of old English hospitality. He is a tolerable specimen of what you will rarely meet with now-a-days in its purity, the old English country gentleman; for our men of fortune spend so much of their time in town, and fashion is carried so much into the country, that the strong rich peculiarities of ancient rural life are almost polished away. My father, however, from early years, took honest Peacham* for his text book, instead of Chesterfield; he determined in his own mind, that there was no condition more truly honourable and enviable than that of a country gentleman on his paternal lands, and, therefore, passes the whole of his time on his estate. He is a strenuous advocate for the revival of the old rural games and holyday observances, and is deeply read in the writers, ancient and modern, who have treated of the subject. Indeed, his favourite range of reading is among the authors who flourished at least two centuries since, who, he insists, wrote and thought more like true Englishmen than any of their successors. He even regrets sometimes that he had not been born a few centuries earlier, when England was itself, and had its peculiar manners and customs. As he lives at some distance from the main road, in rather a lonely part of the country, without any rival gentry near him, he has that most enviable of all blessings to an Englishman, an oppor-

---

*Peacham's Compleat Gentleman, 1622.

tunity of indulging the bent of his own humour, without molestation. Being representative of the oldest family in the neighbourhood, and a great part of the peasantry being his tenants, he is much looked up to, and, in general, is known simply by the appellation of 'The Squire;' a title which has been accorded to the head of the family since time immemorial. I think it best to give you these hints about my worthy old father, to prepare you for any little eccentricities that might otherwise appear absurd."

We had passed for some time along the wall of a park, and at length the chaise stopped at the gate. It was in a heavy magnificent old stile; of iron bars, fancifully wrought at top into flourishes and flowers. The huge square columns that supported the gate were surmounted by the family crest. Close adjoining was the porter's lodge, sheltered under dark fir trees, and almost buried in shrubbery.

The post boy rung a large porter's bell, which resounded through the still frosty air, and was answered by the distant barking of dogs, with which the mansion house seemed garrisoned. An old woman immediately appeared at the gate. As the moonlight fell strongly upon her, I had a full view of a little primitive dame, dressed very much in the antique taste, with a neat kerchief and stomacher, and her silver hair peeping from under a cap of snowy whiteness. She came curtseying forth, with many expressions of simple joy at seeing her young master. Her husband, it seemed, was up at the house keeping Christmas eve, in the servants' hall; they could not do without him, as he was the best hand at a song and story in the household.

My friend proposed that we should alight and walk through the park to the hall, which was at no great distance, while the chaise should follow on. Our road wound through a noble avenue of trees, among the naked branches of which the moon glittered as she rolled through the deep vault of a cloudless sky: the lawn beyond was sheeted with a slight covering of snow, which here and there sparkled as the moon beams caught a frosty chrystal; and at a distance might be seen a thin transparent vapour, stealing up from the low grounds, and threatening gradually to shroud the landscape.

My companion looked round him with transport:—"How often," said he, "have I scampered up this avenue, on returning home on school vacations. How often have I played under these trees when a boy. I feel a degree of filial reverence for them as we look up to those who have cherished us in childhood. My father was always scrupulous in exacting our holydays, and having us around him on family festivals. He used to direct and superintend our games with the strictness that some parents do the studies of their children. He was very particular

The Gate of the Family Mansion

Randolph J. Caldecott illustration from the 1875 edition of *Old Christmas* (London: Macmillan & Company).

that we should play the old English games according to their original form, and consulted old books for precedent and authority for every 'merrie disport.' Yet I assure you there never was pedantry so delightful. It was the policy of the good old gentleman to make his children feel that home was the happiest place in the world, and I value this delicious home feeling as one of the choicest gifts a parent could bestow."

We were interrupted by the clamour of a troop of dogs of all sorts and sizes, "mongrel, puppy, whelp and hound, and curs of low degree," that, disturbed by the ringing of the porter's bell, and the rattling of the chaise, came bounding open mouthed across the lawn.

> ———The little dogs and all,
> Tray, Blanch and Sweetheart, see, they bark at me!

cried Bracebridge, laughing. At the sound of his voice, the bark was changed into a yelp of delight, and in a moment he was surrounded and almost overpowered by the caresses of the faithful animals.

We had now come in full view of the old family mansion, partly thrown in deep shadow, and partly lit up by the cold moonshine. It was an irregular building of some magnitude, and seemed to be of the architecture of different periods. One wing was evidently very ancient, with heavy stone shafted bow windows jutting out and over run with ivy, from among the foliage of which the small diamond shaped panes of glass glittered with the moonbeams. The rest of the house was in the French taste of Charles the Second's time, having been repaired and altered, as my friend told me, by one of his ancestors, who returned with that monarch at the restoration. The grounds about the house were laid out in the old formal manner of artificial flower beds, clipped shrubberies, raised terraces, with heavy stone ballustrades, ornamented with urns, a leaden statue or two, and a jet of water. The old gentleman, I was told, was extremely careful to preserve this obsolete finery in all its original state. He admired this fashion in gardening; it had an air of magnificence, was courtly and noble, and befitting good old family style. The boasted imitation of nature in modern gardening had sprung up with modern republican notions, but did not suit a monarchical government; it smacked of the levelling system. I could not help smiling at this introduction of politics into gardening, though I expressed some apprehension that I should find the old gentleman rather intolerant in his creed. Frank assured me, however, that it was almost the only instance in which he had ever heard his father meddle with politics, and he believed that he had got this notion from a member of parliament who once passed a few weeks with him. The

Squire was glad of any argument to defend his clipped yew trees and formal terraces, which had been occasionally attacked by modern landscape gardeners.

As we approached the house, we heard the sound of music, and now and then a burst of laughter, from one end of the building. This, Bracebridge said, must proceed from the servants' hall, where a great deal of revelry was permitted, and even encouraged, by the Squire, throughout the twelve days of Christmas, provided every thing was done conformably to ancient usage. Here were kept up the old games of hoodman blind, shoe the wild mare, hot cockles, steal the white loaf, Bob apple, and snap dragon: the Yule clog, and Christmas candle, were regularly burnt, and the misletoe, with its white berries, hung up, to the imminent peril of all the pretty housemaids.*

So intent were the servants upon their sports, that we had to ring repeatedly before we could make ourselves heard. On our arrival being announced, the Squire came out to receive us, accompanied by his two other sons; one a young officer of the army, home on leave of absence, the other an Oxonian, just from the university. The Squire was a fine healthy looking old gentleman, with silver hair curling lightly round an open florid countenance, in which a physiognomist, with the advantage, like myself, of a previous hint or two, might discover a singular mixture of whim and benevolence.

The family meeting was warm and affectionate; as the evening was far advanced, the Squire would not permit us to change our travelling dresses, but ushered us at once to the company, which was assembled in a large old fashioned hall. It was composed of different branches of a numerous family connexion, where there were the usual proportions of old uncles and aunts, comfortable married dames, superannuated spinsters, blooming country cousins, half fledged striplings, and bright eyed boarding school hoydens. They were variously occupied: some at a round game of cards; others conversing around the fire place; at one end of the hall was a group of the young folks, some nearly grown up, others of a more tender and budding age, fully engrossed by a merry game; and a profusion of wooden horses, penny trumpets, and tattered dolls, about the floor, showed traces of a troop of little fairy beings, who, having frolicked through a happy day, had been carried off to slumber through a peaceful night.

While the mutual greetings were going on between young Bracebridge and his relatives, I had time to scan the apartment. I have

*The misletoe is still hung up in farm houses and kitchens at Christmas; and the young men have the privilege of kissing the girls under it, plucking each time a berry from the bush. When the berries are all plucked, the privilege ceases.

The Family Gathering

Randolph J. Caldecott illustration from the 1875 edition of *Old Christmas* (London: Macmillan & Company).

called it a hall, for so it had certainly been in old times, and the Squire had evidently endeavoured to restore it to something of its primitive state. Over the heavy projecting fire place was suspended a picture of a warrior in armour, standing by a white horse, and on the opposite wall hung a helmet, buckler and lance. At one end an enormous pair of antlers were inserted in the wall, the branches serving as hooks on which to suspend hats, whips and spurs; and in the corners of the apartment were fowling pieces, fishing rods, and other sporting implements. The furniture was of the cumbrous workmanship of former days, though some articles of modern convenience had been added, and the oaken floor had been carpeted, so that the whole presented an odd mixture of parlour and hall.

The grate had been removed from the wide overwhelming fire place, to make way for a fire of wood, in the midst of which was an enormous log glowing and blazing, and sending forth a vast volume of light and heat: this I understood was the Yule clog, which the Squire was particular in having brought in and illumined on a Christmas eve, according to ancient custom.*

It was really delightful to see the old Squire, seated in his hereditary elbow chair, by the hospitable fireside of his ancestors, and looking around him like the sun of a system, beaming warmth and gladness to every heart. Even the very dog that lay stretched at his feet, as he lazily shifted his position and yawned, would look fondly up in his master's face, wag his tail against the floor, and stretch himself again to sleep, confident of kindness and protection. There is an emanation

---

*The *Yule clog* is a great log of wood, sometimes the root of a tree, brought into the house with great ceremony, on Christmas eve, laid in the fire place, and lighted with the brand of the last year's clog. While it lasted, there was great drinking, singing, and telling of tales. Sometimes it was accompanied by Christmas candles; but in the cottages the only light was from the ruddy blaze of the great wood fire. The Yule clog was to burn all night; if it went out it was considered a sign of ill luck.

Herrick mentions it in one of his songs:

> Come bring with a noise,
> My merrie, merrie boyes,
> The Christmas Log to the firing;
> While my good dame, she
> Bids ye all be free,
> And drink to your hearts desiring.

The Yule clog is still burnt in many farm houses and kitchens in England, particularly in the north, and there are several superstitions connected with it among the peasantry. If a squinting person come to the house while it is burning, or a person bare footed, it is considered an ill omen. The brand remaining from the Yule clog is carefully put away to light the next year's Christmas fire.

from the heart in genuine hospitality, which cannot be described, but is immediately felt, and puts the stranger at once at his ease. I had not been seated many minutes by the comfortable hearth of the worthy old cavalier, before I found myself as much at home as if I had been one of the family.

Supper was announced shortly after our arrival. It was served up in a spacious oaken chamber, the pannels of which shone with wax, and around which were several family portraits decorated with holly and ivy. Besides the accustomed lights, two great wax tapers, called Christmas candles, wreathed with greens, were placed on a highly polished beaufet among the family plate. The table was abundantly spread with substantial fare; but the Squire made his supper of frumenty, a dish made of wheat cakes, boiled in milk with rich spices; being a standing dish in old times, for Christmas eve. I was happy to find my old friend, minced pie, in the retinue of the feast, and finding him to be perfectly orthodox, and that I need not be ashamed of my predilection, I greeted him with all the warmth wherewith we usually greet an old and very genteel acquaintance.

The mirth of the company was greatly promoted by the humours of an eccentric personage whom Mr. Bracebridge always addressed with the quaint appellation of Master Simon. He was a tight brisk little man, with the air of an arrant old Bachelor. His nose was shaped like the bill of a parrot; his face slightly pitted with the small pox, with a dry perpetual bloom on it, like a frost bitten leaf in autumn. He had an eye of great quickness and vivacity, with a drollery and lurking waggery of expression that was irresistible. He was evidently the wit of the family, dealing very much in sly jokes and innuendoes with the ladies, and making infinite merriment by harpings upon old themes, which, unfortunately, my ignorance of the family chronicles did not permit me to enjoy. It seemed to be his great delight during supper, to keep a young girl next him in a continual agony of stifled laughter, in spite of her awe of the reproving looks of her mother, who sat opposite. Indeed, he was the idol of the younger part of the company, who laughed at every thing he said or did, and at every turn of his countenance. I could not wonder at it; for he must have been a miracle of accomplishments in their eyes. He could imitate Punch and Judy; make an old woman of his hand, with the assistance of a burnt cork and pocket handkerchief; and cut an orange into such a ludicrous caricature, that the young folks were ready to die with laughing.

I was let briefly into his history by Frank Bracebridge. He was an old bachelor, of a small independent income, which, by careful management, was sufficient for all his wants. He revolved through the family system like a vagrant comet in its orbit, sometimes visiting one branch, and sometimes another quite remote, as is often the case with gentlemen of extensive connexions and small fortunes, in England. He had a chirping, buoyant disposition, always enjoying the present moment; and his frequent change of scene and company prevented his acquiring those rusty, unaccommodating habits, with which old bachelors are so uncharitably charged. He was a complete family chronicle, being versed in the genealogy, history, and intermarriages of the whole house of Bracebridge, which made him a great favourite with the old folks; he was a beau of all the elder ladies and super-annuated spinsters, among whom he was habitually considered rather a young fellow, and he was master of the revels among the children; so that there was not a more popular being in the sphere in which he moved, than Mr. Simon Bracebridge. Of late years, he had resided almost entirely with the Squire, to whom he had become a factotum, and whom he particularly delighted by jumping with his humour in respect to old times, and by having a scrap of an old song to suit every occasion. We had presently a specimen of his last mentioned talent; for no sooner was supper removed, and spiced wines and other beverages peculiar to the season introduced, than Master Simon was called on for a good old Christmas song. He bethought himself for a moment, and then, with a sparkle of the eye, and a voice that was by no means bad, excepting that it ran occasionally into a falsetto, like the notes of a split reed, he quavered forth a quaint old ditty.

> Now Christmas is come,
> Let us beat up the drum,
> And call all our neighbours together;
> And when they appear,
> Let us make them such cheer,
> As will keep out the wind and the weather. &c.

The supper had disposed every one to gayety, and an old harper was summoned from the servants' hall, where he had been strumming all the evening, and to all appearance comforting himself with some of the Squire's home brewed. He was a kind of hanger on, I was told, of the establishment, and though ostensibly a resident of the village, was oftener to be found in the Squire's kitchen than his own home; the old gentleman being fond of the sound of "Harp in hall."

The dance, like most dances after supper, was a merry one: some of the older folks joined in it, and the Squire himself figured down several couple with a partner with whom he affirmed he had danced at every Christmas for nearly half a century. Master Simon, who seemed to be a kind of connecting link between the old times and the new, and to be withal a little antiquated in the taste of his accomplishments, evidently piqued himself on his dancing, and was endeavouring to gain credit by the heel and toe, rigadoon, and other graces of the ancient school; but he had unluckily assorted himself with a little romping girl from boarding school, who, by her wild vivacity, kept him continually on the stretch, and defeated all his sober attempts at elegance:— such are the ill sorted matches to which antique gentlemen are unfortunately prone!

The young Oxonian, on the contrary, had led out one of his maiden aunts, on whom the rogue played a thousand little knaveries with impunity; he was full of practical jokes, and his delight was to tease his aunts and cousins; yet, like all mad cap youngsters, he was a universal favourite among the women. The most interesting couple in the dance was the young officer, and a ward of the Squire's, a beautiful blushing girl of seventeen. From several shy glances which I had noticed in the course of the evening, I suspected there was a little kindness growing up between them; and, indeed, the young soldier was just the hero to captivate a romantic girl. He was tall, slender, and handsome; and, like most young British officers of late years, had picked up various small accomplishments on the continent—he could talk French and Italian—draw landscapes—sing very tolerably—dance divinely; but, above all, he had been wounded at Waterloo:—what girl of seventeen, well read in poetry and romance, could resist such a mirror of chivalry and perfection!

The moment the dance was over, he caught up a guitar, and lolling against the old marble fire place, in an attitude which I am half inclined to suspect was studied, began the little French air of the Troubadour. The Squire, however, exclaimed against having any thing on Christmas eve but good old English; upon which the young minstrel, casting up his eye for a moment, as if in an effort of memory, struck into another strain, and with a charming air of gallantry, gave Herrick's "night piece to Julia."

> Her eyes the glow-worm lend thee,
> The shooting stars attend thee,
>   And the elves also,
>   Whose little eyes glow
> Like the sparks of fire, befriend thee.
>
> No Will o' th' Wisp mislight thee;
> Nor snake or slow worm bite thee;

> But on, on thy way,
> Not making a stay,
> Since ghost there is none to affright thee.
>
> Then let not the dark thee cumber;
> What though the moon does slumber?
> The stars of the night
> Will lend thee their light,
> Like tapers clear without number.
>
> Then Julia, let me woo thee,
> Thus, thus, to come unto me;
> And when I shall meet
> Thy silvery feet,
> My soul I'll pour into thee.

The song might or might not have been intended in compliment to the fair Julia, for so I found his partner was called: she, however, was certainly unconscious of any such application; for she never looked at the singer, but kept her eyes cast upon the floor; her face was suffused, it is true, with a beautiful blush, and there was a gentle heaving of the bosom, but all that was doubtless caused by the exercise of the dance: indeed, so great was her indifference, that she was amusing herself with plucking to pieces a choice boquet of hot house flowers, and by the time the song was concluded, the nosegay lay in ruins on the floor.

The party now broke up for the night with the kind hearted old custom of shaking hands. As I passed through the hall, on my way to my chamber, the dying embers of the yule clog still sent forth a dusky glow, and had it not been the season when "no spirit dares stir abroad," I should have been half tempted to steal from my room at midnight, and peep, whether the fairies might not be at their revels about the hearth.

My chamber was in the old part of the mansion, the ponderous furniture of which might have been fabricated in the days of the giants. The room was pannelled, with cornices of heavy carved work, in which flowers and grotesque faces were strangely intermingled, and a row of black looking portraits stared mournfully at me from the walls. The bed was of rich, though faded damask, with a lofty tester, and stood in a niche opposite a bow window. I had scarcely got into bed when a strain of music seemed to break forth in the air just below the window. I listened, and found it proceeded from a band, which I concluded to be the waits from some neighbouring village. They went round the house, playing under the windows. I drew aside the curtains to hear them more distinctly. The moon beams fell through the upper part of the casement, partially lighting up the antiquated apartment. The sounds as they receded, became more soft and aerial, and seemed to accord with the quiet and moon light. I listened and listened—they became more and more tender and remote, and as they gradually died away, my head sunk upon the pillow, and I fell asleep.

CHRISTMAS DAY

Dark and dull night flie hence away,
And give the honour to this day
That sees December turn'd to May.

* * * *

Why does the chilling winter's morne
Smile like a field beset with corne?
Or smell like to a meade new-shorne,
Thus on the sudden?—Come and see
The cause why things thus fragrant be.

HERRICK.

When I awoke the next morning, it seemed as if all the events of the preceding evening had been a dream, and nothing but the identity of the ancient chamber convinced me of their reality. While I lay musing on my pillow, I heard the sound of little feet pattering outside of the door, and a whispering consultation. Presently a choir of small voices chaunted forth an old Christmas carol, the burden of which was

Rejoice, our Saviour he was born
On Christmas day in the morning.

I rose softly, slipt on my clothes, opened the door suddenly, and beheld one of the most beautiful little fairy groups that a painter could imagine. It consisted of a boy and two girls, the eldest not more than six, and lovely as seraphs. They were going the rounds of the house and singing at every chamber door, but my sudden appearance frightened them into mute bashfulness. They remained for a moment playing on their lips with their fingers, and now and then stealing a shy glance from under their eyebrows, until as if by one impulse, they scampered away, and as they turned an angle of the gallery, I heard them laughing in triumph at their escape.

Every thing conspired to produce kind and happy feelings in this strong hold of old fashioned hospitality. The window of my chamber looked out upon what in summer would have been a beautiful landscape. There was a sloping lawn, a fine stream winding at the foot of it, and a tract of park beyond, with noble clumps of trees, and herds of deer. At a distance was a neat hamlet, with the smoke from the cottage chimneys hanging over it; and a church with its dark spire in strong relief against the clear cold sky. The house was surrounded with evergreens, according to the English custom, which would have given almost an appearance of summer; but the morning was extremely frosty; the light vapour of the preceding evening had been precipitated by the cold, and covered all the trees and every blade of grass with its fine chrystalizations. The rays of a bright morning sun had a dazzling effect among the glittering foliage. A robin perched upon the top of a mountain ash that hung its clusters of red berries just before my window, was basking himself in the sunshine, and piping a few querulous notes, and a peacock was displaying all the glories of his train, and strutting with the pride and gravity of a Spanish grandee on the terrace walk below.

I had scarce dressed myself, when a servant appeared to invite me to family prayers. He showed me the way to a small chapel in the old wing of the house, where I found the principal part of the family already assembled in a kind of gallery, furnished with cushions, hassocks, and large prayer books; the servants were seated on benches below. The old gentleman read prayers from a desk in front of the gallery, and Master Simon acted as clerk and made the responses, and I must do him the justice to say that he acquitted himself with great gravity and decorum.

The service was followed by a Christmas carol, which Mr. Bracebridge himself had constructed from a poem of his favourite author, Herrick; and it had been adapted to an old church melody by Master Simon. As there were several good voices among the household, the effect was extremely pleasing; but I was particularly gratified by the exaltation of heart, and sudden sally of grateful feeling, with which the worthy Squire delivered one stanza, his eye glistening, and his voice rambling out of all the bounds of time and tune.

> 'Tis thou that crown'st my glittering hearth
>   With guiltlesse mirth,
> And giv'st me Wassaile Bowles to drink
>   Spic'd to the brink.
> Lord, 'tis thy plenty-dropping hand
>   That soiles my land;
> And giv'st me, for my bushell sowne,
>   Twice ten for one.

I afterwards understood that early morning service was read on every Sunday and saint's day throughout the year, either by Mr. Bracebridge or by some member of the family. It was once almost universally the case at the seats of the nobility and gentry of England, and it is much to be regretted that the custom is falling into neglect; for the dullest observer must be sensible of the order and serenity prevalent in those households, where the occasional exercise of a beautiful form of worship in the morning gives, as it were, the key note to every temper for the day, and attunes every spirit to harmony.

Our breakfast consisted of what the Squire denominated true old English fare. He indulged in some bitter lamentations over modern breakfasts of tea and toast, which he censured as among the causes of modern effeminacy and weak nerves, and the decline of old English heartiness: and though he admitted them to his table to suit the palates of his guests, yet there was a brave display of cold meats, wine, and ale, on the sideboard.

After breakfast, I walked about the grounds with Frank Bracebridge and Master Simon, or Mr. Simon, as he was called by every body but the Squire. We were escorted by a number of gentleman like dogs, that seemed loungers about the establishment, from the frisking spaniel to the steady old stag hound, the last of which was of a race that had been in the family time out of mind: they were all obedient to a dog whistle which hung at Master Simon's button hole, and in the midst of their gambols would glance an eye occasionally upon a small switch he carried in his hand.

The old mansion had a still more venerable look in the yellow sunshine than by pale moonlight; and I could not but feel the force of the Squire's idea, that the formal terraces, heavily moulded ballustrades, and clipped yew trees, carried with them an air of proud aristocracy. There appeared to be an unusual number of peacocks about the place, and I was making some remarks upon what I termed a flock of them that were basking under a sunny wall, when I was gently corrected in my phraseology by Master Simon, who told me that, according to the most ancient and approved treatise on hunting, I must say a *muster* of peacocks. "In the same way," added he, with a slight air of pedantry, "we say a flight of doves or swallows, a bevy of quails, a herd of deer, of wrens or cranes, a skulk of foxes, or a building of rooks." He went on to inform me that, according to Sir Anthony Fitzherbert, we ought to ascribe to this bird "both understanding and glory; for, being praised, he will presently set up his tail, chiefly against the sun, to the intent you may the better behold the beauty thereof. But at the fall of the leaf, when his tail falleth, he will mourn and hide himself in corners, till his tail come again as it was."

I could not help smiling at this display of small erudition on so whimsical a subject; but I found that the peacocks were birds of some consequence at the hall; for Frank Bracebridge informed me that they were great favourites with his father, who was extremely careful to keep up the breed, partly because they belonged to chivalry, and were in great request at the stately banquets of the olden time; and partly because they had a pomp and magnificence about them, highly becoming an old family mansion. Nothing, he was accustomed to say, had an air of greater state and dignity than a peacock perched upon an antique stone ballustrade.

Master Simon had now to hurry off, having an appointment at the parish church with the village choristers, who were to perform some music of his selection. There was something extremely agreeable in the cheerful flow of animal spirits of the little man; and I confess I had been somewhat surprised at his apt quotations from authors, who certainly were not in the range of every day reading. I mentioned this last circumstance to Frank Bracebridge, who told me with a smile that Master Simon's whole stock of erudition was confined to some half a dozen old authors, which the Squire had put into his hands, and which he read over and over, whenever he had a studious fit, as he some-times had of a rainy day, or a long winter evening. Sir Anthony Fitz-herbert's book of Husbandry; Markham's Country Contentments; the Tretyse of Hunting, by Sir Thomas Cockayne, Knight; Isaac Walton's Angler, and two or three more such ancient worthies of the pen, were his standard authorities; and, like all men who know but a few books, he looked up to them with a kind of idolatry, and quoted them on all occasions. As to his songs, they were chiefly picked out of old books in the Squire's library, and adapted to tunes that were popular among the choice spirits of the last century. His practical application of scraps of literature, however, had caused him to be looked upon as a prodigy of book knowledge by all the grooms, huntsmen, and small sportsmen of the neighbourhood.

While we were talking, we heard the distant toll of the village bell, and I was told that the Squire was a little particular in having his household at church on Christmas morning; considering it a day of pouring out of thanks and rejoicing, for, as old Tusser observed,

> At Christmas be merry, *and thankful withal,*
> And feast thy poor neighbours, the great with the small.

"If you are disposed to go to church," said Frank Bracebridge, "I can promise you a specimen of my cousin Simon's musical achieve-ments. As the church is destitute of an organ, he has formed a band from the village amateurs, and established a musical club for their improvement; he has also sorted a choir, as he sorted my father's pack of hounds, according to the directions of Jervaise Markham, in his Country Contentments; for the bass he has sought out all the 'deep, solemn mouths,' and for the tenor the 'loud ringing mouths' among the country bumpkins; and for 'sweete mouths,' he has culled with curious taste among the prettiest lasses in the neighbourhood, though these last, he affirms, are the most difficult to keep in tune, your pretty female singer being exceedingly wayward and capricious, and very liable to accident."

As the morning, though frosty, was remarkably fine and clear, the most of the family walked to the church, which was a very old building of grey stone, and stood near a village, about half a mile from the park gate. Adjoining it was a low snug parsonage, which seemed coeval with the church. The front of it was perfectly matted with a yew tree, that had been trained against its walls; through the dense foliage of which, apertures had been formed to admit light into the small antique lattices. As we passed this sheltered nest, the parson issued forth, and preceded us.

I had expected to see a sleek well conditioned pastor, such as is often found in a snug living in the vicinity of a rich patron's table, but I was disappointed. The parson was a little, meagre, black looking man, with a grizzled wig that was too wide, and stood off from each ear, so that his head seemed to have shrunk away within it, like a dried filbert in its shell. He wore a rusty coat with great skirts and pockets that would have held the church bible and prayer book; and his small legs seemed still smaller, from being planted in large shoes, decorated with enormous buckles.

I was informed by Frank Bracebridge, that the parson had been a chum of his father's at Oxford, and had received this living shortly after the latter had come to his estate. He was a complete black letter hunter, and would scarcely read a work printed in the Roman character. The editions of Caxton and Wynkin de Worde were his delight, and he was indefatigable in his researches after such old English writers as have fallen into oblivion from their worthlessness. In deference, perhaps, to the notions of Mr. Bracebridge, he had made diligent investigations into the festive rites and holyday customs of former times, and had been as zealous in the inquiry, as if he had been a boon companion; but it was merely with that plodding spirit, with which men of adust temperament follow up any track of study, merely because it is denominated learning, indifferent to its intrinsic nature, whether it be the illustration of the wisdom or of the ribaldry and obscenity of antiquity. He had pored over these old volumes so intensely, that they seemed to have been reflected into his countenance, which, if the face be, indeed, an index of the mind, might be compared to a title page of black letter.

On reaching the church porch, we found the parson rebuking the gray headed sexton for having used misletoe among the greens with which the church was decorated. It was, he observed, an unholy plant; profaned by having been used by the Druids in their mystic ceremonies, and though it might be innocently employed in the festive ornamenting of halls and kitchens, yet it had been deemed by the fathers of the church as unhallowed, and totally unfit for sacred purposes. So tenacious was he on this point, that the poor sexton was obliged to strip down a great part of the humble trophies of his taste, before the parson would consent to enter upon the service of the day.

The interior of the church was venerable, but simple: on the walls were several mural monuments of the Bracebridges; and just beside the altar was a tomb of ancient workmanship, on which lay the effigy of a warrior in armour, with his legs crossed, a sign of his having been a crusader. I was told it was one of the family who had signalized himself in the holy land, and the same whose picture hung over the fire place in the hall.

During service, Master Simon stood up in the pew, and repeated the responses very audibly; evincing that kind of ceremonious devotion punctually observed by a gentleman of the old school, and a man of old family connexions. I observed, too, that he turned over the leaves of a folio prayer book with something of a flourish, possibly to show off an enormous seal ring which enriched one of his fingers, and which had the look of a family relique. But he was evidently most solicitous about the musical part of the service, keeping his eye fixed intently on the choir, and beating time with much gesticulation and emphasis.

The orchestra was in a small gallery, and presented a most whimsical grouping of heads, piled one above the other, among which I particularly noticed that of the village taylor, a pale fellow with a retreating forehead and chin, who played on the clarionet, and seemed to have blown his face to a point; and there was another, a short pursy man, stooping and labouring at a bass viol, so as to show nothing but the top of a round bald head, like the egg of an ostrich. There were two or three pretty faces among the female singers, to which the keen air of a frosty morning had given a bright rosy tint; but the gentlemen choristers had evidently been chosen, like old Cremona fiddles, more for tone than looks; and as several had to sing from the same book,

The Choir at Christmas Service

Randolph J. Caldecott illustration from the 1875 edition of *Old Christmas* (London: Macmillan & Company).

there were clusterings of odd physiognomies, not unlike those groups of cherubs we sometimes see on country tombstones.

The usual services of the choir were managed tolerably well, the vocal parts generally lagging a little behind the instrumental, and some loitering fiddler now and then making up for lost time by travelling over a passage with prodigious celerity, and clearing more bars than the keenest fox hunter, to be in at the death. But the great trial was an anthem that had been prepared and arranged by Master Simon, and on which he had founded great expectations. Unluckily, there was a blunder at the very outset; the musicians became flurried; Master Simon was in a fever; every thing went on lamely and irregularly until they came to a chorus beginning "Now let us sing with one accord," which seemed to be a signal for parting company: all became discord and confusion, each shifted for himself, and got to the end as well, or, rather, as soon as he could, excepting one old chorister in a pair of horn spectacles, bestriding and pinching a long sonorous nose, who, happening to stand a little apart, and being wrapped up in his own melody, kept on a quavering course, wriggling his head, ogling his book, and winding all up by a nasal solo of at least three bars duration.

The parson gave us a most erudite sermon on the rites and ceremonies of Christmas, and the propriety of observing it, not merely as a day of thanksgiving, but of rejoicing; supporting the correctness of his opinions by the earliest usages of the church, and enforcing them by the authorities of Theophilus of Cesarea, St. Cyprian, St. Chrysostom, St. Augustine, and a cloud more of saints and fathers, from whom he made copious quotations. I was a little at a loss to perceive the necessity of such a mighty array of forces to maintain a point which no one present seemed inclined to dispute; but I soon found that the good man had a legion of ideal adversaries to contend with, having, in the course of his researches on the subject of Christmas, got completely embroiled in the sectarian controversies of the revolution, when the Puritans made such a fierce assault upon the ceremonies of the church, and poor old Christmas was driven out of the land by proclamation of Parliament.* The worthy parson lived but with times past, and knew but little of the present.

Shut up among worm eaten tomes in the retirement of his antiquated little study, the pages of old times were to him as the gazettes of the

*From "The Flying Eagle," a small Gazette published December 24th, 1652.— "The House spent much time this day about the businesse of the Navy for settling the affairs at sea, and before they rose were presented with a terrible remonstrance against Christmas day, grounded upon divine Scriptures, 2 Cor. v. 16. 1 Cor. xv. 14.17; and in honour of the Lord's day, grounded upon these Scriptures, John, xx. 1.

day; while the era of the Revolution was mere modern history. He forgot that nearly two centuries had elapsed since the fiery persecution of poor Mince pie throughout the land; when plum porridge was denounced as "mere popery," and roast beef as antichristian; and that Christmas had been brought in again triumphantly with the merry court of King Charles at the restoration. He kindled into warmth with the ardour of his contest, and the host of imaginary foes with whom he had to combat; had a stubborn conflict with old Prynne and two or three other forgotten champions of the round heads, on the subject of Christmas festivity; and concluded by urging his hearers, in the most solemn and affecting manner, to stand to the traditionary customs of their fathers, and feast and make merry on this joyful anniversary of the church.

I have seldom known a sermon attended apparently with more immediate effects; for on leaving the church the congregation seemed one and all possessed with the gayety of spirit so earnestly enjoined by their pastor. The elder folks gathered in knots in the church yard, greeting and shaking hands, and the children ran about crying Ule! Ule! and repeating some uncouth rhymes,* which the parson, who had joined us, informed me had been handed down from days of yore. The villagers doffed their hats to the Squire as he passed, giving him the good wishes of the season with every appearance of heartfelt sincerity, and were invited by him to the hall, to take something to keep out the cold of the weather; and I heard blessings uttered by several of the poor, which convinced me that, in the midst of his enjoyments, the worthy old cavalier had not forgotten the true Christmas virtue of charity.

On our way homeward, his heart seemed overflowing with generous and happy feelings. As we passed over a rising ground which commanded something of a prospect, the sounds of rustic merriment now and then reached our ears; the Squire paused for a few moments, and looked around with an air of inexpressible benignity. The beauty of the day was, of itself, sufficient to inspire philanthropy. Notwithstanding the frostiness of the morning, the sun in his cloudless journey had

---

Rev. i. 10.   Psalms, cxviii. 24.   Lev. xxiii. 7.11.   Mark. xvi. 8.   Psalms, lxxxiv. 10. In which Christmas is called Antichrist's masse, and those Masse-mongers and Papists who observe it, &c. In consequence of which Parliament spent some time in consultation about the abolition of Christmas day, passed orders to that effect, and resolved to sit on the following day, which was commonly called Christmas day."

*"Ule! Ule!
  Three puddings in a pule;
  Crack nuts and cry ule!"

acquired sufficient power to melt away the thin covering of snow from every southern declivity, and to bring out the living green which adorns an English landscape even in mid winter. Large tracts of smiling verdure, contrasted with the dazzling whiteness of the shaded slopes and hollows. Every sheltered bank, on which the broad rays rested, yielded its silver rill of cold and limpid water, glittering through the dripping grass; and sent up slight exhalations to contribute to the thin haze that hung just above the surface of the earth. There was something truly cheering in this triumph of warmth and verdure over the frosty thraldom of winter: it was, as the Squire observed, an emblem of Christmas hospitality breaking through the chills of ceremony and selfishness, and thawing every heart into a flow. He pointed with pleasure to the indications of good cheer reeking from the chimneys of the comfortable farm houses, and low thatched cottages. "I love," said he, "to see this day well kept by rich and poor; it is a great thing to have one day in the year at least, when you are sure of being welcome wherever you go, and of having, as it were, the world all thrown open to you; and I am almost disposed to join with poor Robin, in his malediction on every churlish enemy to this honest festival."

> Those who at Christmas do repine
> And would fain hence despatch him,
> May they with old duke Humphry dine,
> Or else may Squire Ketch catch 'em.

The Squire went on to lament the deplorable decay of the games and amusements which were once prevalent at this season among the lower orders, and countenanced by the higher. When the old halls of castles and manor houses were thrown open at daylight; when the tables were covered with brawn, and beef, and humming ale; when the harp and the carol resounded all day long, and when rich and poor were alike welcome to enter and make merry.* "Our old games and local customs," said he, "had a great effect in making the peasant fond of his home, and the promotion of them by the gentry made him fond of his lord. They made the times merrier, and kinder, and better, and I can truly say with one of our old poets,

---

*"An English gentleman at the opening of the great day, i.e. on Christmas day in the morning, had all his tenants and neighbours enter his hall by day break. The strong beer was broached, and the black jacks went plentifully about with toast, sugar, nutmeg, and good Cheshire cheese. The Hackin (the great sausage) must be boiled by daybreak, or else two young men must take the maiden (i.e. the cook,) by the arms and run her round the market place till she is ashamed of her laziness." —Round about our Sea-coal Fire.

I like them well—the curious preciseness
And all pretended gravity of those
That seek to banish hence these harmless sports,
Have thrust away much ancient honesty.

"The nation," continued he, "is altered; we have almost lost our simple, true hearted peasantry. They have broken asunder from the higher classes, and seem to think their interests are separate. They have become too knowing, and begin to read newspapers, listen to ale house politicians, and talk of reform. I think one mode to keep them in good humour in these hard times, would be for the nobility and gentry to pass more time on their estates, mingle more among the country people, and set the merry old English games going again."

Such was the good Squire's project for mitigating public discontent: and, indeed, he had once attempted to put his doctrine in practice, and a few years before had kept open house during the holydays in the old style. The country people, however, did not understand how to play their parts in the scene of hospitality: many uncouth circumstances occurred; the manor was overrun by all the vagrants of the country, and more beggars drawn into the neighbourhood in one week than the parish officers could get rid of in a year. Since then, he had contented himself with inviting the decent part of the neighbouring peasantry to call at the hall on Christmas day, and with distributing beef, and bread, and ale, among the poor, that they might make merry in their own dwellings.

We had not been long home when the sound of music was heard from a distance. A band of country lads without coats, their shirt sleeves fancifully tied with ribands, their hats decorated with greens, and clubs in their hands, were seen advancing up the avenue, followed by a large number of villagers and peasantry. They stopped before the hall door, where the music struck up a peculiar air, and the lads performed a curious and intricate dance, advancing, retreating, and striking their clubs together, keeping exact time to the music; while one, whimsically crowned with a fox's skin, the tail of which flaunted down his back, kept capering round the skirts of the dance, and rattling a Christmas box with many antic gesticulations.

The Squire eyed this fanciful exhibition with great interest and delight, and gave me a full account of its origin, which he traced to the times when the Romans held possession of the island, plainly proving that this was a lineal descendant of the sword dance of the ancients. "It was now," he said, "nearly extinct, but he had accidentally met with traces of it in the neighbourhood, and had encouraged its revival, though, to tell the truth, it was too apt to be followed up by rough cudgel play, and broken heads, in the evening."

After the dance was concluded, the whole party was entertained with brawn and beef, and stout home brewed. The Squire himself mingled among the rustics, and was received with awkward demonstrations of deference and regard. It is true, I perceived two or three of the younger peasants, as they were raising their tankards to their mouths, when the Squire's back was turned, making something of a grimace, and giving each other the wink, but the moment they caught my eye they pulled grave faces, and were exceedingly demure. With Master Simon, however, they all seemed more at their ease. His varied occupations and amusements had made him well known throughout the neighbourhood. He was a visiter at every farm house and cottage, gossipped with the farmers and their wives, romped with their daughters, and like that type of a vagrant bachelor, the humble bee, tolled the sweets from all the rosy lips of the country round.

The bashfulness of the guests soon gave way before good cheer and affability. There is something genuine and affectionate in the gayety of the lower orders, when it is excited by the bounty and familiarity of those above them; the warm glow of gratitude enters into their mirth, and a kind word, and a small pleasantry frankly uttered by a patron, gladdens the heart of the dependant more than oil and wine. When the Squire had retired, the merriment increased, and there was much joking and laughter; particularly between Master Simon and a hale ruddy faced white headed farmer, who appeared to be the wit of the village, for I observed all his companions to wait with open mouths for his retorts, and burst into a gratuitous laugh before they could well understand them.

The whole house indeed seemed abandoned to merriment: as I passed to my room to dress for dinner, I heard the sound of music in a small court, and looking through a window that commanded it, I perceived a band of wandering musicians with pandean pipes and tambourine: a pretty coquettish housemaid was dancing a jig with a smart country lad, while several of the other servants were looking on. In the midst of her sport the girl caught a glimpse of my face at the window, and colouring up, ran off with an air of roguish affected confusion.

THE CHRISTMAS DINNER

Lo, now is come our joyful'st feast!
    Let every man be jolly,
Eache roome with yvie leaves is drest,
    And every post with holly.
Now all our neighbours' chimneys smoke
    And Christmas blocks are burning;
Their ovens they with bak't meats choke,
    And all their spits are turning.
        Without the door let sorrow lie,
        And if, for cold, it hap to die,
        Wee'le bury 't in a Christmas pye,
        And ever more be merry.
                WITHERS' JUVENILIA.

I had finished my toilet, and was loitering with Frank Bracebridge in the library, when we heard a distant thwacking sound, which he informed me was a signal for the serving up of the dinner. The Squire kept up old customs in kitchen as well as hall, and the rolling pin struck upon the dresser by the cook, summoned the servants to carry in the meats.

Just in this nick the cook knock'd thrice,
And all the waiters in a trice
    His summons did obey;
Each serving man, with dish in hand,
March'd boldly up, like our train band,
    Presented, and away.*

The dinner was served up in the great hall, where the Squire always held his Christmas banquet. A blazing, crackling fire of logs had been heaped on to warm the spacious apartment, and the flame went sparkling and wreathing up the wide mouthed chimney. The great picture of the crusader and his white horse had been profusely decorated with greens for the occasion, and holly and ivy had likewise been wreathed round the helmet and weapons on the opposite wall, which I understood were the arms of the same warrior. I must own, by the by, I had strong doubts about the authenticity of the painting and armour as having belonged to the crusader, they certainly having the stamp

*Sir John Suckling.

of more recent days; but I was told that the painting had been so considered time out of mind; and that, as to the armour, it had been found in a lumber room, and elevated to its present situation by the Squire, who at once determined it to be the armour of the family hero; and as he was absolute authority on all such subjects in his own household, the matter had passed into current acceptation. A sideboard was set out just under this chivalric trophy, on which was a display of plate that might have vied (at least in variety) with Belshazzar's parade of the vessels of the temple: "flagons, cans, cups, beakers, goblets, basins, and ewers;" the gorgeous utensils of good companionship, that had gradually accumulated through many generations of jovial housekeepers; before these stood the two yule candles beaming like two stars of the first magnitude; other lights were distributed in branches, and the whole array glittered like a firmament of silver.

We were ushered into this banqueting scene with the sound of minstrelsy; the old harper being seated on a stool beside the fireplace, and twanging his instrument, with a vast deal more power than melody. Never did Christmas board display a more goodly and gracious assemblage of countenances; those who were not handsome, were, at least, happy; and happiness is a rare improver of your hard favoured visage. I always consider an old English family as well worth studying as a collection of Holbein's portraits or Albert Durer's prints. There is much antiquarian lore to be acquired; much knowledge of the physiognomies of former times. Perhaps it may be from having continually before their eyes those rows of old family portraits, with which the mansions of this country are stocked; certain it is, that the quaint features of antiquity are often most faithfully perpetuated in these ancient lines; and I have traced an old family nose through a whole picture gallery, legitimately handed down from generation to generation, almost from the time of the conquest. Something of the kind was to be observed in the worthy company around me. Many of their faces had evidently originated in a gothic age, and been merely copied by succeeding generations; and there was one little girl in particular, of staid demeanour, with a high Roman nose, and an antique vinegar aspect, who was a great favourite of the Squire's, being, as he said, a Bracebridge all over, and the very counterpart of one of his ancestors who figured in the court of Henry VIII.

The parson said grace, which was not a short familiar one, such as is commonly addressed to the deity, in these unceremonious days; but a long, courtly, well worded one, of the ancient school. There was now a pause, as if something was expected, when suddenly the Butler entered the hall, with some degree of bustle: he was attended by a servant on each side with a large wax light, and bore a silver dish, on which was an enormous pig's head, decorated with rosemary, with a lemon in its mouth, which was placed with great formality at the head of the table. The moment this pageant made its appearance, the harper struck up a flourish; at the conclusion of which the young Oxonian, on receiving a hint from the Squire, gave, with an air of the most comic gravity; an old carol, the first verse of which was as follows:

> Caput apri defero
> Reddens laudes Domino.
> The boar's head in hand bring I,
> With garlands gay and rosemary.
> I pray you all synge merily
> Qui estis in convivio.

Though prepared to witness many of these little eccentricities, from being apprized of the peculiar hobby of mine host; yet, I confess, the parade with which so odd a dish was introduced, somewhat perplexed me, until I gathered from the conversation of the Squire and the parson, that it was meant to represent the bringing in of the boar's head, a dish formerly served up with much ceremony, and the sound of minstrelsy and song, at great tables on Christmas day. "I like the old custom," said the Squire, "not merely because it is stately and pleasing in itself, but because it was observed at the college at Oxford, at which I was educated. When I hear the old song chanted, it brings to mind the time when I was young and gamesome—and the noble old college hall—and my fellow students loitering about it in their black gowns, many of whom, poor lads, are now in their graves!"

The parson, however, whose mind was not haunted by such associations, and who was always more taken up with the text than the sentiment, objected to the Oxonian's version of the carol, which he affirmed was different from that sung at college. He went on with the dry perseverance of a commentator, to give the college reading, accompanied by sundry annotations, addressing himself at first to the company at large; but finding their attention gradually diverted to other talk and other objects, he lowered his tone as his number of auditors diminished, until he concluded his remarks in an under voice, to a fat headed old gentleman next him, who was silently engaged in the discussion of a huge plate full of turkey.*

---

*The old ceremony of serving up the boar's head on Christmas day is still observed in the hall of Queen's College Oxford. I was favoured by the parson with a copy of the carol as now sung, and as it may be acceptable to such of my readers as are curious in these grave and learned matters, I give it entire.

Christmas Dinner

Randolph J. Caldecott illustration from the 1875 edition of *Old Christmas* (London: Macmillan & Company).

The table was literally loaded with good cheer, and presented an epitome of country abundance, in this season of overflowing larders. A distinguished post was allotted to "ancient sirloin," as mine host termed it, being, as he added, "the standard of old English hospitality, and a joint of goodly presence, and full of expectation." There were several dishes quaintly decorated, and which had evidently something traditionary in their embellishments, but about which, as I did not like to appear over curious, I asked no questions.

I could not, however, but notice a pie, magnificently decorated with peacock's feathers, in imitation of the tail of that bird, which over-shadowed a considerable tract of the table. This the Squire confessed, with some little hesitation, was a pheasant pie, though a peacock pie was certainly the most authentical; but there had been such a mortality among the peacocks this season, that he could not prevail upon himself to have one killed.*

The boar's head in hand bear I,
Bedeck'd with bays and rosemary;
And I pray you, my masters, be merry
 Quot estis in convivio.
  Caput apri defero
  Reddens laudes Domino.

The boar's head, as I understand,
Is the rarest dish in all this land,
Which thus bedeck'd with a gay garland
 Let us servire cantico.
  Caput apri defero, &c.

Our steward hath provided this
In honour of the King of bliss,
Which on this day to be served is
 In Reginensi Atrio.
  Caput apri defero,
   &c. &c. &c.

*The peacock was anciently in great demand for stately entertainments. Some-times it was made into a pie, at one end of which the head appeared above the crust in all its plumage, with the beak richly gilt; at the other end the tail was displayed. Such pies were served up at the solemn banquets of chivalry, when Knights errant pledged themselves to undertake any perilous enterprize, whence came the ancient oath, used by Justice Shallow, "by cock and pye."

The peacock was also an important dish for the Christmas feast, and Massinger in his City Madam gives some idea of the extravagance with which this, as well as other dishes, was prepared for the gorgeous revels of the olden times:—

Men may talk of Country-Christmasses,
Their thirty pound butter'd eggs, their pies of carps' tongues;
Their pheasants drench'd with ambergris; *the carcasses of three fat
 wethers bruised for gravy to make sauce for a single peacock!*

It would be tedious, perhaps, to my wiser readers, who may not have that foolish fondness for odd and obsolete things to which I am a little given, were I to mention the other make shifts of this worthy old humourist, by which he was endeavouring to follow up, though at humble distance, the quaint customs of antiquity. I was pleased, however, to see the respect shown to his whims by his children and relatives, who, indeed, entered readily into the full spirit of them, and seemed all well versed in their parts, having doubtless been present at many a rehearsal. I was amused, too, at the air of profound gravity with which the butler and other servants executed the duties assigned them, however eccentric. They had an old fashioned look, having, for the most part, been brought up in the household, and grown into keeping with the antiquated mansion, and the humours of its lord, and most probably looked upon all his whimsical regulations, as the established laws of honourable housekeeping.

When the cloth was removed, the butler brought in a huge silver vessel of rare and curious workmanship, which he placed before the Squire. Its appearance was hailed with acclamation; being the Wassail Bowl, so renowned in Christmas festivity. The contents had been prepared by the Squire himself; for it was a beverage in the skilful mixture of which he particularly prided himself; alleging that it was too abstruse and complex for the comprehension of an ordinary servant. It was a potation, indeed, that might well make the heart of a toper leap within him; being composed of the richest and raciest wines, highly spiced and sweetened, with roasted apples bobbing about the surface.*

The old gentleman's whole countenance beamed with a serene look of indwelling delight, as he stirred this mighty bowl. Having raised it to his lips, with a hearty wish of a merry Christmas to all present, he sent it brimming round the board, for every one to follow his example, according to the primitive style; pronouncing it, "the ancient fountain of good feeling, where all hearts met together."†

*The Wassail Bowl was sometimes composed of ale instead of wine; with nutmeg, sugar, toast, ginger, and roasted crabs: in this way the nut brown beverage is still prepared in some old families, and round the hearths of substantial farmers at Christmas. It is also called Lamb's wool, and is celebrated by Herrick in his Twelfth Night:

> Next crowne the bowle full
> With gentle Lamb's wooll,
> Add sugar, nutmeg, and ginger,
> With store of ale too;
> And thus ye must doe
> To make the Wassaile a swinger.

†"The custom of drinking out of the same cup gave place to each having his cup. When the steward came to the doore with the Wassel, he was to cry three

There was much laughing and rallying as the honest emblem of Christmas joviality circulated, and was kissed rather coyly by the ladies. When it reached Master Simon he raised it in both hands, and with the air of a boon companion struck up an old Wassail chanson:

> The brown bowle,
> The merry brown bowle,
> As it goes round about-a,
> > Fill
> > Still
> Let the world say what it will
> And drink your fill all out-a.
>
> The deep canne,
> The merry deep canne,
> As thou dost freely quaff-a,
> > Sing
> > Fling
> Be as merry as a king,
> And sound a lusty laugh-a.*

Much of the conversation during dinner turned upon family topics, to which I was a stranger. There was, however, a great deal of rallying of Master Simon about some gay widow, with whom he was accused of having a flirtation. This attack was commenced by the ladies; but it was continued throughout the dinner by the fat headed old gentleman next the parson, with the persevering assiduity of a slow hound; being one of those long winded jokers, who, though rather dull at starting game, are unrivalled for their talents in hunting it down. At every pause in the general conversation, he renewed his bantering in pretty much the same terms; winking hard at me with both eyes, whenever he gave Master Simon what he considered a home thrust. The latter, indeed, seemed fond of being teased on the subject, as old bachelors are apt to be, and he took occasion to inform me, in an under tone, that the lady in question was a prodigiously fine woman, and drove her own curricle.

The dinner time passed away in this flow of innocent hilarity, and though the old hall may have resounded in its time with many a scene of broader rout and revel, yet I doubt whether it ever witnessed more

---

times *Wassel, Wassel, Wassel,* and then the chappel (chaplain) was to answer with a song." ARCHÆOLOGIA.

*From Poor Robin's Almanack.

honest and genuine enjoyment. How easy it is for one benevolent being to diffuse pleasure around him; and how truly is a kind heart a fountain of gladness, making every thing in its vicinity to freshen into smiles. The joyous disposition of the worthy Squire was perfectly contagious; he was happy himself, and disposed to make all the world happy; and the little eccentricities of his humour did but season, in a manner, the sweetness of his philanthropy.

When the ladies had retired, the conversation, as usual, became still more animated: many good things were broached which had been thought of during dinner, but which would not exactly do for a lady's ear; and though I cannot positively affirm that there was much wit uttered, yet I have certainly heard many contests of rare wit produce much less laughter. Wit, after all, is a mighty tart, pungent ingredient, and much too acid for some stomachs; but honest good humour is the oil and wine of a merry meeting, and there is no jovial companionship equal to that, where the jokes are rather small, and the laughter abundant.

The Squire told several long stories of early college pranks and adventures, in some of which the parson had been a sharer; though in looking at the latter, it required some effort of imagination to figure such a little dark anatomy of a man, into the perpetrator of a mad cap gambol. Indeed, the two college chums presented pictures of what men may be made by their different lots in life: the Squire had left the university to live lustily on his paternal domains, in the vigorous enjoyment of prosperity and sunshine, and had flourished on to a hearty and florid old age, whilst the poor parson, on the contrary, had dried and withered away, among dusty tomes, in the silence and shadows of his study. Still there seemed to be a spark of almost extinguished fire, feebly glimmering in the bottom of his soul; and as the Squire hinted at a sly story of the parson and a pretty milkmaid whom they once met on the banks of the Isis, the old gentleman made an "alphabet of faces," which, as far as I could decypher his physiognomy, I verily believe was indicative of laughter;—indeed, I have rarely met with an old gentleman that took absolute offence at the imputed gallantries of his youth.

I found the tide of wine and wassail fast gaining on the dry land of sober judgment. The company grew merrier and louder as their jokes grew duller. Master Simon was in as chirping a humour as a grasshopper filled with dew; his old songs grew of a warmer complexion, and he began to talk maudlin about the widow. He even gave a long song about the wooing of a widow, which he informed me he had gathered from an excellent black letter work entitled "Cupid's Solicitor for Love;" containing store of good advice for Bachelors, and which he promised to lend me; the first verse was to this effect:

> He that will woo a widow must not dally,
>   He must make hay while the sun doth shine;
>   He must not stand with her, shall I, shall I,
>   But boldy say, Widow thou must be mine.

This song inspired the fat headed old gentleman, who made several attempts to tell a rather broad story out of Joe Miller, that was pat to the purpose; but he always stuck in the middle, every body recollecting the latter part except himself. The parson, too, began to show the effects of good cheer, having gradually settled down into a doze, and his wig setting most suspiciously on one side. Just at this juncture we were summoned to the drawing room, and I suspect, at the private instigation of mine host, whose joviality seemed always tempered with a proper love of decorum.

After the dinner table was removed, the hall was given up to the younger members of the family, who, prompted to all kind of noisy mirth, by the Oxonian and Master Simon, made its old walls ring with their merriment, as they played at romping games. I delight in witnessing the gambols of children, and particularly at this happy holiday season, and could not help stealing out of the drawing room on hearing one of their peals of laughter. I found them at the game of blind-man's-buff. Master Simon, who was the leader of their revels, and seemed on all occasions to fulfil the office of that ancient potentate, the Lord of Misrule,* was blinded in the midst of the hall. The little beings were as busy about him as the mock fairies about Falstaff, pinching him, plucking at the skirts of his coat, and tickling him with straws. One fine blue eyed girl of about thirteen, with her flaxen hair all in beautiful confusion, her frolick face in a glow, her frock half torn off her shoulders, a complete picture of a romp, was the chief tormentor; and from the slyness with which Master Simon avoided the smaller game, and hemmed this wild little nymph in corners, and obliged her to jump shrieking over chairs, I suspected the rogue of being not a whit more blinded than was convenient.

When I returned to the drawing room, I found the company seated round the fire, listening to the parson, who was deeply ensconced in a high backed oaken chair, the work of some cunning artificer of yore,

---

*At christmasse there was in the Kinges house, wheresoever hee was lodged, a lorde of misrule, or mayster of merie disportes, and the like had ye in the house of every nobleman of honor, or good worshippe, were he spirituall or temporall. STOW.

which had been brought from the library for his particular accommodation. From this venerable piece of furniture, with which his shadowy figure and dark weazen face so admirably accorded, he was dealing forth strange accounts of the popular superstitions, and legends of the surrounding country, with which he had become acquainted in the course of his antiquarian researches. I am half inclined to think that the old gentleman was himself somewhat tinctured with superstition, as men are very apt to be, who live a recluse and studious life in a sequestered part of the country, and pore over black letter tracts, so often filled with the marvellous and supernatural. He gave us several anecdotes of the fancies of the neighbouring peasantry, concerning the effigy of the crusader, which lay on the tomb by the church altar. As it was the only monument of the kind in that part of the country, it had always been regarded with feelings of superstition by the good wives of the village. It was said to get up from the tomb and walk the rounds of the church yard of stormy nights, particularly when it thundered; and one old woman whose cottage bordered on the church yard had seen it, through the windows of the church, when the moon shone, slowly pacing up and down the aisles. It was the belief that some wrong had been left unredressed by the deceased, or some treasure hidden, which kept the spirit in a state of trouble and restlessness. Some talked of gold and jewels buried in the tomb, over which the spectre kept watch; and there was a story current of a sexton in old times who endeavoured to break his way to the coffin at night; but just as he reached it, received a violent blow from the marble hand of the effigy, which stretched him senseless on the pavement. These tales were often laughed at by some of the sturdier among the rustics, yet when night came on, there were many of the stoutest unbelievers that were shy of venturing alone in the footpath that led across the church yard.

From these and other anecdotes that followed, the crusader appeared to be the favourite hero of ghost stories throughout the vicinity. His picture, which hung up in the hall, was thought by the servants to have something supernatural about it; for they remarked that, in whatever part of the hall you went, the eyes of the warrior were still fixed on you. The old porter's wife too, at the lodge, who had been born and brought up in the family, and was a great gossip among the maid servants, affirmed, that in her young days she had often heard say, that on midsummer eve, when it is well known all kinds of ghosts, goblins, and fairies, become visible and walk abroad, the crusader used to mount his horse, come down from his picture, ride about the house, down the avenue, and so to the church to visit the tomb; on which occasion the church door most civilly swung open of itself: not that he needed it; for he rode through closed gates and even stone walls, and had been seen by one of the dairy maids to pass between two bars of the great park gate, making himself as thin as a sheet of paper.

All these superstitions I found had been very much countenanced by the Squire, who, though not superstitious himself, was very fond of seeing others so. He listened to every goblin tale of the neighbouring gossips with infinite gravity, and held the porter's wife in high favour on account of her talent for the marvellous. He was himself a great reader of old legends and romances, and often lamented that he could not believe in them, for a superstitious person, he thought, must live in a kind of fairy land.

Whilst we were all attention to the parson's stories, our ears were suddenly assailed by a burst of heterogeneous sounds from the hall, in which were mingled something like the clang of rude minstrelsy, with the uproar of many small voices and girlish laughter. The door suddenly flew open, and a train came trooping into the room, that might almost have been mistaken for the breaking up of the court of Fairy. That indefatigable spirit, Master Simon, in the faithful discharge of his duties, as lord of misrule, had conceived the idea of a Christmas mummery, or masqueing; and having called in to his assistance the Oxonian and the young officer, who were equally ripe for any thing that should occasion romping and merriment, they had carried it into instant effect. The old housekeeper had been consulted; the antique clothes presses and wardrobes rummaged, and made to yield up the reliques of finery that had not seen the light for several generations; the younger part of the company had been privately convened from parlour and hall, and the whole had been bedizened out, into a burlesque imitation of an antique masque.*

Master Simon led the van, as "Ancient Christmas," quaintly apparelled in a ruff, a short cloak, which had very much the aspect of one of the old housekeeper's petticoats, and a hat that might have served for a village steeple, and must indubitably have figured in the days of the Covenanters. From under this his nose curved boldly forth, flushed with a frost bitten bloom, that seemed the very trophy of a December blast. He was accompanied by the blue eyed romp, dished up as "Dame Mince Pie," in the venerable magnificence of faded brocade, long stomacher, peaked hat, and high heeled shoes. The young officer ap-

---

*Masquings or mummeries were favourite sports at Christmas in old times; and the wardrobes at halls and manor houses were often laid under contribution to furnish dresses and fantastic disguisings. I strongly suspect Master Simon to have taken the idea of his from Ben Jonson's Masque of Christmas.

peared as Robin Hood, in a sporting dress of Kendal green, and a foraging cap with a gold tassel. The costume, to be sure, did not bear testimony to deep research, and there was an evident eye to the picturesque, natural to a young gallant in the presence of his mistress. The fair Julia hung on his arm in a pretty rustic dress, as "Maid Marian." The rest of the train had been metamorphosed in various ways; the girls trussed up in the finery of the ancient belles of the Bracebridge line, and the striplings bewhiskered with burnt cork, and gravely clad in broad skirts, hanging sleeves, and full bottomed wigs, to represent the characters of Roast Beef, Plum Pudding, and other worthies celebrated in ancient masquings. The whole was under the control of the Oxonian, in the appropriate character of Misrule; and I observed that he exercised rather a mischievous sway with his wand over the smaller personages of the pageant.

The irruption of this motley crew, with beat of drum, according to ancient custom, was the consummation of uproar and merriment. Master Simon covered himself with glory by the stateliness with which, as Ancient Christmas, he walked a minuet with the peerless, though giggling, Dame Mince Pie. It was followed by a dance of all the characters, which, from its medley of costumes, seemed as though the old family portraits had skipped down from their frames to join in the sport. Different centuries were figuring at cross hands and right and left; the dark ages were cutting pirouettes and rigadoons; and the days of Queen Bess jigging merrily down the middle, through a line of succeeding generations.

The worthy Squire contemplated these fantastic sports, and this resurrection of his old wardrobe, with the simple relish of childish delight. He stood chuckling and rubbing his hands, and scarcely hearing a word the parson said, notwithstanding that the latter was discoursing most authentically on the ancient and stately dance of the Paon, or peacock, from which he conceived the minuet to be derived.* For my part, I was in a continual excitement from the varied scenes of whim and innocent gayety passing before me. It was inspiring to see wild eyed frolick and warm hearted hospitality breaking out from among the chills and glooms of winter, and old age throwing off its apathy, and catching once more the freshness of youthful enjoyment. I felt also

---

*Sir John Hawkins, speaking of the dance called the Pavon, from pavo, a peacock, says, "It is a grave and majestic dance; the method of dancing it anciently was by gentlemen, dressed with caps and swords, by those of the long robe in their gowns, by the peers in their mantles, and by the ladies in gowns with long trains, the motion whereof, in dancing, resembled that of a peacock." HISTORY OF MUSIC.

an interest in the scene, from the consideration that these fleeting customs were posting fast into oblivion, and that this was, perhaps, the only family in England in which the whole of them was still punctiliously observed. There was a quaintness too, mingled with all this revelry that gave it a peculiar zest: it was suited to the time and place; and as the old manor house almost reeled with mirth and wassail, it seemed echoing back the joviality of long departed years.*

But enough of Christmas and its gambols: it is time for me to pause in this garrulity. Methinks I hear the question asked by my graver readers, "To what purpose is all this—how is the world to be made wiser by this talk?" Alas! is there not wisdom enough extant for the instruction of the world? And if not, are there not thousands of abler pens labouring for its improvement?—It is so much pleasanter to please than to instruct—to play the companion rather than the preceptor. What, after all, is the mite of wisdom that I could throw into the mass of knowledge; or how am I sure that my sagest deductions may be safe guides for the opinions of others? But in writing to amuse, if I fail, the only evil is my own disappointment. If, however, I can by any lucky chance, in these days of evil, rub out one wrinkle from the brow of care, or beguile the heavy heart of one moment of sorrow; if I can now and then penetrate through the gathering film of misanthropy, prompt a benevolent view of human nature, and make my reader more in good humour with his fellow beings and himself, surely, surely, I shall not then have written entirely in vain.

*At the time of the first publication of this paper, the picture of an old fashioned Christmas in the country was pronounced by some as out of date. The author had afterwards an opportunity of witnessing almost all the customs above described, existing in unexpected vigor on the skirts of Derbyshire and Yorkshire, where he passed the Christmas Holydays. The reader will find some notice of them in the author's account of his sojourn at Newstead Abbey.

LONDON ANTIQUES

> ———I do walk
> Methinks like Guido Vaux, with my dark lanthorn,
> Stealing to set the town o' fire; i' th' country
> I should be taken for William o' the Wisp,
> Or Robin Goodfellow.
>
> FLETCHER.

I am somewhat of an antiquity hunter and am fond of exploring London in quest of the reliques of old times. These are principally to be found in the depths of the city, swallowed up and almost lost in a wilderness of brick and mortar; but deriving poetical and romantic interest from the commonplace prosaic world around them. I was struck with an instance of the kind in the course of a recent summer ramble into the city; for the city is only to be explored to advantage in summer time; when free from the smoke and fog, and rain and mud of winter. I had been buffeting for some time against the current of population setting through Fleet Street. The warm weather had unstrung my nerves and made me sensitive to every jar and jostle and discordant sound. The flesh was weary, the spirit faint and I was getting out of humor with the bustling busy throng through which I had to struggle, when in a fit of desperation I tore my way through the crowd, plunged into a bye lane, and after passing through several obscure nooks and angles emerged into a quaint and quiet court with a grass plot in the centre overhung by elms, and kept perpetually fresh and green by a fountain with its sparkling jet of water. A student with book in hand was seated on a stone bench, partly reading, partly meditating on the movements of two or three trim nursery maids with their infant charges.

I was like an Arab who had suddenly come upon an oasis amid the panting sterility of the desert. By degrees the quiet and coolness of the place soothed my nerves and refreshed my spirit. I pursued my walk and came, hard by, to a very ancient chapel with a low browed saxon portal of massive and rich architecture. The interior was circular and lofty, and lighted from above. Around were monumental tombs of ancient date, on which were extended the marble effigies of warriors in armour. Some had the hands devoutly crossed upon the breast; others grasped the pummel of the sword—menacing hostility even in the tomb!—while the crossed legs of several indicated soldiers of the Faith who had been on crusades to the Holy Land.

I was in fact, in the chapel of the Knights Templars, strangely situated in the very centre of sordid traffic; and I do not know a more impressive lesson for the man of the world than thus suddenly to turn aside from the high way of busy money seeking life, and sit down among these shadowy sepulchres, where all is twilight, dust and forgetfulness.

In a subsequent tour of observation I encountered another of these reliques of a "foregone world" locked up in the heart of the city. I had been wandering for some time through dull monotonous streets, destitute of any thing to strike the eye or excite the imagination, when I beheld before me a gothic gate way of mouldering antiquity. It opened into a spacious quadrangle forming the court yard of a stately gothic pile the portal of which stood "invitingly open."

It was apparently a public edifice, and as I was antiquity hunting I ventured in, though with dubious steps. Meeting no one either to oppose or rebuke my intrusion I continued on until I found myself in a great hall with a lofty arched roof and oaken gallery, all of gothic architecture. At one end of the hall was an enormous fireplace with wooden settles on each side; at the other end was a raised platform or dais, the seat of state, above which was the portrait of a man in antique garb, with a long robe, a ruff and a venerable grey beard.

The whole establishment had an air of monastic quiet and seclusion, and what gave it a mysterious charm was, that I had not met with a human being since I had passed the threshold.

Encouraged by this loneliness I seated myself in a recess of a large bow window which admitted a broad flood of yellow sunshine, chequered here and there by tints from panes of colored glass; while an open casement let in the soft summer air. Here leaning my head on my hand and my arm on an old oaken table I indulged in a sort of reverie about what might have been the ancient uses of this edifice. It had evidently been of monastic origin; perhaps one of those collegiate establishments built of yore for the promotion of learning, where the patient monk, in the ample solitude of the cloister, added page to page and volume to volume, emulating in the productions of his brain the magnitude of the pile he inhabited.

As I was seated in this musing mood a small panneled door in an arch at the upper end of the hall was opened and a number of grey headed old men, clad in long black cloaks, came forth one by one; proceeding in that manner through the hall, without uttering a word, each turning a pale face on me as he passed, and disappearing through a door at the lower end.

I was singularly struck with their appearance; their black cloaks and antiquated air comported with the style of this most venerable and mysterious pile. It was as if the ghosts of the departed years about which I had been musing were passing in review before me. Pleasing myself with such fancies, I set out, in the spirit of Romance, to explore what I pictured to myself a realm of shadows, existing in the very centre of substantial realities.

My ramble led me through a labyrinth of interior courts and corridors and delapidated cloisters, for the main edifice had many additions and dependencies, built at various times and in various styles; in one open space a number of boys who evidently belonged to the establishment, were at their sports; but every where I observed those mysterious old grey men in black mantles, sometimes sauntering alone; sometimes conversing in groups: they appeared to be the pervading genii of the place. I now called to mind what I had read of certain colleges in old times where judicial astrology, geomancy, necromancy and other forbidden and magical sciences were taught. Was this an establishment of the kind—and were these black cloaked old men really professors of the black art?

These surmises were passing through my mind as my eye glanced into a chamber, hung round with all kinds of strange and uncouth objects: implements of savage warfare; strange idols and stuffed alligators; bottled serpents and monsters decorated the mantelpiece; while on the high tester of an old fashioned bed stead grinned a human scull, flanked on each side by a dried cat.

I approached to regard more narrowly this mystic chamber, which seemed a fitting laboratory for a necromancer, when I was startled at beholding a human countenance staring at me from a dusky corner. It was that of a small, shrivelled old man, with thin cheeks, bright eyes, and grey wiry projecting eyebrows. I at first doubted whether it were not a mummy curiously preserved, but it moved and I saw that it was alive. It was another of these black cloaked old men, and, as I regarded his quaint physiognomy, his obsolete garb, and the hideous and sinister objects by which he was surrounded, I began to persuade myself that I had come upon the Arch Mago, who ruled over this magical fraternity.

Seeing me pausing before the door he rose and invited me to enter. I obeyed, with singular hardihood, for how did I know whether a wave of his wand might not metamorphose me into some strange monster, or conjure me into one of the bottles on his mantel piece. He proved, however, to be any thing but a conjuror, and his simple garrulity soon dispelled all the magic and mystery with which I had enveloped this antiquated pile and its no less antiquated inhabitants.

It appeared that I had made my way into the centre of an ancient asylum for superannuated tradesmen and decayed householders, with which was connected a school for a limited number of boys. It was founded upwards of two centuries since on an old monastic establishment, and retained somewhat of the conventual air and character. The shadowy line of old men in black mantles who had passed before me in the hall, and whom I had elevated into magi, turned out to be the pensioners returning from morning service in the chapel.

John Hallum the little collector of curiosities whom I had made the arch magician, had been for six years a resident of the place, and had decorated this final nestling place of his old age with reliques and rarities picked up in the course of his life. According to his own account he had been somewhat of a traveller; having been once in France and very near making a visit to Holland. He regretted not having visited the latter country, "as then he might have said he had been there."—He was evidently a traveller of the simple kind.

He was aristocratical too in his notions; keeping aloof, as I found, from the ordinary run of pensioners. His chief associates were a blind man who spoke Latin and Greek, of both which languages Hallum was profoundly ignorant; and a broken down gentleman who had run through a fortune of forty thousand pounds left him by his father, and ten thousand pounds, the marriage portion of his wife. Little Hallum seemed to consider it an indubitable sign of gentle blood as well as of lofty spirit to be able to squander such enormous sums.

P.S. The picturesque remnant of old times into which I have thus beguiled the reader is what is called the Charter House, originally the Chartreuse. It was founded in 1611 on the remains of an ancient convent by Sir Thomas Sutton, being one of those noble charities set on foot by individual munificence, and kept up with the quaintness and sanctity of ancient times amidst the modern changes and innovations of London. Here eighty broken down men, who have seen better days, are provided, in their old age, with food, clothing, fuel and a yearly allowance for private expenses. They dine together as did the monks of old, in the hall which had been the refectory of the original convent. Attached to the establishment is a school for forty four boys.

Stow, whose work I have consulted on the subject; speaking of the obligations of the grey headed pensioners, says, "They are not to intermeddle with any business touching the affairs of the hospital; but to attend only to the service of God, and take thankfully what is provided for them, without muttering, murmuring or grudging. None to wear weapon, long hair, colored boots, spurs or colored shoes; feathers in their hats, or any ruffian like or unseemly apparel, but such as becomes hospital men to wear." "And in truth," adds Stow, "happy are they that are so taken from the cares and sorrows of the world, and fixed in so good a place as these old men are; having nothing to care for, but the good of their souls, to serve God and to live in brotherly love."

For the amusement of such as have been interested by the preceding sketch, taken down from my own observation, and who may wish to know a little more about the mysteries of London, I subjoin a modicum of local history, put into my hands by an odd looking old gentleman in a small brown wig and a snuff colored coat, with whom I became acquainted shortly after my visit to the Charter House. I confess I was a little dubious at first, whether it was not one of those apocryphal tales often passed off upon inquiring travellers like myself; and which have brought our general character for veracity into such unmerited reproach. On making proper inquiries, however, I have received the most satisfactory assurances of the author's probity; and, indeed, have been told that he is actually engaged in a full and particular account of the very interesting region in which he resides; of which the following may be considered merely as a foretaste.

LITTLE BRITAIN

What I write is most true. * * * * I have a whole booke of cases lying by me, which if I should sette foorth, some grave auntients (within the hearing of Bow bell) would bee out of charity with me.

NASHE.

In the centre of the great City of London lies a small neighbourhood, consisting of a cluster of narrow streets and courts, of very venerable and debilitated houses, which goes by the name of LITTLE BRITAIN. Christ Church School and St. Bartholomew's Hospital bound it on the west; Smith Field and Long Lane on the north; Aldersgate Street, like an arm of the sea, divides it from the eastern part of the city; whilst the yawning gulph of Bull and Mouth Street separates it from Butcher Lane, and the regions of New Gate. Over this little territory, thus bounded and designated, the great dome of St. Paul's, swelling above the intervening houses of Paternoster Row, Amen Corner, and Ave-Maria Lane, looks down with an air of motherly protection.

This quarter derives its appellation from having been, in ancient times, the residence of the Dukes of Britany. As London increased, however, rank and fashion rolled off to the west, and trade creeping on at their heels, took possession of their deserted abodes. For some time Little Britain became the great mart of learning, and was peopled by the busy and prolific race of booksellers: these also gradually deserted it, and emigrating beyond the great strait of New Gate Street, settled down in Paternoster Row and St. Paul's Church Yard; where they continue to increase and multiply even at the present day.

But though thus fallen into decline, Little Britain still bears traces of its former splendour. There are several houses, ready to tumble down, the fronts of which are magnificently enriched with old oaken carvings of hideous faces, unknown birds, beasts, and fishes; and fruits and flowers which it would perplex a naturalist to classify. There are also, in Aldersgate Street, certain remains of what were once spacious and lordly family mansions, but which have in latter days been subdivided into several tenements. Here may often be found the family of a petty tradesman, with its trumpery furniture, burrowing among the relics of antiquated finery, in great rambling time stained apartments, with fretted ceilings, gilded cornices, and enormous marble fireplaces. The lanes and courts also contain many smaller houses, not on so grand a scale, but, like your small ancient gentry, sturdily maintaining their claims to equal antiquity. These have their gable ends

197

to the street; great bow windows, with diamond panes set in lead; grotesque carvings; and low arched door ways.*

In this most venerable and sheltered little nest have I passed several quiet years of existence; comfortably lodged in the second floor of one of the smallest, but oldest edifices. My sitting room is an old wainscotted chamber, with small pannels, and set off with a miscellaneous array of furniture. I have a particular respect for three or four high backed claw footed chairs, covered with tarnished brocade; which bear the marks of having seen better days; and have doubtless figured in some of the old palaces of Little Britain. They seem to me to keep together, and to look down with sovereign contempt upon their leathern bottomed neighbours; as I have seen decayed gentry carry a high head among the plebeian society with which they were reduced to associate. The whole front of my sitting room is taken up with a bow window; on the panes of which are recorded the names of previous occupants for many generations; mingled with scraps of very indifferent, gentleman like poetry, written in characters which I can scarcely decipher; and which extol the charms of many a beauty of Little Britain, who has long, long since, bloomed, faded, and passed away. As I am an idle personage, with no apparent occupation, and pay my bill regularly every week, I am looked upon as the only independent gentleman of the neighbourhood; and being curious to learn the internal state of a community so apparently shut up within itself, I have managed to work my way into all the concerns and secrets of the place.

Little Britain may truly be called the heart's core of the city; the strong hold of true John Bullism. It is a fragment of London as it was in its better days, with its antiquated folks and fashions. Here flourish in great preservation many of the holyday games and customs of yore. The inhabitants most religiously eat pan cakes on Shrove Tuesday; hot cross buns on Good Friday, and roast goose at Michaelmas: they send love letters on Valentine's Day; burn the Pope on the Fifth of November, and kiss all the girls under the misletoe at Christmas. Roast beef and plum pudding are also held in superstitious veneration, and port and sherry maintain their grounds as the only true English wines; all others being considered vile outlandish beverages.

Little Britain has its long catalogue of city wonders, which its inhabitants consider the wonders of the world; such as the great bell of St. Paul's, which sours all the beer when it tolls; the figures that strike the hours at St. Dunstan's clock; the Monument; the lions in the

---

*It is evident that the author of this interesting communication has included in his general title of Little Britain, many of those little lanes and courts that belong immediately to Cloth Fair.

Tower; and the wooden giants in Guildhall. They still believe in dreams and fortune telling, and an old woman that lives in Bull and Mouth Street makes a tolerable subsistence by detecting stolen goods, and promising the girls good husbands. They are apt to be rendered uncomfortable by comets and eclipses; and if a dog howls dolefully at night, it is looked upon as a sure sign of a death in the place. There are even many ghost stories current, particularly concerning the old mansion houses; in several of which it is said strange sights are sometimes seen. Lords and ladies, the former in full bottomed wigs, hanging sleeves and swords, the latter in lappets, stays, hoops, and brocade, have been seen walking up and down the great waste chambers, on moonlight nights; and are supposed to be the shades of the ancient proprietors in their court dresses.

Little Britain has likewise its sages and great men. One of the most important of the former is a tall dry old gentleman, of the name of Skryme, who keeps a small apothecary's shop. He has a cadaverous countenance, full of cavities and projections; with a brown circle round each eye, like a pair of horn spectacles. He is much thought of by the old women, who consider him as a kind of conjuror, because he has two or three stuffed alligators hanging up in his shop, and several snakes in bottles. He is a great reader of almanacks and newspapers, and is much given to pore over alarming accounts of plots, conspiracies, fires, earthquakes, and volcanic eruptions; which last phenomena he considers as signs of the times. He has always some dismal tale of the kind to deal out to his customers, with their doses; and thus at the same time puts both soul and body into an uproar. He is a great believer in omens and predictions; and has the prophecies of Robert Nixon and Mother Shipton by heart. No man can make so much out of an eclipse, or even an unusually dark day; and he shook the tail of the last comet over the heads of his customers and disciples until they were nearly frightened out of their wits. He has lately got hold of a popular legend or prophecy, on which he has been unusually eloquent. There has been a saying current among the ancient Sybils, who treasure up these things, that when the grasshopper on the top of the Exchange shook hands with the dragon on the top of Bow Church steeple, fearful events would take place. This strange conjunction, it seems, has as strangely come to pass. The same architect has been engaged lately on the repairs of the cupola of the Exchange, and the steeple of Bow Church; and, fearful to relate, the dragon and the grasshopper actually lie, cheek by jole, in the yard of his workshop!

"Others," as Mr. Skryme is accustomed to say, "may go star gazing, and look for conjunctions in the heavens, but here is a conjunction on the earth, near at home, and under our own eyes, which surpasses all the signs and calculations of astrologers." Since these portentous weathercocks have thus laid their heads together, wonderful events had already occurred. The good old king, notwithstanding that he had lived eighty two years, had all at once given up the ghost; another king had mounted the throne; a royal duke had died suddenly—another, in France, had been murdered; there had been radical meetings in all parts of the kingdom; the bloody scenes at Manchester; the great plot in Cato Street;—and, above all, the Queen had returned to England! All these sinister events are recounted by Mr. Skryme with a mysterious look, and a dismal shake of the head; and, being taken with his drugs, and associated in the minds of his auditors with stuffed sea monsters, bottled serpents, and his own visage, which is a title page of tribulation, they have spread great gloom through the minds of the people in Little Britain. They shake their heads whenever they go by Bow Church, and observe, that they never expected any good to come of taking down that steeple, which in old times told nothing but glad tidings, as the history of Wittington and his Cat bears witness.

The rival oracle of Little Britain is a substantial cheesemonger, who lives in a fragment of one of the old family mansions, and is as magnificently lodged as a round bellied mite in the midst of one of his own Cheshires. Indeed he is a man of no little standing and importance; and his renown extends through Huggin Lane, and Lad Lane, and even unto Aldermanbury. His opinion is very much taken in affairs of state, having read the Sunday papers for the last half century, together with the Gentleman's Magazine, Rapin's History of England, and the Naval Chronicle. His head is stored with invaluable maxims which have borne the test of time and use for centuries. It is his firm opinion that "it is a moral impossible," so long as England is true to herself, that any thing can shake her: and he has much to say on the subject of the national debt; which, some how or other, he proves to be a great national bulwark and blessing. He passed the greater part of his life in the purlieus of Little Britain, until of late years, when, having become rich, and grown into the dignity of a Sunday cane, he begins to take his pleasure and see the world. He has therefore made several excursions to Hampstead, Highgate, and other neighbouring towns, where he has passed whole afternoons in looking back upon the metropolis through a telescope and endeavouring to descry the steeple of St. Bartholomew's. Not a stage coachman of Bull and Mouth Street, but touches his hat as he passes; and he is considered quite a patron at the coach office of the Goose and Gridiron, St. Paul's Church yard. His family have been very urgent for him to make an expedition to Margate, but he has great doubts of those new gim-cracks the steam boats, and indeed thinks himself too advanced in life to undertake sea voyages.

Little Britain has occasionally its factions and divisions, and party spirit ran very high at one time in consequence of two rival "Burial Societies" being set up in the place. One held its meeting at the Swan and Horse Shoe, and was patronized by the cheesemonger; the other at the Cock and Crown, under the auspices of the apothecary: it is needless to say that the latter was the most flourishing. I have passed an evening or two at each, and have acquired much valuable information as to the best mode of being buried; the comparative merits of church yards; together with diverse hints on the subject of patent iron coffins. I have heard the question discussed in all its bearings as to the legality of prohibiting the latter on account of their durability. The feuds occasioned by these societies have happily died of late; but they were for a long time prevailing themes of controversy, the people of Little Britain being extremely solicitous of funeral honours and of lying comfortably in their graves.

Besides these two funeral societies there is a third of quite a different cast, which tends to throw the sunshine of good humour over the whole neighbourhood. It meets once a week at a little old fashioned house, kept by a jolly publican of the name of Wagstaff, and bearing for insignia a resplendent half moon, with a most seductive bunch of grapes. The whole edifice is covered with inscriptions to catch the eye of the thirsty wayfarer; such as "Truman, Hanbury, and Co's. Entire," "Wine, Rum, and Brandy Vaults," "Old Tom, Rum and Compounds, &c." This indeed has been a temple of Bacchus and Momus from time immemorial. It has always been in the family of the Wagstaffs, so that its history is tolerably preserved by the present landlord. It was much frequented by the gallants and cavalieros of the reign of Elizabeth, and was looked into now and then by the wits of Charles the Second's day. But what Wagstaff principally prides himself upon, is, that Henry the Eighth, in one of his nocturnal rambles, broke the head of one of his ancestors with his famous walking staff. This however is considered as rather a dubious and vain glorious boast of the landlord.

The club which now holds its weekly sessions here, goes by the name of "the Roaring Lads of Little Britain." They abound in old catches, glees and choice stories, that are traditional in the place, and not to be met with in any other part of the metropolis. There is a mad cap undertaker who is inimitable at a merry song; but the life of the club, and indeed the prime wit of Little Britain, is bully Wagstaff himself. His ancestors were all wags before him, and he has inherited with the inn a large stock of songs and jokes, which go with it from generation to generation as heir looms. He is a dapper little fellow, with bandy legs and pot belly, a red face with a moist merry eye, and a little shock of grey hair behind. At the opening of every club night he is called in to sing his "Confession of Faith," which is the famous old drinking trowl from Gammer Gurton's Needle. He sings it, to be sure with many variations, as he received it from his father's lips; for it has been a standing favourite at the Half Moon and Bunch of Grapes ever since it was written; nay, he affirms that his predecessors have often had the honour of singing it before the nobility and gentry at Christmas mummeries, when Little Britain was in all its glory.*

*As mine host of the Half moon's Confession of Faith may not be familiar to the majority of readers, and as it is a specimen of the current songs of Little Britain, I subjoin it in its original orthography. I would observe that the whole club always join in the chorus with a fearful thumping on the table and clattering of pewter pots.

> I cannot eate but lytle meate,
>   My stomacke is not good,
> But sure I thinke that I can drinke
>   With him that weares a hood.
> Though I go bare take ye no care,
>   I nothing am a colde,
> I stuff my skyn so full within,
>   Of joly good ale and olde.

Chorus.   Backe and syde go bare, go bare,
>   Booth foote and hand go colde,
> But belly, God send thee good ale ynoughe,
>   Whether it be new or olde.

> I love no rost, but a nut browne toste,
>   And a crab laid in the fyre;
> A little breade shall do me steade,
>   Much breade I not desyre.
> No frost nor snow, nor winde, I trowe,
>   Can hurte mee if I wolde,
> I am so wrapt and throwly lapt
>   Of joly good ale and olde.

Chorus.   Back and syde go bare, go bare, &c.

> And Tyb my wife, that, as her lyfe,
>   Loveth well good ale to seeke,
> Full oft drynkes shee, tyll ye may see,
>   The teares run downe her cheeke.

It would do one's heart good to hear on a club night the shouts of merriment, the snatches of song, and now and then the choral bursts of half a dozen discordant voices, which issue from this jovial mansion. At such times the street is lined with listeners, who enjoy a delight equal to that of gazing into a confectioner's window, or snuffing up the steams of a cook shop.

There are two annual events which produce great stir and sensation in Little Britain; these are St. Bartholomew's Fair, and the Lord Mayor's day. During the time of the Fair, which is held in the adjoining regions of Smithfield, there is nothing going on but gossiping and gadding about. The late quiet streets of Little Britain are overrun with an irruption of strange figures and faces, every tavern is a scene of rout and revel. The fiddle and the song are heard from the tap room, morning, noon, and night; and at each window may be seen some group of boon companions, with half shut eyes, hats on one side, pipe in mouth and tankard in hand, fondling, and prozing, and singing maudlin songs over their liquor. Even the sober decorum of private families, which I must say is rigidly kept up at other times among my neighbours, is no proof against this saturnalia. There is no such thing as keeping maid servants within doors. Their brains are absolutely set madding with Punch and the Puppet Show; the Flying Horses; Signior Polito; the Fire Eater; the celebrated Mr. Paap; and the Irish Giant. The children too lavish all their holyday money in toys and gilt ginger bread, and fill the house with the Lilliputian din of drums, trumpets and penny whistles.

But the Lord Mayor's day is the great anniversary. The Lord Mayor is looked up to by the inhabitants of Little Britain as the greatest

---

        Then doth shee trowle to me the bowle,
          Even as a mault-worme sholde,
        And sayth, sweete harte, I tooke my parte
          Of this joly good ale and olde.

Chorus.   Back and syde go bare, go bare, &c.

        Now let them drynke, tyll they nod and winke,
          Even as goode fellowes should doe,
        They shall not mysse to have the blisse,
          Good ale doth bring men to.
        And all poore soules that have scowred bowles,
          Or have them lustily trolde,
        God save the lyves of them and their wives,
          Whether they be yonge or olde.

Chorus.   Back and syde go bare, go bare, &c.

potentate upon earth; his gilt coach with six horses as the summit of human splendour; and his procession, with all the Sheriffs and Aldermen in his train, as the grandest of earthly pageants. How they exult in the idea, that the King himself dare not enter the city, without first knocking at the gate of Temple Bar, and asking permission of the Lord Mayor: for if he did, heaven and earth! there is no knowing what might be the consequence. The man in armour who rides before the Lord Mayor, and is the city champion, has orders to cut down every body that offends against the dignity of the city; and then there is the little man with a velvet porringer on his head, who sits at the window of the state coach and holds the city sword, as long as a pike staff—Od's blood! if he once draws that sword, Majesty itself is not safe!

Under the protection of this mighty potentate, therefore, the good people of Little Britain sleep in peace. Temple Bar is an effectual barrier against all interior foes; and as to foreign invasion, the Lord Mayor has but to throw himself into the tower, call in the train bands, and put the standing army of Beef eaters under arms, and he may bid defiance to the world!

Thus wrapped up in its own concerns, its own habits, and its own opinions, Little Britain has long flourished as a sound heart to this great fungous metropolis. I have pleased myself with considering it as a chosen spot, where the principles of sturdy John Bullism were garnered up, like seed corn, to renew the national character, when it had run to waste and degeneracy. I have rejoiced also in the general spirit of harmony that prevailed throughout it; for though there might now and then be a few clashes of opinion between the adherents of the cheesemonger and the apothecary, and an occasional feud between the burial societies, yet these were but transient clouds, and soon passed away. The neighbours met with good will, parted with a shake of the hand, and never abused each other except behind their backs.

I could give rare descriptions of snug junketting parties at which I have been present; where we played at All-Fours, Pope-Joan, Tom-come-tickle-me, and other choice old games; and where we sometimes had a good old English country dance to the tune of Sir Roger de Coverly. Once a year also the neighbours would gather together and go on a gypsey party to Epping Forest. It would have done any man's heart good to see the merriment that took place here as we banqueted on the grass under the trees. How we made the woods ring with bursts of laughter at the songs of little Wagstaff and the merry undertaker! After dinner too, the young folks would play at blind-man's-buff and hide and seek; and it was amusing to see them tangled among the briars, and to hear a fine romping girl now and then squeak from among the bushes. The elder folks would gather round the cheese-monger and the apothecary, to hear them talk politics; for they generally brought out a newspaper in their pockets, to pass away time in the country. They would now and then, to be sure, get a little warm in argument; but their disputes were always adjusted by reference to a worthy old umbrella maker in a double chin, who, never exactly comprehending the subject, managed, some how or other, to decide in favour of both parties.

All empires, however, says some philosopher or historian, are doomed to changes and revolutions. Luxury and innovation creep in; factions arise; and families now and then spring up, whose ambition and intrigues throw the whole system into confusion. Thus in latter days has the tranquillity of Little Britain been grievously disturbed, and its golden simplicity of manners threatened with total subversion by the aspiring family of a retired butcher.

The family of the Lambs had long been among the most thriving and popular in the neighbourhood: the Miss Lambs were the belles of Little Britain, and every body was pleased when Old Lamb had made money enough to shut up shop, and put his name on a brass plate on his door. In an evil hour, however, one of the Miss Lambs had the honour of being a lady in attendance on the Lady Mayoress, at her grand annual ball, on which occasion she wore three towering ostrich feathers on her head. The family never got over it; they were immediately smitten with a passion for high life; set up a one horse carriage, put a bit of gold lace round the errand boy's hat, and have been the talk and detestation of the whole neighbourhood ever since. They could no longer be induced to play at Pope-Joan or blind-man's-buff; they could endure no dances but quadrilles, which no body had ever heard of in Little Britain; and they took to reading novels, talking bad French, and playing upon the piano. Their brother too, who had been articled to an attorney, set up for a dandy and a critic, characters hitherto unknown in these parts; and he confounded the worthy folks exceedingly by talking about Kean, the Opera and the Edinbro' Review.

What was still worse, the Lambs gave a grand ball, to which they neglected to invite any of their old neighbours; but they had a great deal of genteel company from Theobald's Road, Red lion Square, and other parts towards the west. There were several beaux of their brother's acquaintance from Grays inn Lane and Hatton Garden; and not less than three Aldermen's ladies with their daughters. This was not to be forgotten or forgiven. All Little Britain was in an uproar with the smacking of whips, the lashing of miserable horses, and the rattling and jingling of hackney coaches. The gossips of the neighbourhood might be seen popping their night caps out at every window, watching the crazy vehicles rumble by; and there was a knot of virulent old crones, that kept a look out from a house just opposite the retired butcher's, and scanned and criticized every one that knocked at the door.

This dance was a cause of almost open war, and the whole neighbourhood declared they would have nothing more to say to the Lambs. It is true that Mrs. Lamb, when she had no engagements with her quality acquaintance, would give little hum drum tea junkettings to some of her old cronies, "quite," as she would say, "in a friendly way;" and it is equally true that her invitations were always accepted, in spite of all previous vows to the contrary. Nay the good ladies would sit and be delighted with the music of the Miss Lambs, who would condescend to strum an Irish melody for them on the piano; and they would listen with wonderful interest to Mrs. Lamb's anecdotes of Alderman Plunket's family of Portsoken ward, and the Miss Timberlakes, the rich heiresses of Crutched Friars; but then they relieved their consciences, and averted the reproaches of their confederates, by canvassing at the next gossiping convocation every thing that had passed, and pulling the Lambs and their rout all to pieces.

The only one of the family that could not be made fashionable was the retired butcher himself. Honest Lamb, in spite of the meekness of his name, was a rough hearty old fellow, with the voice of a lion, a head of black hair like a shoe brush, and a broad face mottled like his own beef. It was in vain that the daughters always spoke of him as "the old gentleman," addressed him as "papa," in tones of infinite softness, and endeavoured to coax him into a dressing gown and slippers, and other gentlemanly habits. Do what they might, there was no keeping down the butcher. His sturdy nature would break through all their glozings. He had a hearty vulgar good humour that was irrepressible. His very jokes made his sensitive daughters shudder; and he persisted in wearing his blue cotton coat of a morning, dining at two o'clock, and having a "bit of sausage with his tea."

He was doomed, however, to share the unpopularity of his family. He found his old comrades gradually growing cold and civil to him; no longer laughing at his jokes; and now and then throwing out a fling at "some people," and a hint about "quality binding." This both nettled and perplexed the honest butcher; and his wife and daughters, with the consummate policy of the shrewder sex, taking advantage of the circumstance, at length prevailed upon him to give up his afternoon's pipe and tankard at Wagstaff's; to sit after dinner by himself and take his pint of port—a liquor he detested—and to nod in his chair in solitary and dismal gentility.

The Miss Lambs might now be seen flaunting along the streets in French bonnets, with unknown beaux; and talking and laughing so loud that it distressed the nerves of every good lady within hearing. They even went so far as to attempt patronage, and actually induced a French dancing master to set up in the neighbourhood; but the worthy folks of Little Britain took fire at it, and did so persecute the poor Gaul, that he was fain to pack up fiddle and dancing pumps, and decamp with such precipitation, that he absolutely forgot to pay for his lodgings.

I had flattered myself, at first, with the idea that all this fiery indignation on the part of the community, was merely the overflowing of their zeal for good old English manners, and their horror of innovation; and I applauded the silent contempt they were so vociferous in expressing, for upstart pride, French fashions, and the Miss Lambs. But I grieve to say that I soon perceived the infection had taken hold; and that my neighbours, after condemning, were beginning to follow their example. I overheard my landlady importuning her husband to let their daughters have one quarter at French and music, and that they might take a few lessons in the quadrille. I even saw, in the course of a few Sundays, no less than five French bonnets, precisely like those of the Miss Lambs, parading about Little Britain.

I still had my hopes that all this folly would gradually die away; that the Lambs might move out of the neighbourhood; might die, or might run away with attornies' apprentices; and that quiet and simplicity might be again restored to the community. But unluckily a rival power arose. An opulent oil man died and left a widow with a large jointure and a family of buxom daughters. The young ladies had long been repining in secret at the parsimony of a prudent father which kept down all their elegant aspirings. Their ambition being now no longer restrained broke out into a blaze, and they openly took the field against the family of the butcher. It is true that the Lambs, having had the first start, had naturally an advantage of them in the fashionable career. They could speak a little bad French, play the piano, dance quadrilles, and had formed high acquaintances; but the Trotters were not to be distanced. When the Lambs appeared with two feathers in their hats, the Miss Trotters mounted four, and of twice as fine colours. If the Lambs gave a dance, the Trotters were sure not to be behind hand; and though they might not boast of as good company, yet they had double the number and were twice as merry.

The whole community has at length divided itself into fashionable factions, under the banners of these two families. The old games of Pope-Joan and Tom-come-tickle-me are entirely discarded; there is no such thing as getting up an honest country dance; and, on my attempting to kiss a young lady under the misletoe last Christmas, I was indignantly repulsed; the Miss Lambs having pronounced it "shocking vulgar." Bitter rivalry has also broken out as to the most fashionable part of Little Britain; the Lambs standing up for the dignity of Cross Keys Square, and the Trotters for the vicinity of St. Bartholomew's.

Thus is this little territory torn by factions and internal dissensions, like the great empire whose name it bears; and what will be the result would puzzle the apothecary himself, with all his talent at prognostics, to determine; though I apprehend that it will terminate in the total downfall of genuine John Bullism.

The immediate effects are extremely unpleasant to me. Being a single man, and, as I observed before, rather an idle good for nothing personage, I have been considered the only gentleman by profession in the place. I stand therefore in high favour with both parties, and have to hear all their cabinet counsels and mutual backbitings. As I am too civil not to agree with the ladies on all occasions, I have committed myself most horribly with both parties, by abusing their opponents. I might manage to reconcile this to my conscience, which is a truly accommodating one, but I cannot to my apprehension—if the Lambs and Trotters ever come to a reconciliation and compare notes, I am ruined!

I have determined, therefore, to beat a retreat in time, and am actually looking out for some other nest in this great city, where old English manners are still kept up; where French is neither eaten, drunk, danced nor spoken; and where there are no fashionable families of retired tradesmen. This found, I will, like a veteran rat, hasten away before I have an old house about my ears; bid a long, though a sorrowful adieu to my present abode, and leave the rival factions of the Lambs and the Trotters, to divide the distracted empire of LITTLE BRITAIN.

STRATFORD-ON-AVON

Thou soft flowing Avon, by thy silver stream,
Of things more than mortal sweet Shakespeare would dream;
The fairies by moonlight dance round his green bed,
For hallowed the turf is which pillowed his head.

GARRICK.

To a homeless man, who has no spot on this wide world which he can truly call his own, there is a momentary feeling of something like independence and territorial consequence, when, after a weary day's travel, he kicks off his boots, thrusts his feet into slippers, and stretches himself before an inn fire. Let the world without go as it may; let kingdoms rise or fall, so long as he has the wherewithal to pay his bill, he is, for the time being, the very monarch of all he surveys. The arm chair is his throne; the poker his sceptre, and the little parlour of some twelve feet square, his undisputed empire. It is a morsel of certainty, snatched from the midst of the uncertainties of life; it is a sunny moment gleaming out kindly on a cloudy day; and he who has advanced some way on the pilgrimage of existence, knows the importance of husbanding even morsels and moments of enjoyment. "Shall I not take mine ease in mine inn?" thought I, as I gave the fire a stir, lolled back in my elbow chair, and cast a complacent look about the little parlour of the Red Horse, at Stratford-on-Avon.

The words of sweet Shakespeare were just passing through my mind as the clock struck midnight from the tower of the church in which he lies buried. There was a gentle tap at the door, and a pretty chamber maid, putting in her smiling face, inquired, with a hesitating air, whether I had rung. I understood it as a modest hint that it was time to retire. My dream of absolute dominion was at an end; so abdicating my throne, like a prudent potentate, to avoid being deposed, and putting the Stratford Guide Book under my arm, as a pillow companion, I went to bed, and dreamt all night of Shakespeare, the Jubilee, and David Garrick.

The next morning was one of those quickening mornings which we sometimes have in early spring; for it was about the middle of March. The chills of a long winter had suddenly given way; the north wind had spent its last gasp; and a mild air came stealing from the west, breathing the breath of life into nature, and wooing every bud and flower to burst forth into fragrance and beauty.

I had come to Stratford on a poetical pilgrimage. My first visit was to the house where Shakespeare was born, and where, according to tradition, he was brought up to his father's craft of wool combing. It is a small mean looking edifice of wood and plaster, a true nestling place of genius, which seems to delight in hatching its offspring in bye corners. The walls of its squalid chambers are covered with names and inscriptions, in every language, by pilgrims of all nations, ranks, and conditions, from the prince to the peasant; and present a simple, but striking instance of the spontaneous and universal homage of mankind to the great poet of nature.

The house is shown by a garrulous old lady in a frosty red face, lighted up by a cold blue anxious eye, and garnished with artificial locks of flaxen hair, curling from under an exceedingly dirty cap. She was peculiarly assiduous in exhibiting the relics with which this, like all other celebrated shrines, abounds. There was the shattered stock of the very matchlock with which Shakespeare shot the deer, on his poaching exploit. There, too, was his tobacco box; which proves that he was a rival smoker of Sir Walter Raleigh; the sword also with which he played Hamlet; and the identical lanthorn with which Friar Laurence discovered Romeo and Juliet at the tomb! There was an ample supply also of Shakespeare's mulberry tree, which seems to have as extraordinary powers of self multiplication as the wood of the true cross; of which there is enough extant to build a ship of the line.

The most favourite object of curiosity, however, is Shakespeare's chair. It stands in the chimney nook of a small gloomy chamber, just behind what was his father's shop. Here he may many a time have sat when a boy, watching the slowly revolving spit with all the longing of an urchin; or of an evening, listening to the crones and gossips of Stratford, dealing forth church yard tales and legendary anecdotes of the troublesome times of England. In this chair it is the custom of every one that visits the house to sit: whether this be done with the hope of imbibing any of the inspiration of the bard I am at a loss to say, I merely mention the fact; and mine hostess privately assured me, that though built of solid oak, such was the fervent zeal of devotees, that the chair had to be new bottomed at least once in three years. It is worthy of notice also, in the history of this extraordinary chair, that it partakes something of the volatile nature of the Santa Casa of Loretto, or the flying chair of the Arabian enchanter, for though sold some few years since to a northern princess, yet, strange to tell, it has found its way back again to the old chimney corner.

I am always of easy faith in such matters, and am ever willing to be deceived, where the deceit is pleasant, and costs nothing. I am therefore a ready believer in relics, legends, and local anecdotes of goblins and great men; and would advise all travellers who travel for their gratification to be the same. What is it to us whether these stories be true or false, so long as we can persuade ourselves into the belief of them, and enjoy all the charm of the reality? There is nothing like resolute good humoured credulity in these matters; and on this occasion I went even so far as willingly to believe the claims of mine hostess to a lineal descent from the poet, when, unluckily for my faith, she put into my hands a play of her own composition, which set all belief in her consanguinity at defiance.

From the birth place of Shakespeare a few paces brought me to his grave. He lies buried in the chancel of the parish church, a large and venerable pile, mouldering with age, but richly ornamented. It stands on the banks of the Avon, on an embowered point, and separated by adjoining gardens from the suburbs of the town. Its situation is quiet and retired: the river runs murmuring at the foot of the church yard, and the elms which grow upon its banks droop their branches into its clear bosom. An avenue of limes, the boughs of which are curiously interlaced, so as to form in summer an arched way of foliage, leads up from the gate of the yard to the church porch. The graves are overgrown with grass; the grey tombstones, some of them nearly sunk into the earth, are half covered with moss, which has likewise tinted the reverend old building. Small birds have built their nests among the cornices and fissures of the walls, and keep up a continual flutter and chirping; and rooks are sailing and cawing about its lofty grey spire.

In the course of my rambles I met with the grey headed sexton, Edmonds, and accompanied him home to get the key of the church. He had lived in Stratford, man and boy, for eighty years, and seemed still to consider himself a vigorous man, with the trivial exception that he had nearly lost the use of his legs for a few years past. His dwelling was a cottage, looking out upon the Avon and its bordering meadows; and was a picture of that neatness, order, and comfort, which pervade the humblest dwellings in this country. A low white washed room, with a stone floor carefully scrubbed, served for parlour, kitchen, and hall. Rows of pewter and earthen dishes glittered along the dresser. On an old oaken table, well rubbed and polished, lay the family Bible and Prayer book, and the drawer contained the family library, composed of about half a score of well thumbed volumes. An ancient clock, that important article of cottage furniture, ticked on the opposite side of the room; with a bright warming pan hanging on one side of it, and the old man's horn handled Sunday cane on the other. The fireplace, as usual, was wide and deep enough to admit a gossip knot within

its jambs. In one corner sat the old man's grand daughter sewing, a
pretty blue eyed girl,—and in the opposite corner was a superannuated
crony, whom he addressed by the name of John Ange, and who, I
found, had been his companion from childhood. They had played
together in infancy; they had worked together in manhood; they were
now tottering about and gossiping away the evening of life; and in a
short time they will probably be buried together in the neighbouring
church yard. It is not often that we see two streams of existence
running thus evenly and tranquilly side by side; it is only in such
quiet "bosom scenes" of life that they are to be met with.

I had hoped to gather some traditionary anecdotes of the bard
from these ancient chroniclers; but they had nothing new to impart.
The long interval during which Shakespeare's writings lay in comparative neglect has spread its shadow over his history; and it is his
good or evil lot that scarcely any thing remains to his biographers
but a scanty handful of conjectures.

The sexton and his companion had been employed as carpenters
on the preparations for the celebrated Stratford jubilee, and they
remembered Garrick, the prime mover of the fête, who superintended
the arrangements, and who, according to the sexton, was "a short
punch man very lively and bustling." John Ange had assisted also in
cutting down Shakespeare's mulberry tree, of which he had a morsel
in his pocket for sale; no doubt a sovereign quickener of literary
conception.

I was grieved to hear these two worthy wights speak very dubiously
of the eloquent dame who shows the Shakespeare house. John Ange
shook his head when I mentioned her valuable and inexhaustible
collection of relics, particularly her remains of the mulberry tree; and
the old sexton even expressed a doubt as to Shakespeare having been
born in her house. I soon discovered that he looked upon her mansion
with an evil eye, as a rival to the poet's tomb; the latter having comparatively but few visitors. Thus it is that historians differ at the
very outset, and mere pebbles make the stream of truth diverge
into different channels even at the fountain head.

We approached the church through the avenue of limes, and entered
by a gothic porch, highly ornamented, with carved doors of massive
oak. The interior is spacious, and the architecture and embellishments
superior to those of most country churches. There are several ancient
monuments of nobility and gentry, over some of which hang funeral
escutcheons, and banners dropping piecemeal from the walls. The tomb
of Shakespeare is in the chancel. The place is solemn and sepulchral.
Tall elms wave before the pointed windows, and the Avon, which

runs at a short distance from the walls, keeps up a low perpetual murmur. A flat stone marks the spot where the bard is buried. There are
four lines inscribed on it, said to have been written by himself, and
which have in them something extremely awful. If they are indeed
his own, they show that solicitude about the quiet of the grave, which
seems natural to fine sensibilities and thoughtful minds:

> Good friend, for Jesus' sake, forbeare
> To dig the dust encloased here.
> Blessed be the man that spares these stones,
> And curst be he that moves my bones.

Just over the grave, in a niche of the wall, is a bust of Shakespeare,
put up shortly after his death, and considered as a resemblance. The
aspect is pleasant and serene, with a finely arched forehead; and I
thought I could read in it clear indications of that cheerful, social
disposition, by which he was as much characterized among his co-
temporaries as by the vastness of his genius. The inscription mentions
his age at the time of his decease—fifty three years; an untimely death
for the world: for what fruit might not have been expected from
the golden autumn of such a mind, sheltered as it was from the stormy
vicissitudes of life, and flourishing in the sunshine of popular and
royal favour.

The inscription on the tombstone has not been without its effect.
It has prevented the removal of his remains from the bosom of his
native place to Westminster Abbey, which was at one time contemplated.
A few years since also, as some labourers were digging to make an
adjoining vault, the earth caved in, so as to leave a vacant space
almost like an arch, through which one might have reached into his
grave. No one, however, presumed to meddle with his remains, so
awfully guarded by a malediction; and lest any of the idle or the
curious, or any collector of relics, should be tempted to commit
depredations, the old sexton kept watch over the place for two days,
until the vault was finished and the aperture closed again. He told
me that he had made bold to look in at the hole, but could see neither
coffin nor bones; nothing but dust. It was something, I thought, to
have seen the dust of Shakespeare.

Next to this grave are those of his wife, his favourite daughter Mrs.
Hall, and others of his family. On a tomb close by, also, is a full length
effigy of his old friend John Combe, of usurious memory; on whom
he is said to have written a ludicrous epitaph. There are other monuments around, but the mind refuses to dwell on any thing that is not

connected with Shakespeare. His idea pervades the place: the whole pile seems but as his mausoleum. The feelings, no longer checked and thwarted by doubt, here indulge in perfect confidence: other traces of him may be false or dubious, but here is palpable evidence and absolute certainty. As I trod the sounding pavement, there was something intense and thrilling in the idea, that, in very truth, the remains of Shakespeare were mouldering beneath my feet. It was a long time before I could prevail upon myself to leave the place; and as I passed through the church yard I plucked a branch from one of the yew trees, the only relic that I have brought from Stratford.

I had now visited the usual objects of a pilgrim's devotion, but I had a desire to see the old family seat of the Lucys at Charlecot, and to ramble through the park where Shakespeare, in company with some of the roysters of Stratford, committed his youthful offence of deer stealing. In this harebrained exploit we are told that he was taken prisoner, and carried to the keeper's lodge, where he remained all night in doleful captivity. When brought into the presence of Sir Thomas Lucy, his treatment must have been galling and humiliating; for it so wrought upon his spirit as to produce a rough pasquinade, which was affixed to the park gate at Charlecot.*

This flagitious attack upon the dignity of the Knight so incensed him, that he applied to a lawyer at Warwick to put the severity of the laws in force against the rhyming deer stalker. Shakespeare did not wait to brave the united puissance of a Knight of the Shire and a country attorney. He forthwith abandoned the pleasant banks of the Avon and his paternal trade; wandered away to London; became a hanger on to the theatres; then an actor; and, finally, wrote for the stage; and thus, through the persecution of Sir Thomas Lucy, Stratford lost an indifferent wool comber and the world gained an immortal poet. He retained, however, for a long time, a sense of the harsh treatment of the Lord of Charlecot, and revenged himself in his writings; but in the sportive way of a good natured mind. Sir Thomas is said to be the

---

*The following is the only stanza extant of this lampoon:—

> A parliament member, a justice of peace,
> At home a poor scarecrow, at London an asse,
> If lowsie is Lucy, as some volke miscalle it,
> Then Lucy is lowsie, whatever befall it.
>   He thinks himself great;
>   Yet an asse in his state,
> We allow, by his ears, but with asses to mate.
> If Lucy is lowsie, as some volke miscall it,
> Then sing lowsie Lucy whatever befall it.

original of Justice Shallow, and the satire is slyly fixed upon him by the Justice's armorial bearings, which, like those of the Knight, had white luces° in the quarterings.

Various attempts have been made by his biographers to soften and explain away this early transgression of the poet; but I look upon it as one of those thoughtless exploits natural to his situation and turn of mind. Shakespeare, when young, had doubtless all the wildness and irregularity of an ardent, undisciplined, and undirected genius. The poetic temperament has naturally something in it of the vagabond. When left to itself it runs loosely and wildly, and delights in every thing eccentric and licentious. It is often a turn up of a die, in the gambling freaks of fate, whether a natural genius shall turn out a great rogue or a great poet; and had not Shakespeare's mind fortunately taken a literary bias, he might have as daringly transcended all civil, as he has all dramatic laws.

I have little doubt that, in early life, when running, like an unbroken colt, about the neighbourhood of Stratford, he was to be found in the company of all kinds of odd anomalous characters; that he associated with all the mad caps of the place, and was one of those unlucky urchins, at mention of whom old men shake their heads, and predict that they will one day come to the gallows. To him the poaching in Sir Thomas Lucy's park was doubtless like a foray to a Scottish Knight, and struck his eager, and as yet untamed, imagination, as something delightfully adventurous.†

The old mansion of Charlecot and its surrounding park still remain in the possession of the Lucy family, and are peculiarly interesting from being connected with this whimsical but eventful circumstance in the scanty history of the bard. As the house stood at little more than three miles distance from Stratford, I resolved to pay it a pedestrian visit,

°The luce is a pike, or jack, and abounds in the Avon about Charlecot.

†A proof of Shakespeare's random habits and associates in his youthful days, may be found in a traditionary anecdote, picked up at Stratford by the elder Ireland, and mentioned in his "Picturesque Views on the Avon." About seven miles from Stratford lies the thirsty little market town of Bedford, famous for its ale. Two societies of the village yeomanry used to meet, under the appellation of the Bedford topers, and to challenge the lovers of good ale of the neighbouring villages, to a contest of drinking. Among others, the people of Strat-ford were called out to prove the strength of their heads; and in the number of the champions was Shakespeare, who, in spite of the proverb, that "they who drink beer will think beer," was as true to his ale as Falstaff to his sack. The chivalry of Stratford was staggered at the first onset, and sounded a retreat while they had yet legs to carry them off the field. They had scarcely marched a mile, when, their legs failing them, they were forced to lie down under a crab tree,

that I might stroll leisurely through some of those scenes from which Shakespeare must have derived his earliest ideas of rural imagery.

The country was yet naked and leafless; but English scenery is always verdant, and the sudden change in the temperature of the weather was surprising in its quickening effects upon the landscape. It was inspiring and animating to witness this first awakening of spring. To feel its warm breath stealing over the senses; to see the moist mellow earth beginning to put forth the green sprout and the tender blade; and the trees and shrubs, in their reviving tints and bursting buds, giving the promise of returning foliage and flower. The cold snow drop, that little borderer on the skirts of winter, was to be seen with its chaste white blossoms in the small gardens before the cottages. The bleating of the new dropt lambs was faintly heard from the fields. The sparrow twittered about the thatched eaves and budding hedges; the robin threw a livelier note into his late querulous wintry strain; and the lark, springing up from the reeking bosom of the meadow, towered away into the bright fleecy cloud, pouring forth torrents of melody. As I watched the little songster, mounting up higher and higher, until his body was a mere speck on the white bosom of the cloud, while the ear was still filled with his music, it called to mind Shakespeare's exquisite little song in Cymbeline:

> Hark! hark! the lark at heav'n's gate sings,
>   And Phœbus 'gins arise,
> His steeds to water at those springs,
>   On chaliced flowers that lies.
>
> And winking mary-buds begin,
>   To ope their golden eyes;

---

where they passed the night. It is still standing, and goes by the name of Shakespeare's tree.

In the morning his companions awakened the bard, and proposed returning to Bedford, but he declined, saying he had had enough, having drank with

> Piping Pebworth, Dancing Marston,
> Haunted Hillbro', Hungry Grafton,
> Dudging Exhall, Papist Wicksford,
> Beggarly Broom, and Drunken Bedford.

"The villages here alluded to," says Ireland, "still bear the epithets thus given them; the people of Pebworth are still famed for their skill on the pipe and tabor: Hillborough is now called Haunted Hillborough: and Grafton is famous for the poverty of its soil."

Shakespeare before Sir Thomas Lucy

An engraving reproduced in the Geoffrey Crayon edition of *The Sketch Book* (New York: G. P. Putnam's Sons, 1880).

> With every thing that pretty bin,
> My lady sweet arise!

Indeed the whole country about here is poetic ground: every thing is associated with the idea of Shakespeare. Every old cottage that I saw, I fancied into some resort of his boyhood, where he had acquired his intimate knowledge of rustic life and manners, and heard those legendary tales and wild superstitions which he has woven like witch-craft into his dramas. For in his time, we are told, it was a popular amusement in winter evenings "to sit round the fire, and tell merry tales of errant knights, queens, lovers, lords, ladies, giants, dwarfs, thieves, cheaters, witches, fairies, goblins, and friars."*

My route for a part of the way lay in sight of the Avon, which made a variety of the most fanciful doublings and windings through a wide and fertile valley; sometimes glittering from among willows, which fringed its borders; sometimes disappearing among groves, or beneath green banks; and sometimes rambling out into full view, and making an azure sweep round a slope of meadow land. This beautiful bosom of country is called the vale of the Red Horse. A distant line of un-dulating blue hills seems to be its boundary, whilst all the soft intervening landscape lies in a manner enchained in the silver links of the Avon.

After pursuing the road for about three miles, I turned off into a footpath, which led along the borders of fields and under hedge rows to a private gate of the park; there was a style, however, for the benefit of the pedestrian; there being a public right of way through the grounds. I delight in these hospitable estates, in which every one has a kind of property—at least as far as the footpath is concerned. It in some measure reconciles a poor man to his lot, and what is more, to the better lot of his neighbour, thus to have parks and pleasure grounds thrown open for his recreation. He breathes the pure air as freely, and lolls as luxuriously under the shade, as the lord of the soil; and if he has not the privilege of calling all that he sees his own, he has not, at the same time, the trouble of paying for it, and keeping it in order.

I now found myself among noble avenues of oaks and elms, whose vast size bespoke the growth of centuries. The wind sounded solemnly

---

*Scot, in his "Discoverie of Witchcraft," enumerates a host of these fireside fancies. "And they have so fraid us with bull-beggars, spirits, witches, urchins, elves, hags, fairies, satyrs, pans, faunes, syrens, kit with the can'sticke, tritons, centaurs, dwarfes, giantes, imps, calcars, conjurors, nymphes, changelings, incubus, Robin-good-fellow, the spoorne, the mare, the man in the oke, the hell-waine, the fier drake, the puckle, Tom Thombe, hobgoblins, Tom Tumbler, boneless, and such other bugs, that we were afraid of our own shadowes."

among their branches, and the rooks cawed from their hereditary nests in the tree tops. The eye ranged through a long lessening vista, with nothing to interrupt the view but a distant statue; and a vagrant deer stalking like a shadow across the opening.

There is something about these stately old avenues that has the effect of gothic architecture, not merely from the pretended similarity of form, but from their bearing the evidence of long duration, and of having had their origin in a period of time with which we associate ideas of romantic grandeur. They betoken also the long settled dignity, and proudly concentrated independence of an ancient family; and I have heard a worthy but aristocratic old friend observe, when speaking of the sumptuous palaces of modern gentry, that "money could do much with stone and mortar, but thank heaven there was no such thing as suddenly building up an avenue of oaks."

It was from wandering in early life among this rich scenery, and about the romantic solitudes of the adjoining park of Fulbroke, which then formed a part of the Lucy estate, that some of Shakespeare's commentators have supposed he derived his noble forest meditations of Jaques, and the enchanting woodland pictures in "As you like it." It is in lonely wanderings through such scenes, that the mind drinks deep but quiet draughts of inspiration, and becomes intensely sensible of the beauty and majesty of nature. The imagination kindles into reverie and rapture; vague but exquisite images and ideas keep breaking upon it; and we revel in a mute and almost incommunicable luxury of thought. It was in some such mood, and perhaps under one of those very trees before me, which threw their broad shades over the grassy banks and quivering waters of the Avon, that the poet's fancy may have sallied forth into that little song which breathes the very soul of a rural voluptuary:

> Under the green wood tree,
> Who loves to lie with me,
> And tune his merry throat
> Unto the sweet bird's note,
> Come hither, come hither, come hither,
>   Here shall he see
>   No enemy,
> But winter and rough weather.

I had now come in sight of the house. It is a large building of brick, with stone quoins, and is in the gothic style of Queen Elizabeth's day, having been built in the first year of her reign. The exterior remains very nearly in its original state, and may be considered a fair specimen of the residence of a wealthy country gentleman of those days. A great gateway opens from the park into a kind of court yard in front of the house, ornamented with a grass plot, shrubs, and flower beds. The gateway is in imitation of the ancient barbican; being a kind of outpost, and flanked by towers; though evidently for mere ornament, instead of defence. The front of the house is completely in the old style; with stone shafted casements, a great bow window of heavy stone work, and a portal with armorial bearings over it, carved in stone. At each corner of the building is an octagon tower, surmounted by a gilt ball and weathercock.

The Avon, which winds through the park, makes a bend just at the foot of a gently sloping bank, which sweeps down from the rear of the house. Large herds of deer were feeding or reposing upon its borders; and swans were sailing majestically upon its bosom. As I contemplated the venerable old mansion, I called to mind Falstaff's encomium on Justice Shallow's abode, and the affected indifference and real vanity of the latter:

"*Falstaff.* You have here a goodly dwelling and a rich.
Shallow. Barren, barren, barren; beggars all, beggars all, Sir John:—marry, good air."

Whatever may have been the joviality of the old mansion in the days of Shakespeare, it had now an air of stillness and solitude. The great iron gateway that opened into the court yard was locked; there was no show of servants bustling about the place; the deer gazed quietly at me as I passed, being no longer harried by the moss troopers of Stratford. The only sign of domestic life that I met with, was a white cat stealing with wary look and stealthy pace towards the stables, as if on some nefarious expedition. I must not omit to mention the carcass of a scoundrel crow which I saw suspended against the barn wall, as it shows that the Lucys still inherit that lordly abhorrence of poachers, and maintain that rigorous exercise of territorial power which was so strenuously manifested in the case of the bard.

After prowling about for some time, I at length found my way to a lateral portal which was the every day entrance to the mansion. I was courteously received by a worthy old housekeeper, who, with the civility and communicativeness of her order, showed me the interior of the house. The greater part has undergone alterations, and been adapted to modern tastes and modes of living: there is a fine old oaken staircase; and the great hall, that noble feature in an ancient manor house, still retains much of the appearance it must have had in the days of

Shakespeare. The ceiling is arched and lofty; and at one end is a gallery, in which stands an organ. The weapons and trophies of the chace, which formerly adorned the hall of a country gentleman, have made way for family portraits. There is a wide hospitable fireplace, calculated for an ample old fashioned wood fire, formerly the rallying place of winter festivity. On the opposite side of the hall is the huge gothic bow window, with stone shafts, which looks out upon the court yard. Here are emblazoned in stained glass the armorial bearings of the Lucy family for many generations, some being dated in 1558. I was delighted to observe in the quarterings the three *white luces* by which the character of Sir Thomas was first identified with that of Justice Shallow. They are mentioned in the first scene of the Merry Wives of Windsor, where the Justice is in a rage with Falstaff for having "beaten his men, killed his deer, and broken into his lodge." The poet had no doubt the offences of himself and his comrades in mind at the time, and we may suppose the family pride and vindictive threats of the puissant Shallow to be a caricature of the pompous indignation of Sir Thomas.

"*Shallow.* Sir Hugh, persuade me not: I will make a Star-Chamber matter of it; if he were twenty Sir John Falstaffs, he shall not abuse Robert Shallow, Esq.

Slender. In the county of Gloster, justice of peace, and *coram.*

Shallow. Ay, cousin Slender, and *custalorum.*

Slender. Ay, and *ratalorum* too; and a gentleman born, master parson; who writes himself *Armigero* in any bill, warrant, quittance, or obligation, *Armigero.*

Shallow. Ay, that I do; and have done any time these three hundred years.

Slender. All his successors gone before him have done't, and all his ancestors that come after him may: they may give the dozen *white luces* in their coat.   *   *   *   *   *

Shallow. The council shall hear it; it is a riot.

Evans. It is not meet the council hear of a riot; there is no fear of Got in a riot; the council, hear you, shall desire to hear the fear of Got, and not to hear a riot; take your vizaments in that.

Shallow. Ha! o' my life, if I were young again, the sword should end it!"

Near the window thus emblazoned, hung a portrait by Sir Peter Lely of one of the Lucy family, a great beauty of the time of Charles the Second; the old housekeeper shook her head as she pointed to the picture, and informed me that this lady had been sadly addicted to cards, and had gambled away a great portion of the family estate, among which was that part of the park where Shakespeare and his comrades had killed the deer. The lands thus lost had not been entirely regained by the family even at the present day. It is but justice to this recreant dame to confess that she had a surpassingly fine hand and arm.

The picture which most attracted my attention was a great painting over the fire place, containing likenesses of a Sir Thomas Lucy and his family who inhabited the hall in the latter part of Shakespeare's life time. I at first thought that it was the vindictive knight himself, but the housekeeper assured me that it was his son; the only likeness extant of the former being an effigy upon his tomb in the church of the neighbouring hamlet of Charlecot.* The picture gives a lively idea of the costume and manners of the time. Sir Thomas is dressed in ruff and doublet; white shoes with roses in them; and has a peaked yellow, or, as Master Slender would say, "a cane coloured beard." His lady is seated on the opposite side of the picture in wide ruff and long stomacher, and the children have a most venerable stiffness and formality of dress. Hounds and spaniels are mingled in the family group; a hawk is seated on his perch in the foreground, and one of the children holds a bow;—all intimating the knight's skill in hunting, hawking, and archery—so indispensable to an accomplished gentleman in those days.†

---

*This effigy is in white marble, and represents the Knight in complete armor. Near him lies the effigy of his wife, and on her tomb is the following inscription; which, if really composed by her husband, places him quite above the intellectual level of Master Shallow:

Here lyeth the Lady Joyce Lucy wife of Sr Thomas Lucy of Charlecot in ye county of Warwick, Knight, Daughter and heir of Thomas Acton of Sutton in ye county of Worcester Esquire who departed out of this wretched world to her heavenly kingdom ye 10 day of February in ye yeare of our Lord God 1595 and of her age 60 and three. All the time of her lyfe a true and faythful servant of her good God, never detected of any cryme or vice. In religion most sounde, in love to her husband most faythful and true. In friendship most constant; to what in trust was committed unto her most secret. In wisdom excelling. In governing of her house, bringing up of youth in ye fear of God that did converse with her moste rare and singular. A great maintayner of hospitality. Greatly esteemed of her betters; misliked of none unless of the envyous. When all is spoken that can be saide a woman so garnished with virtue as not to be bettered and hardly to be equalled by any. As shee lived most virtuously so shee died most Godly. Set downe by him yt best did knowe what hath byn written to be true. Thomas Lucye.

†Bishop Earle, speaking of the country gentleman of his time, observes, "his housekeeping is seen much in the different families of dogs, and serving men attendant on their kennels; and the deepness of their throats is the depth of his discourse. A hawk he esteems the true burden of nobility, and is exceedingly ambitious to seem delighted with the sport, and have his fist gloved with his

I regretted to find that the ancient furniture of the hall had disappeared; for I had hoped to meet with the stately elbow chair of carved oak, in which the country Squire of former days was wont to sway the sceptre of empire over his rural domains; and in which it might be presumed the redoubted Sir Thomas sat enthroned in awful state when the recreant Shakespeare was brought before him. As I like to deck out pictures for my entertainment, I pleased myself with the idea that this very hall had been the scene of the unlucky bard's examination on the morning after his captivity in the lodge. I fancied to myself the rural potentate, surrounded by his body guard of butler, pages, and blue coated serving men with their badges; while the luckless culprit was brought in, bedrooped and chapfallen; in the custody of game keepers, huntsmen and whippers in, and followed by a rabble rout of country clowns. I fancied bright faces of curious housemaids peeping from the half open doors, while from the gallery the fair daughters of the Knight leaned gracefully forward, eyeing the youthful prisoner with that pity "that dwells in womanhood."—Who would have thought that this poor varlet, thus trembling before the brief authority of a country Squire, and the sport of rustic boors, was soon to become the delight of princes; the theme of all tongues and ages; the dictator to the human mind; and was to confer immortality on his oppressor by a caricature and a lampoon!

I was now invited by the butler to walk into the garden, and I felt inclined to visit the orchard and arbour where the Justice treated Sir John Falstaff and Cousin Silence, "to a last year's pippen of his own graffing, with a dish of carraways;" but I had already spent so much of the day in my ramblings that I was obliged to give up any further investigations. When about to take my leave I was gratified by the civil entreaties of the housekeeper and butler, that I would take some refreshment: an instance of good old hospitality, which I grieve to say we castle hunters seldom meet with in modern days. I make no doubt it is a virtue which the present representative of the Lucys inherits from his ancestor; for Shakespeare, even in his caricature, makes Justice Shallow importunate in this respect, as witness his pressing instances to Falstaff:

---

jesses." And Gilpin, in his description of a Mr. Hastings remarks, "he kept all sorts of hounds that run buck, fox, hare, otter and badger; and had hawks of all kinds both long and short winged. His great hall was commonly strewed with marrowbones, and full of hawk perches, hounds, spaniels and terriers. On a broad hearth paved with brick, lay some of the choicest terriers, hounds and spaniels."

"By cock and pye, Sir, you shall not away to night * * * *. I will not excuse you; you shall not be excused; excuses shall not be admitted; there is no excuse shall serve; you shall not be excused * * * * * *. Some pigeons, Davy; a couple of shortlegged hens; a joint of mutton; and any pretty little tiny kickshaws, tell William Cook."

I now bade a reluctant farewell to the old hall. My mind had become so completely possessed by the imaginary scenes and characters connected with it, that I seemed to be actually living among them. Every thing brought them, as it were, before my eyes; and as the door of the dining room opened, I almost expected to hear the feeble voice of Master Silence quavering forth his favourite ditty:

> " 'Tis merry in hall, when beards wag all,
> And welcome merry Shrove-tide!"

On returning to my inn, I could not but reflect on the singular gift of the poet; to be able thus to spread the magic of his mind over the very face of nature; to give to things and places a charm and character not their own, and to turn this "working day world" into a perfect fairy land. He is indeed the true enchanter, whose spell operates not upon the senses, but upon the imagination and the heart. Under the wizard influence of Shakespeare I had been walking all day in a complete delusion. I had surveyed the landscape through the prism of poetry, which tinged every object with the hues of the rainbow. I had been surrounded with fancied beings; with mere airy nothings, conjured up by poetic power; yet which, to me, had all the charm of reality. I had heard Jaques soliloquize beneath his oak; had beheld the fair Rosalind and her companion adventuring through the woodlands; and, above all, had been once more present in spirit with fat Jack Falstaff, and his contemporaries, from the august Justice Shallow, down to the gentle Master Slender, and the sweet Anne Page. Ten thousand honours and blessings on the bard who has thus gilded the dull realities of life with innocent illusions; who has spread exquisite and unbought pleasures in my chequered path; and beguiled my spirit, in many a lonely hour, with all the cordial and cheerful sympathies of social life!

As I crossed the bridge over the Avon on my return, I paused to contemplate the distant church in which the poet lies buried, and could not but exult in the malediction, which has kept his ashes undisturbed in its quiet and hallowed vaults. What honour could his name have derived from being mingled in dusty companionship with the epitaphs and escutcheons and venal eulogiums of a titled multitude. What would a crowded corner in Westminster Abbey have been, compared with this reverend pile, which seems to stand in beautiful loneliness as his sole mausoleum! The solicitude about the grave may be but the offspring of an overwrought sensibility; but human nature is made up of foibles and prejudices; and its best and tenderest affections are mingled with these factitious feelings. He who has sought renown about the world, and has reaped a full harvest of worldly favour, will find, after all, that there is no love, no admiration, no applause, so sweet to the soul as that which springs up in his native place. It is there that he seeks to be gathered in peace and honour among his kindred and his early friends. And when the weary heart and failing head begin to warn him that the evening of life is drawing on, he turns as fondly as does the infant to the mother's arms, to sink to sleep in the bosom of the scene of his childhood.

How would it have cheered the spirit of the youthful bard, when, wandering forth in disgrace upon a doubtful world, he cast back a heavy look upon his paternal home; could he have foreseen that, before many years, he should return to it covered with renown; that his name should become the boast and glory of his native place; that his ashes should be religiously guarded as its most precious treasure; and that its lessening spire, on which his eyes were fixed in tearful contemplation, should one day become the beacon, towering amidst the gentle landscape, to guide the literary pilgrim of every nation to his tomb.

TRAITS OF
INDIAN CHARACTER

"I appeal to any white man if ever he entered Logan's cabin hungry, and he gave him not to eat; if ever he came cold and naked, and he clothed him not."

SPEECH OF AN INDIAN CHIEF.

There is something in the character and habits of the North American savage, taken in connexion with the scenery over which he is accustomed to range, its vast lakes, boundless forests, majestic rivers and trackless plains, that is, to my mind, wonderfully striking and sublime. He is formed for the wilderness, as the Arab is for the desert. His nature is stern, simple and enduring; fitted to grapple with difficulties, and to support privations. There seems but little soil in his heart for the growth of the kindly virtues; and yet, if we would but take the trouble to penetrate through that proud stoicism and habitual taciturnity, which lock up his character from casual observation, we should find him linked to his fellow man of civilized life by more of those sympathies and affections than are usually ascribed to him.

It has been the lot of the unfortunate aborigines of America, in the early periods of colonization, to be doubly wronged by the white men. They have been dispossessed of their hereditary possessions by mercenary and frequently wanton warfare; and their characters have been traduced by bigoted and interested writers. The colonist has often treated them like beasts of the forest; and the author has endeavoured to justify him in his outrages. The former found it easier to exterminate than to civilize; the latter to vilify than to discriminate. The appellations of savage and pagan were deemed sufficient to sanction the hostilities of both; and thus the poor wanderers of the forest were persecuted and defamed, not because they were guilty, but because they were ignorant.

The rights of the savage have seldom been properly appreciated or respected by the white man. In peace he has too often been the dupe of artful traffic; in war he has been regarded as a ferocious animal, whose life or death was a question of mere precaution and convenience. Man is cruelly wasteful of life when his own safety is endangered, and he is sheltered by impunity; and little mercy is to be expected from him when he feels the sting of the reptile and is conscious of the power to destroy.

The same prejudices which were indulged thus early, exist in common circulation at the present day. Certain learned societies have, it
is true, with laudable diligence, endeavoured to investigate and record
the real characters and manners of the Indian tribes; the American
government too, has wisely and humanely exerted itself to inculcate a
friendly and forbearing spirit towards them, and to protect them from
fraud and injustice.* The current opinion of the Indian character,
however, is too apt to be formed from the miserable hordes which
infest the frontiers, and hang on the skirts of the settlements. These
are too commonly composed of degenerate beings, corrupted and
enfeebled by the vices of society, without being benefited by its civilization. That proud independence, which formed the main pillar of
savage virtue, has been shaken down, and the whole moral fabric lies
in ruins. Their spirits are humiliated and debased by a sense of
inferiority, and their native courage cowed and daunted by the superior
knowledge and power of their enlightened neighbours. Society has
advanced upon them like one of those withering airs that will sometimes breathe desolation over a whole region of fertility. It has enervated
their strength, multiplied their diseases, and superinduced upon their
original barbarity the low vices of artificial life. It has given them a
thousand superfluous wants, whilst it has diminished their means of
mere existence. It has driven before it the animals of the chase, who
fly from the sound of the axe and the smoke of the settlement, and
seek refuge in the depths of remoter forests and yet untrodden wilds.
Thus do we too often find the Indians on our frontiers to be mere
wrecks and remnants of once powerful tribes, who have lingered in the
vicinity of the settlements, and sunk into precarious and vagabond
existence. Poverty, repining and hopeless poverty, a canker of the
mind unknown in savage life, corrodes their spirits and blights every
free and noble quality of their natures. They become drunken, indolent,
feeble, thievish and pusillanimous. They loiter like vagrants about
the settlements, among spacious dwellings, replete with elaborate comforts, which only render them sensible of the comparative wretchedness
of their own condition. Luxury spreads its ample board before their
eyes, but they are excluded from the banquet. Plenty revels over the
fields, but they are starving in the midst of its abundance; the whole

*The American government has been indefatigable in its exertions to ameliorate
the situation of the Indians, and to introduce among them the arts of civilization,
and civil and religious knowledge. To protect them from the frauds of the white
traders, no purchase of land from them by individuals is permitted; nor is any
person allowed to receive lands from them as a present, without the express sanction
of government. These precautions are strictly enforced.

wilderness has blossomed into a garden; but they feel as reptiles that infest it.

How different was their state while yet the undisputed lords of the soil. Their wants were few, and the means of gratification within their reach. They saw every one round them sharing the same lot, enduring the same hardships, feeding on the same aliments, arrayed in the same rude garments. No roof then rose, but was open to the homeless stranger; no smoke curled among the trees, but he was welcome to sit down by its fire and join the hunter in his repast. "For," says an old historian of New England, "their life is so void of care, and they are so loving also, that they make use of those things they enjoy as common goods, and are therein so compassionate, that rather than one should starve through want, they would starve all; thus do they pass their time merrily, not regarding our pomp, but are better content with their own, which some men esteem so meanly of." Such were the Indians whilst in the pride and energy of their primitive natures; they resemble those wild plants which thrive best in the shades of the forest, but shrink from the hand of cultivation, and perish beneath the influence of the sun.

In discussing the savage character, writers have been too prone to indulge in vulgar prejudice and passionate exaggeration, instead of the candid temper of true philosophy. They have not sufficiently considered the peculiar circumstances in which the Indians have been placed, and the peculiar principles under which they have been educated. No being acts more rigidly from rule than the Indian. His whole conduct is regulated according to some general maxims early implanted in his mind. The moral laws that govern him are, to be sure, but few; but then he conforms to them all;—the white man abounds in laws of religion, morals and manners, but how many does he violate!

A frequent ground of accusation against the Indians is their disregard of treaties, and the treachery and wantonness with which, in time of apparent peace, they will suddenly fly to hostilities. The intercourse of the white men with the Indians, however, is too apt to be cold, distrustful, oppressive, and insulting. They seldom treat them with that confidence and frankness which are indispensable to real friendship; nor is sufficient caution observed not to offend against those feelings of pride or superstition, which often prompt the Indian to hostility quicker than mere considerations of interest. The solitary savage feels silently, but acutely. His sensibilities are not diffused over so wide a surface as those of the white man; but they run in steadier and deeper channels. His pride, his affections, his superstitions, are all directed towards fewer objects; but the wounds inflicted on them are proportionably severe, and furnish motives of hostility which we cannot sufficiently appreciate. Where a community is also limited in number, and forms one great patriarchal family, as in an Indian tribe, the injury of an individual is the injury of the whole; and the sentiment of vengeance is almost instantaneously diffused. One council fire is sufficient for the discussion and arrangement of a plan of hostilities. Here all the fighting men and sages assemble. Eloquence and super-stition combine to inflame the minds of the warriors. The orator awakens their martial ardour, and they are wrought up to a kind of religious desperation, by the visions of the prophet and the dreamer.

An instance of one of those sudden exasperations, arising from a motive peculiar to the Indian character, is extant in an old record of the early settlement of Massachusetts. The planters of Plymouth had defaced the monuments of the dead at Passonagessit, and had plundered the grave of the Sachem's mother of some skins with which it had been decorated. The Indians are remarkable for the reverence which they entertain for the sepulchres of their kindred. Tribes, that have passed generations exiled from the abodes of their ancestors, when by chance they have been travelling in the vicinity, have been known to turn aside from the high way, and, guided by wonderfully accurate tradition, have crossed the country for miles to some tumulus, buried perhaps in woods, where the bones of their tribe were anciently deposited; and there have passed hours in silent meditation. Influenced by this sublime and holy feeling, the Sachem, whose mother's tomb had been violated, gathered his men together, and addressed them in the fol-lowing beautifully simple and pathetic harangue; a curious specimen of Indian eloquence, and an affecting instance of filial piety in a savage.

"When last the glorious light of all the sky was underneath this globe, and birds grew silent, I began to settle, as my custom is, to take repose. Before mine eyes were fast closed, methought I saw a vision, at which my spirit was much troubled; and, trembling at that doleful sight, a spirit cried aloud, 'Behold, my son, whom I have cherished, see the breasts that gave thee suck, the hands that lapped thee warm, and fed thee oft! Canst thou forget to take revenge of those wild people, who have defaced my monument in a despiteful manner, disdaining our antiquities and honourable customs. See now, the Sachem's grave lies like the common people, defaced by an ignoble race. Thy mother doth complain, and implores thy aid against this thievish people, who have newly intruded on our land. If this be suffered, I shall not rest quiet in my everlasting habitation.' This said, the spirit vanished, and I, all in a sweat, not able scarce to speak, began to get some strength, and recollect my spirits that were fled, and determined to demand your counsel and assistance."

I have adduced this anecdote at some length, as it tends to show, how these sudden acts of hostility, which have been attributed to caprice and perfidy, may often arise from deep and generous motives, which our inattention to Indian character and customs prevents our properly appreciating.

Another ground of violent outcry against the Indians is their barbarity to the vanquished. This had its origin partly in policy and partly in superstition. The tribes, though sometimes called nations, were never so formidable in their numbers, but that the loss of several warriors was sensibly felt; this was particularly the case when they had been frequently engaged in warfare; and many an instance occurs in Indian history, where a tribe that had long been formidable to its neighbours, has been broken up and driven away, by the capture and massacre of its principal fighting men. There was a strong temptation, therefore, to the victor to be merciless; not so much to gratify any cruel revenge, as to provide for future security. The Indians had also the superstitious belief, frequent among barbarous nations, and prevalent also among the ancients, that the manes of their friends who had fallen in battle, were soothed by the blood of the captives. The prisoners, however, who are not thus sacrificed, are adopted into their families in place of the slain, and are treated with the confidence and affection of relatives and friends; nay, so hospitable and tender is their entertainment, that when the alternative is offered them they will often prefer to remain with their adopted brethren, rather than return to the home and the friends of their youth.

The cruelty of the Indians towards their prisoners has been heightened since the colonization of the whites. What was formerly a compliance with policy and superstition, has been exasperated into a gratification of vengeance. They cannot but be sensible that the white men are the usurpers of their ancient dominion, the cause of their degradation, and the gradual destroyers of their race. They go forth to battle, smarting with injuries and indignities which they have individually suffered, and they are driven to madness and despair by the wide spreading desolation, and the overwhelming ruin of European warfare. The whites have too frequently set them an example of violence, by burning their villages and laying waste their slender means of subsistence; and yet they wonder that savages do not show moderation and magnanimity towards those, who have left them nothing but mere existence and wretchedness.

We stigmatize the Indians, also, as cowardly and treacherous, because they use stratagem in warfare, in preference to open force; but in this they are fully justified by their rude code of honour. They are early taught that stratagem is praiseworthy: the bravest warrior thinks it no disgrace to lurk in silence, and take every advantage of his foe: he triumphs in the superior craft and sagacity by which he has been enabled to surprize and destroy an enemy. Indeed man is naturally more prone to subtilty than open valour, owing to his physical weakness in comparison with other animals. They are endowed with natural weapons of defence; with horns, with tusks, with hoofs and talons; but man has to depend on his superior sagacity. In all his encounters with these, his proper enemies, he resorts to stratagem; and when he perversely turns his hostility against his fellow man, he at first continues the same subtle mode of warfare.

The natural principle of war is to do the most harm to our enemy with the least harm to ourselves; and this of course is to be effected by stratagem. That chivalrous courage which induces us to despise the suggestions of prudence, and to rush in the face of certain danger, is the offspring of society, and produced by education. It is honourable, because it is in fact the triumph of lofty sentiment over an instinctive repugnance to pain, and over those yearnings after personal ease and security, which society has condemned as ignoble. It is kept alive by pride and the fear of shame; and thus the dread of real evil is overcome by the superior dread of an evil which exists but in the imagination. It has been cherished and stimulated also by various means. It has been the theme of spirit stirring song and chivalrous story. The poet and minstrel have delighted to shed round it the splendours of fiction; and even the historian has forgotten the sober gravity of narration, and broken forth into enthusiasm and rhapsody in its praise. Triumphs and gorgeous pageants have been its reward: monuments, on which art has exhausted its skill, and opulence its treasures, have been erected to perpetuate a nation's gratitude and admiration. Thus artificially excited, courage has arisen to an extraordinary and factitious degree of heroism; and, arrayed in all the glorious "pomp and circumstance of war," this turbulent quality has even been able to eclipse many of those quiet, but invaluable virtues, which silently ennoble the human character, and swell the tide of human happiness.

But if courage intrinsically consists in the defiance of danger and pain, the life of the Indian is a continual exhibition of it. He lives in a state of perpetual hostility and risk. Peril and adventure are congenial to his nature; or rather seem necessary to arouse his faculties and to give an interest to his existence. Surrounded by hostile tribes, whose mode of warfare is by ambush and surprisal, he is always prepared for fight, and lives with his weapons in his hands. As the ship careers in fearful singleness through the solitudes of ocean;—as the bird mingles among clouds, and storms, and wings its way, a mere speck, across the pathless fields of air;—so the Indian holds his course, silent, solitary, but undaunted, through the boundless bosom of the wilderness. His expeditions may vie in distance and danger with the pilgrimage of the devotee, or the crusade of the knight errant. He traverses vast forests, exposed to the hazards of lonely sickness, of lurking enemies and pining famine. Stormy lakes, those great inland seas, are no obstacles to his wanderings: in his light canoe of bark he sports, like a feather, on their waves, and darts, with the swiftness of an arrow, down the roaring rapids of the rivers. His very subsistence is snatched from the midst of toil and peril. He gains his food by the hardships and dangers of the chase; he wraps himself in the spoils of the bear, the panther, and the buffalo, and sleeps among the thunders of the cataract.

No hero of ancient or modern days can surpass the Indian in his lofty contempt of death, and the fortitude with which he sustains its cruelest infliction. Indeed we here behold him rising superior to the white man, in consequence of his peculiar education. The latter rushes to glorious death at the cannon's mouth; the former calmly contemplates its approach, and triumphantly endures it, amidst the varied torments of surrounding foes and the protracted agonies of fire. He even takes a pride in taunting his persecutors, and provoking their ingenuity of torture; and as the devouring flames prey on his very vitals, and the flesh shrinks from the sinews, he raises his last song of triumph, breathing the defiance of an unconquered heart, and invoking the spirits of his fathers to witness that he dies without a groan.

Notwithstanding the obloquy with which the early historians have overshadowed the characters of the unfortunate natives, some bright gleams occasionally break through, which throw a degree of melancholy lustre on their memories. Facts are occasionally to be met with in the rude annals of the eastern provinces, which, though recorded with the colouring of prejudice and bigotry, yet speak for themselves; and will be dwelt on with applause and sympathy, when prejudice shall have passed away.

In one of the homely narratives of the Indian wars in New England, there is a touching account of the desolation carried into the tribe of the Pequod Indians. Humanity shrinks from the cold blooded detail of indiscriminate butchery. In one place we read of the surprisal of an Indian fort in the night, when the wigwams were wrapped in flames, and the miserable inhabitants shot down and slain in attempting to escape, "all being dispatched and ended in the course of an hour."

After a series of similar transactions, "our soldiers," as the historian piously observes, "being resolved by God's assistance to make a final destruction of them," the unhappy savages being hunted from their homes and fortresses, and pursued with fire and sword, a scanty but gallant band, the sad remnant of the Pequod warriors, with their wives and children, took refuge in a swamp.

Burning with indignation, and rendered sullen by despair; with hearts bursting with grief at the destruction of their tribe, and spirits galled and sore at the fancied ignominy of their defeat, they refused to ask their lives at the hands of an insulting foe, and preferred death to submission.

As the night drew on they were surrounded in their dismal retreat, so as to render escape impracticable. Thus situated, their enemy "plied them with shot all the time, by which means many were killed and buried in the mire." In the darkness and fog that preceded the dawn of day some few broke through the besiegers and escaped into the woods: "the rest were left to the conquerors, of which many were killed in the swamp, like sullen dogs who would rather, in their self willedness and madness, sit still and be shot through, or cut to pieces," than implore for mercy. When the day broke upon this handful of forlorn but dauntless spirits, the soldiers, we are told, entering the swamp, "saw several heaps of them sitting close together, upon whom they discharged their pieces, laden with ten or twelve pistol bullets at a time; putting the muzzles of their pieces under the boughs, within a few yards of them; so as, besides those that were found dead, many more were killed and sunk into the mire, and never were minded more by friend or foe."

Can any one read this plain unvarnished tale, without admiring the stern resolution, the unbending pride, the loftiness of spirit, that seemed to nerve the hearts of these self taught heroes, and to raise them above the instinctive feelings of human nature? When the Gauls laid waste the city of Rome, they found the senators clothed in their robes and seated with stern tranquillity in their curule chairs; in this manner they suffered death without resistance or even supplication. Such conduct was, in them, applauded as noble and magnanimous; in the hapless Indians it was reviled as obstinate and sullen. How truly are we the dupes of show and circumstance! How different is virtue, clothed in purple and enthroned in state, from virtue naked and destitute, and perishing obscurely in a wilderness.

But I forbear to dwell upon these gloomy pictures. The eastern tribes have long since disappeared; the forests that sheltered them have been laid low, and scarce any traces remain of them in the thickly settled states of New England, excepting here and there the Indian name of a village or a stream. And such must sooner or later be the fate of those other tribes which skirt the frontiers, and have occasionally been inveigled from their forests to mingle in the wars of white men. In a little while, and they will go the way that their brethren have gone before. The few hordes which still linger about the shores of Huron and Superior, and the tributary streams of the Mississippi, will share the fate of those tribes that once spread over Massachusetts and Connecticut, and lorded it along the proud banks of the Hudson; of that gigantic race said to have existed on the borders of the Susquehanna; and of those various nations that flourished about the Patowmac and the Rappahanoc, and that peopled the forests of the vast valley of Shenandoah. They will vanish like a vapour from the face of the earth; their very history will be lost in forgetfulness; and "the places that now know them will know them no more for ever." Or if, perchance, some dubious memorial of them should survive, it may be in the romantic dreams of the poet, to people in imagination his glades and groves, like the fauns and satyrs and sylvan deities of antiquity. But should he venture upon the dark story of their wrongs and wretchedness; should he tell how they were invaded, corrupted, despoiled; driven from their native abodes and the sepulchres of their fathers; hunted like wild beasts about the earth; and sent down with violence and butchery to the grave; posterity will either turn with horror and incredulity from the tale, or blush with indignation at the inhumanity of their forefathers.—"We are driven back," said an old warrior, "until we can retreat no further—our hatchets are broken, our bows are snapped, our fires are nearly extinguished—a little longer and the white man will cease to persecute us—for we shall cease to exist!"

PHILIP OF POKANOKET

An Indian Memoir

As monumental bronze unchanged his look:
A soul that pity touch'd, but never shook:
Train'd, from his tree-rock'd cradle to his bier,
The fierce extremes of good and ill to brook
Impassive—fearing but the shame of fear—
A stoic of the woods—a man without a tear.

CAMPBELL.

It is to be regretted that those early writers who treated of the discovery and settlement of America, have not given us more particular and candid accounts of the remarkable characters that flourished in savage life. The scanty anecdotes which have reached us are full of peculiarity and interest; they furnish us with nearer glimpses of human nature, and show what man is in a comparatively primitive state, and what he owes to civilization. There is something of the charm of discovery in lighting upon these wild and unexplored tracts of human nature; in witnessing, as it were, the native growth of moral sentiment; and perceiving those generous and romantic qualities which have been artificially cultivated by society, vegetating in spontaneous hardihood and rude magnificence.

In civilized life, where the happiness, and indeed almost the existence, of man depends so much upon the opinion of his fellow men, he is constantly acting a studied part. The bold and peculiar traits of native character are refined away, or softened down by the levelling influence of what is termed good breeding; and he practises so many petty deceptions, and affects so many generous sentiments, for the purposes of popularity, that it is difficult to distinguish his real, from his artificial character. The Indian, on the contrary, free from the restraints and refinements of polished life, and, in a great degree, a solitary and independent being, obeys the impulses of his inclination or the dictates of his judgment; and thus the attributes of his nature, being freely indulged, grow singly great and striking. Society is like a lawn, where every roughness is smoothed, every bramble eradicated, and where the eye is delighted by the smiling verdure of a velvet surface; he, however, who would study nature in its wildness and variety, must plunge into the forest, must explore the glen, must stem the torrent, and dare the precipice.

These reflections arose on casually looking through a volume of early colonial history, wherein are recorded, with great bitterness, the outrages of the Indians, and their wars with the settlers of New England. It is painful to perceive, even from these partial narratives, how the footsteps of civilization may be traced in the blood of the aborigines; how easily the colonists were moved to hostility by the lust of conquest; how merciless and exterminating was their warfare. The imagination shrinks at the idea, how many intellectual beings were hunted from the earth; how many brave and noble hearts, of nature's sterling coinage, were broken down and trampled in the dust.

Such was the fate of PHILIP OF POKANOKET, an Indian warrior, whose name was once a terror throughout Massachusetts and Connecticut. He was the most distinguished of a number of cotemporary Sachems who reigned over the Pequods, the Narrhagansets, the Wampanoags, and the other Eastern tribes, at the time of the first settlement of New England: a band of native untaught heroes; who made the most generous struggle of which human nature is capable; fighting to the last gasp in the cause of their country, without a hope of victory or a thought of renown. Worthy of an age of poetry, and fit subjects for local story and romantic fiction, they have left scarcely any authentic traces on the page of history, but stalk, like gigantic shadows in the dim twilight of tradition.*

When the pilgrims, as the Plymouth settlers are called by their descendants, first took refuge on the shores of the New World, from the religious persecutions of the Old, their situation was to the last degree gloomy and disheartening. Few in number, and that number rapidly perishing away through sickness and hardships; surrounded by a howling wilderness and savage tribes; exposed to the rigours of an almost arctic winter, and the vicissitudes of an ever shifting climate; their minds were filled with doleful forebodings, and nothing preserved them from sinking into despondency but the strong excitement of religious enthusiasm. In this forlorn situation they were visited by Massasoit, chief Sagamore of the Wampanoags, a powerful chief, who reigned over a great extent of country. Instead of taking advantage of the scanty number of the strangers, and expelling them from his terri- tories into which they had intruded, he seemed at once to conceive for them a generous friendship, and extended towards them the rites of primitive hospitality. He came early in the spring to their settlement of New Plymouth, attended by a mere handful of followers; entered

*While correcting the proof sheets of this article, the author is informed, that a celebrated English poet has nearly finished an heroic poem on the story of Philip of Pokanoket.

into a solemn league of peace and amity; sold them a portion of the soil, and promised to secure for them the good will of his savage allies. Whatever may be said of Indian perfidy, it is certain that the integrity and good faith of Massasoit, have never been impeached. He continued a firm and magnanimous friend of the white men; suffering them to extend their possessions and to strengthen themselves in the land; and betraying no jealousy of their increasing power and prosperity. Shortly before his death he came once more to New Plymouth, with his son Alexander, for the purpose of renewing the covenant of peace, and of securing it to his posterity.

At this conference he endeavoured to protect the religion of his forefathers from the encroaching zeal of the missionaries; and stipulated that no further attempt should be made to draw off his people from their ancient faith; but, finding the English obstinately opposed to any such condition, he mildly relinquished the demand. Almost the last act of his life was to bring his two sons, Alexander and Philip (as they had been named by the English,) to the residence of a principal settler, recommending mutual kindness and confidence; and entreating that the same love and amity which had existed between the white men and himself, might be continued afterwards with his children. The good old Sachem died in peace, and was happily gathered to his fathers before sorrow came upon his tribe; his children remained behind to experience the ingratitude of white men.

His eldest son, Alexander, succeeded him. He was of a quick and impetuous temper, and proudly tenacious of his hereditary rights and dignity. The intrusive policy and dictatorial conduct of the strangers excited his indignation; and he beheld with uneasiness their exterminating wars with the neighbouring tribes. He was doomed soon to incur their hostility, being accused of plotting with the Narrhagansets to rise against the English and drive them from the land. It is impossible to say whether this accusation was warranted by facts, or was grounded on mere suspicions. It is evident, however, by the violent and overbearing measures of the settlers, that they had by this time begun to feel conscious of the rapid increase of their power, and to grow harsh and inconsiderate in their treatment of the natives. They dispatched an armed force to seize at once upon Alexander, and to bring him before their court. He was traced to his woodland haunts, and surprised at a hunting house, where he was reposing with a band of his followers, unarmed, after the toils of the chase. The suddenness of his arrest, and the outrage offered to his sovereign dignity, so preyed upon the irascible feelings of this proud savage, as to throw him into a raging fever; he was permitted to return home on condition of sending his son as a pledge for his reappearance; but the blow he had received was fatal, and before he reached his home he fell a victim to the agonies of a wounded spirit.

The successor of Alexander was Metamocet, or King Philip, as he was called by the settlers, on account of his lofty spirit and ambitious temper. These, together with his well known energy and enterprise, had rendered him an object of great jealousy and apprehension, and he was accused of having always cherished a secret and implacable hostility towards the whites. Such may very probably, and very naturally, have been the case. He considered them as originally but mere intruders into the country, who had presumed upon indulgence, and were extending an influence baneful to savage life. He saw the whole race of his countrymen melting before them from the face of the earth; their territories slipping from their hands, and their tribes becoming feeble, scattered and dependent. It may be said that the soil was originally purchased by the settlers; but who does not know the nature of Indian purchases, in the early periods of colonization? The Europeans always made thrifty bargains through their superior adroitness in traffic; and they gained vast accessions of territory, by easily provoked hostilities. An uncultivated savage is never a nice inquirer into the refinements of law, by which an injury may be gradually and legally inflicted. Leading facts are all by which he judges; and it was enough for Philip to know, that before the intrusion of the Europeans his countrymen were lords of the soil, and that now they were becoming vagabonds in the land of their fathers.

But whatever may have been his feelings of general hostility, and his particular indignation at the treatment of his brother, he suppressed them for the present; renewed the contract with the settlers; and resided peaceably for many years at Pokanoket, or, as it was called by the English, Mount Hope,* the ancient seat of dominion of his tribe. Suspicions, however, which were at first but vague and indefinite, began to acquire form and substance; and he was at length charged with attempting to instigate the various eastern tribes to rise at once, and by a simultaneous effort, to throw off the yoke of their oppressors. It is difficult at this distant period to assign the proper credit due to these early accusations against the Indians. There was a proneness to suspicion, and an aptness to acts of violence, on the part of the whites, that gave weight and importance to every idle tale. Informers abounded where tale bearing met with countenance and reward; and the sword

*Now Bristol, Rhode Island.

was readily unsheathed when its success was certain and it carved out empire.

The only positive evidence on record against Philip is the accusation of one Sausaman, a renegado Indian, whose natural cunning had been quickened by a partial education which he had received among the settlers. He changed his faith and his allegiance two or three times, with a facility that evinced the looseness of his principles. He had acted for some time as Philip's confidential secretary and councillor, and had enjoyed his bounty and protection. Finding, however, that the clouds of adversity were gathering round his patron, he abandoned his service and went over to the whites; and in order to gain their favour, charged his former benefactor with plotting against their safety. A rigorous investigation took place. Philip and several of his subjects submitted to be examined, but nothing was proved against them. The settlers, however, had now gone too far to retract; they had previously determined that Philip was a dangerous neighbour; they had publicly evinced their distrust; and had done enough to ensure his hostility; according, therefore, to the usual mode of reasoning in these cases, his destruction had become necessary to their security. Sausaman, the treacherous informer, was shortly after found dead in a pond, having fallen a victim to the vengeance of his tribe. Three Indians, one of whom was a friend and councillor of Philip, were apprehended and tried, and on the testimony of one very questionable witness, were condemned and executed as the murderers.

This treatment of his subjects, and ignominious punishment of his friend, outraged the pride and exasperated the passions of Philip. The bolt which had fallen thus at his very feet awakened him to the gathering storm, and he determined to trust himself no longer in the power of the white men. The fate of his insulted and broken hearted brother still rankled in his mind; and he had a further warning in the tragical story of Miantonimo, a great Sachem of the Narrhagansets, who, after manfully facing his accusers before a tribunal of the colonists, exculpating himself from a charge of conspiracy, and receiving assurances of amity, had been perfidiously dispatched at their instigation. Philip, therefore, gathered his fighting men about him; persuaded all strangers that he could, to join his cause; sent the women and children to the Narrhagansets for safety; and wherever he appeared, was continually surrounded by armed warriors.

When the two parties were thus in a state of distrust and irritation, the least spark was sufficient to set them in a flame. The Indians, having weapons in their hands, grew mischievous, and committed various petty depredations. In one of their maraudings a warrior was fired upon and killed by a settler. This was the signal for open hostilities; the Indians pressed to revenge the death of their comrade, and the alarm of war resounded through the Plymouth colony.

In the early chronicles of these dark and melancholy times we meet with many indications of the diseased state of the public mind. The gloom of religious abstraction, and the wildness of their situation, among trackless forests, and savage tribes, had disposed the colonists to superstitious fancies, and had filled their imaginations with the frightful chimeras of witchcraft and spectrology. They were much given also to a belief in omens. The troubles with Philip and his Indians were preceded, we are told, by a variety of those awful warnings which forerun great and public calamities. The perfect form of an Indian bow appeared in the air at New Plymouth, which was looked upon by the inhabitants as a "prodigious apparition." At Hadley, Northampton, and other towns in their neighbourhood, "was heard the report of a great piece of ordnance, with a shaking of the earth and a considerable echo."* Others were alarmed on a still sunshiny morning by the discharge of guns and muskets; bullets seemed to whistle past them, and the noise of drums resounded in the air, seeming to pass away to the westward: others fancied that they heard the galloping of horses over their heads; and certain monstrous births which took place about the time, filled the superstitious in some towns with doleful forebodings. Many of these portentous sights and sounds may be ascribed to natural phenomena. To the northern lights which occur vividly in those latitudes; the meteors which explode in the air; the casual rushing of a blast through the top branches of the forest; the crash of falling trees or disruptured rocks; and to those other uncouth sounds and echoes which will sometimes strike the ear so strangely amidst the profound stillness of woodland solitudes. These may have startled some melancholy imaginations, may have been exaggerated by the love for the marvellous, and listened to, with that avidity with which we devour whatever is fearful and mysterious. The universal currency of these superstitious fancies, and the grave record made of them by one of the learned men of the day, are strongly characteristic of the times.

The nature of the contest that ensued was such as too often distinguishes the warfare between civilized men and savages. On the part of the whites it was conducted with superior skill and success; but with a wastefulness of the blood, and a disregard of the natural rights of their antagonists: on the part of the Indians it was waged

*The Rev. Increase Mather's History.

with the desperation of men fearless of death, and who had nothing
to expect from peace, but humiliation, dependence and decay.

The events of the war are transmitted to us by a worthy clergyman
of the time; who dwells with horror and indignation on every hostile
act of the Indians, however justifiable, whilst he mentions with applause
the most sanguinary atrocities of the whites. Philip is reviled as a
murderer and a traitor; without considering that he was a true born
prince, gallantly fighting at the head of his subjects to avenge the
wrongs of his family; to retrieve the tottering power of his line; and to
deliver his native land from the oppression of usurping strangers.

The project of a wide and simultaneous revolt, if such had really
been formed, was worthy of a capacious mind, and, had it not been
prematurely discovered, might have been overwhelming in its consequences. The war that actually broke out was but a war of detail; a
mere succession of casual exploits and unconnected enterprizes. Still
it sets forth the military genius and daring prowess of Philip; and
wherever, in the prejudiced and passionate narrations that have been
given of it, we can arrive at simple facts, we find him displaying a
vigorous mind; a fertility in expedients; a contempt of suffering and
hardship; and an unconquerable resolution; that command our sympathy and applause.

Driven from his paternal domains at Mount Hope, he threw himself
into the depths of those vast and trackless forests that skirted the
settlements and were almost impervious to any thing but a wild beast,
or an Indian. Here he gathered together his forces, like the storm
accumulating its stores of mischief in the bosom of the thunder cloud,
and would suddenly emerge at a time and place least expected, carrying
havoc and dismay into the villages. There were now and then indications
of these impending ravages, that filled the minds of the colonists with
awe and apprehension. The report of a distant gun would perhaps be
heard from the solitary woodland, where there was known to be no
white man; the cattle which had been wandering in the woods, would
sometimes return home wounded; or an Indian or two would be seen
lurking about the skirts of the forests, and suddenly disappearing; as
the lightning will sometimes be seen playing silently about the edge
of the cloud that is brewing up the tempest.

Though sometimes pursued and even surrounded by the settlers,
yet Philip as often escaped almost miraculously from their toils, and
plunging into the wilderness would be lost to all search or inquiry, until
he again emerged at some far distant quarter, laying the country
desolate. Among his strong holds were the great swamps or morasses,
which extend in some parts of New England; composed of loose bogs

of deep black mud; perplexed with thickets, brambles, rank weeds, the shattered and mouldering trunks of fallen trees, and overshadowed by lugubrious hemlocks. The uncertain footing and the tangled mazes of these shagged wilds, render them almost impracticable to the white man, though the Indian could thrid their labyrinths with the agility of a deer. Into one of these, the great swamp of Pocasset Neck, was Philip once driven with a band of his followers. The English did not dare to pursue him, fearing to venture into these dark and frightful recesses, where they might perish in fens and miry pits, or be shot down by lurking foes. They therefore invested the entrance to the neck, and began to build a fort, with the thought of starving out the foe; but Philip and his warriors wafted themselves on a raft over an arm of the sea, in the dead of night, leaving the women and children behind; and escaped away to the westward, kindling the flames of war among the tribes of Massachusetts and the Nipmuck country, and threatening the colony of Connecticut.

In this way Philip became a theme of universal apprehension. The mystery in which he was enveloped exaggerated his real terrors. He was an evil that walked in darkness; whose coming none could foresee, and against which none knew when to be on the alert. The whole country abounded with rumours and alarms. Philip seemed almost possessed of ubiquity; for, in whatever part of the widely extended frontier an irruption from the forest took place, Philip was said to be its leader. Many superstitious notions also were circulated concerning him. He was said to deal in necromancy, and to be attended by an old Indian witch or prophetess, whom he consulted, and who assisted him by her charms and incantations. This indeed was frequently the case with Indian chiefs; either through their own credulity, or to act upon that of their followers: and the influence of the prophet and the dreamer over Indian superstition has been fully evidenced in recent instances of savage warfare.

At the time that Philip effected his escape from Pocasset, his fortunes were in a desperate condition. His forces had been thinned by repeated fights, and he had lost almost the whole of his resources. In this time of adversity he found a faithful friend in Canonchet, Chief Sachem of all the Narrhagansets. He was the son and heir of Miantonimo, the great Sachem, who, as already mentioned, after an honourable acquittal of the charge of conspiracy, had been privately put to death at the perfidious instigations of the settlers. "He was the heir," says the old chronicler, "of all his father's pride and insolence, as well as of his malice towards the English;"—he certainly was the heir of his insults and injuries, and the legitimate avenger of his murder. Though he had

forborne to take an active part in this hopeless war, yet he received
Philip and his broken forces with open arms; and gave them the most
generous countenance and support. This at once drew upon him the
hostility of the English; and it was determined to strike a signal blow
that should involve both the sachems in one common ruin. A great
force was, therefore, gathered together from Massachusetts, Plymouth,
and Connecticut, and was sent into the Narrhaganset country in the
depth of winter, when the swamps, being frozen and leafless, could
be traversed with comparative facility, and would no longer afford
dark and impenetrable fastnesses to the Indians.

Apprehensive of attack, Canonchet had conveyed the greater part
of his stores, together with the old, the infirm, the women and children
of his tribe, to a strong fortress; where he and Philip had likewise
drawn up the flower of their forces. This fortress, deemed by the
Indians impregnable, was situated upon a rising mound or kind of
island, of five or six acres, in the midst of a swamp; it was constructed
with a degree of judgment and skill vastly superior to what is usually
displayed in Indian fortification, and indicative of the martial genius
of these two chieftains.

Guided by a renegado Indian, the English penetrated, through
December snows, to this strong hold, and came upon the garrison by
surprize. The fight was fierce and tumultuous. The assailants were
repulsed in their first attack, and several of their bravest officers were
shot down in the act of storming the fortress, sword in hand. The
assault was renewed with greater success. A lodgement was effected.
The Indians were driven from one post to another. They disputed their
ground inch by inch, fighting with the fury of despair. Most of their
veterans were cut to pieces; and after a long and bloody battle, Philip
and Canonchet, with a handful of surviving warriors, retreated from the
fort, and took refuge in the thickets of the surrounding forest.

The victors set fire to the wigwams and the fort; the whole was
soon in a blaze; many of the old men, the women and the children
perished in the flames. This last outrage overcame even the stoicism
of the savage. The neighbouring woods resounded with the yells of
rage and despair, uttered by the fugitive warriors as they beheld the
destruction of their dwellings, and heard the agonizing cries of their
wives and offspring. "The burning of the wigwams," says a contemporary writer, "the shrieks and cries of the women and children,
and the yelling of the warriors, exhibited a most horrible and affecting
scene, so that it greatly moved some of the soldiers." The same writer
cautiously adds, "they were in *much doubt* then, and afterwards seriously

inquired, whether burning their enemies alive could be consistent with humanity, and the benevolent principles of the Gospel."[*]

The fate of the brave and generous Canonchet is worthy of particular mention: the last scene of his life is one of the noblest instances on record of Indian magnanimity.

Broken down in his power and resources by this signal defeat, yet faithful to his ally and to the hapless cause which he had espoused, he rejected all overtures of peace, offered on condition of betraying Philip and his followers, and declared that "he would fight it out to the last man, rather than become a servant to the English." His home being destroyed; his country harassed and laid waste by the incursions of the conquerors; he was obliged to wander away to the banks of the Connecticut; where he formed a rallying point to the whole body of western Indians, and laid waste several of the English settlements.

Early in the spring he departed on a hazardous expedition, with only thirty chosen men, to penetrate to Seaconk, in the vicinity of Mount Hope, and procure seed corn to plant for the sustenance of his troops. This little band of adventurers had passed safely through the Pequod country, and were in the centre of the Narrhaganset, resting at some wigwams near Pautucket river, when an alarm was given of an approaching enemy. Having but seven men by him at the time, Canonchet dispatched two of them to the top of a neighbouring hill, to bring intelligence of the foe.

Panic struck by the appearance of a troop of English and Indians rapidly advancing, they fled in breathless terror past their chieftain, without stopping to inform him of the danger. Canonchet sent another scout, who did the same. He then sent two more, one of whom, hurrying back in confusion and affright, told him that the whole British army was at hand. Canonchet saw there was no choice but immediate flight. He attempted to escape round the hill, but was perceived and hotly pursued by the hostile Indians and a few of the fleetest of the English. Finding the swiftest pursuer close upon his heels, he threw off, first his blanket, then his silver laced coat and belt of peag, by which his enemies knew him to be Canonchet, and redoubled the eagerness of pursuit. At length, in dashing through the river, his foot slipped upon a stone, and he fell so deep as to wet his gun. This accident so struck him with despair, that, as he afterwards confessed, "his heart and his bowels turned within him, and he became like a rotten stick, void of strength."

To such a degree was he unnerved, that, being seized by a Pequod

[*]MS. of the Rev. W. Ruggles.

Indian within a short distance of the river, he made no resistance, though a man of great vigour of body and boldness of heart. But on being made prisoner the whole pride of his spirit arose within him; and from that moment we find, in the anecdotes given by his enemies, nothing but repeated flashes of elevated and prince like heroism. Being questioned by one of the English who first came up with him, and who had not attained his twenty second year, the proud hearted warrior, looking with lofty contempt upon his youthful countenance, replied, "You are a child—you cannot understand matters of war—let your brother or your chief come—him will I answer."

Though repeated offers were made to him of his life, on condition of submitting, with his nation, to the English, yet he rejected them with disdain, and refused to send any proposals of the kind to the great body of his subjects; saying, that he knew none of them would comply. Being reproached with his breach of faith towards the whites; his boast that he would not deliver up a Wampanoag, nor the paring of a Wampanoag's nail; and his threat that he would burn the English alive in their houses; he disdained to justify himself, haughtily answering that others were as forward for the war as himself, "and he desired to hear no more thereof."

So noble and unshaken a spirit, so true a fidelity to his cause and his friend, might have touched the feelings of the generous and the brave: but Canonchet was an Indian; a being towards whom war had no courtesy, humanity no law, religion no compassion—he was condemned to die. The last words of his that are recorded, are worthy of the greatness of his soul. When sentence of death was passed upon him, he observed "that he liked it well, for he should die before his heart was soft, or he had spoken any thing unworthy of himself." His enemies gave him the death of a soldier, for he was shot at Stonington, by three young sachems of his own rank.

The defeat at the Narrhaganset fortress, and the death of Canonchet, were fatal blows to the fortunes of King Philip. He made an ineffectual attempt to raise a head of war, by stirring up the Mohawks to take arms; but though possessed of the native talents of a statesman, his arts were counteracted by the superior arts of his enlightened enemies, and the terror of their warlike skill began to subdue the resolution of the neighbouring tribes. The unfortunate chieftain saw himself daily stripped of power, and his ranks rapidly thinning around him. Some were suborned by the whites; others fell victims to hunger and fatigue, and to the frequent attacks by which they were harassed. His stores were all captured; his chosen friends were swept away from before his eyes; his uncle was shot down by his side; his sister was carried

Capture of Canonchet

An engraving reproduced in the Geoffrey Crayon edition of *The Sketch Book* (New York: G. P. Putnam's Sons, 1880).

into captivity; and in one of his narrow escapes he was compelled to leave his beloved wife and only son to the mercy of the enemy. "His ruin," says the historian, "being thus gradually carried on, his misery was not prevented, but augmented thereby; being himself made acquainted with the sense and experimental feeling of the captivity of his children, loss of friends, slaughter of his subjects, bereavement of all family relations, and being stripped of all outward comforts, before his own life should be taken away."

To fill up the measure of his misfortunes, his own followers began to plot against his life, that by sacrificing him they might purchase dishonourable safety. Through treachery a number of his faithful adherents, the subjects of Wetamoe, an Indian princess of Pocasset, a near kinswoman and confederate of Philip, were betrayed into the hands of the enemy. Wetamoe was among them at the time, and attempted to make her escape by crossing a neighbouring river: either exhausted by swimming, or starved with cold and hunger, she was found dead and naked near the water side. But persecution ceased not at the grave. Even death, the refuge of the wretched, where the wicked commonly cease from troubling, was no protection to this outcast female, whose great crime was affectionate fidelity to her kinsman and her friend. Her corpse was the object of unmanly and dastardly vengeance; the head was severed from the body and set upon a pole, and was thus exposed at Taunton, to the view of her captive subjects. They immediately recognised the features of their unfortunate queen, and were so affected at this barbarous spectacle, that we are told they broke forth into the "most horrid and diabolical lamentations."

However Philip had borne up against the complicated miseries and misfortunes that surrounded him, the treachery of his followers seemed to wring his heart, and reduce him to despondency. It is said that "he never rejoiced afterwards, nor had success in any of his designs." The spring of hope was broken—the ardour of enterprise was extinguished—he looked around, and all was danger and darkness; "there was no eye to pity, nor any arm that could bring deliverance." With a scanty band of followers, who still remained true to his desperate fortunes, the unhappy Philip wandered back to the vicinity of Mount Hope, the ancient dwelling of his fathers. Here he lurked about, like a spectre, among the desolated scenes of former power and prosperity, now bereft of home, of family, and friend. There needs no better picture of his destitute and piteous situation than that furnished by the homely pen of the chronicler, who is unwarily enlisting the feelings of the reader in favour of the hapless warrior whom he reviles. "Philip," he says, "like a savage wild beast, having been hunted by the English forces through the woods above a hundred miles backward and forward, at last was driven to his own den upon Mount Hope, where he retired with a few of his best friends, into a swamp, which proved but a prison to keep him fast till the messengers of death came by divine permission to execute vengeance upon him."

Even in this last refuge of desperation and despair a sullen grandeur gathers round his memory. We picture him to ourselves seated among his care worn followers, brooding in silence over his blasted fortunes, and acquiring a savage sublimity from the wildness and dreariness of his lurking place. Defeated, but not dismayed—crushed to the earth, but not humiliated—he seemed to grow more haughty beneath disaster, and to experience a fierce satisfaction in draining the last dregs of bitterness. Little minds are tamed and subdued by misfortune; but great minds rise above it. The very idea of submission awakened the fury of Philip, and he smote to death one of his followers, who proposed an expedient of peace. The brother of the victim made his escape, and in revenge betrayed the retreat of his chieftain. A body of white men and Indians were immediately despatched to the swamp where Philip lay crouched, glaring with fury and despair. Before he was aware of their approach, they had begun to surround him. In a little while he saw five of his trustiest followers laid dead at his feet; all resistance was vain; he rushed forth from his covert, and made a headlong attempt at escape, but was shot through the heart by a renegado Indian of his own nation.

Such is the scanty story of the brave, but unfortunate King Philip; persecuted while living, slandered and dishonoured when dead. If, however, we consider even the prejudiced anecdotes furnished us by his enemies, we may perceive in them traces of amiable and lofty character, sufficient to awaken sympathy for his fate, and respect for his memory. We find, that amidst all the harassing cares and ferocious passions of constant warfare, he was alive to the softer feelings of connubial love and paternal tenderness, and to the generous sentiment of friendship. The captivity of his "beloved wife and only son" are mentioned with exultation, as causing him poignant misery: the death of any near friend is triumphantly recorded as a new blow on his sensibilities; but the treachery and desertion of many of his followers, in whose affections he had confided, is said to have desolated his heart, and to have bereaved him of all further comfort. He was a patriot attached to his native soil—a prince true to his subjects, and indignant of their wrongs—a soldier, daring in battle, firm in adversity, patient of fatigue, of hunger, of every variety of bodily suffering, and ready to perish in the cause he had espoused. Proud of heart, and with an untameable love of natural liberty, he preferred to enjoy it among the beasts of the forests, or in the dismal and famished recesses of swamps and morasses, rather than bow his haughty spirit to submission, and live dependent and despised in the ease and luxury of the settlements. With heroic qualities and bold achievements that would have graced a civilized warrior, and have rendered him the theme of the poet and the historian; he lived a wanderer and a fugitive in his native land, and went down, like a lonely bark foundering amid darkness and tempest—without a pitying eye to weep his fall, or a friendly hand to record his struggle.

JOHN BULL

An old song, made by an aged old pate,
Of an old worshipful gentleman who had a great estate,
That kept a brave old house at a bountiful rate,
And an old porter to relieve the poor at his gate.

With an old study fill'd full of learned old books,
With an old reverend chaplain, you might know him by his looks,
With an old buttery-hatch worn quite off the hooks,
And an old kitchen that maintained half-a-dozen old cooks,
>   Like an old courtier, &c.
>   OLD SONG.

There is no species of humour in which the English more excel, than
that which consists in caricaturing and giving ludicrous appellations,
or nick names. In this way they have whimsically designated, not merely
individuals, but nations; and in their fondness for pushing a joke, they
have not spared even themselves. One would think, that in personifying
itself, a nation would be apt to picture something grand, heroic, and
imposing; but it is characteristic of the peculiar humour of the English,
and of their love for what is blunt, comic, and familiar, that they have
embodied their national oddities in the figure of a sturdy, corpulent
old fellow, with a three cornered hat, red waistcoat, leather breeches,
and stout oaken cudgel. Thus they have taken a singular delight in
exhibiting their most private foibles in a laughable point of view,
and have been so successful in their delineations, that there is scarcely
a being in actual existence more absolutely present to the public mind,
than that eccentric personage, John Bull.

Perhaps the continual contemplation of the character thus drawn
of them, has contributed to fix it upon the nation; and thus to give
reality to what at first may have been painted in a great measure
from the imagination. Men are apt to acquire peculiarities that are
continually ascribed to them. The common orders of English seem
wonderfully captivated with the *beau ideal* which they have formed
of John Bull, and endeavour to act up to the broad caricature that is
perpetually before their eyes. Unluckily, they sometimes make their
boasted Bull-ism an apology for their prejudice or grossness; and this
I have especially noticed among those truly homebred and genuine
sons of the soil, who have never migrated beyond the sound of Bow
bells. If one of these should be a little uncouth in speech, and apt

to utter impertinent truths, he confesses that he is a real John Bull, and always speaks his mind. If he now and then flies into an unreasonable burst of passion about trifles, he observes, that John Bull is a choleric old blade, but then his passion is over in a moment, and he bears no malice. If he betrays a coarseness of taste, and an insensibility to foreign refinements, he thanks heaven for his ignorance—he is a plain John Bull, and has no relish for frippery and nick-nacks. His very proneness to be gulled by strangers, and to pay extravagantly for absurdities, is excused under the plea of munificence—for John is always more generous than wise.

Thus, under the name of John Bull, he will contrive to argue every fault into a merit, and will frankly convict himself of being the honestest fellow in existence.

However little, therefore, the character may have suited in the first instance, it has gradually adapted itself to the nation, or rather, they have adapted themselves to each other; and a stranger who wishes to study English peculiarities, may gather much valuable information from the innumerable portraits of John Bull, as exhibited in the windows of the caricature shops. Still, however, he is one of those fertile humourists, that are continually throwing out new portraits, and presenting different aspects from different points of view; and often as he has been described, I cannot resist the temptation to give a slight sketch of him, such as he has met my eye.

John Bull, to all appearance, is a plain, downright, matter of fact fellow, with much less of poetry about him than rich prose. There is little of romance in his nature, but a vast deal of strong natural feeling. He excels in humour, more than in wit; is jolly, rather than gay; melancholy, rather than morose; can easily be moved to a sudden tear, or surprised into a broad laugh; but he loathes sentiment, and has no turn for light pleasantry. He is a boon companion, if you allow him to have his humour, and to talk about himself; and he will stand by a friend in a quarrel, with life and purse, however soundly he may be cudgelled.

In this last respect, to tell the truth, he has a propensity to be somewhat too ready. He is a busy minded personage, who thinks not merely for himself and family, but for all the country round, and is most generously disposed to be every body's champion. He is continually volunteering his services to settle his neighbours' affairs, and takes it in great dudgeon if they engage in any matter of consequence without asking his advice, though he seldom engages in any friendly office of the kind without finishing by getting into a squabble with all parties, and then railing bitterly at their ingratitude. He unluckily took lessons in his youth in the noble science of defence, and having accomplished himself in the use of his limbs and his weapons, and become a perfect master at boxing and cudgel play, he has had a troublesome life of it ever since. He cannot hear of a quarrel between the most distant of his neighbours, but he begins incontinently to fumble with the head of his cudgel, and consider whether his interest or honour does not require that he should meddle in the broil. Indeed, he has extended his relations of pride and policy so completely over the whole country, that no event can take place, without infringing some of his finely spun rights and dignities. Couched in his little domain, with these filaments stretching forth in every direction, he is like some choleric, bottle bellied old spider, who has woven his web over a whole chamber, so that a fly cannot buzz, nor a breeze blow, without startling his repose, and causing him to sally forth wrathfully from his den.

Though really a good hearted, good tempered old fellow at bottom, yet he is singularly fond of being in the midst of contention. It is one of his peculiarities, however, that he only relishes the beginning of an affray: he always goes into a fight with alacrity, but comes out of it grumbling even when victorious; and though no one fights with more obstinacy to carry a contested point, yet, when the battle is over, and he comes to the reconciliation, he is so much taken up with the mere shaking of hands, that he is apt to let his antagonist pocket all that they have been quarrelling about. It is not, therefore, fighting that he ought so much to be on his guard against, as making friends. It is difficult to cudgel him out of a farthing, but put him in a good humour, and you may bargain him out of all the money in his pocket. He is like a stout ship, which will weather the roughest storm uninjured, but roll its masts overboard in the succeeding calm.

He is a little fond of playing the magnifico abroad; of pulling out a long purse; flinging his money bravely about at boxing matches, horse races, and cock fights, and carrying a high head among "gentlemen of the fancy;" but immediately after one of these fits of extravagance, he will be taken with violent qualms of economy; stop short at the most trivial expenditure; talk desperately of being ruined, and brought upon the parish; and in such moods, will not pay the smallest tradesman's bill, without violent altercation. He is, in fact, the most punctual and discontented paymaster in the world; drawing his coin out of his breeches' pocket with infinite reluctance, paying to the uttermost farthing, but accompanying every guinea with a growl.

With all his talk of economy, however, he is a bountiful provider, and a hospitable housekeeper. His economy is of a whimsical kind, its chief object being to devise how he may afford to be extravagant, for he will begrudge himself a beef steak and pint of port one day, that he may roast an ox whole, broach a hogshead of ale, and treat all his neighbours, on the next.

His domestic establishment is enormously expensive, not so much from any great outward parade, as from the great consumption of solid beef and pudding, the vast number of followers he feeds and clothes, and his singular disposition to pay hugely for small services. He is a most kind and indulgent master, and, provided his servants humour his peculiarities, flatter his vanity a little now and then, and do not peculate grossly on him before his face, they may manage him to perfection. Every thing that lives on him seems to thrive and grow fat. His house servants are well paid, and pampered, and have little to do. His horses are sleek and lazy, and prance slowly before his state carriage, and his house dogs sleep quietly about the door, and will hardly bark at a house breaker.

His family mansion is an old castellated manor house, grey with age, and of a most venerable though weather beaten appearance. It has been built upon no regular plan, but is a vast accumulation of parts, erected in various tastes and ages. The centre bears evident traces of Saxon architecture, and is as solid as ponderous stone and old English oak can make it. Like all the reliques of that style, it is full of obscure passages, intricate mazes, and dusky chambers; and though these have been partially lighted up in modern days, yet there are many places where you must still grope in the dark. Additions have been made to the original edifice from time to time, and great alterations have taken place; towers and battlements have been erected during wars and tumults; wings built in times of peace, and outhouses, lodges, and offices, run up according to the whim or convenience of different generations, until it has become one of the most spacious, rambling tenements imaginable. An entire wing is taken up with the family chapel, a reverend pile that must once have been exceedingly sumptuous, and, indeed, in spite of having been altered and simplified at various periods, has still a look of solemn religious pomp. Its walls within are storied with the monuments of John's ancestors, and it is snugly fitted up with soft cushions and well lined chairs, where such of his family as are inclined to church services, may doze comfortably in the discharge of their duties.

To keep up this chapel has cost John much money; but he is staunch in his religion, and piqued in his zeal, from the circumstance that many dissenting chapels have been erected in his vicinity, and several of his neighbours, with whom he has had quarrels, are strong papists.

To do the duties of the chapel, he maintains, at a large expense, a pious and portly family chaplain. He is a most learned and decorous personage, and a truly well bred christian, who always backs the old gentleman in his opinions, winks discreetly at his little peccadilloes, rebukes the children when refractory, and is of great use in exhorting the tenants to read their bibles, say their prayers, and above all, to pay their rents punctually, and without grumbling.

The family apartments are in a very antiquated taste, somewhat heavy, and often inconvenient, but full of the solemn magnificence of former times; fitted up with rich though faded tapestry, unwieldy furniture, and loads of massy gorgeous old plate. The vast fire places, ample kitchens, extensive cellars, and sumptuous banquetting halls, all speak of the roaring hospitality of days of yore, of which the modern festivity at the manor house is but a shadow. There are, however, complete suites of rooms apparently deserted and time worn; and towers and turrets that are tottering to decay, so that in high winds there is danger of their tumbling about the ears of the household.

John has frequently been advised to have the old edifice thoroughly overhauled, and to have some of the useless parts pulled down, and the others strengthened with their materials; but the old gentleman always grows testy on this subject. He swears the house is an excellent house—that it is tight and weather proof, and not to be shaken by tempests—that it has stood for several hundred years, and, therefore, is not likely to tumble down now—that as to its being inconvenient, his family is accustomed to the inconveniences, and would not be comfortable without them—that as to its unwieldy size and irregular construction, these result from its being the growth of centuries, and being improved by the wisdom of every generation—that an old family, like his, requires a large house to dwell in; new, upstart families may live in modern cottages and snug boxes, but an old English family should inhabit an old English manor house. If you point out any part of the building as superfluous, he insists that it is material to the strength or decoration of the rest, and the harmony of the whole, and swears, that the parts are so built into each other, that if you pull down one, you run the risk of having the whole about your ears.

The secret of the matter is, that John has a great disposition to protect and patronize. He thinks it indispensable to the dignity of an ancient and honourable family, to be bounteous in its appointments, and to be eaten up by dependants; and so, partly from pride, and partly from kind heartedness, he makes it a rule always to give shelter and maintenance to his superannuated servants.

The consequence is, that like many other venerable family establishments, his manor is incumbered by old retainers whom he cannot turn off, and an old style which he cannot lay down. His mansion is like a great hospital of invalids, and, with all its magnitude, is not a whit too large for its inhabitants. Not a nook or corner but is of use in housing some useless personage. Groups of veteran beef eaters, gouty pensioners, and retired heroes of the buttery and the larder, are seen lolling about its walls, crawling over its lawns, dozing under its trees, or sunning themselves upon the benches at its doors. Every office and out house is garrisoned by these supernumeraries and their families, for they are amazingly prolific; and when they die off, are sure to leave John a legacy of hungry mouths to be provided for. A mattock cannot be struck against the most mouldering, tumble down tower, but out pops, from some cranny or loop hole, the gray pate of some superannuated hanger on, who has lived at John's expense all his life, and makes the most grievous outcry, at their pulling down the roof from over the head of a worn out servant of the family. This is an appeal that John's honest heart never can withstand; so that a man, who has faithfully eaten his beef and pudding all his life, is sure to be rewarded with a pipe and tankard in his old days.

A great part of his park, also, is turned into paddocks, where his broken down chargers are turned loose, to graze undisturbed for the remainder of their existence—a worthy example of grateful recollection, which, if some of his neighbours were to imitate, would not be to their discredit. Indeed, it is one of his great pleasures to point out these old steeds to his visiters, to dwell on their good qualities, extol their past services, and boast, with some little vain glory, of the perilous adventures and hardy exploits, through which they have carried him.

He is given, however, to indulge his veneration for family usages, and family incumbrances, to a whimsical extent. His manor is infested by gangs of gipsies, yet he will not suffer them to be driven off, because they have infested the place time out of mind, and been regular poachers upon every generation of the family. He will scarcely permit a dry branch to be lopped from the great trees that surround the house, lest it should molest the rooks, that have bred there for centuries. Owls have taken possession of the dovecote; but they are hereditary owls, and must not be disturbed. Swallows have nearly choked up every chimney with their nests; martins build in every frieze and cornice; crows flutter about the towers, and perch on every weather cock; and old gray headed rats may be seen in every quarter of the house, running in and out of their holes undauntedly, in broad daylight. In short, John has such a reverence for every thing that has been long in the family, that he will not hear even of abuses being reformed, because they are good old family abuses.

All these whims and habits have concurred wofully to drain the old gentleman's purse; and as he prides himself on punctuality in money matters, and wishes to maintain his credit in the neighbourhood, they have caused him great perplexity in meeting his engagements. This too has been increased, by the altercations and heartburnings which are continually taking place in his family. His children have been brought up to different callings, and are of different ways of thinking; and as they have always been allowed to speak their minds freely, they do not fail to exercise the privilege most clamorously in the present posture of his affairs. Some stand up for the honour of the race, and are clear that the old establishment should be kept up in all its state, whatever may be the cost; others, who are more prudent and considerate, entreat the old gentleman to retrench his expenses, and to put his whole system of housekeeping on a more moderate footing. He has, indeed, at times seemed inclined to listen to their opinions, but their wholesome advice has been completely defeated by the obstreperous conduct of one of his sons. This is a noisy rattle pated fellow, of rather low habits, who neglects his business to frequent ale houses—is the orator of village clubs, and a complete oracle among the poorest of his father's tenants. No sooner does he hear any of his brothers mention reform or retrenchment, than up he jumps, takes the words out of their mouths, and roars out for an overturn. When his tongue is once going, nothing can stop it. He rants about the room, hectors the old man about his spendthrift practices, ridicules his tastes and pursuits, insists that he shall turn the old servants out of doors, give the broken down horses to the hounds, send the fat chaplain packing, and take a field preacher in his place—nay, that the whole family mansion shall be levelled with the ground, and a plain one of brick and mortar built in its place. He rails at every social entertainment and family festivity, and skulks away growling to the ale house whenever an equipage drives up to the door. Though constantly complaining of the emptiness of his purse, yet he scruples not to spend all his pocket money in these tavern convocations, and even runs up scores for the liquor over which he preaches about his father's extravagance.

It may readily be imagined, how little such thwarting agrees with the old cavalier's fiery temperament. He has become so irritable, from repeated crossings, that the mere mention of retrenchment or reform is a signal for a brawl between him and the tavern oracle. As the latter is too sturdy and refractory for paternal discipline, having grown out of all fear of the cudgel, they have frequent scenes of wordy warfare, which at times run so high, that John is fain to call in the aid of his son Tom, an officer who has served abroad, but is at present

living at home, on half pay. This last is sure to stand by the old gentleman, right or wrong; likes nothing so much as a racketing, roystering
life, and is ready, at a wink or nod, to out sabre, and flourish it over
the orator's head, if he dares to array himself against paternal authority.

These family dissensions, as usual, have got abroad, and are rare
food for scandal in John's neighbourhood. People begin to look wise,
and shake their heads, whenever his affairs are mentioned. They all
"hope that matters are not so bad with him as represented; but when
a man's own children begin to rail at his extravagance, things must
be badly managed. They understand he is mortgaged over head and
ears, and is continually dabbling with money lenders. He is certainly
an open handed old gentleman, but they fear he has lived too fast;
indeed, they never knew any good come of this fondness for hunting,
racing, revelling, and prize fighting. In short, Mr. Bull's estate is a
very fine one, and has been in the family a long while; but for all that,
they have known many finer estates come to the hammer."

What is worst of all, is the effect which these pecuniary embarrass-
ments and domestic feuds have had on the poor man himself. Instead
of that jolly round corporation, and smug rosy face, which he used
to present, he has of late become as shrivelled and shrunk as a frost
bitten apple. His scarlet gold laced waistcoat, which bellied out so
bravely in those prosperous days when he sailed before the wind, now
hangs loosely about him like a mainsail in a calm. His leather breeches
are all in folds and wrinkles, and apparently have much ado to hold up
the boots that yawn on both sides of his once sturdy legs.

Instead of strutting about, as formerly, with his three cornered hat
on one side, flourishing his cudgel, and bringing it down every moment
with a hearty thump upon the ground, looking every one sturdily in
the face, and trolling out a stave of a catch or a drinking song, he
now goes about, whistling thoughtfully to himself, with his head
drooping down, his cudgel tucked under his arm, and his hands thrust
to the bottom of his breeches' pockets, which are evidently empty.

Such is the plight of honest John Bull at present; yet for all this,
the old fellow's spirit is as tall and as gallant as ever. If you drop the
least expression of sympathy or concern, he takes fire in an instant;
swears that he is the richest and stoutest fellow in the country; talks
of laying out large sums to adorn his house, or to buy another estate;
and, with a valiant swagger and grasping of his cudgel, longs exceedingly to have another bout at quarter staff.

Though there may be something rather whimsical in all this, yet I
confess I cannot look upon John's situation, without strong feelings of
interest. With all his odd humours, and obstinate prejudices, he is a

sterling hearted old blade. He may not be so wonderfully fine a fellow as he thinks himself, but he is at least twice as good as his neighbours represent him. His virtues are all his own; all plain, homebred and unaffected. His very faults smack of the raciness of his good qualities. His extravagance savours of his generosity; his quarrelsomeness of his courage; his credulity of his open faith; his vanity of his pride; and his bluntness of his sincerity. They are all the redundancies of a rich and liberal character. He is like his own oak; rough without, but sound and solid within; whose bark abounds with excrescences in proportion to the growth and grandeur of the timber; and whose branches make a fearful groaning and murmuring in the least storm, from their very magnitude and luxuriance. There is something, too, in the appearance of his old family mansion, that is extremely poetical and picturesque; and as long as it can be rendered comfortably habitable, I should almost tremble to see it meddled with during the present conflict of tastes and opinions. Some of his advisors are no doubt good architects that might be of service; but many I fear are mere levellers, who when they had once got to work with their mattocks on the venerable edifice, would never stop until they had brought it to the ground, and perhaps buried themselves among the ruins. All that I wish is, that John's present troubles may teach him more prudence in future. That he may cease to distress his mind about other people's affairs; that he may give up the fruitless attempt to promote the good of his neighbours, and the peace and happiness of the world, by dint of the cudgel; that he may remain quietly at home; gradually get his house into repair; cultivate his rich estate according to his fancy; husband his income, if he thinks proper; bring his unruly children into order if he can; renew the jovial scenes of ancient prosperity, and long enjoy, on his paternal lands, a green, an honourable, and a merry old age.

THE
PRIDE OF THE VILLAGE

May no wolf howle; no screech owle stir
A wing about thy sepulchre!
No boysterous winds or stormes come hither,
To starve or wither
Thy soft sweet earth! but like a spring
Love keep it ever flourishing.

HERRICK.

In the course of an excursion through one of the remote counties of England, I had struck into one of those cross roads that lead through the more secluded parts of the country, and stopped one afternoon at a village, the situation of which was beautifully rural and retired. There was an air of primitive simplicity about its inhabitants, not to be found in the villages which lie on the great coach roads. I determined to pass the night there, and having taken an early dinner, strolled out to enjoy the neighbouring scenery.

My ramble, as is usually the case with travellers, soon led me to the church, which stood at a little distance from the village. Indeed, it was an object of some curiosity, its old tower being completely over-run with ivy, so that only here and there a jutting buttress, an angle of grey wall, or a fantastically carved ornament, peered through the verdant covering. It was a lovely evening. The early part of the day had been dark and showery, but in the afternoon it had cleared up, and though sullen clouds still hung over head, yet there was a broad tract of golden sky in the west, from which the setting sun gleamed through the dripping leaves, and lit up all nature into a melancholy smile. It seemed like the parting hour of a good christian, smiling on the sins and sorrows of the world, and giving, in the serenity of his decline, an assurance that he will rise again in glory.

I had seated myself on a half sunken tombstone, and was musing, as one is apt to do at this sober thoughted hour, on past scenes, and early friends—on those who were distant, and those who were dead— and indulging in that kind of melancholy fancying, which has in it something sweeter even than pleasure. Every now and then, the stroke of a bell from the neighbouring tower fell on my ear; its tones were in unison with the scene, and instead of jarring, chimed in with my feelings, and it was some time before I recollected, that it must be tolling the knell of some new tenant of the tomb.

Presently I saw a funeral train moving across the village green; it wound slowly along a lane, was lost, and reappeared through the breaks of the hedges, until it passed the place where I was sitting. The pall was supported by young girls, dressed in white, and another, about the age of seventeen, walked before, bearing a chaplet of white flowers; a token that the deceased was a young and unmarried female. The corpse was followed by the parents. They were a venerable couple of the better order of peasantry. The father seemed to repress his feelings; but his fixed eye, contracted brow, and deeply furrowed face, showed the struggle that was passing within. His wife hung on his arm, and wept aloud with the convulsive bursts of a mother's sorrow.

I followed the funeral into the church. The bier was placed in the centre aisle, and the chaplet of white flowers, with a pair of white gloves, were hung over the seat which the deceased had occupied.

Every one knows the soul subduing pathos of the funeral service; for who is so fortunate as never to have followed some one he has loved to the tomb; but when performed over the remains of innocence and beauty, thus laid low in the bloom of existence—what can be more affecting? At that simple, but most solemn consignment of the body to the grave—"Earth to earth—ashes to ashes—dust to dust!" the tears of the youthful companions of the deceased flowed unrestrained. The father still seemed to struggle with his feelings, and to comfort himself with the assurance, that the dead are blessed which die in the Lord; but the mother only thought of her child as a flower of the field, cut down and withered in the midst of its sweetness; she was like Rachel, "mourning over her children, and would not be comforted."

On returning to the inn, I learnt the whole story of the deceased. It was a simple one, and such as has often been told. She had been the beauty and pride of the village. Her father had once been an opulent farmer, but was reduced in circumstances. This was an only child, and brought up entirely at home, in the simplicity of rural life. She had been the pupil of the village pastor, the favourite lamb of his little flock. The good man watched over her education with paternal care; it was limited, and suitable to the sphere in which she was to move, for he only sought to make her an ornament to her station in life, not to raise her above it. The tenderness and indulgence of her parents, and the exemption from all ordinary occupations, had fostered a natural grace and delicacy of character, that accorded with the fragile loveliness of her form. She appeared like some tender plant of the garden, blooming accidentally amid the hardier natives of the fields.

The superiority of her charms was felt and acknowledged by her companions, but without envy, for it was surpassed by the unassuming gentleness and winning kindness of her manners. It might be truly said of her,

> "This is the prettiest low-born lass, that ever
> Ran on the green-sward: nothing she does or seems,
> But smacks of something greater than herself;
> Too noble for this place."

The village was one of those sequestered spots, which still retain some vestiges of old English customs. It had its rural festivals and holyday pastimes, and still kept up some faint observance of the once popular rites of May. These, indeed, had been promoted by its present pastor; who was a lover of old customs, and one of those simple Christians that think their mission fulfilled by promoting joy on earth and good will among mankind. Under his auspices the May pole stood from year to year in the centre of the village green; on May day it was decorated with garlands and streamers; and a queen or lady of the May was appointed, as in former times, to preside at the sports, and distribute the prizes and rewards. The picturesque situation of the village, and the fancifulness of its rustic fetes would often attract the notice of casual visitors. Among these, on one May day, was a young officer, whose regiment had been recently quartered in the neighbourhood. He was charmed with the native taste that pervaded this village pageant; but, above all, with the dawning loveliness of the queen of May. It was the village favourite, who was crowned with flowers, and blushing and smiling in all the beautiful confusion of girlish diffidence and delight. The artlessness of rural habits enabled him readily to make her acquaintance; he gradually won his way into her intimacy; and paid his court to her in that unthinking way in which young officers are too apt to trifle with rustic simplicity.

There was nothing in his advances to startle or alarm. He never even talked of love; but there are modes of making it, more eloquent than language, and which convey it subtilely and irresistibly to the heart. The beam of the eye, the tone of voice, the thousand tendernesses which emanate from every word, and look, and action—these form the true eloquence of love, and can always be felt and understood, but never described. Can we wonder that they should readily win a heart, young, guileless, and susceptible? As to her, she loved almost unconsciously; she scarcely inquired what was the growing passion that was absorbing every thought and feeling, or what were to be its consequences. She, indeed, looked not to the future. When present, his looks. and words occupied her whole attention; when absent, she thought but of what had passed at their recent interview. She would wander with him through the green lanes and rural scenes of the vicinity. He taught her to see new beauties in nature: he talked in the language of polite and cultivated life, and breathed into her ear the witcheries of romance and poetry.

Perhaps there could not have been a passion, between the sexes, more pure than this innocent girl's. The gallant figure of her youthful admirer, and the splendour of his military attire, might at first have charmed her eye; but it was not these that had captivated her heart. Her attachment had something in it of idolatry. She looked up to him as to a being of a superior order. She felt in his society the enthusiasm of a mind naturally delicate and poetical, and now first awakened to a keen perception of the beautiful and grand. Of the sordid distinctions of rank and fortune, she thought nothing; it was the difference of intellect, of demeanor, of manners, from those of the rustic society to which she had been accustomed, that elevated him in her opinion. She would listen to him with charmed ear and downcast look of mute delight, and her cheek would mantle with enthusiasm; or if ever she ventured a shy glance of timid admiration, it was as quickly withdrawn, and she would sigh and blush at the idea of her comparative unworthiness.

Her lover was equally impassioned; but his passion was mingled with feelings of a coarser nature. He had begun the connexion in levity; for he had often heard his brother officers boast of their village conquests, and thought some triumph of the kind necessary to his reputation as a man of spirit. But he was too full of youthful fervour. His heart had not yet been rendered sufficiently cold and selfish by a wandering and a dissipated life: it caught fire from the very flame it sought to kindle; and before he was aware of the nature of his situation, he became really in love.

What was he to do? There were the old obstacles which so incessantly occur in these heedless attachments. His rank in life—the prejudices of titled connexions—his dependance upon a proud and unyielding father—all forbad him to think of matrimony:—but when he looked down upon this innocent being, so tender and confiding, there was a purity in her manners, a blamelessness in her life, and a beseeching modesty in her looks, that awed down every licentious feeling. In vain did he try to fortify himself, by a thousand heartless examples of men of fashion, and to chill the glow of generous sentiment, with that cold derisive levity with which he had heard them talk of female virtue; whenever he came into her presence, she was still surrounded by that mysterious, but impassive charm of virgin purity, in whose hallowed sphere no guilty thought can live.

The sudden arrival of orders for the regiment to repair to the continent, completed the confusion of his mind. He remained for a short time in a state of the most painful irresolution; he hesitated to communicate the tidings, until the day for marching was at hand; when he gave her the intelligence in the course of an evening ramble.

The idea of parting had never before occurred to her. It broke in at once upon her dream of felicity; she looked upon it as a sudden and insurmountable evil, and wept with the guileless simplicity of a child. He drew her to his bosom, and kissed the tears from her soft cheek, nor did he meet with a repulse, for there are moments of mingled sorrow and tenderness, which hallow the caresses of affection. He was naturally impetuous, and the sight of beauty apparently yielding in his arms, the confidence of his power over her, and the dread of losing her forever, all conspired to overwhelm his better feelings—he ventured to propose that she should leave her home, and be the companion of his fortunes.

He was quite a novice in seduction, and blushed and faltered at his own baseness; but so innocent of mind was his intended victim, that she was at first at a loss to comprehend his meaning;—and why she should leave her native village, and the humble roof of her parents. When at last the nature of his proposals flashed upon her pure mind, the effect was withering. She did not weep—she did not break forth into reproach—she said not a word—but she shrunk back aghast as from a viper, gave him a look of anguish that pierced to his very soul, and clasping her hands in agony, fled, as if for refuge, to her father's cottage.

The officer retired, confounded, humiliated, and repentant. It is uncertain what might have been the result of the conflict of his feelings, had not his thoughts been diverted by the bustle of departure. New scenes, new pleasures, and new companions, soon dissipated his self reproach, and stifled his tenderness. Yet, amidst the stir of camps, the revelries of garrisons, the array of armies, and even the din of battles, his thoughts would sometimes steal back to the scene of rural quiet and village simplicity—the white cottage—the footpath along the silver brook and up the hawthorn hedge, and the little village maid loitering along it, leaning on his arm, and listening to him with eyes beaming with unconscious affection.

The shock which the poor girl had received, in the destruction of all her ideal world, had indeed been cruel. Faintings and hystericks had at first shaken her tender frame, and were succeeded by a settled and pining melancholy. She had beheld from her window the march of the departing troops. She had seen her faithless lover borne off, as if in triumph, amidst the sound of drum and trumpet, and the pomp of arms. She strained a last aching gaze after him, as the morning sun glittered about his figure, and his plume waved in the breeze: he passed away like a bright vision from her sight, and left her all in darkness.

It would be trite to dwell on the particulars of her after story. It was, like other tales of love, melancholy. She avoided society, and wandered out alone in the walks she had most frequented with her lover. She sought, like the stricken deer, to weep in silence and loneliness, and brood over the barbed sorrow that rankled in her soul. Sometimes she would be seen late of an evening sitting in the porch of the village church; and the milkmaids, returning from the fields, would now and then overhear her singing some plaintive ditty in the hawthorn walk. She became fervent in her devotions at church, and as the old people saw her approach, so wasted away, yet with a hectic bloom, and that hallowed air which melancholy diffuses round the form, they would make way for her, as for something spiritual, and, looking after her, would shake their heads in gloomy foreboding.

She felt a conviction that she was hastening to the tomb, but looked forward to it as a place of rest. The silver cord that had bound her to existence was loosed, and there seemed to be no more pleasure under the sun. If ever her gentle bosom had entertained resentment against her lover, it was extinguished. She was incapable of angry passions, and in a moment of saddened tenderness, she penned him a farewell letter. It was couched in the simplest language; but touching from its very simplicity. She told him that she was dying, and did not conceal from him that his conduct was the cause. She even depicted the sufferings which she had experienced; but concluded with saying, that she could not die in peace, until she had sent him her forgiveness and her blessing.

By degrees her strength declined, and she could no longer leave the cottage. She could only totter to the window, where, propped up in her chair, it was her enjoyment to sit all day and look out upon the landscape. Still she uttered no complaint, nor imparted to any one the malady that was preying on her heart. She never even mentioned her lover's name; but would lay her head on her mother's bosom and weep in silence. Her poor parents hung, in mute anxiety, over this fading blossom of their hopes, still flattering themselves that it might again revive to freshness, and that the bright unearthly bloom which sometimes flushed her cheek might be the promise of returning health.

In this way she was seated between them one Sunday afternoon; her hands were clasped in theirs, the lattice was thrown open, and the soft air that stole in, brought with it the fragrance of the clustering honeysuckle, which her own hands had trained round the window.

Her father had just been reading a chapter in the bible; it spoke of the vanity of worldly things, and of the joys of heaven; it seemed to have diffused comfort and serenity through her bosom. Her eye was fixed on the distant village church—the bell had tolled for the evening service—the last villager was lagging into the porch—and every thing had sunk into that hallowed stillness peculiar to the day of rest. Her parents were gazing on her with yearning hearts. Sickness and sorrow, which pass so roughly over some faces, had given to hers the expression of a seraph's. A tear trembled in her soft blue eye.—Was she thinking of her faithless lover?—or were her thoughts wandering to that distant church yard, into whose bosom she might soon be gathered?

Suddenly the clang of hoofs was heard—a horseman gallopped to the cottage—he dismounted before the window—the poor girl gave a faint exclamation, and sunk back in her chair:—it was her repentant lover! He rushed into the house, and flew to clasp her to his bosom; but her wasted form—her death like countenance—so wan, yet so lovely in its desolation, smote him to the soul, and he threw himself in an agony at her feet. She was too faint to rise—she attempted to extend her trembling hand—her lips moved as if she spoke, but no word was articulated—she looked down upon him with a smile of unutterable tenderness, and closed her eyes forever.

Such are the particulars which I gathered of this village story. They are but scanty, and I am conscious have little novelty to recommend them. In the present rage also for strange incident and high seasoned narrative, they may appear trite and insignificant, but they interested me strongly at the time; and, taken in connexion with the affecting ceremony which I had just witnessed, left a deeper impression on my mind than many circumstances of a more striking nature. I have passed through the place since, and visited the church again from a better motive than mere curiosity. It was a wintry evening; the trees were stripped of their foliage; the church yard looked naked and mournful, and the wind rustled coldly through the dry grass. Evergreens, however, had been planted about the grave of the village favourite, and osiers were bent over it to keep the turf uninjured.

The church door was open, and I stepped in. There hung the chaplet of flowers and the gloves, as on the day of the funeral: the flowers were withered, it is true, but care seemed to have been taken that no dust should soil their whiteness. I have seen many monuments, where art has exhausted its powers to awaken the sympathy of the spectator, but I have met with none that spoke more touchingly to my heart, than this simple, but delicate memento of departed innocence.

THE ANGLER

This day dame Nature seemed in love,
The lusty sap began to move,
Fresh juice did stir th' embracing vines,
And birds had drawn their valentines.
The jealous trout that low did lie,
Rose at a well dissembled flie,
There stood my friend, with patient skill,
Attending of his trembling quill.

SIR H. WOTTON.

It is said that many an unlucky urchin is induced to run away from his family, and betake himself to a seafaring life, from reading the history of Robinson Crusoe; and I suspect that, in like manner, many of those worthy gentlemen, who are given to haunt the sides of pastoral streams with angle rods in hand, may trace the origin of their passion to the seductive pages of honest Izaak Walton. I recollect studying his "Complete Angler" several years since, in company with a knot of friends in America, and moreover that we were all completely bitten with the angling mania. It was early in the year; but as soon as the weather was auspicious, and that the spring began to melt into the verge of summer, we took rod in hand and sallied into the country, as stark mad as was ever Don Quixote from reading books of chivalry.

One of our party had equalled the Don in the fullness of his equipments; being attired cap-a-pie for the enterprize. He wore a broad skirted fustian coat, perplexed with half a hundred pockets; a pair of stout shoes, and leathern gaiters; a basket slung on one side for fish; a patent rod; a landing net, and a score of other inconveniencies, only to be found in the true angler's armoury. Thus harnessed for the field, he was as great a matter of stare and wonderment among the country folk, who had never seen a regular angler, as was the steel clad hero of La Mancha among the goatherds of the Sierra Morena.

Our first essay was along a mountain brook, among the highlands of the Hudson; a most unfortunate place for the execution of those piscatory tactics which had been invented along the velvet margins of quiet English rivulets. It was one of those wild streams that lavish, among our romantic solitudes, unheeded beauties, enough to fill the sketch book of a hunter of the picturesque. Sometimes it would leap down rocky shelves, making small cascades, over which the trees threw their broad balancing sprays, and long nameless weeds hung

264

in fringes from the impending banks, dripping with diamond drops. Sometimes it would brawl and fret along a ravine in the matted shade of a forest, filling it with murmurs; and after this termagant career, would steal forth into open day with the most placid demure face imaginable; as I have seen some pestilent shrew of a housewife, after filling her home with uproar and ill humour, come dimpling out of doors, swimming and curtseying, and smiling upon all the world.

How smoothly would this vagrant brook glide, at such times, through some bosom of green meadow land among the mountains; where the quiet was only interrupted by the occasional tinkling of a bell from the lazy cattle among the clover, or the sound of a woodcutter's axe from the neighbouring forest.

For my part, I was always a bungler at all kinds of sport that required either patience or adroitness, and had not angled above half an hour, before I had completely "satisfied the sentiment," and convinced myself of the truth of Izaak Walton's opinion, that angling is something like poetry—a man must be born to it. I hooked myself instead of the fish; tangled my line in every tree; lost my bait; broke my rod; until I gave up the attempt in despair, and passed the day under the trees, reading old Izaak; satisfied that it was his fascinating vein of honest simplicity and rural feeling that had bewitched me, and not the passion for angling. My companions, however, were more persevering in their delusion. I have them at this moment before my eyes, stealing along the border of the brook, where it lay open to the day, or was merely fringed by shrubs and bushes. I see the bittern rising with hollow scream as they break in upon his rarely invaded haunt; the kingfisher watching them suspiciously from his dry tree that overhangs the deep black mill pond, in the gorge of the hills; the tortoise letting himself slip sideways from off the stone or log on which he is sunning himself; and the panic struck frog plumping in headlong as they approach, and spreading an alarm throughout the watery world around.

I recollect also, that, after toiling and watching and creeping about for the greater part of a day, with scarcely any success, in spite of all our admirable apparatus, a lubberly country urchin came down from the hills with a rod made from a branch of a tree; a few yards of twine; and, as heaven shall help me! I believe a crooked pin for a hook, baited with a vile earth worm—and in half an hour caught more fish than we had nibbles throughout the day!

But above all, I recollect the "good, honest, wholesome, hungry" repast, which we made under a beech tree just by a spring of pure sweet water that stole out of the side of a hill; and how, when it was over, one of the party read old Izaak Walton's scene with the milk-maid, while I lay on the grass and built castles in a bright pile of clouds, until I fell asleep. All this may appear like mere egotism, yet I cannot refrain from uttering these recollections, which are passing like a strain of music over my mind and have been called up by an agreeable scene which I witnessed not long since.

In a morning's stroll along the banks of the Alun, a beautiful little stream which flows down from the Welsh hills and throws itself into the Dee, my attention was attracted to a group seated on the margin. On approaching, I found it to consist of a veteran angler and two rustic disciples. The former was an old fellow with a wooden leg, with clothes very much but very carefully patched, betokening poverty, honestly come by, and decently maintained. His face bore the marks of former storms, but present fair weather; its furrows had been worn into an habitual smile; his iron grey locks hung about his ears, and he had altogether the good humoured air of a constitutional philosopher, who was disposed to take the world as it went. One of his companions was a ragged wight, with the skulking look of an arrant poacher, and I'll warrant could find his way to any gentleman's fish pond in the neighbourhood in the darkest night. The other was a tall, awkward, country lad, with a lounging gait, and apparently somewhat of a rustic beau. The old man was busy in examining the maw of a trout which he had just killed, to discover by its contents what insects were seasonable for bait; and was lecturing on the subject to his companions, who appeared to listen with infinite deference. I have a kind feeling towards all "brothers of the angle," ever since I read Izaak Walton. They are men, he affirms, of a "mild, sweet and peaceable spirit"; and my esteem for them has been encreased since I met with an old "Tretyse of fishing with the Angle," in which are set forth many of the maxims of their inoffensive fraternity. "Take good hede," sayth this honest little tretyse, "that in going about your disportes ye open no man's gates but that ye shet them again. Also ye shall not use this forsayd crafti disport for no covetousness to the encreasing and sparing of your money only, but principally for your solace and to cause the helth of your body and specyally of your soule."*

---

*From this same treatise, it would appear that angling is a more industrious and devout employment than it is generally considered.—"For when ye purpose to go on your disportes in fishynge ye will not desyre greatlye many persons with you, which might let you of your game. And that ye may serve God devoutly in sayinge effectually your customable prayers. And thus doying, ye shall eschew and also avoyde many vices, as ydelnes, which is principall cause to induce man to many other vices, as it is right well known."

I thought that I could perceive in the veteran angler before me an exemplification of what I had read; and there was a chearful contentedness in his looks that quite drew me towards him. I could not but remark the gallant manner in which he stumped from one part of the brook to another; waving his rod in the air, to keep the line from dragging on the ground, or catching among the bushes; and the adroitness with which he would throw his fly to any particular place; sometimes skimming it lightly along a little rapid; sometimes casting it into one of those dark holes made by a twisted root or overhanging bank, in which the large trout are apt to lurk. In the meanwhile he was giving instructions to his two disciples; showing them the manner in which they should handle their rods, fix their flies, and play them along the surface of the stream. The scene brought to my mind the instructions of the sage Piscator to his scholar. The country around was of that pastoral kind which Walton is fond of describing. It was a part of the great plain of Cheshire, close by the beautiful vale of Gessford, and just where the inferior Welsh hills begin to swell up from among fresh sweet smelling meadows. The day, too, like that recorded in his work, was mild and sunshiny; with now and then a soft dropping shower, that sowed the whole earth with diamonds.

I soon fell into conversation with the old angler, and was so much entertained, that, under pretext of receiving instructions in his art, I kept company with him almost the whole day; wandering along the banks of the stream, and listening to his talk. He was very communicative, having all the easy garrulity of cheerful old age; and I fancy was a little flattered by having an opportunity of displaying his piscatory lore; for who does not like now and then to play the sage?

He had been much of a rambler in his day; and had passed some years of his youth in America, particularly in Savannah, where he had entered into trade and had been ruined by the indiscretion of a partner. He had afterwards experienced many ups and downs in life, until he got into the navy, where his leg was carried away by a cannon ball, at the battle of Camperdown. This was the only stroke of real good fortune he had ever experienced, for it got him a pension, which, together with some small paternal property, brought him in a revenue of nearly forty pounds. On this he retired to his native village, where he lived quietly and independently, and devoted the remainder of his life to the "noble art of angling."

I found that he had read Izaak Walton attentively, and he seemed to have imbibed all his simple frankness and prevalent good humour. Though he had been sorely buffeted about the world, he was satisfied that the world, in itself, was good and beautiful. Though he had been as roughly used in different countries as a poor sheep, that is fleeced by every hedge and thicket, yet he spoke of every nation with candour and kindness, appearing to look only on the good side of things; and above all, he was almost the only man I had ever met with, who had been an unfortunate adventurer in America, and had honesty and magnanimity enough, to take the fault to his own door, and not to curse the country. The lad that was receiving his instructions I learnt was the son and heir apparent of a fat old widow who kept the village inn, and of course a youth of some expectation, and much courted by the idle, gentleman like personages of the place. In taking him under his care, therefore, the old man had probably an eye to a privileged corner in the tap room, and an occasional cup of cheerful ale free of expense.

There is certainly something in angling, if we could forget, which anglers are apt to do, the cruelties and tortures inflicted on worms and insects, that tends to produce a gentleness of spirit, and a pure serenity of mind. As the English are methodical even in their recreations, and are the most scientific of sportsmen, it has been reduced among them to perfect rule and system. Indeed it is an amusement peculiarly adapted to the mild and highly cultivated scenery of England, where every roughness has been softened away from the landscape. It is delightful to saunter along those limpid streams which wander, like veins of silver, through the bosom of this beautiful country; leading one through a diversity of small home scenery; sometimes winding through ornamented grounds; sometimes brimming along through rich pasturage, where the fresh green is mingled with sweet smelling flowers; sometimes venturing in sight of villages and hamlets; and then running capriciously away into shady retirements. The sweetness and serenity of nature, and the quiet watchfulness of the sport, gradually bring on pleasant fits of musing; which are now and then agreeably interrupted by the song of a bird; the distant whistle of the pheasant; or perhaps the vagary of some fish, leaping out of the still water, and skimming transiently about its glassy surface. "When I would beget content," says Izaak Walton, "and increase confidence in the power and wisdom and providence of Almighty God, I will walk the meadows by some gliding stream, and there contemplate the lilies that take no care, and those very many other little living creatures that are not only created, but fed (man knows not how) by the goodness of the God of nature, and therefore trust in him."

I cannot forbear to give another quotation from one of those ancient champions of angling which breathes the same innocent and happy spirit:

Let me live harmlessly, and near the brink
  Of Trent or Avon have a dwelling-place;
Where I may see my quill, or cork, down sink,
  With eager bite of pike, or bleak, or dace;
And on the world and my creator think:
  Whilst some men strive ill-gotten goods t' embrace;
And others spend their time in base excess
  Of wine, or worse, in war or wantonness.

Let them that will, these pastimes still pursue,
  And on such pleasing fancies feed their fill;
So I the fields and meadows green may view
  And daily by fresh rivers walk at will,
Among the daisies and the violets blue,
  Red hyacinth and yellow daffodil.*

On parting with the old angler I inquired after his place of abode, and happening to be in the neighbourhood of the village a few evenings afterwards, I had the curiosity to seek him out. I found him living in a small cottage, containing only one room, but a perfect curiosity in its method and arrangement. It was on the skirts of the village, on a green bank, a little back from the road, with a small garden in front, stocked with kitchen herbs, and adorned with a few flowers. The whole front of the cottage was overrun with a honeysuckle. On the top was a ship for a weathercock. The interior was fitted up in a truly nautical style, his ideas of comfort and convenience having been acquired on the birth deck of a man of war. A hammock was slung from the ceiling, which, in the day time was lashed up so as to take but little room. From the centre of the chamber hung a model of a ship of his own workmanship. Two or three chairs, a table, and a large sea chest, formed the principal moveables. About the walls were stuck up naval ballads, such as Admiral Hosier's Ghost, All in the Downs, and Tom Bowling, intermingled with pictures of sea fights, among which the battle of Camperdown held a distinguished place. The mantle piece was decorated with sea shells; over which hung a quadrant, flanked by two woodcuts of most bitter looking naval commanders. His implements for angling were carefully disposed on nails and hooks about the room. On a shelf was arranged his library, containing a work on angling, much worn; a bible covered with canvass; an odd volume or two of voyages; a nautical almanack; and a book of songs.

*J. Davors.

His family consisted of a large black cat with one eye, and a parrot which he had caught and tamed, and educated himself, in the course of one of his voyages; and which uttered a variety of sea phrases with the hoarse brattling tone of a veteran boatswain. The establishment reminded me of that of the renowned Robinson Crusoe;—it was kept in neat order, every thing being "stowed away" with the regularity of a ship of war; and he informed me that he "scowred the deck every morning, and swept it between meals."

I found him seated on a bench before the door, smoking his pipe in the soft evening sunshine. His cat was purring soberly on the threshold, and his parrot describing some strange evolutions in an iron ring that swung in the centre of his cage. He had been angling all day, and gave me a history of his sport with as much minuteness as a general would talk over a campaign; being particularly animated in relating the manner in which he had taken a large trout, which had completely tasked all his skill and wariness, and which he had sent as a trophy to mine hostess of the Inn.

How comforting it is to see a cheerful and contented old age; and to behold a poor fellow, like this, after being tempest tost through life, safely moored in a snug and quiet harbour in the evening of his days. His happiness, however, sprung from within himself, and was independent of external circumstances; for he had that inexhaustible good nature, which is the most precious gift of heaven; spreading itself like oil over the troubled sea of thought, and keeping the mind smooth and equable in the roughest weather.

On inquiring further about him, I learnt that he was a universal favourite in the village, and the oracle of the tap room; where he delighted the rustics with his songs, and, like Sindbad, astonished them with his stories of strange lands, and shipwrecks, and sea fights. He was much noticed too by gentlemen sportsmen of the neighbourhood; had taught several of them the art of angling; and was a privileged visitor to their kitchens. The whole tenor of his life was quiet and inoffensive, being principally passed about the neighbouring streams when the weather and season were favourable; at other times he employed himself at home, preparing his fishing tackle for the next campaign, or manufacturing rods, nets, and flies for his patrons and pupils among the gentry.

He was a regular attendant at church on Sundays, though he generally fell asleep during the sermon. He had made it his particular request that when he died he should be buried in a green spot, which he could see from his seat in church, and which he had marked out ever since he was a boy, and had thought of when far from home on the raging sea, in danger of being food for the fishes—it was the spot where his father and mother had been buried.

I have done, for I fear that my reader is growing weary; but I could not refrain from drawing the picture of this worthy "brother of the angle;" who has made me more than ever in love with the theory, though I fear I shall never be adroit in the practice of his art: and I will conclude this rambling sketch, in the words of honest Izaak Walton, by craving the blessing of St. Peter's master upon my reader, "and upon all that are true lovers of virtue; and dare trust in his providence; and be quiet; and go a angling."

THE
LEGEND OF SLEEPY HOLLOW

(Found among the Papers of the late Diedrich Knickerbocker)

> A pleasing land of drowsy head it was,
> Of dreams that wave before the half-shut eye;
> And of gay castles in the clouds that pass,
> Forever flushing round a summer sky.
>   CASTLE OF INDOLENCE.

In the bosom of one of those spacious coves which indent the eastern shore of the Hudson, at that broad expansion of the river denominated by the ancient Dutch navigators the Tappaan Zee, and where they always prudently shortened sail, and implored the protection of St. Nicholas when they crossed, there lies a small market town or rural port, which by some is called Greensburgh, but which is more generally and properly known by the name of Tarry Town. This name was given, we are told, in former days, by the good housewives of the adjacent country, from the inveterate propensity of their husbands to linger about the village tavern on market days. Be that as it may, I do not vouch for the fact, but merely advert to it, for the sake of being precise and authentic. Not far from this village, perhaps about two miles, there is a little valley, or rather lap of land among high hills, which is one of the quietest places in the whole world. A small brook glides through it, with just murmur enough to lull one to repose, and the occasional whistle of a quail, or tapping of a woodpecker, is almost the only sound that ever breaks in upon the uniform tranquillity.

I recollect that when a stripling, my first exploit in squirrel shooting was in a grove of tall walnut trees that shades one side of the valley. I had wandered into it at noon time, when all nature is peculiarly quiet, and was startled by the roar of my own gun, as it broke the sabbath stillness around, and was prolonged and reverberated by the angry echoes. If ever I should wish for a retreat, whither I might steal from the world and its distractions, and dream quietly away the remnant of a troubled life, I know of none more promising than this little valley.

From the listless repose of the place, and the peculiar character of its inhabitants, who are descendants from the original Dutch settlers, this sequestered glen has long been known by the name of SLEEPY HOLLOW, and its rustic lads are called the Sleepy Hollow Boys throughout all the neighbouring country. A drowsy, dreamy influence seems to hang over the land, and to pervade the very atmosphere. Some say that the place was bewitched by a high German doctor during the early days of the settlement; others, that an old Indian chief, the prophet or wizard of his tribe, held his powwows there before the country was discovered by Master Hendrick Hudson. Certain it is, the place still continues under the sway of some witching power, that holds a spell over the minds of the good people, causing them to walk in a continual reverie. They are given to all kinds of marvellous beliefs; are subject to trances and visions, and frequently see strange sights, and hear music and voices in the air. The whole neighbourhood abounds with local tales, haunted spots, and twilight superstitions; stars shoot and meteors glare oftener across the valley than in any other part of the country, and the night mare, with her whole nine fold, seems to make it the favourite scene of her gambols.

The dominant spirit, however, that haunts this enchanted region, and seems to be commander in chief of all the powers of the air, is the apparition of a figure on horseback without a head. It is said by some to be the ghost of a Hessian trooper, whose head had been carried away by a cannon ball, in some nameless battle during the revolutionary war, and who is ever and anon seen by the country folk, hurrying along in the gloom of night, as if on the wings of the wind. His haunts are not confined to the valley, but extend at times to the adjacent roads, and especially to the vicinity of a church at no great distance. Indeed, certain of the most authentic historians of those parts, who have been careful in collecting and collating the floating facts concerning this spectre, allege, that the body of the trooper having been buried in the church yard, the ghost rides forth to the scene of battle in nightly quest of his head, and that the rushing speed with which he sometimes passes along the hollow, like a midnight blast, is owing to his being belated, and in a hurry to get back to the church yard before day break.

Such is the general purport of this legendary superstition, which has furnished materials for many a wild story in that region of shadows; and the spectre is known, at all the country firesides, by the name of The Headless Horseman of Sleepy Hollow.

It is remarkable, that the visionary propensity I have mentioned is not confined to the native inhabitants of the valley, but is unconsciously imbibed by every one who resides there for a time. However wide awake they may have been before they entered that sleepy region, they are sure, in a little time, to inhale the witching influence of the air, and begin to grow imaginative—to dream dreams, and see apparitions.

I mention this peaceful spot with all possible laud; for it is in such little retired Dutch valleys, found here and there embosomed in the great state of New York, that population, manners, and customs, remain fixed, while the great torrent of migration and improvement, which is making such incessant changes in other parts of this restless country, sweeps by them unobserved. They are like those little nooks of still water, which border a rapid stream, where we may see the straw and bubble riding quietly at anchor, or slowly revolving in their mimic harbour, undisturbed by the rush of the passing current. Though many years have elapsed since I trod the drowsy shades of Sleepy Hollow, yet I question whether I should not still find the same trees and the same families vegetating in its sheltered bosom.

In this by place of nature there abode, in a remote period of American history, that is to say, some thirty years since, a worthy wight of the name of Ichabod Crane, who sojourned, or, as he expressed it, "tarried," in Sleepy Hollow, for the purpose of instructing the children of the vicinity. He was a native of Connecticut, a state which supplies the Union with pioneers for the mind as well as for the forest, and sends forth yearly its legions of frontier woodmen and country schoolmasters. The cognomen of Crane was not inapplicable to his person. He was tall, but exceedingly lank, with narrow shoulders, long arms and legs, hands that dangled a mile out of his sleeves, feet that might have served for shovels, and his whole frame most loosely hung together. His head was small, and flat at top, with huge ears, large green glassy eyes, and a long snipe nose, so that it looked like a weathercock perched upon his spindle neck, to tell which way the wind blew. To see him striding along the profile of a hill on a windy day, with his clothes bagging and fluttering about him, one might have mistaken him for the genius of famine descending upon the earth, or some scarecrow eloped from a cornfield.

His school house was a low building of one large room, rudely constructed of logs; the windows partly glazed, and partly patched with leaves of old copy books. It was most ingeniously secured at vacant hours, by a withe twisted in the handle of the door, and stakes set against the window shutters; so that though a thief might get in with perfect ease, he would find some embarrassment in getting out; an idea most probably borrowed by the architect, Yost Van Houten, from the mystery of an eelpot. The school house stood in a rather lonely but pleasant situation, just at the foot of a woody hill, with a brook running close by, and a formidable birch tree growing at one end of it. From hence the low murmur of his pupils' voices conning over their lessons, might be heard of a drowsy summer's day, like the hum of a bee hive; interrupted now and then by the authoritative voice of the master, in the tone of menace or command, or peradventure, by the appalling sound of the birch, as he urged some tardy loiterer along the flowery path of knowledge. Truth to say, he was a conscientious man, and ever bore in mind the golden maxim, "spare the rod and spoil the child."—Ichabod Crane's scholars certainly were not spoiled.

I would not have it imagined, however, that he was one of those cruel potentates of the school, who joy in the smart of their subjects; on the contrary, he administered justice with discrimination rather than severity; taking the burthen off the backs of the weak, and laying it on those of the strong. Your mere puny stripling, that winced at the least flourish of the rod, was passed by with indulgence; but the claims of justice were satisfied, by inflicting a double portion on some little, tough, wrong headed, broad skirted Dutch urchin, who sulked and swelled and grew dogged and sullen beneath the birch. All this he called "doing his duty by their parents;" and he never inflicted a chastisement without following it by the assurance, so consolatory to the smarting urchin, that "he would remember it and thank him for it the longest day he had to live."

When school hours were over, he was even the companion and playmate of the larger boys; and on holyday afternoons would convoy some of the smaller ones home, who happened to have pretty sisters, or good housewives for mothers, noted for the comforts of the cupboard. Indeed, it behooved him to keep on good terms with his pupils. The revenue arising from his school was small, and would have been scarcely sufficient to furnish him with daily bread, for he was a huge feeder, and though lank, had the dilating powers of an Anaconda; but to help out his maintenance, he was, according to country custom in those parts, boarded and lodged at the houses of the farmers, whose children he instructed. With these he lived successively a week at a time, thus going the rounds of the neighbourhood, with all his worldly effects tied up in a cotton handkerchief.

That all this might not be too onerous on the purses of his rustic patrons, who are apt to consider the costs of schooling a grievous burthen, and schoolmasters as mere drones, he had various ways of rendering himself both useful and agreeable. He assisted the farmers occasionally in the lighter labours of their farms, helped to make hay, mended the fences, took the horses to water, drove the cows from pasture, and cut wood for the winter fire. He laid aside, too, all the dominant dignity and absolute sway, with which he lorded it in his little empire, the school, and became wonderfully gentle and in-

gratiating. He found favour in the eyes of the mothers, by petting
the children, particularly the youngest, and like the lion bold, which
whilome so magnanimously the lamb did hold, he would sit with a
child on one knee, and rock a cradle with his foot, for whole hours
together.

In addition to his other vocations, he was the singing master of
the neighbourhood, and picked up many bright shillings by instructing
the young folks in psalmody. It was a matter of no little vanity to
him on Sundays, to take his station in front of the church gallery,
with a band of chosen singers; where, in his own mind, he completely
carried away the palm from the parson. Certain it is, his voice resounded far above all the rest of the congregation, and there are
peculiar quavers still to be heard in that church, and which may even
be heard half a mile off, quite to the opposite side of the mill pond,
of a still Sunday morning, which are said to be legitimately descended
from the nose of Ichabod Crane. Thus, by diverse little make shifts,
in that ingenious way which is commonly denominated "by hook and
by crook," the worthy pedagogue got on tolerably enough, and was
thought, by all who understood nothing of the labour of headwork,
to have a wonderfully easy life of it.

The schoolmaster is generally a man of some importance in the
female circle of a rural neighbourhood, being considered a kind of
idle gentleman like personage, of vastly superior taste and accomplishments to the rough country swains, and, indeed, inferior in learning
only to the parson. His appearance, therefore, is apt to occasion some
little stir at the tea table of a farm house, and the addition of a super-
numerary dish of cakes or sweetmeats, or, peradventure, the parade
of a silver tea pot. Our man of letters, therefore, was peculiarly happy
in the smiles of all the country damsels. How he would figure among
them in the church yard, between services on Sundays; gathering
grapes for them from the wild vines that overrun the surrounding trees;
reciting for their amusement all the epitaphs on the tombstones, or
sauntering, with a whole bevy of them, along the banks of the adjacent
mill pond; while the more bashful country bumpkins hung sheepishly
back, envying his superior elegance and address.

From his half itinerant life, also, he was a kind of travelling gazette,
carrying the whole budget of local gossip from house to house; so
that his appearance was always greeted with satisfaction. He was,
moreover, esteemed by the women as a man of great erudition, for
he had read several books quite through, and was a perfect master
of Cotton Mather's History of New England Witchcraft, in which, by
the way, he most firmly and potently believed.

He was, in fact, an odd mixture of small shrewdness and simple credulity. His appetite for the marvellous, and his powers of digesting it, were equally extraordinary; and both had been increased by his residence in this spell bound region. No tale was too gross or monstrous for his capacious swallow. It was often his delight, after his school was dismissed of an afternoon, to stretch himself on the rich bed of clover, bordering the little brook that whimpered by his school house, and there con over old Mather's direful tales, until the gathering dusk of evening made the printed page a mere mist before his eyes. Then, as he wended his way, by swamp and stream and awful woodland, to the farm house where he happened to be quartered, every sound of nature, at that witching hour, fluttered his excited imagination: the moan of the whip-poor-will* from the hill side; the boding cry of the tree toad, that harbinger of storm; the dreary hooting of the screech owl; or the sudden rustling in the thicket, of birds frightened from their roost. The fire flies, too, which sparkled most vividly in the darkest places, now and then startled him, as one of uncommon brightness would stream across his path; and if, by chance, a huge blockhead of a beetle came winging his blundering flight against him, the poor varlet was ready to give up the ghost, with the idea that he was struck with a witch's token. His only resource on such occasions, either to drown thought, or drive away evil spirits, was to sing psalm tunes;— and the good people of Sleepy Hollow, as they sat by their doors of an evening, were often filled with awe, at hearing his nasal melody, "in linked sweetness long drawn out," floating from the distant hill, or along the dusky road.

Another of his sources of fearful pleasure was, to pass long winter evenings with the old Dutch wives, as they sat spinning by the fire, with a row of apples roasting and sputtering along the hearth, and listen to their marvellous tales of ghosts and goblins, and haunted fields and haunted brooks, and haunted bridges and haunted houses, and particularly of the headless horseman, or galloping Hessian of the Hollow, as they sometimes called him. He would delight them equally by his anecdotes of witchcraft, and of the direful omens and portentous sights and sounds in the air, which prevailed in the earlier times of Connecticut; and would frighten them wofully with speculations upon comets and shooting stars, and with the alarming fact that the world did absolutely turn round, and that they were half the time topsy-turvy!

*The whip-poor-will is a bird which is only heard at night. It receives its name from its note which is thought to resemble those words.

But if there was a pleasure in all this, while snugly cuddling in the chimney corner of a chamber that was all of a ruddy glow from the crackling wood fire, and where, of course, no spectre dared to show its face, it was dearly purchased by the terrors of his subsequent walk homewards. What fearful shapes and shadows beset his path, amidst the dim and ghastly glare of a snowy night!—With what wistful look did he eye every trembling ray of light streaming across the waste fields from some distant window!—How often was he appalled by some shrub covered with snow, which like a sheeted spectre beset his very path!—How often did he shrink with curdling awe at the sound of his own steps on the frosty crust beneath his feet; and dread to look over his shoulder, lest he should behold some uncouth being tramping close behind him!—and how often was he thrown into complete dismay by some rushing blast, howling among the trees, in the idea that it was the gallopping Hessian on one of his nightly scourings.

All these, however, were mere terrors of the night, phantoms of the mind, that walk in darkness; and though he had seen many spectres in his time, and been more than once beset by Satan in diverse shapes, in his lonely perambulations, yet daylight put an end to all these evils; and he would have passed a pleasant life of it, in despite of the Devil and all his works, if his path had not been crossed by a being that causes more perplexity to mortal man, than ghosts, goblins, and the whole race of witches put together, and that was—a woman.

Among the musical disciples who assembled, one evening in each week, to receive his instructions in psalmody, was Katrina Van Tassel, the daughter and only child of a substantial Dutch farmer. She was a blooming lass of fresh eighteen; plump as a partridge; ripe and melting and rosy cheeked as one of her father's peaches, and universally famed, not merely for her beauty, but her vast expectations. She was withal a little of a coquette, as might be perceived even in her dress, which was a mixture of ancient and modern fashions, as most suited to set off her charms. She wore the ornaments of pure yellow gold, which her great great grandmother had brought over from Saardam; the tempting stomacher of the olden time, and withal a provokingly short petticoat, to display the prettiest foot and ankle in the country round.

Ichabod Crane had a soft and foolish heart toward the sex; and it is not to be wondered at, that so tempting a morsel soon found favour in his eyes, more especially after he had visited her in her paternal mansion. Old Baltus Van Tassel was a perfect picture of a thriving, contented, liberal hearted farmer. He seldom, it is true, sent either his eyes or his thoughts beyond the boundaries of his own farm; but within those every thing was snug, happy, and well conditioned. He was satisfied with his wealth, but not proud of it, and piqued himself upon the hearty abundance, rather than the style in which he lived. His strong hold was situated on the banks of the Hudson, in one of those green, sheltered, fertile nooks, in which the Dutch farmers are so fond of nestling. A great elm tree spread its broad branches over it, at the foot of which bubbled up a spring of the softest and sweetest water, in a little well, formed of a barrel, and then stole sparkling away through the grass, to a neighbouring brook, that babbled along among elders and dwarf willows. Hard by the farm house was a vast barn, that might have served for a church; every window and crevice of which seemed bursting forth with the treasures of the farm; the flail was busily resounding within it from morning to night; swallows and martins skimmed twittering about the eaves, and rows of pigeons, some with one eye turned up, as if watching the weather, some with their heads under their wings, or buried in their bosoms, and others, swelling, and cooing, and bowing about their dames, were enjoying the sunshine on the roof. Sleek unwieldy porkers were grunting in the repose and abundance of their pens, from whence sallied forth, now and then, troops of sucking pigs, as if to snuff the air. A stately squadron of snowy geese were riding in an adjoining pond, convoying whole fleets of ducks; regiments of turkeys were gobbling through the farm yard, and guinea fowls fretting about it like ill tempered house-wives, with their peevish discontented cry. Before the barn door strutted the gallant cock, that pattern of a husband, a warrior, and a fine gentleman, clapping his burnished wings, and crowing in the pride and gladness of his heart—sometimes tearing up the earth with his feet, and then generously calling his ever hungry family of wives and children to enjoy the rich morsel which he had discovered.

The pedagogue's mouth watered, as he looked upon this sumptuous promise of luxurious winter fare. In his devouring mind's eye, he pictured to himself every roasting pig running about with a pudding in his belly, and an apple in his mouth; the pigeons were snugly put to bed in a comfortable pie, and tucked in with a coverlet of crust; the geese were swimming in their own gravy; and the ducks pairing cosily in dishes, like snug married couples, with a decent competency of onion sauce; in the porkers he saw carved out the future sleek side of bacon, and juicy relishing ham; not a turkey, but he beheld daintily trussed up, with its gizzard under its wing, and, peradventure, a necklace of savoury sausages; and even bright chanticleer himself lay sprawling on his back, in a side dish, with uplifted claws, as if craving that quarter, which his chivalrous spirit disdained to ask while living.

As the enraptured Ichabod fancied all this, and as he rolled his great green eyes over the fat meadow lands, the rich fields of wheat, of rye, of buckwheat, and Indian corn, and the orchards burthened with ruddy fruit, which surrounded the warm tenement of Van Tassel, his heart yearned after the damsel who was to inherit these domains, and his imagination expanded with the idea, how they might be readily turned into cash, and the money invested in immense tracts of wild land, and shingle palaces in the wilderness. Nay, his busy fancy already realized his hopes, and presented to him the blooming Katrina, with a whole family of children, mounted on the top of a waggon loaded with household trumpery, with pots and kettles dangling beneath; and he beheld himself bestriding a pacing mare, with a colt at her heels, setting out for Kentucky, Tennessee, or the Lord knows where!

When he entered the house, the conquest of his heart was complete. It was one of those spacious farm houses, with high ridged, but lowly sloping roofs, built in the style handed down from the first Dutch settlers. The low, projecting eaves formed a piazza along the front, capable of being closed up in bad weather. Under this were hung flails, harness, various utensils of husbandry, and nets for fishing in the neighbouring river. Benches were built along the sides for summer use; and a great spinning wheel at one end, and a churn at the other, showed the various uses to which this important porch might be devoted. From this piazza the wondering Ichabod entered the hall, which formed the centre of the mansion, and the place of usual residence. Here, rows of resplendent pewter, ranged on a long dresser, dazzled his eyes. In one corner stood a huge bag of wool ready to be spun; in another a quantity of linsey-woolsey just from the loom; ears of Indian corn, and strings of dried apples and peaches, hung in gay festoons along the walls, mingled with the gaud of red peppers; and a door left ajar, gave him a peep into the best parlour, where the claw footed chairs, and dark mahogany tables, shone like mirrors; andirons, with their accompanying shovel and tongs, glistened from their covert of asparagus tops; mock oranges and conch shells decorated the mantle-piece; strings of various coloured birds' eggs were suspended above it; a great ostrich egg was hung from the centre of the room, and a corner cupboard, knowingly left open, displayed immense treasures of old silver and well mended china.

From the moment Ichabod laid his eyes upon these regions of delight, the peace of his mind was at an end, and his only study was how to gain the affections of the peerless daughter of Van Tassel. In this enterprize, however, he had more real difficulties than generally fell to the lot of a knight errant of yore, who seldom had any thing but giants, enchanters, fiery dragons, and such like easily conquered adversaries, to contend with; and had to make his way merely through gates of iron and brass, and walls of adamant, to the castle keep, where the lady of his heart was confined; all which he achieved as easily as a man would carve his way to the centre of a Christmas pie, and then the lady gave him her hand as a matter of course. Ichabod, on the contrary, had to win his way to the heart of a country coquette, beset with a labyrinth of whims and caprices, which were for ever presenting new difficulties and impediments, and he had to encounter a host of fearful adversaries of real flesh and blood, the numerous rustic admirers, who beset every portal to her heart, keeping a watchful and angry eye upon each other, but ready to fly out in the common cause against any new competitor.

Among these, the most formidable, was a burly, roaring, roystering blade, of the name of Abraham, or, according to the Dutch abbreviation, Brom Van Brunt, the hero of the country round, which rung with his feats of strength and hardihood. He was broad shouldered and double jointed, with short curly black hair, and a bluff, but not un-pleasant countenance, having a mingled air of fun and arrogance. From his Herculean frame and great powers of limb, he had received the nick name of BROM BONES, by which he was universally known. He was famed for great knowledge and skill in horsemanship, being as dexterous on horseback as a Tartar. He was foremost at all races and cock fights, and with the ascendancy which bodily strength acquires in rustic life, was the umpire in all disputes, setting his hat on one side, and giving his decisions with an air and tone admitting of no gainsay or appeal. He was always ready for either a fight or a frolick; but had more mischief than ill will in his composition; and with all his overbearing roughness, there was a strong dash of waggish good humour at bottom. He had three or four boon companions, who re-garded him as their model, and at the head of whom he scoured the country, attending every scene of feud or merriment for miles round. In cold weather he was distinguished by a fur cap, surmounted with a flaunting fox's tail, and when the folks at a country gathering descried this well known crest at a distance, whisking about among a squad of hard riders, they always stood by for a squall. Sometimes his crew would be heard dashing along past the farm houses at mid-night, with whoop and halloo, like a troop of Don Cossacks, and the old dames, startled out of their sleep, would listen for a moment till the hurry scurry had clattered by, and then exclaim, "aye, there goes Brom Bones and his gang!" The neighbours looked upon him with a mixture of awe, admiration, and good will; and when any mad cap prank, or rustic brawl, occurred in the vicinity, always shook their heads, and warranted Brom Bones was at the bottom of it.

This rantipole hero had for some time singled out the blooming Katrina for the object of his uncouth gallantries, and though his amorous toyings were something like the gentle caresses and endearments of a bear, yet it was whispered that she did not altogether discourage his hopes. Certain it is, his advances were signals for rival candidates to retire, who felt no inclination to cross a lion in his amours; insomuch, that when his horse was seen tied to Van Tassel's paling, of a Sunday night, (a sure sign that his master was courting, or, as it is termed, "sparking," within,) all other suitors passed by in despair, and carried the war into other quarters.

Such was the formidable rival with whom Ichabod Crane had to contend, and, considering all things, a stouter man than he would have shrunk from the competition, and a wiser man would have despaired. He had, however, a happy mixture of pliability and perseverance in his nature; he was in form and spirit like a supple jack—yielding, but tough; though he bent, he never broke; and though he bowed beneath the slightest pressure, yet, the moment it was away—jerk!—he was as erect, and carried his head as high as ever.

To have taken the field openly against his rival, would have been madness; for he was not a man to be thwarted in his amours, any more than that stormy lover, Achilles. Ichabod, therefore, made his advances in a quiet and gently insinuating manner. Under cover of his character of singing master, he made frequent visits at the farm house; not that he had any thing to apprehend from the meddlesome interference of parents, which is so often a stumbling block in the path of lovers. Balt Van Tassel was an easy indulgent soul; he loved his daughter better even than his pipe, and like a reasonable man, and an excellent father, let her have her way in every thing. His notable little wife too, had enough to do to attend to her housekeeping and manage her poultry, for, as she sagely observed, ducks and geese are foolish things, and must be looked after, but girls can take care of themselves. Thus while the busy dame bustled about the house, or plied her spinning wheel at one end of the piazza, honest Balt would sit smoking his evening pipe at the other, watching the achievements of a little wooden warrior, who, armed with a sword in each hand, was most valiantly fighting the wind on the pinnacle of the barn. In the mean time, Ichabod would carry on his suit with the daughter by the side of the spring under the great elm, or sauntering along in the twilight, that hour so favourable to the lover's eloquence.

I profess not to know how women's hearts are wooed and won. To me they have always been matters of riddle and admiration. Some seem to have but one vulnerable point, or door of access; while others have a thousand avenues, and may be captured in a thousand different ways. It is a great triumph of skill to gain the former, but a still greater proof of generalship to maintain possession of the latter, for a man must battle for his fortress at every door and window. He who wins a thousand common hearts, is therefore entitled to some renown; but he who keeps undisputed sway over the heart of a coquette, is indeed a hero. Certain it is, this was not the case with the redoutable Brom Bones; and from the moment Ichabod Crane made his advances, the interests of the former evidently declined; his horse was no longer seen tied at the palings on Sunday nights, and a deadly feud gradually arose between him and the preceptor of Sleepy Hollow.

Brom, who had a degree of rough chivalry in his nature, would fain have carried matters to open warfare, and have settled their pretensions to the lady, according to the mode of those most concise and simple reasoners, the knights errant of yore—by single combat; but Ichabod was too conscious of the superior might of his adversary to enter the lists against him; he had overheard a boast of Bones, that he would "double the schoolmaster up, and lay him on a shelf of his own school house;" and he was too wary to give him an opportunity. There was something extremely provoking in this obstinately pacific system; it left Brom no alternative but to draw upon the funds of rustic waggery in his disposition, and to play off boorish practical jokes upon his rival. Ichabod became the object of whimsical persecution to Bones, and his gang of rough riders. They harried his hitherto peaceful domains; smoked out his singing school, by stopping up the chimney; broke into the school house at night, in spite of its formidable fastenings of withe and window stakes, and turned every thing topsy-turvy, so that the poor schoolmaster began to think all the witches in the country held their meetings there. But what was still more annoying, Brom took all opportunities of turning him into ridicule in presence of his mistress, and had a scoundrel dog, whom he taught to whine in the most ludicrous manner, and introduced as a rival of Ichabod's, to instruct her in psalmody.

In this way, matters went on for some time, without producing any material effect on the relative situations of the contending powers. On a fine autumnal afternoon, Ichabod, in pensive mood, sat enthroned on the lofty stool from whence he usually watched all the concerns of his little literary realm. In his hand he swayed a ferule, that sceptre of despotic power; the birch of justice reposed on three nails, behind the throne, a constant terror to evil doers; while on the desk before him might be seen sundry contraband articles and prohibited weapons, detected upon the persons of idle urchins, such as half munched apples, popguns, whirligigs, fly cages, and whole legions of rampant little paper game cocks. Apparently there had been some appalling act of justice recently inflicted, for his scholars were all busily intent upon their books, or slyly whispering behind them with one eye kept upon the master; and a kind of buzzing stillness reigned throughout the school room. It was suddenly interrupted by the appearance of a negro in tow cloth jacket and trowsers, a round crowned fragment of a hat, like the cap of Mercury, and mounted on the back of a ragged, wild, half broken colt, which he managed with a rope by way of halter. He came clattering up to the school door with an invitation to Ichabod to attend a merry making, or "quilting frolick," to be held that evening at Mynheer Van Tassel's, and having delivered his message with that air of importance, and effort at fine language, which a negro is apt to display on petty embassies of the kind, he dashed over the brook, and was seen scampering away up the hollow, full of the importance and hurry of his mission.

All was now bustle and hubbub in the late quiet school room. The scholars were hurried through their lessons, without stopping at trifles; those who were nimble, skipped over half with impunity, and those who were tardy, had a smart application now and then in the rear, to quicken their speed, or help them over a tall word. Books were flung aside, without being put away on the shelves; inkstands were overturned, benches thrown down, and the whole school was turned loose an hour before the usual time; bursting forth like a legion of young imps, yelping and racketing about the green, in joy at their early emancipation.

The gallant Ichabod now spent at least an extra half hour at his toilet, brushing and furbishing up his best, and indeed only suit of rusty black, and arranging his looks by a bit of broken looking glass, that hung up in the school house. That he might make his appearance before his mistress in the true style of a cavalier, he borrowed a horse from the farmer with whom he was domiciliated, a choleric old Dutchman, of the name of Hans Van Ripper, and thus gallantly mounted, issued forth like a knight errant in quest of adventures. But it is meet I should, in the true spirit of romantic story, give some account of the looks and equipments of my hero and his steed. The animal he bestrode was a broken down plough horse, that had outlived almost every thing but his viciousness. He was gaunt and shagged, with a ewe neck and a head like a hammer; his rusty mane and tail were tangled and knotted with burrs; one eye had lost its pupil, and was glaring and spectral, but the other had the gleam of a genuine devil in it. Still he must have had fire and mettle in his day, if we may judge from the name he bore of Gunpowder. He had, in fact, been a favourite steed of his master's, the cholerick Van Ripper, who was a furious rider, and had infused, very probably, some of his own spirit into the animal, for, old and broken down as he looked, there was more of the lurking devil in him than in any young filly in the country.

Ichabod was a suitable figure for such a steed. He rode with short stirrups, which brought his knees nearly up to the pommel of the saddle; his sharp elbows stuck out like grasshoppers'; he carried his whip perpendicularly in his hand, like a sceptre, and as his horse jogged on, the motion of his arms was not unlike the flapping of a pair of wings. A small wool hat rested on the top of his nose, for so his scanty strip of forehead might be called, and the skirts of his black coat fluttered out almost to the horse's tail. Such was the appearance of Ichabod and his steed, as they shambled out of the gate of Hans Van Ripper, and it was altogether such an apparition as is seldom to be met with in broad day light.

It was, as I have said, a fine autumnal day, the sky was clear and serene, and nature wore that rich and golden livery which we always associate with the idea of abundance. The forests had put on their sober brown and yellow, while some trees of the tenderer kind had been nipped by the frosts into brilliant dyes of orange, purple, and scarlet. Streaming files of wild ducks began to make their appearance high in the air; the bark of the squirrel might be heard from the groves of beech and hickory nuts, and the pensive whistle of the quail at intervals from the neighbouring stubble field.

The small birds were taking their farewell banquets. In the fullness of their revelry, they fluttered, chirping and frolicking, from bush to bush, and tree to tree, capricious from the very profusion and variety around them. There was the honest cock robin, the favourite game of stripling sportsmen, with its loud querulous note; and the twittering blackbirds flying in sable clouds; and the golden winged woodpecker, with his crimson crest, his broad black gorget, and splendid plumage; and the cedar bird, with its red tipt wings and yellow tipt tail, and its little monteiro cap of feathers; and the blue jay, that noisy coxcomb, in his gay light blue coat and white under clothes, screaming and chattering, nodding, and bobbing, and bowing, and pretending to be on good terms with every songster of the grove.

As Ichabod jogged slowly on his way, his eye, ever open to every symptom of culinary abundance, ranged with delight over the treasures of jolly autumn. On all sides he beheld vast store of apples, some hanging in oppressive opulence on the trees, some gathered into baskets and barrels for the market, others heaped up in rich piles for the cider press. Further on he beheld great fields of Indian corn, with its golden ears peeping from their leafy coverts, and holding out the promise of cakes and hasty pudding; and the yellow pumpkins lying beneath them, turning up their fair round bellies to the sun, and giving ample prospects of the most luxurious of pies; and anon he passed the fragrant buckwheat fields, breathing the odour of the bee hive, and as he beheld them, soft anticipations stole over his mind of dainty slap jacks, well buttered, and garnished with honey or treacle, by the delicate little dimpled hand of Katrina Van Tassel.

Thus feeding his mind with many sweet thoughts and "sugared suppositions," he journeyed along the sides of a range of hills which look out upon some of the goodliest scenes of the mighty Hudson. The sun gradually wheeled his broad disk down into the west. The wide bosom of the Tappaan Zee lay motionless and glassy, excepting that here and there a gentle undulation waved and prolonged the blue shadow of the distant mountain: a few amber clouds floated in the sky, without a breath of air to move them. The horizon was of a fine golden tint, changing gradually into a pure apple green, and from that into the deep blue of the mid-heaven. A slanting ray lingered on the woody crests of the precipices that overhung some parts of the river, giving greater depth to the dark grey and purple of their rocky sides. A sloop was loitering in the distance, dropping slowly down with the tide, her sail hanging uselessly against the mast, and as the reflection of the sky gleamed along the still water, it seemed as if the vessel was suspended in the air.

It was toward evening that Ichabod arrived at the castle of the Heer Van Tassel, which he found thronged with the pride and flower of the adjacent country. Old farmers, a spare, leathern faced race, in homespun coats and breeches, blue stockings, huge shoes and magnificent pewter buckles. Their brisk withered little dames in close crimped caps, long waisted short gowns, homespun petticoats, with scissors and pincushions, and gay calico pockets, hanging on the outside. Buxom lasses, almost as antiquated as their mothers, excepting where a straw hat, a fine ribband, or perhaps a white frock, gave symptoms of city innovation. The sons, in short square skirted coats with rows of stupendous brass buttons, and their hair generally queued in the fashion of the times, especially if they could procure an eel skin for the purpose, it being esteemed throughout the country as a potent nourisher and strengthener of the hair.

Brom Bones, however, was the hero of the scene, having come to the gathering on his favourite steed Daredevil, a creature, like himself, full of mettle and mischief, and which no one but himself could manage. He was in fact noted for preferring vicious animals, given to all kinds of tricks, which kept the rider in constant risk of his neck, for he held a tractable well broken horse as unworthy of a lad of spirit.

Fain would I pause to dwell upon the world of charms that burst upon the enraptured gaze of my hero, as he entered the state parlour of Van Tassel's mansion. Not those of the bevy of buxom lasses, with their luxurious display of red and white: but the ample charms of a genuine Dutch country tea table, in the sumptuous time of autumn. Such heaped up platters of cakes of various and almost indescribable kinds, known only to experienced Dutch housewives. There was the doughty dough nut, the tenderer oly koek, and the crisp and crumbling cruller; sweet cakes and short cakes, ginger cakes and honey cakes, and the whole family of cakes. And then there were apple pies and peach pies and pumpkin pies; besides slices of ham and smoked beef; and moreover delectable dishes of preserved plums, and peaches, and pears, and quinces; not to mention broiled shad and roasted chickens; together with bowls of milk and cream, all mingled higgledy-piggledy, pretty much as I have enumerated them, with the motherly tea pot sending up its clouds of vapour from the midst—Heaven bless the mark! I want breath and time to discuss this banquet as it deserves, and am too eager to get on with my story. Happily, Ichabod Crane was not in so great a hurry as his historian, but did ample justice to every dainty.

He was a kind and thankful creature, whose heart dilated in proportion as his skin was filled with good cheer, and whose spirits rose with eating, as some men's do with drink. He could not help, too, rolling his large eyes round him as he ate, and chuckling with the possibility that he might one day be lord of all this scene of almost unimaginable luxury and splendour. Then, he thought, how soon he'd turn his back upon the old school house; snap his fingers in the face of Hans Van Ripper, and every other niggardly patron, and kick any itinerant pedagogue out of doors that should dare to call him comrade!

Old Baltus Van Tassel moved about among his guests with a face dilated with content and good humour, round and jolly as the harvest moon. His hospitable attentions were brief, but expressive, being confined to a shake of the hand, a slap on the shoulder, a loud laugh, and a pressing invitation to "fall to, and help themselves."

And now the sound of the music from the common room or hall, summoned to the dance. The musician was an old grey headed negro, who had been the itinerant orchestra of the neighbourhood for more than half a century. His instrument was as old and battered as himself. The greater part of the time he scraped away on two or three strings, accompanying every movement of the bow with a motion of the head; bowing almost to the ground, and stamping with his foot whenever a fresh couple were to start.

Ichabod prided himself upon his dancing as much as upon his vocal powers. Not a limb, not a fibre about him was idle, and to have seen his loosely hung frame in full motion, and clattering about the room, you would have thought Saint Vitus himself, that blessed patron of the dance, was figuring before you in person. He was the admiration of all the negroes, who, having gathered, of all ages and sizes, from the farm and the neighbourhood, stood forming a pyramid of shining black faces at every door and window, gazing with delight at the scene, rolling their white eye balls, and showing grinning rows of ivory from ear to ear. How could the flogger of urchins be otherwise than animated and joyous; the lady of his heart was his partner in the dance; and smiling graciously in reply to all his amorous oglings, while Brom Bones, sorely smitten with love and jealousy, sat brooding by himself in one corner.

When the dance was at an end, Ichabod was attracted to a knot of the sager folks, who, with old Van Tassel, sat smoking at one end of the piazza, gossipping over former times, and drawling out long stories about the war.

This neighbourhood, at the time of which I am speaking, was one of those highly favoured places which abound with chronicle and great men. The British and American line had run near it during the war; it had, therefore, been the scene of marauding, and been infested with refugees, cow boys, and all kinds of border chivalry. Just sufficient time had elapsed to enable each story teller to dress up his tale with a little becoming fiction, and in the indistinctness of his recollection, to make himself the hero of every exploit.

There was the story of Doffue Martling, a large, blue bearded Dutchman, who had nearly taken a British frigate with an old iron nine pounder from a mud breastwork, only that his gun burst at the sixth discharge. And there was an old gentleman who shall be nameless, being too rich a mynheer to be lightly mentioned, who in the battle of Whiteplains, being an excellent master of defence, parried a musket ball with a small sword, insomuch that he absolutely felt it whiz round the blade, and glance off at the hilt: in proof of which, he was ready at any time to show the sword, with the hilt a little bent. There were several more who had been equally great in the field, not one of whom but was persuaded that he had a considerable hand in bringing the war to a happy termination.

But all these were nothing to the tales of ghosts and apparitions that succeeded. The neighbourhood is rich in legendary treasures of the kind. Local tales and superstitions thrive best in these sheltered, long settled retreats; but are trampled under foot, by the shifting throng that forms the population of most of our country places. Besides, there is no encouragement for ghosts in most of our villages, for they have scarce had time to finish their first nap, and turn themselves in their graves, before their surviving friends have travelled away from the neighbourhood, so that when they turn out of a night to walk the rounds, they have no acquaintance left to call upon. This is perhaps the reason why we so seldom hear of ghosts except in our long established Dutch communities.

The immediate cause, however, of the prevalence of supernatural stories in these parts, was doubtless owing to the vicinity of Sleepy Hollow. There was a contagion in the very air that blew from that haunted region; it breathed forth an atmosphere of dreams and fancies infecting all the land. Several of the Sleepy Hollow people were present at Van Tassel's, and, as usual, were doling out their wild and wonderful legends. Many dismal tales were told about funeral trains, and mournful cries and wailings heard and seen about the great tree where the unfortunate Major André was taken, and which stood in the neighbourhood. Some mention was made also of the woman in white, that haunted the dark glen at Raven Rock, and was often heard to shriek on winter nights before a storm, having perished there in the snow. The chief part of the stories, however, turned upon the favourite spectre of Sleepy Hollow, the headless horseman, who had been heard several times of late, patroling the country; and it was said, tethered his horse nightly among the graves in the church yard.

The sequestered situation of this church seems always to have made it a favourite haunt of troubled spirits. It stands on a knoll, surrounded by locust trees and lofty elms, from among which its decent, whitewashed walls shine modestly forth, like Christian purity, beaming through the shades of retirement. A gentle slope descends from it to a silver sheet of water, bordered by high trees, between which, peeps may be caught at the blue hills of the Hudson. To look upon its grass grown yard, where the sunbeams seem to sleep so quietly, one would think that there at least the dead might rest in peace. On one side of the church extends a wide woody dell, along which raves a large brook among broken rocks and trunks of fallen trees. Over a deep black part of the stream, not far from the church, was formerly thrown a wooden bridge; the road that led to it, and the bridge itself, were thickly shaded by overhanging trees, which cast a gloom about it, even in the day time; but occasioned a fearful darkness at night. Such was one of the favourite haunts of the headless horseman, and the place where he was most frequently encountered. The tale was told of old Brouwer, a most heretical disbeliever in ghosts, how he met the horseman returning from his foray into Sleepy Hollow, and was obliged to get up behind him; how they gallopped over bush and brake, over hill and swamp, until they reached the bridge, when the horseman suddenly turned into a skeleton, threw old Brouwer into the brook, and sprang away over the tree tops with a clap of thunder.

This story was immediately matched by a thrice marvellous adventure of Brom Bones, who made light of the gallopping Hessian as an arrant jockey. He affirmed, that on returning one night from the neighbouring village of Sing-Sing, he had been overtaken by this midnight trooper; that he had offered to race with him for a bowl of punch, and should have won it too, for Daredevil beat the goblin horse all hollow, but just as they came to the church bridge, the Hessian bolted, and vanished in a flash of fire.

All these tales, told in that drowsy under tone with which men talk in the dark, the countenances of the listeners only now and then receiving a casual gleam from the glare of a pipe, sunk deep in the mind of Ichabod. He repaid them in kind with large extracts from his invaluable author, Cotton Mather, and added many very marvellous events that had taken place in his native state of Connecticut, and fearful sights which he had seen in his nightly walks about Sleepy Hollow.

The revel now gradually broke up. The old farmers gathered together their families in their wagons, and were heard for some time rattling along the hollow roads, and over the distant hills. Some of the damsels, mounted on pillions behind their favourite swains, and their light hearted laughter mingling with the clatter of hoofs, echoed along the silent woodlands, sounding fainter and fainter until they gradually died away—and the late scene of noise and frolick was all silent and deserted. Ichabod only lingered behind, according to the custom of country lovers, to have a tête-a-tête with the heiress; fully convinced that he was now on the high road to success. What passed at this interview I will not pretend to say, for in fact I do not know. Something, however, I fear me, must have gone wrong, for he certainly sallied forth, after no very great interval, with an air quite desolate and chopfallen—Oh these women! these women! Could that girl have

been playing off any of her coquettish tricks?—Was her encouragement
of the poor pedagogue all a mere sham to secure her conquest of his
rival?—Heaven only knows, not I!—Let it suffice to say, Ichabod stole
forth with the air of one who had been sacking a hen roost, rather
than a fair lady's heart. Without looking to the right or left to notice
the scene of rural wealth, on which he had so often gloated, he went
straight to the stable, and with several hearty cuffs and kicks, roused
his steed most uncourteously from the comfortable quarters in which
he was soundly sleeping, dreaming of mountains of corn and oats, and
whole valleys of timothy and clover.

It was the very witching time of night that Ichabod, heavy hearted
and crest fallen, pursued his travel homewards, along the sides of the
lofty hills which rise above Tarry Town, and which he had traversed
so cheerily in the afternoon. The hour was as dismal as himself. Far
below him the Tappaan Zee spread its dusky and indistinct waste of
waters, with here and there the tall mast of a sloop, riding quietly at
anchor under the land. In the dead hush of midnight, he could even
hear the barking of the watch dog from the opposite shore of the
Hudson; but it was so vague and faint as only to give an idea of his
distance from this faithful companion of man. Now and then, too, the
long drawn crowing of a cock, accidentally awakened, would sound
far, far off, from some farm house away among the hills—but it was
like a dreaming sound in his ear. No signs of life occurred near him,
but occasionally the melancholy chirp of a cricket, or perhaps the
guttural twang of a bull frog, from a neighbouring marsh, as if sleeping
uncomfortably, and turning suddenly in his bed.

All the stories of ghosts and goblins that he had heard in the afternoon, now came crowding upon his recollection. The night grew
darker and darker; the stars seemed to sink deeper in the sky, and
driving clouds occasionally hid them from his sight. He had never
felt so lonely and dismal. He was, moreover, approaching the very
place where many of the scenes of the ghost stories had been laid.
In the centre of the road stood an enormous tulip tree, which towered
like a giant above all the other trees of the neighbourhood, and formed
a kind of land mark. Its limbs were gnarled, and fantastic, large enough
to form trunks for ordinary trees, twisting down almost to the earth,
and rising again into the air. It was connected with the tragical story
of the unfortunate André, who had been taken prisoner hard by; and
was universally known by the name of Major André's tree. The common people regarded it with a mixture of respect and superstition,
partly out of sympathy for the fate of its ill starred namesake, and

partly from the tales of strange sights, and doleful lamentations, told concerning it.

As Ichabod approached this fearful tree, he began to whistle; he thought his whistle was answered: it was but a blast sweeping sharply through the dry branches. As he approached a little nearer, he thought he saw something white, hanging in the midst of the tree: he paused and ceased whistling; but on looking more narrowly, perceived that it was a place where the tree had been scathed by lightning, and the white wood laid bare. Suddenly he heard a groan—his teeth chattered, and his knees smote against the saddle: it was but the rubbing of one huge bough upon another, as they were swayed about by the breeze. He passed the tree in safety, but new perils lay before him.

About two hundred yards from the tree, a small brook crossed the road, and ran into a marshy and thickly wooded glen, known by the name of Wiley's Swamp. A few rough logs, laid side by side, served for a bridge over this stream. On that side of the road where the brook entered the wood, a group of oaks and chestnuts, matted thick with wild grape vines, threw a cavernous gloom over it. To pass this bridge, was the severest trial. It was at this identical spot that the unfortunate André was captured, and under the covert of those chestnuts and vines were the sturdy yeomen concealed who surprised him. This has ever since been considered a haunted stream, and fearful are the feelings of the schoolboy who has to pass it alone after dark.

As he approached the stream, his heart began to thump; he, however, summoned up all his resolution, gave his horse half a score of kicks in the ribs, and attempted to dash briskly across the bridge; but instead of starting forward, the perverse old animal made a lateral movement, and ran broadside against the fence. Ichabod, whose fears increased with the delay, jerked the reins on the other side, and kicked lustily with the contrary foot: it was all in vain; his steed started, it is true, but it was only to plunge to the opposite side of the road into a thicket of brambles and alder bushes. The schoolmaster now bestowed both whip and heel upon the starvelling ribs of old Gunpowder, who dashed forward, snuffling and snorting, but came to a stand just by the bridge with a suddenness that had nearly sent his rider sprawling over his head. Just at this moment a plashy tramp by the side of the bridge caught the sensitive ear of Ichabod. In the dark shadow of the grove, on the margin of the brook, he beheld something huge, misshapen, black and towering. It stirred not, but seemed gathered up in the gloom, like some gigantic monster ready to spring upon the traveller.

The hair of the affrighted pedagogue rose upon his head with terror.

What was to be done? To turn and fly was now too late; and besides, what chance was there of escaping ghost or goblin, if such it was, which could ride upon the wings of the wind? Summoning up, therefore, a show of courage, he demanded in stammering accents—"who are you?" He received no reply. He repeated his demand in a still more agitated voice.—Still there was no answer. Once more he cudgelled the sides of the inflexible Gunpowder, and shutting his eyes, broke forth with involuntary fervour into a psalm tune. Just then the shadowy object of alarm put itself in motion, and with a scramble and a bound, stood at once in the middle of the road. Though the night was dark and dismal, yet the form of the unknown might now in some degree be ascertained. He appeared to be a horseman of large dimensions, and mounted on a black horse of powerful frame. He made no offer of molestation or sociability, but kept aloof on one side of the road, jogging along on the blind side of old Gunpowder, who had now got over his fright and waywardness.

Ichabod, who had no relish for this strange midnight companion, and bethought himself of the adventure of Brom Bones with the gallopping Hessian, now quickened his steed, in hopes of leaving him behind. The stranger, however, quickened his horse to an equal pace; Ichabod pulled up, and fell into a walk, thinking to lag behind—the other did the same. His heart began to sink within him; he endeavoured to resume his psalm tune, but his parched tongue clove to the roof of his mouth, and he could not utter a stave. There was something in the moody and dogged silence of this pertinacious companion, that was mysterious and appalling. It was soon fearfully accounted for. On mounting a rising ground, which brought the figure of his fellow traveller in relief against the sky, gigantic in height, and muffled in a cloak, Ichabod was horror struck, on perceiving that he was headless! but his horror was still more increased, on observing, that the head, which should have rested on his shoulders, was carried before him on the pommel of the saddle! His terror rose to desperation; he rained a shower of kicks and blows upon Gunpowder, hoping, by a sudden movement, to give his companion the slip—but the spectre started full jump with him. Away, then, they dashed, through thick and thin; stones flying, and sparks flashing, at every bound. Ichabod's flimsy garments fluttered in the air, as he stretched his long lank body away over his horse's head, in the eagerness of his flight.

They had now reached the road which turns off to Sleepy Hollow; but Gunpowder, who seemed possessed with a demon, instead of keeping up it, made an opposite turn, and plunged headlong down hill to the left. This road leads through a sandy hollow shaded by trees for about a quarter of a mile, where it crosses the bridge famous in goblin story, and just beyond swells the green knoll on which stands the whitewashed church.

As yet the panic of the steed had given his unskilful rider an apparent advantage in the chace, but just as he had got half way through the hollow, the girths of the saddle gave way, and he felt it slipping from under him; he seized it by the pommel, and endeavoured to hold it firm, but in vain; and had just time to save himself by clasping old Gunpowder round the neck, when the saddle fell to the earth, and he heard it trampled under foot by his pursuer. For a moment the terror of Hans Van Ripper's wrath passed across his mind—for it was his Sunday saddle; but this was no time for petty fears: the goblin was hard on his haunches; and (unskilful rider that he was!) he had much ado to maintain his seat; sometimes slipping on one side, sometimes on another, and sometimes jolted on the high ridge of his horse's back bone, with a violence that he verily feared would cleave him asunder.

An opening in the trees now cheered him with the hopes that the Church Bridge was at hand. The wavering reflection of a silver star in the bosom of the brook told him that he was not mistaken. He saw the walls of the church dimly glaring under the trees beyond. He recollected the place where Brom Bones' ghostly competitor had disappeared. "If I can but reach that bridge," thought Ichabod, "I am safe." Just then he heard the black steed panting and blowing close behind him; he even fancied that he felt his hot breath. Another convulsive kick in the ribs, and old Gunpowder sprung upon the bridge; he thundered over the resounding planks; he gained the opposite side, and now Ichabod cast a look behind to see if his pursuer should vanish, according to rule, in a flash of fire and brimstone. Just then he saw the goblin rising in his stirrups, and in the very act of hurling his head at him. Ichabod endeavoured to dodge the horrible missile, but too late. It encountered his cranium with a tremendous crash—he was tumbled headlong into the dust, and Gunpowder, the black steed, and the goblin rider, passed by like a whirlwind.——

The next morning the old horse was found without his saddle, and with the bridle under his feet, soberly cropping the grass at his master's gate. Ichabod did not make his appearance at breakfast—dinner hour came, but no Ichabod. The boys assembled at the schoolhouse, and strolled idly about the banks of the brook; but no schoolmaster. Hans Van Ripper now began to feel some uneasiness about the fate of poor Ichabod, and his saddle. An inquiry was set on foot, and after diligent investigation they came upon his traces. In one part of the road leading to the church, was found the saddle trampled in the dirt; the tracks of horses' hoofs deeply dented in the road, and evidently at furious speed, were traced to the bridge, beyond which, on the bank of a broad part of the brook, where the water ran deep and black, was found the hat of the unfortunate Ichabod, and close beside it a shattered pumpkin.

The brook was searched, but the body of the schoolmaster was not to be discovered. Hans Van Ripper, as executor of his estate, examined the bundle which contained all his worldly effects. They consisted of two shirts and a half; two stocks for the neck; a pair or two of worsted stockings; an old pair of corduroy small clothes; a rusty razor; a book of psalm tunes, full of dog's ears; and a broken pitch pipe. As to the books and furniture of the schoolhouse, they belonged to the community, excepting Cotton Mather's History of Witchcraft, a New England Almanack, and a book of dreams and fortune telling, in which last was a sheet of foolscap much scribbled and blotted, in several fruitless attempts to make a copy of verses in honour of the heiress of Van Tassel. These magic books and the poetic scrawl were forthwith consigned to the flames by Hans Van Ripper, who from that time forward determined to send his children no more to school, observing, that he never knew any good come of this same reading and writing. Whatever money the schoolmaster possessed, and he had received his quarter's pay but a day or two before, he must have had about his person at the time of his disappearance.

The mysterious event caused much speculation at the Church on the following Sunday. Knots of gazers and gossips were collected in the church yard, at the bridge, and at the spot where the hat and pumpkin had been found. The stories of Brouwer, of Bones, and a whole budget of others, were called to mind; and when they had diligently considered them all, and compared them with the symptoms of the present case, they shook their heads, and came to the conclusion, that Ichabod had been carried off by the gallopping Hessian. As he was a bachelor, and in nobody's debt, nobody troubled his head any more about him, the school was removed to a different quarter of the hollow, and another pedagogue reigned in his stead.

It is true, an old farmer, who had been down to New York on a visit several years after, and from whom this account of the ghostly adventure was received, brought home the intelligence that Ichabod Crane was still alive; that he had left the neighbourhood partly through fear of the goblin and Hans Van Ripper, and partly in mortification at having been suddenly dismissed by the heiress; that he had changed his quarters to a distant part of the country; had kept school and studied law at the same time; had been admitted to the bar, turned politician, electioneered, written for the newspapers, and finally had been made a Justice of the Ten Pound Court. Brom Bones too, who, shortly after his rival's disappearance, conducted the blooming Katrina in triumph to the altar, was observed to look exceedingly knowing whenever the story of Ichabod was related, and always burst into a hearty laugh at the mention of the pumpkin; which led some to suspect that he knew more about the matter than he chose to tell.

The old country wives, however, who are the best judges of these matters, maintain to this day, that Ichabod was spirited away by supernatural means; and it is a favourite story often told about the neighbourhood round the winter evening fire. The bridge became more than ever an object of superstitious awe, and that may be the reason why the road has been altered of late years, so as to approach the church by the border of the millpond. The schoolhouse being deserted, soon fell to decay, and was reported to be haunted by the ghost of the unfortunate pedagogue; and the plough boy, loitering homeward of a still summer evening, has often fancied his voice at a distance, chanting a melancholy psalm tune among the tranquil solitudes of Sleepy Hollow.

POSTSCRIPT

Found in the Handwriting of Mr. Knickerbocker

The preceding Tale is given, almost in the precise words in which I heard it related at a corporation meeting of the ancient city of Manhattoes, at which were present many of its sagest and most illustrious burghers. The narrator was a pleasant, shabby, gentlemanly old fellow, in pepper and salt clothes, with a sadly humourous face, and one whom I strongly suspected of being poor, he made such efforts to be entertaining. When his story was concluded, there was much laughter and approbation, particularly from two or three deputy aldermen, who had been asleep the greater part of the time. There was, however, one tall, dry looking old gentleman, with beetling eye brows, who maintained a grave and rather severe face throughout; now and then folding his arms, inclining his head, and looking down upon the floor, as if turning a doubt over in his mind. He was one of your wary men, who never laugh but upon good grounds—when they have reason and the law on their side. When the mirth of the rest of the company had subsided, and silence was restored, he leaned one arm on the elbow of his chair, and sticking the other akimbo, demanded, with a slight, but exceedingly sage motion of the head, and contraction of the brow, what was the moral of the story, and what it went to prove.

The story teller, who was just putting a glass of wine to his lips, as a refreshment after his toils, paused for a moment, looked at his inquirer with an air of infinite deference, and lowering the glass slowly to the table, observed, that the story was intended most logically to prove,

"That there is no situation in life but has its advantages and pleasures, provided we will but take a joke as we find it:

"That, therefore, he that runs races with goblin troopers, is likely to have rough riding of it:

"Ergo, for a country schoolmaster to be refused the hand of a Dutch heiress, is a certain step to high preferment in the state."

The cautious old gentleman knit his brows tenfold closer after this explanation, being sorely puzzled by the ratiocination of the syllogism; while methought the one in pepper and salt eyed him with something of a triumphant leer. At length he observed, that all this was very well, but still he thought the story a little on the extravagant—there were one or two points on which he had his doubts.

"Faith, sir," replied the story teller, "as to that matter, I don't believe one half of it myself." D.K.

L'ENVOY*

Go, little booke, God send thee good passage,
And specially let this be thy prayere,
Unto them all that thee will read or hear,
Where thou art wrong, after their help to call,
Thee to correct in any part or all.
                    CHAUCER's *Belle Dame sans Mercie.*

In concluding a second volume of the Sketch Book, the Author cannot but express his deep sense of the indulgence with which his first has been received, and of the liberal disposition that has been evinced to treat him with kindness as a stranger. Even the critics, whatever may be said of them by others, he has found to be a singularly gentle and good natured race: it is true that each has in turn objected to some one or two articles,—and that these individual exceptions, taken in the aggregate, would amount almost to a total condemnation of his work; but then he has been consoled by observing, that what one has particularly censured, another has as particularly praised; and thus, the encomiums being set off against the objections, he finds his work, upon the whole, commended far beyond its deserts.

He is aware that he runs a risk of forfeiting much of this kind favour by not following the counsel that has been liberally bestowed upon him; for where abundance of valuable advice is given gratis, it may seem a man's own fault if he should go astray. He can only say, in his vindication, that he faithfully determined, for a time, to govern himself in his second volume by the opinions passed upon his first; but he was soon brought to a stand by the contrariety of excellent counsel. One kindly advised him to avoid the ludicrous; another to shun the pathetic; a third assured him that he was tolerable at description, but cautioned him to leave narrative alone; while a fourth declared that he had a very pretty knack at turning a story, and was really entertaining when in a pensive mood, but was grievously mistaken if he imagined himself to possess a spirit of humour.

Thus perplexed by the advice of his friends, who each in turn closed some particular path, but left him all the world beside to range in, he found that to follow all their counsels would, in fact, be to stand still. He remained for a time sadly embarrassed; when, all at once, the thought struck him to ramble on even as he had begun: that his

---

*Closing the second volume of the London edition.

work being miscellaneous, and written for different humours, it could not be expected that any one would be pleased with the whole; but that if it should contain something to suit each reader, his end would be completely answered. Few guests sit down to a varied table with an equal appetite for every dish. One has an elegant horror of a roasted pig; another holds a curry or a devil in utter abomination; a third cannot tolerate the ancient flavour of venison and wild fowl; and a fourth, of truly masculine stomach, looks with sovereign contempt on those knick-knacks, here and there dished up for the ladies. Thus each article is condemned in its turn; and yet, amidst this variety of appetites, seldom does a dish go away from the table without being tasted and relished by some one or other of the guests.

With these considerations he ventures to serve up this second volume in the same heterogeneous way with his first; simply requesting the reader, if he should find here and there something to please him, to rest assured that it was written expressly for intelligent readers like himself; but intreating him, should he find any thing to dislike, to tolerate it, as one of those articles which the author has been obliged to write for readers of a less refined taste.

To be serious.—The author is conscious of the numerous faults and imperfections of his work; and well aware how little he is disciplined and accomplished in the arts of authorship. His deficiencies are also increased by a diffidence arising from his peculiar situation. He finds himself writing in a strange land, and appearing before a public which he has been accustomed, from childhood, to regard with the highest feelings of awe and reverence. He is full of solicitude to deserve their approbation, yet finds that very solicitude continually embarrassing his powers, and depriving him of that ease and confidence which are necessary to successful exertion. Still the kindness with which he is treated encourages him to go on, hoping that in time he may acquire a steadier footing; and thus he proceeds, half venturing, half shrinking, surprized at his own good fortune, and wondering at his own temerity.

THE END.

APPENDIX A

[This "Prospectus" introduced *Sketch Book* Number I in the first three American editions. It is presented here as transcribed from Irving's manuscript, and is emended in two places: (1) line 3 experiment;] 1A; ~, MS1 and (2) line 16 recollections] 1A; recollections MS1] (See p. 367 for an explanation of the abbreviations.)

PROSPECTUS

The following writings are published on experiment; should they please they may be followed by others. The writer will have to contend with some disadvantages. He is unsettled in his abode, subject to interruptions, and has his share of cares and vicissitudes. He cannot therefore promise a regular plan, nor regular periods of publication. Should he be encouraged to proceed, much time may elapse between the appearance of his numbers; and their size must depend on the materials he has on hand. His writings will partake of the fluctuations of his own thoughts and feelings; sometimes treating of scenes before him; sometimes of others purely imaginary, and sometimes wandering back with his recollections to his native country. He will not be able to give them that tranquil attention necessary to finished composition, and as they must be transmitted across the Atlantic for publication, he must trust to others to correct the frequent errors of the press. Should his writings, however, with all their imperfections, be well received, he cannot conceal that it would be a source of the purest gratification; for though he does not aspire to those high honours that are the rewards of loftier intellects; yet it is the dearest wish of his heart to have a secure, and cherished, though humble, corner in the good opinions and kind feelings of his countrymen.

London, 1819

APPENDIX B

[This "Advertisement" was printed at the beginning of Volume I of the first British edition, 1820, and continued to introduce *The Sketch Book* until replaced by the "Preface to the Revised Edition" in 1848. It is presented here as printed in 1E.]

ADVERTISEMENT

The following desultory papers are part of a series written in this country, but published in America. The author is aware of the austerity with which the writings of his countrymen have hitherto been treated by British critics: he is conscious, too, that much of the contents of his papers can be interesting only in the eyes of American readers. It was not his intention, therefore, to have them reprinted in this country. He has, however, observed several of them from time to time inserted in periodical works of merit, and has understood that it was probable they would be republished in a collective form. He has been induced, therefore, to revise and bring them forward himself, that they may at least come correctly before the public. Should they be deemed of sufficient importance to attract the attention of critics, he solicits for them that courtesy and candour which a stranger has some right to claim, who presents himself at the threshold of a hospitable nation.

February, 1820.

EDITORIAL APPENDIX

Textual Commentary,
Discussions, and Lists by
Haskell Springer

EXPLANATORY NOTES

The numbers before all notes indicate page and line respectively. Chapter numbers, chapter or section titles, epigraphs, author's chapter or section summaries, text quotations, and footnotes are included in the line count. Only running heads and rules added by the printer to separate the running head from the text are omitted from the count. The quotation from the text, to the left of the bracket, is the matter under discussion.

Where appropriate, below, a headnote discusses the most direct biographical and literary sources of a sketch and directs the reader to the notebook(s) in which Irving entered ideas, phrases, or whole paragraphs relating to that essay. Irving's life at the time of writing *The Sketch Book*, and the general influences on his work are most usefully presented in Stanley T. Williams' *The Life of Washington Irving* (see particularly Volume I, Chapters VII and VIII and the notes to those chapters); and in two of Irving's notebooks: *Notes While Preparing Sketch Book &c., 1817*, ed. S. T. Williams (New Haven: Yale University Press, 1927); and *Tour in Scotland* (1817), ed. S. T. Williams (New Haven: Yale University Press, 1927). For further scholarly commentary on Irving's sources see Haskell Springer, ed., *Washington Irving: A Reference Guide* (Boston: G. K. Hall Co., 1976).

epigraph "I have no wife...." Burton.] Robert Burton's *The Anatomy of Melancholy*, 1621. The quotation is from the introductory section entitled "Democritus Junior to the Reader."

PREFACE TO THE REVISED EDITION

3.12–13 London Literary Gazette] A weekly review founded in 1817 by Henry Colburn, and edited by William Jerdan; it ceased publication in 1862. Its first selection from *The Sketch Book* appeared in the issue of September 25, 1819. See the Introduction, p. xviii.

4.11 Archibald Constable] (1774–1827), the chief publisher in Edinburgh, who, along with Longman and Rees of London, published the *Edinburgh Review*. See also note 3.12–13.

4.35 a weekly periodical] Scott was offering the editorship of a conservative political journal. Irving was actually his second choice for the post.

5.5 'And for my love...'] *The Merchant of Venice*, I, iii.

5.7 Castle street] Scott lived at 39 Castle Street from 1802 to 1826.

5.10 *crimp*] To impress soldiers or seamen; hence, to entrap.

5.29 Don Cossack] The Don Cossacks are so called because the river Don flows through their homeland in southeast Russia. Irving uses the term again at 281.38.

6.23 John Bunyan's Holy War] Published in 1682.

6.27–28 Blackwood's Edinburgh Magazine] William Blackwood, the Edinburgh publisher, in April, 1817, started *The Edinburgh Monthly Magazine*, which six months later took this title.

6.30 Lockhart] John Gibson Lockhart (1794–1854), a contributor to *Blackwood's Edinburgh Magazine*, who married Scott's daughter, Sophia. His *Life of Scott* was published in 1838.

6.34 Miss Sophia Scott] Scott's oldest daughter.

6.36 "nigromancy"] A form of "necromancy," not a slur on "Negro."

6.42 Walter] (1801–1847), Scott's oldest son. He inherited his father's baronetcy, but the title became extinct with his death.

7.4–5 Your name is up, and may go / From Toledo to Madrid] Unidentified.

7.10 bookseller unknown to fame] John Miller, Burlington Arcade.

7.33 *Sunnyside*] In 1835 Irving bought twenty-four acres on the Hudson River near Tarrytown, and gradually remodeled the small cottage he found there into Sunnyside, a fine house of romantic architecture. Except for a four-year absence while minister to Spain, he lived there from 1836 until his death in 1859.

THE AUTHOR'S ACCOUNT OF HIMSELF

8.8 Lyly's Euphues] John Lyly (1554–1606) published *Euphues, The Anatomy of Wit* in 1578, and *Euphues and His England* in 1580. "Euphuism" derives from the title of the book and describes its style. See also 91.7 and 104.30.

10.4–5 the cascade of Terni] The artificially created falls of the river Velino near the town of Terni in the Italian province of Perugia.

THE VOYAGE

Irving's first voyage to Europe took place in 1804, but then his port was Bordeaux. He embarked from New York for Liverpool on May 25, 1815, but the trip was apparently unpleasant, in contrast to the account in this essay. Judging by his letters, "The Voyage" is probably a composite of the two crossings.

11.12 Old Poem] The fourth stanza of a song, "Halloo my fancie," given in *English Minstrelsy*, 2d ed. (Edinburgh: Ballantyne & Co., 1810), vol. II, song 13.

11.25–26 'a lengthening chain'] Oliver Goldsmith, *The Traveller* (1764), line 10.

12.17 uncouth] strange.

13.11 "and was never heard of more"] Unidentified.

14.6 Deep called unto deep.] "Deep calleth unto deep" (Ps. 42:7).

15.34 the land of my forefathers] Irving's father was a native of the Orkney Isles.

ROSCOE

Preliminary jottings for this essay appear in Irving's *Notes While Preparing Sketch Book &c., 1817* (see index).

16.1 *ROSCOE*] William Roscoe (1753–1831). His most important works are: *The Life of Lorenzo de'Medici*; and *The Life and Pontificate of Leo the Tenth*. Irving met him in 1815 when Roscoe was at the peak of his fame, and the two became well acquainted.

16.7 THOMSON] James Thomson (1700–1748), wrote *The Seasons* and *The Castle of Indolence*. This quotation is from a tragedy, *Sophonisba*, II, i. See also note 272.8.

16.9 the Athenaeum] Originally "the temple of Athena" at Athens, in which poets and learned men read their works. In modern times a literary and scientific club.

17.3–4 stony places of the world] See Matt. 13:5.

17.31 living streams of knowledge] See Cant. 4:15 and Rev. 7:17.

17.31 "daily beauty in his life,"] *Othello*, V, i.

18.3 Lorenzo De Medici] (1449–1492), called "il Magnifico"; Florentine statesman, patron of arts and letters, scholar, poet.

18.42 *Address on the opening of the Liverpool Institution.] The Royal Institution. Roscoe was the prime mover behind its establishment in 1817. It was the central literary institution in Liverpool.

19.22 "... dispersed about the country"] The catalog of the sale of Roscoe's library (printed by J. M'Creery, London, 1816) lists 1,813 items. According to contemporary marginal notations in the copy in the Kenneth Spencer Research Library of the University of Kansas, the auction brought a total of £5003 13s. Irving apparently did not know that Roscoe's friends purchased £600 of his books at the sale, and offered them to him as a gift. He refused it, and they gave them to the Liverpool Athenaeum to form a "Roscoe Collection."

19.31–32 black letter] A heavy-faced type used in the earliest printed books. The term occurs repeatedly in *The Sketch Book*.

20.23 Pompey's column at Alexandria] Erected in honor of the Emperor Diocletian in 302.

20.30 To My Books] This sonnet was first published in the *Gentleman's Magazine,* vol. 86, p. 256.

THE WIFE

Irving's *Notes While Preparing Sketch Book &c., 1817,* pp. 68–69, contains the germ of this essay and a draft of its climactic passage.

22.8 Middleton] Thomas Middleton (1570–1627), dramatist. The quotation is from *Women, Beware Women,* III, i. See also 56.2–6.

23.5 Leslie] Charles Leslie, a painter and writer, was one of Irving's close friends. The husband in the sketch is called George, but Irving originally wrote "Charles" and then altered the name in the MS. The incident is supposed to be from the life of another painter friend, Washington Allston. (See STW, I, 429.)

RIP VAN WINKLE

Irving reportedly wrote "Rip Van Winkle" at great speed in June, 1818, at the home of his sister, Sarah Van Wart, in Birmingham. His immediate literary source was "Peter Klaus" in Otmar's *Volkssagen,* but his own observation of Dutch families in New York, his reading from Riesbeck's *Travels Through Germany,* and his interest in American and European folklore are also apparent in the story.

28.11 black letter] See note to 19.31–32.

28.13 a history of the province] Irving's *A History of New York . . .* by Diedrich Knickerbocker appeared in 1809.

28.28 ". . . more in sorrow than in anger,"] *Hamlet,* I, ii.

28.34 Waterloo medal] Issued by George IV as regent to every officer and soldier who took part in the actions of June 16, 17, and 18, 1815.

28.34–35 Queen Anne's farthing] These farthings were struck in 1713–1714 on the recommendation of Jonathan Swift. They are falsely thought to be very rare.

29.6 thylke] *The,* or *that same.*

29.8 Cartwright] William Cartwright (1611–1643), clergyman, poet, and dramatist. The quotation is unidentified. See also 159.10.

29.28 Peter Stuyvesant] He was governor of New Netherlands from 1647 to 1664.

29.38 Fort Christina] A Swedish fort on the Delaware, taken by Stuyvesant in 1655. The incident is described in the *History of New York,* bk. 6, chap. 7.

30.6 curtain lecture] "A reproof given by a wife to her husband in bed" (Johnson's *Dictionary*).

31.8 galligaskins]   Loose breeches.

34.23 hanger]   According to the *Oxford English Dictionary*, a kind of short sword, originally hung from the belt.

34.43 hollands]   A gin manufactured in Holland.

37.9–10 a red night cap]   The Phrygian cap, worn by slaves freed by the Romans and later adopted as the symbol of liberty in the French Revolution.

38.22 Stoney Point]   On July 16, 1779, General Anthony Wayne reported to Washington that he had captured the English fort at Stony Point, on the Hudson.

38.23 Antony's Nose]   A promontory on the Hudson near Stony Point. In the *History of New York* Irving facetiously derives the name from the nose of Antony Van Corlear, Peter Stuyvesant's trumpeter (see bk. 6, chap. 4).

40.5 the historian of that name]   Adriaen Van Der Donck (1620–1655?), colonist and lawyer. He wrote *Beschrijvinge van Niew Nederlant*, a descriptive history of the Dutch colony, first published in Amsterdam in 1655, and in colonial America (in English) in 1656. An edition has recently been published by Syracuse University Press (1968).

40.12 Hendrick Hudson]   Henry Hudson (d. 1611) was English, not Dutch as Irving's rendering of the name is meant to imply.

41.23–24 emperor Frederick *der Rothbart*, and the Kypphauser mountain]   Holy Roman Emperor Frederick I (1152–1190), also known as Frederick Barbarossa, sleeps, according to legend, in a cave of the Kyffhäuser mountain in central Germany. When Barbarossa's red beard has thrice encircled the table at which he sleeps, he will awake and make Germany the preeminent state of the world.

ENGLISH WRITERS ON AMERICA

43.6 ON THE LIBERTY OF THE PRESS]   That is, *Areopagitica* (1644).

48.21 Knowledge is power]   ("Nam et ipsa scientia potestas est.") The quotation is from Francis Bacon's *Essayes. Religious Meditations. Places of Perswasion and Disswasion* (1597).

RURAL LIFE IN ENGLAND

The material for this essay was gathered, at least in part, while Irving was touring in the vicinity of Birmingham in 1816.

50.5 COWPER]   William Cowper (1731–1796); the quotation is from *The Task*, bk. III, lines 290–92; "pleasure" should be "leisure."

50.11 wakes]   These were annual festivals to commemorate the completion of the parish church.

53.28 "The Flower and the Leaf"]   Dryden attributed it to Chaucer, but its authorship is still unknown.

55.14–15 *From a poem on the death of the Princess Charlotte, by the Reverend Rann Kennedy, A. M.]   She was the daughter of George IV. There was a great outburst of grief at her death, because the nation had eagerly anticipated her succession to the throne. Reverend Rann Kennedy (1772–1851) of St. Paul's Chapel, Birmingham, was a friend of Coleridge and Irving. I have not discovered the title of the poem.

THE BROKEN HEART

Irving outlined this essay in his journal *Tour in Scotland* (pp. 116–18).

56.6 MIDDLETON]   from *Blurt, Master Constable*, III, i. See also 22.8.

56.37–38 the wings of the morning]   Ps. 139:9.

56.38 "fly to the uttermost part of the earth, and be at rest."]   Pss. 139:10, 55:6.

57.18 "dry sorrow drinks her blood,"]   *Romeo and Juliet*, III, v, "Dry sorrow drinks our blood."

57.22 "darkness and the worm."]   "The deep damp vault, the darkness, and the worm" (Edward Young, *Night Thoughts*, Night IV, line 11).

57.41 young E———]   Robert Emmet (1778–1803) planned to capture Dublin Castle and the lord lieutenant; after his failure he was tried and hanged. He made moving speeches before being sentenced, and on the gallows. Irving copied Emmet's last speech into *Tour in Scotland*; see pp. 114–16.

58.11–12 the daughter of a late celebrated Irish Barrister]   Sarah, the youngest daughter of John Philpot Curran, a famous Irish lawyer and judge.

59.2 "heeded not the song of the charmer...."]   "Which will not hearken to the voice of charmers, charming never so wisely" (Ps. 58:5).

59.34 Moore]   Thomas Moore (1779–1852). He was a friend of Irving's and Lord Byron's and wrote a biography of Byron (1830). The poem, whose first line is also its title, is in *Irish Melodies*, as is the famous song, "Believe Me, if All Those Endearing Young Charms."

THE ART OF BOOK MAKING

61.2 Synesius]   A bishop of Cyrene at the time of Theodosius the younger, ca. 375–413. I cannot identify the work to which Burton refers.

62.23 "pure English undefiled"]   The allusion is to Spenser, *The Faerie Queen*, bk. 2, canto 2, stanza 32: "Dan Chaucer, well of English undefiled," but may also owe something to the Bible. See James 1:27: "Pure religion and undefiled...." See also 104.1.

63.1-2 line upon line, precept upon precept, here a little and there a little.] See Isa. 28:10.

63.3–5 witches' caldron . . . "slab and good."] *Macbeth*, IV, i, is the source for these lines. "Toe of frog," "blind-worm's sting," and "baboon's blood" are accurate, but "slab and good" is an inadvertent conflation of "thick and slab," line 32, and "firm and good," line 38.

64.22 "The Paradise of dainty Devices,"] (1576) A popular verse miscellany. It was the first successor to A *Mirror for Magistrates* (1559). See note 104.28–29.

64.36 an arcadian hat] Any rustic hat. Arcadia, a pastoral region in the Peloponnesus, is supposed to be typical of rural simplicity.

64.38 Primrose hill] North of Regent's Park, it commands a fine view of London.

64.41 "babbling about green fields."] *Henry V*, II, iii. Falstaff on his deathbed "babbled of green fields."

65.15 Beaumont and Fletcher] Francis Beaumont (ca. 1584–1616), and John Fletcher (1579–1625), Elizabethan dramatists chiefly noted for the plays they wrote together. Fletcher also collaborated with several other playwrights, including Shakespeare and Ben Jonson.

65.15–16 Castor and Pollux] The Dioscuri or Twins. Perhaps the reference is to the battle of Lake Regillus (see Macaulay's *Lays of Ancient Rome*).

65.16 Ben Jonson] (1572–1637). The famous playwright and poet is supposed to have killed an enemy in single-handed combat while serving with the English army in the Netherlands. See note 106.17.

65.20 the dead body of Patroclus.] See the *Iliad*, bks. 16–18.

65.28–29 "chopped bald shot,"] *Henry IV, Part II*, III, ii. Falstaff: "O, give me always a little, lean, old, chapt, bald shot."

65.31–32 learned Theban] *King Lear*, III, iv.

A ROYAL POET

67.8 FLETCHER] The quotation is unidentified. Fletcher could be the dramatist or one of the many poets of that name.

67.25 Sir Peter Lely] (1618–1680), a Dutch artist; First Painter to Charles II.

67.26 "large green courts,"] Surrey's "Prisoned in Windsor, he recounteth his pleasure there passed," line 6.

67.28–29 hapless Surrey] Henry Howard, earl of Surrey (ca. 1517–1547). He was beheaded on a charge of treason.

67.30 the Lady Geraldine] The "Fair Geraldine" of Surrey's poetry was apparently inspired by Lady Elizabeth Fitzgerald, but she was a child at the time, and the lady in the poetry is no doubt largely imaginary.

67.31–32 "With eyes cast up...."] "Prisoned in Windsor...," lines 7, 8.

67.34 James the First] (1394–1437). He became king in 1406, and was assassinated on February 20 or 21, 1437. His widow, Joan Beaufort, a granddaughter of John of Gaul, had no difficulty bringing the murderers to justice. Irving's picture of him, though romanticized, is, in historical detail, largely correct.

68.41 Buchanan] George Buchanan (1506–1582), *Rerum Scotticarum Historia*, bk. 10 (vol. II, p. 148, in the Edinburgh edition of 1821).

68.42 *Ballenden's Translation of Hector Boyce.] bk. 16, chap. 16. A free translation into the Scottish vernacular, by John Ballenden or Ballentyne (1533–1587), of a history of Scotland written in ancient Latin by Hector Boece, or Boethius (1465–1536).

69.22 Tasso in his dismal cell] The Italian poet (1544–1595) was confined for seven years in a hospital for lunatics because he offended the duke of Ferrara.

69.40 †Roger l'Estrange] This is stanza 11 of "Loyalty Confined," found in David Lloyd's *Memoirs of Those that Suffered in the Cause of Charles I* (London, 1668), and reprinted in Bishop Percy's *Reliques of Ancient English Poetry*, vol. II, bk. 3, song 12. Percy attributes it to Sir Roger L'Estrange (1616–1704), loyalist and Tory journalist who, after the Restoration, became licenser of the press and acted strongly in favor of government censorship. L'Estrange's authorship of this song, though, has not been proven.

70.17–18 "Cynthia rinsing...."] A very free translation.

71.21–22 ...his perpetual blindness] See the sonnets "When I consider how my light is spent," and "Cyriac, this three years' day"; see also *Paradise Lost*, bk. 3, lines 1–55.

74.28 gilliflower] Used to designate any of several flowers, including the stock and clove pink.

75.24 Gower] John Gower (ca. 1330–1408) wrote the *Confessio Amantis*.

75.41–42 morning stars] "When the morning stars sang together, and all the sons of God shouted for joy." Job 38:7.

76.1–2 captivating fiction] The allusion is to Sir Walter Scott.

77.37 "Christ's Kirk of the Green,"] Its authorship is uncertain.

78.6 Vaucluse] Near Avignon, it was for many years the home of Petrarch.

78.6–7 the shrine at Loretto] The Santa Casa at Loreto, Italy, according to tradition, is the house in which Mary had been born, brought up, and received the Annunciation. Because of threatened destruction by the Turks in the thirteenth century the building was supposedly carried away by angels and ultimately placed where it now stands. Irving refers to it again at 210.36–37.

THE COUNTRY CHURCH

79.6 BEGGAR's BUSH] A comedy (1615–1622) by John Fletcher and Philip Massinger. The quotation is from II, iii.

82.42 rapt out of sight in a whirlwind] See Elijah in 2 Kings 2:1.

THE WIDOW AND HER SON

Preliminary notes for this sketch appear in Irving's journal, *Tour in Scotland*, pp. 118–19.

83.4 MARLOWE's TAMBURLAINE] The preceding passage is from part I, V, ii, in C. F. Tucker Brooke's edition.

83.14–15 Sweet day, so pure. . . .] Lines 1 and 2 of "Virtue" in *The Temple*, by George Herbert (1593–1633).

87.20–21 "that looked on his childhood,"] Unidentified.

A SUNDAY IN LONDON

Although first published in 1848, this sketch was, at least in part, composed much earlier. See *Notes While Preparing Sketch Book &c., 1817*, p. 54, and STW, I, 421.

89.40 *Part of a sketch. . . .] The manuscript of this piece gives no clue about the "sketch" to which Irving refers. It apparently never became part of *The Sketch Book*.

THE BOAR'S HEAD TAVERN, EAST CHEAP

The only early jottings for this essay appear to be in *Notes While Preparing Sketch Book &c., 1817*, where Irving copied out Robert Preston's epitaph, and wrote "Tallow Chandler" and "Mr. Kash/Hairdresser."

91.7 MOTHER BOMBIE] John Lyly's last comedy. See note 8.8.

91.37 a great German critick] No doubt August Wilhelm von Schlegel, whose *Lectures on Dramatic Art and Literature* appeared in English in 1815.

92.18–19 old Jack Falstaff. . . .] Falstaff describes himself in these terms in *Henry IV, Part I*, II, iv.

92.26 Dame Quickly] Hostess of the Boar's Head Tavern. She appears in *The Merry Wives of Windsor*, both parts of *Henry IV*, and *Henry V*.

92.28 smelling to] Colloquial.

92.32 haunted regions of Cock-lane] Alluding to the reported appearance of a ghost in a Cock Lane house in 1762. Samuel Johnson was instrumental in exposing the spirit as a fraud.

92.33–34 Cateaton Street and Old Jewry] Cateaton Street is now Gresham Street. The name "Old Jewry" derives from the Jewish quarter which existed there before the expulsion of the Jews from England in 1290.

92.34–35 Guildhall and its two stunted Giants]   The council hall of the city of London; its "giants" are large figures of Gog and Magog. (See Ezekiel 38–39, and Rev. 20:8. See also Caxton's translation of the *Recuyell of the Historyes of Troye* [ca. 1474] for the mythical connection of Gog and Magog with the history of Britain.)

92.36 London Stone]   Probably a fragment of the great central milestone of the Romans, from which all distances were measured.

92.37 Jack Cade]   The leader of a rebellion in 1450, during the reign of Henry VI.

92.41 old Stow]   John Stowe, or Stow, historian and antiquary, published a *Survey of London* in 1598. It is our most valuable source book on medieval and Renaissance London. Irving alludes to or quotes from it several times in *The Sketch Book.*

93.1 sawtrie]   psaltry.

93.22 the Monument]   A stone column built by Sir Christopher Wren to commemorate the great fire of 1666. Irving refers to it again at 198.39.

93.29–30 the great fire of London]   It began on September 2, 1666, lasted five days, and virtually destroyed the city.

94.15 Milton's angels]   The allusion is no doubt to *Paradise Lost,* bk. 2, lines 557–61: "Others apart sat on a Hill retir'd, / In thoughts more elevate, and reason'd high / Of Providence, Foreknowledge, Will, and Fate, / Fixt Fate, Free will, Foreknowledge absolute, / And found no end, in wand'ring mazes lost."

94.29 Turenne]   Henri Vicomte de Turenne (1611–1675); French general.

94.32–33 William Walworth . . . Wat Tyler]   Walworth, Mayor of London, in 1381 killed Wat Tyler, one of the leaders of a revolt, while Tyler was speaking to the King.

94.35 Sovereigns of Cockney]   Irving uses "Cockney" here to mean London. More exactly, it refers to someone born "within the sound of Bow Bells," the bells of the church of St. Mary le Bow, Cheapside. See notes 197.2–5, 199.38–40, 200.17–18, 248.37–38.

95.15–16 the "mirre garland of captain Death"]   Unidentified.

95.16 sundry train-band captains]   The train-bands or trained-bands were a militia established in 1327. They were discontinued in 1662, except for those of London, which were reorganized in 1794 as the City of London Militia.

96.23 Miles Lane]   A corruption of St. Michael's Lane.

96.25 "bully Rock"]   Or "bully-rook," now archaic. *The Merry Wives of Windsor,* I, iii, 2: "What says my bully-rook?" and three times in

II, i. Bully-rock apparently means either (1) a jovial comrade or (2) a blustering gallant.

98.3 the learned Scriblerius. . . .] See Chapter 3 of *Memoirs of the Extraordinary Life, Works and Discoveries of Martinus Scriblerus*, a burlesque on pedantry, written by members of the Scriblerus Club which included Pope, Arbuthnot, Gay, and Swift. Published by Pope in 1741.

98.14 Bardolph] He appears in *Henry IV*, parts 1 and 2, *Henry V*, and *The Merry Wives of Windsor*.

98.42 II.ᵈ Part. Henry IV.] II, i.

99.18 a "tedious brief" account] *A Midsummer Night's Dream*, V, i: " 'A tedious brief scene of young Pyramus and his love Thisbe; very tragical mirth.' "

99.35 the far famed Portland vase.] An ancient funeral urn, loaned in 1810 to the British Museum by the duke of Portland. In 1845 it was smashed, but it has since been restored.

THE MUTABILITY OF LITERATURE

100.11 DRUMMOND OF HAWTHORNDEN] William Drummond of Hawthornden (1585–1649) generally wrote graceful poetry imitative of French and Italian models. The quotation (inaccurate in several places) consists of lines 1–3 and 5–8 of an untitled sonnet from his *Poems* (1616). The last line should read: "And that nought lighter is than airy praise."

100.25 doomsday book] Properly *Domesday Book*. The great survey of England, ordered by William the Conqueror. It was originally in the royal treasury at Winchester, and is now in the Public Record Office, Chancery Lane, London.

100.33 An ancient picture] Apparently of John Williams (1582–1650), dean of Westminster and a key political figure before the Puritan Revolution.

102.40 Robert Grosteste of Lincoln] Usually spelled Grosseteste (ca. 1175–1253). He was bishop of Lincoln, and wrote many works on theology, philosophy, and husbandry. A reformer, he was occasionally in conflict with Henry III and the pope.

103.2–3 Gyraldus Cambrensis] Gerald of Wales (1146–1220?). A turbulent churchman and topographer who wrote a number of works on various subjects.

103.5–6 Henry of Huntingdon] (1084?–1155), archdeacon. He wrote a *Historia Anglorum* and *De Contemptu Mundi*.

103.8 Joseph of Exeter] (ca. 1190). Author of a Latin poem in six books, *De Bello Trojano*, and a number of other works in Latin. Some of the writings with which he is credited may never have existed.

103.13 John Wallis, the Franciscan] John Waleys or Wallensis, regent master of the Franciscan schools at Oxford before 1260, and author of theological works. He also taught in Paris, where he was known as "Arbor Vitae" ("The Tree of Life").

103.14 William of Malmsbury] (ca. 1090–1143). Librarian of Malmesbury Abbey. His *Gesta Regum Anglorum* is based on ballads which he collected.

103.14 Simeon of Durham] (ca. 1130), precentor of Durham. He wrote a history of Durham Cathedral and other compilations.

103.14–15 Benedict of Peterborough] (d. 1193), abbot of Peterborough. He wrote histories of the Passion, and of the miracles of St. Thomas à Becket.

103.15 John Hanvill of St. Albans] Born probably before 1180, and known as John of St. Giles, John Giles, or John of St. Albans. He was a Dominican monk and physician, and archdeacon of Oxford. His only extant work is *Experimenta Joannis de S. Aegideo*.

103.20 Wynkyn de Worde] (d. 1534). He was a Belgian pupil of William Caxton, and became the second printer in London. See 173.33.

103.32 Robert of Gloucester] (ca. 1260–1300). Known only from the metrical *Chronicle* of England (to 1270) which bears his name.

103.37 *Chaucer's Testament of Love*] The *Testament of Love* was actually written by Thomas Usk, a contemporary of Chaucer.

103.38 Holinshed] Raphael Holinshed (d. 1580) published his *Chronicles of England, Scotland, and Ireland* in 1577. The passage is unlocated.

103.40 John Scogan] (ca. 1480). Fool at the court of Edward IV. "It is not improbable that his biography, which is supplied in his 'Jests,' said to have been compiled by Andrew Boorde ... is apocryphal and that Scogan is a fictitious hero" (*Dictionary of National Biography*).

103.40 John Lydgate, monke of Berrie] (ca. 1370–1449). He wrote well over 100,000 lines of poetry, much of it justly forgotten. At the age of fifteen he became a monk at the abbey of Bury St. Edmunds.

103.42 John Jewell, Bishop of Sarum] John Jewel (1522–1571) was bishop of Salisbury (formerly Sarum). Hooker was among his protégés, and Fuller edited his works.

103.42–43 John Fox] John Foxe wrote *The Acts and Monuments of the Church* (1563), better known as "The Book of Martyrs."

104.1 ... Spenser's 'well of pure English undefiled,'] See note 62.23.

104.18 As unintelligible ... as an Egyptian obelisk] Champollion's discovery of the meaning of Egyptian hieroglyphics was not made public until 1822, at least three years after Irving wrote the sketch.

104.19 Runic inscriptions said to exist in the deserts of Tartary] Unidentified.

104.22 Xerxes] See Herodotus, *The Histories*, bk. 7, par. 44–46.

104.28–29 Sackville's stately plays, and Mirror for Magistrates] Thomas Sackville, earl of Dorset (1536–1608), wrote an "Induction" and one of the stories for the second edition of the collection of rhymed narratives called *A Mirror for Magistrates* (1563). The "Induction" is one of the best English poems between the *Canterbury Tales* and *The Faerie Queen*. He also collaborated in the first blank verse tragedy, *Gorboduc*, later entitled *Ferrex and Porrex*.

104.30 "unparalelled John Lyly."] In 1632 Edward Blount collected six of Lyly's plays, and published them as *Sixe Court Comedies*... Written By the onely Rare Poet of that Time, The Witie, Comicall, Facetiously-Quicke and Unparalelld: John Lilly, Master of Arts. See note 8.8.

104.42 Bellona] Roman goddess of war.

104.42 Suada] Roman goddess of persuasion.

104.43 *Harvey's Pierces's Supererogation*] Gabriel Harvey (1545?–1630), fellow of Cambridge, friend of Spenser, lecturer, rhetorician. *Pierce's Supererogation* (1593) was one of his contributions to a long and vicious pamphlet war between Gabriel and his brother Richard on one side, and Robert Greene and Thomas Nashe on the other. It was occasioned by Nashe's attack on the Harveys in *Pierce Penniless his Supplication to the Divell* (1592). The complex and vitriolic controversy was finally ended when the archbishop of Canterbury in 1599 prohibited reprinting of Nashe's and Harvey's books and ordered all copies confiscated.

105.15 groan with rank and excessive vegetation] See *Comus*, lines 720–31. Irving also quotes from *Comus* at 151.31.

105.31 fountains of thought...broken up] See Gen. 7:11.

106.3 checks on population...economists] Thomas Malthus published his much discussed *Essay on Population* in 1798. A revised and greatly enlarged edition appeared in 1803.

106.17 knew little of Latin, and nothing of Greek] See Ben Jonson's poem, "To the Memory of Mr. W. Shakespeare," which was prefaced to the First Folio.

107.7 faithful portrayer of nature] See *Hamlet*, III, ii: "to hold, as 't were, the mirror up to nature."

107.44 CHURCHYARD] Thomas Churchyard (1520?–1604), soldier and minor poet. The quotation is unidentified.

RURAL FUNERALS

One passage in *Notes while preparing Sketch Book &c., 1817* closely parallels this essay. It reads: "The silence with which every melancholy rite concerning the deceased is performed the mute and noiseless tread of attendants—suppressed voices as if they feared disturbing the everlasting sleep of the deceased—Gloomy chambers. The air seems to catch the Deaths stillness."

Irving reported writing the essay, which derives from his travels in the English midlands and in Germany, in a churchyard. He told Pierre M. Irving that the passages on death were inspired by Matilda Hoffman; and Rebecca Gratz said she saw in it reference to Matilda's death.

109.7 CYMBELINE] IV, ii.

109.23–27 White his shroud. . . .] *Hamlet*, IV, v (inaccurately quoted).

110.1 says Bourne] In *Antiquitates Vulgares*, chap. 3. Henry Bourne (1696–1733), divine and antiquary. See Acts 20:24.

110.25 Sir Thomas Overbury] (1581–1613). The brief descriptions in prose of different character types which were appended to Overbury's didactic poem, *A Wife*, were known as "characters," and were written by a number of other authors as well as by Overbury. The sketch of "the faire and happy milkmaid" is most likely by John Webster, the dramatist.

110.30 "The Maid's Tragedy,"] First published in 1619. The lines quoted are in I, i. The maid cannot marry her lover and so laments. See also 178.14 and note 65.15.

110.38 Herrick] Robert Herrick (1591–1674), major Cavalier poet and apparently one of Irving's favorite authors. The passage is stanza 2 of "The Dirge of Jephthah's Daughter," Number 83 in *Noble Numbers*. See notes 113.17, 163.33–38, 169.2–11, 170.31–38, and 257.3–9.

111.4 says Evelyn, in his Sylva] John Evelyn (1620–1706), famous for the *Diary* which bears his name. His *Sylva* (1664) is a plea for reforestation in England.

111.31 "Corydon's Doleful Knell,"] Stanzas 5 to 7. See Percy's *Reliques*, vol. II, bk. 2, song 27.

112.14 Camden . . . Britannia] William Camden (1551–1623), antiquary, historian, and teacher of Ben Jonson. The *Britannia* is a Latin survey of the British Isles. The passage quoted by Irving was apparently added by Bishop Gibson in his edition of the *Britannia* (1772).

112.21 Thomas Stanley, Esq.] (1625–1678), lyric poet.

112.29 "The Maid's Tragedy,"] The passage is in II, i.

113.13–16 "Lay her i' the earth," . . . violets spring!] *Hamlet*, V, i.

113.17 "Dirge of Jephtha,"] "The Dirge of Jephtha's Daughter," stanzas 11 and 13. See note 110.38.

114.3–9 With fairest flowers. . . .] *Cymbeline*, IV, ii.

114.27 Jeremy Taylor] (1613–1667). Bishop and author. He wrote *Holy Living, Holy Dying, The Liberty of Prophesying*, and some outstanding sermons. The quotation is from his *Funeral Sermon on the Countess of Carbery*.

115.9–12 Each lonely place shall him restore. . . .] A free rendering
of the last stanza of a poem by William Collins (1721–1759), entitled
"Dirge in Cymbeline."

117.32 Bright, in his travels in Lower Hungary] Richard Bright, M.D.
(1789–1858), discoverer of Bright's disease, and physician to Queen
Victoria. He wrote *Travels from Vienna through Lower Hungary*
(Edinburgh, 1818).

118.1 Iffland] August Wilhelm Iffland (1759–1814). German actor and
dramatist.

THE INN KITCHEN

119.2 Shall I not take mine ease in mine inn?] *Henry IV, Part I*, III,
iii. See also 209.19–20.

119.5 *Pomme d'Or*] Golden Apple.

119.6 *table d'hote*] A fixed-price meal at a specified time.

120.24 *écume de mer*] meerschaum.

THE SPECTRE BRIDEGROOM

Gottfried Bürger's ballad "Lenore" is the probable literary source for
this story.

121.8 SIR EGER, SIR GRAHAME, AND SIR GRAY-STEEL] The story appears
in *Early Metrical Tales, &c.* (Edinburgh: W. and D. Laing, 1826).
These lines do not appear in the much shorter version, "Eger and
Grime," in *Bishop Percy's Folio MSS* (London: Trubner and Co.,
1867). Irving's source is unknown.

121.34 a little French anecdote] Unidentified.

122.12 the Heldenbuch] Collection of thirteenth century German epic
poetry. Its literary value is not great.

122.18 Minne-lieders] Irving means *Minnesingers*, the German trouba-
dours of the twelfth and thirteenth centuries who sang *Minnelieder*,
or love songs.

122.32 wasting their sweetness] See Gray's "Elegy Written in A Country
Church-Yard," line 56.

124.14 the fatted calf had been killed] An allusion to Luke 15:11–32,
the parable of the prodigal son.

124.16 *Rhein-wein*] Rhein wine.

124.17 *Ferne-wein*] Properly *Firne-wein*, old but inferior wine, tasting
of the barrel. Irving apparently mistook the meaning of the term.

124.17 the great Heidelburg tun] The Great Tun (20 feet high by
31 feet long, and holding 49,000 gallons) is kept in the castle of
Heidelberg, the German university town. It was built in 1751, and
is thus an anachronism in the story.

124.19 *Saus und Braus*]   revelry and riotous living.

128.14 Hoch-heimer]   Hochheimer is a famous Rhine wine.

128.38–40 Leonora . . . world]   Lenore is the name of the heroine of a popular ballad by Gottfried August Bürger (1747–1794), who is carried off by the ghost of her dead lover.

129.42 the wild huntsman]   See Bürger's "Der Wilde Jäger," which was translated by Sir Walter Scott.

WESTMINSTER ABBEY

Perhaps the only direct literary source for this essay is James Hervey's *Meditations and Contemplations*. Only one phrase from "Westminster Abbey," namely, "their very monument becomes a ruin," is found in Irving's notebooks (see *Tour in Scotland*, p. 127).

134.16 CHRISTOLERO's EPIGRAMS, BY T. B. 1598.]   *Chrestoleros: Seven Bookes of Epigrams,* written by Thomas Bastard (1566–1618), depicts the manners of the time and is sometimes very bitter.

135.14–15 Vitalis . . . Gislebertus . . . Laurentius. . . .]   Vitalis was a Norman; Gislebertus (Gilbert Crispin) exhumed the body of Edward the Confessor in 1102; Laurentius obtained the canonization of Edward in 1163. "Abbas" means "Abbot." The lettering on their tombs is now virtually obliterated.

136.11 Addison]   Joseph Addison (1672–1719). He and Richard Steele wrote *The Tatler* and *The Spectator*.

137.2–3 that fabled city, where every being had been suddenly transmuted into stone.]   Unidentified.

137.32–33 "all the brothers. . . ."]   See the full inscription on p. 146.

137.36–37 the tomb of Mrs. Nightingale, by Roubillac]   Lady Elizabeth Nightingale (d. 1731). Louis Roubillac (1695–1762) was a French sculptor, whose monument for Mrs. Nightingale was erected in 1758.

140.3–7   For in the silent grave . . . endless darkness.]   Unidentified.

140.33 Edward the Confessor]   Edward, king of England and later a saint, ruled from 1042 to his death in 1066, the year of the Norman Conquest.

140.40 "beds of darkness."]   See Job 17:13: "I have made my bed in the darkness."

142.7–9 "Our fathers," says Sir Thomas Brown. . . .]   *Hydriotaphia, Urne Buriall* (1658), chap. 5. Sir Thomas Browne (1605–1682), a physician, also wrote *Religio Medici.*

142.16–18 "The Egyptian mummies. . . ."]   Sir Thomas Browne, *Hydriotaphia,* chap. 5. See preceding note.

142.17 Cambyses]   Son of Cyrus the Great, king of Persia. In 525 B.C. he conquered Egypt.

142.17 Mizraim] One of the sons of Ham. See Gen. 10:6. The name signifies Egypt.

142.28 as a tale that is told.] Ps. 90:9.

142.33–34 Pope Gregory the Great] Pope from 590–604. One of the four great doctors of the Western Church. He sent Augustine to England in 596.

144.18 A curious narrative] *A True and Perfect Narrative of the Strange and Unexpected Finding the Crucifix and Gold-Chain of that Pious Prince, St. Edward, The King and Confessor, which was found after 620 Years' Interment: and Presented to His Most Sacred Majesty, King James the Second,* by Charles Taylour, Gent. (London, 1688). Irving follows the narrative closely.

144.19 Paul Pry] A busybody in a comedy of the same name by John Poole, which was produced at Haymarket on September 13, 1825.

145.41 Malcolm. Lond. Rediv.] *Londinium Redivivum,* by James Peller Malcolm, 1802 (in four volumes). The quoted passage is supposedly in vol. I, p. 94.

146.1 *Inscription on a monument....*] The allusion is on p. 137. The orthography and punctuation are generally modernized.

146.29 one of the Pultneys.] Daniel Pulteney, a lord of the Admiralty, who died in 1731.

CHRISTMAS

147.5 HUE AND CRY AFTER CHRISTMAS] From the anonymous pamphlet "Arraignment, Conviction and Imprisoning of Christmas: ... with An Hue and Cry after Christmas...." (London, 1645).

148.10 OLD SONG] This is reported to be stanza 7 of "Time's Alteration," found in Joseph Ritson's *Select Collection of English Songs* (1783).

149.24–25 "live abroad and every where."] Unidentified.

150.36 sherris sack] a dry white Spanish wine. See "sherry."

151.21 Waits] Bands of musicians and singers who at Christmas time went from house to house.

151.24 "when deep sleep falleth upon man,"] See Job 4:13 and 33:15.

151.31 "telling the night watches..."] *Comus,* line 34, "Count the night watches to his feathery Dames." See note 105.15.

151.33–39 "Some say that ever..."] *Hamlet,* act I, sc. 1.

152.9 Stranger and sojourner] See Ps. 39:12. There are several similar combinations of the words, as in Lev. 25:23.

THE STAGE COACH

153.2–7 Omne benè...deponendi.] Unknown origin; similar to the verses in the *Carmina Burana,* set to music by Carl Orff. A rendering which catches the spirit of the piece might be as follows: Every pleasure / No more pain / Now it's time for play. / The hour has come / To set aside / Our books without delay.

153.35 Bucephalus] Favorite horse of Alexander the Great.

156.1–11 "Now capons and hens . . . lick his fingers."] The passage quoted is from the December section in Nicholas Breton's *The Fantasticks* (1626).

156.9–10 Dice and cards benefit the butler] It was customary for the players to give part of their winnings to the butler.

157.8 a smoke jack] A device for turning a roasting-spit.

157.39 Poor Robin's Almanack, 1684] *Poor Robin* was one of many prophetical almanacs originating in the seventeenth and eighteenth centuries, and differs from most in its humorous attitude toward its own prophecies. "The earliest volume published under the pseudonym of 'Poor Robin' was an almanac 'calculated from the meridian of Saffron Walden,' which is said to have been originally issued in 1661 or 1662. No copy earlier than 1663 now survives. It was taken over by the Stationers' Company, and it was continued annually by various hands till 1776" (*Dictionary of National Biography*). The original author was no doubt William Winstanley (ca. 1628–1690), a well-known scribbler from Saffron Walden. Also referred to at 177.18–23, 185.5–18, and 185.39.

CHRISTMAS EVE

Apparently only two entries in Irving's notebooks refer to the Christmas sketches; both anticipate Squire Bracebridge's old-fashioned ideas as set forth in this essay. One (*Notes While Preparing Sketch Book &c., 1817*, p. 81) calls Isaac D'Israeli "a goodnatured sociable old gentleman" who "is a great admirer of old fashioned gardening—thinks it gives a greater idea of opulence and grandeur." The other (*Tour in Scotland*, p. 121) refers to "Old style of gardening—flight of steps artificial terraces —statues—urns—cumbrous balustrades of stone with occasionally a peacock with its long fluttering train—."

159.10 CARTWRIGHT] These lines are from *The Ordinary*, III, i, a comedy by William Cartwright (1611–1643), poet, dramatist, and preacher. See also 29.8.

159.23 Peacham] Henry Peacham (1576–1644?). His *Compleat Gentleman* (1622) deals with manners, geometry, poetry, music, military arts, and other matters thought relevant to the education of a gentleman.

159.24 Chesterfield] Philip Dormer Stanhope, fourth earl of Chesterfield (1694–1773) wrote *Letters to His Son* (1774) addressed to his illegitimate son, Philip. The letters, not originally intended for publication, counsel sophistication and the keeping up of appearances rather than moral behavior.

161.3 'merrie disport.'] Stow's *Survey of London*, 1603 edition, p. 98. See note 92.41.

161.8 "mongrel, puppy, whelp...."] From "An Elegy on the Death of a Mad Dog," in Chapter 17 of *The Vicar of Wakefield* (1766), by Oliver Goldsmith (1730–1774).

161.11–12 "—The little dogs and all...."] *King Lear*, III, vi.

162.9–11 the old games of hoodman blind, shoe the wild mare, hot cockles, steal the white loaf, Bob apple, and snap dragon] *Hoodman blind*: Blind Man's Buff. *Shoe the wild mare*: The player chosen to be the wild mare was allowed a head start, and then chased by the other players. In trying to escape, the mare probably kicked enthusiastically. In a Scottish version the player chosen had to perform stunts upon a beam strung between two ropes. If he did not fall off he successfully shod the "auld" mare. *Hot cockles*: One player had to kneel down blindfolded, and, being struck, had to guess who hit him. *Steal the white loaf*: Undiscovered. *Bob apple*: The player had to try to catch in his mouth an apple swinging at the end of a string. (A bob is the weight at the end of a plumb-line.) *Snap dragon*: The object is to snatch raisins from a tray of blazing brandy, and eat them without burning oneself.

163.33–38 Come, bring with a noise....] Robert Herrick, "Ceremonies for Christmasse," stanza 1, from *Hesperides* (1648). See note 110.38.

164.15–16 perfectly orthodox] Minced pie, also called "Christmas pie," was in disfavor with those of Puritan predilections, who did not observe Christmas.

165.25–30 Now Christmas is come, / Let us beat up the drum....] Unidentified.

165.37 "Harp in hall."] Unidentified.

166.29 the little French air of the Troubadour] Unidentified.

167.27–28 "no spirit dares stir abroad,"] *Hamlet*, I, i. See also note 151.33–39.

168.1 waits] See note 151.21.

CHRISTMAS DAY

169.2–10 Dark and dull night....] From stanzas 1, 3, and 4 of Herrick's "A Christmas *Caroll* sung to the King in his Presence at *White-Hall*," Number 96 in *Noble Numbers*. See note 110.38.

169.18–19 Rejoice ... morning.] The varying refrain of a carol, "The Sunny Bank," found in *Songs of the Nativity*, pp. 23-24, published without a date by J. C. Hotten.

170.31–38 'Tis thou that crown'st....] "A Thanksgiving to God, for His House," *Noble Numbers*, 47, lines 37–44. This verse, despite the Squire's work on it, is Herrick's, word for word. See note 110.38.

171.36 Sir Anthony Fitzherbert] (1470–1538), judge and author. His *Booke of Husbandrie* is a practical manual for farmers.

172.21 Markham's Country Contentments] Gervase (or Jervaise) Markham (1568–1637), scholar, poet, dramatist, horsebreeder, and agriculturist. *Country Contentments* (1611) is a book for sportsmen. See also 173.4–6.

172.21–22 the Tretyse of Hunting, by Sir Thomas Cockayne, Knight] Sir Thomas Cokayne (1519?–1592), a country gentleman who devoted himself to hunting, published *A Short Treatise of Hunting, compyled for the Delight of Noblemen and Gentlemen* in 1591.

172.22–23 Isaac Walton's Angler] Izaak Walton (1593–1683) wrote *The Compleat Angler* (1653) and a collection of lives of his contemporaries. See note 264.2–10 in "The Angler," where Walton is repeatedly cited.

172.35 old Tusser] Thomas Tusser (ca. 1525–1580) became the poet laureate of the farm. He composed a *Hundred Good Points of Husbandry Married to as Many of Good Huswifery*. The verse is unlocated.

173.4–6 'deep, solemn mouths,'...] The passage Irving quotes from concerns choosing dogs for "sweetnesse of cry." See note 172.21.

173.31 black letter] See note 19.31–32.

173.33 Caxton] William Caxton (ca. 1422–1491) set up the first printing press in England in 1476. Among his best productions are the *Morte Darthur* and *Canterbury Tales*.

173.33 Wynkin de Worde] See note 103.20.

175.24 ... Theophilus of Cesarea] It is not at all clear which Theophilus Irving is referring to. The most likely candidate is Theophilus, patriarch of Alexandria (385–428), though his extant writings apparently do not contain a defense of Christmas.

175.24 St. Cyprian] (ca. 200–258), bishop of Carthage.

175.24 St. Chrysostom] (345?–407), archbishop of Constantinople; the most famous Greek father.

175.25 St. Augustine] (354–430), bishop of Hippo. The greatest of the Latin fathers of the Church. Author of the *City of God* and *Confessions*.

175.25 a cloud more] See Heb. 12:1: "a cloud of witnesses."

176.8 Prynne] William Prynne (1600–1669), Puritan pamphleteer who compiled an enormous book attacking the theater, entitled *Histrio-Mastix*. He later adopted the cause of Charles II, and after the Restoration of the monarchy was made keeper of the records in the Tower of London.

176.9 round heads] That is, Puritans.

176.40–42 *"Ule! Ule! / Three puddings in a pule; / Crack nuts and cry ule!"] Unidentified.

177.18–23 Poor Robin … catch 'em] See note 157.39.

177.22 duke Humphry] To dine with Duke Humphrey meant to fast. The *Dictionary of the Vulgar Tongue* (London, 1811), explains: "In old St. Paul's church was an aisle called Duke Humphrey's walk (from a tomb vulgarly called his, but in reality belonging to John of Gaunt), and persons who walked there, while others were at dinner, were said to dine with Duke Humphrey."

177.23 Squire Ketch] Usually "Jack Ketch," meaning the hangman, after a famous one of the seventeenth century. According to the *Dictionary of the Vulgar Tongue*, the appellation "Squire" given to a hangman, was "a mark that he had beheaded some state criminal for high treason; an operation which, according to custom from time out of mind, has always entitled the operator to that distinction."

177.37 black jacks] Large leather beer cups or jugs, coated with tar.

177.41 *Round about our Sea-coal Fire*] The quotation is from *Round about our Coal Fire, or Christmas Entertainments* (chap. 1, p. 1), an eighteenth-century pamphlet.

178.1–4 I like them well … honesty.] Unidentified.

178.35 a Christmas box] An earthenware box in which apprentices and others collected contributions at Christmas. The box was later broken and the contents shared.

179.23 oil and wine] A frequently repeated biblical phrase. See also 186.15.

THE CHRISTMAS DINNER

180.14 WITHERS' JUVENILIA] George Wither or Withers (1588–1667), poet and pamphleteer. The collection of pieces for which he is remembered, called *Juvenilia* was first issued in 1622. This is the first stanza of "A Christmas Carol," *Juvenilia*, pt. 3.

180.21–26 Just in this nick. . . .] Stanza 15 of "A Ballad upon a wedding," published in *Fragmenta Aurea* (1646). Sir John Suckling (1609–1642), royalist poet and playwright, was highly admired for his wit, and clear, crisp style.

181.8–9 Belshazzar's parade of the vessels. . . .] The incident, but not the quotation, is found in Dan. 5:1–4. On May 21, 1817, Washington Irving wrote to his painter friend Washington Allston, and mentioned a painting Allston was working on: "I have been much struck with your conception of the Warning of Belchazzar [*sic*]. It is grand and poetical; affording scope for all the beauties and glories of the pencil. . . ."

181.22 Holbein's portraits] Hans Holbein the Younger (1497–1543), German painter who painted the portraits of many of the chief men of England, including King Henry VIII.

181.22 Albert Durer's prints] Albrecht Dürer (1471–1528), German painter and graphic artist. His prints are among the finest ever made.

182.8–13 Caput apri defero . . . convivio] One of at least four known versions of the "Boar's Head Carol." This one was first printed in Wynkyn de Worde's *Christmasse Carolles* (1521). Translation: "The boar's head I bring, giving praises to the Lord . . . who are present at the feast."

183.5 full of expectation] *Henry IV, Part I*, II, iii, "a good plot, good friends, and full of expectation."

183.25 servire cantico] Serve with a song.

183.30 In Reginensi Atrio] In the king's hall.

183.38 . . . ancient oath, used by Justice Shallow, "by cock and pye."] *Henry IV, Part II*, v, i, and *Merry Wives of Windsor*, I, i, "Cock" is a corruption of "God," and "pye" is the service book of the pre-Reformation church.

183.39 Massinger in his City Madam] Philip Massinger (1583–1640), the dramatist. The quotation is from *City Madam*, II, i.

184.37–42 Next crowne . . . a swinger] From Herrick's "Twelfe night, or King and Queen," lines 19–24. F. Max Patrick's *Complete Poetry of Robert Herrick* annotates "Lamb's Wool" as "apple pulp," and "a swinger" as "a whopper."

185.5–18 The brown bowle, / The merry brown bowle, / . . . . / And sound a lusty laugh-a.*] The second stanza of a poem for June beginning "The Black Jack, / The merry Black Jack," in Tutin's *Poor Robin's Almanack: Selected Verses* (n.d.) (see note 157.39).

185.24 slow hound] sleuth hound.

185.38 Archæologia] *Archaeologia: or, Miscellaneous Tracts Relating to Antiquity, Published by the Society of Antiquaries of London*, was first published in 1773.

186.31–32 an "alphabet of faces,"] Thomas Nashe, *Pierce Penilesse His Supplication to the Divell* (1592); R. W. McKerrow, ed., *The Works of Thomas Nashe*, I, 167, line 35.

186.42–187.1 "Cupid's Solicitor for Love;"] The verse is from "Song upon the wooing of a Widow," in *Cupid's Solicitor of Love* (ca. 1640), by Richard Crimsall.

187.8 Joe Miller] (1684–1738) was a comic actor at Drury Lane, but *Joe Miller's Jests, or the Wit's Vade Mecum*, published after his death, was a collection of jokes by John Mottley, a dramatist.

187.26 mock fairies about Falstaff] *Merry Wives of Windsor*, V, v.

187.40 Stow] The note is from Stow's *Survey of London,* 1603 edition, p. 98. See note 92.41.

189.34 Covenanters] Those who supported the Scottish National Covenant of 1638, or the English Parliament's Solemn League and Covenant of 1643, which were directed toward the extirpation of Catholicism and Episcopacy.

190.37 Sir John Hawkins] (1719–1789). His *General History of the Science and Practice of Music* appeared in 1776.

191.25–30 At the time of . . . Newstead Abbey.] Irving spent Christmas of 1831 at Barlborough Hall, Derbyshire, and then visited at Newstead Abbey which had been bought from Byron by his former schoolmate, Colonel Wildman. (See the "Plough Monday" chapter in *Newstead Abbey,* and STW, II, 25, 334.)

LONDON ANTIQUES

192.2–6 ————I do walk . . . Fletcher] I cannot find which of the many poets named Fletcher wrote this verse. "Guido Vaux" is Guy Fawkes, a chief conspirator in the Gunpowder Plot, which almost succeeded in blowing up both houses of Parliament and King James I on November 5, 1605. See also 198.31–32. "William o'the Wisp" (or Will-o'-the-wisp) is a malicious sprite who misled travelers; Robin Goodfellow (Puck) is a mischievous elf.

192.39 Knights Templars] The most famous of the three great military orders founded in the twelfth century. They originated in the Holy Land after the first crusade, and took their name from the so-called Temple of Solomon in Jerusalem where they were quartered.

193.7 "foregone world"] Unidentified.

193.12 "invitingly open."] Unidentified.

195.26 an ancient convent] The original Carthusian monastery was established here in 1371.

195.27 Sir Thomas Sutton] (1532–1611). He made a fortune from coal mines.

195.35–196.5 Stow . . . brotherly love."] Stow died six years before the hospital was founded. The quotations are not from Stow but from John Strype's edition of Stow's *Survey* (London, 1754), bk. 1, chap. 27. See note 92.41.

LITTLE BRITAIN

197.2–5 What I write. . . . Nashe] From Thomas Nashe's prose work, *Christ's Tears Over Jerusalem. Whereunto is annexed a comparative admonition to London,* published in 1593. See also notes 94.35 and 104.43.

198.29 eat pan cakes on Shrove Tuesday] Shrove Tuesday is the day before Ash Wednesday, on which, in the middle ages, sins were confessed in preparation for Lent. The eating of pancakes derives from the need to use up eggs and fat, which were prohibited during Lent.

198.30 Michaelmas] The feast of the archangel Michael, September 29.

198.31–32 burn the Pope on the Fifth of November] November 5 is Guy Fawkes Day, celebrating the discovery of the Gunpowder Plot. See note 192.2–6.

198.38–39 the figures that strike the hours at St. Dunstan's clock] One of London's most popular sights were the two savages (or Hercules) which struck the hours of the clock of St. Dunstan's-in-the-West. When the church was razed in 1630, the figures were sold to the marquis of Hertford and taken to his villa at Regent's Park, still known as St. Dunstan's.

198.39 the Monument] See note 93.22.

198.39; 199.1 lions in the Tower] Stow's *Survey of London* says: "Henry I built his manor of Woodstock. . . . He placed therein . . . divers strange beasts . . . such as . . . lions, leopards, lynxes . . . and such other." Since the time of Henry III "these lions and others have been kept in a part of this bulwark, now called the Lion Tower. . . ." In 1834, however, the large menagerie was moved to the Zoological Gardens in Regent's Park. For Stow see note 92.41.

199.1 the wooden giants in Guildhall] See note 92.34–35.

199.27–28 Robert Nixon] Known as the Cheshire prophet, he was apparently an idiot who at intervals delivered oracles. His dates and even his existence are in doubt.

199.28 Mother Shipton] She was a supposed witch and prophetess who, according to tradition, lived in the late fifteenth century in Yorkshire.

199.34–35 the grasshopper on the top of the Exchange] The grasshopper was the crest of Sir Thomas Gresham, who founded the Royal Exchange, and a figure of one stood on top of the building.

199.38–40 repairs . . . workshop] These took place in 1820. On the church of St. Mary le Bow, see note 94.35.

200.4–6 The good old king . . . had all at once given up the ghost; another king had mounted the throne] George III died January 29, 1820, and his son was crowned George IV.

200.6 a royal duke had died suddenly] Edward, duke of Kent, fourth son of George III, and father of Queen Victoria, died January 23, 1820.

200.6–7 another, in France, had been murdered] The Duc de Berri, son of Charles X, was murdered as he left the Paris Opera House on February 14, 1820.

200.7 there had been radical meetings] Agitation for reform, on such issues as universal suffrage and annual parliaments, led to frequent radical meetings between 1816 and 1819, especially in northern England.

200.8 the bloody scenes at Manchester] The Manchester or "Peterloo" massacre of August 16, 1819, when a huge meeting of working people, held to demand Parliamentary reform, was charged by cavalry. A dozen people were killed and hundreds were injured.

200.8–9 the great plot in Cato Street] The foiled conspiracy of Arthur Thistlewood and twenty-three other Radicals to assassinate the members of the English Cabinet, while they were at dinner on February 23, 1820, resulted in the hanging of Thistlewood and four others.

200.9 the Queen had returned to England] Caroline, wife of George IV, had been excluded from court while her husband was regent, and had been living in Italy. On George's accession to the throne in 1820 she returned to England to claim her rights as queen.

200.17–18 that steeple... Wittington and his Cat] Richard Whittington (d. 1423) was an extremely wealthy man, and several times mayor of London. Popular legend has him a poor orphan who makes his fortune by capitalizing on the rat-catching abilities of his cat, and by heeding the sound of Bow bells. See note 94.35.

200.26 Gentleman's Magazine] Founded by its publisher, Edward Cave, in 1731. Samuel Johnson later joined the staff. The bulk of the magazine, which appeared monthly until 1907, consisted of excerpts and condensations from the newspapers.

200.26 Rapin's History of England] Paul de Rapin (1661–1725) wrote a *History of England* (1723–1725) to the time of William and Mary. It was the standard history until supplanted by David Hume's of the same title, the first volume of which was published in 1754.

200.27 Naval Chronicle] A history of the Royal Navy, containing original papers on nautical matters. It appeared between 1799 and 1818.

201.1 Margate] A seaside resort on the Isle of Thanet, in Kent; about sixty miles by water from London.

201.25–26 "Truman, Hanbury, and Co's. Entire,"] "Entire" or "Entire butt" was a mixture of ale, beer, and twopenny, similar to what is now referred to in England as "Porter."

201.26 Old Tom] A strong English gin.

201.27 Bacchus and Momus] In classical mythology Bacchus is god of wine and intoxication while Momus is god of mockery and censure.

201.31–32 Charles the Second's day] That is, from 1660 to 1685.

202.7 trowle] Now spelled troll. A song whose parts are sung in succession, a round. "Trowle" in the third stanza of the song means "pass."

202.7 Gammer Gurton's Needle]   One of the earliest English comedies, written probably by William Stevenson about 1559, and performed at Christ's College, Cambridge. The "Confession of Faith" opens act 2.

202.18–25; 203.28–41 I cannot eate. . . .]   Nut browne toste: "nut browne and tost: ale"; crab: crab apple; mault-worme: "malt worm: one who loves malt liquor." (Definitions are from the *Oxford English Dictionary*.)

203.8 St. Bartholomew's Fair]   King Henry I granted a charter to Royer or Rahere, the king's minstrel, founder and first prior of the Priory and Hospital of St. Bartholomew, Smithfield, to hold an annual fair and use the proceeds for his institution. In the early eighteenth century the Fair became notoriously immoral. It was last proclaimed in 1854. Ben Jonson's comedy, *Bartholomew Fair*, gives a fine picture of the event. The following notes on shows at the Fair come from H. Morley's *Memoirs of Bartholomew Fair* (1859).

203.8–9 Lord Mayor's day]   November 9, the date of inauguration of the Lord Mayor of London.

203.21 the Flying Horses]   Horse shows were quite popular at such fairs, but this particular act is unidentified. See, for example, Dickens' *Hard Times*.

203.22 Signior Polito]   The owner of a famous menagerie or Wild Beast Show.

203.22 the Fire Eater]   Madame Josephine Girardelli, the "Fireproof Lady" or the "Female Salamander," was a well-known "fire-eater" at the Fair in the years before Irving wrote "Little Britain."

203.22 the celebrated Mr. Paap]   The Dutch dwarf, Sampoeman, known as Simon Paap. He was shown at the Fair in 1815, and later presented to the Royal Family. At the time, he was 26 years old, weighed 27 pounds, and measured 28 inches in height.

203.22–23 the Irish Giant]   Perhaps Patrick O'Brien, who was last exhibited in 1804. Other "giants" were on display in later years.

204.5 Temple Bar]   One of the gates of the city of London, at the junction of the Strand and Fleet Street. The last actual gateway was removed in 1878. The sovereign ceremonially halts there to receive permission from the Lord Mayor to enter the City.

204.17 train bands]   See note 95.16.

204.34 All-Fours]   a card game.

204.34 Pope-Joan]   Unidentified.

204.34–35 Tom-come-tickle-me]   Apparently a kind of a tag game. Iona and Peter Opie's *Children's Games in Street and Playground* (London: Oxford University Press, 1969), mentions Tom Tickler, Tom Tickle, and Tom Tiddler's Ground.

204.36–37 the tune of Sir Roger de Coverly] Unidentified.

204.38 Epping Forest] About 16 miles from Little Britain.

205.35 Kean] Edmund Kean (1787–1833), perhaps England's greatest tragic actor. His portrayals of Shylock and Lear in particular are landmarks in theatrical history.

205.35 the Edinbro' Review] The *Edinburgh Review* was the great Whig publication founded in 1802, and edited by Francis Jeffrey until 1829. It was liberal in politics and conservative in literary taste. See also note 3.12–13.

STRATFORD-ON-AVON

Irving visited Stratford-on-Avon with James Renwick in 1815.

209.6 GARRICK] David Garrick (1717–1779), the famous actor. The quotation is the first stanza of Air VI of his "Ode" composed for the Stratford Jubilee of 1769, which he was instrumental in organizing.

209.19–20 "Shall I not take mine ease in mine inn?"] *Henry IV, Part I*, III, iii. See also 119.2.

209.31–32 the Jubilee, and David Garrick] See note 209.6.

210.10 a garrulous old lady] Mrs. Mary Hornby, who lived at the birthplace from 1793 to 1820.

210.20 Shakespeare's mulberry tree] This tree stood in the garden of Shakespeare's house, New Place, though there is no proof that he himself planted it. It was cut down in 1758 and numerous artifacts made from the wood.

210.36–37 the Santa Casa of Loretto] See note 78.6–7.

210.37 the flying chair of the Arabian enchanter] Possibly a reference to King Housain's magic Persian carpet in the *Arabian Nights*. The carpet would carry anyone sitting on it to any place he desired. There is also a legend that King Solomon owned such a carpet.

210.38 sold . . . to a northern princess] Known as Shakespeare's chair, the original relic was sold in 1790 to Princess Czartoryska, who took it to Poland. But there were at least three other oak chairs for sale among Mrs. Hornby's relics.

211.8 a play of her own composition] *The Battle of Waterloo*, a tragedy (Stratford-upon-Avon, 1819).

211.26 Edmonds] William Edmonds (d. 1823). It is unlikely that he was more than 75 at the time of Irving's visit, at which time he was clerk of the parish.

212.1 grand daughter] Sally Kite (afterward Trinder).

212.3 John Ange] Joseph Ainge, an almsman of the borough.

212.10 "bosom scenes"] Unidentified.

213.7–10 Good friend. . . .] The spelling is modernized here, and the third line is altered; it actually reads "Bleste be ye man y^t spares thes stones."

213.36–37 Mrs. Hall]   His first child, Susanna, who married Dr. John Hall. She was actually buried in the churchyard, not in the church.

213.38 John Combe, of usurious memory]   The charge of usury probably derives from John Aubrey (1626–1697), collector of anecdotes, and appears to be unfair. John Combe, a wealthy Stratford bachelor, died in 1614 and 'left Shakespeare £5 in his will. The "ludicrous epitaph" supposedly written by Shakespeare can be found in Aubrey's *Brief Lives.*

214.17–18 Sir Thomas Lucy]   (1532–1600), owner of Charlecote Hall. The Lucys did not own a deer park during Shakespeare's youth, though they did much later. The legend owes most to Nicholas Rowe's biography of Shakespeare prefaced to his six-volume edition of the plays (1709).

214.31 revenged himself in his writings]   This supposed revenge is in *The Merry Wives of Windsor,* I, i. See 220.12.

214.34–42 A parliament member. . . .]   Although these lines were attributed to the poet by an old man who lived near Stratford and died in 1703, they are probably not authentic.

215.32–33 a traditionary anecdote . . . Avon."]   *Picturesque Views on the Warwickshire Avon* was published in 1795 by Samuel Ireland after a visit to Stratford to gather material for the book. His escort, John Jordan, Stratford poet and forger of Shakespeariana, apparently invented numerous village customs for his benefit, such as this one. Samuel was the father of William Henry Ireland the infamous forger of Shakespeare manuscripts, etc., and although apparently innocent of his son's activities, died in disgrace in 1800.

216.21–27; 217.1–2 song in Cymbeline . . . lady sweet arise!]   II, iii.

217.9–11 "to sit round the fire . . . goblins, and friars."]   Unidentified.

217.35 *Scot, in his "Discoverie of Witchcraft,"]   Published in 1584, this scholarly work was written by Reginald Scot (d. 1599) to reveal the folly of persecuting witches. Shakespeare's witches in *Macbeth* in part derive from it. The passage is from bk. 7, chap. 15.

218.19 meditations of Jaques]   See *As You Like It,* II, vii.

218.30–37 Under the green wood tree . . . winter and rough weather.]   *As You Like It,* II, v. The second and third lines should read: "And turn his merry note / Unto the sweet bird's throat."

218.40 the first year of her reign]   1558.

219.18–20 "*Falstaff* . . . good air."]   *Henry IV, Part II,* V, iii.

220.38–39 a portrait by Sir Peter Lely]   The portrait is actually by Sir Godfrey Kneller, a native of Holstein, who was invited to England in 1674. He was court painter from 1680 until his death in 1723. For Lely, see note 67.25.

221.16 as Master Slender would say, "a cane-coloured beard."] It is Simple, not Slender, who, in *The Merry Wives of Windsor*, I, iv, speaks of a "cane [or 'Cain'] coloured beard."

221.41 *Bishop Earle] John Earle (1601–1665), chaplain to Charles II in exile, wrote *Micro-cosmographie, or, A Peece of The World Discovered; In Essayes and Characters* (1628). The quotation is from Number 17, An Upstart Knight.

222.17 with that pity "that dwells in womanhood."] Unidentifed.

222.18–19 brief authority] "Man, proud man! dressed in a little brief authority." *Measure for Measure*, II, ii.

222.25–26 "to a last year's pippin of his own graffing, with a dish of carraways;"] *Henry IV, Part II*, V, iii.

222.36 Gilpin, in his description of a Mr. Hastings] Henry Hastings (1551–1650) son of the fourth earl of Huntingdon. Anthony Ashley Cooper, the first earl of Shaftesbury, inscribed on Hastings' portrait an account of his life, which was later reprinted in various publications. The passage in Shaftesbury's account is practically identical to the one quoted. I cannot identify Gilpin, to whom Irving attributes the quotation in his note.

223.1–6 "By cock and pye, Sir. . . ."]..*Henry IV, Part II*, V, i. "kickshaws," from the French *quelque chose*, means fancy dishes. See also note 183.38.

223.13–14 " 'Tis merry in hall. . . ."] *Henry IV, Part II*, V, iii.

223.18 "working day world"] *As You Like It*, I, iii.

223.24 airy nothings] "The poet's pen . . . gives to airy nothing / A local habitation and a name." *A Midsummer Night's Dream*, V, i.

223.26 I had heard Jaques soliloquize beneath his oak] *As You Like It*, II, vii.

223.27–28 the fair Rosalind . . . woodlands] In *As You Like It*.

223.29–30 Falstaff . . . Justice Shallow . . . Master Slender . . . Anne Page] They are all characters in *The Merry Wives of Windsor*; and, as the preceding quotations indicate, the three men also appear in *Henry IV*, Parts I and II.

TRAITS OF INDIAN CHARACTER

Irving read a number of works on the early history of the colonies when preparing "Traits of Indian Character" and its companion essay "Philip of Pokanoket" for publication first in the *Analectic Magazine* in 1814 and later in *The Sketch Book* (see pp. 360–64 in the Textual Commentary). Some of his sources are identifiable, others are conjectural, and some may no longer be extant. His *Notes While Preparing Sketch*

Book &c., *1817* shows that he had read and taken notes on more material than he made use of in his published writing.

The major source for these *Sketch Book* essays is apparently Reverend William Hubbard's *A Narrative of the Troubles with the Indians in New-England* (Boston, 1677), though Irving also relied on Increase Mather's *A Brief History of the War with the Indians in New England* (Boston, 1676). Another important one, at least for "Traits of Indian Character," is Thomas Morton's *New English Canaan* (Amsterdam, 1637). For a discussion of the connection and Morton's effect on Irving see Donald F. Connors, *Thomas Morton* (New York: Twayne Publishers, 1969). The only other source specifically identifiable from the text of the essays is the "MS. of the Rev. W. Ruggles." This manuscript, however, was apparently never published and may not be extant. It is of course possible that Irving had access to other manuscripts as well, now either lost or unidentified.

Other possibilities for Irving's source reading, some more likely than others, include Thomas Hutchinson's *The History of the Colony of Massachusetts-Bay* (London, 1760), Cotton Mather's *Magnalia Christi Americana* (London, 1702), Increase Mather's *A Relation of the Troubles which have hapned in New-England, By Reason of the Indians there* (Boston, 1677), Benjamin Church's *Entertaining Passages Relating to Philip's War which Began in the Month of June, 1675* (Boston, 1716), and some of the narratives since published in two collections: *The Old Indian Chronicle; being a Collection of Exceeding Rare Tracts*, edited by Samuel G. Drake (Boston, 1836); and *Narratives of the Indian Wars, 1675–1699*, edited by Charles H. Lincoln (New York, 1913).

225.3–5 "I appeal to any white man. . . ."] Logan, or Tahgahjute (ca. 1725–1780) was a Cayuga who acquired great influence with the Shawnee after marrying into their tribe. As the result of the murder of his sister and other relatives by whites in 1774, Logan declared war. The Indians were finally defeated at Point Pleasant on the Ohio, but Logan refused to attend the peace council with Lord Dunmore. He sent instead the speech which begins with these words. The authenticity of the speech has been questioned.

226.37–42 The American government has been indefatigable. . . .] The government's sincerity and fairness have in recent times been seriously questioned.

227.9–15 "For," says an old historian. . . . meanly of."] The passage is quoted almost word for word from Thomas Morton's *New English Canaan* (1637), bk. 1, p. 178.

228.12–13 an old record of the early settlement] Morton's *New English Canaan*. The incident occurs in bk. 3, pp. 169–71, and Irving's report of the sachem's speech closely follows Morton's.

230.32–33 glorious "pomp and circumstance of war,"]   *Othello*, III, iii: "pomp and circumstance of glorious war!"

231.36–38 one of the homely narratives . . . Pequod Indians.]   A *Narrative of the Troubles with the Indians in New-England* (Boston, 1677) by the Reverend William Hubbard (1621–1704), who emigrated to New England in 1635.

233.9–10 that gigantic race said to have existed on the borders of the Susquehanna]   Unidentified.

233.14–15 "the places that now know them will know them no more for ever."]   Unidentified.

233.25–28 "We are driven back . . . to exist."]   Source unidentified.

PHILIP OF POKANOKET

For the history and genesis of this essay, see the introductory explanatory note to "Traits of Indian Character," above, as well as the Textual Commentary, pp. 360–64.

234.9 CAMPBELL]   Thomas Campbell (1777–1844), Scottish poet, is remembered mainly for his war songs such as "Hohenlinden," and "Ye Mariners of England." The quotation is from "Gertrude of Wyoming" (1809), a poem in Spenserian stanzas focusing on a Mohawk raid on the Pennsylvania settlement of Wyoming. See pt. 1, stanza 23, lines 3–9.

235.1–2 a volume of early colonial history]   Unidentifiable.

235.11 PHILIP OF POKANOKET]   He died in 1676. Irving is essentially correct in the details of his life.

235.41 a celebrated English poet]   Robert Southey (1774–1843), who became poet laureate of England in 1813. The poem Irving refers to is "Oliver Newman, A New England Tale" (1837).

237.4 Metamocet]   Actually Metacomet.

239.34 one of the learned men of the day]   That is, Increase Mather.

239.41 *The Rev. Increase Mather's History]   A *Brief History of the War with the Indians in New England* (1676) by Increase Mather (1639–1723), the father of Cotton Mather, for whom see note 276.41.

240.3–4 a worthy clergyman of the time]   The Reverend William Hubbard. See note 231.36–38.

241.39–41 "He was . . . English;"]   Hubbard.

243.9–10 "he would fight it out . . . English."]   Hubbard.

243.33 peag]   Beads made from shell, strung together and used by the Indians as money.

243.38–39 "his heart and his bowels . . . of strength."]   Hubbard.

243.41 *MS. of the Rev. W. Ruggles]   This manuscript is apparently no longer extant, and its author cannot be identified.

244.5–10 Being questioned . . . answer."]   Hubbard.

244.19–20 "and he desired to hear no more thereof."] Hubbard.

244.27–28 "that he liked it well . . . himself."] Hubbard.

244.29 Stonington] in Connecticut.

245.2–8 "His ruin . . . away."] Hubbard.

245.18–19 where the wicked . . . troubling] Job 3:17: "There the wicked cease from troubling; and there the weary be at rest."

245.26 "most horrid and diabolical lamentations."] Hubbard.

245.29–33 "he never rejoiced afterwards . . . deliverance."] Hubbard.

245.41–246.5 "Phillip," he says . . . upon him."] Hubbard.

246.33 "beloved wife and only son"] Hubbard.

JOHN BULL

248.1 JOHN BULL] Law is a Bottomless Pit, or the History of John Bull (1712), a satire by Dr. John Arbuthnot (1667–1735), contained a character named "John Bull" who allegorically stood for England. The name soon gained popularity and was applied to the nation or a particular Englishman. Irving's friend James K. Paulding wrote The Diverting History of John Bull and Brother Jonathan, and sent Irving a copy of it in 1812.

248.11 OLD SONG] Unidentified.

248.37–38 beyond the sound of Bow bells.] See note 94.35.

250.31–32 "gentlemen of the fancy;"] Those who fancy a particular sport or amusement, especially boxing.

253.4 beef eaters] Here referring to soldiers.

254.16–17 obstreperous conduct of one of his sons] Perhaps an allusion to "Orator Hunt," a popular agitator of the time who always managed to keep himself out of trouble.

254.42 Tom, an officer] Tommy Atkins, the nickname given to British soldiers. At the end of the Napoleonic Wars in 1815, many British officers were on half pay.

255.10–11 he is mortgaged over head and ears] The national debt had grown from a hundred and thirty million pounds before the American Revolution to seven hundred million after the Napoleonic Wars.

255.32 pockets . . . empty] From 1797 to 1821 Bank of England notes were not redeemable in gold.

THE PRIDE OF THE VILLAGE

257.3–9 May no wolfe howle. . . . HERRICK] Stanza 12 of "The Dirge of Jephthah's Daughter." See note 110.38.

258.24 flower of the field] Ps. 103:15; Isa. 40:6.

258.25–26 Rachel, "mourning . . . comforted."] See Jer. 31:15 and Matt. 2:18.

259.3–6 "This is the prettiest . . . place."] *The Winter's Tale*, IV, iv.

262.19 the silver cord] Eccles. 12:6.

THE ANGLER

In a letter to Henry Brevoort (June 16, 1816) Irving reports meeting a fisherman-philosopher such as described here, while traveling in Wales. Some of the language of the sketch may be found in that letter.

264.2–10 This day dame Nature. . . . Sɪʀ H. Wᴏᴛᴛᴏɴ] Sir Henry Wotton (1568–1639), ambassador, poet, provost of Eton College. His works are collected under the title *Reliquiae Wottonianae*. These lines are from a poem quoted by Izaak Walton in *The Compleat Angler*, pt. 1, chap. 1. See note 172.22–23.

264.16–17 Izaak Walton . . . "Complete Angler"] See note 172.22–23.

264.21–22 we took rod in hand . . . country.] Irving and several friends went on this excursion, near Peekskill, New York, in the summer of 1810. Henry Brevoort was the one so fully equipped.

264.31 La Mancha . . . Sierra Morena] *Don Quixote*, pt. 1, bk. 3, chap. 9.

265.15 before I had completely "satisfied the sentiment,"] See Irving to his brother Peter (June 30, 1822): "Like Trim I have satisfied the sentiment." Corporal Trim is Uncle Toby's servant in Sterne's *Tristram Shandy*, but I have not been able to locate the allusion.

265.40–41 "good honest, wholesome, hungry" repast] *The Compleat Angler*, pt. 1, chap. 4.

266.1–2 Izaak Walton's scene with the milkmaid] *The Compleat Angler*, in pt. 1, chap. 2.

266.26 "brothers of the angle,"] A reiterated phrase in *The Compleat Angler*.

266.27 "mild, sweet and peaceable spirit"] *The Compleat Angler*, pt. 1, chap. 1.

266.28–29 "Tretyse of fishing with the Angle,"] *A Treatyse of Fysshynge wyth an Angle*, by Dame Juliana Berners (about whom nothing is known), was the first English book on fishing. It was printed by Wynkyn de Worde in 1496. This quotation is from the next-to-last page, and is followed by the passage quoted in Irving's note.

267.14 instructions of the sage Piscator to his scholar] In *The Compleat Angler*.

267.33 battle of Camperdown] On October 11, 1797, Admiral Duncan defeated the Dutch fleet off Camperdown on the Dutch coast.

267.38 the "noble art of angling."] Irving is presumably quoting again from Walton.

268.33–39 "When I would . . . him"] *The Compleat Angler*, pt. 1, end of chap. 21.

269.1–14 Let me live . . . daffodil.] The opening lines of a poem quoted in *The Compleat Angler*, pt. 1, chap. 1. The book from which the quotation comes was published in 1613 and was written by John Dennys (d. 1609), not J. Davors.

269.30–31 naval ballads, such as Admiral Hosier's Ghost] Admiral Hosier (1673–1727) was stationed in the West Indies when he and four thousand of his men died in a fever epidemic. Richard Glover (1712–1785) wrote this ballad which says that Hosier died of a broken heart. It is printed in Percy's *Reliques*, vol. 2, bk. 3, song 25.

269.31 All in the Downs] Better known as "Sweet William's Farewell to Black-eyed Susan," by John Gay (1685–1732), who wrote *The Beggar's Opera*. It begins, "All in the Downs the fleet was moored."

269.31 Tom Bowling] A song by Charles Dibdin (1745–1814), playwright and songwriter. It is based on Lieutenant Tom Bowling, Roderick's uncle in Tobias Smollett's *Roderick Random*.

271.8 St. Peter's master] That is, Jesus.

271.9–10 "and upon all that . . . go a angling."] A similarly worded passage closes Chapter 13 of Part 1 of *The Compleat Angler*.

THE LEGEND OF SLEEPY HOLLOW

"The Legend of Sleepy Hollow," like "Rip Van Winkle," has distinct literary and biographical antecedents, transmuted by the author's imagination. Bürger's "Der wilde Jäger" is an important literary source, while the chase and throwing of the false head are found in the Rübezahl legends of Germany. More than one person named "Ichabod Crane" has been pointed to by scholars in search of Irving's original, as has Irving's schoolteacher friend, Jesse Merwin. Other people and places in the story also appear to have more than literary reality.

272.8 Castle of Indolence] By James Thomson; canto 1, stanza 6. See also note 16.7.

272.12–13 implored the protection of St. Nicholas] St. Nicholas was the protector of shipwrecked sailors, and others in hazardous trades.

272.31–34 If ever I should wish . . . little valley.] See note 7.33.

273.6 Hendrick Hudson] See note 40.12.

273.14–15 the night mare, with her whole nine fold] See *King Lear*, III, iv.

275.5–6 "spare the rod and spoil the child."] Samuel Butler's *Hudibras* (1663–1678), bk. 2, canto 1, line 844. See Prov. 13:24, "He that spareth the rod hateth his son."

276.2–3 the lion bold . . . hold] In the *New England Primer* (ca. 1683) the couplet accompanying the letter L read, "The lion bold / The lamb doth hold."

276.17–18 "by hook and by crook,"] The phrase apparently dates back to the fourteenth century, but its origin is unknown.

276.41 Cotton Mather's History of New England Witchcraft] Cotton Mather (1663–1728), the son of Increase Mather (see note 239.41), was the most famous of the Mather dynasty of ministers. Irving's reference is probably to *Memorable Providences Relating to Witchcrafts and Possessions* (1689), though Mather also wrote on witchcraft in two other major works: *Magnalia Christi Americana*, and *The Wonders of the Invisible World*.

277.21 token] Apparently a sign or warning.

277.25 "in linked sweetness . . ."] "Of linked sweetness long drawn out," Milton, *L'Allegro*, line 140.

278.33 Saardam] A town about five miles northwest of Amsterdam; also called Zaandam.

281.37 Don Cossacks] See note 5.29.

282.3 rantipole] wild, disorderly.

282.17 supple jack] A climbing shrub with strong stems from which walking sticks are often made.

285.36 monteiro] *Montero*, a round huntsman's cap with a flap.

286.12–13 "sugared suppositions,"] Unidentified.

287.14–15 oly koek, and . . . cruller] oly koek: sweetened dough fried in lard; kruller: dough twisted into various shapes, and crisply fried in lard or oil.

288.33 Doffue Martling] Unidentified. He may be Irving's invention.

288.38 Whiteplains] General Howe was defeated by the Americans at White Plains, north of New York City, on October 28, 1776.

289.23 Major André] The British officer (1751–1780) who was involved in Benedict Arnold's attempt to betray West Point. Despite much popular sympathy for the personable André, he was hanged as a spy.

291.11 the very witching time of night] *Hamlet*, III, ii.

294.23 "If I can but reach that bridge,"] Alluding to the belief that supernatural beings could not cross running water.

296.3 Ten Pound Court] That is, small claims court.

L'ENVOY

298.7 CHAUCER's *Belle Dame sans Mercie*] Although formerly attributed to Chaucer, *La Belle Dame sans Mercie* is a mid-fifteenth-century translation by Sir Richard Ros of a poem by Alain Chartier.

TEXTUAL COMMENTARY

THE MANUSCRIPTS

Irving's small parcels of manuscript for the first edition of *The Sketch Book* passed individually through the hands of Ebenezer Irving, Henry Brevoort, Van Winkle and his compositors (or Murray and his printer), and an unknown number of later holders, and now, not surprisingly, the early *Sketch Book* manuscript exists only in part. Surviving are Numbers I, II, and III, with the strange exception of one page containing the first few lines of the introductory note to "Rip Van Winkle."[1] In addition, four leaves of "The Legend of Sleepy Hollow," only partly in Irving's hand, are extant. All the MS for the first three numbers but "The Broken Heart" and "The Wife" is tipped into a large collector's binding, gold stamped on cover and spine.[2] The front cover reads: "WASHING-TON IRVING/ [rule]/ THE SKETCH BOOK/ [rule]/ ORIGINAL AUTOGRAPH MANUSCRIPT." The bookplates are of Boies Penrose II and Clifton Waller Barrett.

The manuscript proper consists of 212 leaves written on the rectos only, except for frequent false starts and experimental lines on the versos.[3] It is preceded by Irving's "Directions for the Printer," a folio sheet, written on both sides of the first leaf. The manuscript is in ink, which varies in color from light brown to brown-black and changes slightly within sketches. The pages show pinholes where Irving himself evidently sewed together his sketches.[4] Because they are sometimes composite or cut-down sheets, Irving's pages vary from 10⅛ x 4⁹⁄₁₆ to 3⅝ x 4⁷⁄₁₆ inches, while the average one-piece page varies between 7½ x 4⁹⁄₁₆ and 7⅜ x 4⁷⁄₁₆ inches.

---

1. This may be the one page once owned by Irving bibliographer William Langfeld and now in unknown hands. See William R. Langfeld, *Washington Irving: A Bibliography* (New York, 1935), p. 23; hereafter cited as Langfeld.

2. The Clifton Waller Barrett Library, University of Virginia.

3. Irving used four kinds of wove, watermarked paper. In order of first appearance they are: (1) R BARNARD / 1816; (2) J GREEN / 1817; (3) [ornate capital]/ 18[ ] [only one sheet]; and (4) SS/ 1818. In addition, some of the many unwatermarked leaves are embossed with seals in one corner. Three or perhaps four different seal papers were used, but some of the designs are too indistinct to distinguish from one another. The most common in the manuscript, and the most distinct as well, exhibits a crown above BATH, all enclosed in an octagonal border.

4. He mentions stitching up *Sketch Book* No. III in a letter to Brevoort, July 28, 1819, now in the New York Public Library. Other existing Irving manuscripts show evidence of similar stitchings, some of them still intact.

Twenty-seven of these manuscript leaves are made of two or three pieces of paper glued together where Irving used scissors and paste to revise his work. The most extensive use of such revision involves manuscript pages 10–13 in "English Writers on America" (46–47). In these pages and the others similarly revised it is impossible to reconstruct the original sheets or their possible positions in the text before revision. Irving's changes in all such instances evidently were in rewriting, not rearranging, a conclusion supported not only by the inability to match the fragments in the manuscript, but by the several instances in which recovery of a few words hidden by the pasted on segment shows them to be identical with the readings on the substitute pieces. Irving made his cuts, revisions, or additions at these points before sewing, since the pinholes of composite sheets match those of the unaltered ones. A few sketches are evidently written on only one kind of paper, but neither this fact nor even the general chronological sequence of the appearance of the watermarked paper indicates an approximate order of composition; for the general neatness of Irving's page (in contrast to his journals and notebooks), the several instances of eyeskip, and the many words crossed out and then written more clearly, all indicate that this manuscript is fair copy which Irving transcribed from a rougher form of his text.

There are a few obvious nonauthorial entries in the manuscript, but most are not particularly enlightening. They include the following: (1) On page 4 of the "Directions for the Printer" folio are "Monday [illegible] Van that ga" in pencil, and in ink the number 59497. (2) On the verso of page 2 of the "Prospectus" are listed the numbers 25 and 23. (3) At intervals throughout are notations similar to that on page 7 of "The Author's Account of Himself" where a bracket is inserted into the text while on the facing verso appears "Sig. 2. Page 9." These notations accord in every case with the signatures and pagination of the first American edition, and, in conjunction with inky fingerprints, indicate that this manuscript was printer's copy. (4) In the left margin of page 80 of "Rip Van Winkle" are the initials "HB," very likely Henry Brevoort. Perhaps they mark a spot where Brevoort interrupted his reading of the manuscript. In the same sketch, on page 85 verso, is a highly ornate word that appears to be "Perambulator." (5) On the verso of page 66 of "The Art of Book Making" is "end of No 2." (6) On the verso of page 77 of "The Boar's head Tavern, East cheap" appears "End of No III."

The autograph manuscript of "The Broken Heart" exists as a separate, unbound, sewn unit of twelve leaves.[5] The first two leaves make up one folio, but all the succeeding are separate. The manuscript is written

5. The Clifton Waller Barrett Library, University of Virginia.

in brown-black ink on the rectos only, of wove paper watermarked on eight of the twelve leaves J GREEN/ 1817, and measuring on the average 7½ x 4½ inches. Only the last leaf is composite, and is folded to the length of the others. The pages were once sewn together, apparently by Irving and again by a later hand. On the verso of the last leaf Irving wrote "To Elizabeth B. Bull/ from Washington Irving/ New York." The year "1825–" in pencil and in another hand precedes this note, while pasted on the same page just below Irving's inscription is a slip written in ink in still another hand and reading "This original Manuscript/ is presented/ To Miss Mary Beach/ by her friend, Hetty M. Bull/ Hartford, 23ª August, A. D. 1876."; and stamped in red just above the bottom fold is "MISS MARY E. BEACH/ VINE HILL/ WEST HARTFORD, CONN."

On the fifth leaf of this sketch is inserted a bracket, and in the margin a signature and page notation similar to those in the larger manuscript, and again corresponding to the first American edition. No other nontextual matter is written on the manuscript leaves, but on the verso of the first leaf is pasted a clipping from the New York *Daily Post* of a funeral poem by "a friend" of Irving's, "himself eminent in the world of letters," entitled "Sunnyside" and dated December 1, 1859, three days after Irving's death.[6] In faded ink in the margin of the clipping is written "Life of Columbus—Visit to Abbotsford—Washington's/ how gracefully the allusion is made. [brace] Life=/ N. P. Willis.[7]

Comparative measurement of the pinholes in this separate sketch shows that it was once sewn together with the other sketches in *Sketch Book* Number II; it is obviously of a piece with those bound in the large manuscript book described above.

The last segment of these *Sketch Book* manuscripts from which the first edition was printed is the holograph transcription of "The Wife," nineteen unbound, unsewn leaves written in ink on the rectos only.[8] It corresponds in all physical details with the other manuscripts and was no doubt originally sewn in with the packet sent to America as *Sketch Book* Number I. Only the first leaf is composite: the top 3¼ inches of the original leaf, containing the epigraph, was torn off, and another

6. The unidentified author was Henry Theodore Tuckerman, the journalist cousin of Frederick Goddard Tuckerman. Though known to Irving, he was most likely not "a friend." See E. A. Duyckinck, compiler, *Irvingiana: A Memorial of Washington Irving* (New York, 1860), p. 1; STW, II, 206, 390.

7. Willis, an ardent admirer and imitator of Irving, was often a visitor at Sunnyside, Irving's home.

8. Edited and presented here by permission of the Harvard College Library.

piece of paper pasted on in its place. A fragment of a letter just below the tear line does not match anything in the last line of the present epigraph, and therefore suggests that Irving may have originally used a different introductory quotation. The only nonauthorial entries are two printer's notations of line and signature, in different hands. As in the other manuscripts these accord exactly with the signing and pagination of the first edition.[9]

All three of these manuscripts contain many authorial alterations of a more usual kind than the cutting and pasting noted above. Irving made several hundred substitutions of one word for another, and a large number of changes involving whole phrases inserted, deleted, or revised. He corrected many of his own errors in number and tense, as well as punctuation and spelling, and often rewrote for greater clarity. These changes, though sometimes a bit difficult to read, would not have created great problems for his printer; and, indeed, collation with the first edition shows that the compositors were less likely to make errors at a point of correction than where the text is unaltered and clear. (Cancellations, insertions, and mendings of the extant manuscripts are reported in "Alterations in the Manuscripts," beginning on page 467.)

There is another extant manuscript or group of manuscripts. In the Lowell Collection at the Houghton Library, Harvard, is a copy of the Author's Revised Edition, 1848, into which are bound forty-three leaves of manuscript and four pages of print, all of which served as printer's copy for various portions of the Author's Revised Edition of *The Sketch Book.*

The holograph manuscripts are "A Sunday in London" and "London Antiques," entire; the "Postscript" to "Rip Van Winkle," and "Notes Concerning Westminster Abbey" (the complete notes). Two and one-half pages of "The Widow and Her Son" are also included, as are the concluding footnote to "The Christmas Dinner" and a note to "London Antiques."[10] These manuscript leaves vary in size from 7⅞ to 8⅛ inches in the uncut pieces, and several of them are composite—the result of Irving's scissors and paste revisions. The independent sketches, notes, etc., are numbered separately.

The pages of print, from a yet unidentified printing, include one leaf (numbered 89–90) from "Rip Van Winkle." On page 90 is the holograph alteration of the printed "Ah, poor man, his name was Rip Van Winkle" to "Ah poor man! Rip Van Winkle was his name but." The third page

9. The manuscript fragment of "The Legend of Sleepy Hollow," discussed below, has no printer's markings of any kind.

10. "London Antiques" includes an end note which, until ARE, was an introductory note to "Little Britain." In this manuscript Irving rewrote the first, long sentence of that note and attached to it the remainder of the original in printed form.

is from "A Royal Poet," is numbered 187, and includes Irving's deletion of "do not, however, let us always consider what is romantic," with his substitution of "let us not, however, reject every romantic incident." The last page of print included is the first page of "L'Envoy," on which Irving footnoted his title: "*Closing the second volume of the London Edition."

One frustration in the editorial work for this Twayne edition has been the inability, despite extensive search, to identify the edition from which these printed pages come. Examination on the Hinman machine reveals that they are line-for-line resettings of the Baudry-Didot edition, published in Paris in 1823, and are set in the same font as that first French edition. The only textual differences between these pages and the corresponding ones in the 1823 edition are on page 89: the Lowell page contains a reversed quotation mark on line 4 (38.34), and reads "by-standers" on line 23 as against the 1823 "byestanders" (39.4). Irving apparently annotated and gave to Putnam's a copy of a reprint edition based on the Paris edition of 1823, and from this copy, plus the manuscript material in the Lowell volume—the Author's Revised Edition was set. If we make the logical assumption that Irving did not have with him, in 1847–1848, a copy of the 1823 edition, his choice of this reprint makes good sense, since it derives ultimately from the Murray edition of 1822, the last revision of the text before 1848.[11] We cannot be sure, however, that Irving knew he was thus perpetuating his substantive emendations of 1822.

"A Sunday in London" consists of six leaves inscribed in ink on the rectos only.[12] It is headed with Irving's note: "To follow the Widow & her Son." The number 141, corresponding to the page in the Author's Revised Edition on which the sketch begins, is inserted in another hand just above the title, and the signature of a compositor named Wood appears twice.[13] Irving made a number of substantive changes in the manuscript of this sketch before turning it over to the printer, and he did the same with the other pieces added in 1848. He canceled phrases and changed his mind about whole sentences, as he did, for example,

11. See the Introduction, p. xxi.
12. All the manuscripts in this group are so inscribed.
13. The signatures of two other compositors, "Smith" and "Poor," occur elsewhere in these manuscripts. Despite the ten preserved signatures, however, no conclusions can be drawn through analysis of stints because the material of these documents is scattered throughout *The Sketch Book*, because some stints are fragmentary, and because there are too few of them on which to base conclusions about a man's accuracy. Wood's name also appears twice in the forty-three surviving pages of manuscript from which *Mahomet* was set in 1849–1850, in the same print shop. See *Mahomet and His Successors*, ed. Henry A. Pochmann and E. N. Feltskog (Madison: University of Wisconsin Press, 1970), p. 582.

when he deleted his "Now the brisk dapper shopman and apprentice," started again with "Satyrists may say what they please," and then canceled again in the same sentence, "parks and green fields swarming with the populace" ("A Sunday in London," folio 5 [90.12–16]). These late additions to *The Sketch Book*, in general, were given to the printer in a somewhat less finished form than were the surviving manuscripts for the first edition.

"London Antiques" consists of fourteen manuscript leaves. At the head stands Irving's note: "To follow the article entitled The Christmas Dinner," and, in another hand, the number 299, indicating the page of the Author's Revised Edition on which the sketch begins. Similarly, the "Postscript" to "Rip Van Winkle," five leaves, is noted: "(To follow the note on P 97)"—97 was the page number in the printer's copy; "63" at the top of this page is someone's indication of the location of this postscript in the Author's Revised Edition.

The other fragments in this group of manuscripts are of a piece with those described, and need no further description; but included among them is a note written by Irving, apparently to someone at Putnam's: "I must retain the other proofs for a day or two to / make alterations and additions. / There will be no extracts in the appendix / The preface will not make more than a / couple of pages if as much[.]" This note is puzzling since there is no new appendix to the 1848 edition of *The Sketch Book*, and since the new "Preface" comes to six full pages of print. A look at the pagination at the beginning of the Author's Revised Edition answers the latter question: the "Preface" is numbered [vii]–xii, but the first page of the text proper is [9]. If Irving had held himself to the two pages promised in his note, the last page of the peface would have been viii and the first sketch would have correctly begun with [9]. Apparently Putnam's wanted to avoid delay, and on the receipt of this note ordered the pagination of the text on the assumption of a two-page preface. When Irving handed in six pages instead, it was too late to make the pagination of the prefatory matter and the body of the book consecutive.

The note's reference to an "appendix" suggests that Irving might have been planning a new conclusion to the book, since he would not have thus alluded to "L'Envoy" which was part of the printer's copy-text he gave to Putnam's. No evidence of such an addition, however, is extant. Apparently the only other possible referent is "Notes Concerning Westminster Abbey," which in 1848 appeared with the sketch itself, but in editions after Irving's death was sometimes placed at the end of the book. In the absence of further evidence, however, speculation is fruitless.

A separate and somewhat enigmatic MS is in the Berg Collection of the New York Public Library. It is the only known surviving fragment of "The Legend of Sleepy Hollow" and is mostly in the hand of an amanuensis. It consists of four leaves, the second and third of which are consecutive, and is written in brownish ink on the rectos only. The paper is watermarked, half on page 1 and half on page 8, "BASTED MILL/ 1817." The first three of these leaves measure 7⅜ x 4⁷⁄₁₆ and the fourth, made up of two pieces of paper, is 9¹³⁄₁₆ x 4½.

The first leaf, numbered "1," contains from the title of the story to "by the name of" (272.15). The second, numbered "7" covers "passes along the hollow" to "entered that sleepy" (273.30–40), and the third, numbered "8," contains "region" to "straw and bubble" (273.40–274.8). The fourth MS leaf is torn where the number should be. It covers "-hive and" to "hanging uselessly" (286.8–25). All four leaves show apparent needle holes for sewing up the MS into a fascicle, but whether they were actually sewed together is impossible to tell. The portion of this fragment in Irving's hand is only one quarter of the whole. He inscribed the title, subtitle, and epigraph, deleted three words and added seven in the first sentence (see Alterations in the Manuscripts, p. 492), and wrote a sixty-seven word passage describing Ichabod Crane on his way to the party, beginning "-hive and as he," and ending "The sun" (286.8–15).

The exact role of this MS fragment in *The Sketch Book*'s textual history is uncertain. Its substantive readings agree with those of 1A, not the later, variant 1E; and the portions of the text inscribed by Irving contain two commas and a hyphen not in 1A, while 1A has two commas and a hyphen missing in the corresponding portions of the MS. The leaves show no sign of having been handled by a printer. On the MS evidence as a whole (what there is of it) it seems reasonable to conjecture that this fragment is all that survives of a copy of the MS Irving sent to the United States, from which "The Legend of Sleepy Hollow" was first printed. That this MS was not printer's copy for 1A is further argued by the existence in 1A of one of Irving's characteristic dashes where the MS (not in Irving's hand) has a semicolon.

This MS fragment, then, remains more of a curiosity than a useful textual tool. It contains a very small portion of the whole story, few of the MS accidentals are definitely Irving's, and its relationship to 1A is uncertain. As a result, editorial emendation of the copy-text's accidentals according to this fragment is not justified.

THE EDITIONS[14]

The following identifying symbols have been adopted as convenient shortened forms of reference.

1A   First American edition (Van Winkle, 1819–1820)

2A   Second American edition (Van Winkle, 1819–1820)

3A   Third American edition (Van Winkle, 1822–1823)

1E   First British edition: Volume I (John Miller/John Murray, 1820); Volume II (John Murray, 1820)

2E   Second British edition (John Murray, 1820)

22E "New Edition" (John Murray, 1822)

1F   First French edition (Baudry and Didot, 1823)

1G   First German edition (Montucci, 1823)

ARE "Author's Revised Edition" (G. P. Putnam, 1848)

The first American edition (1A) of *The Sketch Book*, in seven paperbound numbers, was printed in New York by C. S. Van Winkle and published simultaneously in New York, Boston, Philadelphia, and Baltimore.[15] The first number was officially published on June 23, 1819, and the last on September 13, 1820.[16] Two thousand copies each of Numbers I–IV were printed, and though evidence is lacking, the same is probably true of Numbers V–VII. Holograph manuscript was printer's copy for Numbers I–VI, but not, supposedly, for Number VII. Pierre M. Irving writes: "On the 28th of June [1820], after the printers had commenced upon the English edition of the second volume of the 'Sketch Book,' Mr. Irving transmitted to his brother Ebenezer the sheets for the seventh

14. The considerable bibliographical complications of *The Sketch Book*, particularly of the early American printings, will be treated in the bibliography volume of this Irving edition, and are therefore not elaborated here. The interested reader is referred to the discussions and descriptions in Langfeld and Jacob Blanck, *Bibliography of American Literature* (New Haven: Yale University Press, 1969), Vol. 5; hereafter cited as *BAL*.

15. Cornelius S. Van Winkle apparently ran a rather small print shop, since he generally handled items of less than one hundred and twenty pages. The second edition (1827) of his *The Printer's Guide* (first published in 1818) lists him as printer to New York University, and he was also, apparently as early as 1811, associated with the College of Physicians and Surgeons as a printer of "inaugural dissertations" for the M.D. degree. His first commercial imprint, according to the records of the New York Historical Society, was a three-act farce in 1813. From 1814–1817 his imprints usually read "Van Winkle and Wiley."

16. No. I copyright May 15, published June 23, 1819; No. II July 26 and August 1, 1819; No. III August 11 and September 13, 1819; No. IV October 12 and "not later than November 30," 1819 (Langfeld, p. 15); No. V December 16, 1819 and January 1, 1820; No. VI February 10 and March 15, 1820; No. VII August 12 and September 13, 1820. The contents of the individual numbers are to be found in the chart on page 355.

number. . . ."[17] From this account one would assume that Irving's "sheets" were British proof sheets or final sheets, and that this part of 1A was set from print. The internal evidence, however, appears to dispute Pierre's statement about the copy sent to the American printer for the sketches in Number VII. As background for this evidence, one should keep in mind that the order of publication for most of *The Sketch Book* was 1A–2A–1E, and that some sketches (depending on the unknown exact dates of publication of parts of 2A) may have appeared in 1A–1E–2A order; but only for the sketches in Number VII was the sequence 1E–1A–2A. Time of appearance, however, does not truly reflect the progressive stages of authorial revision.

1A and 1E disagree, in the four sketches of Number VII, in a large number of accidentals—in many more than one would expect to find in an edition set from printed copy rather than from manuscript.[18] 1A and 1E also disagree in about forty substantive readings, most of them clearly authorial variants. The second American edition (2A) and 1E, however, agree in all substantive readings, showing that the 1E readings postdate those in 1A. In addition, 1A contains one of Irving's characteristic misspellings, corrected in 1E. That this error ("reccollections"), made several times previously in the *Sketch Book* manuscripts, should have passed unnoticed by both the British and American compositors is less likely than that the mistake was perpetuated by the American shop alone, printing from Irving's incorrect manuscript. Finally, if Irving had sent proof sheets for Number VII to America, the sensible thing to do—the practice he apparently adopted with his manuscripts for the previous numbers—would have been to make duplicate emendations in two sets of sheets and send one while retaining the other. But the accidental and substantive differences between 1A and 1E show that he did not do so. The evidence, then, suggests that Irving hurriedly sent, as soon as the British printer was through with it, the Number VII manuscript itself to New York on June 28, 1820 (six months after the dispatch of Number VI). His conjectural haste can be explained by the unprecedented time lag between Numbers VI and VII. If this reconstruction and analysis is essentially correct, the substantive departures of 1E from 1A are Irving's alterations in proof for 1E. That is, the readings in 1E are later, deliberate revisions of those in 1A.[19]

---

17. PMI, I, 458.

18. A comparison of accidentals between earlier parts of 1A and 1E, and between 1A and 2A, for example, reveals much less divergence than between No. VII 1A and 1E.

19. Though this conclusion has critical importance, it does not affect the readings of the Twayne text, which, in cases of conflicting authority, places the unperpetuated readings in the apparatus to the text (see the section on treatment of substantives).

The Sketch Book, A History of Relevant Forms

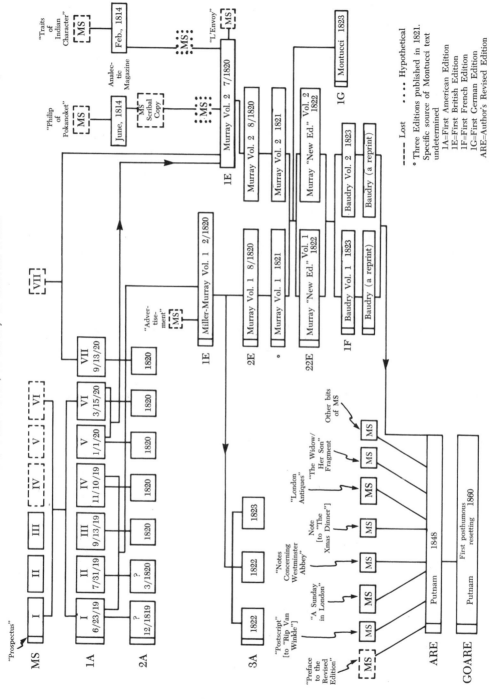

Judging from a comparison of the extant manuscript with 1A, Numbers I–III, the American compositors had no difficulty reading Irving's hand, and were quite accurate in following his intentions—so long as they approved of his spelling, punctuation or usage. Collation of the manuscript with the print clearly shows that though the compositors in Van Winkle's shop did indeed adhere to the general rule of their profession and "follow the copy" in its substantives, they felt little or no compunction in altering Irving's often erratic accidentals. These alterations, however, went beyond mere and legitimate correction in fulfillment of the injunctions in "Directions for the Printer," as Irving noted when he wrote to Brevoort about the over-punctuation, and wondered if his manuscript were at fault (see Introduction). Irving's diffidence was characteristic of him but the fault was not his; the first three printed numbers alone add close to one thousand commas and semicolons to his text, and repeatedly alter perfectly acceptable words ("shew" to "show," "towards" to "toward," for example).[20] The typesetting and proofreading were reasonably careful, though, and as a result there are very few textual differences among separate copies of the individual *Sketch Book* numbers.

Machine collation reveals that all seven parts were printed from type metal and that on many pages the type loosened considerably during the printing. Loose type, however, provides no major reading problems in any of the copies examined. Either loosened type or stop-press correction of compositorial error accounts for a reading in Number III, page 240, line 12, where two copies have "ont he" and the others "on the." In only one instance, moreover, did a type fall out or otherwise fail to be printed. Of the four copies of *Sketch Book* Number IV collated on the Hinman machine, two read "When" on page 313, line 1, while the others show "hen." In Number IV also, the difference between "open—" and "open," (286.5, 116.2); between "corselets" and "corslets" (320.10, 127.29); or between "Bridegroom" and "bridegroom" (320.17, 127.33) probably resulted in the first and third instances from mending of the type pages, and in the second from unnecessary correction of a supposed spelling error. Stop-press correction no doubt also explains "gaze"/ "graze" and "pedagouge"/"pedagogue" in Number VI (19.15, 253.20; 108.1, 292.42).

The two states of the entire signature 8 in Number I are, however, more puzzling. One state of this gathering, found in three copies, contains three commas missing from the other state: "lore," (57.9, 28.8); "now," (58.4, 28.22); and "memory," (58.5, 28.23). Otherwise, their

20. " '*Follow the copy*' is a maxim with compositors, and too many aspire at nothing more; but this is degrading their profession below the meanest handicraft." C. S. Van Winkle, *The Printer's Guide* (New York, 1827), p. 28.

readings are identical. It could be that for some reason the printer found it expedient or more economical to set this gathering in duplicate; or perhaps too few of the sheets were printed at first, and the deficiency noted only at the time of binding, after the type had been distributed.

Since the copy-text manuscript contains the two commas on page 58, their existence or omission in the print is purely academic. But "lore," on page 57 is another matter, since that word occurs in the one manuscript page from Numbers I–III now in unknown hands. Similar constructions in the manuscript suggest that Irving most likely did not use a comma in such a case, and comparison with 1A shows that his printer often inserted one. The Twayne text therefore omits the comma.

A different sort of phenomenon, and one which validates Jacob Blanck's warning in *BAL* about madeup copies, appears in one copy of *Sketch Book* Number I. In this University of Virginia copy (.A1/1819/copy 2) pages 35–40 (leaves $8_{[2]}$–$8_{[4]}$ are second-edition insertions into a previously imperfect first-edition copy. That the leaves in question might have been legitimately inserted by the binder either by accident or to make up a deficiency in one of the last bound first-edition copies is disputed by external evidence: Brevoort reported to Irving that the first edition was completely sold out before the second went to print. Internal evidence more directly contradicts the possibility of legitimacy, since the printer undoubtedly would have inserted a full signature-gathering of eight pages. Rather, leaf $8_{[1]}$ is first edition; only the other three are second edition. Consequently, leaves $8_{[1]}$ and $8_{[4]}$ are separate; whereas, if the sheets had been assembled before binding, they would of course be conjugate, as are $8_{[2]}$ and $8_{[3]}$. The three second-edition leaves are neatly pasted into place, not held by the thread for that gathering, which itself is inconspicuously pasted flat into the back and serves no function.

The only reasonable explanation of the evidence is that this copy of *Sketch Book* Number I was found in a mutilated state and sophisticated in order to enhance its value sometime after it had become a valuable collector's item. Since the original paperbound numbers of *The Sketch Book* are quite rare, it is reasonable to suppose that copies of any of its numbers may be similarly madeup. In this case the urge to sophisticate must have been particularly great, since the lacuna was in "Rip Van Winkle," the literary importance and popularity of which make it of prime concern to any prospective buyer.

The second American edition (2A), again printed by Van Winkle in seven numbers, began to appear in late 1819 (probably in December) and concluded in the latter part of 1820 (Number I is dated 1819, and II–VII 1820). Each number in this edition is reset, generally line for line. Several physical characteristics distinguish the first and second editions: rebound copies usually require collation for identification, but with copies in original wrappers one may note that the street address of the Van Winkle shop on the covers of all parts of 1A is hyphenated, while for 2A it is not. In addition, the first five parts of 1A are paged consecutively and the last two separately, while in 2A the first two parts are consecutive and the last five separately paged.[21] This second edition was set from copies of 1A which Irving, still in England, emended and returned to New York. Irving apparently made duplicate emendations in two copies of 1A and retained one while sending the other to the States. The evidence for this procedure is found in 1E, whose accidentals accord with those of 1A, but many of whose substantive departures from 1A are mirrored in 2A. That is, in almost every instance where 2A differs from 1A, 1E contains the 2A reading.

Usually, after having made his changes in the 1A text, and sent one copy to America, Irving then made further changes either in the retained copy of 1A or in proof for 1E. Thus 1E contains the 2A substantive readings but also has many other departures from 1A not present in 2A. This pattern does not pertain to Numbers I and II of 2A, however. These two numbers contain several substantive departures from 1A which do not appear in 1E, while 1E, as elsewhere, departs from 1A in some readings absent from 2A. What Irving apparently did was to make the duplicate emendations; but before sending one copy of each number to New York, he introduced further changes into that one copy only. Why he should have done so is conjectural. Perhaps the most likely explanation, and the simplest as well, is that at the time he made the later changes, he had with him only one copy each of the previously emended 1A Numbers I and II. This conjecture is strengthened by the occurrence in 1E of several readings similar to but not exactly the same as some in 2A. It would appear that later, before publishing in England, Irving remembered having made changes at these points in the one copy, and from memory tried to reproduce his emendations.

Another interesting illustration of the hazards of trans-Atlantic publication in 1820, and an insight into Irving's revision of *Sketch Book Number V*, is provided by a fragmentary letter from Irving, most likely to his brother Ebenezer:

P.S. In publishing a second edition of No. 5. The Manuscript addition may be got onto the same quantity of paper by omitting the blank leaves or rather half titles between the articles—They are not necessary where the number is made up of one general article,

21. See Langfeld for additional descriptive detail.

such as Christmas. P.S. In page 429. of No. 5. I have restored the passage relating to the peacock pie but I cannot find the note belonging to it, among my copies of the Mss. You of course must have it among the Mss scraps which were omitted—I wish it to be restored—& put at the bottom of the page as in the original Mss:[22]

The additions made to Number V for 2A, referred to in the first postscript, were almost all in "The Christmas Dinner," and Irving's suggestion to omit the half-title leaves was adopted. The passage alluded to in the second postscript is at 183.9–15; "429" is the number of the 1A page into which Irving inserted it, no doubt by attaching a manuscript slip to the copy. Irving's reference to omitted scraps of manuscript suggests that he had previously written to Brevoort after having dispatched manuscript for Number V, and asked him to delete particular passages before the manuscript went to the printer. Though we have no further evidence, it is possible that he did the same with other numbers.

The footnote to the peacock passage, also referred to in the second postscript, appears in different forms in 2A and 1E: the 1E note adds several phrases. Either Irving subsequently found the lost manuscript note and elaborated it, or 2A Number V was printed early enough to be sent to him before printing of 1E Volume II began.[23]

Number VII of 2A, whose sketches are, in order, "Westminster Abbey," "The Angler," "Stratford-on-Avon," and "Little Britain," has its own peculiarities. A comparison of accidentals in Number VII among 1A, 2A, and 1E shows that "Westminster Abbey" and "Little Britain" were, like the sketches in Numbers I–VI, set from 1A printer's copy. That is, in accidentals they agree overwhelmingly with 1A rather than 1E. But "The Angler" and "Stratford-on-Avon" show peculiar patterns of accidentals. In 2A "The Angler" begins by agreeing in all accidental features with 1A (and thus disagreeing with 1E). But after two pages it begins showing the 1E accidentals and disagreeing with 1A. And so it continues until the end of the sketch. "Stratford-on-Avon," which follows "The Angler," begins by agreeing in almost all accidentals with

22. From a manuscript book owned by Mr. Irving B. Kingsford.

23. Since 1A No. V was copyrighted on December 16, 1819, copies could have reached Irving by mid-January, 1820 (a one month gap between dispatch and receipt is common in the Irving-Brevoort correspondence). He need not have sent it back to New York in revised state until the beginning of March. 2A No. V could then have been printed by early or mid-May and could have reached him in June, in time for him to expand the peacock note and add it to the revised copy of 1A No. V he gave to Murray for printer's copy for the volume published in July.

1E for eighteen pages and then for seven pages shows virtually total agreement with 1A, after which the concluding twelve pages show mixed accidentals, with either 1A's or 1E's dominant on a particular page. What appears to have happened with Number VII, 2A, is that "The Angler" and "Stratford-on-Avon" were somehow heavily damaged, either in the revised 1A copy Irving sent to New York, or in type. Apparently all but the first two pages of "The Angler" were rendered unusable to the printer, and a sizeable part of "Stratford-on-Avon" was too.

The first British edition (1E) of *The Sketch Book* appeared in two volumes. One thousand copies of Volume I, containing *Sketch Book* Numbers I–IV, were printed from type metal by W. Pople, 67 Chancery Lane, and five hundred of these were published with the imprint of John Miller, Burlington Arcade, in February, 1820. Miller went bankrupt within the next two months, though, and John Murray took over publication: his cancel title leaf for the five hundred remaining sets of sheets he bought, reads, "Second Edition . . . John Murray, Albemarle-Street." All such "second edition" Murray copies of Volume I, therefore, are actually first British edition, and vary from the copies with the Miller imprint in title leaf only. Collation of three copies, two Miller and one Murray, on the Hinman machine, shows no textual differences. Volume II of 1E, containing *Sketch Book* Numbers V–VII, was published by John Murray in July, 1820. Its title page contains no edition number, but is merely dated 1820. One thousand copies were printed from type metal by "C. Roworth, Bell-yard, Temple-bar." Machine collation of two copies reveals no textual variations.

Irving made more revisions in his text for 1E than he did for any other edition. He did so, as noted in the discussion of the American editions above, by annotating copies of *Sketch Book* Numbers I–VI, 1A, from which 1E was printed. For "A Royal Poet," "The Angler," "Stratford-on-Avon," "Little Britain," and "Westminster Abbey," however, Irving presented the British printer with manuscript. Should we make the reasonable assumption that the manuscript from which the British compositors set type resembled the surviving manuscript in its characteristic mechanical details, we can conclude that house-styling was rather heavy and somewhat inconsistent here, as in the American numbers. In addition to his extensive revisions, Irving added to *The Sketch Book* at this point in its history the rewritten "Philip of Pokanoket" and "Traits of Indian Character," and the newly written "L'Envoy." At the head of Volume I he substituted a new, short "Advertisement" for the "Prospectus" which had prefaced the first American number. It was for this edition also that he changed the order of the sketches in Volume

II. Though he was to add two more sketches twenty-eight years later, he did no further shuffling of the parts of his book after 1E.[24]

Irving made perhaps as many as one hundred additional revisions in *The Sketch Book* for John Murray in "A New Edition," 1822 (22E); these changes occur throughout the book rather than concentrated in a few sketches. This two-volume printing is apparently the only illustrated edition of *The Sketch Book* published by Murray during the 1820's.[25] No textual differences were revealed by machine check of two copies.

Because it was the source of the unidentified printer's copy for the Author's Revised Edition, 1848, and thus plays a role in the direct transmission of the text, the first French edition (1F) should also be considered here. Printed by Jules Didot, Senior, "Printer to His Majesty," and published in Paris by Didot and Baudry, it appeared in two volumes in 1823. Its text derives from the Murray "New Edition," 1823, and thus includes Irving's 1822 revisions. It contains a number of errors likely due to compositorial ignorance of the English language, but is generally well printed and follows its copy. Another, apparently distinct edition, published by A. and W. Galignani in Paris and dated 1824, is actually printed from the same type as the Baudry-Didot 1823 imprint. There is no evidence of Irving's hand in either of these issues.

The Author's Revised Edition (ARE), copyrighted by Irving and published by Putnam in New York in 1848, is the last authorially revised edition of *The Sketch Book*. On it have been based, ultimately, almost all modern printings of the text. The volume was printed from stereotype plates by "Leavitt, Trow & Co., *Printers and Stereotypers*, 49 Ann-street, N.Y.," and appeared in at least two formats: (1) page size 8½ x 5¾ inches; text enclosed by single-line frame; illustrated by F. O. C. Darley; added, engraved title page with view of Sunnyside. (2) page size 7¼ x 4¾ inches; no line-frame; no illustrations; page numbers and running heads reset; added title page: "The Works of Washington Irving. New Edition, Revised. Vol. II." Williams and Edge report an edition of fifty copies dated 1848, apparently in the first format. A copy of format (1) has been seen, and another reported to the editor, with extra illustrations pasted in. In these copies the list of illustrations contains the extra items. Machine collation of two copies of format (1) with one of format (2) reveals no textual discrepancies among them, though repair of plate batter occurs in several places. Further machine collation of one of these format (1) copies with a copy in format (1)

24. See the chart on page 355.

25. The two examined copies, the only ones located, have two entirely different sets of illustrations whose bibliographical significance is unknown. The illustrations in one copy are by Irving's friend, Charles Leslie.

THE ORDER OF THE SKETCHES

Number*	1A	2A	1E	ARE
	Prospectus	Prospectus		
			Advertisement	
				Preface
	Account	Account	Account	Account
I	Voyage	Voyage	Voyage	Voyage
	Roscoe	Roscoe	Roscoe	Roscoe
	Wife	Wife	Wife	Wife
	Rip	Rip	Rip	Rip
	Writers	Writers	Writers	Writers
II	Rural Life	Rural Life	Rural Life	Rural Life
	Broken Heart	Broken Heart	Broken Heart	Broken Heart
	Bookmaking	Bookmaking	Bookmaking	Bookmaking
	Royal Poet	Royal Poet	Royal Poet	Royal Poet
III	Church	Church	Church	Church
	Widow	Widow	Widow	Widow
				Sunday
	Boar's Head	Boar's Head	Boar's Head	Boar's Head
	Mutability	Mutability	Mutability	Mutability
	Funerals	Funerals	Funerals	Funerals
IV	Inn Kitchen	Inn Kitchen	Inn Kitchen	Inn Kitchen
	Spectre Bridegroom	Spectre Bridegroom	Spectre Bridegroom	Spectre Bridegroom
			West. Abbey	West. Abbey
	Christmas	Christmas	Christmas	Christmas
V	Stage Coach	Stage Coach	Stage Coach	Stage Coach
	Christmas Eve	Christmas Eve	Christmas Eve	Christmas Eve
	Christmas Day {	Christmas Morning	Christmas Day	Christmas Day
		Christmas Dinner	Christmas Dinner	Christmas Dinner
				Antiques
			Little Britain	Little Britain
			Stratford	Stratford
			Traits	Traits
			Philip	Philip
VI	John Bull	John Bull	John Bull	John Bull
	Pride	Pride	Pride	Pride
			Angler	Angler
	Sleepy Hollow	Sleepy Hollow	Sleepy Hollow	Sleepy Hollow
	West. Abbey	West. Abbey		
	Angler	Angler		
VII	Stratford	Stratford		
	Little Britain	Little Britain		
			L'Envoy	L'Envoy

*The parts of the first and second American editions.

dated 1849 shows a number of corrections, and more repairs in the plates. *The Sketch Book* continued to be printed from these plates at least until Irving's death in 1859. A check against the first Putnam resetting, 1860, reveals a number of substantive differences, all of which appear to have originated in the print shop.

In The Author's Revised Edition first appeared "A Sunday in London" and "London Antiques." The "Postscript" to "Rip Van Winkle" and the "Notes Concerning Westminster Abbey" were also new, as was the long "Preface to the Revised Edition." Irving made numerous other changes; and the book was heavily styled by the printer: hyphens abound and American spellings predominate. Though it is difficult to separate them from authorial emendations, several changes in wording, apparently for correctness and idiomatic usage, were also made by Putnam's or by the printer.

From 1850 until the editing of the text for the Twayne edition, the history of *The Sketch Book* was one of progressive corruption. As reprint was printed from reprint for over one hundred years (the Williams-Edge bibliography lists at least eighty separate editions or reprints of the complete *Sketch Book* in English from 1860 to 1935), such corruption was inevitable. Most of this progressive error has been, of course, minor and relatively inconsequential. But a number of unauthoritative substantive changes have taken place as well. In this century, then, despite a few attempts at "editing" the book—that is, comparing printer's copy with, apparently, the text as printed in 1848— *The Sketch Book* has been available only in highly untrustworthy texts.

THE INDIVIDUAL SKETCHES

This section of the Textual Commentary deals with those sketches which, because of involved textual history, difficult questions of copy-text, heavy revision, or other distinctive features, require further comment or separate treatment.

"Preface to the Revised Edition"

This preface was written in 1848 for the Author's Revised Edition and takes the place of the "Prospectus" of 1A, 2A, and 3A, and of the "Advertisement" heading all editions from 1E up to ARE. These two superseded prefatory notes are appended to this edition.

"A Royal Poet"

This is the most heavily revised sketch in the book: Irving completely reworked it after its appearance in 1A, Number III. The 1E and 2A versions resulting from this revision, though essentially the same, vary in ways that show "A Royal Poet" to be unique in *The Sketch Book*. Comparison of accidentals in 1E and 2A shows that neither derives from the other. Instead there are many accidental differences (in addition to the seventy substantive ones), and 1E, moreover, contains characteristic Irving spellings such as "shewn," which are missing in 2A. Further evidence is supplied by two extant pages of manuscript agreeing with the 2A version, and apparently the only surviving part of the printer's copy from which 2A was set. The inference from the evidence is clear: the 2A and 1E versions were set from separate manuscripts.

The process by which the setting from two manuscripts came about can be tentatively reconstructed on the basis of known information. Copies of 1A Number III, published September 13, 1819, probably reached Irving by early October (since Henry Brevoort did not send Irving copies of at least the first four numbers until just before or even after publication date). Irving could have sent back a revised copy—including the new manuscript for "A Royal Poet"—during November. We know that he sent revised copies of 1A Numbers I and II to New York on September 21, 1819, and that on November 9 Henry Brevoort reported receiving them, saying that printing of the new editions would begin in a week. 2A Number I was probably not published until late December, 1819, and Number II is dated 1820. 2A Number III, then, the date of whose printing and publication are not known, would in all likelihood not have been printed early enough for a copy to have made its way to England in time for Irving to revise and use it as printer's copy for 1E Volume I, published in mid-February, 1820. It evidently was not early enough, since Irving apparently did with manuscript for "A Royal Poet" what for the other sketches he did with print: he further touched up and gave to the British printer his copy of the "Royal Poet" manuscript he had sent to New York as printer's copy for 2A.

Since Irving personally saw 1E (set from his manuscript) through the press and since all later versions of "A Royal Poet" derive from the 1E text, it has been chosen as copy-text. Substantive variations between 1E and 2A are contained in a separate list in the textual apparatus (see pages 372–73 for a discussion of this procedure), and the lists of emendations and rejected substantives record the history of "A Royal Poet" from 1E through ARE. The revision of the sketch accomplished in the dual manuscripts, though, is too extensive and complex to list.

The chief feature of the thorough rewriting of the piece for its appearance in 2A and 1E is Irving's expansion of it from eighteen (1A) to twenty-nine pages. The two versions (1E, 2A) are substantially the same, and so can be discussed as one. More than half of the increase consists of the elaboration and extension of passages present in the first version, as, for example:

1A	1E
He did all in his power to soften and refine the spirit of his countrymen.	He did every thing in his power to win his countrymen to the gay, the elegant, and gentle arts, which soften and refine the character of a people, and wreathe a grace round the loftiness of a proud and warlike spirit.

Between four and five pages, though, were completely new. The longest added passage, almost two and one-half pages in 1E, relates the events following "the departure of the lady Jane from the garden" (74.6–76.40). The combined additions and revisions replace objective or general observations with the personal comments of Geoffrey Crayon, and convey more precisely the mood and tone of the piece. Irving also replaced with further details of the story such extraneous and artificial passages as, "the whole history of this...prince is...too well known to need particular relation," and "I find I am insensibly swelling this story beyond my original intention." In addition, he expanded his footnotes (including the glossary), thus clarifying some former obscurities; and he improved his organization: his transitions are firmer and the order of details more logical.

This transformation of his essay shows Irving as a painstaking craftsman whose effects are the result of attention to all the aspects of his art. The first two manuscript pages of the 2A version are extant, and, when compared with the original version and the copy-text (identical to the Twayne text in this passage), epitomize his alteration of the essay as a whole:

First Version MS	Revised Version MS
On a soft sunny morning in the month of May, I made an excursion to Windsor to visit the castle. It is a proud old pile, stretching its irregular walls and massive towers along the brow of a lofty ridge, waving its royal banner in the clouds, and looking down with a lordly air upon the surrounding world. It is a place that I love to	On a soft sunny morning in the genial month of May, I made an excursion to Windsor Castle. It is a place full of storied and poetical associations. The very external aspect of the proud old pile is enough to inspire high thought; rearing its irregular walls and massive towers like a mural crown round the brow of a lofty ridge, waving its royal

visit for it is full of storied and poetical associations. On this morning the weather was of that soft vernal kind that calls forth the latent romance of a man's temperament, and makes him quote poetry and dream of beauty. In wandering through the magnificent saloons and long echoing galleries of the old castle I felt myself most disposed to linger in the chamber where hang the portraits of the beauties that once flourished in the gay court of Charles the Second.

banner in the clouds, and looking down with a lordly air upon the surrounding world. On this morning the weather was of that voluptuous vernal kind which calls forth all the latent romance of a man's temperament, filling his mind with music and causing him to quote poetry and dream of beauty. In wandering through the magnificent saloons and long echoing galleries of the old castle, I passed with indifference by whole rows of warriors and statesmen, but lingered in the chamber where hang the portraits of the beauties that once flourished in the gay court of Charles the Second; and as I gazed upon them, each depicted with amorous half dishevelled tresses, and the sleepy eye of love, I blessed the pencil of Sir Peter Lely that had thus enabled me to bask in the reflected rays of beauty.

"The Widow and Her Son"

Irving rewrote the opening of this sentimental piece for the Author's Revised Edition, and the two and one-half pages of manuscript constituting that revision are extant. They have been integrated with the manuscript of the rest of the sketch (inscribed thirty years earlier), and the composite manuscript is copy-text. The textual lists contain only the changes beyond this rewritten section, which, in its original form (1A–1F), reads as follows:

During my residence in the country I used frequently to attend at the old village church. Its shadowy aisles, its mouldering monuments, its dark oaken panellings, all reverend with the gloom of departed years, seemed to fit it for the haunt of solemn meditation. A Sunday too in the country is so holy in its repose: such a pensive quiet reigns over the face of nature, that every restless passion is charmed down, and we feel all the natural religion of the soul gently springing up within us.

> Sweet day, so pure, so calm, so bright,
> The bridal of the earth and sky!—

I do not pretend to be what is called a devout man, but there are feelings that visit me in a country church, amidst the beautiful serenity of nature, which I experience no where else; and if not a more religious, I am certainly a better man on Sunday, than on any other day of the seven.

But in this church I found myself continually thrown back upon the world by the frigidity and pomp of the poor worms around me. The only being that seemed thoroughly to feel the humble and prostrate piety of a true Christian, was a poor, decrepid old woman, bending under the weight of years and infirmities.

Irving made one change in this passage for 22E. In that edition and in 1F the line after the quotation reads: "I cannot lay claim to the merit of being a devout man. . . ."

"Westminster Abbey"
Copy-text for the sketch proper is 1E, which was set from manuscript; but copy-text for the "Notes" to the sketch, added in 1848, is the extant manuscript. No single text could serve as copy-text for both except the Author's Revised Edition, and it is unsuitable for the same reasons cited in rejecting it as copy-text for the whole book (365).

"Christmas Day" and "The Christmas Dinner"
These two essays began, in 1A, as one—under the title "Christmas Day." But for 2A Irving broke the essay in two, calling the first segment "Christmas Morning," and the second "The Christmas Dinner." He introduced a new epigraph for "Christmas Morning" and placed the epigraph which formerly began "Christmas Day" at the head of the newly created "Christmas Dinner." Then for 1E he brought his original title back into the book by using it in place of "Christmas Morning." The division of the sketches remained the same and the titles underwent no further transformations.

"Philip of Pokanoket" and "Traits of Indian Character"
These two sketches are most advantageously discussed together because they present textual problems unique to The Sketch Book. Both essays were printed in the American Analectic Magazine in 1814, while Irving was its editor, and were first included in The Sketch Book in 1E, Volume II.[26] Both were heavily revised for their appearance in The

26. "Traits of Indian Character" appeared in Analectic Magazine 3 (February, 1814), 145–56; "Philip of Pokanoket" was printed in 3 (June, 1814), 502–15.

Sketch Book: in fact they are the most extensively revised essays in the book except for "A Royal Poet."

On March 5, 1816, less than a year after he had arrived in England, Irving wrote to Brevoort: "I wish you would send me the numbers of the Analectic Mag. that have the traits of Indian character—& the story of King Philip. . . ."[27] No other reference to the matter appears in the Irving-Brevoort correspondence until September 9, 1819, when Irving writes:

> By the bye—I break off in the middle of my letter lest I should again forget a matter on which I have intended to speak for these two years. You once sent me a Mss: copy of my article about Philip of Pokanoket—copied by Miss Goodrich, and I have been ungallant enough never to acknowledge so very marked a kindness. It has perpetually slipped my memory when I have been writing and has now in an unaccountable way popped into my brain. Will you make her my very best acknowledgements—and apologize for the tardiness with which they are made—and at the same time present her with a copy of the Sketch Book & continue to send her the numbers, as the only return a poor devil of an author can make. I feel the more obliged to Miss Goodrich for the trouble she took as I had no claim on the score of acquaintanceship to such an act of civility.[28]

Apparently Brevoort had been able to find a spare copy of the *Analectic* "Traits" but not one of "Philip."

Because they are so thoroughly revised, it is difficult to judge the exact stages through which these essays passed before they entered *The Sketch Book*; but it appears safe to assume that the Murray edition of "Traits," in which many passages are rewritten, four pages of the original excised, and the remainder heavily revised, was set from a new author's manuscript: the revisions in many instances are too thoroughgoing to have been interlined or marginally noted in a copy of the *Analectic* version. Certainly the first few pages of the sketch were given to the printer in manuscript, and at least several other heavily revised pages were too; though Irving may possibly have given the printer mixed manuscript and print from which to work. The early history of "Traits," then, can be summarized as: [manuscript]→*Analec-*

27. Stanley T. Williams, ed., *Notes While Preparing Sketch Book, &c.* (New Haven: Yale University Press, 1927), p. 52.

28. Irv-Bvt, II, 116–17. Brevoort corrected Irving's mistaken notion of a debt to Miss Goodrich in a letter of November 9, 1819: "I cannot help remarking on what you say respecting Miss G⸺ that to the best of my recollection I paid her brother $2 for copying Philip" (Bvt-Irv, p. 119).

tic→[new, revised manuscript (or manuscript plus print)]→1E. The text of "Philip of Pokanoket" also suggests a new manuscript: it is extremely doubtful that a compositor could have set type from a document as confused as Miss Goodrich's manuscript emended by Irving's one hundred and ninety substantive changes for "Philip" because, though "Philip" does not contain wholly rewritten pages as does "Traits," its substantive emendations are more regularly distributed. The essay is significantly and repeatedly revised on every page (averaging 5.3 substantive changes per 1E page). The conjectural history of "Philip," then, looks like this: [manuscript]→*Analectic*→[Miss Goodrich's manuscript]→[new, revised manuscript]→1E.

Because they largely involve a few words or phrases each, the early, extensive revisions in "Philip of Pokanoket" are presented as a list of pre-copy-text variants in the apparatus for this Twayne edition. The complexity of the emendations in "Traits of Indian Character," however, prevents their merely being listed; they must instead be described.

Irving's original essay had been occasioned by events in 1812–1813—specifically by the slaughter wreaked on certain tribes as a result of their involvement in the War of 1812, and by Andrew Jackson's brutal handling of the Indian uprising in Florida. These were matters of great interest in America at the time, but when in 1820 Irving prepared the essay for British publication, changes had to be made. He began by deleting the first half of his introductory paragraph and replacing it with the paean to "the North American Savage" which still introduces the sketch. He had originally written:

> In the present times, when popular feeling is gradually becoming hardened by war, and selfish by the frequent jeopardy of life or property, it is certainly an inauspicious moment to speak in behalf of a race of beings, whose very existence has been pronounced detrimental to public security. But it is good at all times to raise the voice of truth, however feeble; to endeavour if possible to mitigate the fury of passion and prejudice, and to turn aside the bloody hand of violence. Little interest, however, can probably be awakened at present, in favour of the misguided tribes of Indians that have been drawn into the present war.

The second half of that original first paragraph he retained; it appears as paragraph three of the revised essay.

All in all, Irving deleted about one thousand words in revising "Traits of Indian Character" for *The Sketch Book*. The longest deletion specifically dealt with events of import in 1814: following the comparison of Indian behavior with that of the Roman senators (232), Irving had included more than two pages, first castigating "sober-thoughted men, far from the scenes of danger" who "discuss the *policy* of extirpating thousands," and then describing in detail the massacre of the Creeks in Florida by General Coffee, under orders of General Andrew Jackson. Irving's removal of this passage probably was due to at least three factors: its lack of immediate relevance in 1820, Irving's position as a patriotic American—albeit an anglophilic one—writing to a British audience, and his desire to tone down the moral indignation of the piece (perhaps because the speaking voice was now Geoffrey Crayon's), evident in a number of other changes throughout the essay, such as:

Analectic	*1E*
deadly hostilities	hostilities
hideous appellations	appellations
intrusion	colonization
savage delight	pride

Similarly, he excised a paragraph attacking the behavior of Christians as compared to that of the Indians:

It is a common thing to exclaim against new forms of cruelty, while, reconciled by custom, we wink at long established atrocities. What right does the generosity of our conduct give us to rail exclusively at Indian warfare. With all the doctrines of christianity, and the advantages of cultivated morals, to govern and direct us, what horrid crimes disgrace the victories of christian armies. Towns laid in ashes; cities given up to the sword; enormities perpetrated, at which manhood blushes, and history drops the pen. Well may we exclaim at the outrages of the scalping knife; but where, in the records of Indian barbarity, can we point to a violated female?

In conjunction with these deletions he added a few passages (such as the one at 230.42–231.15) praising the Indians for their prime virtues. The effect, then, of the 1E version is still to attack the white man's treatment of the Indian, but the tone is somewhat gentler, and the attack is conducted more by comparisons, contrasts, and explanations of Indian behavior, than by outright condemnation of the whites as previously. Further mitigation is supplied by the added footnote, and sentence to which it applies (226), in which Irving, in 1820, praised the Indian policies of the American government.

Irving's only other notable deletion was of the passage originally following "imagination." at 230.23. In it he exemplified the sort of courage he had just referred to:

This may be instanced in the case of a young British officer of great pride, but delicate nerves, who was going for the first time into battle. Being agitated by the novelty and awful peril of the scene, he was accosted by another officer of a rough and boisterous character—"What, Sir," cried he, "do you tremble?" "Yes Sir," replied the other, "and if you were half as much afraid as I am you would run away." This young officer signalized himself on many occasions by his gallantry, though, had he been brought up in savage life, or even in a humbler and less responsible situation, it is more than probable he could never have ventured into open action.

The one hundred other alterations in the essay are diverse and difficult to classify. Irving added the obligatory epigraph, but otherwise generally made stylistic changes of no great import. In these emendations he was once again "re-dressing" his work.

THE COPY-TEXT

The textual intent in this critical edition of *The Sketch Book* has been to come as close as possible to fulfilling Washington Irving's intentions. To that end it follows the general guidelines set forth in the *Statement of Editorial Principles and Procedures* of the Modern Language Association's Center for Editions of American Authors (1972), derived from the work of what is often called the Greg-Bowers school of textual criticism. Though *The Sketch Book* presents particular problems not foreseen by the *Statement*, its editing does not violate the basic assumptions or principles of that document. Rather, in accord with its authorities, this edition of *The Sketch Book* is conservative and eclectic.

The choice of copy-text, the editor's most basic choice, is a particularly vexed one for *The Sketch Book*, since the surviving documents and the circumstances of publication do not permit choosing any one form of the text for the entire book. Following the accepted principle that copy-text should be the author's manuscript, or, in its absence, the edition set from manuscript (unless unusual factors dictate the choice of a later edition), copy-text for *The Sketch Book* has been chosen sketch by sketch. This is not to say that each of the thirty-four sketches is edited from a different basic text; as it happens, the application of the principle results in five copy-texts, pertinent to different sections of the work.

The key reason for this procedure is that *The Sketch Book* is a miscellany—a collection of textually independent essays. Except for a few details in the Christmas sketches, Irving wrote and revised each sketch independently: some coming in for heavy revision in one edition, most lightly revised in several editions, one completely reshaped, two originally published elsewhere and partly rewritten, some appearing first in England, some in America, and two published almost thirty years after the rest. The only single text which could possibly have been chosen for copy-text is the Author's Revised Edition of 1848, revised and proofread by Irving. It was not chosen, however, because it is based on an unauthoritative French edition, and because its heavy house-styling consistently violates Irving's preferences evident in his manuscripts—thus destroying the flavor of his British spellings, archaic forms, and idiosyncratic punctuation. Although it was revised and proofread by Irving, 1E is also rejected as the basic text because it is not complete (Irving added sketches in ARE), it too is heavily styled and violates manuscript practice, and it is largely based on 1A rather than manuscript. In the face of an existing printer's copy manuscript for three-sevenths of the whole, no one printed form could legitimately serve as copy-text unless it could be shown that Irving had for that edition so thoroughly revised his entire text in accidentals as well as in substantives that he had superseded the original manuscript and the edition(s) set directly from manuscript. Such is not the case with *The Sketch Book*. Instead, the chosen copy-texts (presented in tabular form on page 366) are as follows.[29]

The first thirteen sketches in the book ("The Author's Account of Himself" through "The Boar's Head Tavern") plus "London Antiques" and "A Sunday in London" survive in printer's copy manuscript.[30] These fifteen sketches are therefore edited from manuscript, with the exception of "A Royal Poet" which was so thoroughly revised for 2A and 1E that it is virtually a new essay. 1E, set from manuscript, supervised by Irving, and the source of all later versions of "A Royal Poet," is copy-text for this sketch. The sketches which originally appeared in Numbers IV–VI of 1A, set from Irving's manuscript, are edited from that edition. They are "The Mutability of Literature" through "The Spectre Bridegroom," the five Christmas sketches (that is, including "The Stage Coach"), plus "John Bull," "The Pride of the Village," and "The Legend of Sleepy Hollow."[31] Four more sketches are those which first appeared in 1E and were set in England from holograph manu-

29. The reader should refer to the discussions of the individual sketches for detailed treatment of the choice of copy-text in complex cases.

30. One page of manuscript, containing the first few lines of the introductory note to "Rip Van Winkle" is missing. These lines (28.1–14) are edited from 1A.

31. The five Christmas sketches were four in 1A, before Irving split the long "Christmas Day" into two essays for 2A and 1E.

script.[32] These sketches, subsequently *Sketch Book* Number VII, are "Westminster Abbey," "Little Britain," "Stratford-on-Avon," and "The Angler." All are edited from 1E except for the "Notes Concerning Westminster Abbey," which were not added to the essay until 1848. The manuscript for this appendix to the sketch is extant, and serves as

COPY-TEXT

	MS	Analectic	1A	1E	ARE
Preface					x ✿
Author's Account	✔ ✿		x		
Voyage	✔ ✿		x		
Roscoe	✔ ✿		x		
Wife	✔ ✿		x		
Rip	✔ ✿		x #		
English Writers	✔ ✿		x		
Rural Life	✔ ✿		x		
Broken Heart	✔ ✿		x		
Book Making	✔ ✿		x		
Royal Poet	✔		x	✿	
Country Church	✔ ✿		x		
Widow	✔ ✿		x		
Sunday	✔ ✿				x
Boar's Head	✔ ✿		x		
Mutability			x ✿		
Rural Funerals			x ✿		
Inn Kitchen			x ✿		
Spectre Bridegroom			x ✿		
West. Abbey	✔ #			x ✿	
Christmas			x ✿		
Stage Coach			x ✿		
Christmas Eve			x ✿		
Christmas Day			} x ✿		
Christmas Dinner					
London Antiques	✔ ✿				x
Little Britain				x ✿	
Stratford-on-Avon				x ✿	
Traits		x		✿	
Philip		x		✿	
John Bull			x ✿		
Pride			x ✿		
Angler				x ✿	
Sleepy Hollow	✔		x ✿		
L'Envoy				x ✿	

✔ = extant manuscript or partial manuscript; ✿ = copy-text
x = first appearance in print; # = copy-text for part of a sketch

32. Though 1A No. VII was also apparently set from manuscript, 1E *undoubtedly* was, and shows Irving's emending hand as well. Therefore, 1E is chosen rather than 1A.

its copy-text. Four sketches remain. Two are the Indian essays, which appeared in 1814 in the *Analectic Magazine* and, heavily revised, were first incorporated into *The Sketch Book* in 1E. Though they differ in their textual histories, and though the revision in each is somewhat different, the decision has been to use 1E as copy-text for both sketches on the grounds that Irving in effect created new essays. In both cases the emendations involve so much of the essay and so many of its accidentals that an attempt to integrate them into an *Analectic* base text would be unwarranted.[33] Although it is not strictly a sketch, the "Preface to the Revised Edition" is Irving's final choice of prefatory remarks for the book, and begins the Twayne text. It is edited from its first appearance in the Author's Revised Edition. The final sketch, "L'Envoy," is the last in the book. It was first printed in 1E and is edited from that text.

This use of multiple copy-texts results, of course, in some unevenness of texture in the book as a whole. Although this variance in accidentals from sketch to sketch might be noticeable to an attentive reader, there is no way to avoid it except by emending the text on manuscript model or the model of one of the authoritative editions. This procedure, because it would be based on mere guesswork in the former case and would inevitably impose unauthoritative readings on the entire text in the latter, is indefensible. Irving's compulsive habit of "correcting" and "re-dressing" (as he called it), evident in *The Sketch Book* and elsewhere, is responsible for the complexity and eclecticism of the text as he left it, and thus for the unavoidable choice of multiple copy-texts.

List of Items Collated

MS1 Author's MS, *Sketch Book* Numbers I–III, 1818–1819
MS2 Author's MS, additional material, 1848
Anal *Analectic Magazine* ("Traits of Indian Character," February, 1814, and "Philip of Pokanoket," June, 1814)
1A First American edition (Van Winkle, 1819–1820)
2A Second American edition (Van Winkle, 1819–1820)
3A Third American edition (Van Winkle, 1822–1823)
4A Fourth American edition (Van Winkle, 1824)
5A Fifth American edition (Van Winkle, 1826)

33. The conjectured existence of a new author's manuscript for 1E need not necessarily lead one to pick 1E as copy-text, of course. It is not the existence of that hypothetical manuscript that is crucial, but the nature and extent of the changes it would have contained. Even if it could be shown that there was no new authorial manuscript for either sketch, the copy-text decisions would still stand.

7A   Seventh American edition (Carey, Lea, & Carey, 1829)
1E   First English edition (Miller/Murray, 1820)
2E   Second English edition (Murray, 1820)
21E   "New Edition" (Murray, 1821)
4E   "Fourth Edition" (Murray, 1821)
5E   "Fifth Edition" (Murray, 1821)
22E   "New Edition" (Murray, 1822)
23E   "New Edition" (Murray, 1823)
24E   "New Edition" (Murray, 1824)
1F   First French edition (Baudry & Didot, 1823)
1G   First German edition (Montucci, 1823)
46F   French edition (Baudry, 1846)
ARE   "Author's Revised Edition" (G. P. Putnam, 1848)
60ARE First posthumous edition (Putnam, 1860)
64ARE Putnam, 1864

Machine Collations

(1) $1A^{34}$
(2) $1E^{35}$
(3)   22E
(4)   23E vs. 24E
(5)   ARE

34. The following copies were used in collating the individual numbers: UVa1: U. of Virginia °PS2066/.A1/1819a/v.1 [Nos. I–IV]; UVa2: U. of Virginia °PS2066/.A1/1819a/v.2 [Nos. V–VII]; UVa3: U. of Virginia °PS2066/.A1/1819/copy 4 [Nos. I–IV]; UVa4: U. of Virginia °PS2066/.A1/1819/v.1 [Nos. I–IV]; UVa5: U. of Virginia °PS2066/.A1/1819/v.2 [Nos. V–VII]; UVa6: U. of Virginia °PS2066/.A1/1819/copy 3 [Nos. V–VII; only No. VI is first edition]; UVa7: U. of Virginia °PS2066/.A1/1819/copy 2 [seven separate numbers in original wrappers]; Tx: U. of Texas (unnumbered) [Nos. I–VII]. The collation of each separate number was as follows: No. I: UVa1 vs. UVa3, 4, 7 and Tx; No. II: UVa1 vs. UVa3, 4, 7 and Tx; No. III: UVa1 vs. UVa 3, 4, 7 and Tx; No. IV: UVa2 vs. UVa3, 4 and Tx; No. V: UVa2 vs. UVa5, 7 and Tx; No. VI: UVa2 vs. UVa5, 6 and Tx; No. VII: UVa5 vs. Tx.

35. The following copies were used for the remaining machine collations: 1E: U. of Wisconsin-Milwaukee (Rare) PS2066/.A1/1820a vs. Haskell Springer's copy, inscribed "Mary Tierny" (Volumes 1 and 2), plus additional collation of Springer copy, Volume 2 vs. U. of Virginia °PS2066/.A1/1820c/v.2. 22E: Yale U., Iw/Ir8/819bbc vs. U. of Texas (unnumbered), illustrations by Charles Leslie (Volumes 1 and 2). 23E and 24E: U. of Pennsylvania AC8./Ir844/.819s/1823, v.1, v.2 vs. U. of Wisconsin C16890 and C16891. ARE: Haskell Springer's copy, inscribed "N. D. Wilkins" vs. U. of Southern California 810/I724/ts.7/1848; plus Springer copy vs. Yale U. Iw/Ir8/819cg; plus Springer copy vs. U. of Virginia PS2050/1848/v.2/copy 1.

Sight Collations[36]

The following are full-scale collations, recording all variants, substantive and accidental, unless otherwise noted.

(1)   MS1 vs. 1A
(2)   1A vs. 2A
(3)   1A vs. ARE (substantives)
(4)   3A vs. ARE (substantives)
(5)   Anal vs. 1E
(6)   1A vs. 1E
(7)   1E vs. ARE
(8)   1E vs. 23E
(9)   1F vs. ARE
(10)   1G vs. ARE
(11)   MS2 vs. ARE

The following are partial collations, made principally to check textual cruces already noted in collations 1–11, and to locate possible authorial emendation.

36. Items sight collated are as follows: (1) MS1: U. of Virginia vs. 1A: U. of Virginia °PS2066/.A1/1819/copy 2; (2) 1A: U. of Virginia °PS2066/.A1/1819a vs. 2A: U. of Virginia °PS2066/.A1/1819/copy 3 [Nos. 1-5]; 1A: U. of Virginia °PS2066/.A1/1819a vs. 2A: U. of North Carolina PS2066/.A1/1819 [No. 6]; 1A: U. of Texas Ww/.Ir86/819sb./v.7 vs. 2A: U. of Texas Parsons °1119 [No. 7]. [The difficulty of obtaining complete sets of the original seven numbers of 1A and 2A accounts for the use of different copies in collating the separate numbers here and in other collations.] (3) 1A: U. of Virginia °PS2066/.A1/1819a vs. ARE: Haskell Springer's copy, inscribed "N. D. Wilkins"; (4) 3A: Yale U. Iw/Ir8/819bb vs. ARE: Springer copy; (5) Anal: Early American Periodicals microfilm series, Roll 61 vs. 1E: Haskell Springer's copy, inscribed "Mary Tierney"; (6) 1A: U. of Virginia °PS2066/.A1/1819/Part 7, copy 2 vs. 1E: Springer copy; (7) 1E: Springer copy vs. ARE: U. of Virginia PS2050/1848/v.2, copy 1; (8) 1E: Springer copy vs. 23E: Haskell Springer's copy, inscribed "Arthur Ramsay" [Volume 2 only]; (9) 1F: Yale U. Za./Iw/Ir8/819bc vs. ARE: Springer copy; (10) 1G: Yale U. Za./Ir8./819sch vs. ARE: Springer copy; (11) MS2: Harvard U. vs. ARE: Springer copy; (12) 1E: Springer copy vs. 4A: U. of Virginia °PS2066/.A1/1824; (13) 1E: Springer copy vs. 5A: U. of Virginia °PS2066/.A1/1826; (14) 1E: Springer copy vs. 7A: Yale U. Iw/Ir8/819bg; (15) 1E: Springer copy vs. 2E: U. of Virginia PS2066/.A1/1820c; (16) 1E: Springer copy vs. 21E: Haskell Springer's copy (no identifying markings); (17) 1E: Springer copy vs. 4E: Haskell Springer's copy (no identifying markings); (18) 1E: Springer copy vs. 5E: U. of Wisconsin C33810 and C33811; (19) 1E: Springer copy vs. 22E: U. of Texas, uncataloged [Volume 1], and U. of Texas, Bartfield [Volume 2]; (20) 1E: Springer copy vs. 24E: U. of Wisconsin C16890; (21) 1F: Yale U. Iw/Ir8/819bc vs. Haskell Springer's copy (no identifying markings); (22) ARE: Springer copy vs. 60ARE: Haskell Springer's copy (no identifying markings); (23) ARE: Springer copy vs. 64ARE: Yale U. Iw/Ir8/819f; (24) ARE: Edwin Bowden's copy, inscribed "From WP Marshall To Cornelia E. Marshall" and "J.P.M April/89" vs. T: page proof.

(12)   1E vs. 4A
'(13)   1E vs. 5A
(14)   1E vs. 7A
(15)   1E vs. 2E
(16)   1E vs. 21E
(17)   1E vs. 4E
(18)   1E vs. 5E
(19)   1E vs. 22E
(20)   1E vs. 24E
(21)   1F vs. 46F
(22)   ARE vs. 60ARE
(23)   ARE vs. 64ARE
(24)   ARE vs. T (substantives)

TREATMENT OF SUBSTANTIVES

Manuscript substantives present no real difficulty except for one missing word, explained on p. 383 (item 33.43). Print is another matter entirely. The five key editions in which Irving definitely emended his work (1A, 2A, 1E, 22E, and ARE) contain about eleven hundred substantive changes, hundreds of which are clearly Irving's, while hundreds of others might just as easily be someone else's. The lists of emendations and rejected substantives are full of these latter, mostly inconsequential changes: *this* becomes *the, our* changes to *a, cracking* to *smacking, glistering* to *glistening, that* to *which, indications* to *indication*; an *and* or a *the* or a *had* creeps in or drops out, and words are transposed (*is it—it is*). Such alterations occur in every essay, and it is literally impossible most of the time to tell which are Irving's.

A chief reason for the emendations Irving included in his letters to Henry Brevoort as well as of many other small changes made later, was his uneasiness about his inability to read proof for 1A and 2A. He expressed his concern in a letter to Brevoort:

I find in the printed copy of No. 1. three or four inaccuracies in language in addition to those already pointed out, but I have not the number by me to correct them. These errors will take place whenever an author has not the advantage of correcting the proofs where he sees his sentiments fairly printed and brought out in a final compass under his eye. I wish you would keep an eye to see that grammatical inaccuracies do not occur. I often alter my sentiments after they are written out, which is apt to make these errors.[37]

37. August 2, 1819. Irv-Bvt, II, 105.

Ten days later he again wrote to Brevoort and included a number of corrections for *Sketch Book* Number I. At the end of his list he once more showed his uneasiness:

> But I will not plague you with these petty troubles. These are all such corrections as an author makes when he has proof-sheets to look over—and for want of that final revision I must expect to appear ungrammatical & awkward occasionally.[38]

When, for 1E, he finally got the chance to read proof and make changes he did so with a vengeance: 1E has as many small substantive changes as 2A, 22E, and ARE combined. Irving knew that the success of *The Sketch Book* probably owed as much to *how* he wrote as to *what* he said; he rightly feared the reaction of the British critics to an American writer; and he had seen criticism of his style in American reviews. This accounts for the heavy revision of 1E.[39]

In looking over Irving's emendations of the books as a whole, from 2A to ARE, we must admit that, stated bluntly, he was an inveterate piddler. He seems to have been compulsive about making a few more changes each time he got the opportunity. If Irving had had a discernible plan behind all these changes, an editor probably could, in most cases, separate the authoritative ones from the corruptions. But for the most part he was just touching up. Even in the few essays such as "English Writers on America," where we can see a pattern of altered meaning in the emendations as a group, many of the changes, as one might guess from Irving's epistolary comments, are neutral in effect and might just as well have been made by a compositor or a publisher's reader.

In some few instances, however, authorial and nonauthorial changes can be discriminated. By isolating the individual sketches and analyzing the changes made in each sketch for each edition, it is sometimes possible to argue that Irving was not likely to have made certain small changes in an essay to which he paid little attention for a particular edition. Or, by looking at one edition as a whole we can sometimes identify instances of house-styling. For example, the expression *from whence* occurs a number of times in the text, until ARE, where it is consistently changed to *whence*. From the very consistency of the change and its limitation to this edition we can reasonably assume that it is not authorial. But even this degree of certainty is rare. We note that in ARE the word *that* is often changed to *which*, sometimes in places where emendation appears superfluous. But we notice the same

---

38. August 12, 1819. Irv-Bvt, II, 110.
39. No doubt Murray's readers as well as the compositors of 1E also took part in this process of emendation; but Irving's role is clearly dominant.

change taking place to a lesser degree in the other editions as well, and we read Irving's letter to Brevoort (July 28, 1819) where he emends the "Prospectus" to 1A: "for 'those high honours *that* are' read— 'those high honours *which* are.'" Since several other similarly undistinctive emendations occur in Irving's letters, an editor can never be sure that such changes anywhere in the book are not Irving's as well—even though a number of them are bound to be unauthoritative. Under these circumstances, there is no álternative but to accept virtually all substantive changes made in those editions in which Irving had a hand. While this procedure no doubt perpetuates a number of readings introduced by other hands, it avoids the greater danger of eliminating from the text alterations made by Irving himself.

The conservatively rejected substantives include: (1) all readings originating in unauthoritative editions, unless they correct errors; (2) all outright errors, no matter where they originate; (3) all violations of Irving's own practice and manner, as evident in his manuscripts; (4) all changes superseded by further emendation in a later authoritative edition; (5) shifts from unusual, archaic, or otherwise striking readings to undistinguished, plebeian ones; (6) changes which come under suspicion because of their excessive awkwardness or their confusion rather than clarification of their contexts. Rejections under (5) and (6) are few, cautious, and always explained.

One final category of rejected substantives should be mentioned separately, namely, (7) substantive changes originating in an authoritative edition, but dying out with that edition. These are not cases of supersession by subsequent emendation, but rather alterations which, because of peculiarities of *The Sketch Book*'s textual history were not perpetuated.

Several times, as has been explained in the history of the text, Irving made substantive changes for a particular edition but did not use that emended edition when revising again. His subsequent revisions, therefore, were sometimes made without regard to the earlier ones, and at times were in conflict with them. Such discrepancies occurred when he made a number of changes in copies of 1A, Numbers I and II, and sent them to the United States as printer's copy for 2A. When preparing copy for 1E, Irving apparently tried to reconstruct some of the changes from memory, but could not do so exactly; others he forgot. Since all later editions derive ultimately from 1E, a number of 2A readings got no farther than 2A. A similar situation exists with "A Royal Poet": 2A and 1E were printed from different manuscripts; and, again, all later editions derive from 1E. Many readings of 2A, therefore, were not perpetuated. Other such dead-end readings were produced when Irving revised a copy of Murray's 1821 edition of *The Sketch Book* for the Montucci, Dresden edition of 1823. Consequently, in the Twayne edition all these authoritative but, so to speak, neglected readings, are preserved in the apparatus but not included in the text. The differences between 2A and 1E, "A Royal Poet," are contained in a separate list, but all others are to be found in the list of rejected substantives which concludes with an addendum containing those readings unique to the Montucci edition.

An interesting illustration of one way certain readings became part of the text while others did not, is found in "The Voyage." The most significant emendation made in this sketch was originally ordered in a letter to Henry Brevoort, written shortly after Irving had first seen a copy of *Sketch Book* Number I. The description of Geoffrey Crayon's first view of the British Isles, as originally written, contained "a passage which is rather strongly expressed...."[40] Irving had written, "I question whether Columbus, when he discovered the new world, felt a more delicious throng of sensations, than rush into an American's bosom, when he first comes in sight of Europe." He asked Brevoort to see that the second edition of *Sketch Book* Number I read instead: "no one that has not felt them can conceive the delicious sensations &c." But the second edition of the essay was printed from a corrected copy of the first edition, and in that copy, emended at least a month after he had written his letter, Irving revised his passage more adroitly: "None but those who have experienced it can imagine the delicious throng of sensations that rushes...." Still not content, Irving touched up the passage a bit more for 1E, and in that form (14.34–36) it now stands.

TREATMENT OF ACCIDENTALS

The use of multiple copy-text obviously requires more than one group of standards in the handling of the accidentals of *The Sketch Book*. In the editing of this text, two sets of procedures have been applied: one for manuscript, the other for print.

Manuscripts

Because these documents are fair copy manuscripts they present relatively few difficulties in transcription compared to Irving's journals and letters; but Irving, though writing with some care, had orthographic quirks which make a number of specific readings difficult to render with certainty. Often, for example, where a comma is obviously intended, he touched his pen to the paper but left merely a dot. Since Irving often wrote fragmentary sentences (an accepted contemporary

40. Irving to Brevoort, July 28, 1819, in the Seligman Collection of the New York Public Library.

practice), confusion between commas and periods can have serious effects on meaning. Similar problems arise with his periods and dashes: he sometimes did not lift his pen from the paper soon enough, and inadvertently made short dashes out of periods. Therefore, though he intentionally ended many sentences with a dash, he did not do so as often as one might think from scanning the manuscript.

Another practice of Irving's, intended to clarify his usage, is the inscription of a double hyphen in conjunction with a hyphen at the end of a manuscript line, to indicate that he did not intend the printer to retain the hyphen ("hope-/=ful"). But, as with virtually every other kind of accidental, his system here is inconsistent and not an infallible guide to his intent—though the great infrequency of hyphenated constructions makes the resolution of these instances relatively simple. In word division too, difficulties in transcription arise. Irving sometimes ran obviously independent words together, and did not go back to separate them. This problem is sometimes complicated by his opposing habit of lifting his pen in the middle of a single word, leaving a gap which appears to indicate two distinct words.

In all these cases of transcription difficulty, decisions were reached only after repeated readings of the manuscripts for the purpose of classifying their characteristics. Where Irving is inconsistent in his spelling, word division, or punctuation, this edition does not emend to make the text uniform unless Irving is in error or his meaning is obscured. Such inconsistency is a recurring feature of the various editions of *The Sketch Book*, as well as of the manuscript, and it does not seem appropriate to impose a modern sense of uniformity on the manuscript copy-text.

The same reluctance to emend applies to the most common difficulty presented by the accidentals of the *Sketch Book* manuscripts: capitalization. Irving frequently capitalized incorrectly, or neglected to capitalize where it would normally be required. National designations such as "English" or "Dutch" usually appear without capitals. "Primrose hill," "bunkers hill," and "Regents Park" give some idea of the variance in place names. He is often completely capricious, as in a title: "The Country church"; a list: "paintings, music, Horses, dogs"; and elsewhere: "[the young ladies'] Brothers were tall. . . ." But while the manuscript capitalization is often incorrect, some of the eccentricity seems to be intentional, as, for example, in "The Country Church," where Irving's reference to "the Coachman" (as distinct from "a fat coachman" a page earlier) parallels his use of "the Banker" and "the Author" elsewhere, and is apparently meant to be a title accentuated by capitalization. This "Irvingesque" usage should be distinguished from the other, careless capitalization or lack of it, and in this edition is preserved.

A further problem in rendering capitalization is the frequent inability to tell some of Irving's lower case letters from his capitals. In general the editorial decision is based on the distinctive form of the letter, if it has one, and on the size or height of the letter compared to its context; absolute size, however, usually means nothing. In many cases these criteria are insufficient and Irving is given the benefit of the doubt. The validity of crediting him with correctness is supported by his transcriptions in notebooks and commonplace books of German passages, in which he clearly capitalized all nouns, common and proper, as the language requires. He took this care in all cases but for *o* and *s*. Not that he was making exceptions of these letters, but he tended not to distinguish clearly between the capital and lower case *o* or *s*, even when he evidently intended to do so.[41]

There is a good deal of error of all sorts in the accidentals of the *Sketch Book* manuscripts, and it calls for emendation. Almost all such correction was accomplished by Irving's printers, but this edition differs significantly from those set from Irving's manuscript one hundred and fifty years ago. Then, the printers tried to regularize everything but failed because of their own recognition of the contemporary acceptability of variant usage; now, this edition tries to preserve as much of the character and feel of Irving's writing as possible, while recognizing that he did not want his work to be highly idiosyncratic. Unlike some authors, Irving not only expected but asked for the help of his printers and, at times, of his friends. His letters show clearly that he did not regard his spelling, punctuation, or grammatical usage as final or inviolate; he knew his manuscripts contained errors and infelicities of various kinds, and repeatedly asked that they be corrected. To retain, therefore, all eccentricities on the ground that they are the author's own and, besides, are "Irvingesque," would be only pedantry. But here an editor may go too far, as Irving's printers did, for many of the instances of unusual spelling and punctuation (in addition to the capitalization cited above) are not incorrect, and do impart a distinct flavor to the prose.

Such spellings as *ancle* for *ankle, chace* for *chase, gulph* for *gulf,* do not justify emendation since they were acceptable, though picturesque or antiquarian at the time.[42] Similarly, though Irving's punctuation is often confused or wrong, neither modern practice nor an analysis of American punctuation in the earlier nineteenth century provides an

41. These observations are based on the findings of the editors of Irving's journals and notebooks for the Twayne edition.

42. For a discussion of contemporary dictionaries and Irving's possible use of them, see the Textual Commentary to *Mahomet and His Successors* (Madison, 1970), pp. 607–9. The authority of the O.E.D. is recognized in decisions to accept or reject Irving's unusual spellings in *The Sketch Book.*

adequate guide for emendation. Irving punctuated (usually quite sparingly) by feel, by a sense of rhythm, perhaps oral rhythm; and the "corrections" made by his printers, in the form of nearly one thousand added commas and semicolons in the sections of the text for which manuscript is extant, are usually not justified by greater clarity or significantly improved rhythm, though they almost always are, in the strictest sense, correct. Consequently the editorial path, in the case of punctuation, is a slippery one. The responsibility to act for the author comes more strongly into play here than elsewhere, since it would not be sufficient to emend merely all cases of error. Often an added comma or dash will clarify a correct but rather confusing sentence, and in such a case the editor would be rejecting his responsibilities as Irving's agent were he to refuse to accept a sensible emendation made in the edition set from manuscript, or in rare instances to propose an emendation superior to the one made by a printer and perpetuated in later editions.

No inflexible rule for emendation of manuscript punctuation can, therefore, be followed. Instead, this edition tries to implement a guiding principle applicable to all questions of emendation, but particularly pertinent here: emend conservatively and consistently, on strong grounds, in line with the stated or implied desires of the author. Where the principle proves inadequate as a guide, editorial judgment, based on intimate knowledge of Irving's hand and habits, is the legitimate guide for emendation. That in its effect this policy is quite conservative can be verified by a glance at the List of Emendations, and a reading of the part of the text edited from manuscript.

Emendations of the manuscript accidentals can be summarized as follows: (1) all misspellings have been corrected, but acceptable early nineteenth-century variants of the common forms have been retained; (2) errors in punctuation have been corrected, but acceptable though idiosyncratic usage, such as Irving's frequent dash, has not been altered;[43] (3) missing punctuation deemed necessary or highly desirable is supplied, but not so as to alter Irving's intended meaning; (4) Irving's oversights in beginning a new paragraph for each change of speaker in a conversation are corrected.

In addition to these changes, which are all found in the List of Emen-

---

43. "The Wife" is unique in the *Sketch Book* manuscripts for its use of a long dash in addition to Irving's frequent short one. The three instances (24.23, 24.34, 24.42), on three successive manuscript pages, occur at moments of emotional stress in conversation, and, heavily inscribed, measure almost exactly $\frac{7}{16}$ of an inch while Irving's ordinary dash is usually no larger than $\frac{1}{8}$ inch. The Twayne edition preserves these idiosyncratic marks of punctuation since they clearly are Irving's indication of unusually long pauses at those points.

dations, two types of generic emendation have been made. (1) The merely orthographic eccentricities, M^r, D^r, &, S^t (or S$^{\underline{t}}$ as it sometimes appears), having no bearing on meaning, are normalized, as they were in every edition during Irving's lifetime.[44] (2) Irving used a "d" rather than "ed" preterit ending seventeen times in the extant manuscripts. It is sometimes a space-saving device at the end of a line, but, even when used in midline, never more than an inconsistent orthographic practice. All instances are normalized.[45]

Printed Texts

1A, 2A, 1E, and ARE all serve as copy-texts for various parts of Irving's eclectic *Sketch Book,* and the discrepancies in their handling of accidentals tempt the editor to impose some sort of consistency upon them all. The temptation must be resisted, however, since such a practice would in many places inevitably take the text a step farther from the lost manuscript rather than bring it closer. One instance of spelling and one type of punctuation do, however, call for editorial alteration. Apart from these, the text is emended only to correct errors.

1A, 2A, and 1E all agree with Irving's manuscript in generally spelling after the British fashion. Though Irving sometimes used American spellings, they are very few, and are usually written elsewhere in the British form as well. Consequently, since the texture of spellings in manuscript, 1A, 2A, and 1E is virtually of a piece, no effort to impose greater consistency on them has been made. ARE, however, using Webster as a guide, spells almost completely in the American fashion, though because British and American spellings were not so thoroughly distinct then as they have been more recently, it contains a few spellings like *centre, connexion,* and *practised.* ARE is copy-text for the "Preface to the Revised Edition," and in the "Preface" the only word which Irving would have spelled differently is "favorable." He was consistent in using the *-our* spelling in all forms of "favour" (*favourite, favourable, ill favoured,* etc.). Therefore, this edition emends the two occurrences in the "Preface" to "favourable."

44. The emendations under this heading occur as follows: Mr. *from* M^r *at* 16.36, 17.8, 17.25, 18.17, 18.23, 18.40, 19.19, 19.33, 20.2, 20.13, 20.25, 41.7, 41.22, 98.1, 98.36; St. *from* S^t *at* 10.4, 93.35, 93.40, 94.31, 99.25, 143.25, 143.31, 144.6; St. *from* S$^{\underline{t}}$ *at* 94.23 and 96.14; Reverend *from* Rev^d *at* 55.14; and *from* & *at* 10.2, 11.10, 13.14, 14.21, 14.25, 14.27, 14.28, 18.14, 20.26, 32.17, 35.7, 40.20, 40.34, 41.37, 44.20, 46.36, 55.2, 58.4, 80.32, 82.6.

45. The words are: 13.29 uttered; 14.28 decked; 15.1 reconnoitered; 19.18 shattered; 22.23 shattered; 23.33 altered; 28.34 stamped; 31.3 conditioned; 37.28 bewildered; 46.31 uttered; 51.38 sequestered; 54.21 sheltered; 59.31 entered; 64.27 tattered; 65.28 chopped; 98.26 entertained. Irving's old medial *s* (*ſ*) is routinely transcribed as *s* and not .annotated.

Though it is obviously unwise in general to attempt emending the punctuation of a printed text on manuscript model, *The Sketch Book* calls for one type of such emendation. The reason is that in the hyphenation of compounds or possible compounds Irving's own practice is almost contradictory to the practice of his British and American printers.

For the purpose of making a point, one might exaggerate a bit and say that Irving did not hyphenate. To be more accurate, the surviving manuscripts for *The Sketch Book,* equivalent to approximately 285 pages of print in the first American edition, contain (excluding direct quotation) exactly thirteen hyphenated constructions. That is an average of *one* for every twenty-two pages. By contrast, the first American edition has an average of one for every 2.8 pages; and this disparity is slightly greater in both the Miller-Murray edition and the Author's Revised Edition.[46] Even this large manuscript-to-print ratio of almost one to ten is not truly indicative of the degree of variance, however. First of all, five of the manuscript hyphens are, idiosyncratically, in one sketch. So if we exclude that atypical sketch from our count we have eight hyphens in 260 pages or one per 32.5 pages—perhaps a more accurate ratio. Second, four of Irving's thirteen hyphens are in constructions he elsewhere spelled as two words. "Cock-lane" (in "The Boar's Head Tavern"—the atypical sketch) is one of these: a few pages later he renders it "cock lane"; and though he uses many other street names in this essay and others, nowhere else in the manuscripts does he hyphenate one. Similarly inconsistent are "train-band" and "train band" in the manuscript of the same sketch, one coming just a few lines after the other. And though elsewhere he wrote "lookers-on," he also inscribed the parallel "hanger on." Finally, "Boars-head" appears eleven other times as "Boars head."

Excluding these four inconsistent cases, we have nine remaining constructions which might be taken to reveal Irving's practice. Four of these are words whose parts are not independent and so require a hyphen unless spelled as one word: they are "lack-a-daisical," "purblind," "re-echoed," and "ultra-fashionables." Two others are nautical terms: "Aye-aye," and "mid-ships"; "san-greal" and "Kaaters-kill" are foreign; and "dear-dear" is an intensification ("my dear-dear mother"). The manuscripts do not contain constructions of these types in unhyphenated form. We may say, then, that Irving hyphenated only in certain special situations; this edition of his book, therefore, should be similarly restrained.

The fact that Irving's British and American printers added hun-

46. In the manuscript material added by Irving to his text in 1848 there are thirty-one possibly compound, two-word constructions (school boy, old fashioned, memorandum book, Fleet Street, etc.). The ARE hyphenated all thirty-one.

dreds of hyphens to his text is clear evidence that Irving's own practice was at great variance with the custom of the day. What he did do
virtually all the time, of course, was to spell such constructions as
either one word or two; and he greatly preferred the latter. He used
the two-word form approximately 3.5 times as often as the one-word
(though he sometimes spelled the same word both ways). Furthermore,
it is significant that the compositors introduced hyphens into Irving's
two-word items far more often than they did into the one-word. The
point is that Irving and the compositor came much closer to agreement on what was a one-word form than they did on the two-word.
Consequently, a hyphenated word in the print was, by the odds, two
words in the manuscript.

In light of all this evidence, hyphenated constructions in the printed
copy-texts have been handled quite simply: all of the hyphens have
been deleted except for foreign terms ("billet-doux," "Hoch-heimer");
compounds whose parts are not independent ("now-a-days"); and constructions without parallel or equivalent in the manuscripts, including
some proper nouns ("blind-man's-buff," "Tom-come-tickle-me"), and
reduplications ("nick-nacks"). The altered constructions then stand as
two words unless the manuscripts give some hint that they should be
one word. If in the manuscripts Irving wrote the word both ways, his
dominant usage is adopted; if no dominant form is discernible, it is
rendered here as two words. If it appears as both one word and hyphenated, but not two words, and there is no equivalent in the manuscripts,
then the hyphenated form is made one word. The possibility if not
the inevitability of some error exists in this procedure, of course, but
the logic behind it is this: it is almost a certainty that Washington
Irving did not write these hyphens; therefore, even if the editorial
choice in a specific case might be wrong, the hypothetical error is well
within the limits of Irving's own practice, and is not the deliberate per-
petuation of mere house style outside those limits. The hyphenation
list contains a full record of these changes.

Finally, although Irving's text is faithfully and critically rendered,
no effort is made to reproduce exactly the so-called appurtenances of
the text—that is, such typographical details as the precise arrangement
of the title and half-title pages and other preliminary matter, pagination and lineation, footnote symbols, display capitals and the capitalized
text letters following them, or the exact typography of the sketch titles
and running heads.

DISCUSSIONS OF ADOPTED READINGS

These notes generally present the rationale for editorial decisions to emend, or not to emend, the copy-text. An *E* or an *R* following an entry directs the reader to the List of Emendations or to the List of Rejected substantives, where the textual situation being commented on is to be found. Further, many of the discussions here explain and justify seemingly incorrect readings in the Twayne text which are in fact correct; in addition, some other readings are discussed which, for a variety of reasons, deserve annotation.

A number of comments, such as, "The rejected reading originates in the unauthoritative 21E" are included because there were so many forms of the text during Irving's lifetime that to present in tabular form all the sources of significant error in *The Sketch Book* would be more confusing than helpful. These items, then, supplement the entries in the List of Emendations and List of Rejected Substantives.

To the left of the bracket are the page, line, and reading of the Twayne text; to the right the commentary. Symbols used in these discussions are as follows:

MS1	Author's manuscript of *Sketch Book* Numbers I–III
MS2	Author's manuscripts of material added for the "Author's Revised Edition"
1A	First American edition (Van Winkle, 1819–1820)
2A	Second American edition (Van Winkle, 1819–1820)
1E	First British edition: Volume I (John Miller/John Murray, 1820); Volume II (John Murray, 1820)
2E	Second British edition (Murray, 1820)
21E	"New Edition" (Murray, 1821)
4E	"Fourth Edition" (Murray, 1821)
5E	"Fifth Edition" (Murray, 1821)
22E	"New Edition" (Murray, 1822)
23E	"New Edition" (Murray, 1823)
1F	First French edition (Baudry and Didot, 1823)
ARE	"Author's Revised Edition" (G. P. Putnam, 1848)
T	Twayne edition

THE AUTHOR'S ACCOUNT OF HIMSELF

8.21 from whence] Irving's "from whence" is repeatedly changed to "whence" in ARE, and only in ARE. The change is clearly a matter of house-style, and is rejected in every instance. *R*

9.14 beside] The rejected reading, "besides," originates in the unauthoritative 2E. Even had it been introduced in an edition overseen by Irving, however, it would still be rejected as compositorial in origin. As in this instance, so in several others, the *s* is added and then drops off again in a later edition. *R*

9.39 when I look over, however,] The rejected "when, however, I look over" originates in 2E. *R*

THE VOYAGE

11.31 gulph] Irving uses this spelling twice within a few lines. It was definitely archaic or even obsolescent, and the dictionaries preferred "gulf"; but "gulph" appears in Samuel Johnson's citations as late as Pope. Irving must have known he was using an old spelling.

11.38 all that was] The unique ARE reading, "all," is unusually awkward for Irving, and thus is a suspected compositorial error. *R*

12.12 gently] The rejected "gentle" originates in the unauthoritative 21E. *R*

12.29 earth] The rejected "world" originates in 21E. *R*

13.15 which] This change from "that" to "which," and many others exactly like it in 2A, 1E, 22E, and ARE, might merely be the result of house-styling. But Irving was diffident about his use of "that," ordered at least one such change in a letter, and could very well be responsible for many (though surely not all) of them. Except where other evidence suggests the wisdom of rejection, all these changes are accepted. *E*

13.28 'a sail ahead!'] Though Irving's manuscript "a head" was corrected to read "ahead" in 1A, the necessary emendation to single quotation marks rather than double was not made until ARE. *E*

13.30 the] The rejected "her" originates in the unauthoritative 2E. *R*

13.31 a mid-ships] Irving's manuscript reads "a mid-ships," while both 1A and 1E read "a-mid-ships." Neither Johnson's, Webster's, nor Walker's dictionaries include the word, and the *O.E.D.* gives only two forms in its eighteenth- and nineteenth-century citations: "amidships," and "amidships." Because of the apparant lack of a standard spelling, no emendation is called for.

14.6 deep.] "deep—" is the manuscript reading. Irving had originally intended to go on with the same sentence, as the cancellation of the following word "while" indicates. He changed his mind, however, and began a new sentence, apparently neglecting to change his dash to a period.

14.21 side] Since the copy-text reading is more literally correct, the addition of an *s* in ARE is deemed compositorial. *R*

14.31 *Paragraph* I] In his manuscript Irving created an appropriate pause at this point by writing "—I"; but 1A–1F all omitted the dash. He apparently chose the longer pause of a new paragraph for ARE.

ROSCOE

16.9 contains] The rejected "it contains" originates in the unauthoritative 4E. *R*

17.19 They, however,] Irving often placed commas before and after "however," but he just as often left out one or both. He evidently recognized the need for them, but, as with so many other kinds of punctuation, was careless and/or erratic. The Twayne text supplies all missing commas with Irving's "however," and records each instance. *E*

18.10 gardens] The changes in the text of "Roscoe" which originate in ARE are, as in a number of other sketches, almost surely nonauthorial. Three of the four readings here (18.10, 19.26 and 20.11) are clearly inferior to those of the copy-text, and the fourth (19.38) is more likely to be compositorial than authorial. This sort of evidence, occurring in more than a third of the sketches, shows that Irving did not for ARE review the whole text as he had for 1B. The evidence in other sketches is often more conclusive than in this one, and justifies the rejection of all or virtually all the ARE readings in particular essays. *R*

18.33 with posterity] The rejected "posterity" originates in 4E. *R*

19.8 blending] The rejected "blended" originates in the unauthoritative 23E. *R*

19.18 with] This emendation and the ones at 19.25 and 19.26, all originating in 1A, are accepted on the grounds that, together, they suggest the author's, rather than a compositor's hand. It is quite possible that Irving ordered these changes in a letter no longer extant. *E*

THE WIFE

22.17 supporter] The dropping of *er* in ARE destroys the parallelism of "comforter and supporter," and is therefore most likely not Irving's own alteration. *R*

24.1 day,] Irving's comma before "one," one word earlier, indicates his intention to set off "one day." *E*

24.2 had heard] This omission of a word is one of four readings new to ARE. Rejection here, as with 26.18 and 26.31, is on the basis of Irving's inattention to this sketch in 1848. *R*

26.37 around] This is one of many instances in which "round" and "around" become interchanged. These changes are scattered, inconsistent, and indiscriminate, and surely compositorial. They are all rejected. *R*

27.1 by] The rejected "with" originates in the unauthoritative 23E. *R*

27.27 bosom—he] This emendation is accepted because the extended parallelism of the passage suggests that Irving intended no new sentence at this point. *E*

RIP VAN WINKLE

28.34 to being] The rejected form "to the being" is due either to the misconstruction of "being" as a noun, or to an unnecessary grammatical sophistication. *R*

28 *Footnote omitted*] Irving removed this note when it was no longer timely. 1A expanded his abbreviation and wrote out "G. C. Verplanck." *E*

32.26 and call] Irving's transcription of this part of the sentence is obviously in error, and he would presumably have corrected it for the first appearance had he noticed it. He apparently made the correction for 2A and 1E. *E*

32.26 naught] According to the citations in the *O.E.D.*, contemporary usage permitted "naught," Irving's spelling, in this construction. 1A unnecessarily emends to "nought." See 64.17.

32.31 the clamor] Because the pattern of emendations in constructions such as this one indicates an authorial intention to strengthen parallelism, not weaken it; and because this unusual alteration in 22E could easily be a compositorial error, it is rejected. *R*

33.2 herbage,] The comma is needed to indicate that the "knoll" rather than the "herbage" "crowned the brow of a precipice." *E*

33.43 or rather] In the manuscript an ink blot conceals the brief word between "ravine" and "rather." All relevant editions concur that "or" is the only reasonable reading. *E*

35.5 awaking] This change and others like it (waken / awaken, wake / awake) occur several times, in different editions, and are rejected as nonauthorial. *R*

35.26 arose] As with "waking" / "awaking" above, this change from "arose" to "rose," and others such as "arise" to "rise," are judged to be details Irving would not have bothered with. They are rejected as nonauthorial. *R*

35.36 and tendrils] The change to "or" originates in the unauthoritative 23E. *R*

37.1 rung] Irving's characteristic, repeated use of the usually past perfect "rung," "sunk," "sprung," etc., for the simple past tense, is consistently altered, usually in 1E. Irving's usage, however, was more archaic than incorrect, and so the emendations are rejected. *R*

37.9 on top] The rejected "on the top" originates in the unauthoritative 21E. *R*

38.19 rotted] The rejected "rotten" originates in the unauthoritative 4E. *R*

39.9 likely looking] The rejected "comely" originates in 21E. *R*

40.34 village] Irving's sentence originally ended at this point, but he added another clause, forgetting to cancel his period. 1A rendered the uncanceled period as a comma, but a comma is unnecessary. *E*

ENGLISH WRITERS ON AMERICA

44.5 prejudiced] In this sketch, ARE varies from the other texts in only six readings, two of which (46.34, 49.32) are rejected as undoubtedly unauthoritative. Two of the other four departures (44.12, 46.31) are exactly the sorts of changes one would expect to originate with the printer or publisher's reader, and one is almost certainly an error (46.31). Since Irving apparently paid little if any attention to this sketch when revising for ARE, these three readings, namely, "prejudicial," "indication" (44.12), and "from" (46.31) are rejected. The only new ARE reading accepted as at all likely to be authorial is "generally" (47.9) in place of "collectively." *R, E*

49.27–28 english . . . english] Irving wrote the first word as "english," changed *e* to *E* and then restored *e*. Clearly, though his motive is obscure, he meant the adjective to be uncapitalized. The second is clearly written "english," and although elsewhere emendation to "English" is called for, the MS spelling is accepted here since Irving apparently had some deliberate intent—possibly whimsical or satirical.

49.32 from thence] As with "from whence" / "whence," this change is limited to ARE, and is judged nonauthorial. *R*

RURAL LIFE IN ENGLAND

50.4 pleasure] The poem actually reads "leisure," rather than "pleasure"; it is therefore unlikely that "pleasures," originating in 22E, is Irving's work rather than a compositor's. *R*

50.4 pass'd] The rejected "past" originates in the unauthoritative 23E. *R*

50.18 circles] Though "classes" could be a change ordered by Irving in a letter before 1A was printed, it looks like an "improvement" made by someone else on the suspicion that "circles" was not strictly correct. *R*

51.12–13 character—its] The comma is clearly inadequate here, even by Irving's standards. Though the manuscript appears to be clear at this point, Irving's commas and dashes are sometimes almost indistinguishable, and a dash is the logical emendation. E

51.18 conveniencies ... elegancies] These and their singulars "conveniency" and "elegancy" were acceptable contemporary forms (O.E.D.).

52.18–25 The trim ... mind] Punctuation in this sentence is entirely Irving's. His use of semicolons rather than commas to separate parallel phrases (a common practice for him) is not truly correct, but neither does it obscure his meaning. Emendation here would be mere guesswork, and is therefore avoided.

52.43 gentry, small landed proprietors,] Here Irving's inconsistent punctuation leads to confusion: in the manuscript ("Gentry—small landed proprietors;") the gentry appear to be defined as "small landed proprietors," but they are a separate class, one in the list of five. 1A clears up the confusion with the least possible emendation, and its reading is adopted. E

53.15 wave] This form of "waive" was acceptable contemporary usage (O.E.D.).

53.24–29 To this ... dewy landscape.] The two colons in this sentence are unusual, and one could perhaps argue that at least one of them is in error; but the manuscript reading is clear, and so is the meaning of the sentence. Therefore, emendation is not justified.

54.17 style] This alternate form of "stile" was acceptable contemporary usage (O.E.D.).

54.23–24 scene.—All] The passage from 54.16 to 54.27 is punctuated several ways in the different editions, and this last item in the series is set off from the others differently in each of the six key editions. Irving wrote the elements in the series as separate sentences, but then incorrectly set off the last element with only a comma. Reference to similar constructions in the manuscripts indicates that in such cases Irving usually set off the last item with an added dash: the reading, in this instance, of 1E. Since this is a frequent practice of the author's (see 15.33–36, 26.33–40, 51.33–42 for example), just as frequently tampered with by compositors; and since Irving gave more attention to revision of "Rural Life in England" in 1E than in any other edition, its reading is adopted. E

THE BROKEN HEART

56.17 doctrines—Shall] It is impossible to tell whether Irving wrote "doctrines—shall" or "doctrines—Shall." The best sense is made by adopting the latter, as did 1A.

56.27–28 The heart. ... treasures.] Here, as at 53.24–27 the unusual colons are clear in the manuscript and do not obscure meaning; no emendation is called for.

56.39 and a]   The omission of the "a" adversely affects the parallelism of the sentence and is therefore unlikely to be an authorial emendation. *R*

57.2 love,]   The manuscript semicolon after "love" is incorrect and confusing, and therefore calls for emendation. *E*

57.36 deaths]   Because the plural is more appropriate, the change to singular is more likely the work of a compositor than of the author. *R*

58.13–15 When ... sufferings.]   Although the sentence is syntactically faulty, the manuscript and all editions contain identical readings. Since emendation would require major revision without documentary evidence, none is attempted.

58.26 parching]   The rejected "parting" is clearly an error and originates in the unauthoritative 23E. *R*

58.37 loves]   The use of the plural to denote one person's love for another was idiomatic, and all editions agree with the manuscript.

59.40 song]   The rejected "songs" originates in the unauthoritative 21E. *R*

THE ART OF BOOK MAKING

61.3 labors]   The rejected singular originates in the unauthoritative 4E. *R*

63.16 writers]   The rejected "authors" originates in 4E. *R*

63.17 authors]   The rejected "writers" originates in 4E. *R*

63.32 passes]   The erroneous "pass," originating in 1E, was corrected in 21E. *R*

63.33 continues]   The rejected "continue" originates in the unauthoritative 21E. *R*

64.16 exceeding]   The rejected "exceedingly" is judged to be a compositorial attempt to correct Irving's more characteristic form. *R*

64.32 catch]   The rejected "to catch" originates in 21E. *R*

64.35 should]   The rejected "shall" originates in 4E. *R*

65.7 walls]   The rejected "wall" originates in 4E. *R*

65.12 their plunder]   The reading "the plunder" in 22E–1F originates in 21E. The ARE reading, "plunder," could conceivably be an authorial emendation, but it is awkward and clearly inferior to the unauthoritative alternative (21E). The dropped "the" of ARE is judged a compositorial error, and the copy-text reading is retained. *R*

A ROYAL POET

67.22 that]   In this instance the change from "that" to "which" is unjustified grammatically and is therefore rejected as a mistaken compositorial "improvement." See note 13.15 above. *R.*

68.21 servants]   The change to singular could, of course, easily be a compositorial error. It is rejected, though, primarily on the grounds that the King of Scotland would not have only one servant waiting on him. *R*

69.4 powerfully]   The rejected "powerful" originates in the unauthoritative 4E. *R*

69.6 others grow morbid]   This change and the sentence added at 69.21–26 are the only two emendations of 1E (aside from correction of error) that agree with 2A. The changes appear in 22E, revised by Irving, who must have compared the British version with 2A when revising for 22E, and added one word here and the long sentence at 69.21–26. *E*

69.30 peculiar]   The addition of the article "a" in ARE changes the sense of "peculiar" from *particular* to *strange*. Because it thus destroys Irving's intended meaning it is judged unauthoritative and rejected. *R*

70.4 meditate]   This is one of three substantive readings originating in 22E, none of them distinctly authorial. One (74.28) is a correction of error and is accepted, but this one and the third (76.29) are unnecessary though correct syntactical clarifications which would be accepted were there textual evidence that Irving revised this sketch for 22E. In the absence of such evidence they are rejected. *R*

71.26 exhilarating]   This correction of 1E originates in 21E. *E*

72.25 lapses]   Since there is no *re*lapse involved here, the ARE reading ("relapses") is judged in error. *R*

74.14 vent to a]   This correction of 1E originates in 21E. *E*

75.34 lives]   The sense of Irving's comment is best rendered by the 2A reading. The past tense in 1E appears to be a misguided nonauthorial attempt at improvement, or an error in manuscript transcription. *E*

76.6 its interests]   The rejected "its own interests" originates in the unauthoritative 21E. *R*

76.34 broke]   The copy-text error was corrected in 21E. *E*

77.26 fellow man]   The rejected "fellow men" originates in 21E. *R*

78.3 stream]   The rejected "streams" originates in 21E. *R*

THE COUNTRY CHURCH

79.12 county]   The rejected reading originates in the unauthoritative 21E. *R*

79.24–25 doors;—the]   The unnecessary addition of "of" here, and again before "the poor" later in the same sentence, to make the series exactly parallel, seems far too formal an emendation to have been made by Irving. *R*

79.31 county]   "The Country Church," in 22E, contains only three substantive departures from 1E: "county" / "country," "cracking" / "smacking," "the" / "that the." It is highly unlikely, on this evidence, that Irving paid any attention to this sketch when revising for 22E. The three are therefore rejected. *R*

81.1 of the horses]   The error in 1F ("the of horses") was corrected in ARE by removing the "of"; but though its reading is reasonable, it is, in light of the other readings originating in ARE, most likely not authorial. The copy-text reading is therefore retained. *R*

81.10 footmen]   The rejected "footman" originates in 21E. *R*

81.10–11 alight, open the door, pull]   This omission of a phrase is judged compositorial because the readings originating in ARE, as a group, suggest that Irving did not revise "The Country Church" for ARE. *R*

81.24 ultra-fashionables]   The unlikelihood of Irving's altering this strong and appropriate plural, and the high probability of its being a compositorial error are reason enough for rejecting the singular. *R*

82.7 by]   The rejected "with" originates in 21E. *R*

82.8 soul;]   The word occurs at the end of a manuscript line, a point at which Irving occasionally omitted necessary punctuation. *E*

82.19 whisper; . . . finery,]   The punctuation of the manuscript interferes with the sentence. Exchanging the punctuation marks, as in 1A–ARE, correctly conveys Irving's sense. *E*

THE WIDOW AND HER SON

84.39 through, therefore,]   As with "however" (see item 17.19, this list), Irving often sets off "therefore" from its context. When he neglects to include the clarifying punctuation, the Twayne text supplies it. All such emendations are listed. *E*

86.11 likely]   The word "comely" does not fit the context, and appears to be a substitution by a British hand for the more colloquial "likely." The nonauthorial substitution of "comely" for "likely looking" also took place (at 39.9) in 21E. *R*

87.11 returned,]   This is the second of a pair of commas setting off a dependent clause and is accepted because the manuscript omission causes confusion and was probably unintentional. *E*

A SUNDAY IN LONDON

89.5 Babel, London]   Irving's use of commas with appositives is inconsistent. Here, because of the awkwardness of the phrase, the ARE emendation is accepted. *E*

89.37 cleansing]   The ARE "elevating" is a compositorial misreading of Irving's manuscript. *R*

90.12 Satyrists]   The *O.E.D.* supports the validity of Irving's spelling.

THE BOAR'S HEAD TAVERN, EAST CHEAP

91.17 hang]   This rejected reading appears to be a misguided attempt at correction of Irving's subjunctive by someone in Van Winkle's shop. R

92.1 Fourth]   All editions read "IV," but there is no compelling reason to change Irving's designation except by capitalization. E

92.2 Boar's head]   Except in two places, Irving always spells this as "Boars head." An apostrophe is called for, but though all editions also capitalized "Head," Irving's eleven uncapitalized spellings clearly indicate his preference, which, because it is not strictly in error, is not emended. E

92.3 Tavern]   The five capitalizations of "Tavern" (as a proper noun) in the manuscript of this sketch indicate that in this instance and at 97.36 Irving's lowercase spelling is unintentional and deserves emendation. E

92.8 East cheap]   Irving consistently spells this as two words, suggesting perhaps his recognition that the name means "East market." As with "Boar's head," he never capitalizes the second word. His unusual form is not emended.

92.10 who]   The reference is to "hero," not "fiction," and the change to "that" appears to be an error made in Van Winkle's shop. R

92.11 who]   The same reasoning applies here as in the previous note. R

92.33 ran]   The manuscript reading might be a carelessly inscribed "ran." "Run" is, if not strictly incorrect, at least awkward and possibly confusing; the emendation of 1A is therefore accepted. E

92.34 Street]   Irving often capitalized "Street," "Lane," etc., indicating his recognition that capitalization was called for, except, in the practice of the day, where a hyphen was used: "Cock-lane." Irving's oversights in such capitalizations are emended. E

93.10 scite]   Irving's spelling is supported by citations in the O.E.D. See also 144.9.

93.11 empire]   1F, in error, omits "empire." Since Irving was working with a reprint of 1F when revising for ARE, the reprint probably perpetuated the error. In 1848, Irving or the printer supplied "abode," which also appeared a few lines above in the printer's copy. Since the reading of ARE is awkwardly repetitive and since there is no clear textual evidence that Irving paid any attention to this sketch when revising in 1848, the ARE reading is rejected in favor of the undoubtedly authoritative "empire." R

94.11 twinkle]   The rejected "twinkling" originates in the unauthoritative 23E. R

94.23 Michael]   The misreading in 1A ("Michael's") was no doubt due to the manuscript's lack of clarity at this point. Irving had originally written "Michael's," but had mended it to "Michael." R

94.26–27 Fishmonger] The word is capitalized because that seems to have been Irving's intention—as seen in three other instances in this sketch. *E*

94.35 Sovereigns] All printings follow 1A, which corrected Irving's spelling but removed his capitalization, which T retains. *E*

95.2 windows] In only one reading in "The Boar's head Tavern" besides this one does ARE directly depart from the other editions and *not* create an error. The other reading, at 96.23, is questionable, but is probably a legitimate correction. The change from "windows" to "window," then, is suspicious, and most likely unauthoritative. *R*

96.23 Miles] "Miles" is a corruption of "Michael's." Irving no doubt might have known the street as "Mile Lane," but "Miles" is accepted because of its correctness and the slim possibility that it may be authorial. *E*

96.24 Mason's] The manuscript reads "Masons." "Masons'," the reading of 1A, upon which 2A and 1E directly depend, is unauthoritative, and, on balance, 22E is the better choice. *E*

96.24 Mason's arms] Here, as with "Boar's head," Irving's lack of capitalization of the second word appears to be intentional and is therefore not emended.

97.9 Parlour] Irving's unusual capitalization of two items in this series of three: "Kitchen, parlour and Hall," suggests that he meant all three to be capitalized, not made lowercase as was done in 1A and subsequent editions. *E*

97.28 Tobacco] Irving's clear capitalization of "Tobacco" three times in the next few pages must be intentional. This instance is therefore regarded as an oversight on his part, and emended. *E*

98.40 of Windsor] "Of," not "at," is the reading in the play. *R*

THE MUTABILITY OF LITERATURE

100.6 period] ARE gives the correct reading of the poem at this point. *E*

101.4 cloister] The rejected "cloisters" originates in the unauthoritative 21E. *R*

103.15 Peterborough] This correction of "Petersborough" originates in 5E. *E*

103.39 and] The rejected "and of" originates in 21E. *R*

104.38 silver] Harvey's pamphlet contains the copy-text reading. *R*

104.42 spirite] The rejected "sprite" originates in the unauthoritative 4E. *R*

105.6 the fragments] The rejected "fragments" originates in 21E. *R*

105.26 and pursued] The rejected "pursued" originates in 4E. *R*

105.39 and four]   The rejected "or four" originates in the unauthoritative 23E. *R*

106.9 scarce]   The change from "scarce" to "scarcely" occurs a number of times in different sketches. It is almost certainly a nonauthorial "correction," and each occurrence is rejected and listed. *R*

106.38 into a short]   The rejected "in a" originates in 21E. *R*

107.1 I felt]   The rejected "that I felt" originates in 21E. *R*

RURAL FUNERALS

111.14 He noticed]   The new paragraph originates in the unauthoritative 21E. *R*

111.17 seen in]   The omitted "in" after "seen" in 1E was supplied in 2E. *R*

111.24 says]   The rejected "said" originates in the unauthoritative 4E. *R*

112.26 yewe]   This correction ("yewe" for "ewe") originates in 21E. *E*

113.4 funereal]   The rejected "funeral" originates in the unauthoritative 2E. *R*

117.36 transcribe]   The rejected "describe" originates in 2E, and the context favors the manuscript reading. *R*

THE SPECTRE BRIDEGROOM

121.34–35 of a circumstance]   The six readings in "The Spectre Bridegroom" new to ARE show no distinct evidence of Irving's hand, and only one (128.38–39) could be argued to be an improvement. While the dropping of an "of" or the addition of an "a" would probably be accepted as authoritative in the context of other, more clearly authorial changes, here, in the absence of such evidence, the six are rejected. *R*

124.13 of a]   The rejected "on a" originates in the unauthoritative 21E. *R*

125.36 this]   It is not the mission of Von Altenburg that is being referred to, but rather the favor he asks of Starkenfaust; thus the copy-text "this" is more appropriate than "his," and is not emended. *R*

126.1 engagement]   The rejected plural originates in the unauthoritative 23E. *R*

132.2 to scour]   The rejected "scour" originates in 21E. *R*

WESTMINSTER ABBEY

134.26 massy]   It is unlikely that Irving would change his own, unusual "massy" to the ordinary "massive." Instead, the change is most likely to have been a misguided attempt at correction by a compositor. *R*

135.3 dusty]   The change from "dusty" to "dusky" in ARE appears to be a sensible though not necessary emendation, but there is no textual evidence that Irving revised the body of "Westminster Abbey" for ARE. The four other changes originating in ARE consist of an error (139.26), two rather inappropriate words (136.14, 137.16), and a dubious inversion ("eye gazes" / "eyes gaze," 135.29–30). On this evidence of Irving's highly probable neglect of the sketch proper, all readings introduced in ARE are rejected as unauthoritative. *R*

135.27 *Paragraph* I]   The omission of a new paragraph originates in the unauthoritative 23E. *R*

135.42 *No paragraph* And yet]   The rejected creation of a new paragraph originates in 23E. *R*

136.8 Poets']   The more appropriate spelling, "Poets'," occurs once in the copy-text, and occurs in that same place in 1A, independently set from the same manuscript. It is most likely, then, that in all the other instances the manuscript merely read "Poets" as would be normal with Irving, but that in one instance, "Poets'," he remembered the apostrophe. The three *'s* spellings of the copy-text are therefore emended to *s'*. *E*

136.14 remain]   The sense of Irving's general observation is better rendered by the copy-text "remain" than the past tense in ARE. *R*

138.21 leads]   The rejected "lead" originates in 23E. *R*

140.28 around]   The rejected "round" originates in 23E. *R*

141.30 Poets']   The rejected "Poet's" originates in the unauthoritative 4E. *R*

141.35 falling]   The rejected "fallen" originates in 23E. *R*

142.24 those]   The rejected "these" originates in the unauthoritative 5E. *R*

NOTES CONCERNING WESTMINSTER ABBEY

143.35 onto]   The rejected "into" is a misreading of the manuscript. *R*

144.37 rest]   Compositorial misreading of the manuscript accounts for the ARE's "rust." *R*

146.20 Dean]   Irving's capitalization of "Dean" twice earlier and once later in the "Notes" suggests that this lowercase inscription was an oversight. *E*

CHRISTMAS

149.35 pleasures]   Though it is likely that Irving changed the opening words of this essay when revising for ARE, nowhere else in the sketch is his hand evident. Rather, of the five readings (not counting the opening) new to the sketch in ARE, three are singular/plural discrepancies, one is the change of a single letter in an unusual phrase to make it more ordinary (149.40), and the last (150.4) changes an Irvingesque "into" to the more usual "in." On the likelihood that these five are nonauthorial, they are rejected. *R*

THE STAGE COACH

153.24 in]   It is not at all likely that Irving is responsible for the readings new to "The Stage Coach" in 22E. Of the four new readings including this one, only one (154.38) suggests authorial revision—though it too could easily have originated with the printer. Another (157.14) is clearly inferior to the one it replaces; a third (157.18) is a recurring compositorial change rejected elsewhere; and the present one removes a repetition but is not distinctively authorial. On this negative evidence the four readings are rejected as nonauthorial. *R*

153.27 plans of pleasure of the]   Once again the readings new to the text in ARE are in all probability nonauthorial. This one appears to be a compositor's error caused by the repetition of "of"; the deletion of "whole" before "world" at 154.2–3 is also best explained as a print shop oversight; the change from "in" to "into" at 154.39 is not distinctive; and "alongs" for "along" at 155.12 is an error. At 155.38–39 a previously unnoticed spelling error is corrected. On this strong evidence that Irving did not revise this sketch for ARE, all these readings except 155.38–39 are rejected. *R*

156.8 pack]   This correction of "pair" originates in 4E. *E*

156.8 even]   Since the word "even" is perfectly acceptable, the emendation to "eve" in 1E is rejected. *R*

156.18 head]   The rejected "end" originates in the unauthoritative 22E. *R*

156.21 shagged]   This change to "shaggy" was also made in 22E, at 241.4. Both these substitutions of the ordinary for the unusual form are undoubtedly due to hands other than Irving's and are rejected. *R*

CHRISTMAS EVE

159.12 cracked]   In "The Country Church" "cracking" (to describe the sound of a whip) was in 22E unauthoritatively changed to "smacking." Here "cracked" (with the same meaning) becomes "smacked," also in 22E. The change is almost certainly not Irving's, and so is rejected. *R*

159.13 upon a]   The rejected "on a" originates in the unauthoritative 2E. *R*

160.7 any little]   This dropping of a word, two errors (161.16, 166.41), a change from "a" to "the" (162.20), the substitution of "assorted" for "sorted" (166.9), and the replacement of "was amusing" with "amused" (167.20–21) are the readings new to this sketch in ARE. Only the last suggests possible authorial emendation, but even it is not truly distinctive. This evidence leads to the conclusion that Irving did not emend "Christmas Eve" for ARE; therefore, the ARE readings are rejected. *R*

160.11 stile]   This was an acceptable alternate spelling for "style" (*O.E.D.*).

160.15 rung]   See the note to 37.1.

161.9 ringing]   The rejected "ring" originates in the unauthoritative 23E. R

161.27 with heavy]   The rejected "and heavy" obscures rather than clarifies the meaning, and is therefore judged non-authorial. R

162.1 Squire]   The two capitalizations of "Squire" in this sketch, along with Irving's known failure to distinguish clearly between capital and lowercase s, and his evident capitalization of "Baron" in "The Spectre Bridegroom," justify the acceptance of the uniform capitalization of "Squire" in 1E. Since the separate listing of each emendation would be a burden to the reader of the List of Emendations, the first occurrence in this sketch (and in the next two) is entered, and then, in a note, the locations of all other such emendations in the sketch are listed together. The two capitalizations in the copy-text of "Christmas Eve" are at 160.4 and 165.34. All the other, originally lowercase spellings, are emended. They are at 162.8, 162.16, 162.18, 162.24, 163.2, 163.16, 163.19, 164.12, 165.15, 165.36, 165.39, 166.16, 166.30. E

162.17 of the army]   The rejected "in the army" originates in the unauthoritative 23E. R

162.27 proportions]   The copy-text plural is preferred to the emendation in 22E because of the preceding plural verb. R

163.28 the last]   The rejected "last" originates in the unauthoritative 21E. R

164.9 Besides]   This emendation and several other similarly undistinguished ones from 22E are accepted because the changes at 167.14–168.6 suggest that Irving did touch up the sketch for 22E. E

165.20 Master]   Irving's erratic capitalization no doubt accounts for the occurrence of both "Master" and "master" in this sketch and the next two. In order to fulfill Irving's apparent intention, all instances are capitalized in the Twayne text. Since the separate listing of each emendation would be a burden to the reader of the List of Emendations, the first occurrence in each sketch is entered and then, in a note, the locations of all other such emendations are listed together. E

CHRISTMAS DAY

170.20 Master]   See the note to 165.20. The other instances of a copy-text "master" emended to "Master" in "Christmas Day" are at 170.25, 174.22, 175.8, 175.10, 179.10, 179.24. E

170.29 Squire]   See the note to 162.1. The other instances of a copy-text "squire" emended to "Squire" in this sketch are at 171.8, 171.17, 171.26, 172.18, 172.27, 172.33, 176.21, 176.31, 177.10, 177.24, 178.13, 178.36, 179.4, 179.8, 179.23. E

171.21 at Master]   The change from "at" to the much more awkward "to" in 1E was probably due to the influence of the other "to" a few words earlier. *R*

171.35 of wrens or cranes] No word is missing. In archaic usage a flock of wrens or cranes was a "herd."

172.20 of a rainy] The copy-text reading is the more Irvingesque (see 54.28), and the substitution of "on" or some other word for "of" in such a construction (done in at least six other instances) is undoubtedly a gratuitous compositorial emendation of Irving's somewhat unusual usage. *R*

172.22 Cockayne] This spelling originates in 21E and so is not authorial. It is accepted, however, as a correction. *E*

172.34 Christmas] The rejected "a" before "Christmas" originates in the unauthoritative 2E. *R*

175.9 expectations] The rejected singular reading originates in 2E. *R*

175.16–17 who, happening] The evidence shows that Irving did not revise this sketch for ARE. In addition to this infelicitous change, ARE introduces two errors (177.6, 179.2) and one dubious grammatical emendation (178.28). All four readings are rejected. *R*

176.8 had a] The rejected "he had a" is suspicious because the addition of the pronoun affects the parallelism of the second and third clauses in the sentence. *R*

176.36 Mark. xvi] The rejected "xv" originates in the unauthoritative 23E. *R*

THE CHRISTMAS DINNER

180.17 Squire] See the note for 162.1. The other emendations of copy-text "squire" to "Squire" in this sketch are at 180.27, 181.4, 182.6, 182.21, 186.4, 186.18, 186.23, 186.29, 189.6, 190.26. *E*

183.7 traditionary] The four readings introduced in 22E show no evidence of the author's hand, and two, including this one, are patently nonauthorial (the other is at 187.12). All four are rejected. *R*

185.21 Master] See the note to 165.20. The other instances of copy-text "master" emended to "Master" in this sketch are at 185.29, 187.18, 187.31, 189.19. *E*

187.10 except] The rejected "excepting" is no improvement, and is more likely due to the influence of "recollecting," two words earlier, than to Irving's emending hand. *R*

188.4 forth] Except for adding the note at 191.7 Irving apparently did not emend this sketch for ARE. Three of the five other readings new to ARE are errors (190.10, 190.24, 190.30); the remaining two (190.4 and this one) are undistinctive and no doubt nonauthorial. Only one (190.4), because it is a correction, is accepted. *R, E*

188.16 of stormy]   See the note to 172.20. *R*

189.28 parlour]   The rejected "the" before "parlour" originates in the unauthoritative 21E. *R*

190.2 *No paragraph* The costume]   The rejected new paragraph originates in the unauthoritative 2E. *R*

190.35 its apathy]   The rejected "his apathy" originates in the unauthoritative 4E. *R*

LONDON ANTIQUES

192.22 crowd, plunged]   The addition of a comma in ARE is accepted since Irving's omission of it confuses the sense on first reading. *E*

193.12 "invitingly open."]   Irving mistakenly omitted the period in the manuscript. ARE corrected the error, but failed to print Irving's quotation marks. *E*

193.20 robe, a ruff]   Irving almost always separated the items in a series (except for the last) with commas. His omission of this comma is regarded as an oversight and the ARE emendation accepted. *E*

193.38 without]   The word is split on two manuscript lines: "with/ out." Irving elsewhere in the *Sketch Book* manuscripts spells it as one word, but here apparently neglected to write "with–/=out." *E*

194.10 those]   The ARE reading is accepted since it might be Irving's emendation, for he appears to have revised this essay in ARE proof. See 195.30 below. *E*

194.20 idols and]   Irving inserted the "and" as an afterthought, but neglected to delete the semicolon which no longer made grammatical sense. *E*

194.22 scull]   Irving's spelling is supported by the Walker dictionaries of 1815 and 1826, as well as by Webster, 1806.

195.30 have seen]   This emendation is of a piece with the three that follow it. Irving apparently changed the tense of the passage in proof, in order to make clear that the establishment still existed at the time of writing. *E*

196.6–11 For the amusement . . . Charter House]   "London Antiques" was added to *The Sketch Book* in 1848. This particular emendation is in the brief appendix to the essay, which was originally a preface to "Little Britain," but which Irving transferred, with revisions, to "London Antiques" for the ARE.

LITTLE BRITAIN

199.32 a popular]   The three readings in "Little Britain" introduced in ARE do not in themselves, or in light of Irving's practice for the whole edition, suggest that they are authorial. Rather, they appear to be the kinds of compositorial changes seen so often in ARE. *R*

200.34 into]   Some of the twelve readings introduced in 22E are questionable, and a few are in error; but on the whole they do suggest
the possibility of authorial emendation. They are generally accepted,
though with hesitation, on the grounds that it is better to perpetuate
a nonauthorial change which Irving let stand than to omit a revision
he made himself. *E*

206.5 crones]   The rejected reading originates in the unauthoritative
23E. *R*

208.4 misletoe]   The adopted spelling is the acceptable contemporary
one used elsewhere in 1E. *E*

STRATFORD-ON-AVON

210.27 crones]   The rejected "cronies" originates in the unauthoritative
23E. *R*

211.26 Edmonds]   Since all but one (223.26 Jaques) of the other readings new to this sketch in ARE contain errors or infelicities justifying
their rejection, the introduction of the sexton's name here is the only
clear indication that Irving looked over this sketch for ARE. *E*

213.15–16 cotemporaries]   The rejected "contemporaries" originates in
the unauthoritative 4E. *R*

222.7 my]   The rejected "my own" originates in 23E. *R*

222.12 bedrooped]   Irving apparently wrote "bedrooped," but it was
printed as "bedroofed" (Irving's *p* sometimes looks like an *f*). The
change to "forlorn" in 22E might be a compositorial substitution for
"bedroofed" or an authorial emendation of an obvious error; but on
the strong supposition that Irving originally intended "bedrooped,"
supported by the reading "bedrooped" in the Montucci edition (1G),
it is adopted here as a legitimate editorial correction of copy-text. *E*

222.15 open]   The rejected "opened" originates in the unauthoritative
21E. *R*

TRAITS OF INDIAN CHARACTER

225.14 growth]   The four new readings in ARE are no doubt unauthoritative. This one is apparently due to an inadvertent repetition of the
same word on the previous line. The change from plural to singular
at 232.36 is not as appropriate as the original, and the two others
(225.23, 226.25) are the sorts of compositorial changes one expects
to find in a resetting. They are all rejected. *R*

227.13 thus do]   Though Irving may have read proof of this sketch
for 22E, this loss of a word in a quotation is not at all likely to be
Irving's deletion—he had no source with which to compare his text. *R*

227.17 resemble]   The rejected "resembled" originates in the unauthoritative 23E. *R*

230.31 arisen] The rejected "risen" originates in the unauthoritative 21E. *R*

231.18 infliction] The rejected "affliction" originates in 23E. *R*

232.24 their pieces] The rejected "the pieces" originates in 23E. *R*

232.40 upon] The rejected "on" originates in 21E. *R*

233.26 further] The rejected "farther" originates in the unauthoritative 4E. *R*

PHILIP OF POKANOKET

235.13 cotemporary] The rejected "contemporary" originates in the unauthoritative 4E. *R*

236.36 seize at once] Ten substantive differences in this sketch, including this one, originate in the unauthoritative 23E. All but one are rejected. The eight other rejected readings are the ones at 236.37, 239.27, 240.19, 241.2, 243.17, 243.35, 244.29, 246.23. *R*

237.29 many] No authorial emendations were made in "Philip of Pokanoket" after its first appearance in *The Sketch Book*. In the absence of textual evidence of Irving's emending hand, all postcopy-text variants, such as this one, are rejected. *R*

239.17 sunshiny] This correction of "sunshine" originates in 23E. *E*

241.4 shagged] See the note to 156.21. *R*

245.32–33 "there . . . deliverance."] The quotation marks disappeared, one at a time, in 21E and 4E. *R*

JOHN BULL

248.6 *Stanza* With an old study] Irving paid no attention at all to this sketch for ARE. This loss of a stanza break and the introduction of an error (249.21) are the only readings new to "John Bull" in ARE. *R*

250.22–23 all that they] A number of emendations such as this occur in "John Bull." This one and several others do not appear to be authorial, but because Irving did make so many changes in the sketch in the British editions, one must accept virtually all of the new substantive readings. *E*

250.31 and cock] The reading of 22E–ARE ("cock") is rejected because Irving would not have made a series such as this without an "and" before the last item. The loss of the copy-text "and" is therefore considered compositorial. *R*

251.27 times] The rejected "time" originates in the unauthoritative 23E. *R*

255.37 to buy] The rejected "by" originates in 23E. *R*

256.18 the] The rejected "this" originates in 23E. *R*

THE PRIDE OF THE VILLAGE

261.22 proposals] The rejected "proposal" originates in the unauthoritative 21E. *R*

261.33 scene] This, the only reading originating in 22E, is certainly not authorial. *R*

262.30 and she] The rejected "that she" originates in the unauthoritative 4E. *R*

263.13 was heard] The emendation originates in 4E. *E*

THE ANGLER

265.39 we had] Because it cannot be shown, with any degree of certainty, that Irving is not responsible for the readings originating in 22E, they are, with some hesitation, accepted as authoritative. *E*

267.18 fresh sweet smelling] The rejected "fresh-smelling" originates in 23E. *R*

268.31 the pheasant] All editions agree in "peasant," but it is highly unlikely that Irving would speak generically of "the peasant" in this construction. Moreover, he is describing a woodsy scene and referring to birds and fish; "peasant" would be an intrusion. It is therefore judged to be a compositorial error, or error in manuscript transcription. *E*

269.25 birth deck] The *O.E.D.* indicates that either "birth" or "berth" was acceptable at the time.

270.34 at other] The rejected "and at other" originates in 23E. *R*

THE LEGEND OF SLEEPY HOLLOW

274.41 pupils'] The correction was made in 5E. *E*

274.42 of a drowsy] In five places in this sketch, 1E changes Irving's characteristic "of" to something apparently less colloquial, more formally correct (see also 276.15, 277.6, 282.10, 289.11). As elsewhere, these changes are rejected. *R*

276.16 diverse] The rejected "divers" originates in the unauthoritative 21E. *R*

277.9 of evening] The rejected "of the evening" originates in the unauthoritative 4E. *R*

278.18 diverse] The rejected "divers" originates in 21E. *R*

282.10–11 (a ... within,)] The parentheses disappeared, one at a time, in 21E and 4E. *R*

283.37 situations] The rejected "situation" originates in the unauthoritative 23E. *R*

286.3 Further] The rejected "Farther" originates in 4E.

288.3 scraped away] The rejected "scraped" originates in 23E. R
288.23 drawling] The rejected "drawing" originates in 23E. R
289.9 scarce] The rejected "scarcely" originates in 23E. R
289.11 the] The rejected "their" originates in 21E. R
289.21 mournful] The rejected "mourning" originates in 23E. R
290.25 many very] The rejected "many" originates in 4E. R

L'ENVOY

298.23 can only] The rejected "only can" originates in the unauthoritative 21E. R
298.37 on even as] The rejected "on as" originates in 21E. R

LIST OF EMENDATIONS

In this list of departures from the copy-text, the following symbols are used to designate the sources of the readings:

MS1	Author's manuscript of *Sketch Book* Numbers I–III
MS2	Author's manuscripts of material added for the "Author's Revised Edition"
1A	First American Edition (Van Winkle, 1819–1820)
2A	Second American Edition (Van Winkle, 1819–1820)
1E	First British Edition: Volume I (John Miller/John Murray, 1820); Volume II (John Murray, 1820)
2E	Second British Edition (Murray, 1820)
21E	"New Edition" (Murray, 1821)
4E	"Fourth Edition" (Murray, 1821)
5E	"Fifth Edition" (Murray, 1821)
22E	"New Edition" (Murray, 1822)
23E	"New Edition" (Murray, 1823)
1F	First French Edition (Baudry and Didot, 1823)
ARE	"Author's Revised Edition" (G. P. Putnam, 1848)
T	Twayne Edition

These notes identify all emendations of the copy-text, substantive and accidental. The numbers before each note indicate the page and line in this edition. Only running heads and rules added by the printer to separate running heads from the text or to mark spaces are omitted from the line count.

The matter to the left of the bracket is the reading of the Twayne edition, and is an accepted emendation of the copy-text. The text or texts containing the reading are identified by symbol after the bracket. Where the entry represents merely a correction of error, only the earliest edition containing that correction is listed. Accidental differences among texts containing the same substantive departure from copy-text are not recorded.

The reading after the semicolon is the rejected reading of the copy-text and any other text in which it occurs. Accidental differences among texts agreeing substantively with the copy-text are not recorded. The first symbol following the reading designates the copy-text. If other alternatives occur they are recorded following a second semicolon.

When, as is usually the case, texts are listed inclusively ("1A–22E," for example), only the key texts, i.e., MS1 (or MS2), 1A, 2A, 1E, 22E, 1F, and ARE, in chronological order, are so included. Thus, MS1–ARE = MS1, 1A, 2A, 1E, 22E, 1F, ARE.

The swung (wavy) dash ∼ represents the same word or words that appear before the bracket, and is used in recording punctuation variants; the caret ∧ indicates that a mark of punctuation is omitted. T signifies that a decision to emend or not to emend has been made on the authority of the editor of the Twayne edition. Some of these editorial decisions as well as other emendations which might need elucidation are explained in the Discussions of Adopted Readings; discussion in that section is indicated by an asterisk preceding the page number.

PREFACE TO THE REVISED EDITION

4.15–16	favourable] T; favorable ARE
5.7	Castle street] T; Castle-street ARE
7.19	favourable] T; favorable ARE

THE AUTHOR'S ACCOUNT OF HIMSELF

8.1	*AUTHOR'S*] 1A; *AUTHORS* MS1
8.8	LYLY's] 1A; LYLIES MS1
8.17	seen] 1E–ARE; been seen MS1–2A
8.20	journeyed] 1A; journied MS1
8.20	summer's] 1A; summers MS1
8.34	its] 1E–ARE; for its MS1, 1A; for 2A
8.37	thundering] 1A; thundring MS1
9.3	the] ARE; all the MS1–1F
9.22	thought I, must therefore] 1E–ARE; therefore, thought I, must MS1–2A
9.27	thought] 1E–ARE; therefore, thought MS1–2A
9.40	at finding] 1E–ARE; to find MS1–2A
10.4	Peter's] 1A; Peters MS1

THE VOYAGE

11.18	as in] 1E–ARE; in MS1–2A
11.25	separation] 1A; seperation MS1
11.27	last] ARE; last of them MS1–1F
11.32	rendering] ARE; that makes MS1–1F
12.10	summer's] 1A; summers MS1

12.21	watery] 1A; watry MS1
12.23	of those] 1E–ARE; those MS1–2A
12.26	speculation.] 1A; ~∧ MS1
12.28	invention; which has in a manner] ARE; invention, that has thus MS1–2A
13.9	may] ARE; shall MS1–1F
13.10	may] ARE; shall MS1–1F
*13.15	which] ARE; that MS1–1F
13.21	which] ARE; that MS1–1F
*13.28	'a sail ahead'] ARE; "a sail a head" MS1
13.41	cruised] 1A; cruized MS1
14.2	more!–"] T; ~!–∧ MS1
14.8	lightning] 1A; lightening MS1
14.8	which] ARE; that MS1–1F
14.10	were] 1E–ARE; seemed MS1–2A
14.14	appeared] 1E–ARE; seemed MS1–2A
*14.31	*Paragraph* I] ARE; *No paragraph* I MS1–1F
14.34–35	None but those who have experienced it can form an idea of the delicious throng of sensations which rush] 1E–ARE; I question whether Columbus, when he discovered the new world, felt a more delicious throng of sensations than rush MS1, 1A; None but those who have experienced it can imagine the delicious throng of sensations that rushes 2A
14.36	American's] 1A; Americans MS1
14.43	Welsh] 1A; welsh MS1
15.1	interest.] 1A; ~∧ MS1
15.12	him] ARE; to him MS1–1F
15.15	I] 1E–ARE; But I MS1–2A
15.26	was] 1E–ARE; is MS1–2A

ROSCOE

16.4	mind's] 1A; minds MS1
16.9	Athenæum] 1A; Athanæum MS1
16.17	Roman] 1A; roman MS1
16.31	their] 1E–ARE; their own MS1–2A
16.33	find, therefore, the elegant historian of the Medici] 1E–ARE; find the elegant historian of the Medici, therefore MS1–2A
16.39	irresistible] 1A; irrisistible MS1
16.40	assiduities] 2A–ARE; cherishing assiduities MS1, 1A
17.12	achieved] 1A; atchieved MS1

*17.19	They, however,] 1A; ~∧ ~∧ MS1
17.19	in general live but] 2A–ARE; live but in general MS1, 1A
17.23	to revel] 1E–ARE; revel MS1–2A
17.26	nor] 1E–ARE; or MS1–2A
17.29	opened] 1E–ARE; established MS1–2A
17.35	man's] 1A; mans MS1
17.35–36	which, unfortunately, are not exercised by many, or this world would be] 22E–ARE; but which few men exercise, or this world would be MS1, 1A; and which, if generally exercised, would convert this world into 2A; but which not many exercise, or this world would be 1E
17.41	nor] 1E–ARE; or MS1–2A
18.1–2	done for a place in hours of leisure, by one master spirit,] 2A–ARE; done, in hours of leisure, by one master spirit, for a place MS1, 1A
18.1	leisure] 1A; liesure MS1
18.5	interwoven] 2A–ARE; woven MS1, 1A
18.6	has made] 1E–ARE; made MS1–2A
18.11	effected] 2A–ARE; brought into effect MS1, 1A
18.12	recommended] 1A; reccommended MS1
18.17	have all been] 1E–ARE; all MS1–2A
18.23	we know Mr. Roscoe only] 2A–ARE; we only know Mr. Roscoe MS1, 1A
18.28	reverses] 22E–ARE; mutations MS1–1E
19.4	delightful.] 1A; ~∧ MS1
19.9	horizon.] 1A; ~∧ MS1
19.10	Roscoe's] 1A; Roscoes MS1
*19.18	with] 1A–ARE; and MS1
19.21	Italian] 1A; italian MS1
19.23	vessel] 1E–ARE; wreck MS1, 1A; ship 2A
19.25	we might imagine] 1A–ARE; there must have been MS1
19.26	the armoury] 1A–ARE; over the armoury MS1
19.28	We might picture to ourselves] 1E–ARE; To notice MS1, 1A; We might figure to ourselves 2A
19.33	Roscoe's] 1A; Roscoes MS1
19.34	which cannot fail to interest] 1E–ARE; that will be appreciated by MS1, 1A; that cannot fail to interest 2A
19.38	season] 2A–1F; time MS1, 1A; seasons ARE
19.43	which] 2A–ARE; that MS1, 1A
20.2	themselves] 22E–ARE; to themselves MS1–1E
20.7	misfortunes,] 1A; ~∧ MS1
20.8	most expressive] 1E–ARE; expressive MS1–2A

20.12	which] 1E–ARE; that MS1–2A
20.13	Roscoe's] 1A; Roscoes MS1
20.15	surpassed,] 1A; ~∧ MS1
20.16	that] 1E–ARE; the MS1–2A
20.17	character] 1E–ARE; his character MS1–2A
20.22	existence] 1A; existance MS1
20.23	Pompey's] 1A; pompeys MS1
20.29	writer's] 1A; writers MS1
20.34	affliction's] 1A; afflictions MS1

THE WIFE

22.20	about] 1E–ARE; around MS1–2A
22.24	dependent] 1A; dependant MS1
22.31	children. If] 1E–ARE; ~–if MS1–2A
22.34	a married man] 2A–ARE; married men MS1, 1A
22.34	is more] 2A–ARE; are more MS1, 1A
22.34	his] 2A–ARE; their MS1, 1A
22.35	a single one] 1E–ARE; single men MS1, 1A; a single man 2A
22.35	he is] 2A–ARE; they are MS1–1A
22.37	him] 2A–ARE; them MS1, 1A
22.37	his] 2A–ARE; their MS1, 1A
22.38	his] 2A–ARE; their MS1, 1A
22.40–23.1	love at home, of which he is the monarch] 1E–ARE; love, of which they are the monarchs MS1; love, of which they are monarchs 1A; love, of which he is the monarch 2A
23.7	true,] 1A; ~∧ MS1
23.10	life,"] 1A; ~∧" MS1
23.13	combination. He] T; ~∧ ~ MS1
23.24	misfortune] 22E–ARE; mishap MS1–1E
23.25	property] 22E–ARE; fortune MS1–1E
*24.1	day,] 1A; ~∧ MS1
24.4	God's] 1A; gods MS1
24.15	reserve: it feels] 1E; reserve, but feels MS1, 1A; reserve, but will feel 2A; reserve; it feels 22E–ARE
24.40	her,"] 1A; ~∧" MS1
24.42	God] 1A; god MS1
24.42	God] 1A; god MS1
25.6	woman's] 1A; womans MS1
25.27	round] 1E–ARE; around MS–2A
25.31	suffers no loss] 1E–ARE; experiences no want MS1–2A

25.32	nor] 1E–ARE; or MS1–2A
25.35	"But," said I,] 1A; "~ₐ" ~ ~ₐ MS1
26.8	wife's] 1A; wifes MS1
26.22	he, darting] 1A; ~ₐ "~ MS1
26.29	girl!] 1A; ~!, MS1
26.29	I. "You] 1A; ~, ₐ~ MS1
26.37	destitute of] 1A; ~ of of MS1
26.38	elegant,—almost of every thing convenient] 1E–ARE; elegant, and almost convenient MS1–2A
*27.1	by] MS1–22E; with 1F, ARE
27.10	singing, in a style of the most touching simplicity, a little air] 2A–ARE; in a style of the most touching simplicity singing a little air MS1, 1A
27.12	Leslie's] 1A; Leslies MS1
27.19	George," cried she,] 1A; ~ₐ" ~ ~ₐ MS1
27.22	strawberries] 1A; strawberrys MS1
27.24	she, putting] 1A; ~ₐ "~ MS1
27.26	happy] 2A–ARE; snug MS1, 1A
*27.27	bosom—he] 1A–ARE; ~—He MS1
27.28	round] 1E–ARE; around MS1–2A
27.31	has, indeed, been] 1E–ARE; has been MS1–2A
27.32	more exquisite] 22E–ARE; such unutterable MS1–1E

RIP VAN WINKLE

28.5	lie] 1E–ARE; lay MS1–2A
28.14	Dutch] 1A; dutch MS1
28.24	He, however,] 1A; ~ₐ ~ₐ MS1
28.28	anger,] 1E–ARE; ~,* MS1–2A
28.30	by many] 22E–ARE; among ~ MS1–1E
28.31	particularly by] 22E–ARE; particularly MS1–1E
28.32	biscuit] 1A; buiscuit MS1
28.34	Waterloo] 1A; waterloo MS1
28.35	Anne's] 1A; Annes MS1
*28	*Footnote omitted*] 1E–ARE; *Vide the Excellent discourse of G. V. Esq. before the N York Hist. Society MS1–2A
29.10	mountains] 1A; Mountains MS1
29.10–11	Appalachian] 1A; appalachian MS1
29.22	descried] 1A; descryed MS1
29.26	Dutch] 1A; dutch MS1
29.30–31	built of small yellow bricks brought from Holland, having latticed windows and gable fronts, surmounted

	with weathercocks.] 1E–ARE; with lattice windows, gable fronts surmounted with weathercocks, and built of small yellow bricks brought from Holland. MS1–2A
29.38	inherited, however,] 1A; ∼∧ ∼∧ MS1
30.4	discipline] 1A; dicipline MS1
30.22	Rip's] 1A; Rips MS1
30.23	from] 1E–ARE; for MS1–2A
30.23	of] 1A–ARE; either of MS1
30.25	Tartar's] 1A; tartars MS1
30.29	pigeons] 1A; pidgeons MS1
30.29	never] 1E–ARE; never even MS1–2A
30.29	even in] 1E–ARE; in MS1–2A
30.31	Indian] 1A; indian MS1
30.34	body's] 1A; bodys MS1
30.35	he found it] 1E–ARE; it was MS1–2A
30.37	was of] 1E–ARE; was MS1–2A
31.7	mother's] 1A; mothers MS1
31.8	father's] 1A; fathers MS1
31.8	off] 1A; of MS1
31.10	Winkle,] 1A; ∼∧ MS1
31.25	Rip's] 1A; Rips MS1
31.28	going so often] 1E–ARE; so often going MS1–2A
31.31	woman's] 1A; womans MS1
31.35	he would] 1E–ARE; would MS1–2A
31.38	edged] 1E–ARE; edge MS1–2A
31.38	with] 1E–ARE; by MS1–2A
31.41	which] 1E–ARE; that MS1–2A
31.42	inn] 1A; Inn MS1
31.42	rubicund] 1A; rubicond MS1
31.43	Third] 1A; third MS1
31.43	through] ARE; of MS1–1F
31.43–32.1	summer's] 1A; summers MS1
32.1	talking] 2A–ARE; talk MS1, 1A
32.1	telling] 2A–ARE; tell MS1, 1A
32.2	statesman's] 1A; statesmans MS1
32.9	place.] 1A; ∼∧ MS1
32.16	adherents,] 1A; ∼∧ MS1
32.16–17	adherents),] ARE; ∼)∧ MS1
32.19	to send] 1E–ARE; send MS1–2A
*32.26	and call] 2A–ARE; call MS1, 1A
*32.26	naught;] 1E; ∼, MS1
32.35	Wolf,] 1A; ∼∧ MS1
32.36	dog's] 1A; dogs MS1

32.36	whilst] 1E–ARE; while MS1–2A
32.38	master's] 1A; masters MS1
*33.2	herbage,] 1A; ~∧ MS1
33.6	with the] 1E–ARE; the MS1–2A
33.8	highlands.] 1A; ~∧ MS1
33.21	air:] T; ~∧ MS1
33.22	–at] 1A; ∧~ MS1
33.23	master's] 1A; masters MS1
33.24	a vague] 1A; a a vague MS1
33.32	stranger's] 1A; strangers MS1
33.34	Dutch] 1A; dutch MS1
33.35	breeches] 1A; Breeches MS1
*33.43	or rather] 1A–ARE; rather MS1
34.4	amphitheatre] 1A; ampitheatre MS1
34.12	amphitheatre] 1A; ampitheatre MS1
34.16	most of them] 1E–ARE; most MS1–2A
34.20	cock's] 1A; cocks MS1
34.25	Flemish] 1A; flemish MS1
34.26	parson] 1A–ARE; parson's MS1
34.27	Holland] 1A; holland MS1
34.38	keg] 1A; Keg MS1
34.38	flagons] 1A; flaggons MS1
34.39	trembling;] 1A; ~∧ MS1
34.41	Rip's] 1A; Rips MS1
35.2	flagon] 1A; flaggon MS1
35.9–10	"Surely," thought Rip, "I . . . night."] 1A; ∧~∧∧ ~ ~ ∧ ∧~ . . . ~·∧ MS1
35.11	a] 1E–ARE; the MS1–2A
35.11	keg] 1A; Keg MS1
35.12	flagon] 1A; flaggon MS1
35.12–13	flagon . . . flagon] 1A; flaggon . . . flaggon MS1
35.21	him and shouted] 1E–ARE; him, shouted MS1–2A
35.24	evening's] 1A; evenings MS1
35.27	me,] 1A; ~∧ MS1
35.29	Dame] 1A; dame MS1
35.30	gully] 1A; gulley MS1
35.33	He, however,] 1A; ~∧ ~∧ MS1
35.35	hazel] 1A; hazle MS1
35.39	amphitheatre] 1A; ampitheatre MS1
36.4	man's] 1A; mans MS1
36.6	for want of] 2A–ARE; for MS1, 1A
36.11	whom] 2A–ARE; that MS1, 1A
36.15	their eyes] ARE; eyes MS1–1F

.

36.20–21	an old acquaintance] 1E–ARE; his old acquaintances MS1–2A
36.21	was altered] 1E–ARE; seemed ~ MS1–2A
36.25–27	now misgave him; he began to doubt whether both he and the world around him were not bewitched.] 1E–ARE; began to misgive him, that both he and the world around him were bewitched. MS1, 1A; began to misgive him; he doubted whether both he and the world around him were not bewitched. 2A
36.30	flagon] 1A; flaggon MS1
36.30–31	night," thought he, "has] 1A; ~∧∧ ~ ~∧ ∧~ MS1
36.32	that he] 1E–ARE; he MS1–2A
36.38	My] 1A; my MS1
36.38	dog,] 1A; ~∧ MS1
36.40	truth, Dame] 1A; ~∧ dame MS1
36.41	apparently] 1A; apparantly MS1
37.3	village] 1E–ARE; little village MS1–2A
37.8	Dutch] 1A; dutch MS1
37.12	sign,] 1A; ~∧ MS1
37.15	held] 1E–ARE; stuck MS1–2A
37.19	recollected] 1A; reccollected MS1
37.26	elections] 1E–ARE; election MS1–2A
37.27	Congress] T; congress MS1
37.27	Bunker's] 1A; bunkers MS1
37.28	which] ARE; that MS1–1F
37.31	an] ARE; the MS1–1F
37.31	at] ARE; that had gathered at MS1–1F
37.32	tavern] 1A; Tavern MS1
37.34–35	on which] 2A–ARE; which MS1, 1A
37.36	rising] 1E–ARE; raising MS1–2A
37.42	cane,] 1A; ~∧ MS1
38.2	gentlemen,] 1A; ~∧ MS1
38.4	God] 1A; god MS1
38.5	A tory] 1A; ~ Tory MS1
38.10	him] 1E–ARE; them MS1–2A
38.14	Where's] 1A; Wheres MS1
38.20	Where's] 1A; Wheres MS1
38.20	Dutcher?"] 1A; ~?∧ MS1
38.22	storming] 1E–ARE; battle MS1–2A
38.22	Stoney Point] 1A; stoney point MS1
38.23	Nose] 1A; nose MS1
38.23	don't] 1A; dont MS1
38.25	Where's] 1A; Wheres MS1

38.28	Rip's] 1A; Rips MS1
38.31	Congress] T; congress MS1
38.31	Stoney Point] 1A; stoney point MS1
38.33	despair,] 1A; ~∧ MS1
38.35	that's] 1A; thats MS1
38.37	apparently] 1A; apparantly MS1
38.40	hat] 1A; ~, MS1
38.42	knows,] 1A; ~∧ MS1
38.42	wit's] 1A; wits MS1
38.43	that's me] 1A; thats me MS1
38.43	that's somebody] 1A; thats somebody MS1
39.2	thing's] 1A; things MS1
39.3	can't] 1A; cant MS1
39.3	what's] 1A; whats MS1
*39.9	likely looking] 1E; likely MS1–2A; comely 22E–ARE
39.11	Rip," cried she,] 1A; ~∧" ~ ~∧ MS1
39.12	won't] 1A; wont MS1
39.14	recollections] 1A; reccollections MS1
39.14	woman?"] 1A; ~?∧ MS1
39.17	*Paragraph* "And] 1A; *No paragraph* "And MS1
39.17	father's] 1A; fathers MS1
39.18	Rip Van Winkle was his name, but] ARE; his name was Rip Van Winkle, its MS1; his name was Rip Van Winkle; but 1E–1F
39.18	it's] 1A; its MS1
39.23	faltering] 1A; faultering MS1
39.25	Where's] 1A; Wheres MS1
39.26	Oh] 1A; oh MS1
39.28	intelligence.] 1A; ~∧ MS1
39.35	Sure] 1A; sure MS1
39.38	Rip's] 1A; Rips MS1
40.3	determined, however,] 1A; ~∧ ~∧ MS1
40.8	recollected] 1A; reccollected MS1
40.12	country] 1A; Country MS1
40.16	Dutch] 1A; dutch MS1
40.18	distant] 1E–ARE; long MS1–2A
40.21	Rip's] 1A; Rips MS1
40.23	recollected] 1A; reccollected MS1
40.24	Rip's] 1A; Rips MS1
40.31	*No paragraph* Having] MS1; *Paragraph* Having 1A–ARE
40.32	be idle] ARE; do nothing MS1–1F
*40.34	village] T; ~. MS1
40.35	war.] 1A; ~∧ MS1

40.40	Third] 1A; third MS1
40.42	him; but] 2A–ARE; ~. But 1A; ~∧ But MS1
41.2	tyranny] 1A; tyrrany MS1
41.3	mentioned,] 1A; ~∧ MS1
41.7	Doolittle's] 1A; Doolittles MS1
41.14	Dutch] 1A; dutch MS1
41.14	inhabitants, however,] 1A; ~∧ ~∧ MS1
41.20	Winkle's] 1A; Winkles MS1
41.20	flagon] 1A; flaggon MS1
41.23	German] 1A; german MS1
41.23–24	the emperor Frederick *der Rothbart*] 1E–ARE; Charles V. MS1, 1A; the Emperor Frederick 2A
41.24	Mountain;] 1A; ~∧ MS1
41.24	note,] 1A; ~∧ MS1
41.29	Dutch] 1A; dutch MS1
41.31	Hudson] 1A; hudson MS1
41.38	doubt. D. K."] 1A; ~." ~. ~∧" MS1
41.39–42.40	POSTSCRIPT ... Kaaters-kill.] ARE; *omitted* MS1–1F
42.9	Catskills] ARE; Catskill's MS2
42.33	surface.] ARE; ~∧ MS2
42.35	precincts] ARE; prescincts MS2
42.37	seized] ARE; siezed MS2

ENGLISH WRITERS ON AMERICA

43.7	observe] 1E–ARE; have noticed MS1–2A
43.9	United States] 1A; united states MS1
43.13	no people] 1E–ARE; none MS1–2A
43.13	whom] 1E–ARE; which MS1–2A
43.14	British] 1A; british MS1
43.14	public] 1E–ARE; people MS1–2A
43.14	entertain more numerous] 1E–ARE; more MS1–2A
43.19	when either] 1E–ARE; when MS1–2A
43.19	interest] 1E–ARE; interests MS1–2A
43.20	country comes] 1E–ARE; nation come MS1–2A
43.20	that] 1E–ARE; those MS1–2A
43.22	splenetic remark] 22E–ARE; spleen MS1–1E
43.24–25	Englishman's] 1A; englishmans MS1
43.25	Nile] 1A; nile MS1
43.26	India] 1E–ARE; Africa MS1–2A
43.32	It has also been] 1E–ARE; But it has been MS1–2A
43.34	sent] 22E–ARE; envoys MS1–1E
43.35	deserts] 1A; desarts MS1
43.37–44.1	it has been left ... in which] 1E–ARE; it is left ...

America—to treat of a country . . . where MS1, 1A; her oracles concerning America are the broken down tradesman, the scheming adventurer, the wandering mechanic, the Manchester and Birmingham agent: from such sources she draws her information respecting a country in a singular state of moral and physical development; where 2A

43.38   Manchester] 1A; manchester MS1
43.39   Birmingham] 1A; birmingham MS1
44.1   development] 1A; developement MS1
44.4   to] 1E–ARE; for MS1–2A
44.11   which] 1E–ARE; that MS1–2A
44.16   personal gratifications] 1E–ARE; gratifications MS1–2A
44.19   earn] 1E–ARE; make MS1–2A
44.21   comforts, however,] 1A; ~∧ ~∧ MS1
44.22   which] 1E–ARE; and they MS1–2A
44.25   They may, perhaps,] 1E–ARE; Or perhaps they MS1–2A
44.28   sagacity; and where] 1E–ARE; sagacity. Where MS1–2A
44.31   Such persons] 1E–ARE; They MS1–2A
44.33   must win] 1E–ARE; that he must win MS1–2A
44.34   contend] 2A–ARE; compete MS1, 1A
44.36   Perhaps] 1E–ARE; Or perhaps MS1–2A
44.36   mistaken] 22E–ARE; mistake MS1–1E
44.36   or from the] 22E–ARE; or the MS1–1E
44.39   and having been accustomed] 1E– ARE; and, accustomed MS1–2A
44.40   below the surface of good society] 1E–ARE; many strata below the surface of society MS1, 1A; below the surface of society 2A
45.4   desirable] 1A; desireable MS1
45.10   vigilance] 1A; vigilence MS1
45.11   English] 1A; english MS1
45.11   examine] 2A–ARE; test MS1, 1A
45.13   pyramid,] 1A; ~; MS1
45.15   inaccuracy] 2A–ARE; discrepancy MS1, 1A
45.19   Nay, they will even] 1E–ARE; Nay, what is worse, they will MS1–2A
45.27   woven] 2A–ARE; wove MS1, 1A
45.31–33 All the writers . . . combination] 1E–ARE; All the writers of England united MS1, 1A; The combined misrepresentations of all the writers of England, if we could conceive of such great spirits united in so despicable an attempt 2A

45.34	They could not] 2A–ARE; ∼ cannot MS1, 1A
45.35	also to] 1E–ARE; to MS1–2A
45.37	which give] 1E–ARE; that give MS1–2A
46.1	nation's] 1A; nations MS1
46.1	nation's] 1A; nations MS1
46.2–3	national disgrace] 1E–ARE; disgrace MS1–2A
46.5	whether England does] 1E–ARE; whether England do MS1, 1A; how we are estimated in England, or whether she does 2A
46.8	strength.] 1A; ∼∧ MS1
46.10–11	provoked rivalship, and irritated hostility] 2A–ARE; provoked that rivalship and irritated that hostility MS1, 1A
46.12	much] 1E–ARE; completely MS1–2A
46.13	control.] 1A; controul∧ MS1
46.16	longest] 1E–ARE; most sorely and permanently MS1, 1A; most sorely 2A
46.17	render it morbidly sensitive] 1E–ARE; make it morbidly sensitive MS1, 1A; produce a morbid sensibility 2A
46.18	collision] 1A; collission MS1
46.18	but seldom that any one overt act] 1E–ARE; not so much any one overt act that MS1–2A
46.22	mischievous] 1A; mischevious MS1
46.22	mercenary writers] 1E–ARE; writers MS1–2A
46.27	control] 1A; controul MS1
46.29	England] 1A; england MS1
46.31	English] 1A; english MS1
46.38	she, however,] 1A; ∼∧ ∼∧ MS1
47.5	England] 1A; england MS1
47.6–7	errors which] 1E–ARE; errors that MS1–2A
47.7	propagated] 1A; propogated MS1
47.9	English] 1A; english MS1
47.9	generally] ARE; collectively MS1–1F
47.11	union,] 1A; ∼∧ MS1
47.11–12	an absurd degree of bigotry] 1E–ARE; a degree of bigotry that was absurd MS1–2A
47.17	repository of] 1A; repository of of MS1
47.21	to possess] 1E–ARE; of possessing MS1–2A
47.21	which] 2A–ARE; whom MS1, 1A
47.24	our country] 1E–ARE; the country MS1–2A
47.28	Perhaps] 1A; perhaps MS1
47.29	dispel] 1A; dispell MS1
47.29	vassallage;] 1A; ∼.– MS1

47.29–30   vassallage; which might have interfered] 22E–ARE; vas-
            sallage—interfered MS1–1E
47.35   repel] 1E–ARE; not permit MS1–2A
47.37–38   Short sighted and unjudicious, however, as the conduct
            of England may be] 1E–ARE; But however short
            sighted and unjudicious may be the conduct of Eng-
            land MS1–2A
47.40   nor] 22E–ARE; or MS1–1E
48.1   evil] 1E–ARE; injury MS1–2A
48.1   the wrong] 1E–ARE; it MS1–2A
48.2   an unprofitable] 22E–ARE; unprofitable MS1–1E
48.7   beware of] 1E–ARE; not follow MS1–2A
48.9   have we] 1E–ARE; can we have MS1–2A
48.13   retaliation, and] 1E–ARE; retaliation. But MS1–2A
48.14   England; they fall] 1E–ARE; England, and fall MS1–2A
48.17   blossoms. What] 1E–ARE; blossoms; but what MS1–2A
48.17   through] 2A–ARE; over MS1, 1A
48.18   excite] 1E–ARE; produce MS1–2A
48.23   country's] 1A; countrys MS1
48.24   The members of a republic] 1E–ARE; Republicans MS1–
            2A
48.24–25   candid and dispassionate] 1E–ARE; characterized by
            candour and clearness of thinking MS1, 1A; character-
            ized by candour and purity of thinking 2A
48.25–26   sovereign . . . sovereign] 1A; sovreign . . . sovreign MS1
48.27   and unbiassed] 1E–ARE; unbiassed MS1–2A
48.28–29   we must . . . than with] 1E–ARE; also, we must have
            more frequent questions of a difficult and delicate
            character arising between us than with MS1, 1A; also,
            questions of a difficult and delicate character must
            occur more frequently than between us and 2A
48.31–32   and as . . . be determined] 1E–ARE; and as these must
            ultimately be determined MS1, 1A; and as in their
            discussion our government must be influenced 2A
48.34–35   strangers from every portion of the earth] 1E–ARE; all
            nations of the earth MS1, 1A; the persecuted or un-
            fortunate of every country 2A
48.35   receive] 1E–ARE; receive them MS1–2A
48.40   What] 1E–ARE; Indeed, what MS1–2A
48.40   prejudices?] 1A; ~. MS1
48.41   contracted] 1E–ARE; that have crept into their habits
            of thinking MS1–2A
48.43   We, on the contrary,] 1E–ARE; But we MS1–2A

49.4	forego] 1E–ARE; discredit MS1, 1A; are unworthy of 2A
49.9–11	necessarily an imitative one, and must take our examples and models, in a great degree, from the existing] 1E–ARE; and an imitative one, and will form ourselves upon the older MS1, 1A; and an imitative one, and take our models and exemplars from the older 2A
49.11	more] 1E–ARE; as MS1–2A
49.12	than] 1E–ARE; as MS1–2A
49.14–15	those subjects which] 1E–ARE; all subjects that MS1–2A
49.15	charities] 1A; charaties MS1
49.16	congenial] 1E–ARE; most congenial MS1–2A
49.16–17	all intrinsically excellent;] 1E–ARE; most worthy in themselves: MS1, 1A; most intrinsically excellent: 2A
49.20–21	solid in the basis...unshaken amidst] 1E–ARE; solid in its basis, and admirable in its materials, to uphold it so long unshaken by MS1, 1A; solid in the basis, admirable in the materials, and stable in the construction of an ediface, that so long has stood and even towered unshaken amidst 2A
49.23	Let it be the pride] 1E–ARE; It should be the endeavour MS1–2A
49.23	writers,] 1A; ~∧ MS1
49.24	retaliate] 1E–ARE; be affected by MS1–2A
49.24	British] 1A; british MS1
49.25	English nation without prejudice] 1E–ARE; nation dispassionately MS1–2A
49.27	our] 1E–ARE; their MS1–2A
49.28	let them frankly] 1E–ARE; they should MS1–2A
49.30–31	are recorded sound deductions from ages of experience] 1E–ARE; the sound deductions of ages of experience are recorded MS1–2A
49.33	and to embellish] 1E–ARE; and embellish MS1–2A
49.34	character.] 1A; ~∧ MS1

RURAL LIFE IN ENGLAND

50.7	metropolis] 1A; Metropolis MS1
50.8	country] 1A; Country MS1
50.20	indulged] 1E–ARE; passed MS1, 1A; enjoyed 2A
50.20	carnival] 1A; carnaval MS1
50.21	orders] 1E–ARE; strata MS1–2A
50.21	are therefore] 1E–ARE; ,therefore, are MS1–2A
50.25	quick] 1E–ARE; keen MS1–2A
50.25	keen relish] 1E–ARE; relish MS1–2A

50.27   in] 1E–ARE; with MS1–2A

50.33   enterprise] 1E–ARE; operation MS1–2A

50.36–39   In the most dark and dingy quarters of the city, the
                 drawing room window resembles frequently a bank
                 of flowers; every spot capable of vegetation, has its
                 grass plot and flower bed; and every square its mimic
                 park] 1E–ARE; In the dark and dingy lanes of the
                 metropolis every drawing room window is like a bank
                 of flowers; wherever also there is a spot capable of
                 vegetation, the grass plot and flower bed are culti-
                 vated, and every square has its mimic park MS1–2A

51.8   he is] 1E–ARE; is MS1–2A

51.9   in] 22E–ARE; to MS1–1E

51.9–10   An immense metropolis] 2A–ARE; A vast place MS1, 1A

*51.12–13   character–its] 1A; ~, ~ MS1

51.14   It] 1E–ARE; But it MS1–2A

51.17   manages to collect] 1E–ARE; contrives to assemble MS1,
                 1A; contrives to draw 2A

51.21   horses] 1A; Horses MS1

51.25   English] 1A; english MS1

51.26   called] 1E–ARE; termed MS1–2A

51.38   natural] 22E–ARE; the most natural MS1–1E

51.40   and the] 1E–ARE; the MS1–2A

51.41   sylvan statue] 1E–ARE; statue of nymph MS1–2A

51.43   scenery; but] 1E–ARE; scenery which indeed is too well
                 known to need description. But MS1–2A

52.1   English] 1A; english MS1

52.5   seizes] 1A; siezes MS1

52.9   nice] 1E–ARE; delicate MS1–2A

52.12   delicate] 1E–ARE; nice MS1–2A

52.22   to throw] 22E–ARE; throw MS1–1E

52.23   semblance] 1E–ARE; gleam MS1, 1A; look 2A

52.26   English] 1A; english MS1

52.27   fondness for] 1E–ARE; proneness to MS1–2A

52.29   English] 1A; english MS1

52.30   most] 1E–ARE; some MS1–2A

52.34–35   produce also] 1E–ARE; also, produce MS1–2A

52.36–37   even the follies and dissipations of the town cannot easily
                 pervert, and can never entirely destroy] 1E–ARE; not
                 even the follies and dissipations of the town can easily
                 pervert MS1, 1A; not even the follies and dissipations
                 of the town can easily pervert or ever entirely de-
                 stroy 2A

52.40	marked] 2A–ARE; strong MS1, 1A
°52.43	gentry, small landed proprietors,] 1A; Gentry–~ ~ ~; MS1
52.43	and substantial] 1E–ARE; substantial MS1–2A
53.2	infused into] 1E–ARE; implanted in MS1–2A
53.2	rank] 2A–ARE; link MS1, 1A
53.6	These,] 1A; ~∧ MS1
53.14	when he casually mingles with] 1E–ARE; in MS1, 1A; when casually mingling with 2A
53.15	wave the distinctions] 1E–ARE; doff the attributes MS1, 1A; doff the badges and wave the privileges 2A
53.16	to enter] 1E–ARE; enter MS1–2A
53.20	they are in] 2A–ARE; in MS1, 1A
53.24	may also] 1E–ARE; also, may MS1–2A
53.25	British] 1A; british MS1
53.26	descriptions] 1A; discriptions MS1
53.27	British] 1A; british MS1
53.32	British] 1A; british MS1
53.33	caprices] 2A–ARE; characteristics MS1, 1A
53.41	rather level] 22E–ARE; level MS1–1E
53.43	palaces] 1A; pallaces MS1
54.6	English] 1A; english MS1
54.8	sober well established] 1E–ARE; calm and settled MS1, 1A; sound and settled 2A
°54.23–24	scene.–All] 1E; ~, all MS1
54.38	English] 1A; english MS1
55.2	roof'd] 1A; roofd MS1

THE BROKEN HEART

56.5	spring's] 1A; springs MS1
56.7-10	practice . . . poets] 1E–ARE; thing to laugh at all love stories, and to treat the tales of romantic passion as mere fictions of poets and novelists, that never existed in real life. 1A
56.11	induced me to think otherwise. They have convinced] 1E–ARE; convinced me of the contrary, and have satisfied MS1–2A
56.13–16	or cultivated . . . effects.] 1E–ARE; and the pleasures of society; still there is a warm current of affection running through the depths of the coldest heart, that prevents its being utterly congealed. MS1–2A
56.19	not, however,] 1A; ~∧ ~∧ MS1

56.25	world's] 1A; worlds MS1
56.26	woman's] 1A; womans MS1
56.34	may] 22E–ARE; can MS1–1E
56.35	or may] 22E–ARE; or MS1–1E
56.38	"fly to the uttermost parts of the earth, and be at rest."] 22E–ARE; ₐ~ ... ~.ₐ MS1–1E
*57.2	love,] 1A; ~; MS1
57.9	is it] 22E–ARE; it is MS1–1E
57.15	which gladden] 1E–ARE; that gladden MS1–2A
57.19	slightest] 1E–ARE; least MS1–2A
57.19	injury] 1E–ARE; assailment MS1–2A
57.22	so speedily] 1E–ARE; now MS1–2A
57.23	casual] 1E–ARE; slight MS1–2A
57.24	of the] 22E–ARE; the MS1–2A
57.24	which] ARE; that MS1–1F
57.28	heart] 1E–ARE; core MS1–2A
57.29	luxuriant] 1A; luxurient MS1
57.32	recollect] 1A; reccollect MS1
57.40	manner in which] 1E–ARE; manner MS1–2A
57.41	recollect] 1A; reccollect MS1
57.42	Irish] 1A; irish MS1
57.42	it] 2A–ARE; for it MS1, 1A
58.4	intrepid] 1A; intreped MS1
58.9–10	it would be impossible to describe] 1E–ARE; it would be in vain to describe MS1, 1A; no tongue nor pen could describe 2A
58.12	woman's] 1A; womans MS1
58.17	image!] 1A; ~. MS1
58.23	soothe] 1A; sooth MS1
58.25	which] ARE; that MS1–1F
58.29	father's] 1A; fathers MS1
58.37–38	which scathe] ARE; that ~ MS1–1F
58.38	which penetrate] ARE; that ~ MS1–1F
58.40	but] ARE; but she MS1–1F
58.41	solitude; walking] ARE; solitude. She walked MS1–1F
59.18	enthusiasm.] 1A; ~ₐ MS1
59.19	paid] 1A; payed MS1
59.22	He, however,] 1A; ~ₐ ~ₐ MS1
59.27	another's] 1A; anothers MS1
59.34	distinguished Irish] 1E–ARE; irish MS1; Irish 1A, 2A
59.41	he] 1E–ARE; she MS1–2A
60.9	o'er] 1A; oer MS1

THE ART OF BOOK MAKING

61.3	men's] 1A; mens MS1
61.6	comes] 1E–ARE; came MS1–2A
61.7	barrenness] 1A; barreness MS1
61.7	should teem] 22E–ARE; yet teemed MS1–2A; yet teem 1E
61.8	man travels on, however, in the journey of life] 1E–ARE; man, however, jogs on in life MS1, 1A; man, however, advances in life 2A
61.10	Thus have I chanced] 1E–ARE; Thus it has been my hap MS1–2A
61.11	peregrinations] 1A; perigrinations MS1
61.11	metropolis] 1A; Metropolis MS1
61.13	an end to my astonishment] 1E–ARE; my astonishment on this head at an end MS1–2A
61.14	summer's] 1A; summers MS1
61.18	nearly] 2A–ARE; about MS1, 1A
61.19	allegorical] 1A; alegorical MS1
61.19	ceilings] 1A; cielings MS1
61.19	Whilst] 1E–ARE; While MS1–2A
61.26	strait] 1A; straight MS1
61.26	beyond] ARE; that lay beyond MS1–1F
61.27	that] ARE; all that MS1–1F
61.31	black] 22E–ARE; quaint black MS1–1E
61.31–32	About the room were placed long tables, with stands for reading and writing] 1E–ARE; Long tables with stands for reading and writing were placed about MS1–2A
61.33	studious] 22E–ARE; cadaverous MS1–1E
61.35	A] ARE; The most MS1–1F
62.7	The scene reminded me of an old Arabian tale,] 1E–ARE; The scene called to mind an Eastern tale I had read, MS1–2A
62.8	shut] ARE; who was shut MS1–1F
62.9	which] ARE; that MS1–1F
62.9	opened only] 1E–ARE; only opened MS1–2A
62.10	bring him books] ARE; obedient to his commands, to bring him books MS1, 1A; obey his commands, bring him implements of study, and books 2A; obey his commands, and bring him books 1E–1F
62.13	to control] 1E–ARE; controul MS1; control 1A, 2A
62.18	and in] ARE; and were in MS1–1F
62.21	read: one of] ARE; read. To MS1–1F

62.22	to which] ARE; therefore, do many MS1–1F
62.23	English] 1A; english MS1
62.35	determine.] 1A; ∼∧ MS1
62.36	dapper little] 1E–ARE; old MS1–2A
62.40	which] 1E–ARE; that MS1–2A
63.3	witches'] 1A; witches MS1
63.4	worm's] 1A; worms MS1
63.5	baboon's] 1A; baboons MS1
63.14	nature's] 1A; natures MS1
63.19	metempsychosis] 1A; metemphychosis MS1
63.32	posterity] 1E–ARE; their posterity MS1–2A
63.37	Whilst] 1E–ARE; While MS1–2A
63.41	grievously] 1A; greviously MS1
63.43	mind's] 1A; minds MS1
64.5	the] 22E–ARE; that MS1–1E
64.6	Monmouth Street] 1A; Monmouth street MS1
64.6	seized] 1A; siezed MS1
64.9	noticed, however,] 1A; ∼∧ ∼∧ MS1
64.13	portly] 1E–ARE; dapper MS1–2A
64.13	whom] 1E–ARE; who MS1–2A
64.20	Queen] 1A; queen MS1
64.22	Devices,] 1A; ∼∧ MS1
64.23	Sidney's] 1A; Sidneys MS1
64.28	scraps of parchment] 1E–ARE; leaves MS1–2A
64.28	Latin] 1A; latin MS1
64.31	seemed] 1E–ARE; only seemed MS1–2A
64.32	merely to] 1E–ARE; to MS1–2A
64.35–36	in drab breeches and gaiters, and an arcadian hat] 1E–ARE; of an arrant cockney demeanor MS1–2A
64.38	Regent's] 1A; Regents MS1
65.3	Greek] 1A; greek MS1
65.3	majestically] 1E–ARE; stately MS1–2A
65.17	dapper little] 1E–ARE; gossipping MS1–2A
65.24	Greek] 1A; greek MS1
65.27	some strip of raiment was peeled away] 1E–ARE; some strip of raiment was peeled off of him MS1, 1A; they peeled off some strip of raiment 2A
65.37	the] 1E–ARE; my MS1–2A

A ROYAL POET

In the list for this sketch, 2A is considered pre–copy–text and so is not included among the symbols in the historical record of departures from copy-text.

67.36	large] 22E–ARE; huge 1E
68.4	which had] ARE; which I was told had 1E–1F
*69.6	others grow morbid] 22E–ARE; others, morbid 1E
69.21	dungeon.] 22E–ARE; prison house 1E
69.21–26	Such was … prison house.] 22E–ARE; *omitted* 1E
70.15	which] ARE; that 1E–1F
70.17	fire]' ARE; the fire 1E–1F
71.7	nor] ARE; or 1E–1F
71.26	refulgence] ARE; effulgence 1E–1F
*71.26	exhilarating] 22E–ARE; exhiliarating 1E
72.30	beings] ARE; of beings 1E–1F
73.10	eye] ARE; eyes 1E–1F
73.25	splendent] 5E; splendant 1E
74.8	charm] 2E; cuarm 1E
74.10	unattainable] 2E; unattainble 1E
*74.14	vent to a] 22E–ARE; vent a 1E
74.28	is written] 22E–ARE; are written 1E
74.39	*Estate*] 1F; *State* 1E
75.7–8	let us not, however, reject every romantic incident] ARE; do not, however, let us always consider whatever is romantic 1E–1F
75.9	those] ARE; such 1E–1F
75.10	poem] ARE; poem as were 1E–1F
75.11	written] ARE; which was 1E–1F
75.32	current] ARE; which are current 1E–1F
*75.34	lives] 2A; lived 1E–ARE
75.35	James] ARE; James in fact 1E–1F
76.33	together with Sir Robert Graham] 22E–ARE; Sir Robert Graham 1E
*76.34	broke] 22E–ARE; brake 1E

THE COUNTRY CHURCH

79.6	Beggar's] 1A; Beggars MS1
79.11	English] 1A; english MS1
79.29	near] 1E–ARE; close by MS1–2A
79.37	at another person's threshold,] 1E–ARE; at the threshold of another, MS1–2A
80.10	an engaging] 1E–ARE; engaging MS1–2A
80.11	brothers] 1A; Brothers MS1
80.32	laced,] 1A; ~∧ MS1
80.34	Danish] 1A; danish MS1
81.8	suddenness] 1A; suddeness MS1

81.12	first emerged] 1E–ARE; would first emerge MS1– 2A
81.21	mayor's] 1A; mayors MS1
81.23	had] 2A–ARE; there was MS1, 1A
81.23	supercilious] 1A; superscilious MS1
81.30	burly] 1A; burley MS1
81.30	nobleman's] 1A; noblemans MS1
81.37	*No paragraph* They] 2A–ARE; *Paragraph* They MS1, 1A
81.40	phrase] 1A; phraze MS1
81.42	disciplined] 1A; diciplined MS1
82.2	supercilious] 1A; superscilious MS1
82.8	soul;] 1A; ∼∧ MS1
82.8	artificial] 1E–ARE; these artificial MS1–2A
82.15	nobleman's] 1A; noblemans MS1
*82.19	whisper; . . . finery,] 1A; ∼, . . . ∼; MS1
82.22	standing] 2A–ARE; stood MS1, 1A
82.23	uttering] 2A–ARE; uttered MS1, 1A
82.32	swallow publicly] 1E–ARE; publicly swallow MS1–2A

THE WIDOW AND HER SON

83.3	raign'd.] MS1; rain'd∧ MS2; rain'd. ARE
83.4	Marlowe's] ARE; Marlows MS2
83.31	being in the whole congregation who appeared] ARE; being that seemed MS1–1F
84.4	palsied] 1A; palzied MS1
84.5	would not] 2A–ARE; could not MS1, 1A
84.6	I felt persuaded that] 1E–ARE; I felt that MS1–2A
84.6	faltering] 1A; faultering MS1
84.18	from] 1E–ARE; by MS1–2A
84.33	now] 1E–ARE; sometimes MS1–2A
84.35	from] 1E–ARE; out of MS1–2A
84.37	service, however,] 1A; ∼∧ ∼∧ MS1
*84.39	through, therefore,] 1A; ∼∧ ∼∧ MS1
84.40	moved but a few steps] 1E–ARE; scarcely moved ten steps MS1–2A
84.42	that sublime and touching] 2A–ARE; that awfully sublime and tenderly touching MS1, 1A
85.7	mother's] 1A; mothers MS1
85.8	Preparations] 22E–ARE; The service being ended, preparations MS1–1E
85.9	which] 1E–ARE; that MS1–2A
85.17	endeavouring] 1E–ARE; endeavoured MS1–2A
85.18	don't] 1A; dont MS1

85.23	justling] 1E–ARE; jolting MS1–2A
85.40	but a] 22E–ARE; but as a MS1–1E
85.43	indeed] 1E–ARE; the MS1–2A
86.13	one's] 1A; ones MS1
86.15	George's] 1A; Georges MS1
86.16	man's] 1A; mans MS1
86.22	tidings] 1E–ARE; the tidings MS1–2A
86.27	being one] 2A–ARE; one MS1, 1A
86.35	which] 1E–ARE; that MS1–2A
86.37	seaman's] 1A, ARE; seamans MS1; seamen's 2A–1F
86.39	faltering] 1A; faultering MS1
86.42	don't] 1A; dont MS1
87.6	Nature, however,] 1A; $\sim_\wedge \sim_\wedge$ MS1
87.8	on which] 1E–ARE; where MS1–2A
*87.11	returned,] 1A; $\sim_\wedge$ MS1
87.13	He was too weak, however,] 1E–ARE; He, however, was too weak MS1–2A
87.14	thanks,] 1A; $\sim_\wedge$ MS1
87.18	languished] 1E–ARE; suffered MS1–2A
87.22	her] ARE; a MS1–1F
87.27	misfortune] 22E–ARE; adversity MS1–1E
87.28	overtake] 2A–ARE; overtakes MS1, 1A
87.28	from] 22E–ARE; by MS1–1E
87.29–30	him in spite of his disgrace; and] 22E–ARE; him; and MS1–1E
87.32	known what] 22E–ARE; known well what MS1–1E
87.36	and look] 1E–ARE; look MS1–2A
87.37	her bending] 22E–ARE; her venerable form bending MS1–1E
88.1	other's] 1A; others MS1
88.6	on] 1A; one MS1
88.18	by] 1E–ARE; at MS1–2A
88.23	had gone] 1E–ARE; gone MS1–2A

A SUNDAY IN LONDON

89.5	Babel, London] ARE; $\sim_\wedge \sim$ MS2
89.8	extinguished] ARE; extenguished MS2
89.9	streets. The] ARE; $\sim_\wedge \sim$ MS2
89.11	leisurely] ARE; liesurely MS2
89.19	morocco] ARE; morrocco MS2
89.30	shepherd's] ARE; shepherds MS2
89.34	praise. Never] ARE; $\sim_\wedge \sim$ MS2
90.17	mother's] ARE; mothers MS2

THE BOAR'S HEAD TAVERN, EAST CHEAP

91.1	*BOAR'S*] 1A; *BOARS* MS1
91.8	Catholic] 1A; catholic MS1
91.18	smoking] 1A; smoaking MS1
91.18	that in] 1E–ARE; in MS1–2A
91.23	to rescue] 2A–ARE; rescue MS1, 1A
91.27	incense] 1A; insense MS1
91.29	brethren] 1A; bretheren MS1
91.31	time,] 1A; ~∧ MS1
92.1	casually opened] 1E–ARE; happened MS1, 1A; opened 2A
*92.1	Fourth] T; fourth MS1
*92.2	Boar's head] T; Boars-head MS1
*92.3	Tavern] 1A; tavern MS1
92.7	poet's] 1A; poets MS1
92.16	inherit] 1A; ~, MS1
92.23–24	East cheap,"] 1A; ~ ~∧" MS1
92.24	Boar's] 1A; Boars MS1
*92.33	ran] 1A–ARE; run MS1
*92.34	Street] 1A; street MS1
92.38	say, that] 1E–ARE; say, however, that MS1–2A
92.40	Lane] 1A; lane MS1
92.41	Stow,] 1A; ~∧ MS1
93.7	Dame] 1A; dame MS1
93.8	boar's] 1A; Boars MS1
93.12	chandler's] 1A; chandlers MS1
93.27	information, however,] 1A; ~∧ ~∧ MS1
93.28	Boar's] 1A; Boars MS1
93.35	Michael's] 1A; Michaels MS1
93.35	Lane] 1A; lane MS1
93.39–40	but she informed me that] 2A–ARE; but MS1, 1A
93.40	Michael's] 1A; Michaels MS1
94.12	hazard] 1E–ARE; venture MS1–2A
94.15	Milton's] 1A; Miltons MS1
94.17	English] 1A; english MS1
94.23	Lane,] 1A; ~∧ MS1
94.23	standing] 22E–ARE; standing at MS1–1E
*94.26–27	Fishmonger] T; fishmonger MS1
94.31	Michael's] 1A; Michaels MS1
*94.35	Sovereigns] T; Sovreigns MS1
95.1	cemetery] 1A; cemetry MS1
95.2	Boar's] 1A; Boars MS1
95.3	whilom] 1A; whilome MS1

95.10	frightened] 1A; frightned MS1
95.13	Boar's] 1A; Boars MS1
95.16	Death"] 1A; ~∧ MS1
95.23	Cock Lane] 1A; cock lane MS1
95.25	frightened] 1A; frightned MS1
95.38	error] 1A; Error MS1
95.39	"Whereas," saith he,] 1A; "~∧" ~ ~∧ MS1
95.44	&c."] T; ~·∧ MS1
96.3	Preston's] 1A; Prestons MS1
96.14	Michael] 1E; Michaels MS1; Michael's 1A–2A
96.19	Boar's] 1A; Boars MS1
96.21	establishment,] 1A; ~∧ MS1
96.21	tavern] 1A; Tavern MS1
*96.23	Miles] ARE; Mile MS1–1F
96.23	Lane] 1A; lane MS1
*96.24	Mason's] 22E–ARE; Masons MS1; Masons' 1A–1E
96.33	Boar's] 1A; Boars MS1
96.38	inclin'd] 1A; inclind MS1
*97.9	Parlour] T; parlour MS1
97.11	which bespeaks] 1E–ARE; that bespeaks MS1–2A
97.12	English] 1A; english MS1
97.14	boxes] 1A; Boxes MS1
97.25	oblige,] 1A; ~∧ MS1
97.25	and hurrying up] 2A–ARE; hurried up MS1, 1A
97.26–27	she returned] 1E–ARE; and returned MS1, 1A; returned 2A
*97.28	Tobacco] T; tobacco MS1
97.34	Boar's] 1A; Boars MS1
97.34	Tavern] 1A; tavern MS1
97.34–35	was to be seen the] 2A–ARE; the MS1, 1A
97.38	Lest, however,] 1A; ~∧ ~∧ MS1
97.40	chairs.] 1A; ~∧ MS1
97.43	Boar's] 1A; Boars MS1
98.3	Roman] 1A; roman MS1
98.4	Round Table] 1A; round table MS1
98.9	Boar's] 1A; Boars MS1
98.10	Wythers,] 1A; ~∧ MS1
98.13	whom] 1A–ARE; who MS1
98.13	suspected of being] 22E–ARE; suspect to be MS1–1E
98.16	don't] 1A; dont MS1
98.34	extant] 1A; Extant MS1
98.35	Mason's] 22E–ARE; masons MS1; Masons' 1A–1E
98.36	Irish] 1A; irish MS1

98.39–40   Wednesday ... Whitsun ... Windsor] 1A; wednesday ...
              whitsun ... windsor MS1
99.1   Boar's] 1A; Boars MS1
99.1   Jack's] 1A; Jacks MS1
99.16   Lane] 1A; lane MS1
99.17   copper] 1A; Copper MS1
99.23   biographies] 1A; Biographies MS1
99.24   some] 1A; Some MS1
99.25   Michael's] 1A; Michaels MS1
99.25   the history] 1A; The history MS1

THE MUTABILITY OF LITERATURE

*100.6   period] ARE; periods 1A–1F
100.25   in which] 1E–ARE; where 1A, 2A
101.5   echoing] ARE; soberly echoed 1A; echoed soberly 2A;
              that echoed 1E–1F
101.7   a profound] 1E–ARE; the most profound 1A; a most
              profound 2A
101.12   lifeless] 2A–ARE; noiseless 1A
101.37   which] 1E–ARE; that 1A, 2A
102.1   about merit] 2A–ARE; merit 1A
102.11   Dean?] 1E; ~. 1A
102.20   your] ARE; their 1A–1F
102.33   their longevity] 2A–ARE; it 1A
102.34   harems] 2A; harams 1A
*103.15   Peterborough] 22E–ARE; Petersborough 1A–1E
103.23   English."] 2E; ~.ʌ 1A
103.25   have had] 2A–ARE; had 1A
103.25   in rendering] 1E–ARE; to render 1A, 2A
103.33   Even now] 2A; ~, ~ 1A
104.1   'well of ... undefiled,'] 22E; "well of ... undefiled," 1A
104.15   such, he] 2A; ~ʌ ~ 1A
104.15   own work,] 2A–ARE; work. 1A
104.17–18   shall become] 1E–ARE; becomes 1A, 2A
104.30   unparalelled] 1E; unparraleld 1A
104.30   'unparalelled John Lyly.'"] 1F, ARE; "~ ~ ~.ʌ" 1A–
              22E
105.6   that some] 1E–ARE; some 1A, 2A
105.7   curious.] ARE; ~." 1A–1F
105.10   of authors] 1E–ARE; authors 1A, 2A
105.19–20   overstock the world,] 2A–ARE; overwhelm the world
              with productions 1A
105.36   augmented] 1E–ARE; grown 1A, 2A

105.40   the press] 1E–ARE; a press 1A, 2A

105.41   number?] 1E; ∼. 1A

105.42   unforeseen] 1E; unforseen 1A

107.1–2   which, however, I pardoned on account of] 22E–ARE; which I ascribed to 1A–1E

107.9   pages are] 22E–ARE; pages 1A–1E

107.23   do we] 2A–ARE; we 1A

107.41   drop] ARE; drops 1A–1F

108.2   and have] 22E–ARE; and 1A–1E

RURAL FUNERALS

109.12–14   having been observed among the Greeks and Romans, and frequently mentioned by their writers] 1E–ARE; being mentioned in the classic writers 1A, 2A

109.14   were no doubt] 2A–ARE; no doubt were 1A

110.7–12   Thus, thus . . . thy stone*] 1E–ARE; *omitted* 1A, 2A

110.38   *Herrick] 1E–ARE; *omitted* 1A, 2A

111.2–8   and about them . . . but it may still] 1E–ARE; and evergreens and flowers were planted about them. This has now become extremely rare, but it may occasionally 1A, 2A

111.9   retired] 1E–ARE; the little retired 1A, 2A

111.10   at the] 1E–ARE; in the 1A, 2A

111.10   which] 1E–ARE; that 1A, 2A

111.11–14   I have . . . the grave.] 1E–ARE; *omitted* 1A, 2A

111.14–20   He noticed . . . tomb stones.] 1E–ARE; *omitted* 1A, 2A

111.21   formerly a melancholy fancifulness] 1E–ARE; a melancholy fancy 1A, 2A

111.22–27   The rose . . . thorns and crosses."] 1E–ARE; *omitted* 1A, 2A

111.29   had often a particular reference to] 1E–ARE; were emblematical of 1A, 2A

111.30   or were expressive of] 1E–ARE; or 1A, 2A

112.10–17   Evelyn tells us . . . now full of them."] 1E–ARE; *omitted* 1A, 2A

112.18–20   When the . . . melancholy colours] 1E–ARE; Those who had been unhappy in their loves had emblems of a more gloomy character, such as the yew, the cypress, and flowers of melancholy colour 1A, 2A

*112.26   yewe] 22E–ARE; ewe 1A–1E

112.29   a pathetic little air is introduced] 1E–ARE; also, is introduced a pathetic little air 1A, 2A

112.30   this mode] 1E–ARE; the mode 1A, 2A
113.2–3   and the unaffected elegance of thought which pervaded]
                1E–ARE; that pervades 1A, 2A
113.4   observances.] 1E–ARE; observances; though confined to
                the inferior classes of society. 1A, 2A
113.5   employed.] 1E–ARE; used on these occasions. 1A, 2A
113.6   intention] 1E–ARE; object 1A, 2A
113.8–9   with ·the most delicate and beautiful objects] 1E–ARE;
                with what is most delicate and beautiful 1A, 2A
113.12   those refined associations] 1E–ARE; the associations of
                refinement 1A, 2A
113.17–32   Herrick, also ... thine urn] 1E–ARE; *omitted* 1A, 2A
113.36   necessary. I cannot however] 1E–ARE; necessary; and
                yet I cannot 1A, 2A
113.38–114.1   at the same time] 2A–ARE; which 1A
114.17   has disappeared] 1E–ARE; should have disappeared 1A,
                2A
114.17   exists] 1E–ARE; exist 1A, 2A
114.31   effaces] 2A–ARE; efface 1A
114.33   solemnly] 1E–ARE; always more 1A, 2A
114.35   passing] 1E–ARE; death 1A, 2A
114.36   hill] 22E–ARE; every hill 1A–1E
115.3   the grove] 22E–ARE; every grove 1A–1E
115.29   so is it] 2A–ARE; so it is 1A
115.30   true affection] 2A–ARE; truly human affection 1A
115.31   manifests] 2A–ARE; shows 1A
115.31–33   impulse of ... the soul] 2A–ARE; attachment of the
                brute; for the love of the animal must be continually
                refreshed by the presence of its object, but the love
                of the human soul 1A
115.34–39   The mere inclinations ... the survivor.] 2A–ARE; *omitted* 1A
116.4   who] 2A–ARE; that 1A
116.9–10   when he] 2A–ARE; and he 1A
116.11   of consolation that must be] 2A–ARE; consolation that
                was to be 1A
116.19   cloud] 1E–ARE; cloud even 1A, 2A
116.22   remembrance] 2A–ARE; recollection 1A
116.27–28   he should ever have] 2A–ARE; ever he should have 1A
116.30   There] 2A–ARE; Then 1A
116.33   there] 2A–ARE; then 1A
116.38–40   the faint ... existence] ARE; the last fond look of the
                glazing eye, turning upon us even from the threshold

of existence—the faint, faltering accents struggling in
death to give one more assurance of affection 1A–1F

117.10	which] 2A–ARE; that 1A
117.19	henceforth be] 2A–ARE; be 1A
117.21	it was not intended to give] 2A–ARE; there was no intention of giving 1A
117.25	swelled insensibly] 2A–ARE; insensibly swelled 1A
117.26	usages] 2A–ARE; customs 1A
117.28	that this] 1E–ARE; of the prevalence of the 1A, 2A
117.29	flowers prevails] 1E–ARE; flowers 1A, 2A
117.30	observed even] 1E–ARE; observed 1A, 2A
117.31	it is then] 1E–ARE; then it is 1A, 2A
117.31–32	to degenerate] 1E–ARE; degenerate 1A, 2A
118.8	that] 1E–ARE; which 1A, 2A

THE INN KITCHEN

119.16	which] 1E–ARE; that 1A, 2A
119.34	golden] 1E–ARE; gold 1A, 2A
120.1	anecdotes] 2A–ARE; a long history 1A
120.22	readers] ARE; reader 1A–1F

THE SPECTRE BRIDEGROOM

121.11	Main] 4E; Maine 1A
121.23	eagles'] 2A, 22E–ARE; eagle's 1A, 1E
121.36	those] 2A–ARE; these 1A
121.37–38	The appellation . . . fine arm] 1E–ARE; *omitted* 1A, 2A
122.27	in such absolute distrust] 1E–ARE; and distrust 1A, 2A
122.37	that though] 1E–ARE; that 1A, 2A
122.38	thank] 1E–ARE; thanked 1A, 2A
123.15	exceeded even] 1E–ARE; even exceeded 1A, 2A
123.28	time was] 2A–ARE; time 1A
123.31	even been] 2A–ARE; been 1A
123.32	hour when] 2A–ARE; hour 1A
124.41	Herman] 2A; Hermon 1A
125.2	an hereditary] 22E–ARE; a hereditary 1A–1E
125.11	set] 1E; sat 1A
125.24	midst] 22E–ARE; depth 1A–1E
125.39	impressive] 1E–ARE; solemn 1A, 2A
127.24	Baron] 2A; baron 1A
127.33	immediately] 22E–ARE; accidentally 1A–1E
127.39	gravity] 1E–ARE; earnestness 1A, 2A
128.2	that the] 1E–ARE; the 1A, 2A

128.13   but] 1E–ARE; except 1A, 2A
128.13   one; it was always enforced, however,] 1E–ARE; one, but then it was always enforced 1A, 2A
128.23   appear] 2A–ARE; seem 1A
128.24   seemed only] 2A–ARE; only seemed 1A
128.39   which] 1E–ARE; that 1A, 2A
129.9   *Paragraph* The stranger] 22E–ARE; *No paragraph* The stranger 1A–1E
129.22   Baron] 2A; baron 1A
129.22   hollow tone of voice] 2A–ARE; deep voice 1A
129.24   *Paragraph* "Now] 22E–ARE; *No paragraph* "Now 1A–1E
129.37   was lost] 22E–ARE; were lost 1A–1E
130.1   sprites, of] 1E–ARE; sprites 1A, 2A
130.1   of other] 2A–ARE; other 1A
130.5   cavalier] 2A–ARE; cavalier's 1A
130.11   whatever may have been the doubts entertained] 2A–ARE; whatever doubts might have been entertained 1A
130.18   groups] 2A; groupes 1A
130.40   had followed] 2A–ARE; followed 1A
131.22   bird had flown] 2A–ARE; bird flown 1A
131.25   cause] 2A–ARE; causes 1A
131.36–37   many well authenticated histories] 2A–ARE; many histories 1A
131.41   grave] 2A–ARE; tomb 1A
132.8   the Baron's] 2A–ARE; his 1A
132.20   He told how he] 2A–ARE; How that he 1A
133.7   at having] 2A–ARE; to have 1A

WESTMINSTER ABBEY

The order of publication for this sketch was 1E, 1A, 2A, 22E, 1F, ARE.

135.15   1176).] T; ~.) 1E
*136.8   Poets'] T; Poet's 1E
136.32   Poets'] T; Poet's 1E
137.34   Poets'] T; Poet's 1E
138.17   frequent;] 22E–ARE; frequent; the sun had poured his last ray through the lofty windows; 1E–2A
138.41   superbly] 22E–ARE; lofty and superbly 1E–2A
139.16   *Paragraph* When] 22E–ARE; *No paragraph* When 1E–2A
140.37   funeral] 22E–ARE; funereal 1E–2A

NOTES CONCERNING WESTMINSTER ABBEY

142.35   conceived] ARE; and concieved MS2
143.4   religion.] ARE; ~ ∧ MS2

143.21	monastery] ARE; monastary MS2
143.23	Abbey] ARE; abbey MS2
143.41	fisherman's] ARE; fishermans MS2
144.2	fisherman's] ARE; fishermans MS2
144.4	demonstration.] ARE; ∼∧ MS2
144.5	church] ARE; curch MS2
144.8	the reason] ARE; reason MS2
144.16	seizing] ARE; siezing MS2
144.16	revenues.] ARE; ∼∧ MS2
144.28	gossips, however,] ARE; ∼∧ ∼∧ MS2
145.9	time,"] ARE; time∧" MS2
145.17	conceive] ARE; concieve MS2
145.18	Confessor] ARE; confessor MS2
145.27	knees] ARE; Knees MS2
145.32	reposited."] ARE; ∼∧" MS2
145.34	times.] ARE; ∼∧ MS2
145.34	shrine,"] ARE; shrine∧" MS2
145.35	"now] ARE; ∧∼ MS2
145.35	was.] ARE; ∼∧ MS2
145.36	catch] T; catches MS2
145.41	remain."] ARE; ∼.∧ MS2
146.11	*Paragraph* In] ARE; *No paragraph* In MS2
*146.20	Dean] T; dean MS2
146.25	Dean's] ARE; Deans MS2

CHRISTMAS

148.11	Nothing in England exercises] ARE; There is nothing in England that exercises a 1A–1F
148.13	former times] 2A–ARE; antiquity 1A
148.13	They recall the pictures my fancy used to draw] 2A–ARE; They recal the fond picturings of an ideal state of things, which I was wont to indulge 1A
148.16	honest days of yore] 2A–ARE; good old times 1A
149.28	its cloudy] 1E–ARE; cloudy 1A, 2A
150.5	cordial] 1E–ARE; heart-felt 1A, 2A
150.11	hilarity?] 2A–ARE; ∼. 1A
150.13	always been] 1E–ARE; been extremely 1A, 2A
150.14–15	life; and they were, in former days,] 1E–ARE; life, and, in former days, were 1A; life; and were in former days 2A
150.17	antiquaries] 22E–ARE; antiquarians 1A–1E
150.32	the sharp] 1E–ARE; the fine edge, the sharp, 1A, 2A
150.36	become matters] 1E–ARE; matters 1A, 2A

150.40   most attractive] 1E–ARE; greatest 1A, 2A
151.3   has acquired] 2A–ARE; has 1A
151.4   elegant] 1E–ARE; general 1A, 2A
151.10   to the light] 1E–ARE; for the light 1A, 2A
151.14   which holds] 22E–ARE; which seems to hold 1A–1E
151.21   Waits] 1E–ARE; Waits* 1A, 2A
151   *Footnote omitted*] 1E–ARE; *The Waits are bands of music that go about the towns and villages of England, serenading for several nights preceding Christmas, and call, on that day, for a Christmas-box (*i.e.* present) at the houses before which they have played. 1A, 2A
151.28   *Paragraph* How delightfully] 22E–ARE; *No paragraph* How delightfully 1A–1E
151.30   heard sometimes] 22E–ARE; who is sometimes heard 1A–1E
152.4   *Paragraph* The scene] 22E–ARE; *No paragraph* The scene 1A–1E
152.17–18   can sit] 22E–ARE; sit 1A–1E
152.20   but he] 2A–ARE; he 1A

THE STAGE COACH

153.3   poenâ] 2A; poemâ 1A
153.7   deponendi. *omitted*] 1E–ARE; deponendi. / All's well, my brave boys, / Come let's make a noise, / For we shall be beaten no more; / The vacation is come, / We will now return home, / And fling all our books on the floor, /My brave boys. 1A, 2A
153.10–13   am tempted . . . of wisdom,] 2A–ARE; on looking over them, I cannot but smile, as most probably my readers have, at the rhapsody into which I have sometimes run. The article was written on the approach of the festival concerning which it treats, and presents, as indeed most of these sketches do, an accidental current of thought and feeling, set in motion by external circumstances. I am tempted to follow it up by some anecdotes of a Christmas passed in the country, which may serve as practical illustrations of my general remarks: 1A
153.13–14   and to put . . . amusement] 2A–ARE; and, putting on the genuine holyday spirit, which is tolerant of folly, and anxious only for amusement, to attend with all indulgence to the scenes I shall endeavour to represent 1A

153.15	In the course of a December tour in Yorkshire, I rode] 1E–ARE; It was late in the month of December that I was making a tour of Yorkshire, in the course of which I rode 1A, 2A
153.18	by their] 1E–ARE; from their 1A, 2A
154.4–5	on one] 1E–ARE; of one 1A, 2A
154.12	who have] 1E–ARE; for they have 1A, 2A
154.23	has in summer time] 1E–ARE; in summer time has 1A, 2A
154.32–35	He enjoys . . . country lass] 2A–ARE; *omitted* 1A
154.41	Here he is] 1E–ARE; He is 1A, 2A
155.9	Perhaps it might be owing] 1E–ARE; I do not know whether it was owing 1A, 2A
155.10	that] 1E–ARE; but 1A, 2A
155.11–12	carries animation always with] 1E–ARE; always carries animation with 1A, 2A
155.27	to whom] 1E–ARE; to which 1A, 2A
155.29	as the vehicle whirls by] 1E–ARE; to look at the passing sight 1A, 2A
155.38–39	grocer's, butcher's] T; grocers, butchers 1A
156.4	plums] 2A; plumbs 1A
*156.8	pack] 22E–ARE; pair 1A–1E
156.12	roused] 1E–ARE; suddenly roused 1A, 2A
156.27	that they] 1E–ARE; they 1A, 2A
156.28	Off they set] 1E–ARE; Away they set off 1A, 2A
156.32	predominated] 1E–ARE; most predominated 1A, 2A
156.42	reached] 1E–ARE; stopped at 1A, 2A
157.18–25	The scene . . . doth require.*] 1E–ARE; *omitted* 1A, 2A
157.28	a countenance which I thought I knew] 2A–ARE; his countenance. Surely I could not be mistaken 1A
157.28	moved] 1E–ARE; stepped 1A, 2A
157.29	mine.] 2A–ARE; mine. "Mr. Crayon!" exclaimed he, stretching out his hand. 1A
157.39	*Poor Robin's Almanack, 1684.] 1E–ARE; *omitted* 1A, 2A
158.4	preparation] 1E–ARE; preparations 1A, 2A
158.5	loneliness] 1E–ARE; insulated situation 1A, 2A

CHRISTMAS EVE

159.15	arrive] 1E–ARE; get 1A, 2A
159.25–26	a country] 1E–ARE; an English 1A, 2A
159.33	even regrets sometimes] 1E–ARE; sometimes even regrets 1A, 2A
160.6	think] 1E–ARE; thought 1A, 2A

160.13   Close adjoining was] 1E–ARE; Close by the gate was
            1A, 2A
160.28   through] 1E–ARE; slowly through 1A, 2A
160.29   among] 1E–ARE; through 1A, 2A
161.24   as my] 1E–ARE; my 1A, 2A
161.32   The] 21E; This 1A–1E
161.39   that he had got this notion from] 1E–ARE; he got this
            from 1A, 2A
*162.1   Squire] 1E; squire 1A
162.31   around] 1E–ARE; about 1A, 2A
162.38–39   young Bracebridge] 22E–ARE; Bracebridge 1A–1E
163.15   vast volume] 1E–ARE; volume 1A, 2A
163.41–43   If a . . . Christmas fire.] 1E–ARE; omitted 1A, 2A
164.8   around which] 1E–ARE; around 1A, 2A
*164.9   Besides] 22E–ARE; Beside 1A–1E
164.36   Punch and Judy] 1E–ARE; the opera dancers with his
            fingers 1A, 2A
164.41   careful] 1E–ARE; knowing 1A, 2A
165.12   master] 22E–ARE; a master 1A, 2A
*165.20   Master] 1E; master 1A
165.25–30   Now Christmas . . . weather. &c.] 2A–ARE; omitted 1A
166.1   every Christmas] 1E–ARE; Christmas 1A, 2A
166.22   he could] 22E–ARE; could 1A–1E
167.14   might or might not] 22E–ARE; might 1A–1E
167.15   called] 22E–ARE; called, or it might not 1A–1E
168.6   the quiet] 22E–ARE; quiet 1A–1E

                    CHRISTMAS DAY

169.2–11   Dark and dull . . . be. Herrick] 2A–ARE; Lo, now is
            come our joyfuls't feast! / Let every man be jolly, /
            Eache roome with yvie leaves is drest, / And every
            post with holly. / Now all our neighbour's chimneys
            smoke / And Christmas blocks are burning; / Their
            ovens they with bak t meats choke, / And all their spits
            are turning. / Without the door let sorrow lie, / And
            if, for cold, it hap to die, / Wee'le bury't in a Christmas
            pye, / And ever more be merry. / Withers' Juvenilia 1A
169.15   the] 1E–ARE; my 1A, 2A
169.24   and singing] 1E–ARE; , singing 1A, 2A
169.34   and a tract] 1E–ARE; a tract 1A, 2A
170.12–13   Spanish grandee] 1E–ARE; Spaniard 1A, 2A
*170.20   Master] 2A; master 1A

*170.29	Squire] 1E; squire 1A
170.39	read] 1E–ARE; performed 1A, 2A
171.1	or by] 1E–ARE; or 1A, 2A
171.6	worship in the morning] 1E–ARE; worship 1A, 2A
171.7	temper for the] 1E–ARE; temper 1A, 2A
171.10	as among the] 1E–ARE; as the 1A, 2A
171.10	causes] 2E; cause 1A–1E
172.1	that the] 1E–ARE; the 1A, 2A
172.14	somewhat] 2A–ARE; a somewhat 1A
*172.22	Cockayne] 22E–ARE; Cockaine 1A–1E
172.33	that the] 1E–ARE; the 1A, 2A
172.39	a specimen] 2A–ARE; another specimen 1A
172.40	is destitute] 1E–ARE; was destitute 1A, 2A
173.2–5	he has . . . tenor the] 1E–ARE; and for a choir, he has sought out all the 'deep, solempe mouths,' and 1A, 2A
173.10	accident."] 1E–ARE; accident." *Paragraph* Being habitually a little of what is called a church going man, I readily acceded to Bracebridge's proposition. 1A; accident." *Paragraph* I readily acceded to Bracebridge's proposition. 2A
173.32	Roman] 2A; roman 1A
173.40	track] 22E–ARE; tract 1A–1E
174.8	Druids] 1E; druids 1A
174.11–12	So tenacious was he on this point, that the poor sexton] 1E–ARE; The poor sexton therefore 1A, 2A
174.27	which had] 1E–ARE; had 1A, 2A
175.20	erudite] 1E–ARE; learned 1A, 2A
175.28–29	that the good] 1E–ARE; the good 1A, 2A
175.32	Puritans] 2E; puritans 1A
175.34	Parliament.*] 1E–ARE; Parliament. 1A, 2A
175.36	*Paragraph* Shut] 22E–ARE; *No paragraph* Shut 1A–1E
175.36–37	antiquated little] 1E–ARE; little antiquated 1A, 2A
175.38–42; 176.35–39	*From the . . . Christmas day."] 1E–ARE; *omitted* 1A, 2A
176.1	while the era of the Revolution was] 1E–ARE; and as to the era of the revolution, it was 1A, 2A
176.4	"mere popery," . . . antichristian;] 22E–ARE; "∼ ∼, . . . ∼;" 1A–1E
176.9	other] 1E–ARE; more 1A, 2A
176.11	affecting] 1E–ARE; impressive 1A, 2A
176.19	rhymes,*] 1E–ARE; rhymes, 1A, 2A
176.40–42	*"Ule . . . cry ule!"] 1E–ARE; *omitted* 1A, 2A
177.11–12	ceremony and selfishness] 1E–ARE; selfishness 1A, 2A

177.13	reeking] 1E–ARE; that were reeking 1A, 2A
177.17	of having] 1E–ARE; having 1A, 2A
177.27–28	when the tables were] 1E–ARE; the tables 1A, 2A
177.28–29	when the harp] 1E–ARE; the harp 1A, 2A
177.29	when rich] 1E–ARE; rich 1A, 2A
177.30	merry.*] 1E–ARE; merry. 1A, 2A
177.35–41	*"An English . . . *Fire*] 1E–ARE; *omitted* 1A, 2A
177.36	enter] ARE; entered 1E–1F
178.6	broken] 1E–ARE; grown 1A, 2A
178.14	indeed, he had once] 1E–ARE; indeed, Frank Brace-bridge informed me that the old gentleman once 1A, 2A
178.15	before had] 1E–ARE; since 1A, 2A
178.19–20	neighbourhood in one week] 1E–ARE; neighbourhood 1A, 2A
178.22–23	with distributing] 22E–ARE; distributing 1A–1E
178.26	lads without coats, their shirt sleeves] 2A–ARE; lads, in white shirts 1A
179.26	all his companions to wait] 2A–ARE; his companions all waited 1A
179.29	The whole house indeed] 1E–ARE; Indeed, the whole house 1A, 2A
179.29	as] 1E; As 1A

THE CHRISTMAS DINNER

180.1	*THE CHRISTMAS DINNER*] 2A–ARE; *omitted* 1A
180.2–14	Lo, now . . . WITHERS' JUVENILIA.] 2A–ARE; *omitted* 1A
*180.17	Squire] 1E; squire 1A
180.30	mouthed] 2A; ~, 1A
180.31	and his] 1E–ARE; with his 1A, 2A
180.33	which] 1E–ARE; and which 1A, 2A
180.35	authenticity] 1E–ARE; authority 1A, 2A
180.36	having belonged] 1E–ARE; belonging 1A, 2A
181.1	that the painting] 1E–ARE; the painting 1A, 2A
181.8	vied (at least in variety) with] 1E–ARE; vied with 1A, 2A
181.8	Belshazzar's] 1E; Balshazzar's 1A
181.17	twanging his instrument] 1E–ARE; twanging the roast beef of old England, 1A, 2A
181.21–37	I always . . . Henry VIII.] 1E–ARE; *omitted* 1A, 2A
181.38	*Paragraph* The parson] 1E–ARE; *No paragraph* The parson 1A, 2A
182.33–34	talk and other objects, he] 1E–ARE; talk, he 1A, 2A

182.37   turkey.*] 1E–ARE; turkey. 1A, 2A

182.38–42; 183.16–32 *The old ceremony . . . &c. &c. &c.] 1E–ARE;
                  omitted 1A, 2A

183.9–15   I could . . . killed.*] 2A–ARE; *omitted* 1A

183.33–41   *The peacock . . . olden times:–] 1E–ARE; *omitted* 1A;
                  The peacock was anciently in great demand for stately
                  entertainments, and was made into a pie, at one end
                  of which the head appeared above the crust, in all
                  its plumage, the beak richly gilt; at the other end the
                  tail was displayed. It was also served up in gold or
                  silver dishes at the solemn banquets of chivalry, when
                  knights errant pledged themselves to undertake any
                  perilous enterprize, whence the ancient oath, "by cock
                  and pye." The peacock was also an important dish in
                  the Christmas feast, and Massinger, in his City Madam,
                  gives some idea of the extravagance with which these
                  and other dishes were prepared for the gorgeous revels
                  of the olden time. 2A

183.42–45   Men may talk . . . *peacock!*] 2A–ARE; *omitted* 1A

184.16–31; 185.1–18 When the cloth . . . a lusty laugh-a.*] 2A–ARE;
                  omitted 1A

184.32–42   *The Wassail Bowl . . . a swinger.] 1E–ARE; *omitted*
                  1A, 2A

184.36   Twelfth] 4E; Twelvth 1E

184.43–44; 185.37–38 †"The custom . . . ARCHÆOLOGIA.] 1E–ARE; *omit-
                  ted* 1A, 2A

*185.21   Master] 2A; master 1A

185.27   in hunting] 1E–ARE; at hunting 1A, 2A

185.38   ARCHÆOLOGIA] 21E; ARCHÆLOGIA 1E

185.39   *From Poor Robin's Almanack] 1E–ARE; *omitted* 1A, 2A

186.5   disposed] 1E–ARE; seemed disposed 1A, 2A

186.23   left] 2A–ARE; quit 1A

186.33   —indeed] 1E–ARE; and, indeed 1A, 2A

186.37   louder] 1E–ARE; merrier 1A, 2A

187.8   a rather] 1E–ARE; rather a 1A, 2A

188.8   to be] 1E–ARE; to become 1A, 2A

188.31   From these and other] 1E–ARE; Indeed, from other
                  1A, 2A

189.17   train] 1E–ARE; whimsical train 1A, 2A

189.28   bedizened] 1E; bedizzened 1A

189.29   masque.*] 2A–ARE; masque. 1A

189.30–38; 190.1–14 Master Simon led . . . the pageant] 1E–ARE; *omit-
                  ted* 1A; Master Simon led the van as "ancient Christ-

mas," quaintly apparel'd in short cloak and ruff, and a hat that might have served for a village steeple, from under which, his nose curved boldly forth, with a frost bitten bloom that seemed the very trophy of a December blast. He was accompanied by the blue eyed romp, dished up as "Dame mince pie," in the venerable magnificence of faded brocade, long stomacher, peaked hat, and high heeled shoes. The young officer figured in genuine Kendal Green as Robin Hood; the fair Julia in a pretty rustic dress as Maid Marian. The rest of the train had been metamorphosed in various ways; the girls trussed up in the finery of their great grandmothers, and the striplings bewhiskered with burnt cork, and fantastically arrayed to support the characters of Roast Beef, Plum Porridge, and other worthies celebrated in ancient masqueings. The whole was under the control of the Oxonian, in the appropriate character of Misrule, that ancient ring leader of Christmas sports: and I observed that he exercised rather a mischievous sway with his wand, over the smaller personages of the pageant. 2A

189.39–41	*Masquings . . . disguisings.] 2A–ARE; *omitted* 1A
189.42–43	I strongly . . . Christmas.] 1E–ARE; *omitted* 1A; *Vide* a pageant of the kind in Ben Jonson's Masque of Christmas. 2A
190.4	the presence] ARE; presence 1E–1F
190.12	control] 5E; controul 1E
190.15–25	motley crew . . . generations.] 2A–ARE; motley crew, with mock instruments of music, and peals of light hearted laughter, was the consumation of uproar and merriment. 1A
190.36; 191.1–4	I felt . . . observed.] 2A–ARE; *omitted* 1A
191.7	years.*] ARE; years. 1A–1F
191.25–30	*At the time . . . Newstead Abbey.] ARE; *omitted* 1A–1F
191.30	author's] ARE; authors MS2

LONDON ANTIQUES

192.16	buffeting] ARE; buffetting MS2
*192.22	crowd, plunged] ARE; ~∧ ~ MS2
*193.12	"invitingly open."] T; "~ ~∧" MS2; ∧~ ~·∧ ARE
*193.20	robe, a ruff] ARE; ~∧ ~ ~ MS2

*193.38	without] ARE; with out MS2
*194.10	those] ARE; these MS2
194.12	groups] ARE; groupes MS2
*194.20	idols and] ARE; ~; ~ MS2
194.35–36	enter. I] ARE; ~ₐ ~ MS2
194.40	enveloped] ARE; envelloped MS2
194.41	inhabitants.] ARE; ~ₐ MS2
195.25	is what is called] ARE; is called MS2
*195.30	have seen] ARE; had seen MS2
195.30–31	are provided] ARE; were provided MS2
195.32	dine] ARE; dined MS2
195.34	is a] ARE; was a MS2
196.5	love."] ARE; ~ₐ" MS2
196.6–11	For the amusement . . . Charter House.] ARE; The following modicum of local history was lately put into my hands by an odd-looking old gentleman in a small brown wig and snuff-coloured coat, with whom I became acquainted in the course of one of my tours of observation through the centre of that great wilderness the City. 1E, 1A, 2A, 22E, 1F

LITTLE BRITAIN

The order of publication for this sketch was 1E, 1A, 2A, 22E, 1F, ARE.

198.30	Michaelmas] 1A; Michaelmass 1E
*200.34	into] 22E–ARE; unto 1E–2A
201.1	those] 22E–ARE; these 1E–2A
201.15	died] 22E–ARE; died away 1E–2A
201.28–29	Wagstaffs] 21E; Wagstaff's 1E
202.4	belly] 22E–ARE; body 1E–2A
202.7	Needle] 21E; needle 1E
203.24	Lilliputian] 5E; Liliputian 1E
205.27	a bit] 1A; a a bit 1E
205.39	west.] 1A; ~ₐ 1E
205.39	brother's] 22E–ARE; brothers' 1E–2A
206.21	rout] 1A–ARE; route 1E
206.34	"bit] 22E–ARE; "a bit 1E–2A
206.42	sit] 22E–ARE; set 1E–2A
207.3	streets] 22E–ARE; street 1E–2A
207.10	precipitation] 1A; precipition 1E
207.33	No paragraph It is] 22E–ARE; Paragraph It is 1E–2A
*208.4	misletoe] 21E; misseltoe 1E
208.19	counsels] 22E–ARE; councils 1E–2A

| 208.23 | apprehension] 22E–ARE; apprehensions 1E–2A |
| 208.29 | drunk] ARE; drank 1E–1F |

STRATFORD-ON-AVON

The order of publication for this sketch was 1E, 1A, 2A, 22E, 1F, ARE.

209.21	complacent] 22E–ARE; complaisant 1E–2A
210.29–30	of every] 22E–ARE; for every 1E–2A
210.30	be done] 22E–ARE; is done 1E–2A
211.26	rambles] 22E–ARE; ramble 1E–2A
211.26	sexton] 22E–ARE; old sexton 1E–2A
*211.26	Edmonds,] ARE; omitted 1E–1F
213.36	this] 22E–ARE; his 1E–2A
215.41	was] 22E–ARE; were 1E–2A
216.25	On chaliced flowers that lies] 1A–ARE; Each chalic'd flower supplies 1E
218.2–3	a long . . . statue; and] 22E–ARE; long lessening vistas, with nothing to interrupt the view but some distant statue; or 1E–2A
218.19	Jaques] ARE; Jacques 1E
219.26	sign] 22E–ARE; signs 1E–2A
219.29	carcass] 5E, carcase 1E
220.12	mentioned] 1A–ARE; mention 1E
221.13	Charlecot*] ARE; Charlecot 1E–1F
221.23–40	*This effigy . . . Thomas Lucye.] ARE; omitted 1E–1F
222.2	meet with] 22E–ARE; find 1E–2A
*222.12	bedrooped] T; bedroofed 1E–2A; forlorn 22E–ARE
222.12	in the custody] 22E–ARE; in custody 1E–2A
223.19	enchanter] 22E–ARE; necromancer 1E–2A
223.26	Jaques] ARE; Jacques 1E
223.30	Anne] 22E–ARE; Anna 1E–2A

TRAITS OF INDIAN CHARACTER

231.11	rivers] 22E–ARE; river 1E
231.14	buffalo] 5E, buffaloe 1E
233.16	survive] 22E–ARE; survive the lapse of time 1E

PHILIP OF POKANOKET

No changes suggestive of authorial intervention were made in "Philip of Pokanoket" after its first appearance in *The Sketch Book*. In the

absence of textual evidence of Irving's emending hand, all post-copy-text
variants are rejected, except for these three corrections.

*239.17	sunshiny] 1F, ARE; sunshine 1E, 22E
240.2	dependence] 2E; dependance 1E
247.4	dependent] 2E; dependant 1E

JOHN BULL

248.15–16	joke, they have not] 1E–ARE; joke, have not 1A, 2A
248.19	of their] 1E–ARE; their 1A, 2A
248.32	which they] 1E–ARE; they 1A, 2A
249.1	utter] 1E–ARE; say 1A, 2A
249.11	*Paragraph* Thus] 22E–ARE; *No paragraph* Thus 1A–1E
249.12	and will] 1E–ARE; and 1A, 2A
249.14	However little, therefore,] 1E–ARE; However 1A, 2A
249.15	instance,] 1E–ARE; instance therefore, 1A, 2A
249.20	portraits] 22E–ARE; traits 1A–1E
249.26	of romance] 1E–ARE; romance 1A, 2A
249.31	to talk] 1E–ARE; talk 1A, 2A
249.38	takes it] 1E–ARE; is 1A, 2A
249.39	engage in] 1E–ARE; undertake 1A, 2A
249.41	getting into] 1E–ARE; getting in 1A, 2A
*250.22–23	all that they] 1E–ARE; all they 1A, 2A
250.27	a stout ship] 22E–ARE; one of his own ships 1A–1E
251.25	alterations] 1E–ARE; modifications 1A, 2A
251.42	*Paragraph* To do] 1E–ARE; *No paragraph* To do 1A, 2A
252.7	*Paragraph* The family] 1E–ARE; *No paragraph* The family 1A, 2A
252.14	and towers] 1E–ARE; towers 1A, 2A
252.18	and to have] 1E–ARE; to have 1A, 2A
252.26	these] 1E–ARE; they 1A, 2A
252.32	decoration] 1E–ARE; ornament 1A, 2A
252.37	family, to] 1E–ARE; family, like his, to 1A, 2A
253.1	and an] 22E–ARE; and 1A, 2A
253.24	to dwell] 1E–ARE; dwell 1A, 2A
253.37	flutter] 1E–ARE; wheel and caw 1A, 2A
254.13–14	to put] 1E–ARE; put 1A, 2A
254.21	jumps] 1E–ARE; springs 1A, 2A
255.9	own children] 1E–ARE; children 1A, 2A
255.17	these] 1E–ARE; all these 1A, 2A
255.21	which bellied] 1E–ARE; that bellied 1A, 2A
255.24	in folds and wrinkles] 1E–ARE; wrinkles and folds 1A, 2A

255.25   once sturdy legs] 1E–ARE; spindle shanks 1A, 2A
255.26   three cornered] 1E–ARE; *omitted* 1A, 2A
255.27   side] 1E–ARE; side of his head 1A, 2A
255.30   goes] 1E–ARE; crawls 1A, 2A
255.32   breeches'] T; breeches 1A
255.33   *Paragraph* Such] 1E–ARE; *No paragraph* Such 1A, 2A
255.33   honest] 1E–ARE; poor 1A, 2A
255.34   gallant] 1E–ARE; vain-glorious 1A, 2A
255.36   that he] 1E–ARE; he 1A, 2A
255.38   valiant] 1E–ARE; faint 1A, 2A
255.40   may be something rather] 1E–ARE; is something 1A, 2A
256.2   is at least] 1E–ARE; is 1A, 2A
256.3–12   His virtues . . . luxuriance.] 1E–ARE; *omitted* 1A, 2A
256.13   old family mansion] 1E–ARE; mouldering old mansion
            1A, 2A
256.15–20   almost tremble . . . the ruins.] 1E–ARE; grieve to see
            it brought to the ground. 1A, 2A
256.22   people's] 1E; peoples' 1A
256.24   peace and happiness] 1E–ARE; peace 1A, 2A
256.25   gradually get his house into] 1E–ARE; put his house
            in 1A, 2A

THE PRIDE OF THE VILLAGE

257.10   through one] 1E–ARE; in one 1A, 2A
258.9   face] 1E–ARE; countenance 1A, 2A
258.16–17   for who is . . . the tomb;] 1E–ARE; (for who has been
            so fortunate as not to follow some one he has loved
            to the tomb!) 1A, 2A
258.42   it was] 1E–ARE; they were 1A, 2A
259.9   still kept] 1E–ARE; kept 1A, 2A
259.10–26   These, indeed . . . intimacy;] 1E–ARE; On one of these
            occasions, when the villagers had reared the May pole
            on the green, and she, as queen of May, and crowned
            with flowers, was presiding at their sports, she at-
            tracted the notice of a young officer, whose regiment
            had recently been quartered in the neighbourhood. He
            readily found means to make her acquaintance 1A, 2A
259.19   young] 22E–ARE; younger 1E
259.32   of voice] 1E–ARE; of the voice 1A, 2A
259.35   Can we] 1E–ARE; Is it a 1A, 2A
259.36   As to] 1E–ARE; For 1A, 2A
260.8   and the] 1E–ARE; the 1A, 2A
260.8   attire] 2A–ARE; array 1A

260.11	order] 2A–ARE; species 1A
260.15	demeanor] 1E–ARE; appearance 1A, 2A
260.15	manners] 1E–ARE; manner 1A, 2A
260.15	those of the] 1E–ARE; the 1A, 2A
260.41	into her] 1E–ARE; in her 1A, 2A
261.1–2	whose hallowed sphere] 1E–ARE; which 1A, 2A
261.8	occurred] 2A; occured 1A
261.20	was at first] 1E–ARE; at first was 1A, 2A
261.21	parents.] 5E; parents? 1A
261.24	reproach] 1E–ARE; reproaches 1A, 2A
262.10–11	Sometimes she would be seen late of an evening sitting in the porch of the village church] 1E–ARE; She would sometimes be seen sitting in the porch of the village church late of an evening 1A, 2A
262.12	overhear her singing] 1E–ARE; hear her voice singing 1A, 2A
262.14–15	a hectic bloom] 1E–1F; hectic bloom 1A, 2A; a hectic gloom ARE
262.27	which she] 1E–ARE; she 1A, 2A
262.41	theirs] 5E; their's 1A
263.1	which her] 1E–ARE; that her 1A, 2A
263.3	and of the] 1E–ARE; and the 1A, 2A
263.9	hers] 5E; her's 1A
263.10	her soft] 2A; her-soft 1A
*263.13	was heard] 22E–ARE; were heard 1A–1E
263.20	word] 1E–ARE; sound 1A, 2A
263.21	a smile] 1E–ARE; an expression 1A, 2A
263.23–29	They are but . . . striking nature.] 1E–ARE; omitted 1A, 2A
263.36	Paragraph The church] 1E–ARE; No paragraph The church 1A, 2A
263.36	No paragraph There hung] 1E–ARE; Paragraph There hung 1A, 2A

THE ANGLER

The order of publication for this sketch was 1E, 1A, 2A, 22E, 1F, ARE.

265.31	watery] 1A; watry 1E
*265.39	we had] 22E–ARE; we had had 1E–2A
266.1	Izaak] 1A; Izaac 1E
266.22	busy in] 22E–ARE; busied 1E–2A
267.33	real] 22E–ARE; really 1E–2A
268.22	limpid] 22E–ARE; limped 1E–2A

*268.31   the pheasant] T; the peasant 1E, 2A–ARE; a peasant 1A
270.42   had] 22E–ARE; had often 1E–2A
271.1   for the fishes] 22E–ARE; for fishes 1E–2A
271.3   *Paragraph* I have] 22E–ARE; *No paragraph* I have
              1E–2A

THE LEGEND OF SLEEPY HOLLOW

272.9   those] 22E–ARE; the 1A–1E
272.14   generally] 1E–ARE; universally 1A, 2A
272.16   given] 1E–ARE; given it 1A, 2A
272.21   two] ARE; three 1A–1F
272.23   one] 1E–ARE; you 1A, 2A
272.27   walnut] 2A; wallnut 1A
273.2   to pervade] 1E–ARE; pervade 1A, 2A
273.10   are subject to] 1E–ARE; have 1A, 2A
273.10   frequently see] 1E–ARE; see 1A, 2A
273.17   commander in chief] 1E–ARE; commander 1A, 2A
273.21   the country folk] 1E–ARE; various of the country people
              1A, 2A
273.24   church] ARE; church that is 1A–1F
273.29   that the] 1E–ARE; the 1A, 2A
273.37   propensity] 1E–ARE; turn 1A, 2A
273.38–39   unconsciously imbibed] 1E–ARE; imperceptibly ac-
              quired 1A, 2A
273.41   inhale] 1E–ARE; imbibe 1A, 2A
274.3   population] 1E–ARE; populations 1A, 2A
274.4   migration] 1E–ARE; emigration 1A, 2A
274.9   rush] 1E–ARE; rushing 1A, 2A
274.18   as for the] 1E–ARE; as the 1A, 2A
274.25   looked like] 1E–ARE; might have been mistaken for
              1A, 2A
274.38–39   a rather lonely] 1E–ARE; rather a lonely 1A, 2A
274.39   pleasant] 1E–ARE; a pleasant 1A, 2A
*274.41   pupils'] 22E–ARE; pupil's 1A–1E
275.2   in the tone of] 1E–ARE; giving 1A, 2A
275.3   by the] 1E–ARE; the 1A, 2A
275.5   and ever] ARE; that ever 1A–1F
275.14   inflicting] 1E–ARE; giving 1A, 2A
275.14   on] 1E–ARE; to 1A, 2A
275.19–20   "he would . . . live."] 1E–ARE; ∧~ ~ . . . ~.∧ 1A, 2A
275.22–23   the larger boys; and on holyday afternoons would con-
              voy some of the smaller ones home] 1E–ARE; his

	larger boys; and would convoy some of the smaller ones home of a holyday 1A, 2A
275.31	successively] 1E–ARE; alternately 1A, 2A
275.36	as mere] 1E–ARE; mere 1A, 2A
275.38	lighter] 1E–ARE; light 1A, 2A
276.19	all who] 1E–ARE; all those who 1A, 2A
276.20	wonderfully] ARE; wonderful 1A–1F
276.32	their amusement] 1E–ARE; them 1A, 2A
277.7	by his] 1E–ARE; past his 1A, 2A
277.13	whip-poor-will*] 1E–ARE; whip-poor-will 1A, 2A
277.40–41	*The whip-poor-will . . . words.] 1E–ARE; *omitted* 1A, 2A
278.3	dared] 1E–ARE; dare 1A, 2A
278.6	ghastly] 1E–ARE; ghostly 1A, 2A
278.9	like a sheeted] 22E–ARE; like sheeted 1A–1E
279.4	in which] 1E–ARE; into which 1A, 2A
279.7	well] 1E–ARE; kind of well 1A, 2A
279.12	it from morning to night] 1E–ARE; it 1A, 2A
279.21	through] 1E–ARE; about 1A, 2A
279.22	fretting about it like] 1E–ARE; fretting like 1A, 2A
279.28	which he] 1E–ARE; he 1A, 2A
279.32	his belly] ARE; its belly 1A–1F
279.32	his mouth] ARE; its mouth 1A–1F
280.7–8	realized his hopes] 1E–ARE; put him in possession of his hopes 1A, 2A
281.13	burly] 1E; burley 1A
281.23	acquires] ARE; always acquires 1A–1F
281.25	admitting] ARE; that admitted 1A–1F
281.27	but had] ARE; had 1A–1F
281.29	companions] ARE; companions of his own stamp 1A–1F
282.1	occurred] 1E; occured 1A
282.31	her poultry] ARE; the poultry 1A–1F
283.3	captured in] 1E–ARE; captured 1A, 2A
283.6–7	who wins] ARE; that wins 1A–1F
283.15	and have settled] 1E–ARE; and settled 1A, 2A
283.19	a boast] ARE; the boast 1A–1F
283.20	lay] ARE; put 1A–1F
283.20–21	shelf of his own school house] ARE; shelf 1A–1F
283.24	to play] 1E–ARE; play 1A, 2A
284.25	was turned] 1E–ARE; turned 1A, 2A
284.41	a head like a hammer] 1E–ARE; hammer head 1A, 2A
285.3	the name he bore of Gunpowder] ARE; his name, which was Gunpowder 1A–1F

285.7   more of the lurking devil] 22E–ARE; more lurking
             deviltry 1A–1E
285.11   his horse] 22E–ARE; the horse 1A–1E
286.21   the deep] 1E–ARE; a deep 1A, 2A
286.31   breeches] 1E–ARE; small clothes 1A, 2A
286.37   innovation] 22E–ARE; innovations 1A–1E
287.5   for he] 1E–ARE; and 1A, 2A
287.5   unworthy of a] 1E–ARE; unworthy a 1A, 2A
287.17   besides] 1E–ARE; not to mention 1A, 2A
287.17–20   beef; and moreover delectable dishes of preserved
             plums, and peaches, and pears, and quinces; not to
             mention broiled shad and roasted chickens; together
             with] 1E–ARE; beef, together with broiled shad and
             roasted chickens; besides delectable dishes of pre-
             served plums, and peaches, and pears, and quinces;
             with 1A, 2A
287.27   creature] 22E–ARE; toad 1A–1E
287.30   ate] 1E–ARE; eat 1A, 2A
287.35   should dare] 1E–ARE; dared 1A, 2A
287.40   fall] 1E–ARE; reach 1A, 2A
288.18   and smiling] 22E–ARE; she smiled 1A, 2A; and smiled
             1E
288.29   kinds] 1E–ARE; kind 1A, 2A
289.6   are] 1E–ARE; they are 1A, 2A
289.8   in most] 1E–ARE; in the generality 1A, 2A
289.9   finish] 22E–ARE; take 1A–1E
289.13   except] 1E–ARE; excepting 1A, 2A
289.39   there] 1E–ARE; here 1A, 2A
290.7   how he] 1E–ARE; that he 1A, 2A
290.8   how they] 1E–ARE; that they 1A, 2A
290.15   arrant] 1E–ARE; errant 1A, 2A
290.18   should] 1E–ARE; would 1A, 2A
291.2   pedagogue] 1E; pedagouge 1A
291.12   crest fallen] 1E–ARE; bedrooped 1A, 2A
291.27   he had] 1E–ARE; Ichabod had 1A, 2A
291.35   gnarled] 1E–ARE; vast, gnarled 1A, 2A
291.35–37   large enough to form trunks for ordinary trees, twist-
             ing down almost to the earth, and rising again into
             the air.] 1E–ARE; twisting down almost to the earth,
             and rising again into the air, and they would have
             formed trunks for ordinary trees. 1A, 2A
291.38–39   hard by; and was] 1E–ARE; hard by it, and it was
             1A, 2A

291.41	fate] 1E–ARE; memory 1A, 2A
292.1	tales of strange] 1E–ARE; tales, strange 1A, 2A
292.12	lay] 1E–ARE; lay still 1A, 2A
293.3	could 1E–ARE; can 1A, 2A
294.13	(unskilful . . . was!)] 1E–ARE; ,~ . . . ~! 1A, 2A
294.17	asunder.] 2A; ~∧ 1A
294.25	even fancied that] 1E–ARE; fancied 1A, 2A
294.36	with the] 1E–ARE; the 1A, 2A
295.10	two shirts] 1E–ARE; two old shirts 1A, 2A
295.10–11	pair or two of] 1E–ARE; pair of 1A, 2A
295.11–12	stockings; an old . . . pitch pipe] 1E–ARE; stockings with holes in them; an old pair of corduroy small-clothes; a book of psalm tunes full of dog's ears; a pitch pipe out of order; a rusty razor; a small pot of bear's grease for the hair, and a cast-iron comb. 1A, 2A
295.16–17	in several] 1E–ARE; by several 1A, 2A
296.24–25	Manhattoes] ARE; the Manhattoes 1A, 2A; the Manhattoes* 1E–1F

L'ENVOY

298.1	*L'ENVOY.*] ARE; *L'ENVOY.* 1E–1F
298.4	thee will] 2E; theewill 1E
298.32	spirit] ARE; spark 1E–1F
298.38	*Closing the second volume of the London edition.] ARE; *omitted* 1E–1F

LIST OF REJECTED SUBSTANTIVES

In this list, which provides an historical record of substantive variants, in manuscripts and printed texts, which were not adopted for the Twayne text, the following symbols designate the sources of the readings:

MS1   Author's manuscript of *Sketch Book* Numbers I–III

MS2   Author's manuscripts of material added for the "Author's Revised Edition"

1A   First American edition (Van Winkle, 1819–1820)

2A   Second American edition (Van Winkle, 1819–1820)

1E   First British edition: Volume I (John Miller / John Murray, 1820); Volume II (John Murray, 1820)

22E   "New Edition" (Murray, 1822)

1F   First French edition (Baudry and Didot, 1823)

ARE   "Author's Revised Edition" (G. P. Putnam, 1848)

To the left of the bracket is the Twayne reading; to the right the rejected one. An asterisk preceding the page number refers the reader to the Discussion of Adopted Readings.

THE AUTHOR'S ACCOUNT OF HIMSELF

*8.21   from whence] MS1–1F; whence ARE
8.33   a lover] MS1–2A, ARE; influenced by a love 1E–1F
8.34   its] 1E–ARE; for 2A
*9.14   beside] MS1–1E, ARE; besides 22E, 1F
9.17   cast] MS1, 1A, 1E–ARE; have cast 2A
*9.39   when I look over, however,] MS1–1E; when, however, I look over 22E–ARE

THE VOYAGE

*11.38   all that was] MS1–1F; all ARE
*12.12   gently] MS1–1E; gentle 22E–ARE
*12.29   earth] MS1–1E; world 22E–ARE
13.1   *Paragraph* But] MS1; *No paragraph* But 1A–ARE
13.17   that] MS1, 1A, 1E–ARE; which 2A

*13.30   the] MS1–1E; her 22E–ARE
13.30   toward] 1A–1E; towards MS1, 22E–ARE
14.4   lashed up] MS1; lashed 1A–ARE
*14.21   side] MS1–1F; sides ARE
14.35   form an idea of] 1E–ARE; imagine 2A
14.35   which rush] 1E–ARE; that rushes 2A
14.41   that prowled] MS1, 1A, 1E–ARE; prowling 2A
15.20   all] MS1, 1A, 1E–ARE; during 2A

ROSCOE

*16.9   contains] MS1–1E; it contains 22E–ARE
16.35   has been] MS1, 1A, 1E–ARE; is 2A
17.35–36   which, unfortunately, are not exercised by many, or this world would be] 22E–ARE; and which, if generally exercised, would convert this world into 2A; but which not many exercise, or this world would be 1E
*18.10   gardens] MS1–1F; garden ARE
18.21   effected a great benefit to] MS1, 1A, 1E–ARE; conferred a great benefit on 2A
18.32–33   with antiquity] MS1–22E, ARE; in antiquity 1F
*18.33   with posterity] MS1–1E; posterity 22E–ARE
18.33   communions] MS1; communion 1A–ARE
*19.8   blending] MS1–22E; blended 1F–ARE
19.17   finding it] MS1, 2A–ARE; now 1A
19.22   was] MS1, 1A, 1E–ARE; been 2A
19.23   vessel] 1E–ARE; ship 2A
19.26   into] MS1–1F; in ARE
19.28   picture] 1E–ARE; figure 2A
19.30   or] MS1–1E; of 22E–ARE
19.34   which] 1E–ARE; that 2A
19.36   that] MS1, 1A, 1E–ARE; which 2A
19.38   season] 2A–1F; seasons ARE
20.10   mingled up] MS1; mingled 1A–ARE
20.11   and we] MS1–1F; we ARE
20.17   which] MS1, 1A, 1E–ARE; that charm which 2A

THE WIFE

22.11   spirits] MS1; spirit 1A–ARE
*22.17   supporter] MS1–1F; support ARE
22.32   and if] MS1; if 1A–ARE
22.35   one] 1E–ARE; man 2A

22.40–23.1 love at home, of which he is the monarch] 1E–ARE; love, of which they are monarchs 1A; love, of which he is the monarch 2A

*24.2 had heard] MS1–1F; heard ARE

24.15 reserve: it feels] 1E; reserve, but will feel 2A

24.15 when] MS1, 1A, 1E–ARE; if 2A

26.11 leant] MS1; leaned 1A–ARE

26.18 we] MS1–1F; he ARE

26.31 possessed] MS1–1F; possess ARE

26.34 our] MS1; a 1A–ARE

*26.37 around] MS1–1E; round 22E–ARE

*27.1 by] MS1–22E; with 1F–ARE

RIP VAN WINKLE

*28.34 to being] MS1–2A; to the being 1E–ARE

32.3 that] MS1, 1A, 1E–ARE; which 2A

*32.31 the clamor] MS1–1E; clamor 22E–ARE

33.18 around] MS1–1F; round ARE

33.36 shoulder] MS1, 1A, 1E–ARE; shoulders 2A

33.42 that] MS1, 1A, 1E–ARE; which 2A

*35.5 awaking] MS1–2A; waking 1E–ARE

35.5 from whence] MS1–1F; whence ARE

35.12 ah] MS1; Oh 1A–ARE

*35.26 arose] MS1–2A; rose 1E–ARE

*35.36 and tendrils] MS1–22E; or ~ 1F, ARE

36.5 *Paragraph* What] MS1; *No paragraph* What 1A–ARE

36.20 not one] MS1, 1A, 1E–ARE; none 2A

36.25–27 now misgave him; he began to doubt whether both he and the world around him were not bewitched] 1E–ARE; began to misgive him; he doubted whether both he and the world around him were not bewitched 2A

*37.1 rung] MS1–2A; rang 1E–ARE

37.6 printed] MS1; painted 1A–ARE

37.7 that] MS1, 1A, 1E–ARE; which 2A

*37.9 on top] MS1–1E; on the top 22E–ARE

37.16 printed] MS1; painted 1A–ARE

37.33 around] MS1–2A; round 1E–ARE

*38.19 rotted] MS1–1E; rotten 22E–ARE

38.40–41 —what] MS1; and what 1A–ARE

*39.9 likely looking] 1E; comely 22E–ARE

39.18 Rip Van Winkle was his name, but] ARE; his name was Rip Van Winkle; but 1E–1F

40.31	*No paragraph* Having] MS1; *Paragraph* Having 1A–ARE
41.23–24	Frederick *der Rothbart*] 1E–ARE; Frederick 2A
42.22	rugged] MS2; ragged ARE
42.28	in] MS2; on ARE

ENGLISH WRITERS ON AMERICA

43.37–44.1	it has been left . . . in which] 1E–ARE; her oracles concerning America are the broken down tradesman, the scheming adventurer, the wandering mechanic, the Manchester and Birmingham agent: from such sources she draws her information respecting a country in a singular state of moral and physical development; where 2A
*44.5	prejudiced] MS1–1F; prejudicial ARE
44.8	frothings] MS1; frothiness 1A–ARE
44.12	indications] MS1–1F; indication ARE
44.30	that] MS1, 1A, 1E–ARE; which 2A
44.34–35	and the] MS1, 1A, 1E–ARE; and vie with the 2A
44.40	below the surface of good society] 1E–ARE; below the surface of society 2A
45.14	any] MS1, 1A, 1E–ARE; the slightest 2A
45.28	woven round] MS1, 1A, 1E–ARE; wove around 2A
45.31–33	All the writers . . . combination] 1E–ARE; The combined misrepresentations of all the writers of England, if we could conceive of such great spirits united in so despicable an attempt 2A
45.38	which, in fact] MS1, 1A, 22E–ARE; in fact 2A, 1E
46.4	For] MS1, 1A, 1E–ARE; To 2A
46.5	whether England does] 1E–ARE; how we are estimated in England, or whether she does 2A
46.16	longest] 1E–ARE; most sorely 2A
46.17	render it morbidly sensitive] 1E–ARE; produce a morbid sensibility 2A
46.18–19	produces] 1E–ARE; occasions 2A
46.31	from an] MS1–1F; from ARE
46.34	from whence] MS1–1F; whence ARE
47.21	anxious] MS1, 1A, 1E–ARE; desirous 2A
47.21	towards] MS1; toward 1A–ARE
47.39	prompt] MS1; a prompt 1A–ARE
48.24–25	candid and dispassionate] 1E–ARE; characterized by candour and purity of thinking 2A
48.28–29	we must . . . than with] 1E–ARE; also, questions of a

difficult and delicate character must occur more frequently than between us and 2A

48.31–32   and as . . . be determined] 1E–ARE; and as in their
discussion our government must be influenced 2A

48.34–35   strangers from every portion of the earth] 1E–ARE; the
persecuted or unfortunate of every country 2A

49.4   forego] 1E–ARE; are unworthy of 2A

49.9–11   necessarily an imitative one, and must take our examples and models, in a great degree, from the
existing] 1E–ARE; and an imitative one, and take our
models and exemplars from the older 2A

49.16–17   all intrinsically excellent;] 1E–ARE; most intrinsically
excellent: 2A

49.20–21   solid in the basis . . . unshaken amidst] 1E–ARE; solid
in the basis, admirable in the materials, and stable
in the construction of an ediface that so long has stood
and even towered unshaken amidst 2A

49.26   undiscriminating] MS1; indiscriminating 1A–ARE

*49.32   from thence] MS1–1F; thence ARE

49.33   wherewith to strengthen] MS1, 1A, 1E–ARE; to strength-
en 2A

RURAL LIFE IN ENGLAND

*50.4   pleasure] MS1–1E; pleasures 22E–ARE

*50.4   pass'd] MS1–22E; past 1F, ARE

50.11–13   and cope with the people in all their conditions, and
all their habits and humours] MS1, 1A, 1E–ARE;
mingle with the people of all ranks and conditions,
and become familiar with the habits and humours incident to each 2A

*50.18   circles] MS1; classes 1A–ARE

50.20   indulged] 1E–ARE; enjoyed 2A

51.17   manages to collect] 1E–ARE; contrives to draw 2A

51.18   conveniencies] MS1, 22E; conveniences 1A–1E, 1F, ARE

51.43   but a] MS1, 1E–ARE; but 1A; a 2A

52.21   providently] MS1, 2A–ARE; providentially 1A

52.23   semblance] 1E–ARE; look 2A

52.35   a manliness] MS1; and a manliness 1A–ARE

52.36–37   even the follies and dissipations of the town cannot
easily pervert, and can never entirely destroy] 1E–
ARE; not even the follies and dissipations of the town
can easily pervert or ever entirely destroy 2A

53.1   banded] MS1, 1A, 1E–ARE; bound 2A

53.14	when he casually mingles with] 1E–ARE; when casually mingling with 2A
53.15	wave the distinctions] 1E–ARE; doff the badges and wave the privileges 2A
54.8	sober well established] 1E–ARE; sound and settled 2A
54.36	that] MS1, 1A, 1E–ARE; which 2A

THE BROKEN HEART

56.7	It is a common practice] 1E–ARE; It is common to 2A
56.13–16	*Completely revised*] 1E–ARE; which prevents 2A. *See List of Emendations.*
*56.39	and a] MS1–1F; and ARE
*57.36	deaths] MS1–2A; death 1E–ARE
58.5	his] MS1; and his 1A–ARE
58.9–10	it would be impossible to describe] 1E–ARE; no tongue nor pen could describe 2A
58.20	from whence] MS1–1F; whence ARE
*58.26	parching] MS1–22E; parting 1F, ARE
58.35–36	occupations and amusements] MS1; occupation and amusement 1A–ARE
*59.40	song] MS1–1E; songs 22E–ARE

THE ART OF BOOK MAKING

*61.3	labors] MS1–1E; labour 22E–ARE
61.6	seemed] MS1–2A, ARE; seems 1E–1F
61.7	should teem] 22E–ARE; yet teem 1E
61.8	man travels on, however, in the journey of life] 1E–ARE; man, however, advances in life 2A
62.10	bring him books] ARE; obey his commands, bring him implements of study, and books 2A; obey his commands, and bring him books 1E–1F
63.1–2	line upon . . . little.] MS1; "~ ~ . . . ~." 1A–ARE
*63.16	writers] MS1–1E; authors 22E–ARE
*63.17	authors] MS1–1E; writers 22E–ARE
*63.32	passes] MS1–2A, 22E–ARE; pass 1E
*63.33	continues] MS1–1E; continue 22E–ARE
64.6	they] MS1, 1A, 1E–ARE; any one of them 2A
64.8	they] MS1, 1A, 1E–ARE; he 2A
64.8–9	themselves] MS1, 1A, 1E–ARE; himself 2A
*64.16	exceeding] MS1–2A; exceedingly 1E–ARE
64.30	sparkled] MS1–22E, ARE; sparked 1F
*64.32	catch] MS1–1E; to catch 22E–ARE

*64.35   should] MS1–1E; shall 22E–ARE

*65.7   walls] MS1–1E; wall 22E–ARE

*65.12   their plunder] MS1–1E; the plunder 22E–1F; plunder
      ARE

65.27   some strip of raiment was peeled away] 1E–ARE; they
      peeled off some strip of raiment 2A

A ROYAL POET

In the list for this sketch, 2A is considered pre-copy-text and so is not included among the symbols in the historical record of departures from copy-text.

*67.22   that] 1E–1F; which ARE

68.2   which is a gothic] 1E–1F; a gothic ARE

68.4–5   From hence] 1E–1F; Hence ARE

*68.21   servants] 1E–1F; servant ARE

69.4   powerfully] 1E; powerful 22E–ARE

*69.30   peculiar] 1E–1F; a peculiar ARE

*70.4   meditate] 1E; to meditate 22E–ARE

*72.25   lapses] 1E–1F; relapses ARE

*76.6   its interests] 1E; its own interests 22E–ARE

76.18   mingled] 1E–1F; minged ARE

76.29   secret] 1E; with secret 22E–ARE

77.21   round] 1E–1F; around ARE

*77.26   fellow man] 1E; fellow men 22E–ARE

77.30   highly flavored] 1E, 22E, ARE; highly favored 1F

*78.3   stream] 1E; streams 22E–ARE

THE COUNTRY CHURCH

79.11   give] MS1–1F; gives ARE

*79.12   county] MS1–1E; country 22E–ARE

*79.24–25 doors;—the] MS1–2A; doors; of the 1E–ARE

79.26   and the poor] MS1–2A; and of the poor 1E–ARE

*79.31   county] MS1–1E; country 22E–ARE

80.33   around] MS1, 1A; round 2A–ARE

80.39   caught] MS1, ARE; got 1A–1F

80.43   cracking] MS1–1E; smacking 22E–ARE

*81.1   of the horses] MS1–22E; the of horses 1F; of horses ARE

81.1   glistering] MS1; glistening 1A–ARE

*81.10   footmen] MS1–1E; footman 22E–ARE

81.10–11 alight, open the door, pull] MS1–1F; alight, pull ARE

*81.24   ultra-fashionables] MS1–1F; ultra-fashionable ARE

81.32   courtsies] MS1; courtesies 1A–ARE

82.1	denied] MS1; denied them 1A–ARE
*82.7	by] MS1–1E; with 22E–ARE
82.9	the very] MS1–1E; that the very 22E–ARE

THE WIDOW AND HER SON

83.6	pensive] MS2; passive ARE
84.28	corpse] MS1–2A, 22E–ARE; corpe 1E
85.12	awaken] MS1–2A; waken 1E–ARE
85.38	around] MS1–2A; round 1E–ARE
*86.11	likely] MS1–1E; comely 22E–ARE
86.12	round] MS1, 2A, 1E; around 1A, 22E–ARE
86.27	towards] MS1, 1A; toward 2A–ARE
86.37	seaman's] 1A, ARE; seamen's 2A–1F
86.39	towards] MS1, 1A, ARE; toward 2A–1F
88.1	know] MS1, 1A, 1E–ARE; knew 2A

A SUNDAY IN LONDON

| *89.37 | cleansing] MS2; elevating ARE |

THE BOAR'S HEAD TAVERN, EAST CHEAP

*91.17	hang] MS1, 1A; hangs 2A–ARE
92.1	casually opened] 1E–ARE; opened 2A
*92.10	who] MS1, 1A; that 2A–ARE
*92.11	who] MS1, 1A; that 2A–ARE
92.19	he has] MS1, 1A, 1E–ARE; has 2A
93.10	old] MS1–22E, ARE; old old 1F
*93.11	empire] MS1–22E; abode ARE; *omitted* 1F
93.12	widow] MS1–1F; window ARE
93.35	towards] MS1; toward 1A–ARE
*94.11	twinkle] MS1–22E; twinkling 1F, ARE
*94.23	Michael] MS1; Michael's 1A–ARE
94.29	a Turenne] MS1–22E; Turenne 1F, ARE
*95.2	windows] MS1–1F; window ARE
95.38	*No paragraph* An error] MS1; *Paragraph* An error 1A–ARE
*96.24	Mason's] 22E–ARE; Masons' 1A–1E
96.28	*Paragraph* We] MS1; *No paragraph* We 1A–ARE
97.26–27	she returned] 1E–ARE; returned 2A
97.32	on beholding] MS1; at beholding 1A–ARE
98.20	this] MS1–22E, ARE; his 1F

98.35	Mason's] 22E–ARE; Masons' 1A–1E
*98.40	of Windsor] MS1–1F; at Windsor ARE
99.15	good will] MS1–2A; goodness 1E–ARE
99.22	but touched] MS1; touched 1A–ARE

THE MUTABILITY OF LITERATURE

100.7	muses'] 1A–1F; muse's ARE
100.17	irruption] 1A–1F; interruption ARE
100.18	football] 1A–22E; fool-ball 1F
*101.4	cloister] 1A–1E; cloisters 22E–ARE
101.5	echoing] ARE; echoed soberly 2A; that echoed 1E–1F
101.7	a profound] 1E–ARE; a most profound 2A
103.6	beside] 1A–1E; besides 22E–ARE
103.27	you] 1A, 2A; your 1E–ARE
103.38	afterward] 1A, 2A; afterwards 1E–ARE
*103.39	and] 1A–1E; and of 22E–ARE
104.28	Sackville's] 1A–1F; Sacksville's ARE
*104.38	silver] 1A–1E; simple 22E–ARE
*104.42	spirite] 1A–1E; sprite 22E–ARE
104.43	*Harvey's*] 1A–22E; *Harvey* 1F, ARE
*105.6	the fragments] 1A–1E; fragments 22E–ARE
*105.26	and pursued] 1A–1E; pursued 22E–ARE
*105.39	and four] 1A–22E; or four 1F, ARE
*106.9	scarce] 1A; scarcely 2A–ARE
106.22	arise] 1A, 2A; rise 1E–ARE
*106.38	into a short] 1A–1E; in a 22E–ARE
*107.1	I felt] 1A–1E; that I felt 22E–ARE
107.25	separated] 1A–1F; separate ARE

RURAL FUNERALS

*111.14	*No paragraph* He noticed] 1A–1E; *Paragraph* He noticed 22E–ARE
*111.17	seen in] 22E–ARE; seen 1E
*111.24	says] 1E; said 22E–ARE
*113.4	funereal] 1A–1E; funeral 22E–ARE
114.13	around] 1A, 2A; round 1E–ARE
115.36	disgust] 1E–ARE; and disgust 2A
116.35	scene] 1A, 1E–ARE; scence 2A
117.29	besides] 1A, 1E–ARE; beside 2A
117.33	with recesses] 1A, 2A; and recesses 1E–ARE
*117.36	transcribe] 1A–1E; describe 22E–ARE

THE INN KITCHEN

119.24	around] 1A; round 2A–ARE
120.8	travellers'] 1A, 1E–ARE; traveller's 2A

THE SPECTRE BRIDEGROOM

121.23	eagles'] 1A–1F; eagles ARE
*121.34–35	of a circumstance] 1A–1F; a circumstance ARE
121.38	a fine] 1E–1F; her fine ARE
122.26	distance] 1A–1F; a distance ARE
*124.13	of a] 1A–1E; on a 22E–ARE
124.17	had been] 1A–1F; bad been ARE
124.21	forests] 1A–1F; forest ARE
124.36	towards] 1A; toward 2A–ARE
*125.36	this] 1A–1E; his 22E–ARE
*126.1	engagement] 1A–22E; engagements 1F, ARE
126.42	he, however, pacified himself] 1A–1E; he pacified himself, however, 22E–ARE
127.7	his eloquence] 1A–1F; eloquence ARE
127.35	scarce] 1A, 2A; scarcely 1E–ARE
128.38–39	dreadful, but true] 1A–1F; dreadful ARE
*132.2	to scour] 1A–1E; scour 22E–ARE

WESTMINSTER ABBEY

The order of publication for this sketch was 1E, 1A, 2A, 22E, 1F, ARE.

134.3	there] 1E, 2A, 22E–ARE; they 1A
134.22	it seemed] 1E–2A; seemed 22E–ARE
*134.26	massy] 1E–2A; massive 22E–ARE
*135.3	dusty] 1E–1F; dusky ARE
*135.27	*Paragraph* I] 1E–22E; *No paragraph* I 1F, ARE
135.29–30	eye gazes] 1E–1F; eyes gaze ARE
*135.42	*No paragraph* And yet] 1E–22E; *Paragraph* And yet 1F, ARE
136.1	justled] 1E–1F; jostled ARE
*136.14	remain] 1E–1F; remained ARE
137.16	fictions] 1E–1F; fiction ARE
*138.21	leads] 1E–22E; lead 1F, ARE
139.26	other] 1E–1F; others ARE
140.15	and piling] 1E, 1A, 22E–ARE; piling 2A
*140.28	around] 1E–22E; round 1F, ARE
141.17	funeral] 1E–22E; funereal 1F, ARE

°141.30   Poets'] 1E–2A; Poet's 22E–ARE
°141.35   falling] 1E–22E; fallen 1F, ARE
142.14   a tomb] 1E, 1A, 22E–ARE; the tomb 2A
°142.24   those] 1E–2A; these 22E–ARE
142.38   T. Brown] 1E, 1A, 22E–ARE; Thomas Brown 2A

NOTES CONCERNING WESTMINSTER ABBEY

°143.35   onto] MS2; into ARE
°144.37   rest] MS2; dust ARE
145.17   *No paragraph* It is] MS2; *Paragraph* It is ARE

CHRISTMAS

149.31   wrapped] 1A, 1E–ARE; wrapped up 2A
°149.35   pleasures] 1A–1F; pleasure ARE
149.40   living kindness] 1A–1F; loving-kindness ARE
150.4   into a] 1A–1F; in a ARE
150.12   habits] 1A–1F; habit ARE
150.14–15   life; and they were, in former days,] 1E–ARE; life; and
               were in former days 2A
150.27   passenger] 1A–1F; passengers ARE
151.10   were] 1A, 2A; are 1E–ARE

THE STAGE COACH

°153.24   in this] 1A–1E; of this 22E–ARE
°153.27   plans of pleasure of the] 1A–1F; plans of the ARE
154.2–3   whole world] 1A–1F; world ARE
154.34   he seems] 1E–ARE; seems 2A
154.38   drive them] 1A–1E; drive 22E–ARE
154.39   in] 1A–1F; into ARE
155.12   along] 1A–1F; alongs ARE
155.38–39   grocer's, butcher's, and fruiterer's]T; grocers, butchers,
               and fruiterers' 1E–1F; grocers', butchers' and fruiterers'
               ARE
°156.8   even] 1A, 2A; eve 1E–ARE
°156.18   head] 1A–1E; end 22E–ARE
°156.21   shagged] 1A, 2A; shaggy 1E–ARE
157.14   seats] 1A–1E; settles 22E–ARE
157.18   around] 1A–1E; round 22E–ARE
157.38   at a few] 1A, 2A, ARE; a few 1E–1F

CHRISTMAS EVE

°159.12   cracked] 1A–1E; smacked 22E–ARE

*159.13	upon a] 1A–1E; on a 22E–ARE
159.29	of the] 1A, 2A; on the 1E–ARE
160.7	any little] 1A–1F; any ARE
*160.15	rung] 1A–1E; rang 22E–ARE
160.35	round] 1A–1E; around 22E–ARE
*161.9	ringing] 1A–22E; ring 1F, ARE
161.12	Sweetheart] 1A–1F; Sweatheart ARE
161.16	now] 1A–1F; how ARE
*161.27	with heavy] 1A, 2A; and heavy 1E–ARE
*162.17	of the army] 1A–22E; in the army 1F, ARE
162.20	a physiognomist] 1A–1F; the physiognomist ARE
*162.27	proportions] 1A–1E; proportion 22E–ARE
*163.28	the last] 1A–1E; last 22E–ARE
165.24	ditty.] 1A, 1E–ARE; ditty, which he had picked out of one of Poor Robin's almanacks: 2A
165.30	&c.] 1E–ARE; *omitted* 2A
166.9	ill sorted] 1A–1F; ill-assorted ARE
166.23	draw] 1A–22E, ARE; drew 1F
166.41	or slow worm] 1A–1F; nor slow-worm ARE
167.20–21	was amusing] 1A–1F; amused ARE

CHRISTMAS DAY

169.1	*CHRISTMAS DAY*] 1A, 1E-ARE; *CHRISTMAS MORNING* 2A
169.12	awoke] 1A–1E; woke 22E–ARE
170.14	scarce] 1A, 2A; scarcely 1E–ARE
*171.21	at Master] 1A, 2A; to Master 1E–ARE
*172.20	of a rainy] 1A, 2A; on a rainy 1E–ARE
*172.34	Christmas] 1A–1E; a Christmas 22E–ARE
173.10	accident." *omitted*] 1E–ARE; accident." *Paragraph* I readily acceded to Bracebridge's proposition. 2A
*175.9	expectations] 1A–1E; expectation 22E–ARE
*175.16–17	who, happening] 1A–1F; who happened ARE
175.35	but little] 1A, 2A, ARE; but a little 1E–1F
*176.8	had a] 1A–1E; he had a 22E–ARE
176.11	traditionary] 1A–1E; traditional 22E–ARE
176.28	overflowing] 1A–1E; overflowed 22E–ARE
*176.36	Mark. xvi] 1E, 22E; Mark, xv 1F, ARE
177.6	limpid] 1A–1F; limped ARE
177.38	sugar] 1E; sugar, and 22E–ARE
177.40	ashamed] 1E; shamed 22E–ARE
178.19	country] 1A, 2A, 22E–ARE; county 1E

178.28   were] 1A–1F; was ARE
179.2   rough] 1A–1F; the rough ARE

THE CHRISTMAS DINNER

*183.7   traditionary] 1A–1E; traditional 22E–ARE
183.9   *Paragraph* I could] 1E–ARE; *No paragraph* I could 2A
183.9   not, however, but notice] 1E–ARE; not but notice, how-
              ever, 2A
183.33–41   The peacock . . . olden times:–] 1E–ARE; The Peacock
              was anciently in great demand for stately entertain-
              ments, and was made into a pie, at one end of which
              the head appeared above the crust, in all its plumage,
              the beak richly gilt; at the other end the tail was
              displayed. It was also served up in gold or silver
              dishes at the solemn banquets of chivalry, when
              knights errant pledged themselves to undertake any
              perilous enterprize, whence the ancient oath, "by cock
              and pye." The peacock was also an important dish
              in the Christmas feast, and Massinger, in his City
              Madam, gives some idea of the extravagance with
              which these and other dishes were prepared for the
              gorgeous revels of the olden time. 2A
184.20   for it was] 1E–ARE; being 2A
184.20   in the] 1E–ARE; on the 2A
184.23   potation, indeed, that might well] 1E–ARE; potation
              that indeed might 2A
184.24   being composed] 1E–ARE; consisting 2A
184.25   surface.*] 1E–ARE; surface. 2A
184.30   the primitive style] 1E–ARE; primitive custom 2A
184.31   feeling] 1E–ARE; fellowship 2A
184.31   together."†] 1E–ARE; together." 2A
185.2   circulated, and] 1E–ARE; circulated. It 2A
185.3   ladies. When] 1E–ARE; ladies; but when 2A
185.18   lusty laugh-a."] 1E–ARE; lustie laugh a. /Chorus, Sing,/
              Fling, &c. 2A
*187.10   except] 1A, 2A; excepting 1E–ARE
187.11   doze] 1A–22E; dose 1F–ARE
187.12   setting] 1A–1E; sitting 22E–ARE
*188.4   forth] 1A–1F; out ARE
*188.16   of stormy] 1A; on stormy 2A; in stormy 1E–ARE
*189.28   parlour] 1A–1E; the parlour 22E–ARE
189.30–38; 190.1–14 Master Simon . . . the pageant] 1E–ARE; Master
              Simon led the van as "ancient Christmas," quaintly

apparel'd in short cloak and ruff, and a hat that might have served for a village steeple, from under which, his nose curved boldly forth, with a frost bitten bloom that seemed the very trophy of a December blast. He was accompanied by the blue eyed romp, dished up as "Dame mince pie," in the venerable magnificence of faded brocade, long stomacher, peaked hat, and high heeled shoes. The young officer figured in genuine Kendal Green as Robin Hood; the fair Julia in a pretty rustic dress as Maid Marian. The rest of the train had been metamorphosed in various ways; the girls trussed up in the finery of their great grandmothers, and the striplings bewhiskered with burnt cork, and fantastically arrayed to support the characters of Roast Beef, Plum Porridge, and other worthies celebrated in ancient masqueings. The whole was under the control of the Oxonian, in the appropriate character of Misrule, that ancient ring leader of Christmas sports: and I observed that he exercised rather a mischievous sway with his wand, over the smaller personages of the pageant. 2A

189.37	faded] 1A–1F; a faded ARE
189.41–42	I strongly . . . Christmas.] 1E–ARE; *Vide* a pageant of the kind in Ben Jonson's Masque of Christmas. 2A
*190.2	*No paragraph* The costume] 1E; *Paragraph* The costume 22E–ARE
190.10	characters] 2A–1F; character ARE
190.17	stateliness] 1E–ARE; stateliness and indomptible gravity 2A
190.20	costumes] 1E–ARE; quaint costumes 2A
190.24	jigging] 2A–1F; jiggling ARE
190.30	of the Paon] 1A–1F; at the Paon ARE
*190.35	its apathy] 1A–1E; his apathy 22E–ARE
190.36; 191.1	also an interest in the scene,] 1E–ARE; an interest in the scene, also, 2A
191.3	was still] 1E–ARE; were still 2A
191.9	question] 1A–1E; questions 22E–ARE
191.15	*No paragraph* What] 1A–1E; *Paragraph* What 22E–ARE
191.18	my] 1A–22E; in my 1F, ARE
191.29	on the skirts] MS2; in the skirts ARE

LONDON ANTIQUES

196.12	was not] 1E, 2A–ARE; might not be 1A

LITTLE BRITAIN

The order of publication for this sketch was 1E, 1A, 2A, 22E, 1F, ARE.

198.11	sovereign contempt] 1E, 2A–ARE; contempt 1A
198.40–42	interesting communication . . . Cloth Fair.] 1E, 2A–ARE; curious tract includes in the general appellation of Little Britain, many of those odd lanes and nooks that more immediately belong to Cloth Fair. 1A
*199.32	a popular] 1E–1F; popular ARE
200.15	in Little] 1E–1F; of Little ARE
201.17	funeral] 1E–1F; funereal ARE
201.37	holds] 1E–22E, ARE; hold 1F
201.38	They abound] 1E, 22E–ARE; It abounds 1A, 2A
202.30	love] 1E–2A; have 22E–ARE
203.12	every tavern] 1E, 2A–ARE; and every tavern 1A
204.10	with a] 1E, 2A–ARE; with the 1A
*206.5	crones] 1E–22E; cronies 1F–ARE
206.33	morning] 1E, 22E–ARE; morning* 1A, 2A
206	*Footnote omitted*] 1E, 22E–ARE; *The Butchers in England invariably wear blue cotton coats, when attending to their business. 1A, 2A
207.21	the quadrille] 1E–2A; quadrille 22E–ARE
208.3	an honest country dance] 1E, 2A–ARE; a country-dance 1A

STRATFORD-ON-AVON

The order of publication for this sketch was 1E, 1A, 2A, 22E, 1F, ARE.

209.14	of some] 1E–1F; some ARE
210.12	exceedingly] 1E, 2A–ARE; exceeding 1A
210.16	exploit] 1E, 1A; exploits 2A–ARE
*210.27	crones] 1E, 1A, 22E; cronies 2A, 1F, ARE
210.33	fervent] 1E, 22E–ARE; present 1A, 2A
211.6	even so] 1E, 2A–ARE; so 1A
212.39	funeral] 1E, 22E–ARE; funereal 1A, 2A
212.42	pointed] 1E, 22E–ARE; painted 1A, 2A
213.9	be the man] 1E–2A; be he 22E–ARE
*213.15–16	cotemporaries] 1E–2A; contemporaries 22E–ARE
216.8	sprout] 1E–1F; spout ARE
216.30	awakened] 1E–2A; awaked 22E–ARE
217.13	fanciful] 1E–1F; fancy ARE
218.39	quoins] 1E, 22E–ARE; coins 1A, 2A
219.18	have here] 1E–1F; have ARE

219.19	*Shallow*] 1E–1F; "*Shallow* ARE
220.20	Sir John] 1E–1F; John ARE
220.21	Robert] 1E–1F; Sir Robert ARE
221.8	of a Sir] 1E–2A; of Sir 22E–ARE
*222.7	my] 1E–22E; my own 1F, ARE
*222.12	bedrooped] T; forlorn 22E–ARE
222.13	followed] 1E–22E, ARE; fellowed 1F
*222.15	open] 1E–2A; opened 22E–ARE
222.24	arbour] 1E–1F; harbor ARE
222.26	graffing] 1E–1F; grafting ARE
222.33	ancestor] 1E–2A; ancestors 22E–ARE
222.40	spaniels."] 1E–1F; ~·∧ ARE
223.1	"By] 1E–1F; *By ARE
224.23	its lessening] 1E, 22E–ARE; the lessening 1A, 2A

TRAITS OF INDIAN CHARACTER

*225.14	growth] 1E–1F; support ARE
225.22	has often] 1E–1F; often ARE
226.18	breathe] 1E–1F; breed ARE
226.25	mere] 1E–1F; the mere ARE
*227.13	thus do] 1E; thus 22E–ARE
*227.17	resemble] 1E, 22E; resembled 1F, ARE
229.23	place] 1E; the place 22E–ARE
*230.31	arisen] 1E; risen 22E–ARE
*231.18	infliction] 1E, 22E; affliction 1F–ARE
*232.24	their pieces] 1E, 22E; the pieces 1F, ARE
232.36	Indians] 1E–1F; Indian ARE
*232.40	upon] 1E; on 22E–ARE
*233.26	further] 1E; farther 22E–ARE

PHILIP OF POKANOKET

Not one distinctive emendation was made in "Philip of Pokanoket" after its first appearance in *The Sketch Book*. In the absence of textual evidence of Irving's emending hand, all post-copy-text variants are rejected.

235.13	cotemporary] 1E; contemporary 22E–ARE
236.19	same] 1E, 22E, ARE; some 1F
*236.36	seize at once] 1E–22E; seize 1F, ARE
236.37	court] 1E, 22E; courts 1F, ARE
237.29	many] 1E–1F; many many ARE
238.20	after] 1E–1F; afterwards ARE
238.24	as the murderers] 1E, 22E; as murderers 1F, ARE
239.1	upon and] 1E–1F; on and ARE

239.27   falling] 1E, 22E; fallen 1F, ARE
239.27   disruptured] 1E–1F; disrupted ARE
240.19   in expedients] 1E, 22E; of expedients 1F, ARE
241.2   and overshadowed] 1E, 22E; overshadowed 1F, ARE
*241.4   shagged] 1E; shaggy 22E–ARE
241.4   render] 1E; rendered 22E–ARE
243.17   procure] 1E, 22E; to procure 1F, ARE
243.35   *No paragraph* At] 1E, 22E; *Paragraph* At 1F, ARE
244.19   "and he] 1E–1F; and "he ARE
244.29   Stonington] 1E, 22E; Stoningham 1F, ARE
*245.32–33 "there . . . deliverance."] 1E; ∧~ . . . ~.∧ 22E–ARE
245.37   desolated scenes] 1E; scenes 22E–ARE
246.23   at escape] 1E, 22E; to escape 1F, ARE

JOHN BULL

*248.6   *Stanza* With an old study] 1A–1F; *No stanza* With an
           old study ARE
249.21   different] 1A–1F; differents ARE
249.38   neighbours'] 1A–1E; neighbour's 22E–ARE
250.7   broil] 1A, 2A, 22E–ARE; broils 1E
*250.31   and cock] 1A–1E; cock 22E–ARE
250.38   breeches'] 1A–1E; breeches 22E–ARE
*251.27   times] 1A–22E; time 1F, ARE
251.31   must once] 1A–1E; must 22E–ARE
255.19   smug] 1A, 22E–ARE; snug 2A, 1E
*255.37   to buy] 1A–22E; buy 1F, ARE
*256.18   the] 1E, 22E; this 1F, ARE

THE PRIDE OF THE VILLAGE

257.5   come] 1A, 22E–ARE; comes 2A, 1E
257.8   keep] 1A-22E; kept 1F, ARE
258.6   female.] 1E–ARE; female.* 1A, 2A
258   *Footnote omitted*] 1E–ARE; *For some notice of this
           custom, see Sketch Book, No. IV. 1A, 2A
*261.22   proposals] 1A–1E; proposal 22E–ARE
*261.33   scene] 1A–1E; scenes 22E–ARE
262.15   bloom] 1A–1F; gloom ARE
*262.30   and she] 1A–1E; that she 22E–ARE
263.18–19 an agony] 1A–1F; agony ARE

THE ANGLER

The order of publication for this sketch was 1E, 1A, 2A, 22E, 1F, ARE.

264.15	rods] 1E, 2A–ARE; rod 1A
264.21	sallied] 1E, 2A–ARE; sallied forth 1A
264.27	inconveniencies] 1A–22E; inconveniences 1F, ARE
264.33	execution] 1E, 22E–ARE; exercise 1A, 2A
265.4	placid demure face] 1E, 2A–ARE; placid air 1A
265.5	pestilent shrew] 1E, 2A–ARE; shrew 1A
265.20	Izaak] 1E, 2A–ARE; Walton 1A
265.25	was merely] 1E, 2A–ARE; only 1A
265.27	them suspiciously] 1E, 2A–ARE; them 1A
265.29	from off] 1E, 2A–ARE; off from 1A
265.34	part] 1E–1F; parter part ARE
266.30	sayth] 1E, 2A–ARE; says 1A
266.37	it is generally considered] 1E, 2A–ARE; is generally imagined 1A
267.1	that I could perceive] 1E, 2A–ARE; I perceived 1A
°267.18	fresh sweet smelling] 1E–22E; fresh-smelling 1F, ARE
268.4	almost the] 1E, 2A–ARE; the 1A
268.9	of course] 1E, 2A–ARE; accordingly 1A
268.17–18	and are the] 1E, 2A–ARE; and the 1A
268.29	bring] 1E, 2A–ARE; brings 1A
268.31	the pheasant] T; a peasant 1A
268.38	fed] 1E–1F; feed ARE
269.15	after his] 1E, 2A–ARE; his 1A
269.18	containing only] 1E, 2A–ARE; consisting of 1A
°269.25	birth deck] 1E–1F; berth-deck ARE
269.27	lashed up] 1E, 2A–ARE; "lashed up," 1A
269.30	walls] 1E–2A; wall 22E–ARE
269.31	Downs, and Tom] 1E, 2A–ARE; Downs; the Arethusa, and Tom 1A
269.37	containing] 1E, 2A–ARE; comprising 1A
270.4–5	The establishment reminded me of that of the renowned Robinson Crusoe; it] 1E, 2A–ARE; The whole establishment 1A
270.6	being] 1E, 2A–ARE; was 1A
270.12	cage.] 1E, 2A–ARE; cage. The scene brought to mind Robinson Crusoe's picture of himself seated in royal state among his subjects. 1A
270.12	*No paragraph* He] 1E, 2A–ARE; *Paragraph* He 1A
°270.34	at other] 1E–22E; and at other 1F, ARE

270.39   particular] 1E, 2A–ARE; peculiar 1A
271.1   sea] 1E, 2A–ARE; seas 1A

THE LEGEND OF SLEEPY HOLLOW

*274.42   of a drowsy] 1A, 2A; in a drowsy 1E–ARE
275.36   burthen] 1A–1F; burden ARE
276.15   of a still] 1A, 2A; on a still 1E–ARE
*276.16   diverse] 1A–1E; divers 22E–ARE
277.6   of an] 1A, 2A; in the 1E–ARE
277.9   dusk] 1A, 1E–ARE; dust 2A
*277.9   of evening] 1A–1E; of the evening 22E–ARE
277.29   sputtering] 1A–1F; spluttering ARE
*278.18   diverse] 1A–1E; divers 22E–ARE
278.36   toward] 1A–1F; towards ARE
279.8   babbled] 1A–1F; bubbled ARE
279.9   elders] 1A–1E; alders 22E–ARE
279.18   from whence] 1A–1F; whence ARE
279.29   this sumptuous] 1A–1F; his sumptuous ARE
280.16   formed] 1A–1E; forming 22E–ARE
280.22   wondering] 1A–1E, 1F, ARE; wonderful 22E
281.15   rung] 1A–1F; rang ARE
281.19   frame] 1A, 2A, 1F, ARE; fame 1E, 22E
281.37   whoop] 1A–1F; hoop ARE
282.10   of a Sunday] 1A, 2A; on a Sunday 1E–ARE
*282.10–11   (a . . . within,)] 1A–1E; ∧～ . . . ～,∧ 22E–ARE
*283.37   situations] 1A–22E; situation 1F, ARE
283.39   from whence] 1A–1F; whence ARE
*286.3   Further] 1A–1E; Farther 22E–ARE
287.2   mettle] 1A–1F; metal ARE
*288.3   scraped away] 1A–22E; scraped 1F, ARE
288.18   and smiling] 22E–ARE; and smiled 1E
*288.23   drawling] 1A–22E; drawing 1F, ARE
288.28   been infested] 1A, 2A; infested 1E–ARE
288.35   mud] 1A–22E, ARE; muddy 1F
288.42   more who] 1A–1E; more that 22E–ARE
*289.9   scarce] 1A–22E; scarcely 1F, ARE
289.11   of a] 1A, 2A; at 1E–ARE
*289.11   the] 1A–1E; their 22E–ARE
*289.21   mournful] 1A–22E; mourning 1F, ARE
290.23   sunk] 1A–1F; sank ARE
*290.25   many very] 1A–1E; many 22E–ARE

292.24–25	he, however, summoned up] 1A, 2A; he summoned up, however, 1E–ARE
292.32	alder] 1A, 22E–ARE; elder 2A, 1E
293.8	tune] 1A–22E, ARE; tone 1F
294.26	sprung] 1A–1F; sprang ARE
296.23	words in] 1A–22E, ARE; words it 1F
296.24–25	Manhattoes] ARE; the Manhattoes* 1E–1F
296	*Footnote omitted*] ARE; *New York 1E–1F
296.39	and] 1A, 1E–ARE; but 2A
296.39–297.1	a slight] 1A, 1E–ARE; slight 2A

L'ENVOY

| *298.23 | can only] 1E; only can 22E–ARE |
| *298.37 | on even as] 1E; on as 22E–ARE |

MONTUCCI EDITION (DRESDEN, 1823)

To the left of the brackets in this list are the Twayne page and line numbers and readings; to the right the rejected readings of the Montucci edition (1G) (Dresden, 1823). For a discussion explaining the rejection of all 1G substantives, see pp. 372.29–373.6.

9.37	bring] to bring
16.26	have communed] had communed
16.27	our] my
20.23	is like] stands like
26.34	our humble] an humble
28.9	happened upon] chanced to find
28.16	truth] private truth
28.24	He, however, was apt to] He was apt, however, to
31.43	through] during
32.20	puffs] whiffs
33.34	pair] pairs
34.6	so that you only caught] merely allowing
34.28	folks] folk
35.15	place] the place
35.33	He, however, made shift] He made shift, however,
37.5–6	broken, and mended with old hats and petticoats] broken, with old hats and petticoats stuffed into the chasms
39.26	Oh she too had died] "Oh, she died
41.23	superstition] legend

41.31	were] are
43.35	the deserts] deserts
48.7	her] following her
50.29	tact] turn
54.19	immemorial] immemorable
56.35	may] can
58.14	fortune, and] fortune; when
58.39–40	never objected] did not object
62.4	shortly] shortly after
63.5	"slab and good."] thick and slab
67.10	place] proud old pile
67.11	associations. The] interest, and its
67.11	of the proud old pile is enough] is sufficient
67.12	high thought] a train of fanciful and romantic associ-
	ations
69.21	irradiate] to irradiate
70.29	lay] may lay
73.23	is a] may be considered as a
74.5	advance.] advance,
74.28	is] was
76.13	in] on
79.23	cushioned] cushioned and
79.38	by making] in making
81.33	acquaintences] acquaintance
83.19	*Nothing comparable*] I do not pretend to claim the
	character of
84.30	a humble] an humble
85.19	not to] not
86.19	craft] crafts
87.28	from] through
91.4	great, great grandfather] great grandfather
91.5	great grandfather] great, great-grandfather
92.27–28	the toper] which the toper
92.33	in] at
98.4	san] saint
99.4	further] farther
104.17	shall] should
117.21	intended] pretended
126.21	dinner] feast
127.33	immediately] just
138.33	richly carved of oak] of oak richly carved
141.1	rudely carved of oak] of oak rudely carved
150.41	has become] is become

160.1	the bent] in the bent
160.23	seemed] seems
197.12	Butcher] Butcher's Hall
206.9	engagements] engagement
206.14	Lambs] Lamb's
206.31	glozings] glossings
210.21–22	self multiplication as . . . line.] self-multiplication.
215.9	of the vagabond] of vagabond
216.14	hedges] edges
217.2	*Omitted*] Arise! arise!
218.1	from] for
231.6	or] with
231.36	homely] early
240.9	retrieve] detrieve
246.28	of] of an
248.28	thus to give] has thus given
250.13	startling] starting
262.5	after story] after's story
270.30	gentlemen] gentleman
281.6	contrary] country
286.23	their] her
289.25	shriek] shrink
298.38	*Closing the second volume of the London edition.] *The Author here alludes to the first edition of this Work, which was published in two Volumes; but the second came out some time after the first; and began with the Article at page 220 of the present Edition. Note of the Editor.

ALTERATIONS IN THE MANUSCRIPTS

Listed below are the changes made by Irving himself in his manuscripts. Only emendations which seem to indicate a change of mind are listed here; the many alterations made merely for legibility are omitted. Interlineations above and below canceled matter are distinguished, as are those with and without carets; for "interlined" by itself, read "interlined above." When Irving drew a line through a word or phrase, or completely blacked it out, this appendix reads "deleted." When he deliberately smeared the still wet ink, it reads "wiped out." Where a letter or punctuation mark is reshaped into another, or a word is altered by being partially overwritten, the indication is "mended."

A slash is inserted before or after a word to indicate the beginning or end of a manuscript line, where such indication helps clarify the alteration. "[ ]" indicates illegible letters; "[abc]" shows doubtful letters. The two columns of page and line numbers are, from left to right, to the manuscript and to the Twayne edition. Line numbers out of sequence in the Twayne list are the result of Irving's having transposed paragraphs or larger blocks of material, while a missing page or line number indicates that nothing similar to the manuscript reading remains in the text.

This list is in two sections: the first, headed "MS1," treats the manuscript of *Sketch Book* Numbers I–III, published in 1819; the second, headed "MS2," contains the readings of the surviving manuscript material added to the text in 1848 for the Author's Revised Edition. An addendum, headed "Sleepy Hollow," sets forth the readings of the only known MS fragment of that story.

MS1

THE AUTHOR'S ACCOUNT OF HIMSELF

3.11	8.8	Lylies Euphues] this page is made of two pieces of paper, the seam running just below these words; immediately below the seam, on the lower piece, are deleted "Lilies Euphues"
3.19	8.13	town] interlined above deleted "town"
4.1	8.16–17	or robbery] interlined with a caret
4.2	8.17	I] followed by deleted "we[ ]"

6.6	9.6	custom] originally "customs"; the *s* is mended to form a tail for the *m*
9.1	10.1	vagrant] preceded by deleted "inclination"
9.3	10.3	accordingly] interlined with a caret
9.5	10.3	obscure] preceded by deleted *g*
9.7	10.4	cascade] preceded by deleted "falls"
9.7	10.5	Terni] preceded by deleted "Ter[ni]"

THE VOYAGE

10.10	11.10	wealthy] mended from "wealth" and followed by deleted "of"
10.19	11.16	The] mended from "the" and preceded by deleted / "In traversing"
11.15	11.26	the] preceded by deleted / "then"
11.21	11.29	secure] interlined above deleted / "moorings and"
12.19	12.1	may] interlined with a caret above deleted "shall"/
12.20	12.2	may] interlined with a caret above deleted "shall"
12.21	12.3	childhood?] followed by deleted / "Or if he does return, may not his very / home have become strange to him?"/
13.13	12.11	fancy] preceded by deleted "and"
13.14	12.11	fairy] interlined with a caret above deleted / "unknown"
13.20	12.15	awe] interlined with a caret above deleted "terror"
13.22	12.17	Shoals of] interlined above deleted "The"
14.12	12.26	How] preceded by deleted "To"
14.15	12.27	glorious] preceded by deleted "triumph"
14.16	12.28	invention,] interlined above deleted / "enterprize & skill"
14.24	12.32	thus] interlined with a caret
16.1	13.5	wafted] interlined with a caret above deleted "sent"
16.4	13.7	pored] followed by deleted "with anxious" /
17.18	13.28	was] preceded by "it" interlined with a caret and in turn preceded by interlined deleted "the" above deleted "it"
19.1	14.4	encreased] preceded by deleted / "was encreasing and I"
19.5	14.6	deep—] followed by deleted "while" /
19.6	14.7	volume] interlined with a caret
19.15	14.12	it] preceded by deleted / "sometimes almost"
20.10	14.23	prey] preceded by deleted "prey"

21.4	14.33	cry] interlined with a caret above deleted "sound"
21.11	14.37	with] followed by deleted "that word"
21.11	14.37	name] preceded by deleted "word"
22.1	15.2	cottages] preceded by deleted "engl"
23.6	15.18	countenance] preceded by deleted "form"
23.13	15.22	of late] preceded by deleted "towards"
23.19	15.26	shrouds] preceded by deleted "shrouds"

ROSCOE

25.15	16.12	grave] interlined with a caret above deleted "grave"
26.18	16.26	with] preceded by deleted "who"
27.4	16.31	superior] interlined with a caret above deleted "spiritualized"
27.9	16.33	Medici] the previous line ends in deleted "Med[ici]"
28.7	17.4	brambles] interlined with a caret above deleted "briars"
28.20	17.12	eminence] followed by deleted "& distinction"
28.20	17.12	having] interlined above deleted "while he" /
28.21	17.12	become] preceded by deleted / "has"
29.2	17.15	which] interlined with a caret above deleted "that"
29.9	17.20	pleasures. Their] mended from original "pleasures, their"
29.12	17.21	inconsistency] followed by deleted "But there is a daily / beauty in Mr Roscoes life"
29.15	17.22	of] followed by canceled "the"
29.16	17.23	indulge] preceded by deleted "in" /
29.20	17.26	talent.] followed by deleted / "He has gone into the highways and tho[ ] / thoroughfares"
29.23	17.26	or elysium] interlined with carets above deleted "and paradise" and preceded by a deleted interlined "or"
29.24	17.27	forth] interlined with a caret
30.5	17.30	dust] interlined above deleted "labour"
30.8	17.32	meditate] interlined with a caret above deleted "ponder"
30.9	17.32	It] preceded by deleted "It abounds with"
30.9	17.32	no] followed by deleted "picture of"
30.18	17.38	busy] interlined above canceled "commercial"
30.22–23	17.40–41	exclusive . . . wealth,] interlined with a caret above deleted "cherishing assiduities of literary / leisure"

30.24	17.41	on] followed by deleted "the casual and disin- / terested attentions which"
30.26	17.42	snatched] preceded by interlined deleted / "and"
31.6	18.3	on] preceded by deleted "whose pure example"
31.11	18.6–7	his. . . . Wherever] is the last line on the piece of paper that is the upper half of this page. On the lower half, but hidden by the pasted-over upper piece are: "living streams of knowledge. Wherever"
31.12	18.7	perceive] interlined with a caret above deleted "find"
31.16	18.9	rills] interlined with a caret above deleted "streams"
31.19	18.11	effect] interlined with a caret above deleted "union"
32.10	18.18	that] interlined with a caret before deleted "Liverpool"
33.10	18.32	him] followed by deleted [;]
33.11	18.33	posterity. With] the period mended from original [,] and capital W from lowercase [w]
34.14	19.8	blending] preceded by deleted "blinding"
35.4	19.17	once] followed by deleted "well[e]d"
35.16	19.23	like wreckers] interlined with a caret
35.18	19.24	Did] preceded by deleted "If such [a] thi"
35.20	19.25	strange] interlined with a caret above deleted "sudden"
35.21	19.26	into] preceded by deleted "of the sons of trade"
36.14–15	19.36	could provoke] interlined (the latter with a caret) above deleted "he thought / worthy of"
37.18	20.8	sympathy.] followed by deleted "and regard."
37.20	20.9	of genius] interlined with a caret
37.24	20.12	form] preceded by deleted "must"
38.4	20.14	in] followed by deleted "the"
38.13	20.19	always] interlined with a caret

THE WIFE

40.14	22.12	such] interlined with a caret above deleted "an"
40.16	22.13	it approaches] interlined with carets above deleted "almost arises"
41.4	22.16	rising] followed by deleted "to be the"
41.6	22.17	under] followed by deleted "his"
41.7	22.18	misfortune] mended from "misfortunes"

41.16	22.24	providence] interlined above deleted "nature"
43.3	23.2	abandoned] preceded by deleted "d[e]s"
45.23	23.39	A] mended from "a" and preceded by deleted "In"
45.23	23.39	thought] interlined above deleted "thought he,"
46.5	23.42	like mine] interlined with a caret
46.21	24.9	if imparted] preceded by deleted "it would"
47.6	24.14	mind] preceded by deleted "heart"
47.18	24.21	indigence] interlined above deleted "poverty"
48.1	24.25	neglect!] exclamation point mended from question mark
48.13	24.32	she] preceded by deleted "[th]"
48.14	24.33	may] preceded by deleted "m[a]"
50.14	25.17	result] preceded by deleted "event"
52.24	26.8	he said] interlined
57.8	27.19	George] interlined with a caret above deleted "Charles"
57.19	27.25	within his,] "within" interlined with a caret above deleted "on"; comma inserted before deleted "shoulder,"

[PREFATORY NOTE TO "RIP VAN WINKLE"]

60.15	28.23	much] preceded by deleted "employed"
61.1	28.29	offend. But] interlined with a caret
61.2	28.30	is] preceded by deleted "certainly"
61.3	28.31	folk] preceded by deleted "men"
61.7	28.33	have] interlined with a caret

RIP VAN WINKLE

62.10	29.9	Hudson] followed by deleted "river"
62.11	29.10	Kaatskill] preceded by deleted "Kat" /
63.4	29.17	print] preceded by deleted "seem to print"
63.8	29.19	which] followed by deleted "as the / setting sun pours its last gleams rays ["rays" interlined] on it, / will often"
63.10	29.19–20	in . . . will] interlined
63.12	29.22	descryed] interlined with a caret above deleted "noticed"
63.18	29.26	founded] interlined with a caret above deleted "settled"
63.20	29.27	beginning] interlined above deleted "commencement" /

63.21	29.27–28	government] interlined with a caret above deleted "reign"
63.24	29.30	years;] followed by deleted "with gable fronts, lattice" /
64.1	29.31	surmounted] interlined with a caret
64.5–7	29.32–33	( )] the parentheses cover original commas
64.13	29.37	accompanied him to] interlined above deleted "particularly at"
65.14	30.12	squabbles,] followed by deleted "They"
65.17	30.14	Winkle.] followed by deleted "They used / to employ"
65.21	30.16	them] followed by deleted "how"
65.22	30.17	ghosts,] followed by deleted "and" /
66.7	30.23	either] interlined with a caret
66.7	30.24	perseverance;] followed by deleted "either," /
66.8	30.24	sit] followed by deleted "[for]"
66.18	30.30	and] interlined with a caret
67.3	30.35	doing . . . duty,] interlined above deleted / "taking care of himself and his family" /
67.8	30.38	country;] followed by deleted "and" /
67.12	30.41	get] followed by deleted "in"
67.13	30.41	quicker] interlined above deleted "faster"
67.18	31.1	under his management,] interlined with a caret
67.23	31.4–5	wild . . . nobody.] interlined above deleted / "undisciplined as colts."
68.2	31.7	like] preceded by deleted / "at his"
68.3–4	31.8	cast off galigaskins] interlined with carets above deleted "galligas- / galligaskins cast off breeches"
68.14	31.13	If] preceded by deleted "H[e]"
68.21	31.18	produce] preceded by deleted "provo"
69.14	31.27	as] followed by deleted "g[i]"
70.11	31.39	by] followed by deleted "frequen" /
70.14	31.41	held its sessions] interlined above deleted "as- sembled"
70.15	31.41	bench] followed by deleted "f[a]"
70.15	31.41	before] followed by deleted "the inn,"
70.16	31.42	Inn] interlined above deleted / "public house"
70.16	31.42	rubicond] interlined above deleted "r[ ]f[ ] [d]" /
70.22	32.2	been . . . any] interlined above deleted / "done a"
70.22	32.2	statesmans] followed by deleted "heart good"
70.25	32.4	newspaper] followed by deleted "had"
71.3	32.6–7	a dapper . . . man,] interlined with a caret

71.8	32.10	The . . . by] interlined above deleted /"Over this junto presided"
71.10	32.11	inn,] followed by deleted "though he took no part in its active duties, / which were"
71.16–17	32.15	It . . . speak,] interlined above deleted "He was con- / sidered the wisest man in the neighbourhood / though he never said any thing"
71.22	32.18	that was] interlined with a caret
71.30	32.23	gravely] interlined with a caret
71.33	32.24	by] interlined with a caret above deleted "by"
72.4	32.26–27	that . . . personage] interlined above deleted "the august personage of"
73.7	32.43	gun.] followed by deleted "He was seat / seated"
73.15	33.5	lordly] interlined with a caret above deleted "broad"
73.22	33.9	down] followed by deleted "upon" /
74.3	33.12	some] interlined above deleted "a long"
75.2	33.24	felt a] followed by deleted "th[r]" /
75.5	33.26	strange] preceded by deleted "strange person"
75.12	33.30	yield it.] followed by indented deleted / "as he approached" /
75.18	33.34	fashion,] followed by deleted "with"
75.19	33.34	waist] followed by deleted "a pair Breeches of prodigious / magnitude"
75.21	33.35	ample] preceded by deleted "great"
76.5	33.40–41	the dry] interlined above deleted "formed" /
76.10	33.43	toward] interlined above deleted "which" /
76.15	34.3	in] preceded by deleted / "suddenly" and followed by deleted "these"
76.17	34.4	hollow] followed by deleted "of the moun"
76.23	34.7	time] followed by deleted "that" interlined with a caret
77.9	34.14	ninepins.] followed by deleted / "The fashion of their dresses seemed of similar / date with that of the guide. Some wore" /
77.14	34.15	knives] followed by deleted "or daggers"
77.20	34.19	nose,] followed by deleted "which began / at the top of his head forehead and ended / at his chin,"
77.24	34.20	all] interlined with a caret
78.3	34.22	stout] followed by deleted "burley"
78.18	34.30	withal] mended from original "withall"
79.1	34.33	like] preceded by deleted / "sounded"
79.1	34.33	thunder.] followed by deleted / "and echoed along

		the mountains." / ; "echoing" interlined with a caret and deleted above "echoed"
79.19	34.43	naturally] preceded by deleted "a thirst"
79.23	35.3	at length] interlined with a caret above deleted "by degrees"
80.19	35.13	Dame] followed by deleted "Van Winkle.'" /
80.20	35.14	Van Winkle?"] followed by three deleted lines beginning a new paragraph: / "As he looked about him the place / seemed materially altered. The grass had / had shot up to a great height; there" /
81.1	35.16	him] interlined above deleted "his side" /
81.2	35.16–17	the barrel ... rust;] this phrase, the product of two stages of alteration, first read: "the barrel rusted away" then "the barrel consumed by rust" before the final revision to the present form
81.7	35.20	Wolf] preceded by deleted W
81.7	35.20	too] followed by deleted "was" /
81.8	35.20	had disappeared] interlined with a caret above deleted / "not to be seen"
81.11	35.22	the echoes] preceded by deleted "the echoes"
81.19	35.27	mountain] followed by deleted "be[d]"
81.20	35.27	agree] preceded by deleted "agree"
82.7	35.34	working] interlined with a caret over deleted "making"
82.8	35.35	sassafras] preceded by deleted "and"
82.9	35.35	sometimes] followed by deleted "almost brought to a / stand"
82.11	35.36	their] followed by deleted "fantas- / tic"
82.17	35.39	no] followed by deleted "traces of" interlined with a caret, and deleted "such opening was / remained"
82.20	35.40	wall] followed by deleted "down"
82.21	35.41	tumbling] followed by deleted "down"
82.23	35.42	surrounding] interlined above deleted "over" /
83.4	36.2	overhung a] "a" interlined with a caret above deleted "the"
84.5	36.17	long!] followed by indented deleted / "His mind now began to"
84.18	36.25	faces] followed by deleted "we"
84.23	36.27–28	which ... before.] interlined with a caret

85.3	36.30	been—] interlined with a caret above deleted "stood" /
85.9	36.33	expecting] followed by deleted "to hear"
86.1	36.42	connubial] preceded by deleted "domestic"
86.3	37.1	lonely] preceded by deleted "empty"
86.13	37.7	Doolittle."] followed by deleted "Before / the Inn In pl"
86.16	37.8	reared] interlined with a caret above deleted "erected"
86.21	37.11	incomprehensible.] followed by deleted / "to Rip Van Winkle."
87.6	37.16	printed] preceded by deleted "writ"
87.10	37.19	people] interlined above deleted "populace" /
87.13	37.21	drowsy] interlined with a caret
87.18	37.24	Schoolmaster doling] interlined with carets above deleted "Taylor chaunting"
87.19	37.24	contents] preceded by deleted "stale"
87.21	37.25–26	with . . . bills,] interlined with a caret
87.25	37.28	jargon to] followed by deleted "poor Rip."
88.1	37.30	Rip] preceded by deleted "Van Winkle"
88.9	37.34	drawing him partly] interlined with a caret above deleted "half turning him asi"
88.24	37.42	his keen] preceded by deleted / "and"
89.7	38.3	somewhat dismayed] interlined with a caret above deleted "almost at his wits / end"
89.10	38.4	him!"] followed by a paragraph symbol and "Here a general / shout burst" / , all deleted
89.14–15	38.6	away with him] interlined above deleted "tar and / feather him!"
89.16	38.7	self] interlined with a caret
90.3	38.16	a little while,] interlined with a caret above deleted "a moment,"
90.4	38.16–17	in . . . voice,] interlined with a caret
90.17	38.26	wars] preceded by deleted "army too"
90.22	38.29	himself] interlined above deleted "he was"
91.1	38.31	war] mended from "wars"
91.4	38.32	cried out] preceded by deleted "looking around / him in despair exclaimed"
91.9	38.35	yonder—] dash covers original comma
91.19	38.40–41	—what] dash interlined with a caret above deleted / "and"
91.25	39.2	they've] preceded by deleted / "now"
92.5	39.4	at each] preceded by deleted / "shrewdly"

92.7	39.5–6	There ... also] interlined with a caret above deleted "Someone whispered"
92.17	39.11	his looks] preceded by deleted "the cr[ow]d"
92.20	39.13	air] interlined with a caret above deleted "looks"
92.25	39.16	Judith] preceded by deleted "Am[y]"; interlined above it is erased "Judith"
93.12	39.25	"Wheres] preceded by paragraph symbol
93.12	39.26	Oh] preceded by paragraph symbol
93.14	39.26	she too] preceded by deleted / "she too was gone, she but a short time" /
93.16	39.28	There] preceded by paragraph symbol
93.21	39.30	father] preceded by deleted "father" /
94.11	39.39	some] preceded by deleted "and"
94.13	39.41	self] interlined with a caret
94.14	39.41	man] interlined with a caret above deleted / "gentleman"
94.15	39.41–42	when ... over] interlined above deleted / "had returned by this time"
94.16	39.42	the corners of] interlined with a caret
94.19	40.2	assemblage.] followed by indented, deleted / "The matter however was referred to" /
95.3	40.6	village] followed by deleted / "and a perfect"
95.11	40.11	beings.] preceded by deleted "sight" and followed by deleted / "and apparitions"
95.23	40.17	mountain;] followed by deleted "of a summ" /
95.25	40.18	balls,] followed by deleted "wh" /
96.2–3	40.20–21	& ... election] interlined above deleted "each man with his several / opinion"
96.9	40.24	who] interlined with a caret above deleted "which"
96.10	40.25	was employed] interlined above deleted "assisted" /
96.11	40.26	evinced] followed by deleted "his / father"
96.17–18	40.30	preferred . . . among] interlined above deleted "grew rapidly / into favour with"
96.18	40.30–31	with . . . favour.] interlined below the line
96.21	40.32	with] preceded by deleted "without"
96.24	40.34–35	& . . . war."] interlined below the line
97.12	40.42	despotism] interlined above deleted "tyrrany"
98.7	41.10	related] followed by deleted "and not a man"— the last words on the piece of paper comprising the top fourth of this composite page. The first word on the lower piece of paper is deleted "Hotel,"
98.16	41.15	Even] mended from "even"

98.19	41.17	and his . . . their] interlined with a caret above deleted "is at his"
98.24	41.19	out of] preceded by deleted "of"
99.11	41.27	incredible] this is the first standing word on the lower piece of paper in this composite page; it is preceded by a deleted illegible word fragment and deleted "&"
99.16	41.30	in] interlined above deleted "among"
99.16–17	41.30	in the] followed by deleted "worthy dutch folks / of the"
99.26	41.36	before a] followed by deleted "dutch" /
99.27	41.37	&] interlined

ENGLISH WRITERS ON AMERICA

2.5	43.18	faithful,] followed by deleted "preci"
2.17	43.25	description] mended from "descriptions"
3.7	43.32	be visited by] interlined with a caret above deleted "have"
3.8	43.33	travellers.] followed by deleted "among us."
3.11	43.34	poles,] comma mended from semicolon
3.18–19	43.39	birmingham] "birming-" / interlined above deleted "Birming-" /
4.12	44.9	sound and] interlined with a caret
4.22	44.14	capable] preceded by deleted "but"
4.23	44.15	those] followed by deleted "objects" /
4.24	44.15	matters] interlined with a caret
5.5	44.19	crowded] preceded by deleted / "all"
5.5	44.19	many] followed by deleted "are driven / to"
5.8	44.20	appetite] preceded by deleted / "apetite"
5.8	44.21	These] interlined with a caret
5.18	44.27	an] interlined with a caret above deleted "as some"
5.23	44.30	manner.] followed by deleted "They became embittered agains / against a country"
5.24	44.30	mind] interlined above deleted / "judgement"
7.2	45.4	the truth] interlined with a caret above deleted "correct information" /
7.20	45.13	pyramid;] followed by deleted "the"
8.5	45.18	placed] interlined above deleted "engaged" /
8.13	45.22	topic;] preceded by deleted "subject"
8.20	45.26	They] mended from "the"
8.20	45.26	cannot] interlined with a caret above deleted "tissue" /

9.11	45.35	political] interlined above deleted "civil and political"
10.17	46.9	invidious] interlined with a caret above deleted "inveterate"
10.24	46.13	under its] interlined with a caret
.9	46.18	collission.] interlined above deleted "assailment." This is an unnumbered fragmentary page between pages 10 and 11.
11.23	46.31	sarcasm] interlined with a caret above deleted "aspersion"
11.24	46.32	blight] followed by deleted "the" /
11.25	46.32	add] preceded by deleted "exasperate"
12.6	46.39	The] preceded by deleted "If in America"
13.2	47.5–6	the united States] interlined with a caret above deleted "America"
13.6	47.8	considerable] interlined with a caret above deleted / "some deg[ ] degree of"
13.7	47.8	soreness] preceded by deleted "feeling of"
13.10	47.10	England] partially written over wiped-out "Gre"
13.19	47.15	of enthusiasm] interlined with a caret over deleted "enthusiastic"
13.31	47.21	yearned] preceded by deleted "throbbed"
14.2	47.24	it was the] interlined above deleted "there was a"
14.2	47.24	delight of] of interlined with a caret above deleted "among" /
14.3	47.24	spirits] interlined with a caret above deleted "minds"
14.10	47.29	illusion] followed by deleted "by"
14.12	47.30	—interfered . . . our] interlined with a caret above deleted /"rendered us blind to our"
14.19	47.34	farther and farther] the second "farther" is interlined with a caret above deleted "further"
14.21	47.35	parent,] followed by deleted "that outraged every filial affection." /
15.4	47.39	prompt] preceded by deleted "honest, man"
15.10	47.42	Let] preceded by deleted / "Nothing is so easy a"
15.14	48.2	and sarcasm;] interlined with a caret
16.5	48.11	party] mended from "parties"
16.10	48.14	fall] preceded by deleted "therefore"
16.10	48.14	therefore,] interlined with a caret
16.15	48.17	what . . . worse] interlined with a caret above deleted / "above all"

16.19	48.20	public] interlined with a caret above deleted "national" /
16.21	48.21	purity of the] interlined with a caret
16.21	48.21	mind.] followed by deleted "pure and" /
17.1	48.24	Republicans] above this word is deleted / "The characteris"
17.1	48.24	above] interlined with a caret above deleted "before"
17.10–11	48.29–30	character . . . other] interlined with carets above deleted "nature with her, / than with any"
17.16	48.33	passion] interlined with a caret above deleted "petulance"
17.22	48.37	exercising] preceded by deleted "exhibiting"
19.5	49.13	manners] interlined with a caret above deleted "character"
19.5	49.13	people,] followed by deleted / "notwithstanding their haughtiness and / phlegm"
19.14	49.17	feeling] mended from "feelings"
19.19	49.20	admirable] interlined with a caret above deleted "durable"

RURAL LIFE IN ENGLAND

23.20	50.37	drawing room] preceded by deleted "parlor"
24.10	51.4	therefore] followed by deleted "a continual"
25.15	51.22	himself] preceded by deleted "upon"
25.17	51.23	means] followed by deleted ſ
25.22	51.26	unrivalled.] interlined above deleted "admirable."
26.13	51.34	trees] followed by deleted "that"
27.5	51.42	seclusion. These] separated by a paragraph symbol
27.21	52.8	perceived.] followed by deleted "All is done by"
28.3	52.11	partial] interlined
28.3	52.11	opening] mended from "openings"
28.3	52.11	a] interlined with a caret
28.3	52.11	peep] mended from "peeps"
28.4	52.11	gleam] mended from "gleams"
28.14	52.17–18	narrow] preceded by deleted "scanty"
28.20	52.21	providently] interlined above deleted "carefully" /
29.7	52.30	men . . . in] interlined above deleted "men / of rank and fortune in"
29.15	52.35	spirits,] followed by deleted "[&]"
29.20	52.38	seem] interlined above deleted "appear to me"
30.4–5	52.42	a regular] interlined, the latter with a caret, above deleted "an / imperceptible"

30.16	53.5	and] interlined with a caret above deleted "[in]"
30.17	53.6	annihilated] followed by deleted "some of" /
31.1	53.10	the] followed by deleted "work" /
31.9	53.14	cities.] interlined above deleted "the city." /
31.9	53.14	cities.] following are four deleted lines: / "In the latter there is a mixture of servility / and vanity, obsequiousness and familiarity, / ignorance and pretension, which constitute / what is properly called vulgarity wh[ ] / alone"
31.18	53.17	bring] interlined above deleted "blend"
31.22	53.19	gentry] followed by deleted "of"
32.4	53.24	society] preceded by deleted / "life"
32.6	53.25	literature: the] mended from "literature. The"
32.7	53.26	those] interlined with a caret above deleted "the"
32.10	53.28	"the] mended from " "The" and preceded by deleted / "the flower and"
32.20–21	53.33	her . . . characteristics.] interlined above deleted "her in all her coy / games and capricious moods."
34.3	54.6	charm,] followed by wiped-out "of"
34.11	54.10	of] preceded by deleted / "with"
35.3	54.19	shady] interlined above deleted "green sw[ar]t" /
35.9	54.22	antique] interlined with a caret above deleted "antiquat"
35.10	54.22	standing] preceded by deleted / "surrounded"
35.14	54.24	evince] interlined above deleted "bespeak"
37.8	55.11	But] directly above is deleted / "But heaven" /

THE BROKEN HEART

38.13	56.11	and] interlined with a caret following deleted / "and" and deleted, interlined / "they"
40.4	56.32	pangs–] "–" mended from "[,]"
40.5	56.33	tenderness–] "–" mended from "[,]"
40.6	56.34	but] interlined above deleted "but"
40.9	56.35	pleasure. Or] mended from "pleasure[;] or"
40.16	56.39	life] interlined with a caret
41.10	57.10	affection.] followed by deleted "Even when fortu" /
41.12	57.11	fortunate, she] comma inserted after the words were written.
41.15	57.12	it] preceded by wiped-out "it"
41.18	57.14	failed. The] mended from "failed; the"

41.18	57.14	charm] interlined above deleted "object"
41.19	57.14	end. She] mended from "end; she"
41.23	57.16	veins] interlined above deleted "frame"
42.13	57.24	mental] interlined with a caret above deleted "hidden"
42.16	57.26	tree,] followed by deleted "that" /
42.18	57.26–27	graceful in its form;] interlined above deleted "graceful in its form,"
43.6	57.33	many] interlined with a caret
43.9	57.34	had] mended from "ha[ve]"
43.16	57.38–39	circumstances are] interlined with a caret above deleted "story is"
43.17	57.39	they] interlined with a caret above deleted "it"
43.18	57.40	them] interlined with a caret above deleted "it"
43.18	57.40	they were] interlined above deleted "it was" /
44.3	58.1	on] followed by deleted "the"
44.4–5	58.2	young– . . . – . . . –so brave–] dashes mended from commas
44.11	58.5	vindication] preceded by deleted / "and pathetic"
44.12	58.5–6	his pathetic] interlined with a caret
44.24	58.13	first . . . love.] interlined with a caret above deleted "love."
45.1	58.14	fortune, and] "and" interlined with a caret above deleted "when"
45.21	58.25	nothing to] interlined with a caret above deleted "that"
46.1	58.29	an] followed by deleted "the"
46.2	58.30	the] interlined with a caret
46.14	58.37	was] interlined with a caret above deleted "is"
46.16	58.38	soul; that] followed by deleted "rive / it to the core"
47.8	59.5	find it] "it" interlined with a caret
47.11	59.7	out] interlined with a caret above deleted / "up"
47.21	59.12	insensibility] interlined with a caret above the last two words of deleted "thoughts / were insensible"
47.22	59.12	scene,] followed by deleted "before / her"
47.24	59.13	warble] followed by deleted "out"
48.15	59.21	thoughts were] interlined with a caret above deleted "heart was"
48.17	59.22	suit.] interlined above deleted "addresses." /
48.18	59.23	not] followed by deleted "for"
49.2	59.28	hoping] preceded by deleted "hoping" /

49.4	59.29	was] interlined with a caret above deleted "made"
49.12	59.34	on her] preceded by deleted "to her"

THE ART OF BOOK MAKING

51.2	61.11	blunder] followed by deleted "into a"
51.7	61.15	British] preceded by deleted "b[ ]"
51.12	61.17	hieroglyphics] interlined above deleted / "hyeroglyphics"
51.14	61.19	alegorical] preceded by deleted "allegor"
51.16	61.20	way] preceded by deleted "manner"
51.21	61.22	clothed] preceded by deleted "habited"
52.3	61.25	attempt] preceded by deleted "explore"
52.3	61.26	of] followed by deleted "this" /
52.4	61.26	that] interlined with a caret
52.11	61.30	cases] preceded by deleted "book"
52.15	61.32	stands] interlined with a caret above deleted "desks"
52.17	61.33	poring] preceded by deleted "some"
54.1	62.10	so] preceded by deleted "until"
54.2	62.11	when the] followed by deleted "portal" / and interlined deleted "magic magic"
54.3	62.11	magic portal] interlined with a caret
54.15	62.18	principally] interlined above deleted "all"
57.12	63.13	lawless] interlined with a caret
57.13	63.14	fact] followed by deleted "the carriers / and"
57.16	63.16	ancient] followed by deleted / "writers"
58.2	63.21	philosophical treatise,] interlined with a caret above the first two words of "tract of / philosophy"
58.9	63.25	the] interlined with a caret above deleted "the"
58.14	63.28	descend;] ";" mended from "[.]"
58.14	63.28	they . . . submit] interlined above deleted "It is but conformable"
58.23	63.33	Thus] preceded by deleted "In like man"
59.23	64.4	in] preceded by deleted "the"
60.8	64.8	proceeded] preceded by deleted "proceeded" /
60.16	64.13	a] interlined with a caret above deleted "one"
60.17	64.14	mouldy] interlined with a caret above deleted "old" /
60.18	64.14	writers] interlined above deleted "folios"
60.24	64.17	set] preceded by deleted / "[b]id"
62.4	64.33	too] interlined with a caret

62.7–8	64.35	speak of] interlined, respectively, above deleted "point / out"
62.16	64.40	went about] interlined with a caret
62.21	64.43	robes,] followed by deleted "who entered the room"
63.19	65.12	to] followed by deleted "get off" / , and interlined deleted "escap"
63.20	65.12	escape] interlined with a caret
64.3	65.16	Pollux, and] followed by deleted "as / to"
64.4	65.16	Ben] followed by deleted "Johns"
64.4	65.16	Jonson] followed by deleted ", he"
64.10	65.19	fierce] interlined with a caret above deleted "great"
64.23	65.26	haunches;] followed by deleted "at" /
65.4	65.28	choppd] mended from "chopped"
65.5	65.29	exit] followed by deleted "from the / room"
65.8	65.31	so] followed by deleted "irrisistibly"
65.20	65.37	Nothing] preceded by deleted "No"
66.4	65.41	had a] followed by deleted "regular" /

A ROYAL POET

1.14	67.14	in the clouds] interlined with a caret above deleted "high in air"
1.22	67.19	In] preceded by deleted "As"
1.24	67.19	echoing] followed by deleted "chambe" /
2.8	67.28	tender, the] interlined with a caret
3.3	68.4	hanging . . . wall] interlined with a caret
3.7	68	gobelin] the *e* of this word is interlined with a caret
3.22	68.15	that] interlined with a caret
4.4	68.19	told] followed by deleted "[i]t"
4.19	68.28	proper] preceded by deleted "necessary"
4.21	68.29	advantage,] followed by deleted "to hi[m]"
4.23	68.30	exclusively] interlined above deleted / "intensely"
6.3	69.5	choicest] interlined with a caret
6.6	69.6	morbid] preceded by deleted / "become"
7.3	69.21	was] mended from "w[ere]"
7.15	69	Somerset.] followed by deleted "whom"
7.15	69	Somerset. He] mended from "Somerset, he"
7.15	69	her] interlined
7.15	69	accidentally,] followed by deleted / "and became deeply enamoured of, during / his"
8.3	75.25	writings.] interlined with a caret
8.4	75.25	in one] preceded by deleted / *h*
8.5	75.26	in] interlined with a caret

8.6	75.27	poem] followed by deleted "bear almost too strong a"
8.8	75.28	are] followed by deleted "however"
8.15	75	which] interlined with a caret above deleted "that"
8.16	75.33	generation] followed by deleted "of authors is charac- / terized by the"
8.17	75.33	has] mended from "have"
8.18	75.34	it] interlined above deleted "they" /
9.11	69.38	obliges] preceded by deleted "depend"
9.15	70.1	find] followed by deleted "that"
11.4	71.21	breathes] mended from "breaths"
11.9	70.19	Boetius'] preceded by deleted "Boethi"
11.14	70.24	out . . . writings,] interlined with a caret
12.8	71	was] interlined with a caret above deleted "is"
14.1	72.24	and listens] preceded by indented, deleted / "As he gazes on the scene,"
14.5	72.26	this] mended from "the"
14.5	72.26	season.] period added. Followed by deleted "of spring."
15.11	73.18	Chaucers] C mended from c
16.21		intention,] followed by deleted "James" /
18.2	77	in] interlined with a caret
18.3	77.7	month] preceded by deleted "season of the year"
18.12	77.15	still] preceded by deleted "yet"
18.21	77.21	exquisite] interlined above deleted "delicate" /
19.3	77.24	Others] O mended from o
19.7	77.26	stooping] preceded by deleted / "I have"
19.13	77.41	improved] followed by deleted "with his"
19.15	77	may] followed by deleted "still"
19.16	77.43	still] interlined with a caret above deleted "that are"
19.20	78.3	after ages] interlined with a caret above deleted "posterity"
19.22	78.5	as] interlined with a caret above deleted "when"

THE COUNTRY CHURCH

21.17	79.12	with] followed by deleted "opulent" /
22.1	79.12	ancient] preceded by deleted / "and"
22.15	79.20	which] interlined with a caret above deleted "that"
22.22	79.24	arms] followed by deleted "on"
23.22	79.37	delinquency] followed by deleted "at the threshold" /

24.14	80.5	They] the first word on the lower half of this composite page, inserted in the left hand margin and mended from / "they"
25.6	80.15	souls] preceded by deleted "sp"
25.22	80.24	respect] interlined with a caret above deleted / "deference"
26.16	80.33	close] interlined with a caret above deleted / "short"
26.16	80.33	face,] followed by deleted "according to" /
27.10	81.1	whip—] followed by deleted "sudden" /
28.2	81.8	suddeness] originally "suddenness"—the second *n* deleted with a slash
29.14	81.29	an] mended from /"a" and followed by deleted "cold"
31.8	82.11	trespass] preceded by wiped-out "inter"
31.8	82.11	whereas] preceded by deleted "whereas" /
31.13	82.15	behaviour] interlined above wiped-out "departure" /
31.20	82.18	perpetual] interlined with a caret above deleted "constant"
32.9	82.25	who] interlined with a caret above deleted "that"
32.16	82.29	seemed] preceded by deleted "was"

THE WIDOW AND HER SON

35.12	83.31	thoroughly] interlined above deleted / "truly"
35.18	83.35	appearance.] period mended from comma
36.1	83.37	for she] interlined with a caret
36.9	84.5	could] mended from "would"
36.17	84.9–10	delightfully] interlined with a caret above deleted "beautifully" /
37.12	84.19	indigent] interlined with a caret above deleted "poor"
40.11–12	85.15–16	she . . . grief.] interlined above deleted "all her agony / burst out afresh."
40.18	85.19	hands, as] followed by deleted "if there were no / comfort for her on earth"
42.2	85.37	rise] followed by deleted "abo"
43.9	86.12	lad;] semicolon mended from dash
43.10	86.12	him;] semicolon mended from dash
45.1	86.32	cultivate] preceded by deleted "work"
45.21–46.4	86.42–87.2	It . . . childhood] originally a separate paragraph, later indicated as part of the previous paragraph

47.3	87.15	hand.] possibly mended from "hand[s]." /
47.10	87.19	neglect and] interlined with a caret
47.20	87.25	She] mended from "The" /
47.21	87.25	will] preceded by deleted "mother"
48.10	87.32	in sickness] preceded by deleted "sick" and followed by deleted "and" /
48.14	87.35	her.] period mended from dash
49.7	87.43	do] interlined with a caret

THE BOAR'S HEAD TAVERN, EAST CHEAP

52.15	91.21	immortal] preceded by smeared *m*
52.18	91.23	and] followed by deleted "that without his assis- / tance"
52.19	91.23	oblivion.] interlined with a caret above deleted obscurity."
52.23	91.25–26	at the] followed by deleted "bottom" /
53.1	91.26	bottom] above this word is deleted /"notes at the"/
53.7	91.30	proper] preceded by deleted / "right"
53.9	91.31	bard] preceded by deleted / "poet"
53.10	91.31	puzzled] interlined with a caret above deleted "perplexed"
53.14	91.33	line] interlined with a caret above the second segment of "pas- / sage"
53.17	91.35	amply] interlined with a caret
55.8	92.16	leaf—] mended from "leaf,"
55.11	92.18	But] followed by deleted "sweet"
55.13–14	92.19	human] preceded by deleted "human"
55.19	92.22	mankind] the first syllable is mended from "m[en]"
56.7	92.28	empty] interlined with a caret
56.13	92.32	faded] followed by deleted "G[ ]" /
56.16	92.34	Old] mended from "old"
57.15	93.3	tradesman—] followed by deleted "instead of"
57.16	93.4	sawtry"] followed by deleted "[is]"
57.27	93.10	on] followed by deleted "th[ ]" /
58.7	93.14	her] interlined above the second word of deleted "the good old dame" / ; interlined with a caret above "dame" and also deleted is "lady" /
58.21	93.22	the Monument] interlined with a caret above deleted "Pudding lane"; before "Monument" is deleted "mon"
59.3	93.26	neighbourhood] preceded by deleted "negh"
59.4	93.27	however] interlined with a caret

59.5	93.27	antiquity.] period mended from comma; followed by deleted "and"
59.6	93.28	upon] followed by deleted "that"
59.14	93.33	iniquities] interlined above deleted "sins"
60.14	94.3	cost] preceded by deleted "cost"
60.17	94.4	Crooked] mended from "crooked"
60.18	94.5	elbows] preceded by deleted "turns and"
61.22	94.22	them.] followed by indented deleted / "The church of Sᵗ Michaels crooked lane" /
62.1	94.23	Michael] mended from "Michaels"
62.2	94.23	standing] followed by deleted "on Fish street hill,"
62.2	94	at] followed by deleted "but"
62.17	94.31	ashes] interlined with a caret above deleted "monument"
63.8	94.38	monument] interlined with a caret above deleted "tomb"
64.7	95.6	clearing . . . weeds] interlined with a caret above deleted / "brushing away the dust"
64.8	95.6	little] preceded by smeared "sexton"
65.7	95.14	its] interlined with a caret above deleted "a"
65.8	95.14	club,] followed by deleted "to the discom- / fiture of sundry train band captains— / the dum"
65.17	95.18	in the] followed by deleted "lawful" /
66.1	95.23	with . . . spirits] interlined above deleted "with ghosts"
63.14	95.30	myght] mended from "might"
64.21	95.43	were] preceded by deleted "w[ ]"
66.14	96.1	Falstaff] preceded, on the previous line, by deleted "fa" /
68.14–15	96.17	old Tavern,] interlined above deleted "Boars / head,"
68.16	96.18	which] followed by deleted "were deposited / in the parish club room at a neigh- / bouring tavern, and"
68.19	96.19	times,] followed by deleted "ever since the" /
68.24	96.21	Tavern] preceded by deleted "little"
69.8	96.26	centre of] followed by deleted "[th]" /
69.12	96.29	light] interlined above deleted "day"
69.14	97.1	whose] made from "who" and followed by deleted "exist in a"
69.14	97.1	at best] interlined with a caret
69.21	97.5	O'clock] O mended from o
69.26	97.7	piece] mended from / "peice"

70.6	97.15	little] followed by deleted / "back parlour misshapen back parlour" /
71.12	97.31	vulgar] interlined with a caret above deleted / "other"
71.17	97.33–34	displayed] interlined above second segment of deleted "pour- / trayed"
71.19	97.35	at table] interlined with a caret
72.7	97.42	this] followed by deleted "was"
72.12	98.2	description] preceded by deleted / "inscrip"
73.2	98.6	gaze,] interlined with a caret; preceded by deleted / "While I was meditating on this Tobacco / box" and interlined deleted "it with doting enraptur" / which begins above "meditating"
73.12	98.12	red] preceded by deleted "oil"
73.24	98.19	I] mended from "[it]" /
74.11	98.27–28	-men . . . themselves] interlined with carets above deleted "that has seated itself"
74.15	98.30	lest] followed by deleted "th[e]"
75.22	99.9	eye] interlined with a caret above deleted "gaze"
76.9	99.16	parish] preceded by deleted "who"
76.10	99.16	not forgetting] interlined above deleted "including"
76.15	99.19	for] interlined with a caret
76.21	99.22	but] interlined with a caret and written over wiped-out "just"
77.5	99.25	The history] interlined above deleted "Private anecdotes"
77.6	99.25	little–] dash mended from comma
77.6	99.25	little–] followed by deleted "the histo" /
77.11	99.28	and whom,] interlined with a caret above deleted "who,"
77.16	99.31	mine] followed by deleted "of" /

MS2

"POSTSCRIPT" TO RIP VAN WINKLE

1.4	42.1	Kaatsberg or Catskill] interlined above deleted "Kaatskill (or Catskill)"
2.1	42.8	In times of drought, if] interlined with a caret above deleted "When"
2.6	42.11	float] followed by deleted "high"
2.7	42.11	until] preceded by deleted "these being"
3.2	42.18	Spirit] followed by deleted / "of [ ]" "unfriendly to the"

4.9	42.32	pursue] followed by deleted "[the]"
4.20	42.37	swept] preceded by deleted "dashed"

THE WIDOW AND HER SON

1.8	83.6	Sunday.] followed by deleted "Nature is hushed into a hallowed calm."
1.10	83.7	stroke] interlined above deleted "sound"
1.21	83.12	tints] followed by deleted comma
2.1	83.13	enjoyed the hallowed calm.] interlined above deleted "seemed to enjoy the sanctity of the / day of rest."
2.7	83.17	which] preceded by deleted "of the"
2.13	83.20	that] written over "which"
3.4	83.27	but] interlined with a caret above deleted "yet this,"

A SUNDAY IN LONDON

1.10	89.6	repose] interlined above deleted "quiet"
2.1	89.10	meet] followed by deleted "[ ] / [ ]"
2.4	89.11	are] interlined with a caret
2.15	89.17	then] interlined with a caret
3.10	89.28	feet] followed by deleted "[ ]"
3.17	89.31	hushed;] followed by deleted "not a footfall is to be"
3.18	89.32	is heard] "is" interlined above deleted "are"
4.4	89.36	like a river of joy] interlined with a caret
4.6	89.37	cleansing it] "it" interlined above deleted "them"
4.7	89.38	pollutions] preceded by deleted "[ ]"
4.9	89.39	triumphant] interlined with a caret
4.17	90.4	for] followed by deleted "the"
5.5	90.11	On Sunday] interlined with a caret above deleted "The"
5.5	90.11	the city] "the" written over "is"
5.8	90.12	environs.] followed by deleted "Now the brisk dapper / dapper shopman and apprentice"
5.14	90.14–15	beholding the] followed by deleted "parks and green fields swarming with the populace"

NOTES CONCERNING WESTMINSTER ABBEY

1.1	142.30	Concerning] interlined with a caret above deleted "about"
1.6	142.34	Anglo Saxon] preceded by deleted "Saxon"

1.8	142.35	conceived] followed by deleted "the project of"
1.14	143.2	princes] followed by deleted "was under / the"
1.15	143.2	christian] interlined above deleted "French"
1.16	143.3	and] interlined above deleted "who"
1.17	143.3	that . . . stipulation] interlined with a caret above deleted "allowed" which is preceded by uncanceled but superseded "was"
2.6	143.9	island] preceded by deleted "[Isle]"
2.7	143.10–11	and held . . . open air] interlined
2.9	143.12	magic.] followed by deleted "They held a conference in the open air,"
2.14	143.14	The zeal] preceded by deleted "Augustine"
2.17	143.16	British] followed by deleted "subjects"
2.20	143.17	Segebert or] interlined with a caret above deleted "Si[ ]bert"
3.3	143.20	bishop] preceded by deleted "Bish"
3.4	143.21	in 605,] interlined with a caret
3.6	143.22	on the . . . Apollo] interlined
3.6	143.23	origin of the present] interlined above deleted "present pile"
3.9	143.24	church] preceded by deleted "Monastary"
4.3	143.34	performed] followed by deleted "with [ ]"
4.17	143.41	beheld] followed by deleted "the reliques of a grand ceremony"; interlined above "ceremony" is deleted "ceremonial"
5.11	144.9	scite] preceded by deleted "site"
6.3	144.19	Cathedral,] followed by deleted "of the / finding of the"
6.8	144.21	quietly . . . sepulchre] interlined with a caret above deleted "been interred"
6.17	144.27	seen] preceded by deleted "scene"
6.18	144.28	memory.] followed by deleted "To"
7.1	144.28	abbey] interlined with a caret above deleted "cathedral"
8.8	145.9	he] preceded by deleted "this prying choirister,"
8.19	145.16	dust] followed by deleted quotation mark
8.20	145.16	found."] followed by deleted "Such"
[11].7	146.14	The white] preceded by deleted "The rays"
[11].9	146.15	oaken] preceded by deleted "[slatts]" /
[11].10	146.16	makes] followed by deleted "great masses of shade"
[12].3	146.22	the procession] "the" interlined above deleted "as this"
[12].16	146.25	On entering] preceded by deleted eight-line pas-

		sage: "At the entrance of the Little cloisters / there is a mural monument of a [ ] Pultney / representing a ⟨fig⟩ male figure in white / marble reclining on a tomb; a strong / glare is shed upon it by a ⟨glass⟩ gass light / A distant view of this figure is had through / a dark vaulted passage opening from / the Deans Yard"; the words in ⟨ ⟩ were canceled in the course of writing the passage.
[12].16	146.25	at night from what is called] interlined with a caret above deleted "from"
[13].1	146.28	glare] followed by deleted "is"
[13].6	146.30	The cloisters] preceded by a false start at a new paragraph: "This [ ]"

THE CHRISTMAS DINNER

.6	191.27	witnessing] preceded by deleted "seeing"
.8	191.28	on] mended from "in"
.9	191.28	the skirts] interlined above deleted "parts which"
.12	191.30	the author's] "the" interlined above deleted "[ ]"

LONDON ANTIQUES

1.15	192.11	poetical] preceded by deleted "additional"
1.18	192.12	I] preceded by deleted "An"
2.24	192.25	water.] followed by deleted "Every thing here"
3.2	192.26	bench,] followed by deleted "with nothing / to interrupt his studies but"
3.17	192.34	lofty, and] followed by deleted "dimly"
3.20	192.35	marble] interlined with a caret
4.1	192.37	sword—] the dash covers a semicolon
4.3	192.38	indicated] followed by deleted "th"
4.4	192.38	Faith] preceded by deleted "fai"
5.11	193.14	either to] preceded by deleted "to"
5.14	193.16	hall] followed by deleted "of the same gothic architecture"
6.13	193.27–28	my head on my hand and] interlined with a caret
6.17	193.30	monastic] preceded by deleted "religious"
6.18	193.31	establishments] preceded by deleted "edifices"
8.3	194.7	cloisters,] followed by deleted "with"
8.4	194.8	dependencies] preceded by deleted "[depen- / dences]"
8.7	194.9	space] preceded by deleted "court"

8.8	194.9	evidently] preceded by deleted "appeared to"
8.25	194.19	hung] preceded by deleted "which seemed to be"
9.3	194.20	and stuffed] "and" interlined with a caret
9.11	194.24	I] preceded by deleted "On approaching to regard this strange / collection"
9.14	194.25	startled] followed by deleted "by"
9.16	194.26	corner.] followed by deleted "I at first doubted whether it were not / a mummy curiously preserved, but it / moved and I saw that it was alive."
10.18	194.39	his] preceded by deleted "through"
11.9	195.4	conventual] preceded by deleted "original"
11.11	195.5	men] interlined with a caret, following deleted, interlined "magi" above deleted "which"
11.11	195.5	who] interlined with a caret above deleted "which"
11.12	195.6	hall,] followed by deleted "was composed"
11.13	195.6	whom] interlined above deleted "which"
11.14	195.7	returning] interlined above deleted "coming"
12.11	195.18	Latin] mended from "latin"
13.1	195.24	P.S.] preceded, at the bottom of page 12, by deleted "Having beguiled the reader into this stroll / through the Charter House, I will add"
13.5	195.26	an ancient] preceded by deleted "the"
13.14	195.31	fuel] preceded by deleted "and"
[15].3	196.7	observation] followed by deleted / "I subjoin a modicum of local history / put into"

MS3

SLEEPY HOLLOW

1.13–14	272.11	navigators] followed by deleted "of those waters"
1.14	272.11	Zee] capital Z clarified
1.15	272.12	prudently] interlined with a caret
1.16	272.12–13	and implored the protection of St Nicholas] interlined with a caret
7.12	273.36	The Headless Horseman] initial letters mended to capitals
last leaf.8–9	286.13	a range of hills] interlined with carets above deleted "those lofty hills"
last leaf.10	286.14	Hudson] *H* mended from *h*

PRE-COPY-TEXT VARIANTS

A ROYAL POET, 2A

This list contains all substantive differences between the 1E copy-text and 2A. In a few instances, where 1E is in error, the 2A reading is actually the same as the correction of 1E made in a later edition. A double asterisk indicates a substantive difference between 1E and T, and directs the reader to the List of Emendations. To the left of the bracket is the Twayne page number and the copy-text reading; to the right, the reading of 2A. For a discussion explaining the need for this list see pp. 372–73.

67.12	thought. It rears] thought; rearing
67.13	waves] waving
67.14	looks] looking
67.18	disposing] causing
67.20	castle] old castle
67.20–21	rows of portraits of warriors] rows of warriors
67.22	likenesses] portraits
67.22	that graced] that once flourished in
67.23	depicted] each depicted
67.25	which had] that had
67.26	traversing also the "large green courts,"] traversing the "large green courts," also,
67.33	*No paragraph* In this] *Paragraph* In this
68.4	James] the captive prince
68.15	prisoner] a prisoner
68.18	*No paragraph* "The news,"] *Paragraph* "The news,"
68.32	a lustre] lustre
**69.6	others, morbid] others grow morbid
**69.21–26	prison house. *omitted*] dungeon. Such was the world of pomp and pageant that lived round Tasso in his dismal cell at Ferrara, when he conceived the splendid scenes of his Jerusalem; and we may consider the "King's Quair," composed by James, during his captivity at Windsor, as another of those beautiful breakings forth of the soul from the restraint and gloom of the prison house.
69.27	Beaufort] Beaumont

69	*Omitted*] *Quair, an old term for Book.
69.39–70.1	to find] find
69.40	Roger L'Estrange] Sir Roger L'Estrange
70.9	which are] are
70.14	*Paragraph* Such] *No paragraph* Such
70.14–15	gives of his weariness of spirit and of the incident that first suggested the idea of writing the poem.] gives us of the state of mind and the incident which first induced him to write the poem.
71.3	pleasure] pleasance
71.4	his very] all his
**71.7	or exaggerated] nor overstrained
71.8	and are perhaps] and perhaps are
71.10	meet with] meet
71.23	a deficiency] great deficiency
71.32	fortired] for, tired
71.42	leaves] trees
72.11	set] sat
72.18	his enamoured] enamoured
72.25	lapses] falls
72.29	really be] is really
72.29–30	if it be a boon] a boon
72.36	generally modernized.] modernized to make them more readily understood by the generality of readers.
73.9	go] do go
73.13–14	the moment of loneliness and] a moment of loneliness of heart, yet
73.15	his] all his
73.17	evident resemblance] similarity
73.20	similarity] very similarity
73.21	dwell on] dwell upon
73.23	manner] spirit
73.26	even to] to
73.33	favourite and pet] favourite
73.39	*Gilt*, what injury have I done, &c.] *Gilt,&c.* What injury have I done to him.
74.2	cunning‡ sure] cunning sure,§
**74.14	vent a] vent to a
74.17	allegorically shadowed out] shadowed out in allegory
74.25–26	*No paragraph* Suddenly] *Paragraph* Suddenly
74.34–35	reads it with rapture] he reads it over with rapture an hundred times
74.40	‡*Cunning*, discretion.] §*Cunning sure*, discretion.

75.5	adventures] adventure
**75.7	do not, however, let us] do not let us, however,
75.9	noticed] considered
75.12	that day] the time
75.13	golden] most golden
75.15	urbanity,] urbanity, and the playful fancy
75.18	periods] period
75.19	edifying] likewise edifying
75.20	the nature, refinement,] the refinement
75.22	all its] its
75.25	admirer and studier] studier and admirer
**75.34	lived] lives
75.35	*Paragraph* James] *No paragraph* James
75.35	brilliant] distinguished
75.35	our literary] literary
75.37	Whilst] While
75.39	evidently] undoubtedly
75.40	never-failing] never-fading
76.7	having] and having
76.8	Jane, who] Jane, she
76.13–14	in the] on the
76.18	mingled occasionally] occasionally mingled
76.26	immunities which] immunities
76.36	rushing] rushed
77.29	become] been
78.3	to after] down to after

PHILIP OF POKANOKET

To the left of the bracket is the Twayne page number and the reading of the first British edition (1E), copy-text for "Philip." To the right is the reading of the *Analectic Magazine* article. For a discussion explaining the need for this list, see pp. 360–62.

234	*Omitted*] The following anecdotes, illustrative of Indian character, are gathered from various sources, that have every appearance of being authentic. It was thought needless to encumber the page with references.
234.3–9	As . . . CAMPBELL.] *Omitted*
234.11	America] our country
234.11	particular] frequent
234.13	which] that
234.17	lighting] happening
234.20	cultivated] wrought up

234.22	and indeed almost the existence] and almost existence
234.23	upon the opinion of his fellow men,] public opinion
234.24	constantly] forever
234.24	studied part] part
234.26	petty] amiable
234.27	affects] assumes
234.28–29	real, from his artificial character] real character from that which is acquired or affected
234.30	*Omitted*] and living
234.30	and, in] in
234.30	a solitary] solitary
234.31	independent being] independent,
234.33	a lawn] an artificial lawn
234.34–35	where the] the
235.2	colonial] provincial
235.4	these] those
235.5	may] in this country may
235.6	aborigines] original inhabitants
235.18	in the cause of] for the deliverance of
235.22	tradition.*] tradition.
235.23–24	as the Plymouth settlers are called by their descendants, first] as they are termed, first
235.25	religious persecutions] persecutions
235.25–26	their . . . and disheartening.] they found themselves in the most gloomy and helpless situation.
235.27	through] by
235.30	their minds were filled with doleful forebodings] their hearts were filled with the most gloomy forebodings
235.31	despondency] utter despondency
235.32	were visited by] received from
235.33	a powerful chief, who] the cheering rites of primitive hospitality. This powerful prince, who
235.34	country. Instead] country, came early in the spring, with a small retinue to the new settlement of Plymouth; instead
235.36–39	intruded, he . . . followers; entered] intruded, he entered
235.40–42	*While . . . Pokanoket.] *Omitted*
236.2	for] to
236.3	that the] that nothing appears to impeach the
236.4	Massasoit, have never been impeached. He] Massasoit. He
236.5	magnanimous] generous
236.5	suffering] allowing

236.6   their possessions and] and
236.9   for . . . the] to renew the
236.10   of securing] to secure
236.11   *Paragraph* At this conference] *No paragraph* In this
               treaty
236.12   encroaching zeal of] zealous attacks of
236.12   and] he
236.16–17   Philip (as . . . English,) to] Philip, to
236.23   ingratitude] gratitude
236.24   succeeded him] who succeeded him, soon incurred the
               hostilities of the settlers
236.27   indignation] imagination
236.27   uneasiness] alarm
236.27   their exterminating] their merciless and exterminating
236.28   with] against
236.28–29   He . . . hostility] Whether authorized by fact, or dictated
               by suspicion
236.29   being] he was
236.30–35   It . . . natives] The proceedings of the settlers show the
               rapid increase of their power, and their overbearing
               conduct towards the natives.
236.36   seize at once] seize
236.36   to bring] bring
236.38–39   reposing with a band of his followers, unarmed] repos-
               ing unarmed, with a band of his followers,
237.1   pledge] hostage
237.1   reappearance] appearance
237.2   agonies] exasperations
237.6   These, together with his well-known] The well known
237.6   enterprise] enterprize of his character
237.7   had rendered] made
237.8   having always cherished] of always cherishing
237.9   whites] English
237.10   but mere] mere
237.11   into] in
237.11   had presumed] were presuming
237.12   were extending] extending
237.17   purchases, in the early periods of colonization?] pur-
               chases?
237.17   *Omitted*] The nations were equally despoiled by the
               arts and the arms of the white men.
237.17–18   The Europeans always made] The latter made
237.20   provoked] excited

237.21–22	be gradually and legally] be legally
237.23	the Europeans] Europeans
237.34	and by a simultaneous effort] and make a common effort
237.35	difficult at this distant period to assign] difficult to assign
237.37	to] for
238.1	when] where
238.5	quickened] heightened
238.6	He changed] He had two or three times changed
238.6–7	allegiance two or three times, with] allegiance, with
238.7	evinced the looseness of his principles.] shows great looseness of principle,
238.7–8	He had acted for some time as] and, after having acted as
238.9	and had] and
238.9–11	protection. Finding . . . and went over] protection, he deserted him when he found the glooms of adversity beginning to lower around him, went over
238.11–12	their favour] favor
238.12	charged his] turned against his
238.12	with] and charged him with
238.17	ensure] arouse
238.20	dead] murdered
238.24	the] his
238.27	which had fallen thus] that had thus fallen at
238.30–31	and he . . . tragical story] and he recollected the tragical end
238.33	exculpating] acquitting
238.33	from a charge of conspiracy] of an alleged conspiracy
238.34	amity] their amity
238.35	about] around
238.36	cause] standard
238.39	distrust and irritation] irritation and distrust
238.42	petty depredations. In] depredations, and in
239.1	killed] wounded
239.2	the death of their] their
239.4–5	we meet with many indications] we find symptoms
239.6	gloom] glooms
239.7	among trackless forests,] among the trackless forests
239.8	filled] had filled
239.9	witchcraft and spectrology] witchcraft, spectrology, and omens
239.9–10	They . . . omens.] *Omitted*

239.10–11   Indians were preceded, we are told, by] Indians, we are told, were preceded by
239.12   which] that
239.12   The] At one time the
239.15   in their neighbourhood] thereabouts
239.18   seemed] appeared
239.19   seeming] and seemed
239.20–21   that they heard the galloping of horses] the galloping of troops of horses
239.21   which] that
239.23   Many of these] These
239.23   sights and sounds may be] noises may easily be
239.24–29   phenomena. To the northern ... solitudes. These may] phenomena—to the uncouth sounds and echoes that will sometimes strike the ear amidst the profound stillness of woodland solitudes—to the casual rushing of a blast through the tree tops—the crash of falling wood or mouldering rocks—they may
239.30   imaginations, may have been] imagination—been
239.32–33   The universal currency of these superstitious fancies] The currency of their circulation,
239.33   made of] of
239.36   ensued] ensued with Philip
239.36–37   too often distinguishes] marks
239.39   with a] with
240.3   the] this
240.3   transmitted] minutely transmitted
240.12   of a] a
240.15   casual exploits and unconnected enterprizes] massacres
240.16   genius and daring] skill and prowess
240.17   wherever,] whenever
240.18   arrive] reach
240.19   mind;] genius,
240.19–20   a contempt of suffering and hardship;] *Omitted*
240.22–241.6 he ... deer] compelled to take refuge in the depths of forests, or the glooms and thickets of swamps, and frequently surrounded by the enemy, yet he repeatedly found means to evade their toils, and suddenly emerging with his forces, carried havoc and dismay into the settlements.
241.6–7   Into one of these, the great swamp of Pocasset Neck, was Philip once driven with a band of his followers. The English] At one time he was driven, with a band

	of followers, into the great swamp of Pocasset Neck, where the English forces
241.10	foes. They therefore] foes: they, therefore
241.11	thought] intention
241.12	warriors] companions,
241.12–14	wafted . . . behind;] leaving the women and children behind, wafted themselves on a raft over an arm of the sea, in dead of night
241.17–34	In . . . resources] *Omitted*
241.34–35	In this time of adversity he found a faithful friend in] One of the most faithful friends that Philip had in the time of his adversity, was
241.37–38	who, as already mentioned, after an honourable acquittal of the charge of conspiracy, had been privately put] who had put
241.38	at] by
241.39	settlers. "He] English: "he
241.40	"of all] "of
242.2	broken] shattered
242.3	upon] on
242.5	one] a
242.7	was sent] set
242.8–10	leafless, could be traversed with comparative facility, and would no longer afford dark and impenetrable fastnesses] leafless, no longer afforded impenetrable fortresses
242.11	conveyed] sheltered
242.13	to a] in a
242.16	midst] middle
242.16	it was constructed] constructed
242.17	degree of judgement] judgement
242.17–18	to what is usually displayed in Indian fortification,] to the usual fortifications of the Indians;
242.23	attack, and several] attack; several
242.25	success. A] success; a
242.25–26	effected. The] effected; the
242.26	post] hold
242.26	another. They] another; they
242.27	despair. Most] despair; most
242.30	and took refuge in the thickets] and plunged into the depths
242.31	*Paragraph* The] *No paragraph* The
242.33	outrage] inhuman outrage

242.35–36	the destruction] with anguish of heart, the desolations
242.41	they] They
243.7	which he] he
243.28	that the] the
243.32–33	he threw off, first his blanket] he threw by first his blanket
244.3	prisoner] a prisoner
244.10	him will I] him I will
244.15–16	his boast that he] and that he had boasted he
244.17	and his threat that he] and that he
244.26	soul. When] soul, and challenge a comparison with any speech on a similar occasion in the whole range of history. When
244.35	the superior] superior
244.40–41	stores were all captured] treasures were captured
245.9	misfortunes] misfortune
245.22	body and] body,
245.22	was thus] thus
245.36	dwelling] dwellings
245.38	of family] family
245.40	the feelings] feelings
246.7	gathers] seems to gather
246.11	disaster] the disaster
246.12	experience] receive
246.15	he smote] he even smote
246.30	that amidst] amid
247.8	lonely bark foundering amid] foundering bark, amid
247.9	a pitying eye] an eye

LIST OF COMPOUND WORDS

AT END OF LINE

List I contains all hyphenated Twayne readings which were hyphenated in the printed copy-texts. End-of-line hyphenations of compounds and possible compounds are included, as are those words which were hyphenated in accepted emendations of the copy-texts. Each occurrence of a formerly hyphenated word or words is listed by the page and line numbers of its appearance in the T text.

List II presents all words hyphenated at end of line in the T text which would have been hyphenated had they come in midline. All other end-of-line hyphenations are to be read as simple words, without hyphenation. For commentary on Irving's hyphenation practice see pages 378–79.

LIST I

4.20	all important	115.8	sweet souled
5.7	Castle street	117.34	green house
5.27	weather cock	119.24	hangers on
5.36	good for nothing	119.28	tea kettle
6.19	booksellers	119.32–33	well scoured
7.25	well merited	120.23	akimbo
7.28	golden hearted	122.15	good for nothing
71.32	fortired	122.35	rose bud
71.33	wo begone	123.14	supernatural
75.40	never failing	124.36	jog trot
70.23–24	text book	125.4	warm hearted
100.12	half dreaming	126.9	far famed
100.18	football	126.22	watch tower
103.29–30	book collectors	126.34	son in law
104.29	fine spun	127.27	hard favoured
107.24	heaven illumined	127.32	battle axes
107.24–25	widely separated	127.32	cross bows
109.8	simple hearted	128.1	side long
110.32	broken hearted	128.19	broad faced
113.5	sweet scented	129.29	tomorrow

129.30	tomorrow		173.20	well conditioned
129.36	drawbridge		173.22	black looking
130.1	wood demons		173.31	black letter
131.39	heartrending		174.6	gray headed
131.5	love sick		175.36	worm eaten
131.41	wood demon		176.3	Mince pie
131.41–42	son in law		176.3	plum porridge
131.42	grand children		177.14	farm houses
132.3–4	jack boots		178.8–9	ale house
134.37	key stones		180.30	wide mouthed
135.5	sun gilt		181.20	hard favoured
136.22	fellow men		181.40	well worded
137.26	overwrought		182.2	rosemary
140.20	long drawn		182.35–36	fat headed
142.7	tomorrow		182.37	plate full
142.24	sun beam		183.12	peacock
142.26	fox glove		183.37	knights errant
142.6	today		185.23	fat headed
142.7	tomorrow		185.25	long winded
148.30	heartfelt		186.21–22	mad cap
150.29	oft told		186.25	sunshine
152.6	home dwelling		186.30	milkmaid
154.6	button hole		186.42	black letter
155.1	hangers on		187.7	fat headed
155.3	tap room		187.21	drawing room
155.32	long drawn		187.28	blue eyed
157.9	well scoured		187.37	high backed
157.14	high backed		188.9	black letter
157.26	post chaise		189.35	frost bitten
157.30	good humoured		189.36	blue eyed
160.20–21	over run		190.9	full bottomed
160.25	household		190.33	wild eyed
162.26	old fashioned		190.34	warm hearted
162.29	half fledged		191.7	long departed
162.29–30	bright eyed		191.25	old fashioned
163.42	bare footed		196.9	odd looking
164.24	frost bitten		196.10	snuff coloured
165.18	last mentioned		197.12	Bull and Mouth
165.34	hanger on		197.13	New Gate
166.14	mad cap		197.23	New Gate
167.21	hot house		197.35	time stained
171.14	sideboard		197.37	fireplaces
171.17	gentleman like		198.7–8	high backed

198.8	claw footed	211.37	Prayer book
198.17	gentleman like	211.38	well thumbed
198.29	pan cakes	211.40	warming pan
198.30	hot cross buns	211.41	fireplace
199.2	Bull and Mouth	211.41	horn handled
199.12	moonlight	212.1	grand daughter
199.34	grasshopper	212.2	blue eyed
199.40	grasshopper	212.28	mulberry tree
199.41	star gazing	213.17	fifty three
200.5	eighty two	213.22	tombstone
200.12–13	sea monsters	214.9	church yard
200.39	coachman	214.14–15	deer stealing
200.42	church yard	214.15	harebrained
201.2	steam boats	214.23	deer stalker
201.12	church yards	214.26	hanger on
201.23	half moon	214.29	wool comber
201.41	mad cap	214.32	good natured
202.13	Half moon's	215.19	mad caps
203.10	Smithfield	215.43	crab tree
203.24	ginger bread	216.10	snow drop
204.18	Beef eaters	217.22	footpath
204.30	good will	217.26	footpath
205.5	newspaper	217.35	fireside
205.8	umbrella maker	218.9	long settled
205.36	New York	219.2	court yard
205.38	Red lion	219.3–4	flower beds
205.40	Grays inn	219.5	outpost
206.17	Portsoken ward	219.23	court yard
206.18	Crutched Friars	219.25	moss troopers
206.25	shoe brush	219.34	every day
207.28	oil man	219.39	manor house
208.3	country dance	220.4	fireplace
208.8	Cross Keys	220.5	old fashioned
208.16	good for nothing	220.7	bow window
210.2	wool combing	220.7–8	court yard
210.3	mean looking	221.16	cane coloured
210.16	tobacco box	222.13	game keepers
210.21	self multiplication	222.13	whippers in
210.28	church yard	222.15	half open
211.10	birth place	222.31	castle hunters
211.15–16	church yard	223.4	shortlegged
211.20	tombstones	223.5	kickshaws
211.33	white washed	223.11	dining room

223.18	working day		253.20	broken down
229.35	wide spreading		253.25	vain glory
229.36	overwhelming		253.37–38	weather cock
230.11	fellow man		253.38	gray headed
230.24	spirit stirring		253.39	daylight
231.6	knight errant		254.5	heartburnings
231.38	cold blooded		254.17	rattle pated
232.18–19	self willedness		254.25–26	broken down
232.30	self taught		254.30	ale house
234.23	fellow men		255.1	half pay
234.26	good breeding		255.12	open handed
235.29	ever shifting		255.14	prize fighting
236.33	overbearing		255.20–21	frost bitten
237.6	well known		255.21	gold laced
237.39	tale bearing		255.26	three cornered
238.29	broken hearted		255.39	quarter staff
239.12	forerun		256.1	sterling hearted
240.7	true born		256.3	homebred
242.33	overcame		257.31	half sunken
244.5	prince like		257.31	tombstone
244.7	proud hearted		257.32	sober thoughted
244.7	twenty second		258.9	deeply furrowed
246.8	care worn		258.15	soul subduing
248.14	nick names		259.12–13	good will
248.21	three cornered		259.13	May pole
248.36	homebred		259.14	May day
248.37–38	Bow bells		259.19	May day
249.24	matter of fact		261.16	overwhelm
249.35	busy minded		263.12	church yard
250.9	finely spun		263.17	death like
250.11–12	bottle bellied		264.30	steel clad
250.15	good hearted		264.37	sketch book
250.15	good tempered		265.28	mill pond
250.41	housekeeper		265.30	panic struck
251.1	beef steak		266.1–2	milkmaid
251.2	hogshead		266.15	iron grey
251.17	weather beaten		266.16	good humoured
251.35	well lined		266.19	fish pond
252.16	household		268.10	gentleman like
252.2	well bred		268.12	tap room
253.8	out house		269.25	birth deck
253.13	hanger on		269.25	man of war
253.15	worn out		269.26	day time

269.33	mantle piece	279.27	ever hungry
269.34	woodcuts	280.14	farm houses
270.10	sunshine	280.14	high ridged
270.23	good nature	280.14–15	lowly sloping
270.27	tap room	280.29	claw footed
270.29	sea fights	280.36	well mended
273.14	night mare	280.41	knight errant
273.20	cannon ball	281.20	nick name
273.28	church yard	281.23	cock fights
273.32	church yard	281.27	ill will
273.32	day break	281.34	well known
273.35	firesides	281.37	farm houses
274.3	New York	281.41	mad cap
274.13	by place	281.42	good will
274.31	school house	282.24	gently insinuating
274.38	school house	282.25	farm house
275.1	bee hive	283.17	knights errant
275.15	broad skirted	283.28	school house
275.15	wrong headed	284.2	half munched
276.6	singing master	284.3	fly cages
276.14	half a mile	284.7–8	school room
276.14	mill pond	284.9	tow cloth
276.23	gentleman like	284.10–11	half broken
276.26	farm house	284.13	merry making
276.26	tea table	284.25	overturned
276.28	tea pot	284.36	knight errant
276.30	church yard	284.39	broken down
276.32	tombstones	285.6	broken down
276.34	mill pond	285.31	cock robin
276.41	New England	285.33	woodpecker
277.4	spell bound	286.3	cider press
277.7–8	school house	286.8	bee hive
277.11	farm house	286.10	slap jacks
277.14	tree toad	286.30	leathern faced
277.14–15	screech owl	286.37	square skirted
277.16	fire flies	286.39	eel skin
278.19	daylight	287.5	well broken
278.28	rosy cheeked	287.11	tea table
278.33	great great grandmother	287.14	dough nut
278.40	liberal hearted	287.21	tea pot
278.42	well conditioned	287.42	grey headed
279.9	farm house	288.15	eye balls
279.22	ill tempered	288.33	blue bearded

288.34–35 nine pounder
289.13–14 long established
289.38   grass grown
290.11   tree tops
290.32–33 light hearted
290.34   woodlands
291.11   heavy hearted
291.12   crest fallen
291.18   watch dog
291.21   long drawn
291.35   land mark
291.41   ill starred
293.29   horror struck
294.14   much ado

294.34   whirlwind
294.37–38 dinner hour
295.27   church yard
295.11   small clothes
295.12   pitch pipe
295.14   Witchcraft
295.15   New England
295.36   New York
296.32   dry looking
296.32   eyebrows
296.39   akimbo
297.3   story teller
297.20   story teller

LIST II

64.40–41   lack-a-daisical
98.20–21   parcel-gilt
197.15–16 Ave-Maria
204.34–35 Tom-come-tickle-me

205.29–30 blind-man's-buff
220.19–20 Star-Chamber
283.29–30 topsy-turvy